D1297480

Improving the Measurement of Consumer Expenditures

Studies in Income and Wealth, Volume 74

National Bureau of Economic Research
Conference on Research in Income and Wealth

Improving the Measurement of Consumer Expenditures

Edited by **Christopher D. Carroll, Thomas F. Crossley, and John Sabelhaus**

The University of Chicago Press

Chicago and London

CHRISTOPHER D. CARROLL is professor of economics at Johns
Hopkins University and the chief economist of the Consumer
Financial Protection Bureau. He is a former research associate of
the NBER. THOMAS F. CROSSLEY is professor in the Department
of Economics at the University of Essex. JOHN SABELHAUS is an
economist and chief of the Microeconomic Surveys Section at the
Federal Reserve Board in Washington, DC.

The University of Chicago Press, Chicago 60637
The University of Chicago Press, Ltd., London
© 2015 by the National Bureau of Economic Research
All rights reserved. Published 2015.
Printed in the United States of America

24 23 22 21 20 19 18 17 16 15   1 2 3 4 5

ISBN-13: 978-0-226-12665-4   (cloth)
ISBN-13: 978-0-226-19471-4   (e-book)
DOI: 10.7208/chicago/9780226194714.001.0001

Library of Congress Cataloging-in-Publication Data

Improving the measurement of consumer expenditures / edited by
    Christopher D. Carroll, Thomas F. Crossley, and John Sabelhaus.
        pages cm — (NBER studies in income and wealth ; volume 74)
        ISBN 978-0-226-12665-4 (cloth : alk. paper) — ISBN 978-0-226-
    19471-4 (e-book) 1. Cost and standard of living. 2. Consumption
    (Economics) I. Carroll, Chris. II. Crossley, Thomas F. III. Sabelhaus,
    John Edward. IV. Series: Studies in income and wealth; v. 74.
        HD6983.I57 2015
        339.4'70287—dc23
                                                          2014035488

♾ This paper meets the requirements of ANSI/NISO Z39.48-1992
(Permanence of Paper).

Relation of the Directors to the
Work and Publications of the
National Bureau of Economic Research

1. The object of the NBER is to ascertain and present to the economics profession, and to the public more generally, important economic facts and their interpretation in a scientific manner without policy recommendations. The Board of Directors is charged with the responsibility of ensuring that the work of the NBER is carried on in strict conformity with this object.

2. The President shall establish an internal review process to ensure that book manuscripts proposed for publication DO NOT contain policy recommendations. This shall apply both to the proceedings of conferences and to manuscripts by a single author or by one or more co-authors but shall not apply to authors of comments at NBER conferences who are not NBER affiliates.

3. No book manuscript reporting research shall be published by the NBER until the President has sent to each member of the Board a notice that a manuscript is recommended for publication and that in the President's opinion it is suitable for publication in accordance with the above principles of the NBER. Such notification will include a table of contents and an abstract or summary of the manuscript's content, a list of contributors if applicable, and a response form for use by Directors who desire a copy of the manuscript for review. Each manuscript shall contain a summary drawing attention to the nature and treatment of the problem studied and the main conclusions reached.

4. No volume shall be published until forty-five days have elapsed from the above notification of intention to publish it. During this period a copy shall be sent to any Director requesting it, and if any Director objects to publication on the grounds that the manuscript contains policy recommendations, the objection will be presented to the author(s) or editor(s). In case of dispute, all members of the Board shall be notified, and the President shall appoint an ad hoc committee of the Board to decide the matter; thirty days additional shall be granted for this purpose.

5. The President shall present annually to the Board a report describing the internal manuscript review process, any objections made by Directors before publication or by anyone after publication, any disputes about such matters, and how they were handled.

6. Publications of the NBER issued for informational purposes concerning the work of the Bureau, or issued to inform the public of the activities at the Bureau, including but not limited to the NBER Digest and Reporter, shall be consistent with the object stated in paragraph 1. They shall contain a specific disclaimer noting that they have not passed through the review procedures required in this resolution. The Executive Committee of the Board is charged with the review of all such publications from time to time.

7. NBER working papers and manuscripts distributed on the Bureau's web site are not deemed to be publications for the purpose of this resolution, but they shall be consistent with the object stated in paragraph 1. Working papers shall contain a specific disclaimer noting that they have not passed through the review procedures required in this resolution. The NBER's web site shall contain a similar disclaimer. The President shall establish an internal review process to ensure that the working papers and the web site do not contain policy recommendations, and shall report annually to the Board on this process and any concerns raised in connection with it.

8. Unless otherwise determined by the Board or exempted by the terms of paragraphs 6 and 7, a copy of this resolution shall be printed in each NBER publication as described in paragraph 2 above.

Contents

Prefatory Note

This volume contains revised versions of most of the papers presented at the Conference on Research in Income and Wealth entitled "Improving the Measurement of Consumer Expenditures," held in Washington, DC, on December 2–3, 2011.

We gratefully acknowledge the financial support for this conference provided by the ESRC-funded Centre for Microdata Methods and Practice (ES/I034021/1). Support for the general activities of the Conference on Research in Income and Wealth is provided by the following agencies: Bureau of Economic Analysis, Bureau of Labor Statistics, Census Bureau, Board of Governors of the Federal Reserve System, Internal Revenue Service, and Statistics Canada.

We thank Christopher Carroll, Thomas Crossley, and John Sabelhaus who served as conference organizers and as editors of the volume. Chris, Tom, and John in turn wish to express their thanks to Brett Maranjian and Helena Fitz-Patrick of the NBER, who provided outstanding assistance with the conference and this volume, respectively.

Executive Committee, September 2013

John M. Abowd	Michael W. Horrigan
Susanto Basu	Charles R. Hulten (chair)
Andrew Bernard	Ron Jarmin
Ernst R. Berndt	J. Steven Landefeld
Carol A. Corrado	Brent Moulton
W. Erwin Diewert	Valerie Ramey
Robert C. Feenstra	Mark J. Roberts
John Greenlees	Daniel Sichel
John C. Haltiwanger	William Wascher

Introduction

Christopher D. Carroll, Thomas F. Crossley, and John Sabelhaus

As we write in the fall of 2012, many countries (including the United States) are embarking on ambitious multiyear projects to redesign their surveys of household expenditures. In most countries the decision to rethink has been prompted by a sense that existing methods are failing to achieve the surveys' principal objectives, at a time when the importance of those objectives is clearer than ever.

These concerns fit neatly into a broader agenda of improving the measurement of heterogeneity that has been gathering force for a number of years, reflected, for example, in the widely cited work of the Stiglitz-Sen-Fitoussi commission,[1] in the formation of an Organisation for Economic Co-operation and Development (OECD) International Expert Group for the compilation of micro statistics,[2] and in the recent decision by the US Bureau of Economic Analysis to explore constructing "satellite accounts" to account for microeconomic heterogeneity.

Economic theory suggests that a household's spending patterns reflect its economic circumstances better than any other indicator of resources, with the obvious corollary that accurate measurement of households' differences in spending choices would be among the most useful possible tools for understanding economic heterogeneity. This is why the growing concerns

Christopher D. Carroll is chief economist and director of research at the Consumer Financial Protection Bureau. Thomas F. Crossley is professor of economics at the University of Essex. John Sabelhaus is chief of the Microeconomic Surveys Section of the Division of Research and Statistics of the Board of Governors of the Federal Reserve System.

For acknowledgments, sources of research support, and disclosure of the authors' material financial relationships, if any, please see http://www.nber.org/chapters/c12658.ack.

1. Stiglitz, Sen, and Fitoussi (2009).
2. McCall (2012).

about the accuracy of expenditure data are so pertinent to the agenda of measurement of heterogeneity.

This volume brings together work by some of the world's leading experts on measurement of household spending in order to illuminate the difficulties and opportunities that lie ahead for the scholars and statisticians who will be taking up the challenge of producing better data. In broadest terms, the aim of the volume is to provide a knowledge base for agencies and researchers as they design new systems for improving expenditure measurement using household-level data. The volume's sixteen chapters were prepared by economists working on these issues in both academic and government settings, within the United States and in several other countries. (All chapters are based on papers presented at a Conference on Research in Income and Wealth [CRIW] held in Washington, DC, on December 2 and 3, 2011.)

The volume has four main sections. The first provides a framework for analyzing the issues involved in expenditure measurement, and includes a comprehensive review of what is already known about key methodological issues. The second section reviews the principal goals of collecting household-level expenditure data, outlining the various objectives that such surveys might satisfy, and implicitly or explicitly suggesting which goals are both feasible and important (especially in light of the existence of other data sources, like aggregate retail sales data, that might be able to answer some of the questions now addressed using household expenditure surveys).

The third section covers what is known about the existing Consumer Expenditure (CE) survey in the United States, with a focus on how well the survey tracks aggregate benchmarks, how it compares to similar surveys around the world, and how well it represents the underlying population being studied.

The fourth section reviews new modes of data collection, including the use of scanner data, Internet panels, and administrative data from government and private sources.

Coincident with the conference and the writing of this CRIW volume, the Bureau of Labor Statistics (BLS) sponsored a review by the National Academy of Sciences (NAS) of the CE redesign effort. That review panel began meeting around the same time that the CRIW conference was held, and released a detailed report in October 2012. The NAS panel members and staff had extensive interactions with authors of papers for this volume, and a number of the panelists and staff members attended the December 2011 conference at which preliminary versions of the papers were presented.

The NAS panel ultimately released a 260-page report on possible redesign alternatives that included numerous references to the work contained in this volume, and the panel requested (and received) permission to reproduce some of the exhibits prepared for the papers in this volume.[3] After reading

---

3. National Research Council (2013).

the panel's report, it seems clear that one conclusion upon which all panel members would agree is that a great deal of work remains to be done. Panel members were not able to agree fully on how best to proceed, and as a result the report contains a substantial dissent signed by a majority of the economists on the panel. (The panel included distinguished experts from a number of other fields including survey methodology, political science, and sociology, reflecting the broad scholarly uses to which the CE survey is put and the complexity it faces in achieving its goals.) Below we point out points of contact between the chapters in this volume and the NAS report.

In short, despite the important work undertaken by the panel, the question of how best to measure household-level expenditures remains unanswered, and this CRIW volume provides further evidence that while agreement may exist that fundamental redesign of household expenditure surveys is required, a great deal remains to be learned about what new methods of measurement would work better than those that have been employed in the past.

What Do We Already Know about Collecting Household Expenditure Data?

Chapter 1: "Asking Households about Expenditures: What Have We Learned?" (Thomas F. Crossley and Joachim K. Winter)

The starting point for the volume is a chapter by Thomas Crossley and Joachim Winter that summarizes what has been learned from previous studies about collecting household-level expenditure data. This extensive literature review is oriented around the key dimensions of the data collection process: survey mode, recall versus diary, disaggregation of expenditure categories, defining the response unit and choosing the respondent, reference period, the role of incentives, and the potential for reducing response errors in real time. This chapter's key contribution comes from its comprehensive approach and its global perspective; other chapters relating to data collection methodology per se generally make contributions on only one or two of these issues, and usually for a single country or a small number of countries.

Crossley and Winter are able to draw a number of conclusions about the various design decisions that have to be made in surveys that aim to collect household expenditure data. For example, they report evidence that diaries do not necessarily dominate recall surveys from a reporting perspective, and because there is incremental respondent burden in a diary, recall surveys may be preferable. They also find that research showing that higher levels of disaggregation improve recall may not be appropriate for the CE redesign question, because the CE already has much more detail than other surveys, and recent experiments with more aggregated categories finds aggregates that line up well with the more detailed CE (findings that are confirmed in chapters 13 and 14 by Michael Hurd and Susann Rohwedder later in this volume). Review of the literature on other questions about data collection strategy yield more mixed results, and the authors identify several specific questions where more focused research is warranted.

Crossley and Winter's review describes the state of the international literature on expenditure surveys, as it stood at the time of our conference. Naturally, they describe research in a number of areas that figure prominently in the NAS report. For example, the NAS report suggests that the redesign of the CE must make use of incentives, and discusses the problem of respondents "learning to say no" (also called "motivated underreporting"), particularly when surveys have a cascading structure. Crossley and Winter review research on both these points.

The NAS report is specifically focused on the CE surveys, while the Crossley-Winter chapter is not. Consequently, the former highlights some CE issues that do not get much attention in Crossley-Winter. The most important of these is the sheer cognitive load of the CE interview survey. The CE is very detailed both in terms of the number of expenditure categories collected and in the follow-up information requested on purchases. The NAS report put a great deal of emphasis on the difficulty that respondents face in recalling the information requested by the interview survey. This is undoubtedly an important point, and a key reason why many suggest that the CE needs to be redesigned.

Goals for the Expenditure Survey Redesign

The CRIW conference in December 2011 contained a number of presentations illustrating the multiple goals of collecting household-level expenditure data. Four of those presentations are included as chapters here, providing a useful representation of goals from a number of different user perspectives. The first perspective is from the BLS itself, and aims to illuminate the original goal of the CE in generating weights for the construction of the Consumer Price Index (CPI). The chapter compares the CE against alternative approaches to generating expenditure weights. The other goals represent a range of academic applications, including studying household spending responses in a panel-data framework, using expenditures as an alternative to income when measuring inequality and poverty, and using expenditure data to model household-level spending responses to changes in prices and incomes.

Chapter 2: "Constructing a PCE-Weighted Consumer Price Index" (Caitlin Blair)

This chapter by Caitlin Blair seeks to answer the following question: How would our assessment of consumer price inflation change if we stopped using CE data to construct CPI expenditure weights and instead constructed weights using Bureau of Economic Analysis personal consumption expenditures (PCE)?

The question is important for CE redesign because of well-known divergence in rates of reporting across different types of spending in the CE.

For example, if the particular goods and services that are overweighted in the CE market basket are also the goods and services for which prices rose most rapidly, then the CPI will be biased upward relative to a PCE-weighted index.

Blair shows that the extent of CPI bias depends on the specific question being asked. If we adjust for conceptual and coverage differences between the two possible weighting schemes, then the results for overall inflation are not very different, at least for the time period being studied (2005–2010). If we do not adjust for conceptual differences, then some spending categories that are not well covered in the CE (especially employer-provided medical and spending on education) and that exhibit higher inflation over the study period do raise the overall inflation estimate by a noticeable amount—0.441 percentage points on the average twelve-month index change of 2.013 percentage points. This raises an important philosophical issue about what the CPI should be measuring—for example, do we want the (implicit) cost of employer-provided medical care to affect the CPI?

Chapter 3: "The Benefits of Panel Data in Consumer Expenditure Surveys" (Jonathan A. Parker, Nicholas S. Souleles, and Christopher D. Carroll)

The CE interview survey is unusual among national comprehensive household expenditure surveys in that it has a panel structure. Participating households are asked to complete five quarterly interviews. The first of these is designed primarily to bound recall; the subsequent four interviews are the basis for the data that is produced, yielding up to four observations on households spanning a period of up to a year. ("Up to" because many households do not complete all five interviews.) This chapter, by Jonathan Parker, Nicholas Souleles, and Christopher Carroll, assesses the value of this panel structure. They conclude that there is a strong case for retaining the panel element of the CE survey in any redesign, and that the panel structure of the CE interview survey is of value to both the core missions of the CE survey, such as price-index construction and poverty measurement, and to the research uses that the data serve.

The authors review the ways that the panel structure can improve measurement, for example, by reducing nonsampling error. One important aspect of this is that with a single recall period, surveys designers face a trade-off between greater recall error (with a longer recall period) or greater variability arising from purchase infrequency (with a shorter recall period). A design with repeated interviews on each sampled unit (a panel) relaxes this trade-off.

The authors also consider the role of the panel structure in the CE interview survey in supporting research. The key issues are heterogeneity and dynamics. The authors review how panel data allows for consistent estimation of parameters of interest in the presence of unobserved heterogeneity, and illustrate the argument with the example of studying the impact of stimulus tax rebates on spending. They also discuss how dynamic issues such as habits in spending behavior and the degree of mobility in spending behavior can be studied with panel data on consumption.

The NAS report noted that the CPI does not utilize the panel nature of the current CE. On the other hand, the panel acknowledged that economic research and policy analysis was an important use of the CE and that the panel nature of the data was a key feature that makes the CE useful for such research. Each of the three prototype redesigns put forward in the report includes a panel component, although one of the options has data collection at just two points, and variable response periods (by expenditure category) at each point. This design may not produce data that is very useful for economic research and policy analysis, as the report acknowledges and the dissent to the main report further emphasizes.

Chapter 4: "The Evolution of Income, Consumption, and Leisure Inequality in the United States, 1980–2010" (Orazio Attanasio, Erik Hurst, and Luigi Pistaferri)

An influential set of papers culminating in Meyer and Sullivan (2012) has argued that, among poor households, income is badly mismeasured, while spending is less mismeasured; an obvious implication is that poverty researchers should use data on spending (e.g., from the CE survey) rather than on income to measure household well-being. Separately, a literature sparked by Krueger and Perri (2006) has shown that inequality in spending as measured by data from the interview component of the CE survey remained fairly stable over the past three decades in the United States, even as income inequality has widened dramatically; however, from its inception this literature has been plagued with doubts about whether its main result reflects increasing measurement error rather than true economic patterns.

This is the context for the chapter by Orazio Attanasio, Erik Hurst, and Luigi Pistaferri, who compare changes in US household spending inequality over the past thirty years to changes in measured income inequality over the same period, using data that they argue can (at least partly) overcome the criticisms that have been leveled at the CE data. Using an impressive variety of evidence, Attanasio, Hurst, and Pistaferri show that ever-increasing measurement error in the CE data explains the discrepancy between trends in spending inequality and income inequality. Specifically, they estimate spending inequality by (a) using a simple demand system that allows for measurement error; (b) using data from the diary component of the CE survey for items where past research has shown measurement error to be small; (c) using data on durables purchases, which also arguably have relatively small measurement error; and (d) using spending data from the Panel Study of Income Dynamics, which arguably are better measured than overall expenditures in the CE survey. With all four of these methods they find an increase in spending inequality that roughly matches the increase in income inequality, in sharp contrast to the pattern exhibited in the raw CE interview data. Together with the work of others whom they cite, this chapter provides a compelling illustration of the importance of the growing measurement problems faced by expenditure surveys. The question (growing inequality in household well-being) is of great interest to policymakers and the public, but bad data has the potential to lead to profoundly mistaken conclusions about the nature, causes, and appropriate policy responses to the real economic changes that are taking place.

Chapter 5: "Using the CE to Model Household Demand"
(Laura Blow, Valérie Lechene, and Peter Levell)

The final chapter on CE goals is by Laura Blow, Valérie Lechene, and Peter Levell, and seeks to answer the following question: How does the availability of comprehensive household demographic and labor force data affect estimates of demand system parameters? The demand system parameters of interest are price and income elasticities, which are used extensively in structural policy models. These estimated elasticities are the key to predictions about general equilibrium effects of tax, transfer, and other government policies that affect consumer spending. The importance of this chapter for CE redesign is underscored by the fact that one could never properly estimate these elasticities without using household-level spending data, but one also needs demographic and labor force variables because the estimated demand parameters vary systematically based on those characteristics.

Blow, Lechene, and Levell estimate a number of different demand systems using a two-stage approach and different population subsamples. The commodities in their nondurable goods demand system are food in, food out, entertainment, apparel, utilities, and motor fuel. The authors conclude that the estimated demand system parameters are in fact dependent on the conditioning used to estimate the system, where conditioning refers to number of rooms in the housing unit, labor force participation, and stock of cars. The bottom line conclusion is that we need all the household-level data to be preserved in one place if we want to provide policymakers with appropriate demand system parameters for modeling policy changes.

The NAS panel emphasized the importance of nonexpenditure information collected in the CE, which is important for many types of research conducted using the CE; for example, the demand system estimation described in this chapter. Indeed, one key NAS panel recommendation involves better alignment of the timing for income and expenditure flows, which will improve the reliability of estimates that use income and other nonexpenditure information along with expenditure data.

Evaluating the Existing CE Survey

Much of the impetus for redesigning the CE survey comes from a growing realization that the current BLS methodology leaves much to be desired in representing aggregate household spending. Assessing the extent to which the CE diverges from aggregate benchmarks requires a comprehensive reconciliation of exactly what is being measured, and a comparison of how different approaches using the CE itself (diary versus interview) give different answers. Both the fact that CE aggregates are below aggregate benchmarks and the fact that the discrepancies are worsening has motivated further investigations into whether the same phenomenon is occurring in other similar surveys around the world, and to what extent underrepresentation of the wealthiest families may be affecting comparisons against aggregate totals.

Chapter 6: "Understanding the Relationship: CE Survey and PCE" (William Passero, Thesia I. Garner, and Clinton McCully)

The chapter by William Passero, Thesia I. Garner, and Clinton McCully seeks to answer the following question: How does the new concordance between CE and personal consumption expenditures (PCE) developed by BLS and Bureau of Economic Analysis (BEA) staff affect how well the two data series track each other over time? The authors of this chapter have written extensively about CE versus PCE aggregates in previous papers, and they focus this chapter on the specific issue of how that concordance is affected by the new BEA spending categories introduced a few years ago. The importance of this chapter for CE redesign is paramount, because assessing whether the CE is comprehensively capturing household spending necessarily begins with comparing aggregates across spending categories and time.

Passero, Garner, and McCully focus on two aspects of the question. First, how much conceptual overlap is there between CE and PCE? Second, how do the ratios of comparable CE to PCE aggregates vary across spending categories and time periods? The conceptual differences between the two data sets are significant. As of 2010, only 62 percent of PCE expenditures will, in principle, be captured by the CE, and only 80 percent of CE expenditures will, in principle, show up in the PCE. These comparability ratios are highest (94 percent for both PCE and CE) for nondurable goods and lowest (48 percent for PCE, 73 percent for the CE) for spending on services. Regarding trends over time and focusing on comparable goods and services only, the authors conclude that CE to PCE ratios have steadily decreased. For total comparable goods and services, CE to PCE ratios decreased from 84 percent in 1992 to 74 percent in 2010. The greatest decline in CE to PCE ratios is for durables, with a decrease of 24 percentage points. Ratios for comparable services dropped the least, with a percentage decrease of 10 percentage points. The NAS panel requested (and were granted) the ability to cite numbers from this chapter in their report, as part of the core evidence about deterioration of CE representativeness over time.

Chapter 7: "The Validity of Consumption Data: Are the Consumer Expenditure Interview and Diary Surveys Informative?" (Adam Bee, Bruce D. Meyer, and James X. Sullivan)

This chapter, by Adam Bee, Bruce D. Meyer, and James X. Sullivan, provides an assessment of the quality of the data collected by the current CE surveys. While data generated by the CE surveys has been assessed against various benchmarks before, the key contribution of this chapter is to assess the CE interview survey and CE diary survey separately (past analyses have often assessed a combination of the two). This approach delivers a number of insights. The most of important is that in careful comparisons to the national accounts, the interview survey appears to perform better than the diary survey. Many large categories of expenditure seem to be well measured in the interview survey, in that the ratio of implied aggregate spending to the relevant national accounts figures is close to 1 and stable over time. The authors note that the diary data also contain many more reports of zero expenditure in a consumption category. These zeros, which may be related to purchase infrequency, cause significant problems when using the data to assess levels of poverty and inequality. Overall, the authors argue that for many purposes the interview data may be superior to the diary data.

In additional analysis, the authors show that the CE compares well to external sources on ownership and value of durables, particularly homes and cars. This is important for analysis that requires an imputation of households' total consumption, including service flows from durables. Such a measure is required, for example, in assessing living standards and poverty. They also provide some evidence that the CE interview survey sample is representative of the target population along many dimensions, although they acknowledge concerns about underrepresentation at the top of the income distribution, which are raised in the next chapter.

The main NAS report rejects the central conclusion of this chapter—that by many measures the current CE interview survey data are superior to the data from the diary survey. The report argues that it is not possible to determine which mode is inherently better, and all of the prototype redesigns developed by the panel include a significant diary (or journal) component. Those proposals do, however, include significant changes to the current diary mode of the CE, including the adoption of technologies for self-administered data collection (including tablet computers and home scanners).

Overall, the NAS report calls for a greater, rather than lesser, role for diary modes of data collection. The dissent to the main report, which was cowritten by one of the authors of this chapter, expresses a reservation about a move to greater reliance on diary-based data collection. The dissent points to the evidence in this chapter, and to earlier evidence on the relative quality of diary and recall methods summarized in chapter 1 by Crossley and Winter.

Chapter 8: "Is the Consumer Expenditure Survey Representative by Income?" (John Sabelhaus, David Johnson, Stephen Ash, David Swanson, Thesia I. Garner, John Greenlees, and Steve Henderson)

The underreporting of expenditures was cited as a major motivation for the NAS review of the CE redesign effort. This chapter, by John Sabelhaus, David Johnson, Stephen Ash, David Swanson, Thesia I. Garner, John

Greenlees, and Steve Henderson begins with the observation that under-reporting can arise in two main ways. It could be that high-income, and hence high-spending, households are underrepresented in the CE sample, or it could be that some or all households underreport their spending. Of course, both sources of error could be operative.

The authors bring a valuable new data source to bear on the question of the importance of these two sources of error. This data set links sampled units from the CE interview survey, both those that responded and those that did not, to their zip-code level average adjusted gross income (AGI). This allows the authors to examine directly response rates by AGI percentile income groups. It turns out that the CE response rate is fairly constant between the 10th and 90th percentile of AGI, but that there is less nonresponse in the bottom decile and significantly more nonresponse above the 90th percentile. Households in the top 5 percent of zip code-mean AGI are about 10 percent-age points less likely to respond to the survey. This is the first direct evidence that high-income households are underrepresented in the CE sample.

Nevertheless, the authors argue that the underrepresentation of high-income households in the CE sample cannot close all the gap between national accounts expenditure totals and aggregates derived from CE data: multiplying the missing income by estimates of the marginal propensity to spend for the high-income group does not deliver enough extra spending. Thus it seems that underreporting of spending also plays a role. The authors note that, given income, spending reports of the lowest-income households in the CE survey are implausibly high, and the spending reports of the highest-income households are implausibly low (implying rates of wealth accumulation that are not consistent with wealth surveys).

Thus it seems that both underrepresentation of high-income households and underreporting of spending by high-income households contribute to overall underreporting of spending in the CE survey. The authors conclude that the CE design effort must consider strategies for addressing these twin problems and discuss several, including the oversampling of more affluent households (as in the Survey of Consumer Finances) and the streamlining of the data collection process to make it feasible for high-income households to accurately estimate their spending. The main NAS report and the accompanying dissent both raised the issue of oversampling high-income families, because BLS did not emphasize the importance of that component in the redesign proposals that were given to the panel. The second issue, streamlining data collection, is also a key theme in the NAS recommendations.

Chapter 9: "A Comparison of Micro and Macro Expenditure
Measures across Countries Using Differing Survey Methods"
(Garry Barrett, Peter Levell, and Kevin Milligan)

A final empirical perspective on the current CE is the chapter by Garry Barrett, Peter Levell, and Kevin Milligan. These authors analyze how differences in expenditure data collection methodologies across countries are reflected in differences in the quality of data collected. The measures of data quality that the authors consider include both response rates (fraction of selected respondents who participate in the survey) and coverage rates (ratios of survey spending aggregates to published national account aggregates for the same categories of spending). The coverage rates estimates for the CE are consistent with findings in other chapters in this volume, and also permeate the NAS report. The importance of this chapter for CE redesign is that we may be able to learn something from divergent experiences across countries. Barrett, Levell, and Milligan choose four Anglophone countries for their comparison: Australia, Canada, the United Kingdom, and the United States. Their chapter begins with a concise description of how the four surveys differ, both in terms of how the samples are drawn and how the surveys are conducted. The authors show a general deterioration in survey response rates across all four countries since the 1980s, but a general decline in coverage only for the United Kingdom and the United States. That is, the ratio of survey to aggregate spending in Australia and Canada has not deteriorated over time. One interesting possibility the authors consider is that the decline in coverage rates may be correlated with shifting income distributions. If households in the top 1 percent of the income distribution are less likely to participate in the survey, then an increasing share of income going to the top 1 percent will cause a small drop in response rates but a large drop in coverage. The authors find some evidence that this helps explain differences in coverage trends across countries.

Alternative Approaches to Data Collection

The CRIW conference and this volume were motivated by the prospects of addressing the shortcomings of current data collection methodologies, and at the same time improving the ability to achieve the agreed upon goals for collecting the data in the first place. Simultaneously improving measurement and achieving multiple goals (while still adhering to a statistical agency's budget constraint) will require considering new approaches to collecting data, which means moving beyond the traditional survey setting. Toward that end, the remaining seven chapters in this volume are focused on methodological changes such as real-time cash-flow reconciliation (balance-edit) to help minimize misreporting, combining survey and administrative data, self-interviews using the Internet, the effect of allowing respondents to choose reporting periods, and scanner technologies. Many of these possibilities also received attention in the NAS report, and the report encouraged the testing of new technologies as means of improving particularly self-completed data collection methodologies.

Yet another new way of measuring a household's total spending has emerged from Scandinavian countries in which government agencies collect extensive information about each taxpayer in a centralized database. In principle, if perfect data on wealth and income data over time were available to tax authorities, it would be possible (for example) to compute the amount of an individual's spending by presuming that any non-capital-gains-related increase in wealth reflected a choice to spend less than measured after-tax income (the residual method). Of course, there are many complexities in implementing the residual method in practice, ranging from the difficulty of observing capital gains and losses to the existence of forms of income and wealth that are not reported to the tax authorities.

Both Denmark and Sweden happen to have conducted traditional consumer expenditure surveys during the period when the national registry data are available. And in both cases, scholars contributing to this volume have managed to link the data for participants in those expenditure surveys to the national registry data for the surveyed individuals. These two chapters differ somewhat from the others in this section; while the method is indeed new, it is not one that is likely to be implementable (or at least not very quickly implementable) in countries that have not built national registry systems. For this reason, and because this method does provide the detailed information on expenditure by category that is required for many uses of the CE, this approach did not get much attention in the NAS report. Nevertheless, these chapters are also unique in that they provide the only method we know of for testing the "external validity" of existing survey methods. For this reason, they provide a useful background for the other chapters in this section, so we begin with them.

Chapter 10: "Measuring the Accuracy of Survey Responses Using Administrative Register Data: Evidence from Denmark" (Claus Thustrup Kreiner, David Dreyer Lassen, and Søren Leth-Petersen)

For Denmark, the chapter by Claus Thustrup Kreiner, David Dreyer Lassen, and Søren Leth-Petersen reports an extensive set of comparisons between the registry-based "residual" method of measuring spending and the survey-based method, with the explicit aim of extracting lessons about the pitfalls of surveys. On the whole, they find a disturbingly small correlation between spending as measured using the residual method and spending as measured by the survey; according to one metric, a regression of registry-measured spending on survey-measured spending yields a coefficient of 0.791 with an R^2 of only 0.46.

Among the many other interesting results in this chapter, one stands out as possibly the most important: answers to the expenditure survey's question about the household's total income had remarkably little correlation with income as measured by the tax authorities. The authors make a persuasive case that the data from the tax records are likely to be fairly accurate. This result is disturbing because almost all existing expenditure surveys rely on self-reported measures of income (like the one in the Danish survey) for a host of benchmarking and other purposes. Furthermore, total household income is much easier to compute than many of the other items about which households are questioned on such surveys. If households cannot accurately answer even a (comparatively) simple question like what their income was for the prior year, it is difficult to have confidence that the answers they are giving to other questions are accurate.

The authors examine whether various plausible kinds of confusion (between gross and net income, for example) might explain their disturbing results, but in the end they are not able to resolve the problem. They also show that the errors are nonclassical (that is, they are correlated in ex ante unknowable ways with characteristics of the population), which presents thorny statistical problems in figuring out appropriate methods of correcting for error.

The authors point out that the Danish government has encouraged the use of these data for research purposes, and a growing number of academic studies and statistical analyses have been conducted using them. For researchers who bring appropriate funding to the table, and who can make contact with a collaborator who can gain access to the data (naturally, access to the data is tightly restricted for security reasons), Denmark could become a uniquely useful "laboratory" for conducting experiments on what works and what does not for survey measurement. For example, one question that the Committee on National Statistics panel report highlighted as crucially important, but despaired of as nearly unknowable, was the dynamic properties of survey-response error. That is, if a person makes an error of a given size in a given survey, if that person is reinterviewed at some later date are they likely to make exactly the same error, or an independent error, or something else? As the authors point out, questions of this type could be investigated by commissioning a study using Danish data, where "truth" is known to a reasonable degree of accuracy.

Chapter 11: "Judging the Quality of Survey Data by Comparison with 'Truth' as Measured by Administrative Records: Evidence from Sweden" (Ralph Koijen, Stijn Van Nieuwerburgh, and Roine Vestman)

The chapter by Ralph Koijen, Stijn Van Nieuwerburgh, and Roine Vestman takes up the case of Sweden. In principle, the data available to the Swedish government are even more impressive than in Denmark; this is a legacy of the Swedish wealth tax (which was abolished in 2007). In order to implement such a tax the authorities needed to be able to compute the net worth of each individual. For assessing individual tax obligations, an automatic reporting procedure from financial institutions to the tax authorities was set up, resulting in a mechanism by which highly disaggregated information on the income and wealth of all households flowed to government records. Individual financial asset, mutual fund, and real estate portfolios are provided at the single property and security level during the period covered by the expenditure survey.

Since spending (in this approach) is measured by comparing income to the change in wealth, being able to determine the extent to which wealth has changed as a result of capital gains or losses (and not a result of active saving or dissaving) is a crucial advantage. Other studies (including the Danish registry study) have had to make assumptions about the size of capital gains and losses, typically assuming that a fixed aggregate rate of return applied to all assets of a particular class. (See, e.g., Maki and Palumbo [2001], and chapter 14 of this volume by Hurd and Rohwedder).

The authors find that properly accounting for the idiosyncratic capital gains and losses does make a substantial difference to measured expenditures for many households, and that (intuitively) this problem is larger the greater a household's wealth.

Overall, they find that the mean and median levels of spending are similar in the two sources (their registry computations and the survey). Again, however, at the level of individual households the results are disturbing. Even among the subgroup that the authors identify as likely the best measured in their data (renters measured in December), the correlation between survey-based and registry-based consumption is only about 0.5, and the correlation is substantially lower for other groups of households. Indeed, and somewhat surprisingly, the relation between their registry-based measure of spending and the survey-based measure at the level of individual households is looser than the corresponding relation in the Danish study. This is true even though the authors present evidence that the Swedish registry's information on capital gains and losses does improve the coherence between the Swedish registry-based measure of spending and the survey-based measure. A possible interpretation is that while the Swedish registry-based data is better, the Swedish survey-based data is worse than in Denmark. Or perhaps some other aspect of the Swedish registry data is worse.

One hint that the Swedish survey data may be seriously problematic is that, among persons who are known (from the reliable national registry records) to have purchased a vehicle during the last twelve months before the date of the survey, only 71.2 percent of survey respondents report having purchased this vehicle. Since vehicle purchases have long been viewed as one of the most reliable kinds of data obtained by household surveys, this is surprising, and suggests either that the Swedish survey was unusually inaccurate or that the presumption among researchers that vehicle purchases are measured well is misplaced.

One particular finding resonates with the message of Aguiar and Bils (2011): the authors find that, in the survey, spending is particularly understated for richer households. It is not obvious a priori that the biases in a Swedish spending survey should be similar to those in an American survey, and this result suggests that it is not unreasonable to hope more broadly that lessons obtained in one country may apply to other countries as well.

Chapter 12: "Exploring a Balance Edit Approach in the
Consumer Expenditure Quarterly Interview Survey"
(Scott Fricker, Brandon Kopp, and Nhien To)

Reporting detailed spending is a difficult task for households, and so it is perhaps unsurprising that some, or perhaps many, households underreport their spending. Some comprehensive household spending surveys include a "balance edit" as a data-control measure. A balance edit compares a household's reports of spending, income, and changes in assets and liabilities. These totals are, of course, linked by the household's budget constraint: the difference between income and spending must be flows to or from assets and liabilities. Where the reported elements of a household's budget constraint are out of balance by a predetermined amount, respondents are given the opportunity to review and revise their responses. Early versions of the CE survey had such a measure, but it was eliminated in the major redesign of 1972, in part because it was thought to be infeasible to conduct the balance edit in the context of the quarterly interview survey introduced at that time. However, research based on other surveys suggests that a balance edit can be useful in improving households' reports of spending and income.

This chapter, by Scott Fricker, Brandon Koop, and Nhien To, reports on a small-scale test of a modified version of the CE interview survey with a balance edit procedure. The test was conducted in the Office of Survey Methods Research Laboratory, and this allowed the authors to use cognitive testing methods and participant debriefing to investigate not only if the balance edit works, but how it works.

In the experiment, the balance edit improved the balance for a majority of participants, but only a small fraction of respondents were able to achieve balance. Debriefing revealed very heterogeneous comprehension of, and reaction to, the balance edit. While most respondents understood the measure and had neutral or positive reactions to it, there was a group of respondents who struggled to understand the balance edit and a second group who had a negative reaction to it. The latter included individuals whose spending exceeded their income. The authors conclude that balance edit procedures have some potential for improving data quality, but that there are significant issues to be considered in the design and implementation of any such procedure and the usefulness of the procedure is likely to depend on specific details of a redesigned CE survey.

The use of a balance edit or similar methods to improve data quality did not get much attention in the NAS report. The report does note that this method has recently been dropped from the Canadian Budget Survey, as it transited to greater reliance on diaries. The dissent to the main report felt that the report could have put greater emphasis on ways to monitor data quality, and cited the use of budget balance as one possible approach.

Chapter 13: "Measuring Total Household Spending in a Monthly Internet Survey: Evidence from the American Life Panel" (Michael D. Hurd and Susann Rohwedder)

The first of two chapters by Michael Hurd and Susann Rohwedder presents a potentially revolutionary new measurement tool for household expenditures: an Internet panel. Panel participants agree to answer questions using an Internet-enabled device (they are given such a device if they do not have one) on a regular schedule in exchange for a payment to compensate them for their time and effort. While it seems reasonable to worry about the representativeness of such a sample, at some point, as more and more daily routines of life get integrated into the Internet, it may become more reasonable to question the representativeness of a sample not conducted using Internet tools. (This point is especially compelling given the plummeting response rates for non-Internet-based survey methods.) The proliferation of Internet-based collection methods for such data is creating the knowledge needed to adjust the sample to correct for bias. A proof of the effectiveness of such sample adjustment came from the 2012 elections in the United States: a prominent expert ranked the entirely Internet-based Google Consumer Polls as the second-most accurate among all pollsters using all survey methods.[4]

Hurd and Rohwedder report a host of interesting results obtained by adding a carefully considered set of spending questions (based on experience gained from the Health and Retirement Study) to the financial crisis surveys that they began conducting in the American Life Panel (which interviews about 2,500 households on a regular basis) immediately after the onset of the recent financial crisis. Using a variety of methodological innovations, they produce a measure that appears to capture the bulk of the spending measured by the far more expensive and elaborate CE survey. Furthermore, because of the panel structure of their survey, they can observe changes in spending patterns in response to economic events like movements in the stock market.

In their first financial crisis survey (November 2008), 73 percent of households reported that they had reduced spending because of the economic crisis. Prompted by this striking result, and by their knowledge that understanding the spending response to the crisis would be critical for analyzing it, they began working to establish a monthly interview schedule for spending questions, which was implemented in May 2009, with monthly data available thereafter. A particularly interesting finding is the discrepancy between the recovery in spending at the median and at the mean. They find that both mean and median spending reached a trough in May 2010, but that (by the time the data sample used in their chapter ended) median monthly spend-

---

4. Silver (2012).

ing had recovered only 8 percent from its trough while mean spending had recovered by 11 percent. These are the kinds of high-frequency results that heretofore have been possible to calculate only years later when (for example) the cleaned and edited CE survey becomes available. Their chapter shows the potential for getting at least a rough-and-ready measure of how distributions are changing nearly in real time.

Chapter 14: "Wealth Dynamics and Active Saving at Older Ages" (Michael Hurd and Susann Rohwedder)

A second contribution by Michael Hurd and Susan Rohwedder explores a classic question in the economics of life cycle behavior—Do most people aim to spend their wealth before they die?—using another relatively new tool for measuring spending. Over the past decade, the US Health and Retirement Study (HRS) has added a battery of spending and other questions (the Consumption and Activities Mail Survey [CAMS]) to its core household questionnaire. Hurd and Rohwedder show that the HRS's CAMS data match the spending of similarly aged households in the CE survey reasonably well (especially given the vastly smaller resources employed in the CAMS measurement exercise), with the CAMS measure generally exceeding the corresponding CE measure by between 8 and 16 percentage points. (Since a primary problem of the CE survey is that it misses substantial amounts of spending [cf. Attanasio, Hurst, and Pistaferri in chapter 4, this volume, and the papers cited therein], it is even possible that the CAMS comes closer to the truth than the CE does.)

Turning to the motivating question (do people draw down their wealth as they age), the chapter is able to use the CAMS measure of spending in combination with the HRS's fairly complete measures of income to construct a measure of "active saving" (the difference between income and expenditures). The authors then compare that measure to the results obtained by examining the changes in wealth across survey waves. They find broadly consistent results: while single individuals do appear to be drawing down their wealth, elderly couples continue to save (presumably in order to finance the spending of the survivor when one of them dies).

The chapter illustrates the point that adding carefully considered spending questions to existing surveys may not be as costly as once thought, and that important topics can be studied using such questions. The interesting contrast is between the "bottom up" survey method traditionally employed by CE surveys (asking about spending category-by-category for narrowly defined categories of products), and the more aggregated approach in CAMS-type surveys, which aims at a "big picture" and does not worry about getting spending details. While results from big picture questions may not be useful in constructing basket weights for price indices, the answers to such questions are key for understanding issues of saving, overall inequality, and household finances.

Chapter 15: "Measuring Household Spending and Payment Habits:
The Role of 'Typical' and 'Specific' Time Frames in Survey Questions"
(Marco Angrisani, Arie Kapteyn, and Scott Schuh)

In designing recall expenditure questions, two important issues are the length of the recall period (a week? a month?) and whether the question should refer to a specific period (such as last week) or a "typical" or "usual" period. Survey response theory tells us that different question designs may induce very different response styles. Longer recall periods and typical periods are more likely to lead to rate-based estimation, while respondents are more likely to enumerate when faced with shorter and specific recall periods. Short periods suffer from less recall error, but exhibit higher variability due to purchase infrequency. Specific recall periods may exhibit variability due to purchase infrequency or seasonal effects. How different designs perform is ultimately an empirical question.

This chapter, by Marco Angrisani, Arie Kapteyn, and Scott Schuh, reports on an experimental module in the American Life Panel (ALP). Respondents were asked the number and amount of purchases by different payment methods (debit cards, cash, credit card, and personal check). Respondents were interviewed four times. For each respondent, subsequent interviews switched between typical and specific formats, with the format of the initial interview randomly assigned. Within each interview respondents were asked about different recall periods (a day, a week, a month, and a year), with the order of different periods randomly assigned. Results from the first round of interviews are reported in this chapter.

On average, respondents report higher numbers of payments and greater amounts for short recall periods (a day or a week). For most payment methods, the probability of reporting nonzero payments is higher for typical than for specific periods, but amounts spent are systematically lower for typical periods. These results illustrate the important influence of recall period type and length on reporting behavior.

This chapter shows that type (specific/typical) and length of recall period greatly affect household-reporting behavior. The current CE interview survey uses a three-month recall period for most goods and the NAS report argues that this is very long for actual recall of many items. One of the prototype redesigns moves away from a common reporting period for all expenditure categories. On the other hand, the issue of specific versus typical periods does not seem to have received much attention in the report.

Chapter 16: "The Potential Use of In-Home Scanner Technology for
Budget Surveys" (Andrew Leicester)

Another novel mode of data collection is the use of in-home scanners to record information in individual purchases; market research firms have developed these devices as a tool for measuring the effects of advertising and for other commercial purposes. This chapter by Andrew Leicester considers how scanner data might be used in the context of a comprehensive survey of household expenditures.

His chapter yields a number of insights that could guide future choices by statistical agencies. One disappointing result is that spending patterns of different households within the same store are quite different. This is discouraging because if all consumers had the same spending patterns for a given store, then it would be possible to impute to a household detailed spending patterns by category of goods based just on the distribution of their spending across store types. Leicester's result shows that this would lead to mistakes (at least at the level of an individual household).

Leicester also finds results that could be helpful in understanding differences between survey results from interview surveys (which typically cover an extended time period, like three months) and results from diary surveys (which typically cover a shorter period, like two weeks). For example, over any given two-week period Leicester finds that a high proportion of households buy no fish. If household-specific expenditure weights for a CPI were constructed using such data (as, Leicester reports, has been done), the price of fish would have no effect on the computed household-specific inflation rate for these households. Yet, Leicester shows that when the time frame is extended (at its longest, to a year), the proportion of households who buy no fish is much lower. Broadly speaking, Leicester's results tend to suggest that in order to provide a reasonably accurate measure of a household's "true" spending patterns (for purposes like constructing individual- or group-specific CPIs), it will be necessary to collect data over an extended time interval, perhaps as long as a year. Two-week diary surveys are not adequate for this purpose.

This is an important conclusion, in part because it speaks directly to a major source of dissent among members of the Committee on National Statistics panel that BLS convened to provide advice on revising the CE survey. The dissenting members believed that diary survey approaches should be abandoned because even if the data obtained from them were accurate, the time frame covered by diary surveys is too short for the data to have any meaningful economic use. Leicester's results bolster the dissenters' argument by showing that the expenditures that a household makes over a two-week period are very far from being a good picture of their expenditure patterns over an entire year. Indeed, he shows that patterns of expenditures are markedly different even between the quarterly and the annual frequency. This suggests that to obtain a reasonably useful picture of a household's expenditure patterns it may be necessary to collect data for a period as long as a full year.

References

Aguiar, Mark A., and Mark Bils. 2011. "Has Consumption Inequality Mirrored Income Inequality?" NBER Working Paper no. 16807, Cambridge, MA.
Krueger, Dirk, and Fabrizio Perri. 2006. "Does Income Inequality Lead to Consumption Inequality? Evidence and Theory." *Review of Economic Studies* 73 (1): 163–93.
Maki, Dean M., and Michael G. Palumbo. 2001. "Disentangling the Wealth Effect: A Cohort Analysis of Household Saving in the 1990s." Finance and Economics Discussion Series 2001–21, Board of Governors of the Federal Reserve System.
McCall, Robert. 2012. "Development of International Guidelines and Frameworks for Micro Statistics on Household Income, Consumption and Wealth." Presentation at 32nd General Conference of the International Association for Research in Income and Wealth. http://www.iariw.org/ papers/2012/McCollPaper.pdf.
Meyer, Bruce D., and James X. Sullivan. 2012. "Winning the War: Poverty from the Great Society to the Great Recession." *Brookings Papers on Economic Activity* 45 (2): 133–200.
National Research Council. 2013. *Measuring What We Spend: Toward a New Consumer Expenditure Survey*. Washington, DC: National Academies Press.
Silver, Nate. 2012. "Which Polls Fared Best and Worst in the 2012 Presidential Race?" http://fivethirtyeight.blogs.nytimes.com/2012/11/10/which-polls-fared-best-and-worst-in-the-2012-presidential-race/.
Stiglitz, J. E., A. Sen, and J. P. Fitoussi. 2009. "Report by the Commission on the Measurement of Economic Performance and Social Progress." Council on Foreign Relations. http://www.cfr.org/world/report-commission-measurement-economic-performance-social-progress/p22847.

I

What Do We Already Know about Collecting Household Expenditure Data?

1

Asking Households about Expenditures
What Have We Learned?

Thomas F. Crossley and Joachim K. Winter

1.1 Introduction

The importance of expenditure data to a wide range of important areas of both basic research and policy analysis has been well argued elsewhere (e.g., Deaton and Grosh 2000; Browning, Crossley, and Weber 2003). We believe the case is broadly accepted. At the same time, there is mounting evidence of problems with the household budget surveys conducted by national statistical agencies in many countries. The US Consumer Expenditure Survey exhibits declining response rates and a diminishing correspondence to national account aggregates, and similar patterns have emerged in the budget surveys of other nations (see the evidence in Barrett, Levell, and Milligan, chapter 9, this volume). There is also substantial evidence that survey design and data quality affect substantive conclusions about important research questions. A good example is the study of the evolution of inequality in the United States by Attanasio, Battistin, and Ichimura (2004).

These facts have led to a number of initiatives that investigate what might be done to improve the quality of expenditure data collected and available for research and other purposes. These initiatives include the NBER-CRIW

Thomas F. Crossley is professor of economics at the University of Essex and a research fellow of the Institute for Fiscal Studies. Joachim K. Winter is professor of economics at the University of Munich.

This chapter was written for the Conference on Improving the Measurement of Consumer Expenditures sponsored by the Conference on Research in Income and Wealth and the National Bureau of Economic Research, with support from the Centre for Microdata Methods and Practice. We thank conference participants for many helpful comments. Some of this work on this chapter was cofunded by the ESRC-funded Centre for Microeconomic Analysis of Public Policy at the Institute for Fiscal Studies (CPP, reference RES-544–28–5001). For acknowledgments, sources of research support, and disclosure of the authors' material financial relationships, if any, please see http://www.nber.org/chapters/c12666.ack.

conference to which this chapter is a contribution. Another is the Gemini Project, a multiyear, interdisciplinary research effort initiated by the US Bureau of Labor Statistics in 2009 to inform the redesign of the Consumer Expenditure (CE) surveys. The aim of the CE survey redesign is to improve data quality through a verifiable reduction in measurement error—particularly error caused by underreporting. Papers written for the Gemini Project, or presented at its regular meetings, investigate many of the issues covered in this survey.[1]

In fact, researchers and survey designers have been studying alternative ways of collecting household expenditure data for many years. The resulting literature is very disperse, distributed over many years, many countries, and multiple academic disciplines. Given the renewed attention that the collection of expenditure data is now receiving, it seems timely to try to bring that literature together in an accessible way. This chapter is an attempt to do so.

Like any short survey, this chapter is necessarily selective and circumscribed. It is aimed primarily at economists and researchers that traditionally analyze expenditure data, but who are becoming increasingly involved in the design of data collection. There is experience with the collection of expenditure data in both developed countries and in developing countries. Some of the issues are common and others specific; our focus is tilted toward evidence from developed countries, but we mention evidence from less developed countries when it seems to us particularly useful. Deaton and Grosh (2000) discuss many more results from developing countries.

1.2 The Design of Expenditure Surveys: The Evidence

In this section, we review existing studies on various design choices that arise in expenditure surveys: survey mode, recall versus diary surveys, response formats for recall questions, surveys that predict aggregates from components, the level of aggregation of expenditure items, the definition of the response unit, the reference period, the role of incentives, and approaches to reduce or correct response errors in real time.

1.2.1 Survey Mode

A first important decision in the administration of household surveys concerns the survey mode, the most common options being personal (face-to-face) interviews, telephone interviews, and self-administered questionnaires. All three modes could be based on a paper questionnaire or a computer interface. Other than for self-administered surveys, including "leave behind" questionnaires in personal interviews, the use of paper questionnaires has

---

1. Details on the Gemini Project, including project papers, other materials, and recommendations, can be found online at http://www.bls.gov/cex/geminimaterials.htm (last accessed March 8, 2012).

become rare. Self-administered questionnaires are increasingly administered using the Internet. There is a large literature on how the survey mode affects responses that we certainly cannot review here (see Tourangeau, Rips, and Rasinski [2000] for an overview).[2]

Key aspects of the interaction between survey mode and response behavior that are relevant for expenditure measurement concern the comprehension of survey questions (since an interviewer can provide clarification of difficult questions, should this be allowed by the survey protocol) and the sensitivity or confidentiality of the target quantities (since the presence of an interviewer might increase such concerns). A third consideration is that self-administered surveys make it easier for respondents to look up information on hard-to-recall quantities such as asset holdings, should they be willing to do so. While there is a large literature on mode effects in survey research, there is little systematic evidence when it comes to asking for consumption expenditure.

Models of survey response behavior suggest that written surveys enhance respondents' understanding of survey questions relative to oral presentations. Kemsley (1965) noted that expenditure data collected by self-completed diaries does not exhibit statistically significant interviewer effects, while data collected by recall interviews does (the interviewer still plays a role with the diaries in that they drop off, explain, review, and collect them). While he interpreted this as sign of lower quality (e.g., greater subjectivity) in the latter, there is also the possibility that interviewer presence might have a positive (though uneven) effect on respondent comprehension, or on other steps in the response process.

Confidentiality concerns will be more relevant in personal than in self-administered interviews. This would suggest that personal interviews should result in lower estimates on potentially sensitive goods, such as alcohol, and there is some evidence that this is the case (Silberstein and Scott 1991). On the other hand, a consistent finding of many studies is that response rates to total household expenditure questions are higher than response rates to comparable income questions (Browning, Crossley, and Weber 2003), suggesting that respondents view questions about broad categories of expenditure as being less sensitive than comparable income questions. This interpretation has been corroborated in the recent UK focus group studies summarized by d'Ardenne and Blake (2011).

Essig and Winter (2009) conducted a controlled survey experiment on mode effects in household surveys. In the data from the German SAVE household survey they analyzed, a random group of respondents answered sensitive questions, including those on household income and assets, using a questionnaire that was left behind by the interviewer rather than as part of the main interview so that it could be answered in private and independently of the rest of

---

2. Several chapters in this volume deal with using the Internet to elicit consumption expenditure, so in this chapter we do not discuss issues that are specific to Internet surveys in detail.

the survey interview. In comparison to the computer-assisted personal interview (CAPI) mode, rates of nonresponse were lower in the paper-and-pencil drop-off questionnaire. This effect was pronounced for all six asset categories they analyzed, while there was no significant effect on item nonresponse to the question on household net income. This result suggests that the strength of mode effects is not constant across different target quantities that vary in sensitivity. An alternative interpretation is that households were willing to look up their asset holdings in their records when the leave-behind questionnaire allowed them to do so, the premise being that asset holdings are more difficult to recall from memory during a survey interview than income.

Bonke and Fallesen (2010) offered survey respondents the choice between answering a telephone or an Internet survey (their main research interest was the role of incentives; see below). The study included both expenditure and time-use questions. Overall, they found that response quality was higher when respondents chose to participate in the Internet survey over the telephone interview. Due to the self-selection of respondents, the mode effect cannot, however, be interpreted causally.

Safir and Goldenberg (2008) analyze variation in the mode of administration of the Consumer Expenditure Survey. They argue that while telephone interviewing may impact the quality of CE data relative to that obtained by personal visit interviewing, mode effects can be mitigated by using "recall aids" in both modes (for example, through a mailed information booklet and user-friendly checklists for records and receipts).

An important concern with using a mixed-mode design is that response rates might be different across modes. Shin, Johnson, and Rao (2012) compare unit and item response rates in Web and mail survey modes in the 2008 Gallup Health Panel Survey. They find that the Web survey mode produces a lower unit response rate compared to the mail mode. However, the Web mode elicits higher data quality in terms of item response to both closed and open-ended questions. These mode effects on data quality remain after controlling for sociodemographic characteristics.

Summary. The survey mode influences response behavior via various channels, the most important being comprehension of the questionnaire, ease of recall and information look-up, and confidentiality and sensitivity of the responses. Given that these channels interact, there cannot, in our view, be an easy answer to the question of which survey mode works best when it comes to consumption expenditure. Moreover, while there is a large literature on mode effects in survey research, we are not aware of a systematic, controlled experimental study of how survey mode affects response quality in expenditure surveys along these channels.

1.2.2 Strategies for the Collection of Expenditure Data: Recall versus Diary

A second fundamental design choice in expenditure measurement is whether respondents are asked to report how much they spend on consumption goods in a certain period (the recall approach) or whether they fill in a diary over a certain period of time in which they record every single expense (the diary approach). A final strategy for measuring consumer expenditure is the use of home scanner data; this approach is covered in detail by Leicester (chapter 16, this volume) and therefore not discussed here. Recall surveys of expenditure have typically been conducted by interviewers, raising the mode issues discussed in the last section. However, there have been a number of recent experiments with recall expenditure surveys administered by mail and by Internet (Hurd and Rohwedder 2009, 2010) so that collection mode and collection method are no longer tightly linked. For each of the recall and diary methods, there are additional design choices to be made, such as the length of the reference period (both recall and diary) and the level of disaggregation and the response format. We will review these aspects in the following sections, but first, we review evidence that concerns the choice between recall and diary approaches.

Problems with Recall Methods

The literature on survey response behavior noted early on that questions that require recalling quantities from memory are difficult to answer (Gray 1955). There is now substantial evidence of "forgetting": that memory declines with the length of the recall period, leading to underestimation (see Sudman, Bradburn, and Schwartz [1996] for a review). The situation is complicated by the fact that forgetting does not occur at random, but might be differential across respondents and types of questions.

A key development in the literature on recall expenditure questions was the identification of "telescoping" as a significant problem by Neter and Waksberg (1964). This is the phenomena of respondents erroneously including in their response expenditures that occurred before the specified recall period, leading to an overestimation of expenditure in the recall period. Neter and Waksberg documented this phenomena in the CE (particularly, home alterations and repairs). Telescoping is thought to arise because remembering dates is particularly difficult. This leads to an overestimation of expenditure in the recall period since uncertainty over dates increases as one goes back farther in time. Thus, it is more likely for an older expenditure to be mistakenly placed in the recall period than it is for a more recent expenditure to be mistakenly placed prior to the recall period. This process has been formally modeled (see, e.g., Rubin and Baddeley 1989). Recall answers could therefore be overestimated (because of telescoping) or underestimated (because of forgetting).

Early predecessors of the CE had annual recall but this was abandoned for the 1972 survey, in part because of the work of Neter and Waksberg (1964) and Sudman and Ferber (1971) on recall problems, particularly telescoping (Jacobs and Shipp 1993).

Neter and Waksberg proposed "bounded" recall as a way of minimizing telescoping problems. The idea is that the recall period should be marked by an interview to prevent prior expenditures entering the recall period. This suggestion has been adopted by the current design of the CE. The recall sample is interviewed five times with data from the first interview discarded; the first interview serves to mark the beginning of the first recall period. Data from the current CE is consistent with telescoping. For some categories of expenditure the (normally discarded) data from the first interview suggests significantly higher rates of expenditure for some categories of goods (Silberstein 1990).

Problems with Diary Methods

In principle, a diary with perfect compliance and covering a sufficiently long period should give very good expenditure data. In practice, however, diary collection of expenditure information suffers from a number of problems.

First, respondents are typically asked to keep diaries only for short periods, partly in recognition that careful completion of a diary implies significant respondent burden. For categories of expenditure that are purchased irregularly, or at regular intervals that exceed the duration of diary keeping, infrequency problems will arise. This is a kind of measurement error: a household may over (or under) estimate their true rate of expenditure if the diary-keeping period happens to include (or not include) a major shopping trip or a major purchase. While this may not affect estimates of average expenditure across households, it certainly increases variance and will therefore bias estimates of inequality and poverty; it also causes bias when total expenditure is used as a "right-hand side" variable, as in the estimation of Engel curves.

A second concern is that compliance with diaries is certainly not perfect. In some budget surveys a great deal of diary completion occurs at the time of diary pick-up: interviewers collecting the diary check for completeness and often end up recording additional expenses. Silberstein and Scott (1991) report that this occurs in as many as a quarter of CE diaries. In such cases the distinction between a diary survey and recall survey is not clear.

In addition, evidence from a number of diary surveys with two weekly diaries suggests that compliance declines with the duration of record keeping. Apparent rates of expenditure in the second week of diary keeping are lower, sometimes substantially so. In addition to the between-week differences, within-week responses tend to be significantly larger for the earlier days of either week. These patterns have been reported in the CE (Silberstein and Scott 1991; Stephens 2003), the Canadian Food Expenditure Survey (Statistics Canada 1999; Ahmed, Brzozowski, and Crossley 2010), and the UK Family Expenditure Survey (Tanner 1998). In the 1987 CE, expenditures in the second week of the diary were 11 percent below those in the first week (Silberstein and Scott 1991). These patterns are typically attributed to "diary fatigue" (for example, Silberstein and Scott 1991; Statistics Canada 1999) and they have been known for a long time (e.g., Kemsley 1961; Turner 1961; Sudman and Ferber 1971; McWhinney and Champion 1974).

An intriguing (and alarming) alternative explanation for the drop off in expenditure rates from first-week diaries to second-week diaries is that keeping a diary alters behavior. This would not be entirely surprising: in the popular personal finance literature, making a record of expenditures is routinely advocated as a way of controlling expenditure and increasing saving. We identified only two studies, both from the United Kingdom, that investigate this possibility. Kemsley, Redpath, and Holmes (1980) report on experiments with the UK Family Expenditure Survey. They conclude that behavioral responses to participation in the survey are not systematic or uniform. McKenzie (1983) is an early study of response problems with diaries, undertaken with the cooperation of British Telecom and based on telephone calls (where the diary record can be compared to metered usage). McKenzie concludes that there is no evidence in this study that keeping a diary affects telephone usage. Of course, this result does not necessarily generalize to other categories of expenditure.

Another kind of noncompliance with diaries is nonspecificity (in which the respondent does not record sufficiently detailed information about a purchase). A closely related problem is that respondents sometimes record a single cost or expenditure for multiple items bought together. Silberstein and Scott (1991) report that 7 percent of food purchases in the 1987 CE (totaling 26 percent of food expenditure) suffer from nonspecificity. This nonspecificity often implies that the data analyst needs to allocate non-specific expenditures to specific categories, which is a kind of imputation. Silberstein and Scott note these phenomena are much less of a problem in the interview survey, presumably because of the structure of the interview and the interaction with the interviewer.

A final concern with diaries is that they are expensive to administer. The way in which they are typically now used, with drop off and collection and checking, involves multiple visits to the household.

Direct Comparisons of Diary and Recall Records

McWhinney and Champion (1974) report on early experiments in Canada that compared diary and recall methods of collecting expenditures. The conclusion of those studies was that *annual* recall (in conjunction with a cash-flow reconciliation or "balance edit," to be discussed below) gave data of good quality. The Canadian national budget survey (initially called the Family Expenditure Survey and later the Survey of Household Spending) maintained this design until very recently.

A number of recent studies have sought to compare diary versus recall methods, often for food expenditures. These studies exploit the fact that a number of existing surveys, including the CE and the Canadian Food Expenditure Survey, ask respondents to estimate or recall usual food expenditures before subsequently completing a diary. This provides recall and diary measures for the same households. Using the Canadian data on food expenditure, Ahmed, Brzozowski, and Crossley (2010) show that recall and diary responses are different and the differences between them relate to both the level of expenditure and observable characteristics of the households. This implies that, perhaps unsurprisingly, there is nonclassical measurement error in one or both measures. Battistin and Padula (2009) show that recall and diary food expenditure measures are not rank preserving, meaning that recall and diary measures from the same household do not order those households by expenditure identically. This is important, as rank preservation is among the weakest identification conditions required by econometric models of measurement error. Silberstein and Scott (1991) note that some categories of expenditure (e.g., apparel) exhibit different seasonal patterns in the diary and interview components of the CE.

Of course, it is insufficient to know that recall and diary measures differ; we would like to know which is superior. Recall measures almost always have a longer reference period, and hence will almost always have lower variance; the literature has not considered this a sensible criterion of comparison. Most categories of expenditure are thought to be underreported, so that higher rates of expenditure have been taken to be indicative of less error.

In both the Canadian food survey (Ahmed, Brzozowski, and Crossley 2010) and the CE (Gieseman [1987]; Bee, Meyer, and Sullivan, chapter 7, this volume), the recall measure of food is on average higher than the diary measure. This would be surprising if recall questions on food expenditure suffered from significant forgetting and the diary records were accurate. Telescoping is unlikely to be the explanation for this finding as food expenditures are small and regular, and telescoping is thought to be a problem mostly for large and irregular expenditures. Diary fatigue and noncompliance may be an explanation. Statistics Canada apparently has greater confidence in the level of the recall measure as they routinely inflate the diary data to match the average of recall reports prior to release. Silberstein and Scott (1991) make comparisons for a number of items that are collected in both the interview and diary components of the CE. They report that the diary method produces higher expenditure estimates for some categories (apparel, home furnishings) while the interview produces higher expenditures for others (entertainment and hobbies).

Gieseman (1987) compared food expenditure data from CE interview and diary surveys and finds the former are significantly higher and closer to the PCE numbers from the National Income and Product Accounts (NIPA). Bee, Meyer, and Sullivan (chapter 7, this volume) separately assess the CE interview and diary surveys against PCE benchmarks derived from the NIPA for a range of expenditure categories. They report that for many large categories of expenditure, the ratio of expenditure observed in the interview survey to the PCE benchmark is close to one, and they have not deteriorated over time; this is not true of the diary survey. (See chapter 7 for additional details.)

Mixed Data Collection Methods

As noted in Silberstein and Scott (1991), many national budget surveys use a mix of diary and recall methods. The choice then becomes not which method to use for the survey, but rather which method to use for each category of expenditure.[3] The considerations are similar to those just discussed. Detailed comparisons of expenditure reports in the two sources suggest that there may be some advantage in making these choices at very detailed item levels, but whether that advantage can be realized in practice is open to question. See Silberstein and Scott (1991) for further discussion.

Summary. There appears to be a common view that diary approaches provide more reliable measures of expenditure—it is almost a folk theorem that diary-based budget surveys set a "gold standard" for measuring household expenditures. However, our review of the literature casts doubt on that conclusion. Response effects such as diary fatigue imply that diary-based measures are not necessarily error free, and since they clearly involve a much higher burden on respondents, selective participation might be a more severe concern than for the recall approach.

1.2.3 Response Formats

With both recall and diary methods there are important questions of questionnaire design in general, and response format in particular. A key issue is whether one should employ open-ended (fill-in) formats or closed-response formats such as range card or brackets. At least two aspects are important for this choice. The first is respondent burden—it is easier for the respondent to tick off one of a small number of specified ranges rather than provide a numerical estimate, so different response formats might result in different rates of item nonresponse. The second aspect concerns problems associated with each of the two formats: open-ended questions typically yield rounded or heaped responses, whereas closed formats might induce the respondent to use certain estimation strategies that produce systematic biases.

Pudney (2007) analyzed the responses to questions in the British Household Panel Study (BHPS) about spending on domestic energy (electricity, gas, etc.). He documented that responses are heaped with large proportions of responses at particular focal expenditure levels (i.e., prominent, round numbers such as multiples of 10, 50, or 100). Pudney argues that heaping results from the use of estimation strategies that involve rounding. Some respondents might choose a round number for weekly spending and then scale that up to an annual total, some use rounding at the monthly or annual level, while others do not round at all. (There might be an interest-

---

3. Where both the diary and the interview components of the CE collect information on a category of expenditure, a similar decision is made in determining which data to use in the production of the integrated accounts.

ing interaction between rounding strategies and the choice of the reference period, another important aspect of questionnaire design that we review below.) These results suggest that rounding is differential across respondents. There is also some evidence from controlled experiments that the degree of response rounding is affected by the respondent's uncertainty about the target quantity (Ruud, Schunk, and Winter 2014). Thus, simple strategies to correct for heaped responses in the analysis of the data that have been developed in the statistics literature (such as those that require a "coarsened at random" assumption; Heitjan and Rubin [1991]) are too simplistic (see also Wright and Bray 2003).

One way to avoid the statistical problems associated with heaped responses is to use closed-response formats that provide respondents with a list of brackets (a "range card") from which they choose one. Another advantage of closed-response formats is that they tend to produce lower rates of item nonresponse. But the data obtained from such bracketed questions also come with their problems—when the object of interest is a continuous and cardinal variable, information is lost and regression models require stronger assumptions compared to those that could be estimated with the continuous variable. Moreover, Manski and Tamer (2002) illustrate that these assumptions must be strong since the bounds on parameters of interest that can be identified from bracketed data are large.

Winter (2002), building on work in survey research and social psychology (Schwarz et al. 1985), shows that in addition to these statistical problems, bracketed data might introduce additional systematic biases. In a controlled survey experiment, he assigned respondents either to open-ended or three versions of bracketed questions that used different bracket thresholds; the target quantities were six expenditure items. The four question types delivered response distributions that are statistically different from each other. The response patterns are consistent with psychological theories of response behavior that predict that respondents who are uncertain about their response (here, their true expenditure on an item) use the information provided by the bracket thresholds to determine what the distribution of the target quantity in the population is and then give a relative response. For instance, a person who thinks her consumption is average might tick off the middle category of a range card irrespective of the thresholds used. The biases that arise from such behavior can be large, and they are likely differential across survey respondents.

Similar systematic biases arise when follow-up bracketed questions (sometimes known as "unfolding brackets") are used when respondents give item nonresponse to open-ended questions (e.g., van Soest and Hurd 2008). The underlying psychological mechanism in unfolding questions that require yes-no responses at each step (anchoring) is, however, slightly different from the one that affects range-card-type questions (estimation and response on a relative scale).

There are a number of further issues in the design of diaries, including whether to preprint expenditure categories on the diary, and whether diaries should be organized chronologically (as a journal) or by product or outlet type. Indeed, Silberstein and Scott (1991) argue that questionnaire design issues are likely to be more important with diaries than with recall interviews because of the absence of an interviewer to help with survey comprehension and check for obvious reporting errors. Sudman and Ferber (1971) reported higher expenditure reports in diaries organized by product type in an experimental comparison with journal and outlet formats. Tucker (1992) and Tucker and Bennett (1988) report that preprinting expenditure categories in diaries leads to higher expenditure totals.

Summary. Both open-ended and closed-response format recall questions produce data that are coarsened in nonrandom ways. Thus, they cannot be used with standard regression approaches and, technically, they do not point-identify the parameters of interest (and if bounds are identified, they tend to be wide). It is an open question of whether the biases in open-ended or closed (bracketed) questions are larger. Leaving this choice aside, reducing the respondent's uncertainty about the quantity of interest by appropriate survey design should reduce the response biases and subsequent statistical problems associated with both response formats: respondents who are less uncertain are less likely to use biased estimation strategies when they form their response, an issue to which we return below.

1.2.4 Disaggregation of Expenditure Categories

The issue of how finely survey instruments should disaggregate the components of quantities such as income or expenditure has been studied for a long time. In the following discussion, we focus on a situation in which the researcher is interested in getting an accurate measure of a quantity at an aggregate level, such as total expenditure on nondurable goods in a certain period. If a researcher has substantive interest in a variable at more disaggregate levels, such as food expenditure, that places a natural restriction on how much the components can be aggregated.[4]

Much of the early work on disaggregation we are aware of looks at income rather than consumption questions. Herriot (1977) compared four questionnaire variants and found that the more aggregated the income categories are, the less complete is the reporting of income. More recently, Micklewright and Schnepf (2010) investigated the reliability of single-question measures of income. They compared the distributions of income in two UK surveys—individual income in the Office for National Statistics's Omnibus survey and

---

4. There has been work on "one-shot" questions about total expenditure of a household, particularly for use in general purpose surveys. As our focus here is on dedicated expenditure surveys, and any such survey will surely wish to capture more disaggregated detail, we do not review that literature here. See Browning, Crossley, and Weber (2003) for an introduction.

household income in the British Social Attitudes survey—with those in two other surveys that measure income in much greater detail. They found that the distributions of single-question and more detailed measures compare less well for household income than for individual income.

There has been work on expenditure categories in both developed and developing countries. Joliffe (2001) reports findings from a survey experiment conducted in El Salvador. Longer, more detailed sets of questions resulted in an estimate of mean household consumption that was 31 percent greater than the estimate derived from a condensed version of the questionnaire, and the distributions of household consumption from the long and short questionnaires were also different. Joliffe further shows that the differences in estimated consumption lead to different substantive conclusions about levels of poverty in the population. Pradhan (2009) analyzes data from an experiment that occurred in a national household survey in Indonesia: questions on consumption were asked with different levels of aggregation, and households were randomly assigned to the different designs. Like Joliffe, Pradhan finds that the level of aggregation has a significant effect on the estimate of total consumption.

Turning to expenditure surveys in developed countries, an early study by Reagan (1954) of farm operators found that total expenditure was only about 10 percent lower with fifteen categories than with over 200. Winter (2004) conducted an experimental study with a large, representative sample in a Dutch Internet panel survey (the CentERpanel). Respondents were randomly assigned to either a one-shot question on total monthly nondurables expenditure or to a table with thirty-five disaggregated categories they had to fill in. The two designs produced significantly different distributions of the totals. Moreover, these differences varied with household characteristics. Underreporting was high for the middle income groups and decreased with income. Also, underreporting appeared to be most severe for middle-aged respondents. The findings are consistent with older households' nondurables expenditures being concentrated on few items and therefore easier to recall. Also, and perhaps not surprisingly, underreporting in the one-shot question is smaller for respondents who list "housekeeper" as their occupation.

Focus group results reported by d'Ardenne and Blake (2011) suggest that respondents consider more disaggregated designs to be not only a heavier burden but also more intrusive. This finding may be quite important in some settings or for particular subpopulations of households.

Asking respondents to report their expenditures on a large list of items might have another drawback. The questions on such expenditure items are typically worded identically and presented sequentially. Depending on the survey mode, they often also contain filter questions. For example, in a phone or personal interview, the first question might be "Have you spent money on (item no. 1) last month?" followed by a question on the amount if the first question is answered in the affirmative. Then the questionnaire would loop through the list of items. In such a situation, as they progress through the list of items, respondents might learn that a "no" response to the first question on each item allows them to skip the follow-up question (which they might perceive as burdensome or even intrusive and thus want to avoid). Recent experimental studies by Kreuter et al. (2011, 2012) show that such learning, termed as "motivated underreporting" does indeed happen. This phenomenon obviously results in systematic underreporting, which is differential across items (depending on their sequence) and downward biased aggregates.

Summary. There are several studies that investigate the effects of disaggregation on survey measures of both income and expenditure. These studies suggest that designs that use more disaggregated categories yield higher estimates of the totals, presumably because households do not include some categories in their estimates of totals in one-shot or highly aggregated designs. It is not certain that greater disaggregation always leads to better results, particularly as respondents find more disaggregate demands more intrusive and a greater burden. It is worth noting that most of the studies cited above compare treatments, all of which have less disaggregation than the current CE. There is also evidence (for example, Hurd and Rohwedder, chapter 13, this volume) that less disaggregated collection can capture many of the important life cycle and time-series patterns of expenditure. It may well be that for *research* purposes, a less disaggregated design is sufficient. Finally, even if designs with more questions on more disaggregated categories yield better results, in practice there is still a trade-off between respondent burden and survey cost and response quality. We are not aware of studies that try to quantify this trade-off and find optimal levels of disaggregation under a survey cost or time constraint.

1.2.5 Predicting Aggregates from Components or Other Variables

Given that measuring the aggregate quantity of interest (say, total household expenditure) using a one-shot question might provide unreliable results, and that asking for a longer list of components might not be feasible, an alternative approach is to ask questions on fewer expenditure items and employ them to predict the aggregate quantity using a statistical model. This model would be estimated using a separate, more detailed survey with reliable data on a large number of categories (typically, a household budget survey based on diaries); the estimated coefficients could then be used to predict the aggregate with a subset of the items in another survey. The statistical goal would be to have an unbiased prediction that preserves patterns of variance and covariance. The classic paper in this vein is Skinner (1987) on imputing total consumption of Panel Study of Income Dynamics (PSID) respondents on the basis of the limited expenditure questions in the PSID. There have been a number of proposed refinements to this procedure; recent examples are Blundell, Pistaferri, and Preston (2008), Blundell and Pistafferi (2003), and Battistin, Miniaci, and Weber (2003). Browning and Crossley

(2009) propose a method by which moments of the total expenditure distribution can be recovered from information on just two goods (see also Attanasio, Hurst, and Pistaferri, chapter 4, this volume). Note, however, that these methods all require that information on the relationship between total expenditure and expenditure on categories of goods and services (that is, Engel curves) is available from some other source.

An alternative is to use the intertemporal budget constraint to impute consumption expenditure from data on income and wealth: Browning and Leth-Petersen (2003) report one attempt to do this with Danish data. Interestingly, recent UK focus group evidence (d'Ardenne and Blake 2011) suggests that, when asked a question on total expenditure, many (but by no means all) respondents work out an answer by beginning with income and adjusting for changes in assets (primarily by subtracting savings). The same focus group evidence suggests, though, that using survey questions on income and wealth changes to get total expenditure is unlikely to be a full solution, for a number of reasons. One problem identified in the focus groups is that respondents whose expenditures exceed their incomes find questions about changes in wealth very intrusive.

Summary. Our conclusion is that prediction of expenditure from components or from income and wealth data may be useful in particular contexts, but is not likely to be a major component to any replacement of current national budget surveys. The methods that use components to predict total expenditure require the existence of a budget survey for calibration, and methods based on income and wealth changes are very intrusive for significant subpopulations. Moreover, these methods do not capture the disaggregated spending information necessary for price index construction and many research applications.

1.2.6 Defining the Response Unit (and Choosing the Respondent[s])

Another fundamental design choice for expenditure surveys is: Should we measure household or personal expenditure? This question has various aspects. First, some expenditures arise only at the household level (such as rent and heating) and cannot be easily assigned to individual members, others are typically made at the household level but could, in principle, be assigned to individual members, such as many items purchased during regular trips to the grocery store, and yet others are made individually or can be assigned easily to individuals, such as clothing. Capturing these structures is difficult at the conceptual level and highly expensive to implement in interview surveys since different parts of the instrument would have to be assigned to the members of the household. Even if we aim to collect only the aggregate expenditure of all household members on each item of interest, there remains the practical question of how to collect this information.

In many existing recall expenditures surveys, expenditure questions are given only to one respondent (typically, the person most knowledgeable about household finances) who is asked to provide estimates "for the household" This can lead to two types of problems. First, great care must be taken in communicating the spending about which the question asks. The concept of a household—which economists often do not care to define in plain language, presumably because it is so natural to us—might be misunderstood. Respondents may report individual expenditure even when a question asks about household expenditure (Comerford, Delaney, and Harmon [2009] provide experimental evidence on this problem). D'Ardenne and Blake (2011) report focus group evidence of a different misunderstanding: respondents believe that "household spending" or even "spending of your household" means *only* shared expenses, or expenditures on those goods and services necessary to run the household.

The second kind of problem is that even the member of the household with the best knowledge of household finances may not know or be able to estimate the spending of other members. This can be interpreted as a proxy interview problem, and is likely to be particularly problematic in complex households: those with unrelated adults (sharers) or multiple generations of adults. Browning, Crossley, and Weber (2003) report evidence that nonresponse to household expenditure questions is much higher for such households. However, it is likely to pose difficulties for all types of households, apart from single-person households. Focus group results reported in d'Ardenne and Blake (2011) confirm this conjecture and also suggest that this problem may be more severe the finer the detail to be collected. Individual household members may be able to estimate the total spending of other household members but unable to provide much information on how that spending is broken down by goods and services.

The corresponding issue in diary surveys is how many diaries should be completed. The current CE design involves a single diary for the household, but some national budget surveys (United Kingdom, France, Denmark) have multiple diaries (one for each household member above a minimum age). The choice of one or multiple diaries has been studied (Kemsley and Nicholson 1960; Grooteart 1986) and the evidence is mixed. Multiple diaries give higher totals, suggesting that some expenditures are missed with a single diary, but multiple diaries lead to a higher incidence of noncooperation. Similar findings emerged from a small feasibility study commissioned by the CE in 2006 (Goldenberg and Ryan 2009).

Beyond these difficulties with collecting household-level expenditures, it is undoubtedly the case that the intrahousehold allocation of goods and services to individuals is of considerable interest to researchers and policy makers.[5] Individual diaries (or individual recall interviews) do not necessarily identify individual consumption. We do not know, for example, if one

---

5. See Deaton ([1997], section 4.3 and the references therein) for an introduction to the literature on intrahousehold allocation.

adult's expenditures are for themselves, for another adult, for children in the household, or to be shared. Bonke and Browning (2009) report on successful Danish experiments that collect individual consumptions in household surveys by asking "for whom?" in addition to the standard information collected on each expenditure item.

Summary. Asking one respondent, even the person most knowledgeable, to report expenditures leads to a number of possible response problems and errors. More detailed collection of data on expenditures made by different household members is potentially expensive. But where it is feasible, it may lead to higher-quality data. If it can also be combined with data on who benefited from the expenditure, it opens up rich possibilities for studying allocations within households.

1.2.7 Reference Period

Another fundamental issue in the design of survey instruments that elicit flow variables such as consumption or income is the choice of the reference period. Should we ask respondents for daily, weekly, monthly, or annual amounts? Is the optimal reference period different when measuring income and expenditure? Are there perhaps also differences in optimal reference periods across different expenditure items? Then, whatever the choice of reference period may be, should we ask respondents to provide reports for the past period or for a typical period?

The discussion in section 1.2.2 above suggests that designers of recall questions face a trade-off. Longer periods may lead to greater "forgetting" and hence underreporting. Shorter recall may generate measurement error through the infrequency of purchases. Because diary fatigue seems to lead to decreasing compliance throughout the recording period, designers of diary surveys face a trade-off not unlike that faced by designers of recall surveys. Shorter recording periods will lead to less bias in the estimation of mean expenditures, but, because of infrequency, higher variance. Infrequency will also lead to bias in estimates of dispersion. Longer recording periods will reduce infrequency problems but lead to greater underestimation. There is no reason for diary fatigue and forgetting to follow the same time path, so that even for a given good, the optimal reference periods might also differ between recall and diary approaches.

At least in a recall survey it is quite feasible to vary reference periods by category of expenditure, and it seems obvious that the optimal reference period will be different for different categories of expenditure. Rates of forgetting depend on the frequency and on the salience of purchase (Silberstein and Jacob 1989), which will also differ by category of expenditure.

Bradburn (2010) provides an excellent review of the cognitive processes that occur when survey respondents are asked to recall quantities from memory and maps these processes into the issue of optimal lengths of recall periods. A central conclusion he draws is that "no single recall period will be optimal for all events," but also that there is no general knowledge on what recall periods should be used for which goods, and that "more empirical work is needed to determine the optimum recall periods for different categories of expenditures" (8). Bradburn also discusses how questions with different recall horizons should be grouped within a questionnaire.

Clarke, Fiebig, and Gerdtham (2008) present an interesting approach to estimate the optimal length of recall periods from prior survey data; their application is, however, not expenditure, but the frequency of doctor visits and medical treatments during defined past periods.

Hurd and Rohwedder (2009) report evidence from controlled experiments on the tension between asking about spending over long and short time frames. They conclude that respondents' choice of reference period is related to their household's frequency and level of spending in a particular category. Respondents tend to choose a longer reference period for less frequently purchased items. Also, recall bias is important when using longer reference periods such as "last twelve months." They argue that longer reference periods should be used sparingly with relatively frequently purchased items. Finally, they confirm that short reference periods might provide an unrepresentative snapshot of household spending because of infrequent purchases. In the Consumption and Activities Mail Survey, a component of the Health and Retirement Study (HRS), they adopted an innovative alternative approach that allows respondents to choose from a set of reference periods of different lengths for each item.

Despite the theoretical considerations and evidence just described, not all evidence points to the desirability of different reference periods for different categories of expenditure. The Indian National Sample Survey Organization (NSSO) conducted a detailed experiment with different recall periods using daily visits as a gold standard measure. The study found no uniformly optimal recall length across all goods, but a thirty-day recall period (which was the baseline design) seemed to do reasonably well (Deaton and Kozel 2005). There is also some suggestive evidence (McWhinney and Champion [1974]; see also the discussion in Deaton and Grosh [2000]) that annual recall works well, at least in some contexts. Moreover, recording at different expenditures on different categories of goods and services with different recall periods can lead to important practical difficulties when constructing aggregates.

A further issue related to recall period is whether—given a period length—recall questions should be asked for the last period or for a typical period; the trade-off being between recall accuracy (better for the most recent period) versus missing infrequent expenditure (which will be avoided when asking for a typical period). There is a related literature on measuring the frequency of regular behaviors. Chang and Krosnick (2003), for example, study survey questions on the frequency of news media consumption. They find that "typical week" questions perform better than "last week" questions in that context, but they also conclude that more systematic research is needed on how questions on the frequency of behaviors should be asked in other contexts.

With respect to expenditures, Edgar (2009) reports a cognitive interviewing study (seventy-six participants) that examines four questions about "usual" spending in the CE interview survey: food at home, food away, alcohol at home, and alcohol away. The study revealed a great deal of heterogeneity in the estimation strategies that respondents employed to answer these questions. Respondents seemed to interpret the term "usual" in a variety of ways.

Angrisani, Kapteyn, and Schuh (chapter 15, this volume) designed and fielded an experimental module in a US Internet survey (the American Life Panel) in which they asked individuals to report the frequency of their purchases and the amount spent by debit cards, cash, credit cards, and personal checks. The data show that the type—specific or typical—and length of recall periods can greatly influence household reporting behavior.

Summary. Different reference periods lead to significant differences in the distribution of responses. As noted in Deaton and Kozel (2005) these difference can in turn lead to dramatic differences in objects of interest, like poverty rates. Theoretical considerations and some evidence suggest different reference periods for different categories of expenditure, although some of the evidence we have suggests a uniform reference period may work fairly well. Given the potential importance of design choice, further evidence would be welcome.

There is good evidence that the choice of usual (or typical) versus most recent period has a significant effect on the responses received. But it is not clear, from the evidence we reviewed, which approach is preferable.

2.8 The Role of Incentives

Incentives affect survey response behavior. In a standard neoclassical view of the survey respondent, incentive payments compensate the respondent for the opportunity cost associated with answering the survey. There is, however, also a principal-agent problem: since the survey agency cannot observe the true response, the respondent generally has an incentive to provide too little effort—that is, not to think as hard about the responses as he might. In a series of papers, Philipson (1997, 2001), Philipson and Lawless (1997), and Philipson and Malani (1999) pursue this view using both theoretical models and data from controlled experiments. A general finding of these studies is that measurement error is elastic with respect to the incentive paid, which opens up the possibility of optimally assigning incentive payments to different (groups of) respondents should appropriate conditioning variables be available in sample frame data; however, these ideas have, to our knowledge, not been pursued.

In the context of expenditure surveys, Kemsley and Nicholson (1960) report on a small experiment in which modest cash incentives raised the cooperation rate among households asked to complete a one-week expenditure survey by 15 percentage points. Sudman and Ferber (1971) report on an experiment with small gifts (a flag or a notebook) in the context of a diary-based household expenditure survey. They report that households receiving a gift are significantly more likely to cooperate with the survey and report higher expenditures. Ferber and Sudman reviewed these and several other small studies in the mid-1970s and concluded that the effects of financial incentives in expenditure surveys had not been well studied at the time of their review (Sudman and Ferber 1974).

The CE itself conducted experiments with monetary incentives in both the diary and interview surveys in 2005/2006 (Goldenberg and Ryan 2009). In both cases, a quarter of respondent households received a twenty-dollar debit card and a quarter received a forty-dollar debit card. In the interview survey the forty-dollar incentive improved response rates and a range of measures of data quality. The effects of the twenty-dollar incentive were, in most cases, not statistically significant. In the diary survey, the incentives were less successful. They seemed to improve data quality but had little effect on response rates.

The most recent study that our review of this literature uncovered is Bonke and Fallesen (2010). These authors also show that incentives can increase cooperation of respondents in consumption surveys—in their specific application, they offered larger lottery prices for respondents who were willing to answer a survey over the Internet (which as they argue is the more reliable mode) rather than over the phone.

Summary. The use of incentives in expenditure surveys seems to be an area where additional systematic research would be welcome. Current evidence suggests that incentives can improve the quality of data collected in expenditure surveys, but there is insufficient evidence to draw any conclusions on the optimal form or size of the incentives. A particularly interesting question is whether the optimal size of incentives varies with respondent characteristics and whether it is possible to condition incentives on such variables to the extent they are known from the sampling frame.

1.2.9 Approaches to Reduce or Correct Response Errors in Real Time

Computer-assisted surveys (personal and telephone interviews as well as Internet surveys) offer additional strategies for improving the reliability of consumer expenditure measurement.

A first approach is preloading of information. If data on income or assets are already available, either from earlier interviews or from earlier questions within an interview, these variables can be used to provide the respondents with cues or to check whether a response is reasonable. For instance, if preload information says that disposable monthly income was $2,000, and the respondent says that he spent $4,000 on nondurable consumption items last month, he could be asked whether that amount is indeed correct. Parker, Souleles, and Carroll (chapter 3, this volume) argue that the possibility of preloading information is one of the significant advantages of a longitudinal component in a budget survey. While such approaches can reduce the number of severe response errors and outliers, designing them involves some judgment and to the extent that preload information is itself unreliable, might even exacerbate response errors (e.g., Manski and Molinari 2008; Bollinger and David 2005).

The official budget surveys in Canada have long been based on an intensive interview, annual recall, and a field editing procedure in which budget balance is checked. Households that are too far "out of balance" are asked to review expenditures, incomes, and changes in money balances. This cashflow reconciliation procedure, in fact, significantly predated the move to computer-assisted interviewing. Early predecessors of the CE had a similar balance edit (Jacobs and Shipp 1993) but when the survey was subsequently redesigned in 1972 to address the research indicating problems with recall, the balance edit was dropped as being incompatible with the new design (that is, with a survey without annual recall).

Brzozowski and Crossley (2011) report some evidence on the efficacy of the balance edit in the Canadian survey. They exploit the fact that the balance edit was dropped from the survey design in one year, and then reintroduced the following year. Through comparisons to adjacent years, they show that the main effect of the balance edit appears to be in improving income reports, especially at the bottom of the income distribution.

Hurd and Rohwedder (2010) describe the use of something like a balance edit in the American Life Panel (ALP), which is an Internet panel. They asked households to complete a monthly survey on twenty-five higher-frequency purchase categories and a quarterly survey on eleven lower-frequency categories. At the end of the survey, respondents were presented with a "reconciliation screen" and asked to review and correct the information they had provided. Hurd and Rohwedder report that about 3 percent of entries were corrected and that this led to reductions in item nonresponse and in the size and frequency of outliers.

Fricker, Kopp, and To (chapter 12, this volume) report on a new experiment exploring the feasibility of a cash-flow reconciliation (balance edit) in a revised CE survey. See their chapter for more details. A key finding is that the reconciliation seems to improve responses even when income and expenditures and income are reported over different intervals.

Summary. Evidence from a variety of sources suggests that cash-flow reconciliations and other opportunities for respondents to review their answers improve data in budget surveys. This merits further study and consideration in budget survey design or redesign.

1.3 Where Do We Go from Here?

Surveying this literature, we see three priorities for further research on the collection and analysis of expenditure data. First, while we are accumulating

Table 1.1   Schematic of the survey response process

1. Comprehension
   - → Identify question focus (information sought)
   - → Link key terms to relevant concepts
   Description of the items
2. Retrieval or recall
   - → Generate retrieval strategies and cues
   - → Retrieve specific, generic memories
   - → Fill in missing details
   Effects of the length of the recall period
   Number of categories asked (what we often call aggregation)
3. Judgment
   - → Assess completeness and relevance of memories
   - → Integrate material retrieved
   - → Form estimate based on partial retrieval and other salient information
   Effects of brackets on response (range-card type and unfolding)
4. Response
   - → Map judgment onto response scale
   - → Edit response
   Nonresponse for sensitive items

Source: Tourangeau, Rasinsky, and Rips (2000, 8).

much evidence on the consequences of different design choices in expenditure surveys, we need a theoretical framework to organize and interpret this evidence. Second, we need to begin to think more explicitly about cost-benefit trade-offs. Third, on the analysis side, we need approaches to the data that incorporate what we know about the nature of response behavior and measurement error into structural econometric analysis. We now discuss these three points in turn.

1.3.1 A Conceptual Framework for Understanding Response Behavior

As we have seen, researchers and survey designers have collected considerable evidence on the effects of different design choices in the collection of expenditure information. To move forward, we need to place this evidence in a theoretical framework that allows us to understand the evidence, to guide future experimentation, and to offer at least tentative answers to counterfactual questions about survey design. This is a challenging prescription, but a conceptual model of the response process can be useful as a starting point.

The response process, as a source of measurement error, can be broken down in several distinct stages (or tasks), as in table 1.1. This schematic, adapted from Tourangeau, Rips, and Rasinski (2000), presents the standard conceptualization of the survey response process in psychology.[6] We

---

6. See also Sudman, Bradburn, and Schwarz (1996). The literature contains a number of such schemes, which are similar in their broad conceptualization of the response process but differ in some details.

have added aspects of response behavior in expenditure surveys in italics. Many of the sources of measurement error and consequences of design features outlined above fit naturally into this framework, and it seems to us the natural place to begin to develop a more theoretical perspective on the design of expenditure surveys.[7]

As one example of the utility of such a perspective, consider the puzzling evidence that annual recall may give higher-quality data than shorter recall periods. A possible explanation (Deaton and Grosh 2000), which the conceptualization in table 1.1 highlights, is that the lengthening of the recall period changes the response strategy of the respondent from one of retrieval or "counting" (with the attendant problems of telescoping and forgetting) to a strategy of estimation (based on partial retrieval and other salient information). The respondent's estimation strategy may work well—as well, for example, as diaries, or bounded recall designs. At the same time, the literature on the psychology of social response suggests that where respondents use an estimation strategy, the quality of responses may be quite sensitive to what information is available and salient. For this reason, it could be that the quality of annual recall data described in McWhinney and Champion (1974) may be quite sensitive to particular aspect of the survey design (such as the budget balance perspective imposed on both the interviewer and respondent by the balance edit in the Canadian surveys).

Another example of the application of this kind of conceptualization of the response process as a series of cognitive tasks is the analysis of recall periods in Bradburn (2010). Bradburn uses a conceptualization of the response process to highlight the key considerations in determining recall period length. In our view, this is a fine example of how such questions should be approached.

1.3.2 Systematic Discussions of Survey Costs

Collecting data on expenditures is expensive. For example, Deaton and Grosh (2000) note that the CE costs about five times as much per household as the Current Population Survey (the main income survey in the United States). In the literature survey in section 1.2, there is useful evidence on almost all the aspects of expenditure design we might be interested in. However, what is lacking, in almost all cases, is a systematic comparison of the benefits (in terms of increased reliability of the measures) and costs (monetary costs of administration, implicit costs arising from item, or unit nonresponse and selection).

Groves (1989) provides a classic development of the survey cost versus survey error perspective. Manski and Molinari (2008) are among the

---

7. Hudomiet (2011) attempts to map such a conceptual model into hypotheses that are testable in a structural model of survey responses, and he presents some preliminary estimates using data from the Health and Retirement Study (HRS).

few economists who take such a perspective to survey design. They argue that survey designers "should use an explicit loss function to quantify the trade-off between cost and informativeness of the survey and aim to make a design choice that minimizes loss" (264). The specific design problem they study is the use of "skip sequencing"—whether all respondents should be asked about an item of interest or only a subset, which is determined conditional on earlier responses. The key problem is that skip sequencing reduces survey cost, but since conditioning variables might be mismeasured themselves, it will also tend to increase survey error.

Given the high cost of expenditure surveys, it seems clear to us that more explicit discussion of the trade-offs between cost and quality are needed.

1.3.3 Econometric Models That Reflect Response Behavior

Few studies try to take what we know about structure of measurement error and incorporate this knowledge in structural econometrics (see McFadden et al. 2005). Traditionally, measurement error was dealt with by making the assumption that it is classical, that is, additive and uncorrelated with any other variable in the model of interest (Bound, Brown, and Mathiowetz 2001). This assumption is unrealistic for many variables that are measured in surveys, and in light of the evidence we reviewed in the previous section, it certainly does not hold for survey measures of consumption expenditure. Nevertheless, the assumption that measurement error is classical is often made since it makes the effects tractable, at least in textbook cases.[8] A more recent literature relaxes the assumption of classical measurement error, but its focus is on general results that do not depend on—or take advantage off—what we might know about the structure of measurement error. There are a few papers that are exceptions, and we think these papers lead us in a very useful direction.

Perhaps most relevant for the present research agenda is the paper by Battistin and Padula (2009), who suggest a way to obtain a superior measure of total expenditure at the household level. The methods developed in this paper exploit the structure of the CE (particularly the multiple reports of expenditures available in the survey) in a sophisticated econometric framework. It is a model of how such work can be done.

Pudney (2007) and Ruud, Schunk, and Winter (2014), already mentioned above, model rounding strategies used by respondents when they answer open-ended survey questions. The implication of these papers is that a "coarsening at random" assumption on rounded data should be replaced by a model that uses explicit knowledge of the process that generates rounding,

---

8. In the linear regression model, classical measurement error either leads to inflated variances of the estimated parameters if it affects the dependent variable or to a downward bias in the size of the estimated coefficients if it affects an explanatory variable. In nonlinear models, even for classical measurement error, the predictions are not as clear-cut any more, and the effects are analytically intractable.

for instance, the fact that respondents who are more uncertain about an item might be more likely to round their response. Hoderlein and Winter (2010) study the effects of recall errors in a structural econometric model of household consumption. They show that nonclassical measurement error related from recall errors in consumption, which is the dependent variable, can have grave consequences on model estimates, in contrast to the conventional wisdom, which is based on the fact that classical measurement error in the dependent variable does not bias parameter estimates in a linear regression.

Papers such as these remind us that we need to do both things: get better data and make better use of the data we have (and better use of the knowledge we have of the flaws in the data we have). There should, in general, be more interaction between survey design and analysis methods (McFadden et al. 2005; Browning and Crossley 2009). This interaction, of course, must be mindful of the fact that these are general-use surveys, and should not be tailored for any particular analysis. Nevertheless, we think the potential returns are large.

Those of us who both analyze household expenditure data and think about how to collect it are sometimes in a strange position. We worry that survey respondents may not be able to answer our survey questions, but the models we use the data to estimate imply that they should be able to answer. The problem is symmetric. If we knew more about how households allocate resources over time and goods, we could design better questions. But equally, if we learn about how to ask better expenditure questions, this should also help us develop better models of consumer behavior. The possibilities of two-way exchange between data development and model development seem to us very promising.

References

Ahmed, N., M. Brzozowski, and T. F. Crossley. 2010. "Measurement Errors in Recall Food Consumption Data." Unpublished manuscript, McMaster University, York University, and University of Cambridge.

Attanasio, O., E. Battistin, and H. Ichimura. 2004. "What Really Happened to Consumption Inequality in the US?" NBER Working Paper no. 10338, Cambridge, MA.

Battistin, E., R. Miniaci, and G. Weber. 2003. "What Do We Learn from Recall Consumption Data?" *Journal of Human Resources* 38 (2): 354–85.

Battistin, E., and M. Padula. 2009. "Survey Instruments and the Reports of Consumption Expenditures: Evidence from the Consumer Expenditure Surveys." Unpublished manuscript, University of Padova and University of Venice.

Blundell, R., and L. Pistaferri. 2003. "Income Volatility and Household Consumption: The Impact of Food Assistance Programs." *Journal of Human Resources* 38:1032–50.

Blundell, R., L. Pistaferri, and I. Preston. 2008. "Consumption Inequality and Partial Insurance." *American Economic Review* 98:1887–921.

Bollinger, C. R., and M. H. David. 2005. "I Didn't Tell, and I Won't Tell: Dynamic Response Error in the SIPP." *Journal of Applied Econometrics* 20:563–69.

Bonke, J., and M. Browning. 2009. "The Allocation of Expenditures within the Household: A New Survey." *Fiscal Studies* 30:461–81.

Bonke, J., and P. Fallesen. 2010. "The Impact of Incentives and Interview Methods on Response Quantity and Quality in Diary- and Booklet-Based Surveys." *Survey Research Methods* 4:91–101.

Bound, J., C. Brown, and N. Mathiowetz. 2001. "Measurement Error in Survey Data." In *Handbook of Econometrics*, vol. 5, edited by J. J. Heckman and E. Leamer, 3705–843. Amsterdam: Elsevier.

Bradburn, N. M. 2010. "Recall Period in Consumer Expenditure Surveys Program." Unpublished manuscript, NORC, University of Chicago. http://www.bls.gov/cex/methwrkshp_pap_bradburn.pdf.

Browning, M., and T. F. Crossley. 2009. "Are Two Cheap, Noisy Measures Better than One Expensive, Accurate One?" *American Economic Review, Papers & Proceedings* 99 (2): 99–103.

Browning, M., T. F. Crossley, and G. Weber. 2003. "Asking Consumption Questions in General Purpose Surveys." *Economic Journal* 113:F540–67.

Browning, M., and S. Leth-Petersen. 2003. "Imputing Consumption from Income and Wealth Information." *Economic Journal* 113: F282–301.

Brzozowski, M., and T. F. Crossley. 2011. "Measuring the Well-Being of the Poor with Income or Consumption: A Canadian Perspective." *Canadian Journal of Economics* 44 (1): 88–106.

Chang, L., and J. A. Krosnick. 2003. "Measuring the Frequency of Regular Behaviors: Comparing the 'Typical Week' to the 'Past Week'." *Sociological Methodology* 33:55–80.

Clarke, P. M., D. G. Fiebig, and U.-G. Gerdtham. 2008. "Optimal Recall Length in Survey Design." *Journal of Health Economics* 27:1275–84.

Comerford, D., L. Delaney, and C. Harmon. 2009. "Experimental Tests of Survey Responses to Expenditure Questions." *Fiscal Studies* 30 (3/4): 419–33.

d'Ardenne, J., and M. Blake. 2011. "Developing Expenditure Questions: Findings from Focus Groups." Technical Report, National Centre for Social Research (NatCen), London.

Deaton, A. 1997. *The Analysis of Household Surveys*. Baltimore: Johns Hopkins University Press.

Deaton, A., and M. Grosh. 2000. "Consumption." In *Designing Household Survey Questionnaires for Developing Countries: Lessons from Ten Years of LSMS Experience*, edited by M. Grosh and P. Glewwe, chapter 17. Washington, DC: The World Bank.

Deaton, A., and V. Kozel. 2005. "Data and Dogma: The Great Indian Poverty Debate." *World Bank Research Observer* 20 (2): 177–99.

Edgar, J. 2009. "What Does 'Usual' Usually Mean?" Unpublished manuscript, Bureau of Labor Statistics.

Essig, L., and J. Winter. 2009. "Item Nonresponse to Financial Questions in Household Surveys: An Experimental Study of Interviewer and Mode Effects." *Fiscal Studies* 30:367–90.

Ferber, R., and S. Sudman. 1974. "Effects of Compensation in Consumer Expenditure Surveys." *Annals of Economic and Social Measurement* 3 (2): 21–34.

Gieseman, R. 1987. "The Consumer Expenditure Survey: Quality Control by Comparative Analysis." *Monthly Labor Review* 110 (3): 8–14.

Goldenberg, K., and J. Ryan. 2009. "Evolution and Change in the Consumer Expenditure Surveys: Adapting to Meet Changing Needs." Paper presented at the National Bureau of Economic Research, Summer Institute 2009 Conference on Research on Income and Wealth, July 13.

Gray, P. G. 1955. "The Memory Factor in Social Surveys." *Journal of the American Statistical Association* 50:344–63.

Grooteart, Christian. 1986. "The Use of Multiple Diaries in a Household Expenditure Survey in Hong Kong." *Journal of the American Statistical Association* 81 (396): 938–44.

Groves, R. M. 1989. *Survey Errors and Survey Costs.* New York: Wiley.

Heitjan, D. F., and D. B. Rubin. 1991. "Ignorability and Coarse Data." *Annals of Statistics* 19:2244–53.

Herriot, R. A. 1977. "Collecting Income Data on Sample Surveys: Evidence from Split-Panel Studies." *Journal of Marketing Research* 14 (3): 322–29.

Hoderlein, S., and J. Winter. 2010. "Structural Measurement Errors in Nonseparable Models." *Journal of Econometrics* 157:432–40.

Hudomiet, P. 2011. "Cognition and Survey Behaviour: Evidence from a Validation Study of Earnings." Unpublished manuscript, University of Michigan.

Hurd, M., and S. Rohwedder. 2009. "Methodological Innovations in Collecting Spending Data: The HRS Consumption and Activities Mail Survey." *Fiscal Studies* 30 (3/4): 435–59.

———. 2010. "The Effects of the Financial Crisis and the Great Recession on American Households." NBER Working Paper no. 16407, Cambridge, MA.

Income Statistics Division, Statistics Canada. 1999. *1996 Food Expenditure Survey, Public-Use Microdata Files.* Ottawa: Statistics Canada.

Jacobs, E., and S. Shipp. 1993. "A History of the US Consumer Expenditure Survey: 1935–36 to 1988–89." *Journal of Economic and Social Measurement* 19:59–96.

Jolliffe, D. 2001. "Measuring Absolute and Relative Poverty: The Sensitivity of Estimated Household Consumption to Survey Design." *Journal of Economic and Social Measurement* 27 (1–2): 1–23.

Kemsley, W. F. F. 1961. "The Household Expenditure Enquiry of the Ministry of Labour: Variability in the 1953–1954 Enquiry." *Journal of the Royal Statistical Society, Series C* 10 (3): 117–35.

———. 1965. "Interviewer Variability in Expenditure Surveys." *Journal of the Royal Statistical Society, Series A* 128 (1): 118–39.

Kemsley, W. F. F., and J. L. Nicholson. 1960. "Some Experiments in Methods of Conducting Consumer Expenditure Surveys." *Journal of the Royal Statistical Society, Series A* 123 (3): 307–28.

Kemsley, W. F. F., R. Redpath, and M. Holmes. 1980. *Family Expenditure Survey Handbook.* London: Social Survey Division, OPCS.

Kreuter, F., S. Eckman, A. Jaeckle, A. Kirchner, S. Presser, and R. Tourangeau. 2012. "Mechanisms of Misreporting to Filter Questions." Paper presented at the 67th AAOPR Annual Conference, Orlando, Florida.

Kreuter, F., S. McCulloch, S. Presser, and R. Tourangeau. 2011. "The Effects of Asking Filter Questions in Interleafed versus Grouped Format." *Sociological Methods and Research* 40 (1): 88–104.

Manski, C. F., and F. Molinari. 2008. "Skip Sequencing: A Decision Problem in Questionnaire Design." *Annals of Applied Statistics* 2:264–85.

Manski, C. F., and E. Tamer. 2002. "Inference on Regressions with Interval Data on a Regressor or Outcome." *Econometrica* 70 (2): 519–46.

McFadden, D., A. Bemmaor, F. Caro, J. Dominitz, B. Jun, A. Lewbel, R. Matzkin, F. Molinari, N. Schwarz, R. Willis, and J. Winter. 2005. "Statistical Analysis of Choice Experiments and Surveys." *Marketing Letters* 16 (3–4): 183–96.

McKenzie, J. 1983. "The Accuracy of Telephone Call Data Collected by Diary Methods." *Journal of Marketing Research* 20:417–27.

McWhinney, I., and H. Champion. 1974. "The Canadian Experience with Recall and Diary Methods in Consumer Expenditure Surveys." In *Annals of Economic and Social Measurement* (vol. 3, no.2), edited by S. V. Berg, 113–40. Cambridge, MA: National Bureau of Economic Research.

Micklewright, J., and S. V. Schnepf. 2010. "How Reliable are Income Data Collected with a Single Question?" *Journal of the Royal Statistical Society, Series A* 173: 409–29.

National Sample Survey Organisation. 2000. "Choice of Reference Period for Consumption Data." Report no. 447, Department of Statistics, Government of India.

Neter, J., and J. Waksberg. 1964. "A Study of Response Errors in Expenditures Data from Household Interviews." *Journal of the American Statistical Association* 59:18–55.

Philipson, T. 1997. "Data Markets and the Production of Surveys." *Review of Economic Studies* 64 (1): 47–72.

———. 2001. "Data Markets, Missing Data, and Incentive Pay." *Econometrica* 69 (4): 1099–111.

Philipson, T., and T. Lawless. 1997. "Multiple-Output Agency Incentives in Data Production: Experimental Evidence." *European Economic Review* 41:961–70.

Philipson, T., and A. Malani. 1999. "Measurement Errors: A Principal Investigator-Agent Approach." *Journal of Econometrics* 91:273–98.

Pradhan, M. 2009. "Welfare Analysis with a Proxy Consumption Measure: Evidence from a Repeated Experiment in Indonesia." *Fiscal Studies* 30 (3/4): 391–417.

Pudney, S. 2007. "Heaping and Leaping: Survey Response Behavior and the Dynamics of Self-Reported Consumption Expenditure. Unpublished manuscript, University of Essex.

Reagan, B. B. 1954. *Condensed versus Detailed Schedule for Collection of Family Expenditure Data.* Washington, DC: Agricultural Research Service, US Department of Agriculture.

Rubin, D. C., and A. D. Baddeley. 1989. "Telescoping is not Time Compression: A Model of the Dating of Autobiographical Events." *Memory and Cognition* 17 (6): 653–61.

Ruud, P. A., D. Schunk, and J. Winter. 2014. "Uncertainty Causes Rounding: An Experimental Study." *Experimental Economics* 17 (3): 391–413.

Safir, A., and K. L. Goldenberg. 2008. "Mode Effects in a Survey of Consumer Expenditures." Unpublished manuscript, Bureau of Labor Statistics. http://www.bls.gov/cex/cesrvymethssafir1.pdf.

Schwarz, N., H. J. Hippler, B. Deutsch, and F. Strack. 1985. "Response Categories: Effects on Behavioral Reports and Comparative Judgments." Public Opinion Quarterly 49:388–95.

Shin, E., T. P. Johnson, and K. Rao. 2012. "Survey Mode Effects on Data Quality: Comparison of Web and Mail Modes in a US National Panel Survey." *Social Science Computer Review* 30 (2): 212–28.

Silberstein, A. R. 1990. "First Wave Effects in the US Consumer Expenditure Interview Survey." *Survey Methodology* 16:293–304.

Silberstein, A. R., and C. A. Jacob. 1989. "Symptoms of Repeated Interview Effects in the Consumer Expenditure Survey." In *Panel Surveys*, ed. D. Kasprzyk, G. Duncan, G. Kalton, and M. P. Singh, 289–303. Hoboken, NJ: Wiley.

Silberstein, A. R., and S. Scott. 1991. "Expenditure Diary Surveys and their Associated Errors." In *Measurement Errors in Surveys*, edited by P. P. Biermer, R. M. Groves, L. E. Lyberg, N. A. Mathiowetz, and S. Sudman. Hoboken, NJ: Wiley.

Skinner, J. 1987. "A Superior Measure of Consumption from the Panel Study of Income Dynamics." *Economics Letters* 23:213–16.

Statistics Canada. 1999. *1996 Food Expenditure Survey, Public-Use Microdata Files.* Ottawa: Income Statistics Division, Statistics Canada.

Stephens, M. 2003. "'3rd of the Month': Do Social Security Recipients Smooth Consumption between Checks?" *American Economic Review* 93 (1): 406–22.

Sudman, S., N. M. Bradburn, and N. Schwarz. 1996. *Thinking about Answers*. San Francisco: Jossey-Bass.

Sudman, S., and R. Ferber. 1971. "Experiments in Obtaining Consumer Expenditures by Diary Methods." *Journal of the American Statistical Association* 66:725–35.

Sudman, S., and R. Ferber. 1974. "A Comparison of Alternative Procedures for Collecting Consumer Expenditure Data for Frequently Purchased Products." *Journal of Marketing Research* 11:128–35.

Tanner, S. 1998. "How Much Do Consumers Spend? Comparing the FES and National Accounts." In *How Reliable is the Family Expenditure Survey?*, edited by J. Banks and P. Johnson. London: Institute for Fiscal Studies.

Tourangeau, R., L. J. Rips, and K. Rasinski. 2000. *The Psychology of Survey Response*. Cambridge: Cambridge University Press.

Tucker, C. 1992. "The Estimation of Instrument Effects on Data Quality in the Consumer Expenditure Survey." *Journal of Official Statistics* 8:41–61.

Tucker, C., and C. Bennett.1988. "Procedural Effects in the Collection of Consumer Expenditure Information." *Proceedings of the Section on Survey Research Methods*, American Statistical Association.

Turner, R. 1961. "Inter-Week Variations in Expenditure Recorded during a Two-Week Survey of Family Expenditure." *Journal of the Royal Statistical Society, Series C* 10 (3): 136–46.

van Soest, A., and M. Hurd. 2008. "A Test for Anchoring and Yea-Saying in Experimental Consumption Data." *Journal of the American Statistical Association* 103:126–36.

Winter, J. 2002. "Bracketing Effects in Categorized Survey Questions and the Measurement of Economic Quantities." Discussion Paper no. 02–35, Sonderforschungsbereich 504, University of Mannheim.

Winter, J. 2004. "Response Bias in Survey-Based Measures of Household Consumption." *Economics Bulletin* 3 (9): 1–12.

Wright, D. E., and I. Bray. 2003. "A Mixture Model for Rounded Data." *Statistician* 52 (1): 3–13.

II

Goals for the Expenditure Survey Redesign

Constructing a PCE-Weighted Consumer Price Index

Caitlin Blair

2.1 Introduction

Consumer Expenditure Survey (CE) data are a source of frequent debate in the federal statistical community. Pundits have criticized the household survey with arguments ranging from population and item coverage bias to inaccurate reporting as disadvantages of using CE data.[1] However, alternatives to the Consumer Expenditure Survey are scarce, and CE data have many advantages, including scope and population specificity. A variety of agencies and statistical programs utilize CE data, but one of the most important uses of CE data is in the construction of weights for the US Consumer Price Index (CPI), produced by the Bureau of Labor Statistics (BLS). Reported expenditures in the CE survey are used to calculate the relative importance, or expenditure weight, of each item category in the index. In order for the CPI to be an accurate measure of price change, it is vital that the weight data are accurate and representative of the appropriate population. If there is a systemic bias in the CE weights, there could be a bias in the resulting CPI.

Caitlin Blair wrote this chapter as part of her duties as an economist at the US Bureau of Labor Statistics. She is currently an international economist at the US Department of Commerce.

This chapter was originally prepared for the NBER/CRIW conference on Improving the Measurement of Consumer Expenditures, December 2011. The author would like to thank Rob Cage, Sara Stanley, Josh Klick, Madeleine Saxton, Bill Passero, Ronald Johnson, Anya Stockburger, Charles Mason, and John Greenlees of the Bureau of Labor Statistics and Clinton McCully and Brent Moulton of the Bureau of Economic Analysis for their support and input on this project. The views expressed in this chapter are those of the author and do not necessarily represent the views of the Bureau of Labor Statistics or the Department of Labor. The author takes full responsibility for any errors. Please contact Anya Stockburger of the BLS (stockburger.anya@bls.gov) with any questions related to this chapter. For acknowledgments, sources of research support, and disclosure of the author's material financial relationships, if any, please see http://www.nber.org/chapters/c12661.ack.

1. Garner et al. (2006) provide a brief chronology of work comparing CE and PCE.

This chapter examines CPI weights using an alternate weighting scheme under current CPI methodology. This is done by comparing official 2005–2010 CPI index values with index values derived from secondary source weights. Creating these indexes and comparing them to the published CPI allows us to gain a better understanding of item representativeness and item response accuracy in the CE-sourced CPI aggregation weights. In this study, personal consumption expenditures (PCE) data from the Bureau of Economic Analysis are the secondary source. Ultimately, we find that an index weighted to PCE levels matches the urban Consumer Price Index (CPI-U) very closely in trend and magnitude but grows at an annualized rate that is about 0.1 percent lower than the CPI-U growth rate over the 2005–2010 period. An index weighted to PCE levels that is not adjusted for definitional differences has an annualized five-year growth rate that is 0.3 percent higher than the CPI-U rate.

2.2 Importance of CE in the CPI

One reason that CE data are currently used in CPI production is the level of item, geographic, and population disaggregation available from the survey. The CPI utilizes expenditure values for five distinct population subgroups, which are then combined to create a variety of indexes for specific populations such as "urban," "wage-earner," and "elderly." Detailed demographic data ranging from respondent age to housing tenure to Social Security recipiency status are collected in the CE survey and can be used in index research. In addition, CE data are collected for thirty-eight geographic zones known as index areas, which are the primary level of geographic index aggregation in the CPI. These subnational population and geographic distinctions are possible because in the CE, survey data are collected at the household rather than national level.

The CE collates expense reports for over 200 unique expenditure categories, which can then be used to construct category expenditure estimates. The survey is conducted continuously on a monthly basis, providing users the ability to derive monthly, quarterly, and annual expenditure estimates. In this regard, the CE survey is unique. It is currently the exclusive source of monthly and annual expenditure estimates as required by the CPI program to construct elementary item-area indexes for the CPI.[2]

The alternative source of consumer expenditure data in this report, the PCE component of the National Income and Product Accounts (NIPA), is produced by the Bureau of Economic Analysis (BEA). These data are based on a census of retail establishments conducted every five years and on a variety of other sources rather than on a single survey, and they are

---

2. The CPI methodology is explained in detail in the BLS *Handbook of Methods*, available at http://stats.bls.gov/opub/hom.

widely used as a measure of national consumption expenditures. This chapter examines the accuracy and reliability of CPI data by comparing the official CPI, based on CE expenditure weights, to experimental indexes based on PCE expenditure levels using a PCE/CE spending factor. Because the PCE data are national data and the CE data are available at a local-area level, the PCE/CE spending factor used in the chapter must be applied identically across all areas and population groups. The comparisons that follow discuss indexes created for the years 2005–2010.

Two alternative indexes were constructed for the analysis. The first of these indexes, called PCE-UNADJ, uses PCE expenditure levels with CPI item definitions without adjusting PCE data for coverage differences (for example, the inclusion of expenditures for rural households) or conceptual differences (for example, PCE's inclusion of employer-provided health insurance). The second index, called PCE-ADJ, uses PCE expenditure levels adjusted for CPI item definitions, coverage, and concepts. A PCE alternate-weighting scheme is also useful in providing a check of the two data sources against each other. Both PCE and CE measure consumer expenditures, but they do so with very different approaches.

2.3 Data and Hybrid Index Design

Previous work has studied weighting bias, deflator differences, and expenditure ratios between PCE and CE to stimulate discussion and methodological improvement. This chapter builds upon that body of work by reconstructing CPI aggregation weights using PCE expenditure levels and item definitions to create hybrid indexes. These hybrid indexes use CPI index methodology and CE expenditure data to construct weights as the CPI does; however, CPI expenditures in the hybrid index aggregation weights are multiplied by factors that adjust them to PCE expenditure levels. The following pages discuss the realities of creating such PCE-calibrated CPIs using current CPI methodology and describe both results and drawbacks of such work. Designing a PCE-calibrated CPI is especially valuable to the current discussion of CE design, as it gives us a better idea of whether CE item response is both accurate and representative.[3] The similarity of the CPI-U and PCE-calibrated indexes and item-relative importances provides insight into CE accuracy.

To create PCE-calibrated indexes, a concordance between CPI and PCE item classifications is required. With this concordance, PCE expenditures are approximately matched to CPI item classifications and used to adjust the CPI expenditure weights to the levels where they would be if the CE reported absolute expenditures at the same level as PCE. This constitutes the PCE scope index in this study: an index that is calibrated to PCE expenditure

3. For a description of the current CE redesign project, see http://www.bls.gov/cex/gemini project.htm.

levels in the CPI goods and services categories that correspond to PCE categories. The PCE scope index is referred to as PCE-UNADJ in this chapter.

The other created index goes one step further and tries to account for the fact that some PCE categories match CPI categories in concept but not in expenditure definition; in this index, factors derived from secondary source data are used to adjust PCE expenditures to match CPI definitions in categories where the two data sources differ. For example, both PCE and CPI measure eggs and milk expenditures in the same way, but they measure medical expenditures differently. The CPI only uses out-of-pocket consumer spending for medical goods and services, including insurance premiums, whereas PCE includes all expenditures made both by and on behalf of consumers for medical goods and services, taking into account additional expenditures such as employer and government contributions. Therefore, this index includes a factor that adjusts PCE medical expenditures to include out-of-pocket payments only. This index is referred to as PCE-ADJ for the purposes of this chapter. The methodology section below elaborates on this process.

2.3.1 Previous Consumer Expenditure Data Comparisons

Numerous authors have undertaken important research into the comparison of PCE and CPI data on consumer expenditures to examine the quality and accuracy of CE. This previous work delves further into potential causes of bias and error between PCE and CE. Lebow and Rudd (2003) approached the issue of weighting bias in the CPI after the 1990s brought about tremendous change in CPI methodology.[4] They constructed a set of PCE weights to compare to CPI weights in the same time period by performing a variety of adjustments to PCE data and then aggregating the weights. They excluded out-of-scope items, adjusted medical, housing, and education expenditures to more closely align with CPI values, and they attempted to adjust for population differences between the two data sources using a factor.

Fixler and Jaditz (2002) compared the CPI and the PCE deflator, the BEA's price index computed from PCE data, to derive the magnitude of index difference attributable in 1992–1997 to each type of major difference: formulaic, conceptual, and implementation related.[5] They focused on what they called an "accounting" solution that attempted to adjust for each of the major differences and calculate its ratio of the index discrepancies; Fixler and Jaditz did not try to examine weighting or pricing issues directly.

McCully, Moyer, and Stewart (2007) built on work like that by Fixler and Jaditz to expand the time period addressed forward to 2007 and calculated formula, scope, weight, and "other" effects, such as seasonal adjustment, that cause fundamental differences between the deflator and the CPI.[6]

---

4. See Lebow and Rudd (2003).
5. See Fixler and Jaditz (2002).
6. For more information see McCully, Moyer, and Stewart (2007).

Garner et al. (2006) have produced a variety of papers in which they construct and update expenditure category ratios between PCE and CE data.[7] Those authors constructed ratios for both comparable and noncomparable goods and services categories, taking care to examine each category in their paper and explain the caveats to the comparison and provide some reasons why ratios differ from one. Many other authors, including Clark (2003), Triplett (1978, 1981), and others have also examined the PCE and CPI; the work of the authors mentioned above adds to the debate about differences between the two subjects.

All of the papers discussed above bring to light a variety of fundamental issues in attempting to relate PCE and CE or CPI data. Garner et al. (2006) explain data collection methodology differences between the two. The CE obtains its data through a series of diary and interview surveys of consumers. In contrast, PCE data come from a variety of data sources, but are primarily derived from the quinquennial Economic Census, with data from trade and industry surveys to supplement in the off years (or nonbenchmark years).

Many authors speak of the item-scope differences between the two surveys. As McCully, Moyer, and Stewart (2007) explain, CPI includes out-of-pocket consumer expenditures and PCE includes purchases both by and on behalf of consumers. Two big conceptual differences discussed by Fixler and Jaditz (2002) are population and implementation at the component level. In most cases, they argue, CE data should be a subset of PCE data. The PCE includes expenditures by military personnel and third-party payers, such as employers, that CE does not allow. However, CE and CPI go outside of the bounds of PCE in some areas. The PCE does not include items that it considers coercive, such as vehicle registration and licensing, which are included in both CE and the Consumer Price Index. The PCE also does not include CPI and CE items such as lawn mowers and garden tractors, household maintenance and repairs, and fishing and hunting licenses.

There are even differences in definition between items that match each other in the two indexes, such as apparel and food. In many cases, PCE and CPI categories will be a perfect match, except that the item classification results in CPI arranging items in a way that is slightly different from how it is done in PCE. For example, CPI and PCE apparel categories concord perfectly, except that CPI includes wallets, umbrellas, and purses in apparel under accessories. The PCE includes these items not in apparel, but in luggage. Some of this structure knowledge comes from concordance research conducted as a collaborative effort between the CE, CPI, and PCE offices at the Bureau of Labor Statistics and Bureau of Economic Analysis.[8]

---

7. See Garner et al. (2006).
8. E-mails and concordance discussions with Clinton McCully (BEA), William Passero (BLS), Thesia Garner (BLS), and Rob Cage (BLS), 2011.

Garner et al. (2006) note that previous studies have shown that although underreporting in CE and diminished representativeness or respondent accuracy may be a cause for the difference between PCE and CE results, the magnitude of PCE revisions indicates that there are potential estimation issues coming from those data as well. Issues may also arise in the way that PCE uses a variety of data sources. The general consensus among authors who studied both PCE and CE data was that one could not be chosen as the whole source of bias and difference between the two, and all agreed that there was further work to be done.

2.3.2 Index Methodology

There are two experimental indexes in this study: an index that is PCE-calibrated using PCE valuation of consumption (PCE-UNADJ) and an index that is PCE-calibrated using CPI valuation of consumption (PCE-ADJ). The PCE-UNADJ is created in the following manner:

1. A CPI entry level item[9] (ELI) to PCE series code[10] concordance is created with input from the Bureau of Labor Statistics and the Bureau of Economic Analysis. This is because the CPI uses a proprietary classification system that does not align perfectly with the PCE system: there are many goods and services that are classified in general categories in one system and in disaggregated categories in the other system. There are also goods and services that have different definitions between PCE and CPI and no clear match between their PCE and CPI classification codes. In the concordance, ELIs are assigned to the lowest-level-matching PCE series code publicly available. Although this is sometimes a perfect match, sometimes multiple ELIs matched to one broad PCE code, and sometimes an ELI had to be split between multiple PCE codes in the concordance. Using this concordance, all ELIs are broken down into one of three categories: out of PCE scope, one PCE series code per ELI, and multiple PCE series codes per ELI. One example of an ELI that falls outside the scope of PCE is TF011 (see table 2.1).

The CPI apparel demonstrates an example of the other two types of ELIs, ELIs that match to exactly one PCE series code and ELIs that must be split between multiple PCE series codes (see table 2.2).

The ELI AA021 maps into only one PCE series code, DMBCRC. The AA022, however, maps mostly into DMBCRC but also maps in part to

9. More information on ELIs can be found in the BLS *Handbook of Methods*, chapter 17 (http://stats.bls.gov/opub/hom): "Within each item stratum, one or more substrata, called entry-level items (ELIs), are defined. There are a total of 305 ELIs, which are the ultimate sampling units for items as selected by the BLS national office. They represent the level of item definition from which data collectors begin item sampling within each sample outlet."

10. The PCE series code names and definitions can be found in National Income and Product Accounts (NIPA) Underlying Detail Table 2.4.5U "Personal Consumption Expenditures by Type of Product." Further information about the PCE series structure is available in the NIPA Handbook at http://www.bea.gov/national/pdf/NIPAchapters1–9.pdf.

Table 2.1   **Out-of-scope ELI example**

ELI	ELI description	PCE series code	PCE description	Allocation ratio
TF011	State vehicle registration and driver's license	n/a	n/a	0.00

Table 2.2   **In-scope ELI examples**

ELI	ELI description	PCE series code	PCE description	Allocation ratio
AA021	Men's underwear, hosiery, and nightwear	DMBCRC	Men's and boys' clothing	1.00
AA022	Men's accessories	DMBCRC	Men's and boys' clothing	0.93
AA022	Men's accessories	DLUGRC	Luggage and similar personal items	0.07

DLUGRC. This is because CPI includes wallets and umbrellas in apparel, whereas PCE includes those items in luggage.[11]

2. Allocation ratios are assigned to each ELI-PCE code combination so that all ratios for an ELI summed to one.[12] All ELIs that matched perfectly to one PCE code, regardless of the number of ELIs per PCE code, receive a value of "1" as in the example above for ELI AA021. The ELIs that are not included in the scope of PCE are given a value of "0," as shown above in the TF011 example.[13] All other ELIs are divided into their component PCE series codes using underlying CE expenditure data at the observation level. For most ELIs, this means using data at the CE diary survey level. For the few split ELIs that are only available in the interview portion of CE, an even split ratio is provided for all PCE codes that mapped to the ELI. This is the case in two education ELIs and one other goods and services ELI. In the apparel example above, a scan of all 2003–2008 AA022 diary data

11. The ELI-to-PCE-series-code concordance can be viewed on the CPI website at http://www.bls.gov/cpi/cpipceconcd.pdf.

12. If the ELI did not completely map to PCE, that is, part of but not the entire ELI was out of PCE scope, then the ratios for that ELI would sum to the percentage of ELI expenditures that were within scope for both CE and PCE. For example, the ratios for EE031, "other information services," sum to approximately .98 because a small web services component of that ELI does not map to PCE at all.

13. In some cases, it may be possible to find expenditure data in the National Income and Product Accounts that corresponds to these goods and services. However, this study makes no attempt to supplement PCE expenditure data with secondary source data in such a manner to account for item categories included in the CPI but excluded from PCE. A similar procedure could be implemented in a later version of this chapter.

shows that 7 percent of all AA022 expenditures were wallets and umbrellas, whereas 93 percent of AA022 consists of other accessories. Therefore, the AA022 allocation ratios are 0.93 for DMBCRC and 0.07 for DLUGRC.

3. The ratios are multiplied by CE expenditure data and then summed by PCE code assignment to create a set of total CPI expenditures by PCE code for each year in the period.

4. Using NIPA underlying table 2.4.5U "Personal Consumption Expenditures by Type of Product"[14] and the CPI expenditure data from step number 3, PCE/CPI factors are created for each PCE series code. For example, in a PCE category where PCE reported $200 of expenditures and CE reported $100 of expenditures, the PCE/CPI factor would be two.

5. The factor is applied to expenditure data and then applied to the CE microlevel data to recalibrate CPI aggregation weights to PCE values for the 2003–2008 period. For example, an ELI that matched one-to-one in definition with a PCE series code would have a recalibration factor of one. If PCE reported $200 in expenditures for that PCE code and CPI reported $100 in expenditures for that PCE code, then the factor would be two as in step number 4. Because of the perfect definition match, the PCE calibration for this ELI would simply apply a factor of two to the microlevel data.

6. The adjustments in step number 5 are made for each ELI at the reported CPI expense level. The resulting adjusted costs are then weighted and summed to the elementary CPI item-area category level, annualized for the 2003–2004, 2005–2006, and 2007–2008 expenditure reference periods, and converted into aggregation weights.

7. The new aggregation weights are used to create indexes for 2005–2010 using standard CPI-U methodology.

Because two market basket structure changes have taken place in the CPI over the past few years, the aggregation weights are adjusted depending on the market basket structure used in that year. The final result of this work is a set of annualized biennial expenditure weights by CPI item-area category that are used to create PCE-UNADJ using CPI index aggregation methods. That is, the indexes presented here all employ the same formula and biennial weight update process used in the CPI-U, whereas the PCE indexes published by the BEA use quarterly weights and a Fisher ideal index formula.

An important difference between the CE and PCE weights is that the former are calculated and implemented in the CPI at the item-area level. For example, the CPI employs "apple" category weights for thirty-eight geographic areas and matches them to thirty-eight corresponding area-level basic price indexes. In contrast, PCE weights and indexes exist only at the national level. This chapter uses elementary item-area prices and adjusted weights. Due to data availability, we assume that the PCE/CPI expenditure ratio is uniform across

14. http://www.bea.gov/national/nipaweb.

US areas and create the calibration factors and PCE-ADJ adjustment factors at a national level to apply them to the local thirty-eight-area CPI data.

To create PCE-ADJ, the original recalibration factors are modified by secondary source data to create a new set of factors that not only reflect differences in item definition, but also reflect differences in expenditure definition. The CPI apparel example above is a difference in item definition: CPI wallets and umbrellas are listed in clothing accessories, whereas PCE wallets and umbrellas are included in luggage; the ratios for both PCE-UNADJ and PCE-ADJ are created so that the wallet and umbrella value from CPI apparel is recalibrated by PCE luggage expenditures. An expenditure definition difference can be seen in CPI education: CPI higher education tuition reflects only out-of-pocket payments, whereas PCE higher education tuition reflects all payments—out-of-pocket and third party; the expenditure factor must be adjusted by a constant that represents the average US out-of-pocket spending on college tuition as a percentage of total US spending on college tuition. After this proportion adjustment is made, the process aligns perfectly with the process used to create PCE-UNADJ in steps 4–7 above.

In this project, a variety of adjustments are made to differentiate PCE-ADJ from PCE-UNADJ, or to adjust PCE categories with different expenditure definitions to fit CPI expenditure definitions. In many cases, this adjustment removes third-party payments from PCE expenditure data. Table 2.3 contains the adjustments and affected ELIs.

For PCE-ADJ, student tuition and board expenditures from PCE-UNADJ are adjusted to exclude third-party payments such as grants using National Center for Education Statistics data on total and out-of-pocket costs of college for American students.[15] Medical expenditures that typically include some insurance payment component are adjusted to exclude third-party payments made by employers, government, and others using data from the Agency for Healthcare Research and Quality's Medical Expenditure Panel Survey (2008).[16] Utilities, rent, homeowners' insurance, financial services fees, vehicle insurance, and vehicle maintenance and repair are adjusted using the CE-PCE ratios in Garner et al. (2006) to fit PCE levels.

The homeowners' insurance ratio of 8 is an approximation from the text of the paper rather than an official ratio, and it is used because homeowners' insurance is included in a large-scope ratio of "other household operations" that has a value closer to 1.03. The ratios from Garner et al. (2006) are not ideal for such an index because they include other factors beyond expenditure difference such as item under- or overreporting.[17] However, in these cases,

---

15. The National Center for Education Statistics (NCES) data used is derived from tables 1 and 2 in Wei (2010).

16. The MEPS data comes from the Agency for Healthcare and Research Quality (2008).

17. The goal of this chapter is to produce broad-level PCE/CE ratios to shed a critical light on how the two have changed over the years. These ratios may differ from one for a variety of reasons other than differences in the way category consumer expenditures are measured.

Table 2.3   **PCE-ADJ adjustments by ELI**

ELI(s)	CPI description	PCE code(s)	PCE description	Adjustment factor	Data source
All "EB" ELIs	Tuition, other school fees, and child care	All	All	0.59	NCES[a]
FV051	Board, catered events, and other food away from home	DMSLRC	Meals at schools	0.59	NCES
GD051	Checking accounts and other bank services	DFEERC	Financial service charges and fees	0.08	GJPPV[b]
HA011	Rent of primary residence	All	All	0.98	GJPPV
HD011	Tenants' and household insurance	All	All	8.00	GJPPV
HF011	Electricity	All	All	1.02	GJPPV
HF021	Utility (piped) gas service	All	All	0.86	GJPPV
HG011	Residential water and sewage service	All	All	0.69	GJPPV
MA011 and MF011	Prescription drugs	All	All	0.17	AHRQ[c]
MA090 and MG090	Unsampled rent or repair of medical equipment	DOMORC	All other professional medical services	0.17	AHRQ
All "MC" ELIs	Professional medical services	All	All	0.17	AHRQ
All "MD" ELIs except MD031	Hospital and related services	All	All	0.17	AHRQ
All "ME" ELIs	Health insurance	All	All	0.17	AHRQ
MB023 and MG013	Supportive and convalescent medical equipment	All	All	0.17	AHRQ
All "TD" ELIs	Motor vehicle maintenance and repair	All	All	0.67	GJPPV
TE011	Motor vehicle insurance	All	All	2.11	GJPPV

[a] NCES refers to the National Center for Education Statistics publication "What Is the Price of College? Total, Net, and Out-of-Pocket Prices in 2007–2008" (Wei 2010).

[b] GJPPV refers to Garner et al. (2006).

[c] AHRQ refers to the Agency for Healthcare Research and Quality's Medical Expenditure Panel Survey (2008).

quality national data that separated item costs by the expenditure type needed are unavailable.

2.4 Results

2.4.1 Item Representation

In the 2007–2008 annualized weights (which correspond to the 2010 index values), the mean item stratum PCE-UNADJ-to-CPI-U expenditure ratio is 1.65—this is a simplified approximation of the ratio that was applied to CE data in step number 3 to create weights for PCE-UNADJ and PCE-ADJ. The mean item stratum PCE-ADJ-to-CPI-U expenditure ratio for the same time period is 1.51. It aligns well with the final expenditure totals: at $9.3 trillion, the 2010 final weighted PCE-UNADJ expenditure total was slightly less than twice the CPI-U expenditure total of approximately $5.1 trillion. In contrast, the 2010 final weighted PCE-ADJ expenditure total of $7.5 trillion was 1.46 times the CPI-U total—these expenditure totals correspond with the 2007–2008 annualized weights.

Tables 2.4 and 2.5 show more detail for the items with the highest and lowest CPI-U/PCE-ADJ ratios—this is the inverse of the PCE-ADJ-to-CPI-U ratio discussed previously. These cases in which the adjusted PCE expenditure value differs most from the CPI value can be indicative of item representation issues or of areas where the PCE-ADJ secondary source adjustments could be more finely tuned. "Child care and nursery school," as seen leading table 2.4, is an excellent example of this. Babysitting, a person-to-person component of child care, frequently involves payments between individuals and is therefore more likely to be represented in the CPI. For the purposes of this chapter, child care in one's home has been removed from the ratio allocations to account for this definition difference because that is the lowest accurate level at which the child care and nursery school data can be disaggregated to remove babysitting. However, not all in-home child care is considered to be babysitting, which may be the cause behind the high ratio seen below.

Table 2.5 lists item strata with the lowest CPI-U/PCE-ADJ expenditure ratio—this is equivalent to the highest PCE-ADJ/CPI-U expenditure ratio. Item strata that consistently have much higher PCE-ADJ expenditure levels than CPI-U expenditure levels include "floor coverings," "other video equipment," and "technical and business school tuition and fees." In table 2.4, there are multiple notable medical-item strata, which is indicative of the possibility that the broadly applied medical-expenditure adjustment used in PCE-ADJ may not be a perfect fit for all medical expense categories.

Figures 2.1 and 2.2 show scatterplots of the CPI-U and PCE-ADJ expenditure values for each item stratum, with rent and a few other large expenditures such as tuition and vehicles excluded in figure 2.2 so that all other

Table 2.4 Top five CPI-U/PCE-ADJ expenditure ratio maximums

Item	Item description	2005 ratio	Item	Item description	2007 ratio	Item	Item description	2009 ratio
SEEB03	Child care and nursery school	4.155	SEEB03	Child care and nursery school	4.556	SEEB03	Child care and nursery school	4.182
SEMC03	Eyeglasses and eye care	2.529	SEMC03	Eyeglasses and eye care	2.820	SEMC03	Eyeglasses and eye care	2.708
SEHE02	Other household fuels	2.006	SEHE02	Other household fuels	2.450	SEHE02	Other household fuels	2.640
SEMC02	Dental services	1.806	SEMC02	Dental services	2.112	SEMC02	Dental services	1.986
SEHB02	Other lodging away from home including hotels and motels	1.763	SEHB02	Other lodging away from home including hotels and motels	1.623	SEME03	Health maintenance plans	1.509

Table 2.5 Bottom five CPI-U/PCE-ADJ expenditure ratio minimums

Item	Item description	2005 ratio	Item	Item description	2007 ratio	Item	Item description	2009 ratio
SEGD01	Legal services	0.136	SEFW02	Distilled spirits at home	0.136	SEEE02	Computer software and accessories	0.131
SEEE02	Computer software and accessories	0.133	SEEE02	Computer software and accessories	0.117	SEFW02	Distilled spirits at home	0.131
SEEB04	Technical and business school tuition and fees	0.132	SEMD03	Care of invalids and elderly at home	0.112	SEHH01	Floor coverings	0.117
SERA03	Other video equipment	0.128	SERA03	Other video equipment	0.099	SEEB04	Technical and business school tuition and fees	0.087
SEHH01	Floor coverings	0.100	SEHH01	Floor coverings	0.090	SERA03	Other video equipment	0.087

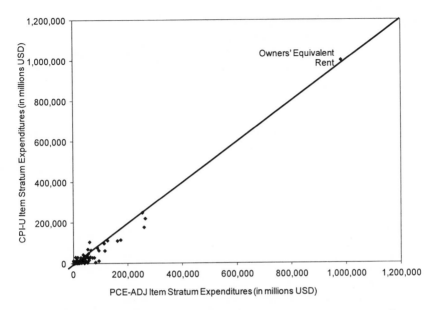

Fig. 2.1 Scatterplot of CPI-U and PCE-ADJ elementary item stratum expenditure estimates, 2005.12

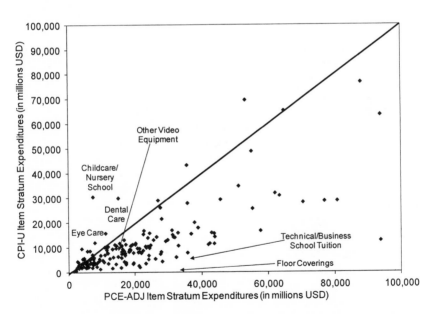

Fig. 2.2 Scatterplot of CPI-U and PCE-ADJ elementary item stratum expenditure estimates, 2005.12 (OER, tuition, and other large expenditures excluded)

Table 2.6   December 2005 item relation importances

	CPI-U (%)	PCE-calibrated indexes	
		PCE-UNADJ (%)	PCE-ADJ (%)
Consumption category			
Food and beverages	15.1	13.8	17.0
Food at home	8.0	7.1	8.7
Food away from home	6.0	4.9	6.0
Alcoholic beverages	1.1	1.8	2.3
Housing	42.4	26.5	32.9
Rent	5.8	3.4	4.1
Owner's equivalent rent	23.4	12.9	15.9
Other housing	13.1	10.2	12.9
Apparel	3.8	4.5	5.5
Medical care	6.2	22.3	5.0
Transportation	17.4	13.9	17.3
Motor vehicles	7.9	5.3	6.5
Gasoline	4.2	3.4	4.3
Other transportation	5.4	5.2	6.5
Education and communication	6.0	5.4	6.7
Recreation	5.6	6.8	8.4
Tobacco	0.7	1.0	1.2
Other goods and services	2.8	5.8	6.0
	100.0	100.0	100.0

item trends may be more easily examined. From these scatterplots, it is easy to see that the expenditure levels used to calculate the PCE-ADJ and CPI-U are similar, because their ratio lies along the 45° line. In other words, after secondary source adjustment to CPI definitions, these items have roughly the same absolute expenditure value in both CE and PCE.

In both figures, a 1:1 ratio line illustrates item stratum expenditure level trends; items below the line have a higher PCE-ADJ expenditure level than CPI-U expenditure level, while items above the line have a higher CPI-U expenditure level than PCE-ADJ expenditure level. A majority of the 211-item strata fall below the line, which indicates, as expected due to the PCE weight adjustments, that overall expenditure levels for most items are higher in the PCE-calibrated CPI-U than in the published CPI-U.

Table 2.6 shows item-category relative importances for the three indexes using December 2005 weights. As expected, there are large differences in medical relative importances between PCE-UNADJ and PCE-ADJ and small differences in these relative importances between the CPI and PCE-ADJ. Shelter relative importances are very different between both PCE indexes and the CPI-U, not because of dramatic differences between the two data sources in housing expenditure levels, but rather because of total expenditure differences in other categories (such as medical care). In other words, although the budget share of housing is smaller using PCE data than

CE data, both PCE and CE agree on how much is spent total on shelter—the share itself changes because other goods and services increase their proportions of total spending in the PCE indexes.

It is also important to note that some items show larger differences between the CPI-U and PCE-ADJ, which could be indicative of an item representation issue in CE. Four categories that are commonly cited as being underrepresented in CE due to respondent behavior are apparel, other goods, tobacco, and alcohol. The evidence from this study supports the expectation that those four categories might have lower CE representation than PCE representation. Tobacco and alcohol, which are believed to be underreported because of their sensitive nature, also have a significantly smaller relative importance in the CPI-U than in PCE-ADJ index. Apparel and other goods may be underreported in CE because of proxy reporting: if only one member reports expenditures for the entire household, they may be more aware of family food, housing, and education purchases than of the clothing and other personal goods purchases made by all household members.[18] Both of those categories also have significantly higher relative importance values in both PCE-calibrated indexes than they do in the CPI-U.

The PCE-UNADJ relative importances are slightly different. Because medical care is measured so differently between the two sources (CE and PCE) and therefore carries a large adjustment in this study, medical care makes up almost a quarter of PCE-UNADJ, but makes up only 5 percent of the CPI-U and PCE-ADJ. In accordance with the other adjustments made to create PCE-ADJ, the PCE-UNADJ transportation and housing categories have lower relative importances than the corresponding CPI-U and PCE-ADJ categories, while PCE-UNADJ education is a bit higher. Slight variations exist in some of the other item categories such as recreation and other goods. This merits further investigation; it is possible that there could be a significant difference in item representation in one of those categories as well.

2.4.2 Index Levels and Change

When the PCE-calibrated indexes and the CPI-U are compared between 2005 and 2010, it is clear how closely the published CPI-U and PCE-ADJ track each other. As shown in figure 2.1, the CPI-U tends to be slightly higher than PCE-ADJ. However, overall the PCE-ADJ five-year annualized growth rate is 0.071 percent lower than the CPI-U five-year annualized growth rate. In contrast, the PCE-UNADJ five-year annualized growth rate is 0.338 percent higher than the CPI-U five-year annualized growth rate.

Lebow and Rudd (2003), constructing an index similar to PCE-ADJ, concluded that the CPI has an upward bias of approximately 0.1 percent per

---

18. Garner et al. (2006) provide an in-depth discussion of underreporting in the context of PCE/CE ratios in their paper.

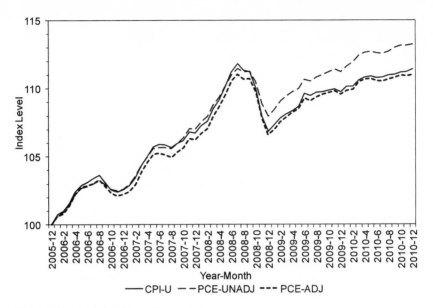

Fig. 2.3 CPI-U and PCE-calibrated index comparisons

year due to inaccurate weights. Their conclusion was based on comparison of indexes using CE and PCE weights over the 1987–2001 period, with those weights computed at the twenty-four-item level. This chapter, using a later time period and a more detailed weight and index decomposition, shows a difference of 0.071 percent, which is of the same magnitude as Lebow and Rudd's results, but slightly lower.

Figure 2.3 demonstrates the shape and direction of the indexes. As previously noted, both indexes containing the CPI definitions (CPI-U and PCE-ADJ) exhibit similar rates of change and rise more slowly than the index that uses PCE expenditure valuation (PCE-UNADJ). The fact that the CPI-U and PCE-ADJ indexes exhibit similar rates of change is logical because their expenditure definitions match in two large categories: medical expenses and education.

Figure 2.3 also shows that the PCE-UNADJ index has risen more quickly than the CPI-U and PCE-ADJ indexes. The PCE-UNADJ index series diverges from the CPI-U and PCE-ADJ index series after October 2008 due to the larger weight given to medical care and education items. From October 2008 to the end of the study period, the all-items CPI-U index increased 1.20 percent while the medical care and education CPI-U indexes increased 7.16 percent and 8.93 percent, respectively. Combined, these categories contribute to a larger rate of inflation for the PCE-UNADJ series compared to the CPI-U and PCE-ADJ series.

Most items in the CPI-U and PCE-ADJ indexes have similar relative importances between the two indexes, with one notable exception. Shelter,

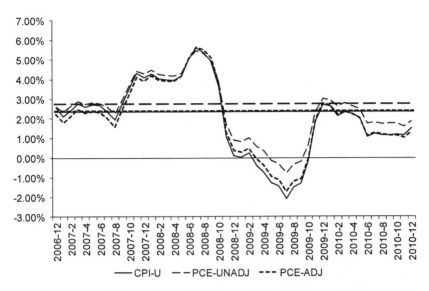

Fig. 2.4 CPI-U and PCE-calibrated twelve-month index change comparisons

the category that has a relative importance almost 10 percentage points higher in the CPI-U than in the PCE-ADJ, might be expected to be the reason that the PCE-ADJ diverges from the CPI-U for most of the time between 2005 and 2010.[19] The shelter CPI-U index increased 0.46 percent from October 2008 through December 2010—a price change lower than the all-items index change. Between October 2008 and December 2010, the average monthly shelter-only CPI-U index change differed from the average monthly CPI-U index change for all items by a mere 0.010 percent. A look at 1998–2010 CPI-U data reveals that the two average monthly CPI-U index change values differed by only 0.015 percent (with the all-items index increasing slightly more rapidly than the shelter-only index) between the two indexes. Despite the difference in weights, shelter price change is more similar to the rest of the CPI than education and medical services, and so it has a lower impact on the experimental index results than the latter two items.

Figure 2.4 shows the twelve-month index change values for each of the three indexes. While the 2006–2010 average twelve-month index change for the CPI-U is approximately 2.013 percent, that value is 0.003 percent lower for PCE-ADJ and 0.441 percent higher for the PCE-UNADJ index. However, the difference between CPI-U and PCE-ADJ twelve-month index change ranges from 0.371 to –0.373 over the 2006–2010 period.

19. Section 4.1 includes a discussion of why shelter-relative importances differ between PCE-ADJ and CPI-U.

2.4.3 Caveats

As mentioned above, there are a variety of ways in which it is nearly impossible to create a perfect PCE-calibrated CPI due to differences in the nature of the data. Although secondary source data make the ratio estimates for education and medical expenses more useful, they are applied broadly in the creation of PCE-ADJ rather than disaggregated down to the item level. It is unlikely that the ratio of medical expenditures paid out-of-pocket by consumers will be identical for the purchase medical specialist services and prescription drugs or primary care doctor visits. It is also possible that the proportions of education expenditures for public and private universities are different between the CPI and the NCES survey from which the tuition ratio is derived. There may be ratios other than those created by Garner et al. (2006) in which the nonconsumer portion of the ratio can be removed in aggregation, although they are difficult to find in secondary sources.

In addition, the populations covered by the aggregate CPI-U and PCE data are very different. The CPI-U data cover urban, nonmilitary, noninstitutional households, whereas PCE data cover domestic consumers including third parties that make purchases on behalf of consumers. The PCE does not include domestic consumers who have been and will be in the country for less than one year.

Across all time periods, the total expenditure values for items HA01 and HC01—the two major CPI shelter categories—are nearly identical for the CPI-U and its PCE-calibrated counterparts. As shown in figure 2.1, owners' equivalent rent falls extremely close to the CPI-U/PCE-ADJ=1 line in 2005. However, the relative importance of housing in the CPI-U is higher than the relative importance of housing in both PCE-UNADJ and PCE-ADJ because CE expenditure levels in housing more closely match PCE expenditure levels than expenditure levels in other item categories do; in many item categories outside of housing, CE expenditure levels are lower than PCE expenditure levels.

Other small discrepancies may arise in specifics of the concordance and in the scope of the two consumption data sets; PCE and CPI both contain items that are out-of-scope in the other consumption data. To produce the two indexes above, four ELIs from the three-market basket structures used had to be removed altogether because they are considered out of scope in PCE and therefore have no expenditure value. Vehicle registration and license fees are seen as coercive and not included in PCE, while gardening and lawn services and inside home maintenance and repair are not included in PCE because they are considered intermediate expenditures of homeowners. Some additional portions of CPI items, such as hunting and fishing licenses, are excluded from PCE. In such cases, the portion of the ELI that is not used in PCE was removed, causing these ELI proportions to sum to less than one. There is also the potential for item definition differences that were not addressed in the concordance used for this study. This is because CE uses survey data, and item definition interpretations can vary from respondent to respondent. For example, PCE disaggregates the CPI "souvenirs" universal classification code (UCC) out to categories that describe the individual components. Guidebooks and programs are included in books, postcards are included in stationery, and T-shirts are a part of apparel. However, determining this disaggregation in the CPI can be nearly impossible because some respondents simply write "$20 souvenirs" rather than "$15 T-shirt, $5 postcards" in the diary portion of the survey.

Finally, an unsolved methodological debate arose during this project that involves the way in which PCE-CPI expenditure ratios were calculated for ELIs that had to be split between PCE codes. Data are PCE calibrated by fitting CPI expenditures into PCE series categories, but the data must then be mapped back into CPI items (one level above ELIs) to construct expenditure weights as CE data are in CPI production. For the purposes of this chapter, data are mapped into the item categories corresponding to the ELIs from which their CPI expenditures originally came. However, a future improvement to this methodology would be to identify the CPI items that best match where the PCE expenditures map so that CPI price quotes are functionally "moved" into the categories that best fit the PCE calibration rather than staying in their original item categories.

2.5 Future Research

The PCE and CE data have been compared for years at the Bureau of Labor Statistics and in the broader federal community.[20] There is still much work to do, however. If anything, this chapter illustrates the need for further analysis in this area. The PCE-calibrated price indexes constructed here explore only a few of the many possibilities that exist in bringing current CPI data closer to the data used in PCE. Although some of these possibilities seem infeasible currently, there is always the hope that more light will be shed on them in future efforts.

One area in which methodological improvements could be made is in population matching. The CE and CPI populations differ from the PCE population, which is a problem rooted in the way the data are collected. The PCE data come primarily from the production side as part of the National Income and Product Accounts and are typically the result of equations that remove all nonconsumer use allocations from the total purchase value of a good or service to create a personal consumption value. The CE (and therefore CPI) data are collected directly from the consumer, a practice that allows for more population-limiting specificity. These data are limited to nonmilitary, noninstitutionalized households and, in the case of the CPI-U,

20. See Lebow and Rudd (2003) or Fixler and Jaditz (2002) for examples of this.

can be further limited to exclude consumption by rural households. Finding a method by which to more closely match the CPI population to the PCE population would allow for more accurate use of PCE weights in an alternate CPI.

Further study into the historical differences between the CPI-U and an index similar to PCE-ADJ would also be very useful. Being able to see ten or more years of comparative data instead of five would help researchers better understand the differences and how they have changed with time and item-structure updates in both the CPI and PCE. The CPI has undergone two item-structure changes in the past few years, and PCE has moved from one benchmark year period to the next. These changes could potentially have a large effect on the data, but also help us more easily identify bias and data inaccuracies as they change from structure to structure or period to period.

A larger-scale update to the methodology used in this chapter lies in the items themselves. Although this concording exercise focuses on the weight side of the Consumer Price Index, it would be beneficial to create a hybrid CPI that matches PCE definitions for both weighting and pricing. Similarly, a set of hybrid indexes created using concorded UCCs rather than concorded ELIs could create a more accurate comparison by fine-tuning the good- and service-level comparisons. The UCC structure can also change, and the methodology used here only focused on item- and ELI-structure changes when determining allocation ratios.

Finally, there are a few ways in which data from the Consumer Price Index can be used to create a more accurate representation of a PCE-calibrated index. An index could be constructed by modifying the level of aggregation in the CPI. A CPI aggregated to the major group (apparel, education and communication, food, other goods, housing, medical, recreation, transportation) level would remove many definitional discrepancies between PCE and CPI, allowing us to focus on the largest differences. Going in the opposite direction, more detailed concording research could be done to break data down for classification at the individual-observation level, causing each data point in the CPI or PCE data to be intentionally mapped to its correct ELI or PCE series code. This would mean the creation of a "true" PCE-UNADJ or PCE-ADJ, but would also involve mapping both NIPA and CPI data to underlying categories.

2.6 Conclusion

This chapter contrasts current BLS Consumer Price Index values with the values derived from PCE-calibrated Consumer Price Indexes adjusted to PCE and CPI good and service definitions. Ultimately, the results indicate that adjusting PCE weights to CPI expenditure definitions yields an index (PCE-ADJ) that closely tracks the CPI-U. However, there are also strong differences between the two indexes, particularly once results are disaggregated to the item level. We see differences in item-relative importance in the apparel, alcohol, and tobacco categories that may be indicative of an item representativeness issue in those categories in the CE survey. Overall, the PCE-UNADJ annualized growth rate over five years is 0.338 percent higher than that of the CPI-U, while the PCE-ADJ annualized growth rate over five years is 0.071 percent lower than that of the CPI-U.

As shown above, there is still a lot of ground to cover in order for this work to accurately represent the two indexes. Some aspects may be more difficult to correct in future work, such as adjustments for population and scope differences between PCE and CPI, while others may provide an excellent opportunity for further research, such as more detailed item concording using further disaggregated data from both the BLS and the BEA. The closer these indexes come to accurately representing the real CPI and a real PCE-valued CPI, the more useful they are in examining the representativeness of CE survey data. Finding that PCE and CE have similar item-level outcomes may be useful in future survey design to reduce respondent burden or allow for detailed data-quality checks. Large differences would indicate that it may be time to reexamine the motivations and methodology in the two consumer expenditure data sets. Although, when using this index data, we cannot show whether match issues are due to CE bias or PCE methods, the above results and future work will help us to better determine how to continue refining our data collection and aggregation methods.

References

Agency for Healthcare and Research Quality. 2008. "Medical Expenditure Panel Survey Table 1: Total Health Services-Median and Mean Expenses per Person with Expense and Distribution of Expenses by Source of Payment: United States, 2008." http://www.meps.ahrq.gov.

Bureau of Economic Analysis. 2009. "Concepts and Methods of the US National Income and Product Accounts." Washington, DC, Bureau of Economic Analysis. http://www.bea.gov/methodologies.

Clark, Todd E. 2003. "A Comparison of the CPI and the PCE Price Index." *Economic Review* 1999 (Q III): 15–29.

Fixler, Dennis, and Ted Jaditz. 2002. "An Examination of the Difference between the CPI and the PCE Deflator." Working Paper no. 361, Bureau of Labor Statistics, June.

Garner, Thesia I., George Janini, William Passero, Laura Paszkiewicz, and Mark Vendemia. 2006. "The CE and the PCE: A Comparison." *Monthly Labor Review* September:20–46.

Lebow, David E., and Jeremy B. Rudd. 2003. "Measurement Error in the Consumer Price Index: Where Do We Stand?" *Journal of Economic Literature* March: 159–201.

McCully, Clinton P., Brian C. Moyer, and Kenneth J. Stewart. 2007. "A Reconciliation between the Consumer Price Index and the Personal Consumption Expenditures Price Index." Working Paper, Bureau of Economic Analysis and Bureau of Labor Statistics. September. http://www.bea.gov/papers/pdf/cpi_pce.pdf.

Triplett, Jack E. 1978. "Reconciliation of Quarterly Changes in Measures of Prices Paid by Consumers." *Survey of Current Business* March:6–9, 24.

———. 1981. "Reconciling the CPI and PCE Deflator." *Monthly Labor Review* September:3–15.

Wei, Christina Chang. 2010. "What Is the Price of College? Total, Net, and Out-of-Pocket Prices in 2007–2008." *Stats in Brief*, National Center for Education Statistics, Institute of Education Sciences, December. http://nces.ed.gov/pubs2011/2011175.pdf.

The Benefits of Panel Data in Consumer Expenditure Surveys

Jonathan A. Parker, Nicholas S. Souleles, and
Christopher D. Carroll

> The Consumer Expenditure Survey (CE) program provides a
> continuous and comprehensive flow of data on the buying
> habits of American consumers. These data are used widely in
> economic research and analysis, and in support of revisions of
> the Consumer Price Index.
> —Bureau of Labor Statistics (2009)

3.1 Introduction

Since the late 1970s, two features have distinguished the US Consumer
Expenditure (CE) Survey from any other American household survey: its
goal is to obtain comprehensive spending data (that is, not just in a few
spending categories and not just over a brief time interval), and it has a panel
structure. It reinterviews households, which enables measurements of how
a given household's spending changes over time.

These two features give the survey great value. This is why, in addition
to satisfying the core mission of measuring the spending basket needed to
construct the Consumer Price Index (CPI), the CE data are widely used by
federal agencies and policymakers examining the impact of policy changes,
and by businesses and academic researchers studying consumers' spending
and saving behavior. These uses are rightly emphasized by the BLS, for example, in the quote that begins this chapter.

It could be argued that the non-CPI-related uses of the survey are becoming more important than its core use in constructing the CPI. After all, spending weights can be constructed from aggregate data without a household

Jonathan A. Parker is the International Programs Professor of Management at MIT's
Sloan School of Management and a research associate of the National Bureau of Economic
Research. Nicholas S. Souleles is the Michael L. Tarnopol Professor and professor of finance
at the Wharton School of the University of Pennsylvania and a research associate of the
National Bureau of Economic Research. Christopher D. Carroll is chief economist and director
of research at the Consumer Financial Protection Bureau.

This chapter was prepared for the NBER CRIW conference on Consumption Measurement
in December 2011. For helpful comments, we thank Karen Dynan and participants at the
NBER CRIW conference. For acknowledgments, sources of research support, and disclosure
of the authors' material financial relationships, if any, please see http://www.nber.org/chapters/
c12674.ack.

survey; many countries use such price indexes (often in the form of a "personal consumption expenditures [PCE] deflator") as their principal (or their only) measure of consumer inflation.[1] Macroeconomic analysis in the United States has moved increasingly toward use of the PCE deflator instead of the CPI.[2]

But national-accounts-based spending weights do not provide any information about how expenditure patterns vary across households with different characteristics (e.g., elderly versus working age, or employed versus unemployed, or any of the myriad other subpopulations whose expenditure patterns might be important to measure). The BLS CE survey home page rightly emphasizes this point: "The CE is important because it is the only federal survey to provide information on the complete range of consumers' expenditures and incomes, as well as the characteristics of those consumers."[3] Furthermore, without expenditure data it is impossible to measure the different rates of inflation experienced by different kinds of households. These purposes provide a compelling case for continued collection of comprehensive spending data at the level of individual households.

The importance of maintaining the second of the CE's two unique features—the *panel* aspect of the survey—is less obvious. Our purpose is to articulate and explore the reasons that the panel aspect of the data is extremely valuable. We argue that panel data contribute greatly to the central mission of the CE survey, construction of the CPI (both the aggregate CPI and the relevant indexes for subgroups), as well as to its other missions, such as helping researchers and policymakers understand the spending and saving decisions of American households.

A panel survey is arguably more expensive and more difficult to conduct than a cross-sectional survey would be,[4] and any redesign of the CE survey must consider costs as well as benefits. We do not have the expertise to estimate the costs of preserving the panel dimension of the survey, so our goal is simply to ensure that the significant benefits of true *panel* data on *comprehensive* spending are clearly recognized. Specifically, we focus on the following benefits and their implications for CE redesign. Collection of panel data:

1. See chapter 2 (Blair) in this volume for a detailed comparison of the US CPI and the PCE deflator.
2. The most recent sign of such a trend is a decision by the Federal Reserve to begin publishing forecasts of consumer inflation as measured by the PCE deflator rather than CPI inflation. A 2010 speech by Federal Reserve Bank of Philadelphia president Charles Plosser argued that the PCE deflator is a more accurate measure of inflation than the CPI because the CE survey overweights housing compared to the "correct" weights.
3. The third sentence on http://www.bls.gov/cex/ (accessed February 1, 2012).
4. It is inarguable that contacting the same households twice is more expensive than contacting them once. However, a proper measure of survey cost is "dollars spent to obtain data of a given informativeness" and if the data-quality benefits of panel measurement methods outweigh the calling-multiple-times costs, a panel survey might have a lower cost in dollars-per-unit-of-data-quality.

1. Improves measurement of expenditure data, feeding into the core mission of the CE survey.

2. Increases the range and quality of group-specific price indexes that can be constructed.

3. Permits reasonably reliable measurement of consumption inequality and relative standards of living.

4. Expands the range and improves the power of analyses of household spending.

5. Allows the measurement of dynamic responses like the propensities to consume that are crucial to the analysis of many economic events and policies.

The rest of the chapter considers each of these benefits in turn. Where we discuss the extant CE survey we focus on the interview survey rather than its (also useful) diary complement. (For reasons that will become clear below, our view is that it is impossible for a diary survey to form the basis for a meaningful panel.)

3.2 How Panel Data Aids Measurement

This section discusses first how, in a redesigned CE survey, repeated interviews can increase the accuracy of any given measure of spending in a period and thus may improve the quality of the comprehensive spending data that virtually every use of the CE survey relies upon, directly or indirectly. Second, this section shows that, because spending has volatile transitory components, understanding the evolution of inequality in true standards of living, or constructing price indexes for households with different patterns of expenditure, requires measurement of spending not just at a point in time, but over a substantial interval of time. Such long-term spending information is best measured by repeated interviews (or by a time-series of administrative data), in part because recall is imperfect.

3.2.1 How Panel Data Affects Accuracy of Expenditure Measurement

Measurement error in the CE threatens all of its missions, and measurement error seems to be increasing. The fact that households are interviewed several times in the collection of panel data offers the potential to reduce the mismeasurement of expenditures for those households who participate in multiple interviews (*nonsampling error*), but it is possible that the added burden of a panel survey increases another kind of error, the *sampling error*, that arises when the participants in a survey differ in systematic but unobservable ways from the population.[5] We discuss these in turn.[6]

---

5. The two types of mismeasurement are not completely separate: some households, rather than being nonparticipants, are instead reluctant participants who report expenditures poorly.

6. See the outline and citations in Safir (2011).

Nonsampling Error is Likely Reduced

Research by BLS staff and others has demonstrated that the expenditure data that are recorded in the survey for a particular household may be inaccurate for a host of reasons, including problems of respondent misinterpretation of the survey questions, incorrect recall, deliberate misrepresentation (for example, about purchases of alcohol or illegal drugs), or as a result of data processing errors due to mistakes in collecting, recording, or coding expenditure information. For all of these categories of error, the benefit of repeated measurement of expenditures is potentially large.

The first benefit of true panel data is that familiarity breeds accuracy. As households are reinterviewed, respondents become familiar with the process and so the quality of the responses is likely to rise. Having gone through at least one expenditure interview, the household can better keep information on hand to improve the accuracy and efficiency/speed of responses. Households may also mentally note purchases during a subsequent recall period that might previously have been forgotten. (Chapter 13 in this volume, by Hurd and Rohwedder, provides evidence supportive of these hypotheses; in the survey literature, these kinds of effects are called "panel conditioning." See Shields and To [2005] for a discussion of some of the less favorable effects of such conditioning.)

It is possible that some of the gains from repeat interviews may be captured by an initial contact interview, as the current CE structure provides. In a household's contact interview, the CE survey procedures are explained to household members and information is collected so that the household can be assigned a population weight. The preparation includes suggestions on record keeping, such as keeping receipts and bills (e.g., utility bills), so that they can be consulted in the subsequent interviews. While surely helpful, such a preview of the survey procedures is unlikely to foster the degree of understanding that is gained by actually participating in the survey.

A second benefit of repeated interviews is that the survey taker has the ability to look for and double-check reporting errors or omissions and so can correct potential mismeasurement.[7] The current computer program that Census Bureau surveyors use during interviews in the field is programmed with various procedures to double-check suspicious entries. The introduction of computer-assisted personal interviews in 2003 may have improved the quality of the CE data.[8]

7. "Dependent interviewing"—see Kalton and Citro (1995) for a discussion, and Manski and Molinari (2008) or Bollinger and David (2005) for critiques.
8. See http://www.bls.gov/opub/hom/pdf/homch16.pdf for a description of the changes associated with the introduction of CAPI interviewing. Cho and Pickering (2006) analyze whether CAPI interviewing improved data quality. First, the amount of spending in (ex ante thought to be) underreported categories rises with CAPI and the amount of spending in (ex ante thought to be) overreported categories falls, although the net effect is an overall fall. At the same time, CAPI increases the number of items reported—higher counts (but not higher expenditures). Finally, there are more high-spending levels for households.

With reinterview panel data, this benefit can be maintained by the new, improved version of the CE. A respondent who previously reported an expenditure on any category of regular spending, such as on mobile telephone service, cable television, mortgage payments, and so forth can be prompted for these categories because the software can add additional prompts based on the reports from the previous interview. Not only can this assist in identifying omitted categories, but it can be used to improve amounts. A household who is guessing about past spending on cell phones, for example, could be prompted with their previous report, or prompted conditional on their previous report having been based on consulting a specific bill.

Repeat interviewing also allows the correction of past responses based on more accurate information in a subsequent interview. For example, respondents who had a water bill to consult when responding in one interview could be asked whether, based on the history on their bill, their previous response was accurate. Or, a respondent who realizes that he is making a wild guess about spending in a particular category in a given interview might pay more attention to spending in that category as subsequent bills arrive, thus leading to a better estimate of spending in subsequent interviews.

Finally, evidence from the survey research literature suggests that memorable events tend to be subject to the "telescoping" problem: they may be remembered as being nearer in time than they actually are (Neter and Waksberg 1964). Thus, a purely cross-sectional CE might overstate spending on automobiles (for example) if respondents tended to remember automobile purchases well but tended to think that they were more recent than they actually were. Here, the benefit of repeated interviews is the ability to check responses against reports from the previous interview to correctly measure the spending during the actual period covered by the interview. For example, the surveyor could remind the household that in their prior interview (say, three months ago) they reported a car purchase and check whether a claim that they had purchased a new vehicle in the last three months really constituted the second purchase of a new vehicle in such a short time.[9]

In sum, when households participate in repeated interviews the accuracy of their responses is likely to improve measurement quality through respondent familiarity, through comparison of responses across interviews, and through checking for errors in temporal recall. These benefits are more likely to be reaped when the interviews are closer together in time.

---

9. The panel structure of the current CE was, in part, designed specifically to address this problem: the first interview is intended to bound the recall period for the second interview, and the data from the first interview is not used because of concerns about telescoping effects. One might argue that the telescoping problem could be addressed in a two-interview survey where the data from the first interview were discarded, but discarding half of the data collected might not be an efficient use of time and money.

Table 3.1   Participation rates for 2008 CE households

Number of completed expenditure interviews	Number of consumer units	Percent	Percent of those with at least one interview
0	3,408	30	
1	1,072	9	13
2	886	8	11
3	1,089	10	14
4	4,957	43	62
Total	11,412	100	100

Source: Calculations by Bureau of Labor Statistics performed for the authors.

Sampling Error Might Rise

One widely acknowledged cost of repeated interviews is an increase in survey fatigue, which leads some households to drop out of the survey without completing all interviews.[10] Table 3.1 provides some statistics on the participation patterns for the 2008 survey (kindly provided to us by the BLS).[11] The table indicates that while about 70 percent of households agreed to the first interview (the first row says 30 percent completed zero interviews), only 43 percent completed all four interviews (last row). This compares with a corresponding full-interview-completion rate of 56.5 percent as recently as the late 1990s reported in Reyes-Morales (2003, 27), who finds that households "who completed all four interviews are larger and older and are more likely to be homeowners and married couples than are [those] who responded only intermittently."

These results suggest the potential for significant bias due to nonparticipation that is correlated with expenditure choices. If the households who complete all four interviews differ from those who complete only some, there can be little doubt that the households who refuse be interviewed at all (the 30 percent in the first row) differ systematically from those who complete at least one interview.[12]

It seems likely that the panel nature of the survey (specifically, the burden associated with reinterviews) increases the degree of sampling mismeasurement

10. There is also evidence that households increasingly respond "no" to lead-in questions ("Have you made any expenditures in [category x]?") even when they have done spending in that broad category (Shields and To 2005), because a "no" response reduces the time they must spend in the interview. We discuss this type of measurement error below.

11. The BLS statistician looked at all addresses that entered the sample in 2008. That is, she looked at all addresses whose first or "bounding" interview was scheduled for 2008. Then she excluded the "type C" addresses (the nonresidential or "bogus" addresses) and got the numbers above for the consumer units at the remaining addresses. Some consumer units moved away and others moved in during the period. Table 3.1 includes the consumer units that were originally there and moved away, but not the ones that moved in later (their replacements). (Personal communication to Christopher Carroll on February 22, 2012.)

12. For further evidence on the characteristics of nonresponders, see Reyes-Morales (2005).

by introducing stronger selection effects than those that would exist for a single cross-sectional survey. To some extent this can be rectified in the construction of appropriate sample weights (for example, by reweighting the households who participate in multiple interviews so that the weighted sample's characteristics match the characteristics of households who complete only a single interview). But to the extent that nonparticipation is both correlated with the expenditure of interest and not perfectly correlated with the observed household characteristics, the measurement of expenditures will be biased even after reweighting.

It is not clear, however, that the set of households who participate in the first interview are meaningfully different from those who would participate in a purely cross-sectional survey. Indeed, until the second interview is conducted, the CE survey *is* a cross-sectional survey.[13] The size of the bias introduced as a result of reinterview-induced attrition might therefore be estimated by comparison of results obtained from a sample that includes only the first interview to results obtained from the complete CE data set. If results are not markedly different, it may be that the reinterview-induced bias is not very large in its practical implications.

3.2.2 How Panel Data Improves Measurement of Standard of Living (and Associated Price Indexes)

The case for measuring well-being using consumption rather than income goes back at least to Friedman (1957), whose famous "permanent income hypothesis" argued that income incorporates both permanent and transitory components, but that households choose their normal level of spending based principally on income's permanent component. Friedman illustrated his argument by observing that households who are paid once a month do not concentrate all their spending on payday; rather, they choose a level of regular monthly expenditure (including mortgage payments, utility bills, etc.) that *on average* matches the regular flow of income that they expect to receive. He then extended this point to annual data. According to Friedman, households who experience transitory shocks to income in a given year will keep their expenditures close to the level of income expected in a "typical" year, smoothing through any temporary shocks to income.[14]

Nevertheless, most work on economic inequality has focused on measuring disparities in household income, not consumption.[15] This is

13. Excepting the initial contact interview in which the expenditure part of the survey is not asked.

14. Because permanent income was not directly measurable, Friedman anticipated that researchers would challenge him to propose a measurable proxy for permanent income. One of his proposals for such a measure was average household income over a three-year period. Friedman was explicit in rejecting the idea that permanent income should be defined as "lifetime" income, as Modigliani and Brumberg (1954) had proposed; this seems to be because he had the (correct) intuition that liquidity constraints and uncertainty could prevent distant future income from influencing current choices (Carroll 2001).

15. See, for example, Piketty and Saez (2003). This is a principal reason that the formal list of the CE's missions has recently been expanded to include the measurement of poverty.

likely because the CE data are not as well measured as the available income data.[16]

What would be required for a redesigned CE to contribute significantly to the measurement of inequality? Two features stand out: comprehensive measures of spending, and measures that cover sufficiently long time periods without requiring recall over extended periods—that is, something like the panel structure of the current CE interview survey.

As Friedman noted, an important part of spending is on durable goods like cars, televisions, suits, and the like, which provide "consumption services" over a period far longer than the annual frequency of the budget survey. The theoretically correct measure of "consumption" would spread out the expenditures on such goods over the time span over which they provide value, rather than recording the entire expenditure as consumption on the date of purchase.

Friedman also emphasized the point that spending on nondurable goods and services may contain nonrepeating or transitory elements that do not reflect the household's perception of its permanent income. For example, emergency vehicle repairs induced by an auto accident should not be confused with permanent elements of consumption.[17]

Friedman's insightful original discussion of these points provides some enduring guidance about the appropriate goals of a redesigned CE survey. For example, it clarifies why spending data that cover a narrow slice of time (like a month or less) may provide a poor picture of both households' true spending patterns across categories of goods and their long-term well-being. In only a short period, a household's spending, even on highly nondurable goods like food, may be seriously distorted by economically meaningless variations like a long holiday or failure to visit the grocery store during one of the four weeks in the month.[18]

Over how long a period should spending be measured?

16. See Aguiar and Bils (2011) for recent evidence of important systematic biases in the CE data, and Attanasio, Battistin, and Ichimura (2004) for some earlier evidence; see Meyer and Sullivan (2009) for comparisons of poverty as measured by income and consumption sources. Meyer and Sullivan (2009) have argued in a number of papers, however, that at the bottom of the distribution consumption is likely *better* measured than income, which may come from informal or irregular sources that are not well captured by the usual survey methods such as the use of income tax returns.

17. Further complications arise from items that may not be classified as durable but that nevertheless are purchased only occasionally because they provide "memories" or other benefits that last a long time; the most compelling example here is holiday travel expenses, but to some extent this category could include spending on entertainment like tickets for plays, sports events, and museums.

18. This point goes to the heart of the debate about the meaning of the conflict between the much larger increases in consumption inequality measured in the CE's diary survey (which covers a two-week period) versus the interview survey (which covers a three-month period). One interpretation of the discrepancy is that with the spread of "big box" retailers, households may be making fewer trips to the store but buying more when they do go. It is possible that over some appropriately extended period (like a year) they buy precisely the same amount as before the advent of the big box stores, but the shift to more diary-survey periods with zero expenditures and fewer with larger expenditures would look like an increase in inequality. See Attanasio, Battistin, and Ichimura (2004) for a discussion.

It seems plausible to propose that three months' worth of spending data would provide a reasonable measure of a household's usual spending on most nondurable goods, including food. For example, using UK scanner data, Leicester (chapter 16, this volume) shows that over a four-week period about 8 percent of households recorded no spending on sugars or confectionary, but over a twelve-week period only about 1 percent reported no spending in these categories. More broadly, he calculates the distribution across households of budget shares on various categories of commodities purchased at grocery stores when the data are aggregated at frequencies ranging from two weeks to a full year. For these highly nondurable goods, the distribution of budget shares for the three-month time interval are not sharply different from those for the yearly time interval, while the distribution of budget shares at the monthly frequency is markedly different. This evidence strongly supports the proposition that a month is not a long enough time interval to reliably measure a household's usual spending behavior.

For more durable goods, Leicester's (chapter 16, this volume) data show that expenditure patterns over even a three-month interval differ markedly from those over a full year. This is perhaps not surprising, since many kinds of spending—holiday travel, school expenses, clothing—vary systematically across households and are highly seasonal, or have a once-a-year character. (This is called the "infrequency of purchase" problem in the survey literature.)

While these points suggest that longer interview time frames might provide better measurement, such a conclusion might not be correct because longer periods might introduce other measurement problems. If respondents had perfect memories, an annual accounting could be accomplished in a single interview, but experience has shown that there are enormous measurement problems associated with long recall periods—forgotten expenditures, misremembered timing of purchases, and problems due to the burden of the length of interview required for such an long recall period.

With cross-sectional surveys there is always a trade-off in the recall period. Longer recall periods have greater recall problems (forgetting, telescoping, and so on), but shorter periods have more problems because of infrequency of purchase. A panel survey with repeated interviews dodges this tradeoff: several interviews over which fluctuations in purchases can be averaged are likely to provide a much better measure of a household's typical budget constraint and standard of living than can be obtained from a single interview.

Credible measurements of permanent expenditures are especially important for the CE's mission of permitting the construction of group-specific price indexes, which are a major advantage of a CE-based CPI over an inflation index constructed from aggregate spending weights.[19] As an important example, an

---

19. Or, to put the point in reverse, if the CE survey does not provide a credible measure of *permanent* consumption expenditure patterns by household type and expenditure category, then it cannot be used to construct a credible measure of the group-specific CPIs, and its advantage over PCE deflators disappears.

expenditure survey that accurately measures permanent consumption can be used to measure price indexes for households at different levels of standards of living. Broda and Romalis (2009), for example, show that high- and low-expenditure households have experienced substantially different changes in the prices of the baskets of the goods that they consume, so that the inequality in the nominal expenditure levels of these different groups of households overstates the increase in inequality in real expenditure between groups.

The mandate to improve the usefulness of the CE for measuring poverty provides another important reason for collecting panel data (as "poverty" defined by expenditure ought to be based on permanent expenditure patterns). When short time intervals are employed, infrequency of expenditure generates spurious dispersion that does not correspond to meaningful variation in standards of living.

A final related point is that the collection of panel data could prove to be important for the CE's ability to meet future needs that are not currently anticipated. A plausible example of such a use might be the construction of a price index for people with "high medical expenses." If only cross-sectional data were available, the price index would inevitably be biased (lumping together, say, people with temporarily high expenses because of an auto accident, with people with permanently high expenses because of a chronic condition). It would be impossible to construct a credible price index for such a group without panel data.

3.3 How Panel Data Aids Research

> The mission of the Consumer Expenditure Survey program (CE) is to collect, produce, and disseminate information that presents a statistical picture of consumer spending for the Consumer Price Index, government agencies, and private data users. The mission encompasses analyzing CE data to produce socioeconomic studies of consumer spending. (Horrigan 2011, 2)

In this section, we more formally lay out some of the advantages of panel data for the research mission of the CE survey: to support government agencies and private users in their study of consumer spending. Studies using the CE data have long been an important source of information for academic and government economists concerned with improving our understanding of national saving, consumption demand, and a variety of policies that operate at least in part through consumer spending and saving. Most of the policies one might consider, theories that one might like to evaluate, or behavioral responses that one might like to measure are dynamic, meaning that they relate to *changing* consumption and saving behavior. This focus comes partly from the core economic theory of the consumer, in which spending levels are based on forward-looking behavior, so that identification of the impact of economic events or policies on spending cannot in general be measured from cross-sectional spending patterns, but only from changes in spending. But the focus also comes partly from the important questions for which expenditure measurement is crucial, which are often about dynamic issues such as price elasticities, national saving, and responses to policies. While some information can be extracted from changes in the cross-sectional distribution (see, for example, Blundell, Pistaferri, and Preston [2008]), this section lays out the advantages of true panel data.[20]

An alternative to true panel data is synthetic panel data. Such data can be useful for some purposes, but the section following this one lays out some of the limitations of synthetic panel data.

3.3.1 General Framework for Studying Expenditures

Consider the following general framework for studying the causal impact of some observed variable $X_{h,t}$ for household h and time t on the expenditure of that household $c_{h,t}$.

$$(1) \qquad c_{h,t} = \beta_0 + \beta_1 X_{h,t} + \varepsilon_{h,t}$$

$$\varepsilon_{h,t} = \alpha_h + \tau_t + u_{h,t}$$

which is a specialization of the more comprehensive framework in Deaton (2000b).

In this statistical model, we assume additivity of the unobserved determinants of spending, denoted $\varepsilon_{h,t}$, and assume that the causal effect, given by β_1, is linear and homogeneous across households and time. Neither assumption is central to the issues we discuss, but both make our points easier to elucidate. Notably, we assume that there is a permanent household-specific component of $\varepsilon_{h,t}$, denoted α_h, and potentially a time-specific component common across households, denoted τ_t.[21]

The analysis of this equation could proceed, given certain strong assumptions, using cross-sectional data alone.

As an alternative, one could, given repeated observations on spending of the same households over time, first-difference equation (1) and analyze the change in spending over time:

$$(2) \qquad \Delta c_{h,t} = \beta_1 \Delta X_{h,t} + \upsilon_{h,t}$$

$$\upsilon_{h,t} = \Delta \tau_t + \Delta u_{h,t}.$$

---

20. See also the more detailed discussion in Deaton (2000a) of applications to development economics.

21. In exercises of this kind, the proportion of household-level consumption expenditures that can be explained by observable variables like the household's demographic characteristics and other standard $X_{h,t}$ variables is modest—the R^2 in regressions of the form of equation (1) is typically far below 0.5, indicating that households' choices are determined much less by observable than by unobservable characteristics (a leading candidate for such an unobservable characteristic is, of course, permanent income).

Notice that the individual effect (α) drops out. The advantages of this equation then stem, first, from the ability to estimate the causal effect β_1 consistently when there is possible correlation between α_h and $X_{h,t}$ in the cross sectional, and, second, from increased power in the first-difference estimation because the variation in α_h generally weakens estimation of the relationship of interest.

An important caveat is that equation (2) will be biased if $\Delta X_{h,t}$ is measured with error. We discuss the implications of such measurement error below, which has varying plausibility for different X variables. But for clarity of exposition we begin with the assumption that X has no measurement error.

3.3.2 Advantage: Consistent Estimation

In many applications, it is unreasonable to expect that persistent, unmodeled differences in household expenditure levels are uncorrelated with the variation in $X_{h,t}$ across households. If $E[\alpha|X] \neq 0$, then cross-sectional estimation of β_1 is inconsistent. Using data on expectations of income and other financial conditions, and subsequent data on realizations of these variables to explicitly measure alpha, Souleles finds that forecast errors are correlated with consumers' demographic characteristics (Souleles 2004). As an example, consider a study of how tax rates are related to expenditures. In a cross section of households, wealthier households will tend to have higher levels of expenditure and higher tax rates, so the relationship uncovered by estimation of equation (1) would be that households with higher tax rates would tend to have higher expenditures, $\beta_1 > 0$. Obviously, it would be a mistake to conclude from this that raising tax rates would raise household expenditures.

One solution would be to try to include measures of permanent income and wealth on the right-hand side of equation (1) to "control for" differences in household-specific spending levels not driven by tax rates. While this might seem straightforward, in order to eliminate the bias, the measure of permanent income used must capture *all* the variation in permanent income. Thus, as already discussed, one needs not just to capture variation in current income and wealth, but enough variables to capture completely any differences in household-specific variation in anticipated future income that might be correlated with tax rates. This is surely impossible (although absorbing most of the variation would eliminate most of the bias).

A common, and better, solution is to focus on the sort of variation that identifies what is probably the effect of interest: how a *change* in taxes *changes* the expenditures of households on average. To do this, one can measure the average relationship between the change in expenditures and the change in tax rates over time, as in equation (2). This relationship removes the household-level effect, α, which is the problematic term causing the inconsistency in equation (1). (Of course, one also might expect the true effect β_1 to differ with household characteristics. But allowing for different effects in different subpopulations is straightforward using equation [2].)

Formally, when $E[\alpha|X] \neq 0$ estimates of β_1 using equation (1) are biased. One can still estimate β_1 consistently if in addition to X one includes a vector of Z_h of persistent household-level characteristics that completely capture all variation in α *and* is orthogonal to u, $E[\varepsilon|X, Z] = 0$. But even this approach is still likely to be less efficient than panel data estimation (as we show below).

Our example may seem special because it focuses on the change in spending over time, rather than the level. But most questions of either academic or policy interest are of the form: "How does some change in the environment change spending?" A topical example important to the macroeconomic outlook as this chapter is being written is the effect of changes in housing prices on spending (the "housing wealth effect"). Cross-sectional data would undoubtedly show that people with greater housing wealth have greater consumption expenditures, controlling for any and all other observable characteristics, but a substantial part of this relationship would surely reflect the fact that people with higher unobserved permanent income have both higher spending and higher wealth. The *causal* effect of house price shocks on spending would remain unknowable. Similarly, the effects on household spending of policy interventions designed to induce mortgage refinancing cannot be plausibly estimated with cross-sectional data, for the same reasons. These examples are the norm, not the exception. Indeed, few variables spring to mind that would be directly related to household consumption expenditures but would *not* also be systematically related to the unobservable determinants of consumption like permanent income.

But a solution comes from the permanent income theory of consumption. The theory implies that for an optimizing consumer the path of spending will satisfy an equation like:

$$c^*_{h,t+1} = c^*_{h,t} + \theta\Delta p_{t+1} + \upsilon_{h,t}$$

or

$$\Delta c^*_{h,t+1} = \theta\Delta p_{t+1} + \upsilon_{h,t}$$

where, for example, Δp_{t+1} might represent the change in the real price of goods between two periods; that is, the real interest rate between these periods. This is the famous "random walk" proposition of Hall (1978). In this analysis, the key question of interest is the coefficient θ, which reveals the effect of the interest rate (say) on consumption growth. More sophisticated versions of the theory allow roles for uncertainty, liquidity constraints, and other variables, but still tend to assign a central role to the *change* in consumption as a measure of the change in circumstances. According to these theories, the *change* in spending is the most fundamental appropriate object of analysis. This key point explains the exalted role that panel data (even when it comes in highly problematic forms like "usual" household food expenditures) has played in the academic and policy literatures.

3.3.3 Advantage: Improved Power

The previous section shows the benefits of panel data when $E[\varepsilon|X] \neq 0$. A next question is whether panel data is important even when $E[\varepsilon|X] = 0$. For the reasons sketched out above, this is typically an implausible assumption, but we maintain it throughout this subsection to illustrate that there can be important improvements in the precision of estimation from using true panel data rather than cross-sectional data in this case. These advantages arise from the ability to eliminate the variation stemming from α across households. (For a comprehensively useful treatment of the issues discussed below and many related ones, see Deaton [2000b]; for a more general-purpose treatment, see Johnson and DiNardo [2000]; and for a clear discussion of panel identification issues, see Moffitt [1993]).[22]

To make this point as concretely as possible, consider cross-sectional (CS) estimation of the effect of interest, denoted β^{CS}, with sample size N, and first-difference (FD) estimation on true panel data, denoted β^{FD}, also with sample size N (for example, two cross sections on the same $N/2$ households).[23]

If $E[\varepsilon|X] = 0$ (and our other assumptions hold), both estimators are unbiased. But the asymptotic approximation to the statistical uncertainty is smaller for the estimator of β_1 using equation (2) and true panel data than for the estimator of β_1 using equation (1) and cross-sectional data if $\text{var}(\hat{\beta}^{FD}) < \text{var}(\hat{\beta}^{CS})$. Assuming (for the moment) that α_h and $u_{h,t}$ are independent and identically distributed across h in each sample, the asymptotic approximations to these variances are:

$$(3) \qquad \text{var}(\hat{\beta}^{CS}) = \frac{1}{N} \frac{\sigma_\alpha^2 + \sigma_u^2}{\text{var}(X_{h,t})}$$

$$\text{var}(\hat{\beta}^{FD}) = \frac{1}{N} \frac{\sigma_{\Delta u}^2}{\text{var}(\Delta X_{h,t})}.$$

To further interpret these equations, assume temporarily that X and u are independent and identically distributed over time so that $\sigma_{\Delta u}^2 = 2\sigma_u^2$ and $\text{var}(\Delta X_{h,t}) = 2\text{var}(X_{h,t})$. Under these (admittedly extreme) assumptions, the panel-data first-difference estimator is more efficient than the cross-sectional data levels estimator if

$$\frac{1}{N} \frac{\sigma_{\Delta u}^2}{\text{var}(\Delta X_{h,t})} < \frac{1}{N} \frac{\sigma_\alpha^2 + \sigma_u^2}{\text{var}(X_{h,t})},$$

---

22. The points we make below are well known to microeconometricians; the purpose of our exposition is to clarify and sharpen the argument, not to break new econometric ground.

23. A more efficient approach still would be to employ a random effects estimator, which optimally combines the variation in the cross section with that over time, but the key features of the power advantage of panel data are readily observable in the comparison of these two estimators.

$$\frac{2\sigma_u^2}{2\text{var}(X_{h,t})} < \frac{\sigma_\alpha^2 + \sigma_u^2}{\text{var}(X_{h,t})},$$

which holds if there are *any* unmodeled persistent differences across households; that is, as long as

$$\sigma_\alpha^2 > 0.$$

While X and u are highly unlikely to be independent over time, the intuition for this result is broadly useful and intuitive: a second observation on a given household provides more information than a first observation on a different household because, as long as there are persistent household effects, the first observation tells you something (and may tell you a lot) about what to expect for the second observation (and vice versa). Intuitively, with less statistical uncertainty surrounding the possible determinants of the expenditures that one is trying to explain with $X_{h,t}$, the role of $X_{h,t}$ is easier to measure.

This conceptual point gains empirical clout from the fact, widely known among microeconomists, that observable X variables have embarrassingly little explanatory power for expenditures, income, wealth, or other similar outcomes in cross-sectional regressions. It is rare to encounter a data set in which a dependent variable relevant to our discussion can be explained with an R^2 greater than 0.5. The traditional interpretation of this fact is that unmeasured variables are hugely important in practice, and it is not implausible to guess that most such variables are highly persistent.

Exploring our setup further, it is also useful to think about the polar alternative to an iid u; if u is perfectly persistent, $\sigma_{\Delta u}^2 = 0$ and $\text{var}(\hat{\beta}^{FD})$ collapses to zero. This implausible result highlights (among other things) the extreme nature of our assumptions that $X_{h,t}$ is measured without error (and, implicitly, that $\Delta X_{h,t}$ has nonzero variance). But it also makes very clear the point that the more important are persistent unmodeled differences in spending, the more useful is panel data for obtaining power in any given inference.

Another lesson of equation (3) is about the great importance (in the panel context) of minimizing or eliminating measurement error in ΔX (though perfectly persistent measurement error in the level of X is not a problem). It is easy to see that such measurement error will bias the estimates of β_1 (toward zero, in the univariate case). Equation (3) makes plain that such error will also bias down the measured variance of the panel estimator. The upshot is that, while good measurement is important in a cross-sectional context, it may be even more important in a panel context. This point could be important in guiding survey designers among the choices they must make. If survey resource constraints force a choice, say, between collecting several variables that have high transitory measurement error and one that has little or no measurement error, the logic of panel estimation would tend to suggest a very high value to collecting the variable with low measurement error.

A few caveats now deserve mention.

First, less persistence in u (a greater value of the household-specific error term $\sigma_{\Delta u}^2$) weakens the panel data estimator. For questions in which expenditures are the object to be explained, classical measurement error will not bias estimates of β_1, but will reduce their precision. In some contexts expenditures are an independent rather than a dependent variable; measurement error could lead to bias there as well.

Second, and in many contexts more problematic, the more persistent X is over time, the less variation there is in ΔX (holding its cross-sectional variance fixed). For many potential X variables (e.g., demographics) first differencing removes all information, since the household's demographic characteristics usually do not change over time. Since the first-difference estimator relies on this variation to identify the effect of interest, it is weaker when there is less variation in this dimension.

A generalized least squares estimator like the random effects estimator would balance these benefits and weight the variation in the different dimensions to produce a still more efficient estimator. But the main point remains that repeated observations on the same households—because each observation provides more information about the other than either would about a third, random household—can enhance the power of estimation in the presence of unmodeled persistent differences in household-spending levels. This logic carries over to a large class of nonlinear and more complex models than considered here.

How important are these issues in practice in the current CE survey? For illustrative purposes, we calculate the variances that affect the power of panel versus cross-sectional estimation using CE interview survey data from the family files in 2007 and 2008. Since no single application is critical, we simply assume that $\beta_0 = 0$ and consider no X in our calculations. Table 3.2 shows the ratio of the variances in equation (3) based on estimation of equations (1) and (2) under the assumption that $\beta_1 = 0$ and u, τ, and α are independent and identically distributed. For the cross-sectional regression, we ignore the panel structure in estimation and inference, treating the data as if there were no repeat interviews of the same household.

Table 3.2 shows that estimates from panel data (would) have roughly half the variance of the corresponding analysis pretending that the data was purely cross-sectional in nature. While the actual improvement will depend on the specific analysis, these results suggest that standard errors on coefficients of interest could be about 70 percent smaller when a first-difference estimator is used and likely smaller still if a random-effects estimator were employed (which would be consistent if the cross-sectional analysis were also consistent). Furthermore, in many applications the assumptions necessary for consistent estimation in cross-sectional data are not met, so that

Table 3.2   **Variances in 2007 and 2008 CE interview survey**

Expenditures	Ratio of total VAR $(\alpha_h + \tau_t + u_{h,t})$ to FD VAR $(\Delta\tau_t + \Delta u_{h,t})$
Food	1.06
Log food	1.78
Nondurable	1.79
Log nondurable	2.87
Total	1.88
Log total	2.49

Source: Author's calculations based on the 2007 and 2008 files of the Consumer Expenditure Interview Survey Family files, processed as described in Parker et al. (2011).

power is irrelevant and the *only* way to make inference at all is to have access to panel data.

A final important point concerns the limits to the advantages of panel data for power. As with the case where $E[\alpha|X] \neq 0$ so that cross-sectional estimation is inconsistent, it is possible to improve power in the cross sectional by modeling α. As in the previous case, any included Z_h must be orthogonal to u to preserve consistency. But these additions can be costly in terms of power. As one introduces more variables in the vector of Z_h, one introduces more parameters to estimate that lowers the precision of the estimator, leading to an (at least partially) offsetting increase in the variance of $\hat{\beta}^{CS}$. Further, to the extent that these additional variables are correlated with X_h their addition further increases in the variance of $\hat{\beta}^{CS}$. The additional variables do this by leaving less independent variation in X from which to identify the effect of X on spending. Finally, it is possible that the additional covariates also reduce the variance of household-specific nonpersistent unmodeled variation; that is, they may reduce the variance of u. To the extent that these covariates reduce this variation, they can actually raise the precision of $\hat{\beta}^{CS}$ and reduce its variance. In this case, if these covariates vary over time, they can also increase the power and reduce the variance of the panel data estimator. In sum, while in theory it is possible to model permanent household-level determinants of spending levels and approach the precision of estimation that exploits the panel dimension of panel data, it is rarely the case in practice that there are sufficiently few actually exogenous determinants of persistent differences to make cross-sectional data on spending as powerful as the comparable data set with a true panel dimension.

3.3.4 Example from the 2007 and 2008 CE Interview Surveys

In this subsection we present an example that illustrates the importance of the benefits of panel data just discussed. We consider how the availability of panel data affects the ability to study the effect of the receipt of a stimulus tax rebate on spending, following Parker et al. (2011).

Parker et al. (2011) use the CE survey to measure the effect of the receipt of a 2008 economic stimulus payment (ESP) on spending during the three months of receipt. The BLS, working with the authors, added a supplement to the standard survey to cover this additional source of household income in sufficient detail to allow the research. The BLS was able to accomplish this extremely rapidly, as the time between the law that enacted the stimulus payment program and the first payments was only a few months.[24] The ESPs were distributed by the federal government from the end of April to the beginning of July 2008. The amount of payment any household received was based on year-2007 taxable income. The timing of the receipt was determined largely by the last two digits of the tax filer's Social Security number and the means of delivery—electronic transfer of funds or mailed paper check.[25]

Parker et al. (2011) estimate the following equation

$$(4) \qquad \begin{matrix} \Delta C_{h,t} \text{ or} \\ \Delta \ln C_{h,t} \end{matrix} = Z_{h,t}\theta + \beta \begin{matrix} \mathrm{ESP}_{h,t} \text{ or} \\ 1(\mathrm{ESP} > 0)_{h,t} \end{matrix} + \varepsilon_{h,t},$$

where the dependent variable is three-month to three-month change in spending or log spending, the control variables, $Z_{h,t}$, are age of household head, change in the number of children, and change in the number of adults, and the key independent variable is either the stimulus payment amount received in that period or an indicator for whether any payment is received in that period.

To illustrate the importance of panel data, we consider instead the estimated effect of receipt of a stimulus payment on spending from a regression that is analogous to equation (4), but in levels instead of first differences:

$$(5) \qquad \begin{matrix} C_{h,t} \text{ or} \\ \ln C_{h,t} \end{matrix} = \tilde{Z}_{h,t}\theta + \beta \begin{matrix} \mathrm{ESP}_{h,t} \text{ or} \\ 1(\mathrm{ESP} > 0)_{h,t} \end{matrix} + \tilde{\varepsilon}_{h,t}$$

where the vector of control variables, $\tilde{Z}_{h,t}$, are age, age-squared, the number of children, and the number of adults.

There are several reasons why estimation in first differences is more likely to lead to consistent estimation of the causal effect of stimulus payments. First, whether a household receives a rebate at all is a function of the previous year's income, which in turn is correlated with standard of living. Thus, in the entire sample, there is a correlation between the level of income and payment receipt that does not reflect the causal effect of the receipt of a payment on spending, but instead partly measures the effect of permanent income on both spending and eligibility for a payment. While there is the

---

24. The BLS has a commendable history of nimbleness in such circumstances; the BLS staff similarly added questions to the 2001 survey to permit analysis of the 2001 economic stimulus (see Johnson, Parker, and Souleles [2006] for the analysis of those data).
25. See Parker et al. (2011) for more details.

Table 3.3   **The effect of economic stimulus payments on spending with and without panel data**

Spending	Nondurable	Total	Nondurable	Total	Log nondurable	Log total
	Using panel data: Dollar change or log change in spending					
ESP	0.121	0.516			2.09	3.24
	(0.055)	(0.179)			(0.94)	(1.17)
1(ESP > 0)			1.215	4.945		
			(0.672)	(2.072)		
	Using cross-sectional data: Level or log spending					
ESP	0.246	0.363			4.54	3.73
	(0.072)	(0.185)			(1.27)	(1.44)
1(ESP > 0)			−94.6	−3.120		
			(0.842)	(2.067)		
Percent difference	103	−30	−178	−163	118	15

Source: Parker et al. (2011).

Note: Regressions on the bottom use the same sample in cross-sectional form, so the dependent variable is level or log consumption and the controls add age squared and are number of kids and number of adults instead of changes. All regressions include a complete set of time dummies.

possibility that this type of problem might arise in first differences, it is less likely. Nevertheless, it is possible that households ineligible for stimulus payments in a given period have different changes in spending (or log spending) than the typical recipient. For this reason, Parker et al. (2011) focus most of their analysis on the subsample of households that report receiving a payment, and we follow this choice and focus only on households that receive stimulus payments at some point in time.

The second reason to estimate in first differences applies to this subsample. The amount of the stimulus payment is determined by household characteristics, such as income (eligibility for receipt of the payment required a minimum income and was phased out at high incomes) and the number of children eligible for the child tax credit. First differencing implies that any correlation between the level of spending and stimulus payment caused by permanent income or usual standard of living is removed from the variation that identifies the causal effect of the payment on spending. There remains a smaller concern that this type of correlation might cause bias even in first differences due to a correlation between spending changes and other factors correlated with household characteristics. To circumvent this concern, the original analysis also considers the effect of stimulus payment receipt; we also do so here.

Table 3.3 shows the results of estimation of equation (4) in the top panel and equation (5) in the bottom panel. The coefficients in the first and third pairs of columns are interpreted as the proportion of the stimulus payment spent during the three-month period in which it is received. The middle two columns show the percent increase in spending upon receipt. The final row shows the percent by which the cross-sectional estimates differ from the panel estimates. These differences are large, in some cases more than 100 percent. They are large and negative for the analysis with a log-dependent variable, despite the fact that these results use only variation in the timing of receipt (the middle pair of columns of results). The bias is larger for nondurable than for durable goods.

3.3.5 Advantage: Dynamics

Many interesting issues in the analysis of spending data involve not just the contemporaneous effect on spending of a contemporaneous change in environment, but the dynamics of this effect over time.

Consider, for example, the research on aggregate consumption expenditures that shows that they are "too smooth" to be explained by standard versions of the canonical permanent-income model. A common response has been to incorporate "habit formation" into the utility function in aggregate models, so that changes in circumstances lead to persistent dynamic changes in spending (because habits slow the adjustment of consumption to changed circumstances). In one of the main models of habits, for example, the strength of the habit formation motivation can be estimated as the coefficient γ_1 in a regression of the form

$$(6) \qquad \Delta C_{t+1} = \gamma_0 + \gamma_1 \Delta C_t + \epsilon_{t+1}.$$

Estimation of this equation using aggregate data typically finds quite large values for γ_1. Across thirteen countries, Carroll, Sommer, and Slacalek (2011) find an average value of $\gamma_1 = 0.7$, with no country having a point estimate below 0.5.

Many other kinds of models (for example, models with sticky expectations or rational inattention) also predict important and extended dynamics of spending. In the economic stimulus example of the previous section, a central question is whether the stimulus-related spending was rapidly reversed so as to provide little net increase in spending over longer periods like six months or nine months. The current panel structure of the CE (with three first differences in expenditures) allowed this to be investigated.

Another (related) set of interesting questions concerns the degree of "mobility" in expenditure patterns. A large literature has measured the degree of income mobility as a proxy for socioeconomic fluidity, but if consumption determines utility, mobility (or the lack of mobility) in spending should be even more interesting than income mobility. Measuring spending mobility in this sense, of course, requires comprehensive panel data on spending over an extended period, at least a few years, which may not be feasible for a CE-type survey. In principle, such questions might be addressed, however, by survey data from sources like the Panel Study of Income Dynamics, using its new questions that attempt to measure broad aggregates of household spending. An improved CE survey with a shorter panel element, however, could play a vital role in calibrating the degree of measurement error versus true mobility that would emerge from a PSID-type study.

Because extended dynamics are central to the questions posed by these models, panel data are indispensable to being able to answer them. Cross-section data offer virtually no ability to estimate parameters like γ_1. Of course, estimation of such a parameter can be problematic even in panel data, because any measurement error or transitory variation in lagged consumption growth should bias the γ_1 coefficient toward zero. But, in principle, careful econometric work (and assumptions about the size and nature of the transitory "noise") could yield estimates of γ_1 that should be comparable to those from macrodata. (See Dynan [2000] for just such an effort.) Without high-quality panel data on household-level spending, it will likely be impossible to distinguish between the competing explanations (habits, sticky expectations, etc.) for the macroeconomic stickiness of consumption growth. This matters, because alternative interpretations have quite different consequences for vitally important questions like the appropriate monetary and fiscal policies during an economic slump.

3.4 Is Synthetic Panel Data a Substitute for True Panel Data?

By grouping or averaging repeated cross-sections on time-invariant household characteristics, a researcher can track group averages over time and conduct panel analysis for cohorts as unit of observation, as for example:

$$(7) \qquad \Delta \overline{c_{c,t}} = \beta_0 + \beta_1 \Delta \overline{X_{c,t}} + \overline{v_{c,t}}$$

$$(8) \qquad \overline{v_{c,t}} = \overline{\Delta \tau_t} + \overline{\Delta u_{c,t}}.$$

Deaton (1985) discusses estimation with such "synthetic" panel data instead of true panel data.

The CE data have been fruitfully used for such analyses by, for example, Attanasio and Weber (1995), Gourinchas and Parker (2002), and Attanasio and Davis (1996). Attanasio and Weber (1995) studies how consumption growth responds to changes in interest rates. In this case, averaging loses the researcher very little within-cohort variation in the key explanatory variables because most of the power of the analysis comes from changes over time. Further, as exemplified by Gourinchas and Parker (2002), in practice, estimation from moments requires that the moments that are available for every household be collapsed to average moments across households in the finite sample (otherwise there are far too many moments for the data size for any hope for generalized method of moments [GMM] asymptotics to apply). When moments like this are employed, even analyses that use true panel data (such as Attanasio and Vissing-Jorgensen [2003], for example) take cross-sectional averages before estimating. In the case of Attanasio and Davis (1996), to match data across unrelated data sets requires the construction of synthetic cohorts in any case, so that true panel data is of less use. Another example is Aaronson, Agarwal, and French (2012), who study the effect of a change in the minimum wage on spending by comparing changes in households' spending around dates when state-specific minimum wages were changed. Since the change in the minimum wage is statewide, no information is lost by collapsing the data across states.

Perhaps the greatest shortcoming of synthetic panel analysis is the enormous loss of variation in the independent variable that could have been used to identify the effect of interest. The significance of this loss depends on the relative variances of the independent variables and the residual in the true panel data and in the synthetic equivalent, that is on $\text{var}(\Delta X_{h,t})$ and $\text{var}(\upsilon_{h,t})$ versus $\text{var}(\overline{\Delta X_{c,t}})$ and $\text{var}(\overline{\upsilon_{c,t}})$. In the extreme case, if there is no variation in ΔX_c that is correlated with cohort characteristics, then one loses identification completely in synthetic cohorts.

Any randomized experiment, like the timing of economic stimulus payments among recipients, has no (asymptotic) variation at the synthetic cohort level. That is, the best possible source of variation—variation that is independent of households' characteristics—is impossible to exploit in a panel dimension using synthetic cohort analysis. In general, in any situation where $\text{var}(\overline{\Delta X_{c,t}}) \to 0$ with the size of the cohorts, there is no exploitable variation in synthetic panel data (but there would be in true panel data).

A second relative shortcoming of synthetic panel data is that it can be impossible (or sometimes difficult, requiring many other assumptions) to identify the change in spending for a time-varying population of interest. For example, researchers have been interested in measuring the consumption of stockholders, or might be interested in measuring the effect of house-price changes on spending. But households' stockholding status can switch over time (if they buy or sell their portfolio), and even more obviously, home-ownership status can change. This significantly impedes analysis. Attanasio and Vissing-Jorgensen (2003) thus use the true panel nature of the CE survey and Attanasio, Banks, and Tanner (2002) need additional information and must make additional assumptions to show that their estimates will be unbiased because they use only cross-sectional data.

3.5 Conclusion

The CE survey can be used to address many economically crucial questions that no other US survey can be used to address. This reflects two important features that are therefore valuable to maintain in any redesign of the CE survey. The first of the CE's unique characteristics is its collection of spending data that is *comprehensive* in both the scope of expenditures and the span of time covered. This need is compelling but obvious, so our chapter focuses on articulating the value provided by the second of the unique features of the CE survey: its provision of household-level *true panel* data on spending.

A reinterviewing process that yields true panel data on spending is critical to the core missions of the CE survey, such as the construction of group-specific price indices or improving the measurement of poverty. Panel data is even more important for the many research purposes to which the survey has been put, such as estimating the marginal propensity to consume out of economic stimulus payments.

The BLS faces formidable challenges in redesigning the survey in a way that preserves its current unique qualities and addresses the growing problems of measurement error. But any redesign would be a large step backward if it did not preserve both the comprehensiveness and the panel features of the current survey.

References

Aaronson, Daniel, Sumit Agarwal, and Eric French. 2012. "The Spending and Debt Response to Minimum Wage Hikes." *American Economic Review* 102 (7): 311–39.

Aguiar, Mark A., and Mark Bils. 2011. "Has Consumption Inequality Mirrored Income Inequality?" NBER Working Paper no. 16807, Cambridge, MA.

Attanasio, Orazio, James Banks, and Sarah Tanner. 2002. "Asset Holding and Consumption Volatility." *Journal of Political Economy* 110 (4): 771–92.

Attanasio, Orazio, Erich Battistin, and Hidehiko Ichimura. 2004. "What Really Happened to Consumption Inequality in the US?" NBER Working Paper no. 10338, Cambridge, MA.

Attanasio, Orazio, and Steven J. Davis. 1996. "Relative Wage Movements and the Distribution of Consumption." *Journal of Political Economy* 104 (6): 1227–62.

Attanasio, Orazio, and Annette Vissing-Jorgensen. 2003. "Stock Market Participation, Intertemporal Subsititution and Risk Aversion." *American Economic Review (Papers and Proceedings)* 93 (2): 383–91.

Attanasio, Orazio, and Guglielmo Weber. 1995. "Is Consumption Growth Consistent with Intertemporal Optimization? Evidence from the Consumer Expenditure Survey." *Journal of Political Economy* 103 (6): 1121–57.

Blundell, Richard, Luigi Pistaferri, and Ian Preston. 2008. "Consumption Inequality and Partial Insurance." *American Economic Review* 98 (5): 1887–921.

Bollinger, C. R., and M. H. David. 2005. "I Didn't Tell, And I Won't Tell: Dynamic Response Error in the SIPP." *Journal of Applied Econometrics* 20 (4): 563–69.

Broda, Christian, and John Romalis. 2009. "The Welfare Implications of Rising Price Dispersion." Unpublished manuscript, University of Chicago.

Bureau of Labor Statistics. 2009. *2008 Consumer Expenditure Interview Survey: Public-Use Microdata User's Documentation.* Division of Consumer Expenditure Surveys, BLS, US Department of Labor. http://www.bls.gov/cex/pumd_2008.htm.

Carroll, Christopher D. 2001. "A Theory of the Consumption Function, With and Without Liquidity Constraints." *Journal of Economic Perspectives* 15 (3): 23–46. http://econ.jhu.edu/people/ccarroll/ATheoryv3JEP.pdf.

Carroll, Christopher D., Martin Sommer, and Jiri Slacalek. 2011. "International Evidence on Sticky Consumption Growth." *Review of Economics and Statistics* 93 (4): 1135–45. http://econ.jhu.edu/people/ccarroll/papers/cssIntlStickyC/.

Cho, Moon J., and Carolyn M. Pickering. 2006. "Effect of Computer-Assisted Personal Interviews in the US" Technical Report, Bureau of Labor Statistics. http://www.bls.gov/osmr/pdf/st060200.pdf.

Deaton, Angus. 1985. "Panel Data from Time Series of Cross Sections." *Journal of Econometrics* 30:109–26.

———. 2000a. *The Analysis of Household Surveys*, 3rd ed. Baltimore: Johns Hopkins University Press.

———. 2000b. *The Analysis of Household Surveys: A Microeconometric Approach to Development Policy*, 3rd ed. Baltimore: Johns Hopkins University Press.

Dynan, Karen E. 2000. "Habit Formation in Consumer Preferences: Evidence from Panel Data." *American Economic Review* 90 (3): 391–406. http://www.jstor.org/stable/117335.

Friedman, Milton A. 1957. *A Theory of the Consumption Function*. Princeton, NJ: Princeton University Press.

Gourinchas, Pierre-Olivier, and Jonathan A. Parker. 2002. "Consumption over the Lifecycle." *Econometrica* 70 (1): 47–89.

Hall, Robert E. 1978. "Stochastic Implications of the Life-Cycle/Permanent Income Hypothesis." *Journal of Political Economy* 86 (6): 971–87. http://www.stanford.edu/~rehall/Stochastic-JPE-Dec-1978.pdf.

Horrigan, Mike. 2011. "Household Survey Producers Workshop Opening Remarks." CNSTAT Panel on the Redesign of the CE, June 1–2, Bureau of Labor Statistics. http://www.bls.gov/cex/hhsrvywrkshp_horrigan.pdf.

Johnson, David S., Jonathan A. Parker, and Nicholas S. Souleles. 2006. "Household Expenditure and the Income Tax Rebates of 2001." *American Economic Review* 96 (5): 1589–610.

Johnston, J., and J. DiNardo. 2000. "Econometric Methods." *Econometric Theory* 16:139–42.

Kalton, G., and C. F. Citro. 1995. "Panel Surveys: Adding the Fourth Dimension." *Innovation: The European Journal of Social Science Research* 8 (1): 25–39.

Manski, C. F., and F. Molinari. 2008. "Skip Sequencing: A Decision Problem in Questionnaire Design." *Annals of Applied Statistics* 2 (1): 264.

Meyer, Bruce D., and James X. Sullivan. 2009. "Five Decades of Consumption and Income Poverty." Working Papers, Harris School of Public Policy Studies, University of Chicago.

Modigliani, Franco, and Richard Brumberg. 1954. "Utility Analysis and the Consumption Function: An Interpretation of Cross-Section Data." In *Post-Keynesian Economics*, edited by Kenneth K. Kurihara. New Brunswick, NJ: Rutgers University Press.

Moffitt, Robert. 1993. "Identification and Estimation of Dynamic Models with a Time Series of Repeated Cross-Sections." *Journal of Econometrics* 59 (1–2): 99–123.

Neter, J., and J. Waksberg. 1964. "A Study of Response Errors in Expenditures Data from Household Interviews." *Journal of the American Statistical Association* 59 (305): 18–55.

Parker, Jonathan A., Nicholas S. Souleles, David S. Johnson, and Robert McClelland. 2011. "Consumer Spending and the Economic Stimulus Payments of 2008." NBER Working Paper no. 16684, Cambridge, MA.

Piketty, Thomas, and Emmanuel Saez. 2003. "Income Inequality in the United States, 1913–1998." *Quarterly Journal of Economics* 118 (1): 1–39.

Reyes-Morales, Sally E. 2003. "Characteristics of Complete and Intermittent Responders in the Consumer Expenditure Quarterly Interview Survey." In *Consumer Expenditure Survey Anthology*, 25–29. Washington, DC: Bureau of Labor Statistics. http://www.bls.gov/cex/anthology/csxanth4.pdf.

———. 2005. "Characteristics of Nonresponders in the Consumer Expenditure Quarterly Interview Survey." In *Consumer Expenditure Survey Anthology*, 18–23. Washington, DC: Bureau of Labor Statistics. http://www.bls.gov/cex/anthology05/csxanth3.pdf.

Safir, Adam. 2011. "Measurement Error and Gemini Project Overview." CNSTAT Panel Briefing, February. http://www.bls.gov/cex/redpanl1_safir2.pdf.

Shields, Jennifer, and Nhien To. 2005. "Learning to Say No: Conditioned Underreporting in an Expenditure Survey." Paper presented at the American Association for Public Opinion Research, American Statistical Association, Proceedings of the Section on Survey Research Methods, Miami Beach, FL.

Souleles, Nicholas S. 2004. "Expectations, Heterogeneous Forecast Errors, and Consumption: Micro Evidence from the Michigan Consumer Sentiment Surveys." *Journal of Money, Credit, and Banking* 36 (1): 39–72.

The Evolution of Income, Consumption, and Leisure Inequality in the United States, 1980–2010

Orazio Attanasio, Erik Hurst, and Luigi Pistaferri

Recent research has documented that income inequality in the United States has increased dramatically over the last three decades. There has been less of a consensus, however, on whether the increase in income inequality was matched by an equally large increase in consumption inequality. Most researchers have studied this question using data from the Consumer Expenditure Survey (CE) and some studies have suggested that the increase in consumption inequality has been modest. Unfortunately, there is now mounting evidence that the CE is plagued by serious nonclassical measurement error, which hinders the extent to which definitive conclusions can be made about the extent to which consumption inequality has evolved over the last three decades.

In this chapter, we use a variety of different techniques to overcome the measurement error problems with the CE. First, we use data from the diary

Orazio Attanasio is a professor in the department of economics at University College London, a research fellow and codirector of the ESRC Research Centre for the Microeconomic Analysis of Public Policy at the Institute for Fiscal Studies, and a research associate of the National Bureau of Economic Research. Erik Hurst is the V. Duane Rath Professor of Economics and the John E. Jeuck Faculty Fellow at the Booth School of Business, University of Chicago, and a research associate of the National Bureau of Economic Research. Luigi Pistaferri is professor of economics at Stanford University, the Ralph Landau Senior Fellow in Economic Growth at the Stanford Institute for Economic Policy Reseach (SIEPR), and a research associate of the National Bureau of Economic Research.

A first version of this chapter was presented at the NBER-CRIW conference on the Consumer Expenditure Survey, Washington, DC, December 2–3, 2011. We are grateful to Angus Deaton, Guglielmo Weber, Thesia Garner, David Johnson, Erich Battistin, and Mario Padula for useful comments. We would also like to thank Peter Levell, Erich Battistin, and Mario Padula for help with the CE data and Andres Otero for efficient research assistance. Attanasio's research was supported by the ESRC Research Centre for the Microeconomic Analysis of Public Policy. As usual, we are responsible for any mistakes. For acknowledgments, sources of research support, and disclosure of the authors' material financial relationships, if any, please see http://www.nber.org/chapters/c12675.ack.

component of the CE, focusing on categories where measurement error has been found to be less of an issue. Second, we explore inequality measures within the CE using the value of vehicles owned, a consumption component that is considered to be measured well. Third, we try to account directly for the nonclassical measurement error of the CE by comparing the spending on luxuries (entertainment) relative to necessities (food). This is similar to the recent approach taken by Browning and Crossley (2009) and Aguiar and Bils (2011). Finally, we use expenditure data from the Panel Study of Income Dynamics (PSID) to explore the dynamics of alternative measures of consumption inequality. All of our different methods yield similar results. We find that consumption inequality within the United States between 1980 and 2010 has increased by nearly the same amount as income inequality.

4.1 Introduction

This chapter studies the evolution of the distribution of well-being over the last thirty years in the United States. Our study has three distinctive features. First, we look at different measures of well-being (e.g., income, consumption, and leisure) to assess whether they paint similar pictures with regard to trends in inequality. This is important not only because variables such as consumption and leisure are likely to affect well-being directly, but also because the joint characterization of the evolution of the distribution of these variables can be informative about the nature of the shocks that have affected individual incomes, about the ability of individual households to buffer them and, ultimately, about the potential need for government interventions. Second, we measure inequality in well-being using different indexes and looking at different population groups, which helps us understand movements in the entire distribution and, in particular, whether the trends we observe tend to be concentrated in certain groups within the population. Finally, we draw our inference from disparate sources of data that differ by the quality and the type of well-being measures available, which is useful to assess the robustness of our conclusions. In summary, our analysis of a variety of different data sources suggests that the well-documented rise in income inequality during the last thirty years was accompanied by an increase in consumption inequality of nearly the same magnitude.

It is a very well-known fact that, starting in the early 1980s, inequality in wages (and earnings) in the United States has increased dramatically, both in absolute terms and within groups defined by observable characteristics such as education, labor market experience, occupation, gender, and race. The rise in inequality has been attributed to a combination of many forces, including skill-biased technology changes (such as the computerization of the labor force), institutional factors (such as the decline in unionization and the falling real value of the minimum wage), and the impact of international trade. Some authors have argued that the rise in wage and earnings inequality has been of a structural or permanent nature; others have noticed that structural factors have been accompanied by a rise in transitory factors of similar or even higher magnitude.[1]

The distinction between temporary and persistent shifts in the wage distribution is important because the nature of the policy interventions aimed at reducing the welfare effects of the rise in inequality depends on identifying correctly what caused it. If the increase in wage inequality is mainly due to unskilled individuals losing ground due to technology shocks making their skills obsolete, policies that try to retrain the unskilled may be effective. In contrast, if the rise in wage inequality is primarily due to transitory forces (such as increased turnover in the labor market), then short-run income support policies are more appropriate to reduce the welfare consequences of increasing inequality.

The distinction between temporary and persistent forces also highlights the usefulness of measures of welfare, such as consumption or leisure, that are likely to depend on long-run (or permanent) income. This consideration has spurred a large and growing literature looking at trends in consumption inequality. A first set of contributions, which includes among others Cutler and Katz (1992), Attanasio and Davis (1996), Slesnick (2001), Attanasio, Battistin, and Ichimura (2007), Krueger and Perri (2006), Meyer and Sullivan (2009), Attanasio, Battistin, and Padula (2010), and Aguiar and Bils (2011), had as a primary objective verifying whether the trends in consumption inequality mirror the trends in wage or earnings inequality. Implicitly, the question that these papers try to answer is whether the worries induced by the well-documented increased dispersion in the wage and earnings distributions were confirmed by observing an increase in consumption inequality of similar magnitude. Another set of contributions, such as Deaton and Paxson (1994), Attanasio and Davis (1996), Blundell and Preston (1998), Krueger and Perri (2006), Blundell, Pistaferri, and Preston (2008), Parker, Vissing-Jorgensen, and Ziebarth (2009), Heathcote, Perri, and Violante (2010), and Attanasio and Pavoni (2011), use information on consumption (and sometimes income) inequality to test a number of theoretical predictions, such as the hypothesis of complete markets, the presence of partial insurance against income shocks, or evidence for endogenous incomplete markets due to asymmetric information or limited commitment.

We complement and extend the existing literature in a number of directions. First, and most importantly, we analyze the evolution of consumption inequality with a variety of empirical strategies, using different consumption measures, and using consumption data from many alternative data sets. When exploring the changing nature of consumption inequality within the United States, most of the studies cited above use nondurable expenditure

---

1. For a detailed discussion of these issues see, for example, Autor, Katz, and Kearney (2008) and the citations within.

data from the Consumer Expenditure Survey (CE). It is now well documented that the CE has measurement problems that are nonclassical in a way that will likely bias the estimates of trends in consumption inequality. For example, many papers document the fact that aggregate measures of expenditure from the CE does a poor job at reproducing the level of expenditure in national account data (see Garner and Maki 2004). The most worrying feature is the fact that the large discrepancy between CE aggregate consumption measures and the personal consumption expenditures (PCE) aggregates has been increasing over time. Additionally, Aguiar and Bils (2011) document that higher-income households are increasingly likely to underreport their expenditures relative to lower-income households. If true, such measurement error will mechanically result in trends in consumption inequality to be increasingly biased downward. This can be one reason why authors who have used CE data have concluded that the rise in consumption inequality during the last thirty years was only a small fraction of the rise in income inequality during the same period (see, for example, Krueger and Perri 2006).

We start the empirical analysis of this chapter by replicating the analysis of consumption inequality in the main (interview) CE survey. However, we also perform many exercises to try to overcome the measurement error problems in the CE data. First, we examine consumption inequality in categories of the CE that have been found to be measured well relative to the PCE in all years of the survey. Using the properties of a simple demand system where the consumption categories are measured with an error structure that we specify, we can then scale up the measures of consumption inequality in these categories by the income elasticity for that category to get a measure of overall consumption inequality.[2] Second, we use data from the diary component of the CE where measurement error in some of the categories have been found to be less problematic. Third, we look at the stock of car owning in the CE and use the imputed value of those vehicles to create an alternative measure of consumption inequality. Finally, we can use expenditure data from the PSID—where systematic changes in measurement error has not been documented—to compute trends in overall consumption inequality.

All of the different methods tell a very similar story. During the last thirty years, consumption inequality evolved very similarly to income inequality. In particular, our estimate of the standard deviation of log income increased by roughly 0.2 log points between 1980 and the latter part of the first decade of the twenty-first century. Depending on our sample and measure of expenditure, our preferred estimates of the increase in the standard deviation of log consumption ranged between 0.15 and 0.2 log points during this time period (depending on the sample and the measure of consumption used). All of these estimates are much larger than the estimates obtained using

---

2. The approach we take is related to ideas in Browning and Crossley (2009) and Aguiar and Bils (2011).

the interview CE survey data, without accounting for the changing nature of measurement error within the survey. The striking feature is how robust these estimates are across the different surveys and consumptions measures we explore.

Our second contribution is to document the evolution of leisure inequality within the United States during the last thirty years. We show that despite the fact that consumption and income inequality increased dramatically between high- and low-educated households during this time period, the change in actual utility differences between the two groups was muted by the fact that low-educated households were spending much more time in leisure relative to their highly educated counterparts.

We also look at different aspects of the change in the distribution of income, consumption and leisure inequality. To do this, we look at trends in inequality both at the top of the distribution (as measured by the 90th–50th percentile difference) and at the bottom of the distribution (as measured by the 50th–10th percentile difference). Lastly, we explore the evolution of leisure inequality during this time period. We find that despite the fact that higher-income individuals experienced a rapid rise in consumption relative to lower-income individuals, higher-income individuals experienced a smaller change in leisure relative to lower-income individuals.

Overall, our results suggest that there has been a substantial rise in consumption and leisure inequality within the United States during the last thirty years. The rise in income inequality translated to an increase in actual well-being inequality during this time period because consumption inequality also increased. Some of this increase, however, was offset by the fact that leisure inequality increased as well, in particular with lower-income individuals taking more leisure relative to their highly educated counterparts.

4.2 A Conceptual Framework

In this section, we expand upon some of the conceptual issues we need to address to assess the changing nature of income, consumption, and leisure inequality. Additionally, we will introduce the conceptual framework we will be using to address the measurement error within the CE data.

4.2.1 Consumption versus Income Inequality

Most analyses of inequality focus on income, not consumption. Partly, this is due to data availability. Data sets containing information on measures of household resources (wages, earnings, income, etc.) are more frequently available, have typically larger samples, and have more consistent variable definitions than data sets containing information on consumption.

While an analysis of income inequality is very valuable, one may argue that analyzing trends in consumption inequality may be even more informative from a welfare point of view. Since individuals' utility is typically defined over consumption of goods rather than income per se, one may argue that measures of consumption inequality get closer to an ideal measure of inequality in household welfare than income inequality. Moreover, large changes in income inequality may reflect transitory variations, and these may have small welfare effects if households can smooth their consumption against transitory shocks. In other words, consumption might be a better proxy of "permanent income." Consumption inequality might therefore provide a more reliable measure of inequality in long-term living standards than income. Finally, a study of consumption inequality allows researchers to study allocation of disposable income to different commodities, which differ in their necessity/luxury characteristics. This analysis may be important insofar as an increase in food-spending inequality is perceived as being more worrying than, say, an increase in the inequality of spending on holidays.

In practice, it may be important to study income and consumption inequality simultaneously. Their joint analysis may be informative about smoothing possibilities available to consumers, as well as distinguishing between external shocks in insurance opportunities as opposed to fundamental changes in the income process caused by, say, labor market reforms, technological changes, and so forth. Moreover, one can distinguish between income- and consumption-based measures of poverty and study their evolution over the business cycle.

While the main focus of this chapter is the analysis of the evolution of consumption inequality, partly because the trends on income inequality are much better known and partly to put the consumption inequality figures into context, we start our result section (4.4) with some discussion on the evolution of income inequality, where income is measured by total household income divided by the number of adult equivalents.

As we discuss in section 4.3, we will be using different data sources, some of which have an established use in the analysis of income and earnings inequality. We will also discuss the fact that different pictures emerge when we consider inequality of consumption measures from different data sources that rely on completely different samples. Comparing income inequality in the same data sources can then be informative about the nature of these differences, with the two main alternatives being the different nature of the consumption information contained in the data sets and the composition of the samples used in the analysis.

4.2.2 Measures of Inequality and Changes in the Distribution

When looking at the evolution of consumption and income inequality, we will start by considering the evolution over time of the standard deviation of the log of both consumption and income in the samples described below. However, the evolution of the standard deviation of log consumption (or income) is only one way to characterize the changing inequality within the distribution of interest. It maybe that a given change in the standard deviation corresponds to a large change in the difference between the top of the distribution and its middle with nothing much happening in the bottom of the distribution. As a result, to provide a more complete picture of what has happened to consumption and income inequality in the last thirty years, we will also be looking at the difference between the 90th percentile and the median as well as the difference between the median and the 10th percentile of the respective distributions.

4.2.3 Inequality in Different Dimensions: Skill and Year of Birth Groups

The statistics mentioned in the previous subsection will be computed on the whole sample we use. It may be of considerable interest, however, to consider the evolution of the distribution over time in other dimensions, as they might suggest direct economic interpretations to what has happened. An important dimension we will be looking at is that of the difference across skill groups (as proxied by the education achievement of the household head). In particular, we will be looking at inequality both across and within different skill groups. The evolution of differences in income and consumption between skill groups might reflect the evolution of the prices of different skills in the labor market, which in turn have been associated to technological progress and other innovations that are likely to be permanent and difficult to insure and smooth out. Inequality within skill groups will reflect both the evolution of unobserved skill prices and other factors. When considering this decomposition, it is clear that the simultaneous analysis of consumption and income inequality can be particularly informative about the nature of the shocks we observe and household ability to smooth them out.

An issue that potentially affects many measures that have been considered in the literature is the fact that when we follow the evolution of inequality measures over time, they might reflect changes in the composition of the sample we are considering. This concern may be particularly salient when exploring the patterns of inequality over long periods of time. This is true for the overall sample and, even more so, in the case of the skill groups, as the fraction of, for instance, high school dropouts declines monotonically over the sample period. To address this issue, one can consider the evolution of inequality within groups whose membership is (approximately) constant over time. For instance, one can define groups by year of birth (of the household head), and by doing so follow the same group of individuals over time.[3] The evolu-

---

3. Groups defined by the year of birth of the household head can change in composition, however, for several reasons. First, it is possible that family formation and dissolution is different for individuals of different economic status. Second, there are strong differences in mortality rates between rich and poor individuals that are likely to make observed cohorts progressively "richer." Finally, it is possible that migration patterns are also related to economic status.

tion of the distribution of a given variable, being consumption or income, in the overall sample can mask very different dynamics for a fixed group of individuals. This is particularly the case in the presence of strong cohort effects. Moreover, theoretical models of insurance of income shocks have specific implications for the evolution of the relative distribution of income and consumption. Following the evolution of these distributions over the life cycle can therefore be particularly interesting. For reason of space, we discuss results related to the evolution of inequality over the life cycle in an appendix available on our website.[4]

4.2.4 Measuring Inequality: Accounting for Measurement Error

As discussed in the introduction, one of the main issues we have to deal with when studying the distribution of consumption and its evolution over time is the presence of large measurement error of the nonclassical type in the CE. The CE, however, contains details on hundreds of commodities that, in turn, can be aggregated into different categories, some of which have been documented as providing a good match to PCE data (see Bee, Meyer, and Sullivan, chapter 7, this volume; Garner and Maki [2004]). One possible approach to study the evolution of the inequality of overall consumption is therefore to focus on consumption categories that are well measured. To get an estimate of the changing nature of total consumption inequality, one simple approach is to compute the extent of consumption inequality using the specific consumption category that is measured well and then scale that measure up by the category's income elasticity. We do this below.

Additionally, we can take a stand on the nature of the measurement error in the consumption data. Let's denote with C_{it} the total consumption of household i in period t. Suppose that total consumption is made of K different categories with $C_{it} = \Sigma_{k=1}^{K} q_{it}^{k}$, where q_{it}^{k} is the spending on consumption category k by household i in period t. Let's consider two commodities that are known to be measured without systematic error, q_{it}^{1} and q_{it}^{2}, and suppose that commodity 2 is a necessity, while commodity 1 is a luxury. As usual, we define a necessity as a commodity whose elasticity with respect to total expenditure is less than one and a luxury as a commodity whose income elasticity is greater than one.

Suppose that in the case of commodities q_{it}^{1} and q_{it}^{2} spending on those categories can be expressed by the following equations:

(1) $$q_{it}^{1} = C_{it}^{\alpha_1} u_{it}^{1} v_{t}^{1}, \, \alpha_1 > 1$$

(2) $$q_{it}^{2} = C_{it}^{\alpha_2} u_{it}^{2} v_{t}^{2}, \, \alpha_2 < 1$$

Equations (1) and (2) represents two Engel curves. They relate the expenditure of each of the two commodities to total expenditure (with α_1 and α_2 being

---

4. See http://www.stanford.edu/pista.

the income elasticities), some aggregate factors v_t^j (with $j = 1, 2$), such as relative prices, and some unobserved idiosyncratic taste shocks (u_{it}^j, $j = 1, 2$). We will assume that the idiosyncratic taste shocks are i.i.d across households and that their distribution is constant through time. Taking the ratio between q_{it}^1 and q_{it}^2 one obtains:

$$(3) \qquad \frac{q_{it}^1}{q_{it}^2} = C_{it}^{\alpha_1 - \alpha_2} \frac{v_t^1 u_{it}^1}{v_t^2 u_{it}^2}.$$

Taking logs of this expression, one gets:

$$(4) \qquad \begin{aligned} \log(q_{it}^1) - \log(q_{it}^2) &= (\alpha_1 - \alpha_2)\log(C_{it}) + (\log(v_t^1) - \log(v_t^2)) \\ &+ (\log(u_{it}^1) - \log(u_{it}^2)) \end{aligned}.$$

Computing the cross-sectional variance of both sides of equation (4) and assuming for the time being that the idiosyncratic taste shocks are uncorrelated with total expenditure, one obtains:

$$(5) \qquad \begin{aligned} \mathrm{Var}(\log(q_{it}^1) - \log(q_{it}^2)) &= (\alpha_1 - \alpha_2)^2 \mathrm{Var}(\log(C_{it})) \\ &+ \mathrm{Var}(\log(u_{it}^1) - \log(u_{it}^2)) \end{aligned}.$$

Expression (5) deserves several comments. First, the aggregate shocks, by their very nature and because they enter additively in equation (4), do not contribute to the variance of the right-hand side. Second, the left-hand side of equation (5) is observed and can be computed in a data set that contains detailed information on consumption. In situations where a reliable measure of total consumption is not available because some of its components are affected by substantial measurement error whose variance is changing over time, the interesting question is the extent to which we can use such a variable as an approximation for the level or the changes in total consumption inequality. Notice that, because of the choice of commodities, $(\alpha_1 - \alpha_2) \neq 0$ so that the left-hand side of equation (5) will be varying with changes in the variance of total expenditure. If one is willing to assume that the variance of the taste shocks is invariant over time, then *changes* in the left-hand side will be driven entirely by *changes* in the variance of total consumption. Indeed, changes in the left-hand-side will be proportional to changes in such a variance, where the factor of proportionality is given by $(\alpha_1 - \alpha_2)^2$. Information on total expenditure elasticities derived from other sources can be used to evaluate the size of such a factor of proportionality.[5]

The approach we propose is similar to the idea discussed in Aguiar and Bils (2011) and even more so to the approach proposed by Browning and Crossley (2009). Browning and Crossley (2009), in particular, consider the

5. Aguiar and Bils (2010) use information on demand systems to address the measurement error problems in the CE in the United States. Our approach is, however, different from theirs in that they attempt to address systematic measurement error within the CE. Like them, we also find that consumption inequality tracks income inequality over this time period.

evolution of the covariance of two "noisy measures" of total consumption. Notice that from components, this would imply considering:

(6) $\mathrm{Cov}(\log(q_{it}^1), \log(q_{it}^2)) = (\alpha_1 \alpha_2)\mathrm{Var}(\log(C_{it})) + \mathrm{Cov}(\log(e_{it}^1), \log(e_{it}^2)),$

where the e's include both the aggregate and individual shocks in equations (1) and (2). Again, assuming that the second term in equation (6) does not change over time, one can use changes in the covariance on the left-hand side of equation (6) and knowledge of the income elasticities to back out the evolution of total consumption.

In what follows, we will look at the ratio of the changing variance of expenditure on entertainment services relative to the changing variance of expenditure on food at home. The latter is a luxury, while the former is a necessity (see Blow, Lechene, and Levell, chapter 5, this volume). Moreover, as indicated, for instance, in the study by Bee, Meyer, and Sullivan (chapter 7, this volume), these components of the CE are relatively well measured over the sample period we study. Moreover, when aggregated up, the ratio of the resulting aggregates to PCE from the national accounts is relatively constant.

4.3 Data: Surveys and Sample Selections

4.3.1 The Consumer Expenditure Survey (CE)

Survey Overview. Studying income and consumption inequality entails nonnegligible measurement issues. The first is data availability. In the United States there is only one data set with a comprehensive measure of consumption, the Consumer Expenditure (CE) Survey. Other data sets include incomplete consumption information, ranging from just food (the Panel Study of Income Dynamics [PSID] before the 1999 redesign, as well as most proprietary scanner data sets), to spending on only child care and rent (the Survey of Income and Program Participation [SIPP]), to measures that have much more details about expenditure but still fall short of covering the entirety of household budget (the PSID after the 1999 redesign). We begin our analysis with the CE data given that it is designed to provide a comprehensive measure of spending for US households. However, as we discuss below, we are aware that the CE has its own limitations.

The CE survey has a long history, dating back to the beginning of the twentieth century. The main purpose of the survey is to collect information to be used in computing the weights for the Consumer Price Index (the CPI). For this reason, the CE survey contains comprehensive and detailed information about consumption expenditure and its components. Until 1980, the CE was performed roughly every ten years. In 1980, however, it was radically redesigned and became a survey that is run continuously. It is made of two separate and independent samples: the Interview and the

Diary surveys. The former is a rotating panel available on a continuous basis since 1980. Households are interviewed every three months for, at most, five quarters. The first interview is a preparatory one and no data pertaining to it are released. From the second interview, the respondent in each household is asked to report detailed expenditures on hundreds of categories in each of the three months preceding the interviews. These categories are almost exhaustive of total consumption, the only exception being personal care items. Some items, however, are extremely aggregated. The best example is food at home, which is a single category. The information on expenditure is then complemented with information on mortgages, cars (including loans to finance their purchases), credit cards, health and education expenditures, and so on. Finally, the interview survey also includes extensive socioeconomic information on the household, ranging from detailed demographic information to labor supply and earning information on each household member, to some information on assets.

A large part of the income and demographic information are also found in the diary survey. The information on expenditure in this sample, however, is collected with a radically different method. In the diary survey, households are asked to fill in a register (a diary) detailing their spending for two continuing weeks. Until 1986, the diary survey contained information only on "frequently purchased items" such as food and personal care items. The information on food is much more detailed than in the interview survey. Starting in 1986, the diary survey becomes an almost exhaustive expenditure survey, with substantial overlap with the interview survey. Despite this overlap, however, the Bureau of Labor Statistics, which runs the survey, uses the diary for some expenditure components and the interview for others. The presumption is that one survey is better at measuring some components and the other is better for others.

The CE survey is a remarkable data source. Given its richness, it is not surprising that over the last twenty years it has been extensively used by economists for a variety of purposes. However, there are well-known issues with the CE. A particular worry is the lack of correspondence between aggregates derived from the CE survey and the personal consumer expenditure series published in the national accounts. Not only does the CE seem to underestimate substantially the level of PCE consumption, but the ratio of CE aggregates to PCE aggregates has declined substantially over time. Moreover, there is now increasing evidence of nonrandom nonresponses and attrition. In what follows, we will use the CE data without referring explicitly to these issues, although the approach we sketched in section 4.2.4 was designed precisely to deal with the fact that comprehensive measures of consumption derived from the CE might be plagued by substantial measurement error with an increasing variance over time. As we show below, the CE data, without adjusting for potential measurement error issues, provides a very different picture of consumption inequality than does the CE where measurement error issues are confronted directly or with the PSID where the measurement issues are not as problematic.

Sample Selection. Within the CE data, we select households whose household head is between age twenty-five and sixty-five. With this choice we want to avoid a number of issues that are relevant for very young households and those that are approaching the last part of the life cycle where retirement and health problems become particularly relevant. Family formation and dissolution, binding liquidity constraints for the young group, pressing health problems for the older one, are only some of the issues we want to avoid. Additionally, given that the CEX excludes households living in rural areas from their sampling frame, we drop such households from the sample in all years of our analysis. Finally, we drop from our sample all households with incomplete income responses. The reason for this is that we want to match the sample documenting consumption inequality with the same sample with which we measure income inequality.

Variable Definitions. There are a number of issues one needs to tackle before even starting to analyze trends in consumption inequality. First, which definition of consumption should we focus on? The distinction between durable and nondurable goods is important as it drives a wedge between the concepts of spending and consumption. For nondurable goods the two concepts coincide, but for durable goods (especially large-ticket items) spending is typically done upfront, but the same good provides services over multiple periods. We will be interested in measuring inequality in consumption, rather than inequality in spending per se, and hence will focus our analysis primarily on nondurable spending. When using the CE diary data, it is only possible to construct a comprehensive measure of nondurable consumption starting in 1986. For the CE interview data our nondurable spending data starts in 1980.

While some items are naturally included (e.g., food) or excluded (e.g., furniture) from the definition of nondurable consumption and services, there are a number of arbitrary choices one needs to make. To make our figures comparable with those of other researchers, we decided to include clothing and footwear in our nondurable expenditures measures. On the other hand, we exclude expenditure on health and education, as we see them more as investment in the stock of human capital. On conceptual grounds, we also exclude payments of interest on loans and mortgages (as well as the repayment of the principal). Finally, and somewhat more arbitrarily, we exclude contributions and donations to charities. A complete definition of our measure is reported in appendix A (on website). In addition to nondurable consumption and services, we also consider two additional flow aggregates: the expenditure on food at home and the expenditure on nondurable entertainment. Nondurable entertainment expenditures include items such as cable television subscriptions, DVDs, music, and so forth.

We do explore inequality patterns using the one durable commodity that is measured in a very rich manner in the CE: the amount of vehicles owned by the household. The CE contains, in a special module, detailed information on the type of cars held by each household. In particular, the make, model, and year is known in addition to a number of car characteristics. Furthermore, if the car has been purchased (new or used) in the twelve months preceding the interview, the purchase price is also reported. We use these data to impute a value for the cars for which no price is reported. Effectively, for the cars for which we have a value, we run an hedonic regression that includes make, model, and year identifiers as well as age and several characteristics. We then use the parameters of this regression to interpolate the value of all the cars in the survey and obtain, for each household, the value of the stock of cars they hold. The procedure is described in detail in appendix B (on website) and is similar to the one used by Padula (1999).[6]

Another relevant issue when we measure inequality in household consumption is that households differ in size and composition, implying important differences in needs as a function of, say, the age and number of children in the households and so forth. To account for these differences we will equivalize household consumption by dividing total consumption by an adult equivalence scale. We use the Organisation for Economic Co-operation and Development (OECD) scale, defined as $S = 1 + 0.7 * (A - 1) + 0.5 * K$ (where A is the number of adults and K the number of children, age eighteen or less, in the household). A final issue is how to deflate monetary variables in our data. One option is to use a global deflator (the CPI), and another is to use commodity-specific deflators, which may be important in the presence of differential trends in relative prices. Here we use the general CPI-Urban deflator (in 1983–1984 USD).[7]

4.3.2 The Panel Study of Income Dynamics

Survey Overview. The PSID is a longitudinal survey of US families that started in 1968 with two subsamples, the Survey Research Center (SRC) sample, which was representative of the US population (60 percent of the initial sample), and the Survey of Economic Opportunity (SEO) sample, which was oversampling poor families (the remaining 40 percent of the initial sample). The main feature of the PSID is that it follows the original survey households as well as households that get formed as a branch of the original ones (e.g., sons or daughters forming their own household unit). Data have been collected yearly from 1968 to 1997, and biannually after that. The latest available survey refers to 2008. The data is primarily geared toward collecting data on labor market items such as labor supply, wages, and so forth. However, the PSID has also collected information on consumption, especially food (at home and away from home) and, in some waves, rent, utilities, and child care. After the 1997 wave the PSID was rede-

---

6. We thank Mario Padula for help with this procedure.
7. For food we use the CPI food deflator.

signed. The survey became biannual and richer in certain interview components (such as expenditure on various commodities, health, wealth, and detailed information on spousal sources of income). For our purposes, the most relevant change was that the PSID started collecting richer and more detailed information on household spending, which now covers 70 percent of total CE spending. See below for a definition.

Sample Selection. Our sample includes all survey households with a head (typically the male) between age twenty-five and sixty-five. We exclude the Latino subsample and keep the SEO subsample, but use sampling weights throughout the analysis. We also exclude observations with outlier records on total household income and food.

Variable Definitions. Similarly to the CE survey, the PSID can also be used to address the dynamics of consumption distributions. To do so, we will look both at direct measures of consumption in the PSID (food, and the post-1997 consumption measure), and imputed consumption measures.

Food consumption is the sum of food at home, food away from home, and the value of food stamps. The post-1997 consumption measure (or "70 percent measure" from now on) includes information on spending on utilities (electricity, heating, water, miscellaneous utilities); home insurance premiums; health (health insurance premiums, nursing care, doctor visits, prescriptions, other health spending); vehicle spending (vehicle insurance premiums, vehicle repairs, gasoline, parking); transportation (bus fares, taxi fares, other transportation expenses); education (tuition, other school expenses); and child care. To match the nondurable consumption definition from the CE, we also consider an alternative measure that excludes spending on education and health.

We adopt two procedures for imputing a measure of total consumption in the PSID. The first measure follows Ziliak (1998) and is based on a simple budget constraint accounting (the "Ziliak measure" from now on). Consumption is defined as the difference between income and the change in assets. Assets are the sum of liquid assets and equity (the difference between the self-reported home value and the remaining principal on the home mortgage). Before 1999, data on asset stocks (with the exception of housing) are reported only every five years (starting in 1984). We thus impute liquid assets by taking the ratio of income from liquid assets (which is available every year) and the return on the T-bill. This imputed measure of consumption is not available for 1981–1982 because no data on equity are available for 1981.[8]

The second measures, based on Blundell, Pistaferri, and Preston (2008), impute consumption using the estimates of a food demand equation from the CEX (the "BPP measure" from now on). In particular, we use the CE data set to estimate (on a sample where the head is age twenty-five to sixty-five

8. Note that this imputation procedure provides more correctly a measure of total consumption, rather than total nondurable consumption.

and for each year for which we have data) a regression of log food onto the number of children, a quadratic in the household head's age, a dummy for self-employment, education dummies, log consumption, and the interaction of the latter with education dummies:

$$\ln f_{it} = X_{it}\beta_t + \ln C_{it}\gamma_t(E_{it}) + \varepsilon_{it.}$$

We then use the estimated coefficients in the CEX to impute a measure of consumption in the PSID:

$$\ln \hat{C}_{it} = \frac{\ln f_{it} - X_{it}\hat{\beta}_t}{\hat{\gamma}_t(E_{it})}.$$

We refer the interested reader to Blundell, Pistaferri, and Preston (2008, 2004) for more technical details about this imputation procedure.

Similarly to what done with CE data, in the PSID we also equivalize household consumption using the OECD scale, and deflate nominal values using the general CPI-Urban deflator or the food CPI when we use just food data (both deflators are expressed in 1983–1984 USD).

4.3.3 Time-Use Surveys

Survey Overview. To examine the trends in leisure inequality during this time period, we use data from the 1985 Americans' Use of Time survey and the 2003–2007 American Time Use Survey. The 1985 Americans' Use of Time survey was conducted by the Survey Research Center at the University of Maryland. The sample of 4,939 individuals was nationally representative with respect to adults over the age of eighteen living in homes with at least one telephone. The survey sampled its respondents from January 1985 through December 1985. The 2003 American Time Use Survey (ATUS) was conducted by the US Bureau of Labor Statistics (BLS). Participants in the ATUS, which includes children over the age of fifteen, are drawn from the existing sample of the Current Population Survey (CPS). The individual is sampled approximately three months after completion of the final CPS survey. At the time of the ATUS survey, the BLS updated the respondent's employment and demographic information. During 2003, roughly 1,700 individuals completed the survey each month, yielding an annual sample of over 20,000 individuals. During the 2004–2007 period, roughly 1,160 individuals were surveyed per month yielding an annual sample of just about 14,000 individuals.[9]

Each survey is based on twenty-four-hour time diaries. Survey personnel assign each activity to a category in a set classification scheme. The more refined the classification scheme, the less the survey needs to rely on the judgment of surveyors in correctly coding activities. The ATUS represents the state of the art of time-use surveys for the United States and reports 406

---

9. See Aguiar and Hurst (2007) for a detailed discussion of both surveys.

detailed time-use categories. The 1985 Americans' Use of Time survey used a scheme that included slightly less than 100 categories.

All data in the surveys are weighted so that they are nationally representative using the provided survey weights. Moreover, we also weight the data so that each day of the week is represented equally.

Sample Selection. For both surveys we restrict the sample to those individuals between the age of twenty-five and sixty-five (inclusive). Given that the data is collected at the individual level, we did not restrict the data to include only household heads. We also restricted the data to include only those households that had complete time diaries in that all twenty-four hours were accounted for and were able to be classified into discrete time-use categories.

Variable Definitions. We break the allocation of time into a number of broad time-use categories. As we have constructed the categories, they are mutually exclusive and they sum to the household's entire day. In other words, each person in the survey has twenty-four hours of nonoverlapping activities. Time spent on an activity includes any time spent on transportation associated with that activity.

In terms of our analysis, we use the time-use surveys to construct measures of leisure. Our definition of leisure follows the definition of Aguiar and Hurst (2007). In particular, we think of leisure time as being the time not allocated to market work or to home production (cooking, cleaning, mowing the lawn, etc.). We also exclude time spent taking care of one's children, time spent allocated to health care (going to the doctor), and time spent in educational attainment from our measure of leisure. Our measure of leisure therefore sums together time spent watching television; socializing (relaxing with friends and family, playing games with friends and family, talking on the telephone, attending/hosting social events, etc.); time spent exercising or participating in sports (playing sports, attending sporting events, exercising, running, etc.); reading (reading books and magazines, reading personal mail, reading personal email, etc.); enjoying entertainment events and hobbies (going to the movies or theatre, listening to music, using the computer for leisure, doing arts and crafts, playing a musical instrument, etc.); and all other similar activities.[10]

4.4 The Evolution of Income Inequality

As mentioned above, the main aim of this chapter is the study of the evolution of the *distribution* of welfare, which we will mainly approximate by the distribution of consumption. Before delving in the evidence on con-

---

10. We exclude the following from our measure of leisure: time spent eating, time spent sleeping, and time spent in personal maintenance (grooming, etc.). Aguiar and Hurst (2007) include such activities in some of their leisure measures. Our results are not sensitive to whether or not we include such activities in our leisure measures.

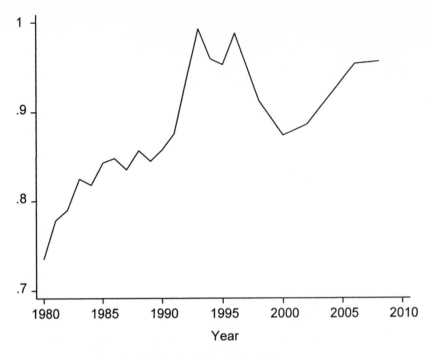

Fig. 4.1 Inequality in (equivalized) family income, PSID

sumption and how its distribution is measured in different data sources and with different definitions of consumption, we provide some evidence on the evolution of the distribution of household income. This piece of evidence is much more familiar and uncontroversial.

Figure 4.1 shows how income inequality, as measured by the standard deviation of logs, has evolved over the 1980–2008 period using PSID data. Our measure of income is before-tax family income, scaled by the OECD equivalence scale. Before-tax family income includes labor earnings, financial income, and public and private transfers received by all household members. All data are deflated using the CPI for urban households (in 1983–1984 USD) and weighted using the PSID longitudinal sampling weights.

The figure summarizes well-known facts. Income inequality, measured by the standard deviation of the logarithms, rises quite rapidly and dramatically over the 1980s until the mid-1990s; it slows down (and it even declines) during the second half of the 1990s before rising again throughout the first decade of the twenty-first century.[11] Between 1980 and 2008, the overall increase in the standard deviation of logs is large, at roughly 0.2.

---

11. We find similar trends using the Gini coefficient, which is less subject to the influence of extreme values.

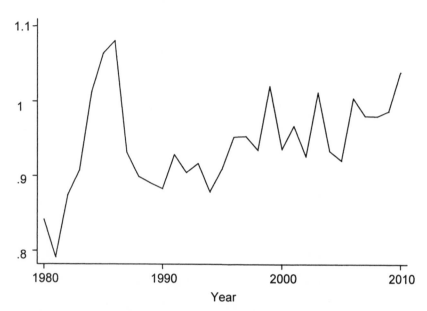

Fig. 4.2 Inequality in (equivalized) family income, CE interview survey

Figure 4.2 illustrates the change in income inequality using income measures from the CE instead of the PSID. In the CE, we use "before-tax family income" as our measure of income. As with the PSID data, we account for family size differences across households by normalizing income by the OECD equivalence scale. As visible from figure 4.2, the overall increase in the standard deviation of log income within the CE during the last thirty years was nearly identical to the similar measure in the PSID data (roughly 0.2). Notice, however, that there are a few differences between the PSID trends and the CE trends. First, the level of inequality in all years is higher in the CE. This is likely due to the fact that the CE income measure is measured with more error in all years. The CE survey is designed to measure consumption, not income. The PSID data, in contrast, has as its primary goal that of measuring income well. Second, the CE data suggests a sharp rise in income inequality in the early 1980s that is not present in the PSID data. The patterns in the PSID match well the patterns found using data from other surveys such as the Current Population Survey (see Autor, Katz, and Kearney 2008).

As we mentioned above, in addition to the evolution of overall inequality, as measured, for instance, by the standard deviation of logs, we also want to consider the evolution of different parts of the distributions of the variables of interest. In figures 4.3 (PSID data) and 4.4 (CE data), we provide some

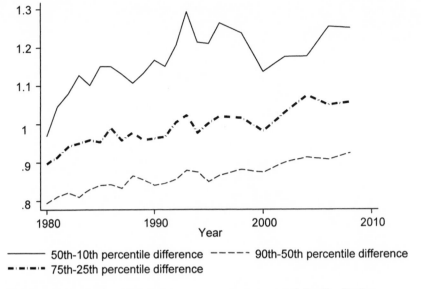

Fig. 4.3 (Equivalized) income inequality in different parts of the distribution, PSID data

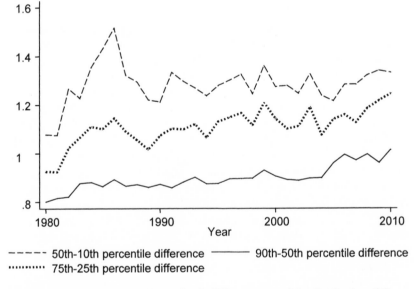

Fig. 4.4 (Equivalized) income inequality in different parts of the distribution, CE interview survey

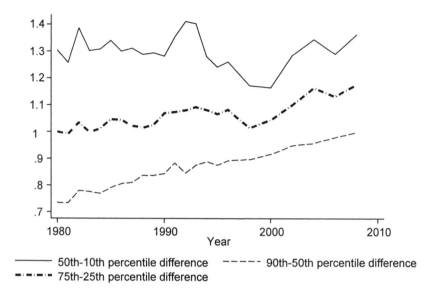

——— 50th-10th percentile difference   — — — 90th-50th percentile difference
— · — · — 75th-25th percentile difference

Fig. 4.5 Inequality in family earnings, various points of the distribution

information on the evolution of income inequality in different parts of the distribution. To this purpose, we plot the 90th–50th, the 50th–10th, and the 75th–25th percentile difference. Focusing our attention on the PSID data in figure 4.3, we first notice that the difference between the 50th and 10th percentile is considerably larger than the difference between the 90th and the 50th and (to a lesser extent) than the difference between the 75th and 25th percentile. The figure also shows that the decline in income inequality of the 1990s comes primarily from a decline in inequality at the bottom of the distribution, while inequality at the top of the distribution increases almost monotonically throughout our sample period. It should also be noted that the PSID does not sample very rich households, and hence substantially underestimates the rise in inequality that has occurred at the very top of the income distribution. Indeed, over the entire period the rise in inequality at the bottom is larger than at the top (measured in log points). When comparing figures 4.3 and 4.4, notice in particular the steady increase, in both data sets, of the 90th–50th and 75th–25th differentials. In both data sets, the largest increases, especially in the first part of the sample, however, are registered for the 50th–10th differential.

Some of the trends in the above figures are induced by the dynamics of public transfers at the bottom of the distribution. We can assess this fact using the PSID data by comparing figure 4.3 with figure 4.5. Figure 4.5 is similar to figure 4.3, except that the income measure is "family earnings" rather than "family income." The family earnings measure does not include transfer payments (and financial income). In figure 4.5, we find that

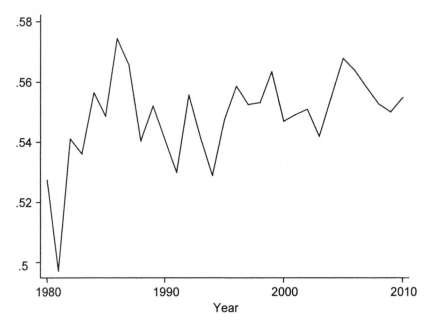

Fig. 4.6 Standard deviation log-equivalized nondurable consumption, CE interview data

inequality in family earnings at the top has risen substantially, while that at the bottom has remained fairly constant (except a drop and a subsequent rise from the mid 1990s to the middle of the first decade of the twenty-first century). Indeed, the main difference between figures 4.3 and 4.5 is the fact that in the former the 50th–10th differential line increases throughout the 1980s and early 1990s, while it is constant in the latter.

4.5 Consumption Inequality: Nondurable Expenditure in the CE Interview Survey

We start our analysis of consumption inequality by looking at data from the interview survey of the CE. We start here because this is often used as a starting point by researchers exploring the evolution of consumption inequality within the United States over the last thirty years. Figure 4.6 reports the standard deviation of log consumption of nondurable commodities and services, as defined in appendix A (on website), and as measured in the interview survey. As with the income data, we adjust the consumption data for differences in family composition using the same OECD scale mentioned above.

The results shown in figure 4.6 are staggering. First of all, we notice that the level of the standard deviation of log consumption is considerably lower than the standard deviation of log household income in all years of the sur-

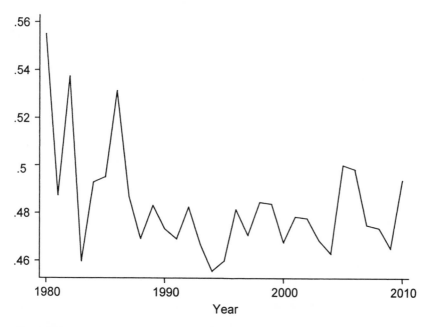

Fig. 4.7 Standard deviation log-equivalized food at home consumption, CE interview data

vey. This, by itself, is not surprising. Some of the variation in income documented in figures 4.1 and 4.2 is transitory. Households are able to smooth out such transitory shocks through borrowing and saving. This implies that the standard deviation in log consumption should be lower, on average, than the variation in log income. The staggering part of figure 4.6 is that the dramatic increase in the standard deviation of log income was not matched by any meaningful increase in the standard deviation of log consumption. Even starting in 1982, where the level of the standard deviation of logs is lowest, the standard deviation of log nondurable consumption as measured in the CE interview survey does not increase by more than 0.06. This is just over a third of the increase witnessed for income. Even this number, however, is likely overstated. Starting in 1983, there was essentially no increase in the standard deviation of log consumption. The bulk of the increase from 1982 through 2010 occurred between 1982 and 1983. This feature of the CE data on consumption inequality has been discussed, among others, by Attanasio, Battistin and Ichimura (2007), Attanasio, Battistin and Padula (2010), Krueger and Perri (2006), Heathcote, Perri, and Violante (2010).

In figure 4.7, we look at the evolution of inequality in (log) consumption of food at home, as measured in the interview survey. Again, we adjust the measure for family size using the OECD equivalence scales. We show these data so as to compare it with the food measures in the CE diary data and

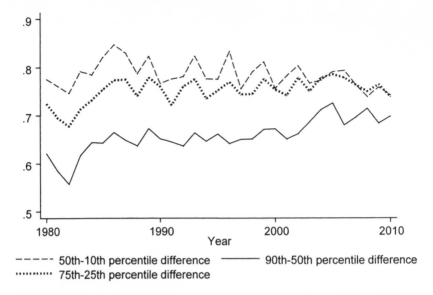

50th-10th percentile difference   **90th-50th percentile difference**
75th-25th percentile difference

Fig. 4.8 Movements in the distribution of nondurable consumption, CE interview data

with the food measures in the PSID data. Not surprisingly, the standard deviation of this variable is always below that of the standard deviation of total nondurable consumption as shown in figure 4.6. Food at home is more of a necessity good and, as a result, varies less in the cross section. Moreover, the evolution over time indicates that it does not change much until early in the first decade of the twenty-first century, when it exhibits a slight increase. Although there is much more noise in the data, the results in figure 4.7 are broadly consistent with the results from figure 4.6. Given the noise over time in this picture, one could conclude that the inequality of food at home has not increased over time and, relative to the early 1980s, it has, if anything, declined. But if the food measure in the CE is plagued with systematic measurement error over time, then consumption inequality measured using food at home data may also be biased downward.

Having described the evolution of overall inequality in our sample, we now look—as we did for income—at the evolution of different parts of the consumption distribution. As in figures 4.3 and 4.4, we now plot the difference between the 90th and 50th percentile, between the 50th and 10th, and between the 75th and 25th for consumption using the CE interview data. These results are shown in figure 4.8.

As with income, of the three differentials, the largest is the one between the 50th and the 10th, followed by that between the 75th and the 25th and then by the one between the 90th and the 50th. The differences between the three lines, however, are much less pronounced that in the case of family income. This is particularly true for the difference between 50th and 10th and 75th and 25th percentile in that the second part of the samples are actually very close to each other.

Interestingly, in the case of consumption, as with income, the last two increase steadily for the sample period, while the first (the difference between the 50th and 10th) is flat. However, while the income differential between the 90th and 50th percentile of household (log) income increases by over 0.2 points, the increase over the whole period is half that size in the case of consumption. The increase in the difference between the 75th and 25th is again about 0.2 points in the case of income and less than 0.1 points for nondurable consumption.

4.6 Consumption Inequality Does Track Income Inequality: Beyond the Aggregate CE Interview Measures of Consumption

Given the measurement error in the CE, which has been widely documented in many studies, we are not sure how much faith to put in the results on consumption inequality in figures 4.6, 4.7, and 4.8. In this section, we use other measures from the CE where measurement error may be less of an issue, as well as data from the PSID. We do this to see if the patterns using these other data sets and consumption measures yield a different story relative to the CE interview data, but a consistent story among themselves. The results again are striking. Across all the other measures we consider—where, to reiterate, measurement error is less of an issue—consumption inequality has increased by only slightly less than the increase in income inequality.

4.6.1 CE Diary Data: Total Expenditure

As we mentioned in the data section, the CE survey is made of two components: the interview survey and the diary survey. While the figures we have considered so far are derived from the former, analogous figures can be constructed using the latter, especially after 1986, when the diary survey became comprehensive and includes virtually all consumption categories. In figure 4.9, we plot the standard deviation of log total consumption for the 1986–2010 period. Again, we adjust the data for differences in family size.

When comparing figures 4.6 and 4.9, two features emerge. First, the level of inequality measured in figure 4.9 is considerably larger. This is not particularly surprising because of the structure of the two surveys: the diary survey covers only two weeks and infrequently purchased items can induce a considerable amount of additional inequality in the cross section. What is most surprising, however, is the increase in inequality is considerably larger and more persistent in the diary survey. This second feature has been discussed extensively in Attanasio, Battistin, and Ichimura (2007) and in Attanasio, Battistin, and Padula (2010). Attanasio, Battistin, and Ichimura (2007), in particular, rule out a number of simple explanations for this differ-

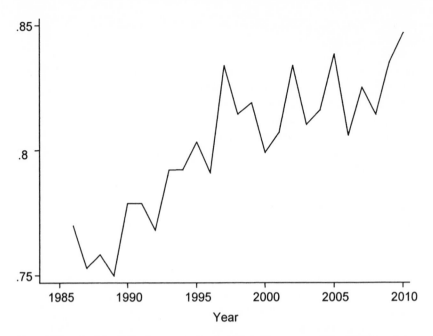

Fig. 4.9 Standard deviation log-equivalized nondurable consumption, CE diary data

ence, including a decrease in the frequency of shopping that could increase the number of zeros in a two-week diary.

The increase in the measure of the standard deviation of log expenditure using the diary data is 0.10, which is about one-half the increase in the measured increase in income inequality. Now, this measure may be understated if the expenditure categories that comprise the diary data are more likely to be necessities (like food). In that case, the increase in the consumption inequality from the diary survey would have to be scaled up by the income elasticity for the goods in the diary survey to get an overall measure of the change in inequality for total consumption. We do not do that here. Instead, we look at specific categories within the diary data, particularly food (and later on, entertainment). We turn to that analysis next. The take away from this section, however, is that within the goods in the diary data, there is a substantial increase in consumption inequality during the last three decades. The timing of the increases in consumption inequality from the diary data also matches closely the timing of the changes in income inequality over this time period.

4.6.2 CE Diary Data: Food

In figure 4.10, we explore the evolution of consumption inequality using food expenditures reported in the diary data. Researchers at the BLS believe that food data in the diary is measured with much less error than in the interview and, indeed, the main motivation for having the diary survey is to mea-

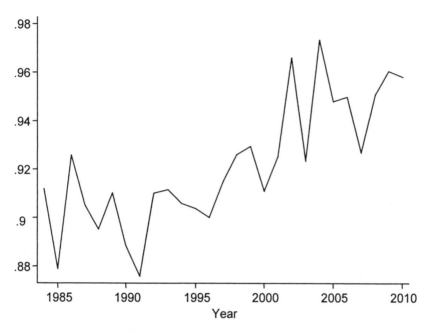

Fig. 4.10 Standard deviation log-equivalized food consumption, diary survey

sure more accurately what the BLS defines "frequently purchased items." As seen in figure 4.10, the standard deviation of log food expenditure at home in the diary data increased by between 6 and 8 percentage points. Estimates from Aguiar and Bils (2011) find that the income elasticity for total food spending is 0.5. Using this estimate, it follows that a simple back-of-the-envelope calculation suggests that total consumption inequality increased by between 12 and 16 percentage points over the period examined.[12]

Two things are of interest from the food results in figure 4.10. First, using the food data, the rise in consumption inequality was roughly 80 percent of the rise in income inequality during the sample period (0.16/0.20). Second, the rise in consumption inequality using the food data in the diary is higher than the rise in consumption using total consumption in the diary (0.16 vs. 0.10). Again, this is likely because the "total" nondurable expenditure measure in the diary is not a complete representation of nondurable expenditures. Given that it likely contains more reports of food expenditures than other nondurable expenditure measures, it may also need to be deflated using the income elasticity. As we show below, the results from the food data in the CE diary matches well the results on consumption inequality from the PSID.

12. This simple back-of-the-envelope calculation assumes that the income elasticity remains constant. If the elasticity is declining over time, our calculation is overestimating the increase in total consumption inequality.

4.6.3 CE Diary Data: Food versus Entertainment Spending

As we discussed in section 4.2.4, one way to deal with measurement error problems that can affect our overall measures of consumption is to focus on components of consumption for which the measurement issues are less severe and, possibly, stable over time. In this section we combine information on two such measures: consumption of food in the home and expenditure on entertainment goods and services (excluding durable goods).

In figure 4.11A, we plot the standard deviation of the log of the ratio of entertainment to food at home expenditure using the measures from the diary data. As argued in section 4.2.4, under certain conditions, this should be proportional to the standard deviation of log nondurable consumption, with the factor of proportionality depending on the difference between the income elasticities of the two commodities. As said, Aguiar and Bils (2011) estimate the income elasticity for total food spending estimates to be 0.5; they also estimate the elasticity for entertainment goods and services to be about 1.9. According to these estimates, one would then adjust the increase in figure 4.11A by a factor of 1.4 (1.9–0.5). The study by Blow, Lechene, and Levell (chapter 5, this volume) reports a similar expenditure elasticity of food at home of 0.5, but their estimate of the expenditure elasticity of entertainment is lower, at 1.5—implying a difference of 1—and hence suggesting that the increase in figure 4.11A would be in no need of adjustment.

As seen from figure 4.11A, the standard deviation of the log ratio of the two commodities increased over the whole sample period by about 0.15.[13] This figure would imply an increase in total nondurable consumption inequality (as measured by the standard deviation of logs) of the same size, if we take the Blow, Lechene, and Levell elasticities (while it would be lower using the Aguiar-Bils estimates). Again, this metric suggests that roughly 75 percent of the increase in income equality has translated to an increase in consumption inequality (0.15/0.20).

The ratio between food at home and entertainment expenditure can also be computed in the interview data. In figure 4.11B, we report the path of the standard deviation of the log of such a ratio, to be compared to figure 4.11A.

We find that, in the case of this ratio, the inequality measure that emerges from the interview CE data is considerably larger than what was obtained with total nondurable consumption expenditure and not inconsistent with the evidence coming from the diary survey. In particular, depending on when one starts counting, the increase in the standard deviation of the log ratio is between 0.15 and 0.25.

These results further suggest that the problems associated with the CE interview survey and the discrepancies between that and the diary survey might be attributed to difficulties in measuring certain specific commodities

---

13. In figure 4.11A, we do not need to adjust our results by changes in family size, as we are considering the (log) of a ratio.

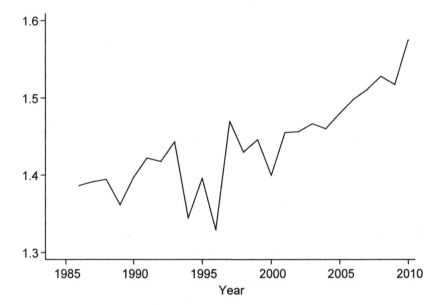

Fig. 4.11A SD log ratio entertainment/food spending, CE diary data

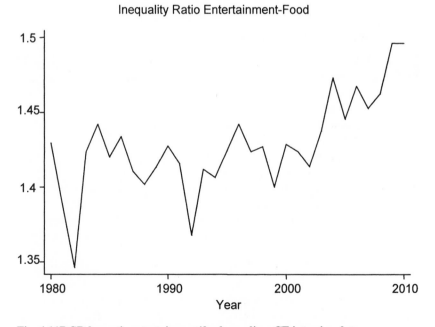

Fig. 4.11B SD log ratio entertainment/food spending, CE interview data

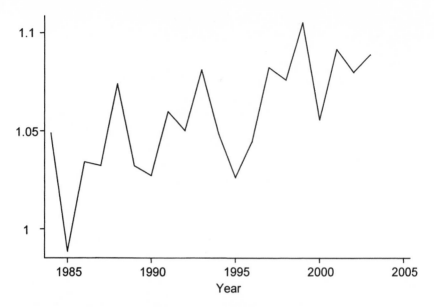

Fig. 4.12 Coefficient of variation stock of cars, CE interview survey

within the interview survey. It may be worth remembering that household income inequality in the CE interview survey increases as much as in other data sets, such as the PSID.

4.6.4 CE Interview Data: Stock of Car Holdings

If it is true that the different conclusions between the CE diary data and the CE interview data arise because some components of the CE interview data are fraught with changing nonclassical measurement error, one ideal exercise would be to find a category within the CE interview data that is measured with less error. To do this, we look at one such measure in the CE: the stock of cars owned by the household. This is an interesting exercise to perform for at least two reasons. First, the data on the value of the car stock in the CE seems to be of excellent quality, both in terms of the expenditure on cars and in terms of the composition of the stock of existing cars. Second, cars are durables and large. Moreover, adjusting the stock of cars is subject to transaction and adjustment costs. One would therefore guess that decisions about cars reflect long-run expectations about permanent income.

When analyzing the stock of cars one has to take into account the fact that there are a number of households that do not own a car. This prevents us from computing the log of the value of cars for these households. To deal with this issue we follow two different approaches. In figure 4.12, we plot the coefficient of variation of the stock of cars, defined as the standard deviation

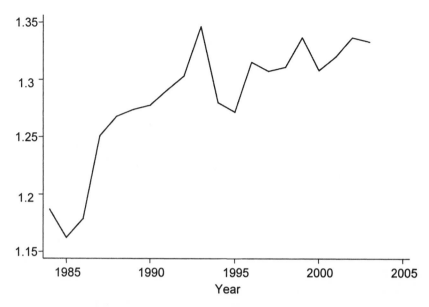

Fig. 4.13 SD log stock of cars, CE interview data

of car values divided by its mean. Both the mean and the standard deviation are computed including the zeros for households who do not own a car. In figure 4.13, instead, we only use households who own at least one car and plot the standard deviation of the log value for these households.

When looking at the coefficient of variation we see an increase of about 0.1, which happens especially in the first part of the sample period. The increase documented in figure 4.12 for the standard deviation of logs is actually larger, at almost 0.2.

4.6.5 PSID Data: Food and Nondurable Expenditures

Figure 4.14 uses PSID data and plots consumption inequality (as measured by the standard deviation of the logs) against time. Here we use the five different consumption measures we can construct from the PSID: (a) food consumption over the 1980–2010 period; (b) the so-called 70 percent measure available over the 1998–2010 period (with spending on health and education); (c) the 70 percent measure excluding spending on health and education;[14] (d) the imputation based on the CEX estimation of the food demand function over the 1980–2010 period (BPP measure), and (e) the imputation based on the difference between income and the change in assets over the 1980–2010 period (Ziliak measure).

14. Attanasio and Pistaferri (2013) use the consumption measure available in the redesigned PSID 1998–2010 to impute consumption inequality for the years before 1999.

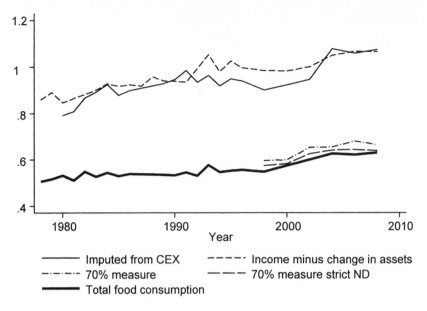

Fig. 4.14 Trends in consumption inequality from the PSID

A number of features of figure 4.14 are worth noting. First, the five measures rank as we might expect: food has less variance than the 70 percent measure, which in turn displays less variance than the imputed (more comprehensive) measures. Second, it is remarkable that the two more comprehensive measures—despite being obtained with two completely different imputation procedures that use completely different modules of the survey—display very similar trends and levels. Third, both imputed measures show a considerable increase in consumption inequality over the 1980s and into the early 1990s, of almost 0.2. In other words, the composite measures from the PSID show that consumption inequality has tracked income inequality nearly exactly.[15] Fourth, the increase in inequality in food consumption in the PSID is nearly identical to the increase in inequality in food consumption from the CE diary survey. This is reassuring given that there is no evidence that systematic measurement error has been changing in the PSID. Fifth, the increase in total consumption inequality based on the PSID food data is 0.2 (0.10/0.5). Again, to get this, we scale up the estimate based upon the total food income elasticity of 0.5. Finally, the consumption inequality measure using the new consumption data available for the 1998–2010 period confirms the general increasing trends.

15. Both imputed measures, of course, do not identify the levels of consumption inequality because of imputation errors. However, if such errors are stationary, then the imputed measures are unbiased estimates of the *change* in consumption inequality over the sample period.

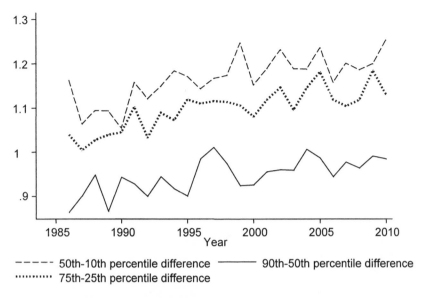

- - - - - 50th-10th percentile difference ———— 90th-50th percentile difference
.... 75th-25th percentile difference

Fig. 4.15 Movements in the distribution of nondurable consumption, CE diary survey

Taken together, the results from the PSID data shown in figure 4.14 is that consumption inequality and income inequality tracked each other nearly identically during this time period. We highlight one more aspect emerging from the PSID data. Given the results in figure 4.1 and the results in figure 4.14, we can compute the simple correlation between the total consumption inequality measures based on the imputation procedures and the income inequality measures from the PSID over this time period. A simple ocular examination of the figures shows that the time-series patterns of the inequality measures are very similar. Both inequality measures (imputed consumption inequality and income inequality) increased during the 1980s, leveled off during the 1990s, and increased further in the first decade of the twenty-first century. This is reflected in the simple correlation measures. For example, the simple time-series correlation between the PSID-imputed consumption inequality measure (based on the CE elasticities) and the PSID income inequality measure was 0.69, and that between the Ziliak measure and the income inequality measure was 0.88.

4.7 Different Dimensions of Inequality

In this section, we use our various other consumption measures within the CE and the PSID to explore the evolution of consumption inequality at different points in the distribution. In figure 4.15, we consider the percentile differentials we have used so far to study the evolution of the distribution of

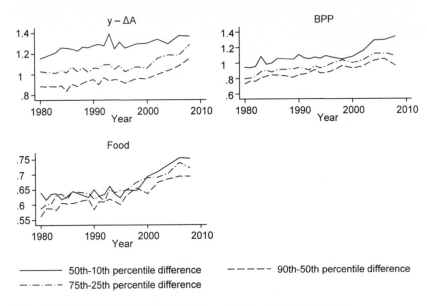

Fig. 4.16 Consumption inequality in different parts of the distribution

consumption. In figure 4.15, we plot the same differentials between percentiles in figure 4.8, but instead use the diary total nondurable consumption measure. Notice the 50/10 differential, which was substantially flatter in figure 4.8 and increases throughout the sample period as does the 75/25 differential. The 90/10 differential, which in figure 4.8 was the one that increases the most, increases but slightly less than the other differentials. Again, the changes in consumption inequality throughout the distribution using the CE diary data better matches the time-series trends in income inequality at similar percentile points.

Figure 4.16 explores whether the changes in consumption inequality within the PSID are coming from the bottom or the top part of the distribution. In the top-left panel, we show the results using the Ziliak measure (defined as the difference between income and the change in assets). First, in the 1980–1995 period the rise in inequality is explained by movements in both tails—the 75th–25th percentile difference is indeed very stable. The rise in inequality at the bottom is, if anything, more pronounced than the rise in inequality at the top. However, in the second half of the sample, the top part of the distribution starts detaching itself more dramatically from the rest—the rise in the 90th–10th percentile difference and in the 75th–25th percentile difference is very pronounced, while the 50th–10th percentile difference remains stable. Interestingly, trends in food consumption inequality (bottom panel) are different—there is less heterogeneity in the movement of different parts of the food consumption distribution. Partly reflecting

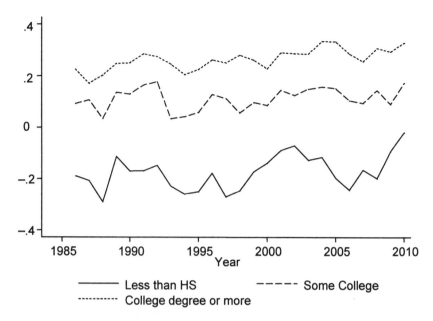

Fig. 4.17 Consumption inequality across skill groups (averages relative to those with a high school degree), CE diary survey

this, the percentile differences computed using the BPP's imputed measure of consumption (top-right panel) display less stark trends.

In addition to the overall sample and its distribution, it is also interesting to cut the sample by skill levels of the household level. We know from a large literature in labor economics that the return to education has increased dramatically over the period we are considering and that, in the case of income and wages, there have been large increases in inequality both across skill level and within skill levels (possibly reflecting changes also in the price of unobservable skills).

In figure 4.17, we divide the CE diary sample into four groups on the basis of the education of the household head: the first group is formed of households headed by an individual with a college degree or more, the second group by households headed by an individual with some college experience, the third by high school graduates, and the fourth by high school dropouts. We then express, for every year, average log consumption as difference from average log consumption of the third group (the high school graduates).

The graphs in figure 4.17 indicate a steady increase in the return to education as measured by the difference between high school graduates and college graduates (the top line). The differential between college graduate and high school graduates increases from about 0.2 to about 0.33 at the end of the sample. These changes in the first part of the sample (across different years of birth cohorts) were studied in Attanasio and Davis (1996) in rela-

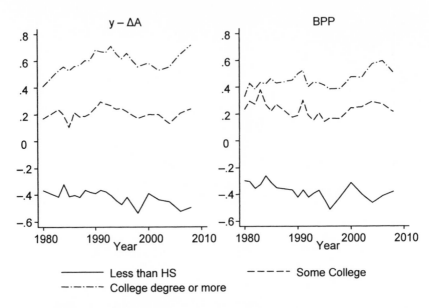

Fig. 4.18 Consumption inequality across skill groups (averages relative to those with a high school degree), PSID consumption measures

tion to similar changes in relative wages. Similar patterns for the PSID are shown in figure 4.18.

Having considered changes across education groups, we now look at changes within education groups. In particular, in figures 4.19 and 4.20, we plot the standard deviation of log consumption within each of the four education groups listed above for the CE diary data and the PSID consumption measures, respectively. Within-skill group consumption inequality increased dramatically across all skill groups in both surveys.

4.8 Leisure Inequality: Time-Use Surveys

The results in the prior section suggest strongly that consumption inequality has tracked income inequality rather closely over the last thirty years. Does this mean that the actual inequality in well-being tracked income inequality over this period? In the standard model, utility is a function of both consumption and leisure time. It is therefore natural to look at the changes in inequality in leisure in conjunction with the changes in inequality in consumption so as to get a better measure of changes in the inequality of total well-being across individuals.[16]

---

16. The inequality in leisure has been explored by Aguiar and Hurst (2007, 2009).

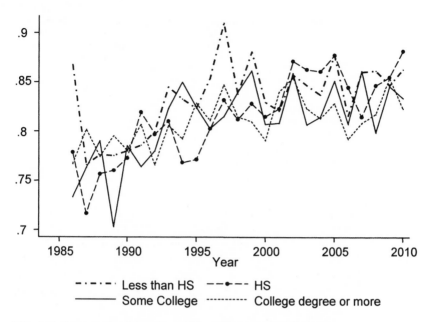

Fig. 4.19 Consumption inequality within skill groups, CE diary survey

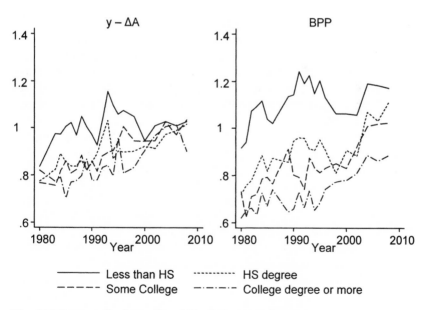

Fig. 4.20 Consumption inequality within skill groups, PSID data

Table 4.1   Leisure measures (hours per week) by group, 1985 and 2003–2007

	Leisure (hours per week)		
Sample	1985	2003–2007	Change
Men			
Low educated	36.6	39.1	2.5
High educated	34.4	33.2	–1.2
Women			
Low educated	35.0	35.2	0.2
High educated	32.2	30.3	–1.9

To make the results from the time-use surveys comparable with some of the results in the prior sections, we explore the changes in leisure inequality across skill groups. Table 4.1 explores the hours per week spent in leisure for low- and high-educated men and women in both 1985 and 2003–2007. As discussed above, our measure of leisure includes the actual time the individual spends in leisurely activities like watching television, socializing with friends, going to the movies, and so forth.

A few things are of note from table 4.1. First, in 1985, low-educated men took only slightly more hours per week of leisure than high-educated men. As above, we define high educated as those with more than twelve years of schooling. A similar pattern holds for women. However, by 2007, the leisure differences between high- and low-educated men are substantial. Specifically, low-educated men experienced a 2.5 hours per week gain in leisure between 1985 and 2007. High-educated men, during the same time period, experienced a 1.2 hour per week decline in leisure. The new effect is that leisure inequality increased dramatically after 1985. Again, similar patterns are found for women.

Figure 4.21 shows the distribution of leisure for low-educated men in 1985 (dashed line) and 2003–2007 (solid line). Figure 4.22 shows similar patterns for higher-educated men. Most of the increase in leisure occurred as a result of changes in the upper tail of the leisure distribution. A greater share of low-educated men in 2003–2007 are taking more than fifty hours per week of leisure than in 1985. This is not the case for higher-educated men. If anything, there is slightly lower proportion of higher-educated men taking more than fifty hours per week of leisure in 2003–2007 than there was in 1985.

The patterns shown in table 4.1 and figures 4.21 and 4.22 show that the overall inequality measures between high- and low-skilled individuals becomes muddied when one combines the results for consumption and leisure. While it is true that the consumption of the highly educated has grown rapidly relative to the consumption of the low educated, it is also true that leisure time of the low educated has grown rapidly relative to the leisure time of the highly educated. In order to make overall welfare calculations,

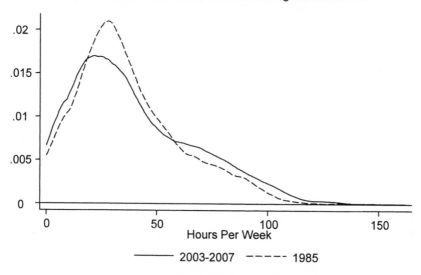

Fig. 4.21 Kernel density of leisure time for low-educated men (1985 and 2003–2007)

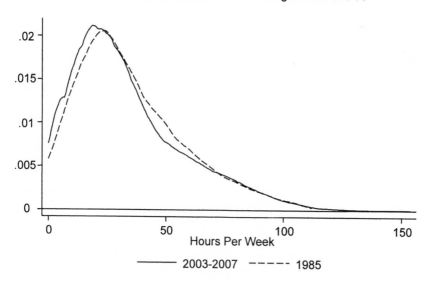

Fig. 4.22 Kernel density of leisure time for highly educated men (1985 and 2003–2007)

one needs to take a stance on how the leisure time is valued. But, as long as leisure has some positive value, the increase in consumption inequality between high- and low-educated households during the past few decades will overstate the true inequality in well-being between these groups.

4.9 Conclusions

In this chapter, we have documented thoroughly that the increase in income inequality was matched by an increase in consumption inequality of comparable magnitude. In particular, between 1980 and 2010, the standard deviation of log income increased by roughly 0.2 percentage points. Across our various preferred measures, the standard deviation of log consumption increased by roughly 0.10 to 0.2 percentage points with most of the estimates being in the 0.15 to 0.20 range.

The main innovation of the chapter is to show that the data on the increase in consumption inequality within the United States is very robust to alternative measures of consumption and across alternative data sets. The one outlier in terms of estimates of consumption inequality is total nondurable expenditure from the CE interview survey (where no attempt is made to adjust for measurement error). For this measure, the standard deviation of log consumption increased by only 0.06 percentage points—with most of the increase coming before 1982. As shown by Aguiar and Bils (2011), the CE interview data is plagued with nonclassical measurement error that biases estimates of consumption inequality downward. Given that many researchers used the nondurable consumption measure from the CE interview data as their primary measure of consumption inequality, they have naturally concluded that consumption inequality has not increased much over the last thirty years. However, some researchers have found rising consumption inequality using other measures. These various estimates have lead researchers to conclude that the extent of the increase in consumption inequality is still an open debate among economists.

Our results in this chapter, however, show that such a conclusion is unwarranted. Across every other measure of consumption we analyzed, consumption inequality increased substantially. Some of these measures came from the CE diary survey, like food and entertainment spending (where measurement error in those categories has been found to be less of a problem). Some measures came from the CE interview survey, like the stock of cars (where quality of data appears fairly high). Finally, some of our measures come from the PSID (where systematic measurement has not been found to be a problem). Not only do these other measures of consumption inequality mirror the overall change in income inequality, the timing of the changes also line up very closely.

Within the context of the CE, it is clear that the interview survey is plagued by some serious measurement problems. These can arise from a variety of sources. In terms of the discussion of inequality, however, the evidence we have presented seems to indicate that these problems are not caused by the specificity of the interview sample and by the fact that it might exclude, for a variety of reasons, households from the extremes of the income distribution. The main evidence we provide in this respect is that we do find evidence of increasing inequality in the interview survey. It is apparent in income, in the value of the car stock, and in the ratio of food at home to entertainment. It is therefore likely that the issue lies with the measurement of specific items or the degree to which expenditures are fully reported by certain groups. This evidence can be valuable in the redesign of the CE survey.

From a methodological point of view, more work is needed to formalize the use of several components of the CE survey, both to do imputation in other data sets and to make inferences about overall (nondurable) consumption. We also believe more work is needed in order to understand the consequences for welfare of changes in relative prices and the consequent shifts in commodity-demand patterns. Finally, if would also be helpful to think about overall measures in well-being by thinking about the overall change in consumption inequality jointly with the overall change in leisure inequality. We think future work should attempt to make a composite change in the inequality of well-being by formally linking the two measures.

References

Aguiar, Mark, and Mark Bils. 2011."Has Consumption Inequality Mirrored Income Inequality?" NBER Working Paper no. 16807, Cambridge, MA.

Aguiar, Mark, and Erik Hurst. 2007. "Measuring Trends in Leisure: The Allocation of Time over Five Decades." *Quarterly Journal of Economics* 122 (3): 969–1006.

———. 2009. *The Increase in Leisure Inequality: 1965–2005*. Washington, DC: American Enterprise Institute for Public Policy Research.

Attanasio, Orazio, Erich Battistin, and Hidehiko Ichimura. 2007. "What Really Happened to Consumption Inequality in the United States?" In *Hard-to-Measure Goods and Services: Essays in Honor of Zvi Griliches*, Studies in Income and Wealth, vol. 67, edited by Ernst R. Berndt and Charles R. Hulten, 515–44. Chicago: University of Chicago Press.

Attanasio, Orazio, Erich Battistin, and Mario Padula. 2010. *Inequality in Living Standards since 1980: Income Tells Only a Small Part of the Story*. Washington, DC: AEI Publishing.

Attanasio, Orazio, and Steven J. Davis. 1996. "Relative Wage Movements and the Distribution of Consumption." *Journal of Political Economy* 104 (6): 1227–62.

Attanasio, Orazio, and Nicola Pavoni. 2011. "Risk Sharing in Private Information Models with Asset Accumulation: Explaining the Excess Smoothness of Consumption." *Econometrica* 79 (4): 1027–68.

Attanasio, Orazio, and Luigi Pistaferri. 2013. "What Do We Know about Consumption Inequality? Some Evidence Using the New PSID Consumption Measure." Working Paper, Stanford University.

Autor, David H., Lawrence F. Katz, and Melissa S. Kearney. 2008. "Trends in US Wage Inequality: Revising the Revisionists." *Review of Economics and Statistics* 90 (2): 300–23.

Blundell, Richard, Luigi Pistaferri, and Ian Preston. 2004. "Imputing Consumption in the PSID Using Food Demand Estimates from the CEX." IFS Working Paper no. W04/27, Institute for Fiscal Studies.

———. 2008. "Consumption Inequality and Partial Insurance." *American Economic Review* 98 (5): 1887–921.

Blundell, Richard, and Ian Preston. 1998. "Consumption Inequality and Income Uncertainty." *Quarterly Journal of Economics* 113 (2): 603–40.

Browning, Martin, and Thomas Crossley. 2009. "Are Two Cheap, Noisy Measures Better Than One Expensive, Accurate One?" *American Economic Review* 99 (2): 99–103.

Cutler, David M., and Lawrence F. Katz. 1992. "Rising Inequality? Changes in the Distribution of Income and Consumption in the 1980s." *American Economic Review* 82 (2): 546–51.

Deaton, Angus, and Christina Paxson. 1994. "Intertemporal Choice and Inequality." *Journal of Political Economy* 102 (3): 437–67.

Garner, Thesia I., and Atsushi Maki. 2004. "The Gap between Macro and Micro Economic Statistics: Estimation of the Misreporting Model Using Micro-Data Sets Derived from the Consumer Expenditure Survey." Working Paper no. 3, Econometric Society.

Heathcote, Jonathan, Fabrizio Perri, and Giovanni L. Violante. 2010. "Unequal We Stand: An Empirical Analysis of Economic Inequality in the United States: 1967–2006." *Review of Economic Dynamics* 13 (1): 15–51.

Krueger, Dirk, and Fabrizio Perri. 2006. "Does Income Inequality Lead to Consumption Inequality? Evidence and Theory." *Review of Economic Studies* 73 (1): 163–93.

Meyer, Bruce D., and James X. Sullivan. 2009. "Five Decades of Consumption and Income Poverty." NBER Working Paper no. 14827, Cambridge, MA.

Padula, Mario. 1999. "Euler Equations and Durable Goods." CSEF Working Paper no. 30, Centre for Studies in Economics and Finance.

Parker, Jonathan, Annette Vissing-Jorgensen, and Nicolas L. Ziebarth. 2009. "Inequality in Expenditure in the Twentieth Century." Working Paper, Northwestern University.

Slesnick, Daniel T. 2001. *Consumption and Social Welfare: Living Standards and Their Distribution in the United States.* Cambridge: Cambridge University Press.

Ziliak, James. 1998. "Does the Choice of Consumption Measure Matter? An Application to the Permanent-Income Hypothesis." *Journal of Monetary Economics* 41 (1): 201–16.

Using the CE to Model Household Demand

Laura Blow, Valérie Lechene, and Peter Levell

5.1 Introduction

The focus of this chapter is to reflect on the interaction between core Consumer Expenditure Survey (CE) goals and fundamental research questions in the area of consumer demand analysis. Demand analysis uses information on household choices and their incomes not only to summarize the variability of responses of demand to prices, incomes, and characteristics, but also to predict responses to changes in the environment and to assess the corresponding changes in welfare. Price and income elasticities predicted from the estimation of demand systems are used, for example, to assess the welfare effects of tax changes, transfers, and so on. Knowing what is needed in survey data to enable a relatively accurate prediction of consumer responses is of fundamental importance.

Demand analysis is done within the conceptual framework of the theory of choice, where the choices that are observed are assumed to correspond to the maximization of an objective subject to constraints. In theory, all information from all periods is pertinent to the current period's choices, and much of demand theory has been devoted to the business of simplifying this framework. For example, the analysis of choices can fruitfully be restricted to the analysis of the allocation of a given budget between different com-

Laura Blow is senior research economist at the Institute for Fiscal Studies. Valérie Lechene is senior lecturer at University College London and a research fellow at the Institute for Fiscal Studies. Peter Levell is research economist at the Institute for Fiscal Studies.

We are very grateful to Orazio Attanasio, Martin Browning, Tom Crossley, Arthur Lewbel, Irina Telyukova, and Frederic Vermeulen for useful discussions on the CE and the analysis of household demand. We also thank John Sabelhaus for his editing comments. For acknowledgments, sources of research support, and disclosure of the authors' material financial relationships, if any, please see http://www.nber.org/chapters/c12676.ack.

modities within one period given only that period's prices under a number of assumptions, some of which are testable. The assumption under which it is possible to concentrate on within-period behavior is that there is intertemporal separability.[1]

Under this assumption there is two-stage budgeting, so that at the top stage the consumer chooses how to allocate income between current consumption and savings and expenditures on durables, and at the bottom stage the individual chooses how to allocate total expenditure within the period between the different goods. Under this assumption, once we observe the budget allocated to a period, only the within-period prices matter for the allocation of that total expenditure between goods rather than all the prices of all the periods. Time-separable models and the analysis of within-period allocation are well developed, starting with the Linear Expenditure model of Richard Stone (1954); the Rotterdam model, developed by Theil (1965); the model of Barten (1966); and the Translog model of Christensen, Jorgenson, and Lau (1975). More recent contributions are the Almost Ideal Demand System (AIDS) of Deaton and Muellbauer (1980) and its extension to Quadratic Almost Ideal Demand System (QUAIDS) by Banks, Blundell, and Lewbel (1997). Many of the early empirical tests of these demand systems rejected the restrictions imposed by demand theory, such as symmetry and homogeneity. However, the data used was aggregate data (for example, Christensen, Jorgenson, and Lau 1975; Deaton and Muellbauer 1980), and it has been argued (see Sabelhaus 1990) that aggregation bias leads to the rejection. When Sabelhaus estimates a time-separable demand system on aggregate US data and on household-level CE data, he finds the restrictions are rejected in the former but not the latter. Here we do not have to worry about aggregation bias and are more focused on whether the separability assumptions need to be relaxed and what the data requirements for doing this are.

A further set of assumptions restrict the aspects of behavior that are considered; for instance, separability between consumption and the use of time is invoked to enable the analysis to be focused on choices between goods, without reference to labor supply. However, it is unlikely that use of time is separable from demand. As Browning and Meghir (1991) argue, casual observation reveals that labor supply affects heating needs during the day, and costs of travel and child care. The formal tests they conduct on data from the UK Family Expenditure Survey confirm the rejection of separability of commodity demands from labor supply.

Similar arguments can be put forward concerning potential links between nondurable expenditures and stocks of durable goods. Consider, for

1. As Hussain (2006) points out, if there is no relative price variation within nondurables, then the composite goods theorem applies, and separability obtains without resorting to behavioral assumptions. However, in this case, there are no substitution effects within the group of nondurables either.

instance, housing stock and utilities. Those living in a larger home are, other things equal, likely to spend more on furnishing and maintaining their properties. This means that we should either condition on the price of housing or on housing stock when we consider the demand for utilities. Stocks of durables such as housing can also be expected to affect nondurable consumption choices when levels of the durable stock are costly to adjust. Building on the seminal work of Grossman and Laroque (1990), these issues are discussed for the case of housing decisions by, for example, Flavin and Yamashita (2002) and Flavin and Nakagawa (2008). Furthermore, if there are unobservables in preferences for utilities that are also correlated with housing stock, then there will be an endogeneity problem that requires addressing even if we condition on housing stock. Another example concerns transport. How much households choose to spend on public transport, petrol, and insurance is likely to be affected by whether or not they own a car. In this case, the price of cars affects the demand for public transport and for other nondurable goods. Padula (1999) examines this question using the CE, and his results indicate that the stock of cars should be included in an analysis of demand. Hussain (2006) shows that separability of demand from labor supply is rejected. He also investigates the relationship between demand and housing stock. Both authors are able to conduct these tests thanks to some unusual features of the CE, which we will come back to below.

Testing for separability of commodity demands from labor supply, for intertemporal separability, and for the other restrictions under which demand is analyzed is a task that would ideally require a data set with all the possible information, so that one could do an estimation "pretending" the information was not available to see what leads to the biggest bias. Although such a data set does not exist, the CE offers good opportunities to examine the assumptions of demand theory. Indeed, the CE is an unusual expenditure survey in that together with demand and income data, it contains data on durables and cars, and also has a short panel element.[2] Thus, we will be able to consider durables and labor supply to discuss whether they can be omitted without biasing the results. More precisely, we test for separability of cars, housing stock, and labor force participation from demand for nondurables, first under the assumption of exogeneity and then allowing for endogeneity of cars. We compute the elasticities obtained in the different models. We also discuss possible instrumenting strategies for housing and labor force participation, but we do not find suitable instruments in the data.

---

2. These features have permitted much research to be conducted on consumption and dynamic aspects of behavior using the CE. Our focus, however, is on the analysis of demand, that is, the choices that take place within a period, and we will have little to say about consumption, intertemporal choices, savings, and other dynamic aspects of behavior per se.

Our results are aligned to those of Padula (1999), who rejects separability for cars in the context of Euler equations, and to those of Hussain (2006), who rejects separability of labor force participation. Regarding housing, Hussain's results are mixed, while we find that separability is unambiguously rejected. We compute elasticities obtained under the different assumptions. We find that income elasticities change with the different modeling assumptions, while price elasticities are more robust.

We have structured the chapter in the following manner. We start in section 5.2 with the model of consumer choice and the functional forms of the associated elasticities. We present the CE data and sample, which we use in this chapter in section 5.3. In section 5.4, we start with a discussion of instrumenting strategies, we then show the first-stage regressions for the endogenous variables, the Engel curves, and finally the demand system estimates under the different assumptions. In the first model, we make the usual assumption of full intertemporal separability between stocks of durables and demand for nondurables, as well as the assumption of separability of time use from nondurable demand. We then relax the separability assumptions and condition on stock variables (cars and housing) and labor force participation, all assumed exogenous. We test for and reject separability, under the assumption of exogeneity. We then show results obtained instrumenting for cars, where separability is again rejected. We are not able to conduct similar tests instrumenting for labor force participation or housing. We contrast the elasticities obtained in the different models.

5.2 Modeling Household Demand

5.2.1 Almost Ideal Demand System and Quadratic Almost Ideal Demand System

Demand analysis starts with the assumption that the consumer, h, has a utility or welfare function, $U^h(\mathbf{q})$ that tells us the level of welfare associated with consuming a vector of goods $\mathbf{q}$. The superscript h reminds us that the welfare function might vary across households. Demand choices are made by maximizing this welfare function subject to the consumer's budget constraint, M^h, and to prices, $\mathbf{p}$:

$$\max U^h(\mathbf{q}) \ s.t. \ \mathbf{p}'\mathbf{q} = M^h,$$

and this results in the (Marshallian) demand functions for each good $q_i^h(\mathbf{p}, M^h)$, where i indexes the good, $i = 1 \ldots I$. An alternative way of modeling the consumer's decision is to use the cost function, $C^h(u,\mathbf{p})$, which tells us the minimum level of expenditure needed to attain a given level of welfare at a given set of prices. That is,

$$C^h(u, \mathbf{p}) = \min_q \mathbf{p}'\mathbf{q} \ s.t. \ U^h(\mathbf{q}) = u.$$

The cost function is often used as the starting point for theoretical demand modeling since it can be shown that

$$\frac{\partial \ln C^h(u, \mathbf{p})}{\partial \ln p_i} = w_i^h(u, \mathbf{p}),$$

where w_i^h is the budget share of the *ith* good for household h, that is,

$$w_i^h(u, \mathbf{p}) = \frac{p_i q_i^h(u, \mathbf{p})}{M^h}.$$

The Almost Ideal Demand (AIDS) model derives from the following specification of the consumer cost function, $\ln C^h(u, p)$

$$\ln C^h(u, p) = \ln a^h(p) + u b^h(p),$$

so that the share, w_{it}^h, of the *ith* good for household h in time period t ($= \partial \ln C^h / \partial \ln p_{it}$) is

$$w_{it} = \frac{\partial \ln a^h(p_t)}{\partial \ln p_{it}} + \frac{\partial b^h(p_t)}{\partial \ln p_{it}} u$$

$$\frac{\partial \ln a^h(p_t)}{\partial \ln p_{it}} + \frac{\partial b^h(p_t)}{\partial \ln p_{it}} \left(\frac{\ln M^h - \ln a^h(p_t)}{b^h(p_t)} \right).$$

$$\frac{\partial \ln a^h(p)}{\partial \ln p_{it}} + \frac{\partial \ln b^h(p)}{\partial \ln p_{it}} [\ln M^h - \ln a^h(p_t)]$$

For the price indices $\ln a^h(p)$ and $b^h(p)$, the forms typically employed in the AI demand system are a translog form for $\ln a^h(p)$ and a Cobb–Douglas form for $b^h(p)$:

$$\ln a^h(p_t) = \alpha_0 + \sum_i \alpha_i^h \ln p_{it} + \frac{1}{2} \sum_i \sum_j \gamma_{ij} \ln p_{it} \ln p_{jt}$$

$$b^h(p_t) = \prod_i p_{it}^{\beta_i^h}$$

where

$$\alpha_i^h = \alpha_{i0} + \sum_k \alpha_{ik} z_k^\alpha$$

$$\beta_i^h = \beta_{i0} + \sum_k \beta_{ik} z_k^\beta,$$

in which the zs denote demographic characteristics such as age of head, number of children, and so on.

The theoretical restriction of additivity implies

$$\sum_i \alpha_{i0} = 1, \sum_i \alpha_{ir} = 0 \; \forall r, \sum_i \beta_{i0} = 0, \sum_i \beta_{ir} = 0 \; \forall r, \sum_i \gamma_{ij} = 0,$$

while that of homogeneity of degree zero implies

$$\sum_j \gamma_{ij} = 0,$$

and finally symmetry implies

$$\gamma_{ij} = \gamma_{ji} \ \forall \ i \neq j.$$

This gives the following form for the share equations:

$$(1) \qquad w_{it}^h = \alpha_i^h + \sum_j \gamma_{ij} \ln p_{jt} + \beta_i^h \ln\left[\frac{M_t^h}{a^h(p_t)}\right].$$

From work starting with Banks, Blundell, and Lewbel (1997), we know that the AIDS assumption of shares that are linear in log expenditure is too restrictive for some goods and the Quadratic Almost Ideal Demand (QUAIDS) model allows, as its name implies, more curvature in the Engel path. The QUAIDS model extends the consumer cost function to the following form:

$$\ln C^h(u, p) = \ln a^h(p) + \frac{ub^h(p)}{1 - ug^h(p)},$$

so that the share, w_{it}^h, of the ith good for household h in time period t ($= \partial \ln C^h \ / \ \partial \ln p_{it}$) is

$$w_{it} = \frac{\partial \ln a^h(p_t)}{\partial \ln p_{it}} + \frac{\partial b^h(p_t)}{\partial \ln p_{it}}\left(\frac{u}{1 - ug^h(p_t)}\right) + \frac{\partial g^h(p)}{\partial \ln p_{it}}\left(\frac{u}{1 - ug^h(p_t)}\right)^2 b^h(p_t)$$

$$= \frac{\partial \ln a^h(p_t)}{\partial \ln p_{it}} + \frac{\partial b^h(p_t)}{\partial \ln p_{it}}\left(\frac{\ln m^h - \ln a^h(p_t)}{b^h(p_t)}\right) + \frac{\partial g^h(p_t)}{\partial \ln p_i}\left(\frac{[\ln m^h - \ln a^h(p_t)]^2}{b^h(p_t)}\right)$$

$$= \frac{\partial \ln a^h(p)}{\partial \ln p_i} + \frac{\partial \ln b^h(p)}{\partial \ln p_i}[\ln M^h - \ln a^h(p_t)] + \frac{\partial g^h(p_t)}{\partial \ln p_{it}}\left(\frac{[\ln M^h - \ln a^h(p_t)]^2}{b^h(p_t)}\right).$$

For the additional (to the AIDS model) price index $g^h(p)$ we follow the specification used in Banks, Blundell, and Lewbel:

$$g^h(p_t) = \sum_i \lambda_i^h \ln p_{it},$$

where

$$\lambda_i^h = \lambda_{i0} + \sum_k \lambda_{ik} z_k^\lambda,$$

and additivity implies

$$\sum_i \lambda_{i0} = 0, \sum_i \lambda_{ir} = 0 \ \forall \ r.$$

This gives the following form for the share equations

$$(2) \qquad w_{it}^h = \alpha_i^h + \sum_j \gamma_{ij} \ln p_{jt} + \beta_i^h \ln\left[\frac{M_t^h}{a^h(p_t)}\right] + \frac{\lambda_i^h}{b^h(p_t)} \ln\left[\frac{M_t^h}{a^h(p_t)}\right]^2,$$

which is a complicated nonlinear function of prices. The estimation procedure in papers such as Banks, Blundell, and Lewbel (1997) exploits the linearity of the share equation *given* $a^h(p_t)$ and $b^h(p_t)$. The procedure is iterative—first, the price and expenditure parameters are estimated for given values of $a^h(p_t)$ and $b^h(p_t)$, then $a^h(p_t)$ and $b^h(p_t)$ are updated using the estimated values of α_i^h, γ_{ij} and β_i^h, and then the procedure is repeated using the updated price indices, continuing until the difference between the current and previous estimates is negligible.[3] An alternative approach often used is to approximate $a^h(p_t)$ with the Stone price index $\Gamma(p_t)$:

$$\ln a^h(p_t) \simeq \Gamma(p_t) = \sum_i w_{it}^h \ln p_{it}.$$

5.2.2 Elasticities from the AIDS and QUAIDS Models

Denote the income elasticity by e_i, then

$$e_i = \frac{\eta_i}{w_i} + 1,$$

where

$$\eta_i \equiv \frac{\partial w_i}{\partial \ln M},$$

which is equal to β_i for AIDS or AIDS with the Stone Approximation and to

$$\beta_i + 2 \frac{\lambda_i}{b(p_t)} \ln\left(\frac{M_t}{a(p_t)}\right)$$

for QUAIDS or QUAIDS with the Stone Approximation.

Denote the elasticity of good i with respect to the price of good k by e_{ik}, then

$$e_{ik} = \frac{\eta_{ik}}{w_i} - \delta_{ik}$$

$$\delta_{ik} = 0 \text{ for } i \neq k \quad ; \quad \delta_{ik}=1 \text{ for } i=k$$

where

$$\eta_{ik} \equiv \frac{\partial w_i}{\partial \ln p_k},$$

and takes the following forms:

Model	η_{ik}
AIDS	$\gamma_{ik} - \eta_i \left[\alpha_k + \sum_j \gamma_{kj} \ln p_j \right]$

---

3. The consistency and asymptotic efficiency of these estimators is described in Blundell and Robin (1999).

AIDS, Stone Approximation $\gamma_{ik} - \eta_i w_{kt}^h$

QUAIDS $\gamma_{ik} - \eta_i \left[\alpha_k + \sum_j \gamma_{kj} \ln p_j \right] - \beta_k \dfrac{\lambda_i}{b(p_t)} \left[\ln \left(\dfrac{M_t}{a(p_t)} \right) \right]^2$

QUAIDS, Stone Approximation $\gamma_{ik} - \eta_i w_{kt}^h$.

By the Slutsky equation, compensated price elasticities, e_{ik}^c, are given by

$$e_{ik}^c = e_{ik} + e_i w_k .$$

5.2.3 Weak Separability

Suppose we divide the goods $\mathbf{q}$ into two mutually exclusive groups, call them $\mathbf{q}_A$ and $\mathbf{q}_B$. We say that goods A are weakly separable in the utility function if we can write

$$U^h(\mathbf{q}_A, \mathbf{q}_B) = U^h(\Psi(\mathbf{q}_A), \mathbf{q}_B),$$

and obviously this can be generalized to further grouping. Weak separability is an important concept because if a given group of goods is weakly separable from all other consumption, then the demand for those goods can be analyzed using only total expenditures on those goods and the prices of those goods. So, in our example, for goods in group A, the demand function $q_{Ai}^h(\mathbf{p}, M^h)$ simplifies to $q_{Ai}^h(\mathbf{p}_A, M_A^h)$ where $M_A^h = \Sigma_{i \in A} p_{Ai} q_{Ai}^h$. So, for example:

- if preferences are weakly separable over time, then we can analyze demand in a given period ignoring what happens in the past or what will happen in the future; and
- if consumption goods are weakly separable from leisure, then we can look at demand for consumption without reference to labor supply and wages.

Thus a simple test of separability, exploited in papers such as Browning and Meghir (1991), is that, conditional on $\mathbf{p}_A$ and M_A^h, demands for goods in group A should not depend on $\mathbf{q}_B$. Browning and Meghir (1991) work with "conditional cost functions," where the conditional cost function for group A would be defined as

$$C_A^{h*}(\mathbf{p}_A, \mathbf{q}_B, u) = \min_{\mathbf{q}_A} \mathbf{p}_A' \mathbf{q}_A \ \ s.t. \ \ U^h(\mathbf{q}_A, \mathbf{q}_B) = u .$$

They show that weak separability also has the following implication for the conditional cost function:

$$U^h(\mathbf{q}_A, \mathbf{q}_B) = U^h(\Psi(\mathbf{q}_A), \mathbf{q}_B)$$

$$\Leftrightarrow$$

$$C_A^{h*}(\mathbf{p}_A, \mathbf{q}_B, u) = C_A^{h*}(\mathbf{p}_A, g(\mathbf{q}_B, u))$$

which illustrates, again, that the conditioning goods $\mathbf{q}_B$ only have income effects on the demands for $\mathbf{q}_A$ and that we can test for this by putting conditioning goods in the demand system. The econometric problem that arises in

Table 5.1	Nondurable goods groupings
Category	Description
Food in	Food and drink purchased for home consumption (excluding alcohol)
Food out	Catered affairs, restaurant meals (excluding alcohol), and school meals
Entertainment	Recreation and sporting activities, rental of vacation vehicles
Apparel	Clothes and shoes
Utilities	Electricity, gas, and water
Motor fuel	Gasoline and motor oils

this test is that the conditioning goods might be endogenous to the system; for example, unobserved tastes for working might be correlated with unobserved tastes for some consumption goods.

5.3 Data and Sample

5.3.1 The CE Data

The CE is the most extensive expenditure survey in the United States. In 2010 it covered roughly 7,000 consumer units (CUs) throughout the country. The CE comprises a diary survey, where households are asked to record their spending over a two-week period, and an interview survey, where households are asked to recall their spending on various categories over the last quarter. The interview survey is a short panel with households asked expenditure questions for four successive quarters (though households may not complete all interviews and can skip interviews). Both surveys include questions on demographic characteristics, labor supply, household resources (including income and assets), building characteristics, and detailed information about cars.

5.3.2 Sample and Goods

To estimate our demand system, we need to know how much households spent on various product categories, as well as the relative prices of these goods over time and across regions. In our case, we combine spending data from the interview survey of the CE with price data from the product-specific series of the Urban Consumer Price Index (CPI) taken from the Bureau of Labor Statistics (BLS) website. We make use of the four regional price indices (for the Northeast, Midwest, South, and West).

We use spending on six different nondurable product categories, chosen to match price categories in the CPI. These are: food in, food out, entertainment, apparel, fuel and utilities, and motor fuel (what these contain is described in more detail in table 5.1).

We draw the spending data from the years 1998–2010, as we do not have monthly prices for some product categories prior to this. We treat spending

Table 5.2   Average income and nondurable expenditure

	Annual income	Monthly expenditure
1998	68,242	1,296
1999	69,525	1,307
2000	69,963	1,335
2001	74,775	1,361
2002	77,574	1,329
2003	78,589	1,305
2004	81,286	1,333
2005	83,590	1,406
2006	78,807	1,444
2007	80,297	1,538
2008	78,459	1,560
2009	80,288	1,434
2010	78,729	1,408

Note: 2010 dollars deflated with the Consumer Price Index.

choices in each interview as separate observations. Each interview covers three months of spending, so for instance, a CU interviewed in April 2010 would be asked about spending in each of the months January, February, and March. We take the average of spending on each category over the three months that are covered by each interview. This is due to the fact that there is likely to be some noise in individual monthly observations (for instance, with infrequently purchased items). The three-month spending averages are linked to an average of monthly prices in the CPI for the same three-month period (see below). To ensure that all households' spending data is a monthly average over a complete quarter, we drop households interviewed in January, February, or March in 1998.

The sample selected for estimation is composed of households in urban areas in which the adults are a couple with any number of dependent children, where the head is between ages twenty-one and sixty-five, who have less than five cars, and in which the husband works. We also trim those in the top and bottom 5 percent of the income and expenditure distribution in each year. This leaves us with 80,838 observations. Average annual incomes, monthly expenditures, and other demographic characteristics are shown in tables 5.2 and 5.3.

Table 5.4 shows how average budget shares of our various goods (out of total spending on these six goods) have been evolving over time. The shares of some goods, such as food at home, have been steadily decreasing over time, while the share spent on motor fuel, for instance, has tended to increase (rising from 12 percent in 1998 to peak at 21 percent in 2008). Inevitably, changes in the survey have led to occasional discontinuities in budget shares. For example, the share spent on food away from home jumped by 4 percentage points between 2006 and 2007. This is likely due to the fact that in 2007

Table 5.3   **Sample mean demographic characteristics**

	Age of head	White head (%)	Adult earners (%)	Own home (%)	Head with degree (%)
1998	42	88	80	77	33
1999	42	88	79	78	34
2000	42	87	79	78	32
2001	43	87	79	79	36
2002	43	87	79	80	36
2003	43	87	78	81	37
2004	44	87	78	82	38
2005	44	85	78	82	36
2006	44	87	78	81	34
2007	44	88	77	81	37
2008	44	87	77	81	37
2009	44	86	77	79	38
2010	44	85	76	78	38

Table 5.4   **Budget shares by year**

	Food in	Food out	Entertainment	Apparel	Utilities	Motor fuel
1998	38.3	12.7	6.5	11.1	19.4	11.9
1999	38.1	12.7	6.5	11.7	19.0	11.9
2000	37.2	12.4	6.5	11.3	18.6	14.0
2001	36.5	12.1	6.7	10.6	20.5	13.5
2002	37.5	11.9	7.1	10.6	19.9	13.0
2003	37.3	12.0	6.3	9.4	21.2	13.8
2004	37.5	11.8	5.8	8.3	21.4	15.2
2005	35.5	11.2	5.7	8.5	21.2	17.9
2006	34.5	11.0	5.7	8.3	21.7	18.7
2007	32.9	15.0	5.7	7.7	20.5	18.3
2008	32.7	13.9	5.4	6.8	20.6	20.6
2009	34.9	14.6	5.8	6.7	22.3	15.6
2010	34.8	14.3	5.6	6.5	22.0	16.8

the survey question for food out changed from asking households to recall their "usual" monthly spending to asking them to recall their usual weekly spending. To try to account for these sorts of changes we employ year dummies in our share equations rather than a time trend, as is sometimes used. Table 5.5 looks in more detail at budget shares in 2010. There is quite wide variation in budget shares of reported expenditure on our chosen goods. Many households report zero spending over the quarter on entertainment (23 percent), apparel (18 percent), and food away from home (10.5 percent). Table 5.6 looks at how budget shares vary according to the labor force participation of the wife. Households where the wife works spend relatively less on food at home (35 percent compared to 39 percent) and slightly less on

Table 5.5   **Budget shares for households interviewed in 2010**

	Food in	Food out	Entertainment	Apparel	Utilities	Motor fuel
Mean	34.8	14.2	5.5	6.7	22.0	16.8
Min.	0.0	0.0	0.0	0.0	0.0	0.0
Max.	93.5	76.7	81.4	63.5	76.3	79.6
Percent zero	0.002	0.105	0.230	0.182	0.009	0.018

Table 5.6   **Budget shares by LFP of wife**

	(Female works, male works)	(0,1)	(1,1)
	Sample size	18,869	61,969
	Food in	39.3	34.9
		(13.6)	(12.6)
	Food out	11.2	13.1
		(9.2)	(9.6)
	Entertainment	5.2	6.4
		(7.0)	(7.4)
	Apparel	8.5	9.1
		(8.5)	(8.6)
	Utilities	21.0	20.6
		(9.7)	(9.0)
	Motor fuel	14.9	15.8
		(8.8)	(8.8)

Note: Standard deviations in parentheses.

utilities (20.6 percent vs. 21 percent), but more on food out, entertainment, apparel, and motor fuel.

5.3.3 Some Remarks about the Data

We cannot discuss demand analysis using the CE without mentioning the well-known issue concerning the discrepancy between the window of time for the income data and the consumption data. Spending refers to the previous quarter, while income and hours worked are given as a total for the last twelve months. Income data is collected only in the first and final of the four interviews. It may also sometimes be collected in the second and third interviews, but only if a CU member over age thirteen is new to the CU or has not worked in previous interviews and has now started working. In each case, however, the question that is asked is how much income has been earned over the last twelve months, not over the last quarter. The same is true for other variables, including hours worked.

This is a most crucial problem for any analysis of this data, and solving it seems to us to be high on the agenda. Indeed, any assumption used by researchers to link income and consumption introduces a bias whose direction and scale, by definition, cannot be known. While one might hope that

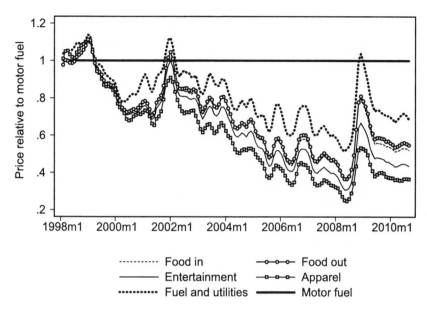

Fig. 5.1 Prices over time (relative to motor fuel)

this is of second order, if the CE data is used to evaluate the effect of policy on choices and welfare, it seems rather problematic.

Other authors have used various methods to get around this problem. For instance, Attanasio et al. (2011) look at separability between consumption and leisure choices over time. In order to be able to link wages in each quarter to quarterly consumption, they divide annual salary income and annual hours (themselves calculated using weeks worked, and typical hours per week) by four. If income or hours are updated in subsequent quarters, they then adjust these to take account of known income changes—for instance if salary is reported in the second quarter, then fourth quarter income is defined as annual income in the fourth quarter less annual income in the second quarter divided by two. Gervais and Klein (2010) implement a more sophisticated method to deal with the mismatch in timing. They construct a proxy for quarterly income by assuming an income process, which they estimate with GMM using the two-income observations they have.

A second data issue we need to raise relates to prices. To estimate price responses it is crucial to have sufficient relative price variation. There are two sources of price variation in our data—variation over time, and variation across regions. As figure 5.1 shows, there is substantial variation in prices across goods and across time (shown relative to motor fuel prices). Prices of motor fuel have been most volatile over the period. All goods have mostly fallen in price relative to motor fuel. Some prices such as food in and food out have tended to move together, with some divergence visible toward the end

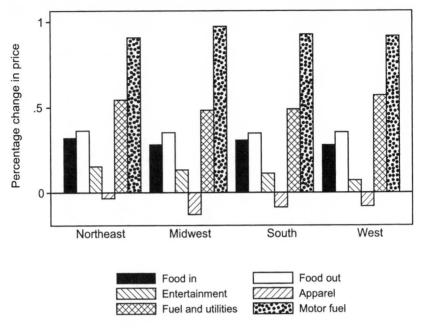

Fig. 5.2 Price changes by region

of the period. Figure 5.2 shows that there has also been important variation across regions. For instance, since 1998 the price of apparel declined by 3.3 percent in the northeast but by 12.8 percent in the midwest, while entertainment increased in price by 7.3 percent in the west compared to 15.4 percent in the northeast over the period.

5.4 Demand System

We estimate six demand systems. In the first model we look at a case where we assume full separability from the "stock" variables (cars and rooms) and labor force participation. In the second and third models, we condition on the number of cars,[4] first assuming them to be exogenous, and then allowing them to be endogenous (instrumenting them with log car prices). In the fourth model, we condition on the number of rooms, and in the fifth we condition on labor force participation of the wife. In the sixth and final model, we condition on all three at once (assuming that all are exogenous). In each case we test for separability, allowing for an effect of the conditioning variable on the intercept of the budget share as well as in the slope of the Engel

4. Ideally, information of the number of cars should be supplemented by information on expenditure on cars.

curve. We discuss instrumenting strategies, first stages and Engel curves, before turning to the demand system estimates and the associated elasticities.

5.4.1 Endogenous Variables and Instruments

In a demand system under separability, it is usual to allow for the endogeneity of total expenditure. There are several reasons why total expenditure might be endogenous in a demand system. It could be that total expenditure is correlated with taste shocks that also affect budget shares. For instance, a shock that increases food spending increases both the budget share of food as well as total expenditure. Another reason for endogeneity is measurement error in total expenditure. To instrument for this, we follow the literature (Banks, Blundell, and Lewbel 1997) by using after-tax income as an instrument for total expenditure.

It should be noted that if labor supply is not separable from commodity demands and is a potentially endogenous variable, then income is not a valid instrument for expenditure (as households who work more will also tend to earn a higher income). As we wish to look at the potential separability of labor force participation, this will be a problem for us. To get around this problem, when estimating a demand system conditional on both total expenditure and labor force participation, Browning and Meghir (1991) and Hussain (2006) use combinations of education, asset income, and average wage by cohort and education as the instrument set rather than total income. However, each of these instruments has its own problem. It is not obvious that the exclusion restriction for education is valid, since as Hussain notes, education is itself a choice variable. Furthermore, for the sample and the period we use, the asset income variable is informed only for 10 percent of the sample. Finally, the CE does not include wage data, and wages must be calculated using measures of salary income and hours and weeks worked (as described above). Tax data is also self-reported and often unreliable, adding further complications to the calculation of marginal net wages.

The other potentially endogenous variables of the system are expenditure on cars (proxied by the number of cars) and on housing (proxied by the number of rooms). The problem of endogeneity arises because households with preferences for larger houses or more cars are likely to have different tastes for the goods included in our demand system. This introduces a correlation between the stocks and a CU's unobserved tastes. We experiment with different instruments to attempt to get around these problems.

For the stock of cars we use the log regional price of cars from the CPI. It is hoped this would affect the number of cars households choose to purchase but be uncorrelated with their tastes. For housing, we employ the log of the regional price of housing services from the CPI, and (following Hussain 2006) a dummy variable for the sex composition of children (1 if children have different sexes, 0 otherwise). The latter instrument is motivated by the belief that households who have a boy and a girl will be more likely to need a separate bedroom for each child (not all of the households in our sample have children, those that do not are assigned a zero for this variable). However, it could also be argued that the exclusion restriction for the sex composition of children is dubious. As we describe in the following section, the instruments for housing do not perform well, and so in the end we estimate the demand system under the assumption that housing is exogenous, despite the potential problems in doing so.

5.4.2 First Stages

In table 5.7 we present results for the first-stage regressions of log expenditure on the various instruments (log of after-tax income, log of after-tax income squared, and the price of cars). The income instruments are highly significant in the first stage (both the linear and quadratic income terms) in all specifications. Model 1 is the demand system under separability. Model 2.1 is the demand system conditional on exogenous cars, and model 2.2 conditional on endogenous cars, using the car CPI as instrument. Model 3.1 is the demand system conditional on exogenous housing, model 4.1 conditional on exogenous labor force participation, and finally model 5 is conditional on cars, housing, and labor force participation. We also estimate model 3.2, where we allow for endogeneity of rooms, but we do not report the estimated coefficients.

In table 5.8, we report the results from the first stages for cars and housing. For cars, the instrument is log regional car prices (homogenized relative to the price of motor fuel in the same way as the other prices we use in the demand system); it is significant at the 5 percent level and has the expected sign (i.e., higher car prices lead to fewer cars). The interaction term with log income is also negative and highly significant. We also estimate two versions of model 3.2, where we allow for endogeneity of housing, in the first instance using the sex composition of the children as instrument and then using the regional shelter CPI. The sex composition variable is significant at the 1 percent level, and it has the expected sign over most of the range of values of income. However, the sex composition of children may also enter the demand system itself, and so not give a truly exogenous source of variation in the number of rooms. We also estimate another version of model 3.2, where we instrument housing with log homogenized regional price of housing. Unlike Hussain (2006), we find that there is a negative relationship between housing price and housing expenditure as proxied by the size of the house. We also investigate an instrument constructed from lagged imputed rents in the region of residence of the household. We do not report the estimated coefficients in this case, because the estimated coefficients of the demand system obtained using this instrument for housing were implausible and we were not sure of the quality of information contained in the imputed rents.

Table 5.7 **First stage for total expenditure on nondurables**

	Model 1	Model 2.1	Model 2.2	Model 3.1	Model 4.1	Model 5
$ln(y)$	−0.86***	−0.96***	−0.87***	−0.83***	−0.90***	−0.92***
	(0.040)	(0.040)	(0.040)	(0.039)	(0.040)	(0.040)
$ln(y)^2$	0.07***	0.08***	0.07***	0.07***	0.07***	0.08***
	(0.002)	(0.002)	(0.002)	(0.003)	(0.003)	(0.003)
lfp					0.26***	0.15***
					(0.036)	(0.036)
$lfp \times ln(y)$					−0.03***	−0.02***
					(0.004)	(0.004)
Cars		0.19***				0.12***
		(0.014)				(0.015)
$cars \times ln(y)$		−0.02***				−0.01***
		(0.002)				(0.002)
Rooms				0.72***		0.58***
				(0.049)		(0.050)
$rooms \times ln(y)$				−0.07***		−0.05***
				(0.006)		(0.006)
$ln(pcars)$			0.53***			
			(0.119)			
$ln(pcars) \times ln(y)$			−0.01**			
			(0.005)			
Age	0.00***	0.00***	0.00***	0.00***	0.00***	0.00***
	(0.000)	(0.000)	(0.000)	(0.000)	(0.000)	(0.000)
White	0.09***	0.08***	0.09***	0.08***	0.09***	0.07***
	(0.003)	(0.003)	(0.003)	(0.003)	(0.003)	(0.003)
Elderly	−0.02*	−0.01	−0.02**	−0.01	−0.02**	−0.01
	(0.009)	(0.009)	(0.009)	(0.009)	(0.009)	(0.009)
$ln(CUsize)$	0.30***	0.28***	0.30***	0.28***	0.30***	0.25***
	(0.005)	(0.006)	(0.005)	(0.005)	(0.005)	(0.006)
Children, 0–2	−0.08***	−0.07***	−0.08***	−0.08***	−0.08***	−0.07***
	(0.003)	(0.003)	(0.003)	(0.003)	(0.003)	(0.003)
Children, 3–15	−0.01***	0.00	−0.01***	−0.01***	−0.01***	0.00**
	(0.002)	(0.002)	(0.002)	(0.002)	(0.002)	(0.002)
Head < college	0.03***	0.03***	0.03***	0.02***	0.03***	0.02***
	(0.003)	(0.003)	(0.003)	(0.003)	(0.003)	(0.003)
Head college	0.05***	0.05***	0.05***	0.03***	0.05***	0.04***
	(0.003)	(0.003)	(0.003)	(0.003)	(0.003)	(0.003)
Wife < college	0.04***	0.04***	0.04***	0.03***	0.04***	0.03***
	(0.003)	(0.003)	(0.003)	(0.003)	(0.003)	(0.003)
Wife college	0.06***	0.05***	0.06***	0.04***	0.06***	0.04***
	(0.003)	(0.003)	(0.003)	(0.003)	(0.003)	(0.003)
Constant	8.82***	9.06***	8.86***	8.10***	8.90***	8.45***
	(0.162)	(0.161)	(0.163)	(0.163)	(0.162)	(0.163)

Notes: Controls include month of interview, year of interview, log prices, and twenty-two state-region dummies. $N = 80{,}838$ and t statistics are in parentheses.
***Significant at the 1 percent level.
**Significant at the 5 percent level.
*Significant at the 10 percent level.

Table 5.8   **First stage for cars and housing**

Instruments	Model 2.2–cars		Model 3.2–housing
	Car CPI	Sex diff.	Shelter CPI
$ln(y)$	1.72***	−0.40***	−0.40***
	(0.136)	(0.035)	(0.035)
$ln(y)^2$	−0.09***	0.03***	0.03***
	(0.008)	(0.002)	(0.002)
$ln(pcars)$	−0.99**		
	(0.408)		
$ln(pcars) \times ln(y)$	−0.08***		
	(0.018)		
Sex diff.		−0.17***	
		(0.043)	
$sexdiff \times ln(y)$		0.02***	
		(0.005)	
$ln(phouse)$			0.00
			(0.069)
$ln(phouse) \times ln(y)$			−0.01**
			(0.006)
Age	0.01***	0.01***	0.01***
	(0.000)	(0.000)	(0.000)
White	0.29***	0.06***	0.06***
	(0.011)	(0.003)	(0.003)
Elderly	−0.17***	−0.04***	−0.04***
	(0.031)	(0.008)	(0.008)
$ln(CUsize)$	0.98***	0.15***	0.15***
	(0.019)	(0.005)	(0.005)
Children, 0–2	−0.36***	0.00	0.00
	(0.010)	(0.003)	(0.003)
Children, 3–15	−0.28***	0.02***	0.02***
	(0.006)	(0.002)	(0.002)
Head < college	0.02**	0.04***	0.04***
	(0.010)	(0.003)	(0.003)
Head college	−0.17***	0.07***	0.07***
	(0.011)	(0.003)	(0.003)
Wife < college	0.12***	0.05***	0.05***
	(0.010)	(0.002)	(0.002)
Wife college	0.04***	0.06***	0.06*** .
	(0.011)	(0.003)	(0.003)
Constant	−7.51***	2.19***	2.22***
	(0.558)	(0.141)	(0.144)

Notes: Controls include month of interview, year of interview, log prices, and twenty-two state-region dummies. $N = 80{,}838$, and t statistics are in parentheses.

***Significant at the 1 percent level.

**Significant at the 5 percent level.

*Significant at the 10 percent level.

5.4.3 Engel Curves

To begin we decide which specification is more appropriate: AIDS or QUAIDS. We estimate QUAIDS and AIDS models on data ignoring the stocks of housing and cars, and using the Stone price index to deflate expenditures. The Engel curves produced from this exercise are displayed in the panels below (figure 5.3). These graph log expenditure against predicted shares. Upward sloping Engel curves indicate that a good is a luxury, while downward sloping curves indicate that goods are necessities or inferior. Unsurprisingly, food out, entertainment, and apparel are luxuries, while food in, utilities, and motor fuel are necessities.

For some goods, a linear model is clearly appropriate (the Engel curves for entertainment and food out are essentially linear). For other goods, the QUAIDS model fits U-shaped Engel curves, though in these cases there does not appear to be much curvature in the center of the spending distribution. The steep U-shaped curves therefore appear to be the natural consequence of allowing for a small amount of curvature in the middle of the distribution (with the effect that the gradient becomes quite steep for very high and very low levels of expenditure). We therefore conclude that a liner model is a more appropriate, and proceed using the AIDS demand system.

5.4.4 Demand System Estimates

In this section we present the estimated coefficients of the various demand systems. We start by estimating a benchmark model, where we assume full separability. We then proceed by conditioning on cars (first exogenous and subsequently allowing for endogeneity), rooms, and the labor force participation of the wife. In our final model, we condition on all of these variables simultaneously.

Table 5.9 presents the results for model 1 where we assume full separability (that is, we do not condition on cars, rooms, or labor force participation).

The first column of tables 5.12 and 5.13 present, respectively, the income and price elasticities obtained from the demand system under full separability. We comment on those below, when we contrast the elasticities obtained with the different models.

In table 5.10, we condition on cars assuming them to be exogenous. In table 5.11, we present results where we instrument for the number of cars, using the car CPI as instrument. The differences in estimated coefficients between specifications translate into differences in the budget and price elasticities (calculated at mean values of all the covariates). The intercept and slope interaction terms for cars enter highly significantly in the share equations for food at home, entertainment, apparel, domestic utilities, and (perhaps unsurprisingly) motor fuel. Thus, it appears that the data strongly reject the separability of cars. Once we allow for the endogeneity of cars, however, the number of cars and its interaction with expenditure enter significantly

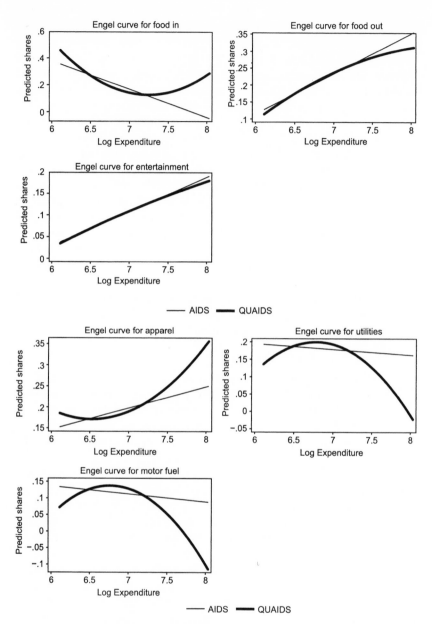

Fig. 5.3 Engel curves (AIDS vs. QUAIDS)

only for food in and for motor fuel (though the intercept and slope terms are jointly significant at the 1 percent level for all goods except food out and entertainment). These differences in the estimated coefficients translate into differences in the estimated elasticities (reported for the basic model, a model including exogenous cars, and a model including endogenous cars in tables 5.12 and 5.13). While the estimated own price elasticities are essentially the same across models, there are some interesting differences in the estimated income elasticities. Apparel becomes more of a luxury when we allow cars to be endogenous (increasing from 1.61 to 1.82). By contrast, utilities become more of a necessity (with the elasticity falling from 0.9 to 0.75). The largest difference is for motor fuel (which rises to 1.1 from 0.7 when we instrument).

In table 5.14, we estimate a demand system conditioning on the number of rooms. The associated elasticities for this model are reported in tables 5.17 and 5.18. The number of rooms and its interaction with expenditure both enter significantly in the share equations of all goods (though for entertainment, it is only the intercept that is significant at the 5 percent level). The intercept shift and slope coefficient are jointly significant in all of the equations of the demand system. Under the assumption that rooms are exogenous, it therefore seems that the data strongly reject separability between the size of the house and commodity demands. However, the elasticities do not vary greatly from the elasticities estimated using the benchmark model (where we assume full separability).

Following the strategy chosen by Hussain (2006) and using the sex composition of the children as an instrument for housing leads to demand system estimates and elasticities that are quite different from what we obtain under the assumption of exogeneity of housing. For instance, entertainment goes from being a luxury to a necessity (income elasticity 0.54) and food out becomes more of a luxury (with an elasticity of 3.57). However, as we explained above, we find the exclusion restriction dubious. We investigate another instrumenting strategy using the housing CPI, and there again the results change substantially. Food becomes an inferior good (with an elasticity of –0.34) while the income elasticity of entertainment increases to 5. These numbers are implausible and we do not believe that we are able to capture the relationship between expenditure on nondurables and total expenditure using this instrumenting strategy for housing. We leave this question for further investigation.

In table 5.15, we include the labor force participation of the wife. Once again, the data strongly reject separability under exogeneity. The intercept shift and slope interaction terms for labor force participation are jointly significant in all equations. The slope interaction terms are also all significant at the 5 percent level, suggesting that labor supply enters the demand system in a nonlinear way.

Table 5.16 shows the results for a demand system conditioning on cars, housing, and labor force participation together. Again, coefficients on the

Table 5.9   Demand system under full separability

	Food in	Food out	Entertainment	Apparel	Utilities	Motor fuel
$\ln(x)$	-0.209***	0.119***	0.0793***	0.0509***	-0.0162***	-0.024***
	(-56.33)	(43.77)	(39.04)	(21.04)	(-6.16)	(-9.57)
$lnpr1$	-0.0645	0.0989**	0.0258	0.0271	-0.0445***	-0.043***
	(-1.42)	(2.94)	(1.06)	(1.45)	(-3.41)	(-6.10)
$lnpr2$	0.0989**	-0.0743	-0.0689**	0.0439**	-0.00348	0.004
	(2.94)	(-1.74)	(-2.67)	(2.70)	(-0.35)	(0.73)
$lnpr3$	0.0258	-0.0689**	0.0763**	-0.0285*	-0.00267	-0.002
	(1.06)	(-2.67)	(2.95)	(-2.39)	(-0.36)	(-0.51)
$lnpr4$	0.0271	0.0439**	-0.0285*	-0.0139	-0.0198*	-0.009
	(1.45)	(2.70)	(-2.39)	(-0.93)	(-2.52)	(-1.96)
$lnpr5$	-0.0445***	-0.00348	-0.00267	-0.0198*	0.0999***	-0.029***
	(-3.41)	(-0.35)	(-0.36)	(-2.52)	(10.36)	(-6.55)
Age	0.00131***	-0.000984***	-0.000311***	0.000769***	0.00114***	0.000***
	(25.26)	(-25.99)	(-10.99)	(-22.84)	(31.08)	(-10.93)
White	0.0154***	-0.000673	0.00746***	-0.00877***	-0.0121***	-0.001
	(11.46)	(-0.68)	(10.14)	(-10.01)	(-12.66)	(-1.50)
Elderly	-0.00296	0.000859	0.00366	0.00533*	0.00454	-0.011***
	(-0.83)	(0.33)	(1.87)	(2.28)	(1.79)	(-4.74)
$\ln(CUsize)$	0.119***	-0.0748***	-0.0414***	-0.0158***	-0.0107***	0.024***
	(46.90)	(-40.17)	(-29.77)	(-9.56)	(-5.95)	(13.78)
Children, 0–2	-0.00601***	-0.00495***	-0.00169*	0.0204***	0.00687***	-0.015***
	(-4.79)	(-5.38)	(-2.47)	(25.00)	(7.73)	(-17.37)
Children, 3–15	0.00165*	0.00142**	0.00708***	0.000584	0.000912	-0.012***
	(2.26)	(2.66)	(17.69)	(1.23)	(1.76)	(-23.67)
Head < college	-0.00857***	0.00351***	0.00522***	0.00195*	-0.000525	-0.002*
	(-7.35)	(4.11)	(8.18)	(2.56)	(-0.63)	(-2.02)

Head college	0.000392	0.00660***	0.0128***	0.00393***	-0.00894***	-0.015***
	(0.30)	(6.91)	(17.92)	(4.62)	(-9.66)	(-16.83)
Wife < college	-0.0108***	0.000834	0.00648***	0.00234**	0.000114	0.001
	(-9.33)	(0.98)	(10.23)	(3.11)	(0.14)	(1.32)
Wife college	-0.00635***	0.00348***	0.0149***	0.00290**	-0.00854***	-0.006***
	(-4.69)	(3.51)	(20.19)	(3.29)	(-8.90)	(-7.07)
Constant	1.633***	-0.600***	-0.447***	-0.159***	0.292***	0.2802***
	(70.26)	(-35.20)	(-35.13)	(-10.47)	(17.74)	(17.93)

Notes: Controls include month of interview, year of interview, log prices, and twenty-two state-region dummies. $N = 80{,}838$ and standard errors are in parentheses.

***Significant at the 1/10 of 1 percent level.

**Significant at the 1 percent level.

*Significant at the 5 percent level.

Table 5.10   Demand system conditional on exogenous cars

	Food in	Food out	Entertainment	Apparel	Utilities	Motor fuel
$ln(x)$	-0.285***	0.123***	0.0764***	0.0419***	0.0401***	0.004
	(-45.59)	(26.40)	(22.01)	(10.15)	(8.97)	(0.9)
Cars	-0.293***	-0.00193	-0.0127	-0.0413***	0.180***	0.308***
	(-17.25)	(-0.15)	(-1.35)	(-3.69)	(14.84)	(23.01)
$cars \times ln(x)$	0.0411***	-0.000166	0.00173	0.00567***	-0.0262***	-0.088***
	(16.69)	(-0.09)	(1.27)	(3.49)	(-14.88)	(-14.85)
$lnpr1$	-0.0593	0.0982**	0.0235	0.0255	-0.0447***	-0.128***
	(-1.31)	(2.93)	(0.97)	(1.37)	(-3.46)	(-9.01)
$lnpr2$	0.0982**	-0.0748	-0.0684**	0.0442**	-0.00336	-0.039***
	(2.93)	(-1.75)	(-2.65)	(2.72)	(-0.34)	(-3.53)
$lnpr3$	0.0235	-0.0684**	0.0774***	-0.0284*	-0.00225	-0.044***
	(0.97)	(-2.65)	(2.99)	(-2.38)	(-0.30)	(-5.00)
$lnpr4$	0.0255	0.0442**	-0.0284*	-0.0138	-0.0192*	-0.068***
	(1.37)	(2.72)	(-2.38)	(-0.92)	(-2.45)	(-7.17)
$lnpr5$	-0.0447***	-0.00336	-0.00225	-0.0192*	0.0990***	0.029***
	(-3.46)	(-0.34)	(-0.30)	(-2.45)	(10.32)	(2.80)
Age	0.00144***	-0.000953***	-0.000301***	-0.000744***	0.00112***	-0.040***
	(28.34)	(-25.28)	(-10.70)	(-22.23)	(30.78)	(-8.83)
White	0.0176***	-0.0000566	0.00764***	-0.00832***	-0.0122***	-0.057***
	(13.33)	(-0.06)	(10.42)	(-9.54)	(-12.94)	(-12.00)
Elderly	-0.00467	0.000383	0.00352	0.00497*	0.00465	-0.044***
	(-1.32)	(0.15)	(1.80)	(2.13)	(1.84)	(-8.18)
$ln(CUsize)$	0.115***	-0.0727***	-0.0413***	-0.0159***	-0.00409*	-0.025***
	(44.68)	(-37.98)	(-28.88)	(-9.38)	(-2.22)	(-4.92)
Children, 0–2	-0.00570***	-0.00583***	-0.00180**	0.0203***	0.00490***	-0.047***
	(-4.56)	(-6.27)	(-2.59)	(24.58)	(5.48)	(-10.27)

	(1)	(2)	(3)	(4)	(5)	(6)
Children, 3–15	0.00155*	0.000583	0.00697***	0.000321	−0.000794	−0.050***
	(2.09)	(1.05)	(16.90)	(0.65)	(−1.49)	(−10.81)
Head < college	−0.00823***	0.00352***	0.00524***	0.00197**	−0.000767	−0.043***
	(−7.16)	(4.12)	(8.22)	(2.60)	(−0.93)	(−9.12)
Head college	−0.00254	0.00592***	0.0126***	0.00326***	−0.00863***	−0.059***
	(−1.95)	(6.12)	(17.45)	(3.79)	(−9.26)	(−12.47)
Wife < college	−0.00973***	0.00110	0.00657***	0.00254***	0.0000524	−0.041***
	(−8.54)	(1.30)	(10.39)	(3.38)	(−0.06)	(−8.67)
Wife college	−0.00597***	0.00345***	0.0150***	0.00288***	−0.00896***	−0.055***
	(−4.47)	(3.47)	(20.22)	(3.28)	(−9.38)	(−11.55)
Constant	2.171***	−0.621***	−0.426***	−0.0929***	−0.0980**	0.067*
	(51.76)	(−19.91)	(−18.27)	(−3.35)	(−3.26)	(2.37)

Notes: Controls include month of interview, year of interview, log prices, and twenty-two state-region dummies. N = 80,838 and standard errors are in parentheses.

***Significant at the 1/10 of 1 percent level.

**Significant at the 1 percent level.

*Significant at the 5 percent level.

Table 5.11   Demand system conditional on endogenous cars

	Food in	Food out	Entertainment	Apparel	Utilities	Motor fuel
$\ln(x)$	-0.767***	0.0545	0.0561	0.0717	0.0188	0.565***
	(-5.94)	(0.74)	(1.03)	(1.10)	(0.26)	(4.66)
Cars	-1.600***	-0.115	-0.0404	-0.0262	0.239	1.763***
	(-5.16)	(-0.65)	(-0.31)	(-0.17)	(1.39)	(6.08)
cars * $\ln(expend)$	0.238***	0.0194	0.00686	0.00101	-0.0309	-0.284**
	(4.95)	(0.71)	(0.34)	(0.04)	(-1.16)	(-2.85)
lnpr1	-0.0214	0.0876*	0.0154	0.0120	-0.0428**	-0.112
	(-0.46)	(2.56)	(0.62)	(0.62)	(-3.15)	(-1.51)
lnpr2	0.0876*	-0.0768	-0.0629*	0.0515**	-0.00315	-0.018
	(2.56)	(-1.79)	(-2.42)	(3.14)	(-0.32)	(-0.25)
lnpr3	0.0154	-0.0629*	0.0789**	-0.0273*	-0.00165	-0.023
	(0.62)	(-2.42)	(3.04)	(-2.27)	(-0.22)	(-0.32)
lnpr4	0.0120	0.0515**	-0.0273*	-0.0129	-0.0175*	-0.042
	(0.62)	(3.14)	(-2.27)	(-0.84)	(-2.17)	(-0.58)
lnpr5	-0.0428**	-0.00315	-0.00165	-0.0175*	0.0975***	0.046
	(-3.15)	(-0.32)	(-0.22)	(-2.17)	(9.96)	(0.65)
Age	0.00123***	-0.00114***	-0.000366***	-0.000584***	0.000860***	-0.018
	(7.32)	(-11.89)	(-5.16)	(-6.84)	(9.22)	(-0.25)
White	0.0117**	-0.00400	0.00631***	-0.00511**	-0.0173***	-0.028
	(3.02)	(-1.80)	(3.86)	(-2.60)	(-8.05)	(-0.39)
Elderly	0.000335	0.00349	0.00458*	0.00245	0.00862**	-0.030
	(0.06)	(1.12)	(1.99)	(0.89)	(2.85)	(-0.41)
$\ln(CUsize)$	0.0420	-0.0909***	-0.0470***	-0.00429	-0.0192	0.081
	(1.74)	(-6.58)	(-4.61)	(-0.35)	(-1.43)	(1.22)
Children, 0–2	0.0198*	0.00149	0.000564	0.0153***	0.0117*	-0.056
	(2.18)	(0.29)	(0.15)	(3.31)	(2.33)	(-0.74)

Children, 3–15	0.0257**	0.00768	0.00930*	−0.00454	0.00603	−0.057
	(2.97)	(1.55)	(2.55)	(−1.03)	(1.26)	(−0.76)
Head < college	−0.00577***	0.00379***	0.00534***	0.00190*	−0.000743	−0.024
	(−3.50)	(4.03)	(7.69)	(2.27)	(−0.81)	(−0.34)
Head college	0.00625	0.0108***	0.0144***	−0.000630	−0.00235	−0.050
	(1.27)	(3.85)	(6.90)	(−0.25)	(−0.86)	(−0.68)
Wife < college	−0.0112***	−0.000472	0.00604***	0.00388***	−0.00220*	−0.017
	(−5.76)	(−0.42)	(7.34)	(3.91)	(−2.03)	(−0.24)
Wife college	−0.000638	0.00433**	0.0153***	0.00243*	−0.00841***	−0.040
	(−0.27)	(3.24)	(15.51)	(2.05)	(−6.48)	(−0.56)
Constant	5.442***	−0.178	−0.295	−0.277	0.0146	−3.706***
	(6.29)	(−0.36)	(−0.81)	(−0.63)	(0.03)	(−4.55)

Notes: Controls include month of interview, year of interview, log prices, and twenty-two state-region dummies. $N = 80,838$ and standard errors are in parentheses.

***Significant at the 1/10 of 1 percent level.

**Significant at the 1 percent level.

*Significant at the 5 percent level.

Table 5.12   Income elasticities

	Full separability	Exog. cars	Endog. cars
Food in	0.42	0.48	0.42
	(0.010)	(0.011)	(0.051)
Food out	1.94	1.97	1.79
	(0.021)	(0.023)	(0.083)
Entertainment	2.30	2.32	2.18
	(0.033)	(0.036)	(0.128)
Apparel	1.57	1.61	1.82
	(0.027)	(0.029)	(0.104)
Utilities	0.92	0.90	0.74
	(0.013)	(0.014)	(0.050)
Motor fuel	0.85	0.69	1.10
	(0.016)	(0.017)	(0.112)

Note: Standard errors are in parentheses.

Table 5.13   Own price elasticities

	Full separability	Exog. cars	Endog. cars
Food in	−0.97	−0.98	−0.85
	(0.126)	(0.126)	(0.133)
Food out	−1.71	−1.71	−1.71
	(0.337)	(0.336)	(0.338)
Entertainment	0.17	0.19	0.22
	(0.424)	(0.424)	(0.426)
Apparel	−1.21	−1.21	−1.22
	(0.166)	(0.166)	(0.171)
Utilities	−0.50	−0.50	−0.48
	(0.047)	(0.046)	(0.048)
Motor fuel	−0.47	−0.45	−0.45
	(0.031)	(0.030)	(0.056)

Note: Standard errors are in parentheses.

conditioning variables are jointly significant in all equations. The estimated elasticities from these sets of models are presented alongside those for conditioning only on rooms in tables 5.17 and 5.18. There are some small differences across models. For instance, when we condition on rooms the estimated income elasticity for apparel is 1.7, but this falls to 1.55 when we condition on labor supply, and the estimated elasticity of utilities goes from around 0.7 when we condition on rooms to just over 0.9 when we condition on labor supply. Once again, the price elasticities do not vary greatly across models.

To illustrate how the differences in our various estimates of price effects translate into differences in forecast budget shares, table 5.19 shows predicted mean budget shares for each of our models following a 25 percent increase in food prices. Confidence intervals are sufficiently tight that all these shares are significantly different to each other and so we do not report standard errors. It is clear that while many of the predicted shares are similar, allowing for the endogeniety of the number of cars has quite a large impact on forecast budget shares.

Endogeneity of labor force participation in the demand system is a concern, but as we discussed above, there is no credible instrument in the CE survey.

5.5 Conclusion

The estimation of demand systems is an exercise that enables researchers to examine a large set of questions of interest to economists and policymakers. Demand system estimates can be used to answer positive questions regarding responses to price changes and thus to policy interventions, as well as measure the welfare impact of price changes, tax reform, or other interventions that change the environment in which households make decisions.

In the United States, the CE is the only survey with which it is possible to carry out such tasks, thanks to the detailed information of expenditures, prices, incomes, and individual and household characteristics it contains. Additional information on labor supply, durables, and asset incomes allows researchers to go further than standard demand analysis and to test for the validity of the assumptions of the standard model.

Using CE data from 1998 to 2010, we estimate demand systems for nondurable goods under standard as well as more general assumptions regarding the behavior of households. We show that estimated elasticities are dependent on conditioning and thus on the assumptions made on behavior. The next step would be to address the rejection of separability, and condition on labor supply and durables in demand systems. However, we argue that it is difficult to address the likely endogeneity of labor supply and durables in the demand system using data from the CE.

Thus, while an invaluable source of quantified information on households, the CE is not without its limitations, and overcoming some of these would allow it better to fulfill its goal of informing government and policymakers of the impact of policy on household behavior and welfare. The limitations we found in the exercise we conducted are to do with the income and expenditure period mismatch, the difficulties in constructing measures of the values of cars and of housing stock, the absence of information on wages, and the sketchy information on asset income. It would be very useful to have information on the value of cars for all households, rather than only those who have bought a car. Better reporting of asset income would, of course, be useful, as well as information on wages to construct instruments for labor supply. Finally, it would be desirable to know more about housing values and the imputed rent.

Table 5.14   Demand system conditional on exogenous rooms

	Food in	Food out	Entertainment	Apparel	Utilities	Motor fuel
$ln(x)$	-0.418***	0.159***	0.0678***	-0.0150	0.148***	0.059***
	(-27.81)	(14.18)	(8.18)	(-1.53)	(14.61)	(5.83)
Rooms	-0.845***	0.0437	-0.0609*	-0.310***	0.862***	0.310***
	(-15.31)	(1.06)	(-2.00)	(-8.58)	(23.25)	(8.29)
$rooms \times ln(x)$	0.122***	-0.0110	0.00815	0.0428***	-0.116***	-0.046***
	(14.99)	(-1.82)	(1.82)	(8.07)	(-21.26)	(-8.33)
$lnpr1$	-0.0565	0.0903**	0.0251	0.0270	-0.0442***	-0.042***
	(-1.24)	(2.67)	(1.03)	(1.44)	(-3.45)	(-5.95)
$lnpr2$	0.0903**	-0.0761	-0.0665*	0.0435**	0.00374	0.005
	(2.67)	(-1.78)	(-2.57)	(2.66)	(0.38)	(0.95)
$lnpr3$	0.0251	-0.0665*	0.0750**	-0.0290*	-0.00267	-0.002
	(1.03)	(-2.57)	(2.90)	(-2.43)	(-0.36)	(-0.48)
$lnpr4$	0.0270	0.0435**	-0.0290*	-0.0147	-0.0190*	-0.008
	(1.44)	(2.66)	(-2.43)	(-0.98)	(-2.46)	(-1.75)
$lnpr5$	-0.0442***	0.00374	-0.00267	-0.0190*	0.0952***	-0.033***
	(-3.45)	(0.38)	(-0.36)	(-2.46)	(10.50)	(-7.72)
Age	0.00142***	-0.000835***	-0.000281***	-0.000669***	0.000744***	0.000***
	(27.93)	(-22.09)	(-10.03)	(-20.13)	(21.78)	(-11.01)
White	0.0151***	-0.000528	0.00748***	-0.00882***	-0.0121***	-0.001
	(11.33)	(-0.53)	(10.16)	(-10.11)	(-13.50)	(-1.28)
Elderly	-0.00387	0.0000948	0.00347	0.00469*	0.00696**	-0.011***
	(-1.09)	(0.04)	(1.77)	(2.02)	(2.92)	(-4.71)
$ln(CUsize)$	0.116***	-0.0759***	-0.0417***	-0.0175***	-0.00547**	0.025***
	(45.38)	(-39.97)	(-29.66)	(-10.49)	(-3.19)	(14.28)
Children, 0–2	-0.00406**	-0.00359***	-0.00138*	0.0217***	0.00242**	-0.015***
	(-3.21)	(-3.82)	(-1.98)	(26.25)	(2.84)	(-17.61)

Children, 3–15	0.00215**	0.00219***	0.00721***	0.00106*	−0.000975*	−0.012***
	(2.95)	(4.03)	(17.93)	(2.23)	(−1.99)	(−23.55)
Head < college	−0.00774***	0.00414***	0.00538***	0.00250***	−0.00261***	−0.002*
	(−6.70)	(4.82)	(8.45)	(3.31)	(−3.36)	(−2.13)
Head college	−0.000653	0.00809***	0.0129***	0.00408***	−0.0105***	−0.014***
	(−0.50)	(8.39)	(18.10)	(4.82)	(−12.05)	(−15.89)
Wife < college	−0.00979***	0.00145	0.00666***	0.00296***	−0.00216**	0.001
	(−8.54)	(1.70)	(10.54)	(3.95)	(−2.81)	(1.13)
Wife college	−0.00612***	0.00439***	0.0151***	0.00333***	−0.0105***	−0.006***
	(−4.57)	(4.42)	(20.50)	(3.81)	(−11.71)	(−6.84)
Constant	3.079***	−0.821***	−0.361***	0.316***	−0.930***	−0.283***
	(30.40)	(−10.91)	(−6.47)	(4.78)	(−13.67)	(−4.13)

Notes: Controls include month of interview, year of interview, log prices, and twenty-two state-region dummies. $N = 80{,}838$ and standard errors are in parentheses.

***Significant at the 1/10 of 1 percent level.

**Significant at the 1 percent level.

*Significant at the 5 percent level.

Table 5.15   Demand system conditional on exogenous female labor force participation

	Food in	Food out	Entertainment	Apparel	Utilities	Motor fuel
$ln(x)$	−0.218***	0.108***	0.0861***	0.0411***	0.00653	−0.024***
	(−38.31)	(25.69)	(27.37)	(10.98)	(1.60)	(−6.24)
lfp	−0.234***	−0.0592	0.0727**	−0.0676*	0.196***	0.282***
	(−5.57)	(−1.90)	(3.12)	(−2.44)	(6.50)	(7.74)
$lfp \times ln(x)$	0.0314***	0.00952*	−0.0105**	0.0104*	−0.0291***	−0.047***
	(5.10)	(2.09)	(−3.07)	(2.56)	(−6.58)	(−5.61)
$lnpr1$	−0.0617	0.0951**	0.0264	0.0255	−0.0433***	−0.092***
	(−1.37)	(2.84)	(1.08)	(1.37)	(−3.35)	(−6.5)
$lnpr2$	0.0951**	−0.0694	−0.0699**	0.0449**	−0.00418	−0.007
	(2.84)	(−1.63)	(−2.71)	(2.77)	(−0.43)	(−0.65)
$lnpr3$	0.0264	−0.0699**	0.0766**	−0.0282*	−0.00288	−0.011
	(1.08)	(−2.71)	(2.96)	(−2.36)	(−0.39)	(−1.31)
$lnpr4$	0.0255	0.0449**	−0.0282*	−0.0130	−0.0203**	−0.036***
	(1.37)	(2.77)	(−2.36)	(−0.87)	(−2.59)	(−3.83)
$lnpr5$	−0.0433***	−0.00418	−0.00288	−0.0203**	0.100***	0.064***
	(−3.35)	(−0.43)	(−0.39)	(−2.59)	(10.39)	(6.2)
Age	0.00114***	−0.000942***	−0.000298***	−0.000748***	0.00113***	−0.006
	(21.95)	(−24.58)	(−10.39)	(−21.88)	(30.40)	(−1.39)
White	0.0137***	−0.000182	0.00755***	−0.00851***	−0.0123***	−0.019***
	(10.32)	(−0.19)	(10.24)	(−9.69)	(−12.83)	(−4.35)
Elderly	−0.00745*	0.00183	0.00408*	0.00584*	0.00450	−0.011*
	(−2.10)	(0.70)	(2.08)	(2.50)	(1.77)	(−2.12)
$ln(CUsize)$	0.114***	−0.0739***	−0.0408***	−0.0155***	−0.0102***	0.010*
	(44.84)	(−39.38)	(−29.04)	(−9.30)	(−5.58)	(1.99)
Children, 0–2	−0.00783***	−0.00440***	−0.00159*	0.0208***	0.00656***	−0.014***
	(−6.29)	(−4.78)	(−2.30)	(25.34)	(7.35)	(−3.3)

Children, 3–15	0.00104	0.00175**	0.00705***	0.000820	0.000559	-0.017***
	(1.43)	(3.26)	(17.53)	(1.71)	(1.07)	(-4.16)
Head < college	-0.00947***	0.00385***	0.00523***	0.00215**	0.000764	-0.008
	(-8.21)	(4.51)	(8.19)	(2.83)	(-0.92)	(-1.93)
Head college	-0.00218	0.00752***	0.0129***	0.00448***	-0.00954***	-0.029***
	(-1.68)	(7.83)	(17.90)	(5.24)	(-10.24)	(-6.58)
Wife < college	-0.00962***	0.000609	0.00635***	0.00222**	.0000869	-0.006
	(-8.40)	(0.72)	(10.01)	(2.94)	(0.11)	(-1.41)
Wife college	-0.00517***	0.00306**	0.0149***	0.00260**	-0.00821***	-0.022***
	(-3.86)	(3.09)	(20.08)	(2.94)	(-8.54)	(-4.97)
Constant	1.721***	-0.532***	-0.495***	-0.0966***	0.140***	0.264***
	(45.88)	(-19.18)	(-23.85)	(-3.90)	(5.19)	(10.34)

Notes: Controls include month of interview, year of interview, log prices, and twenty-two state-region dummies. N = 80,838 and standard errors are in parentheses.

***Significant at the 1/10 of 1 percent level.

**Significant at the 1 percent level.

*Significant at the 5 percent level.

Table 5.16   Demand system conditional on exogenous labor force participation, cars and rooms

	Food in	Food out	Entertainment	Apparel	Utilities	Motor fuel
ln(x)	-0.385***	0.157***	0.0716***	-0.0175	0.167***	0.007
	(-25.28)	(13.58)	(8.33)	(-1.72)	(15.97)	(0.67)
Cars	-0.224***	0.00395	-0.0117	-0.00491	0.0719***	0.069***
	(-12.48)	(0.29)	(-1.15)	(-0.41)	(5.84)	(3.64)
cars × ln(x)	0.0312***	-0.00100	0.00159	0.000426	-0.0107***	-0.199***
	(11.99)	(-0.51)	(1.09)	(0.25)	(-5.97)	(-18.6)
Rooms	-0.514***	0.0562	-0.0645*	-0.292***	0.791***	0.647***
	(-8.99)	(1.30)	(-2.00)	(-7.66)	(20.15)	(14.22)
rooms × ln(x)	0.0731***	-0.0126*	0.00873	0.0405***	-0.106***	-0.277***
	(8.70)	(-1.97)	(1.84)	(7.21)	(-18.30)	(-17.41)
lfp	-0.115**	-0.0381	0.0824***	-0.0420	0.101***	-0.054
	(-2.75)	(-1.20)	(3.49)	(-1.50)	(3.52)	(-1.46)
lfp × ln(x)	0.0144*	0.00641	-0.0119***	0.00673	-0.0152***	-0.183***
	(2.34)	(1.38)	(-3.43)	(1.64)	(-3.61)	(-14.74)
lnpr1	-0.0519	0.0882**	0.0238	0.0243	-0.0431***	-0.251***
	(-1.16)	(2.62)	(0.98)	(1.31)	(-3.41)	(-14.91)
lnpr2	0.0882**	-0.0730	-0.0676**	0.0447**	0.00283	-0.160***
	(2.62)	(-1.71)	(-2.61)	(2.75)	(0.29)	(-10.91)
lnpr3	0.0238	-0.0676**	0.0766**	-0.0286*	-0.00251	-0.171***
	(0.98)	(-2.61)	(2.96)	(-2.40)	(-0.34)	(-13.2)
lnpr4	0.0243	0.0447**	-0.0286*	-0.0133	-0.0194*	-0.194***
	(1.31)	(2.75)	(-2.40)	(-0.89)	(-2.51)	(-14.59)
lnpr5	-0.0431***	0.00283	-0.00251	-0.0194*	0.0953***	-0.105***
	(-3.41)	(0.29)	(-0.34)	(-2.51)	(10.52)	(-7.64)
Age	0.00138***	-0.000773***	-0.000259***	-0.000629***	0.000739***	-0.167***
	(27.57)	(-20.30)	(-9.16)	(-18.74)	(21.42)	(-15.94)
White	0.0159***	0.000513	0.00774***	-0.00814***	-0.0122***	-0.183***
	(12.21)	(0.52)	(10.53)	(-9.34)	(-13.61)	(-17.34)

	(1)	(2)	(3)	(4)	(5)	(6)
Elderly	−0.00894*	0.000726	0.00384	0.00511*	0.00650**	−0.168***
	(−2.57)	(0.27)	(1.96)	(2.19)	(2.71)	(−15.42)
/ln/(CUsize/)	0.111***	−0.0726***	−0.0409***	−0.0158***	−0.00233	−0.149***
	(43.36)	(−37.44)	(−28.40)	(−9.23)	(−1.32)	(−13.84)
Children, 0–2	−0.00648***	−0.00403***	−0.00136	0.0215***	0.00115	−0.177***
	(−5.20)	(−4.26)	(−1.93)	(25.85)	(1.35)	(−16.79)
Children, 3–15	0.000911	0.00159**	0.00708***	0.000761	−0.00223***	−0.178***
	(1.24)	(2.84)	(17.04)	(1.55)	(−4.40)	(−16.91)
Head < college	−0.00845***	0.00441***	0.00541***	0.00268***	−0.00287***	−0.171***
	(−7.47)	(5.13)	(8.48)	(3.55)	(−3.69)	(−16.21)
Head college	−0.00482***	0.00825***	0.0128***	0.00419***	−0.0113***	−0.188***
	(−3.75)	(8.46)	(17.68)	(4.88)	(−12.84)	(−17.8)
Wife < college	−0.00809***	0.00140	0.00658***	0.00291***	−0.00203**	−0.170***
	(−7.21)	(1.64)	(10.41)	(3.89)	(−2.63)	(−16.09)
Wife college	−0.00457***	0.00386***	0.0151***	0.00294***	−0.0105***	−0.184***
	(−3.48)	(3.88)	(20.36)	(3.35)	(−11.65)	(−17.45)
Constant	2.899***	−0.819***	−0.388***	0.329***	−1.060***	0.040
	(28.29)	(−10.54)	(−6.73)	(4.80)	(−15.06)	(0.57)

Notes: Controls include month of interview, year of interview, log prices, and twenty-two state-region dummies. $N = 80{,}838$ and standard errors are in parentheses.

***Significant at the 1/10 of 1 percent level.

**Significant at the 1 percent level.

*Significant at the 5 percent level.

Table 5.17 **Income elasticities**

	Rooms	LFP	Rooms, cars, and lfp
Food in	0.46	0.46	0.53
	(0.012)	(0.010)	(0.012)
Food out	2.09	1.91	2.08
	(0.025)	(0.022)	(0.027)
Entertainment	2.36	2.28	2.35
	(0.039)	(0.034)	(0.041)
Apparel	1.70	1.55	1.70
	(0.031)	(0.028)	(0.033)
Utilities	0.69	0.92	0.70
	(0.014)	(0.013)	(0.015)
Motor fuel	0.84	0.79	0.67
	(0.019)	(0.016)	(0.020)

Note: Standard errors are in parentheses.

Table 5.18 **Own price elasticities**

	Rooms	LFP	Rooms, cars, and lfp
Food in	−0.96	−0.98	−0.98
	(0.127)	(0.125)	(0.125)
Food out	−1.74	−1.66	−1.71
	(0.338)	(0.336)	(0.337)
Entertainment	0.15	0.18	0.17
	(0.424)	(0.424)	(0.423)
Apparel	−1.23	−1.19	−1.21
	(0.166)	(0.166)	(0.166)
Utilities	−0.48	−0.50	−0.48
	(0.044)	(0.047)	(0.044)
Motor fuel	−0.47	−0.46	−0.44
	(0.031)	(0.031)	(0.030)

Note: Standard errors are in parentheses.

Table 5.19 **Predicted budget shares following 25 percent increase in food prices**

	Prior to change	Full separability	Exog. cars	Endog. cars	Rooms	LFP	Rooms, cars, and lfp
Food in	35.9	36.2	37.0	42.3	38.3	36.4	38.1
Food out	12.7	14.1	14.0	14.4	13.5	14.1	13.5
Entertainment	6.1	6.0	6.0	6.0	6.1	6.0	6.1
Apparel	9.0	9.2	9.3	8.7	9.8	9.3	9.8
Utilities	20.7	19.7	19.2	19.5	18.3	19.6	18.1
Motor fuel	15.6	14.7	14.5	9.2	14.0	14.8	14.5

This being said, much research is being done using CE data to investigate questions relating to demand estimation (Hussain 2006; Padula 1999), trends in consumption inequality (Aguiar and Bils 2011; Attanasio, Battistin, and Leicester 2006), tests of the life-cycle hypothesis (Gervais and Klein 2010), and asset pricing (Kocherlakota and Pistaferri 2009).

However, there are still many potentially relevant aspects of the life of households that are typically neglected in demand analysis, such as the impact of extended family, (via transfers, sharing of risk or proximity leading to joint consumption choices), or that of health on contemporaneous choices. We do not examine these in the empirical exercise. However, we know that extended families (Browning and Lechene 2003), habit formation (Browning and Collado 2007), and heterogeneity (Christensen 2007; Lewbel and Pendakur 2009) all matter in determining household demand, and having information on these in the CE together with information on demand would allow much progress in understanding household behavior.

References

Aguiar, M., and M. Bils. 2011. "Has Consumption Inequality Mirrored Income Inequality?" NBER Working Paper no. 16807, Cambridge, MA.

Attanasio, O., E. Battistin, and A. Leicester. 2006. "From Micro to Macro, from Poor to Rich: Consumption and Income in the UK and the US." Working paper, National Poverty Center, Gerald R. Ford School of Public Policy, University of Michigan, http://www.homepages.ucl.ac.uk/~uctpjrt/Files/Attanasio-Battistin-Leicester.pdf.

Attanasio, O., P. Levell, H. Low, and V. Sanchez-Marcos. 2011. "Aggregating Elasticities: Intensive and Extensive Margins of Female Labour Supply." Unpublished manuscript.

Banks, J., R. Blundell, and A. Lewbel. 1997. "Quadratic Engel Curves and Consumer Demand." *Review of Economics and Statistics* 79 (4): 527–39.

Barten, A. P. 1966. "Theorie en Empirie van een Volledig Stelsel van Vraagvergelijkingen." PhD diss., University of Rotterdam.

Blundell, R., and J.–M. Robin. 1999. "Estimation in Large and Disaggregated Demand Systems: An Estimator for Conditionally Linear Systems." *Journal of Applied Econometrics* 14 (3): 209–32.

Browning, M., and M. Dolores Collado. 2007. "Habits and Heterogeneity in Demands: A Panel Data Analysis." *Journal of Applied Econometrics* 22 (3): 625–40.

Browning, M., and V. Lechene. 2003. "Children and Demand: Direct and Non-Direct Effects." *Review of Economics of the Household* 1 (1): 9–31.

Browning, M., and C. Meghir. 1991. "The Effects of Male and Female Labor Supply on Commodity Demands." *Econometrica* 59 (4): 925–51.

Christensen, M. 2007. "Integrability of Demand Accounting for Unobservable Heterogeneity: A Test on Panel Data." IFS Working Paper no. W07/14, Institute for Fiscal Studies.

Christensen, L. R., D. W. Jorgenson, and L. J. Lau. 1975. "Transcendental Logarithmic Utility Functions." *American Economic Review* 65:367–83.

Deaton, Angus, and John Muellbauer. 1980. "An Almost Ideal Demand System." *American Economic Review* 70 (3): 312–26.

Flavin, Marjorie, and Shinobu Nakagawa. 2008. "A Model of Housing in the Presence of Adjustment Costs: A Structural Interpretation of Habit Persistence." *American Economic Review* 98 (1): 474–95.

Flavin, Marjorie, and Takashi Yamashita. 2002. "Owner-Occupied Housing and the Composition of the Household Portfolio." *American Economic Review* 92 (1): 345–62.

Gervais, Martin, and Paul Klein. 2010. "Measuring Consumption Smoothing in CE Data." *Journal of Monetary Economics* 57 (8): 988–99.

Grossman, Sanford J., and Guy Laroque. 1990. "Asset Pricing and Optimal Portfolio Choice in the Presence of Illiquid Durable Consumption Goods." *Econometrica* 58 (1): 25–51.

Hussain, I. 2006. "Consumer Demand and the Role of Labour Supply and Durables." *Economic Journal* 116 (510): C110–29.

Kocherlakota, N., and L. Pistaferri, L. 2009. "Asset Pricing Implications of Pareto Optimality with Private Information." *Journal of Political Economy* 117 (3): 555–90.

Lewbel, A., and K. Pendakur. 2009. "Tricks with Hicks: The EASI Demand System." *American Economic Review* 99 (3): 827–63.

Padula, Mario. 1999. "Euler Equations and Durable Goods." CSEF Working Paper no. 30, Centre for Studies in Economics and Finance.

Sabelhaus, J. 1990. "Testing Neoclassical Theory with Aggregate and Household Data." *Applied Economics* 22 (11): 1471–78.

Stone, Richard. 1954. "Linear Expenditure Systems and Demand Analysis: An Application to the Pattern of British Demand." *Economic Journal* 64 (255): 511–27.

Theil, Henri. 1965. "The Information Approach to Demand Analysis." *Econometrica* 33 (1): 67–87.

III

Evaluating the Existing CE Survey

Understanding the Relationship
CE Survey and PCE

William Passero, Thesia I. Garner, and Clinton McCully

6.1 Introduction

The Consumer Expenditure Survey (CE) data from the Bureau of Labor Statistics (BLS) and the personal consumption expenditures (PCE) data from the Bureau of Economic Analysis (BEA) are two sources of expenditures that focus on households in the United States.[1] Both are used to assess the economic well-being of households in the United States. Comparisons of data from these two sources have been conducted for many years, both within the BEA and BLS and by outside researchers, with resulting studies showing varying degrees of disparities in expenditures from the two sources.

William Passero is supervisory economist at the Bureau of Labor Statistics, US Department of Labor in the Division of Consumer Expenditure Surveys. Thesia I. Garner is senior research economist in the Division of Price and Index Number Research at the Bureau of Labor Statistics, US Department of Labor. Clinton McCully is the former chief of the Research Group in the National Income and Wealth Division, Bureau of Economic Analysis, US Department of Commerce.

A presentation based on this chapter was given at the conference on Improving the Measurement of Consumer Expenditures. That conference was sponsored by the Conference on Research in Income and Wealth and the National Bureau of Economic Research, with support from the Centre for Microdata Methods and Practice, December 2–3, 2011, Grand Hyatt Washington, 1000 H Street, NW, Washington, DC. We thank Brent Moulton, John Greenlees, and others attending the CRIW-NBER conference on Improving Measurement of Consumer Expenditures for helpful comments and discussion, and John Sabelhaus for extensive comments and suggestions after the conference. All views expressed in this manuscript are those of the authors and do not necessarily reflect the policies of the Bureau of Economic Analysis, the Bureau of Labor Statistics, or the views of other staff members. The authors take full responsibility for any errors. For acknowledgments, sources of research support, and disclosure of the authors' material financial relationships, if any, please see http://www.nber.org/chapters/c12659.ack.

1. For a definition of consumer unit, and the Consumer Expenditure Surveys, see the Bureau of Labor Statistics website at http://stats.bls.gov/cex/faq.htm#q3.

Recent studies within the BEA and BLS include those by Garner, McClelland, and Passero (2009); Garner et al. (2006); and McCully (2011). For earlier BLS studies of CE-to-PCE comparisons, see BLS (2008). One of the earliest comparisons by outside researchers was conducted by Houthakker and Taylor (1970). In this work, the authors compared 1960–1961 CE data with PCE aggregate expenditures. Later and more recent related studies, in which CE and PCE are compared, include those by Attanasio, Battistin, and Leicester (2006); Bee, Meyer, and Sullivan (2012); Meyer and Sullivan (2010, 2011); and Slesnick (1992, 1998, 2000). Maki and Garner (2010) conducted a study of CE expenditures relative to PCE; their results suggest that much of the difference in the two is due to measurement error. Barrett, Levell, and Milligan (chapter 9, this volume) also considered a measurement issue in their study of the relationship between declining CE participation rates and declines in CE-to-PCE ratios over time; they compared the US results to those from other countries.[2] The CE and PCE have also been compared to assess economic growth and other economic trends. For example, Attanasio and Weber (1995) used the data to address the question of whether consumption growth is consistent. Parker and Preston (2005) have studied precautionary savings and consumption. Bosworth, Burtless, and Sabelhaus (1991) have studied the decline in savings, and Fernandez-Villaverde and Krueger (2007) have considered consumption over the life cycle. See Meyer and Sullivan (2009, 2011) for a study of consumption and poverty. Blair (chapter 2, this volume) examined differences in the Consumer Price Index (CPI) expenditure weights based on the CE and the PCE (also see McCully, Moore, and Stewart 2007).

    When ratios of CE to PCE aggregate expenditures diverge, many express concern about the quality of the CE data, since the assumption is that both the CE and PCE are designed to measure the same phenomenon, household spending. However, household spending differs for the two. The CE is designed to collect expenditures made by households for goods and services. The PCE is designed to reflect spending by households and by nonprofits on behalf of households. As noted by various researchers (e.g., McCully 2011; Garner, McClelland, and Passero 2009; Bee, Meyer, and Sullivan 2012; Slesnick 1998), some differences in estimates of CE and PCE are expected because of differences in coverage and definition. However, even after accounting for these differences, CE and PCE aggregate expenditures still diverge because of measurement differences. In the first part of this chapter, we try to account for these differences using published CE and PCE data, referring to functional categories of goods and services (e.g., clothing, housing). In the second part, our focus is on building a data concordance at a finer level of detail to develop a series of the most comparable categories of expenditures for the

---

2. Battistin and Padula (2008) examined the role of measurement errors in distributions of expenditures from the Tucker, Biemer, and Meekins (2005) examined levels of underreporting of expenditures using latent class analysis.

CE and PCE by type of product (i.e., durable, nondurable, service). For the concordance, much attention is given to making adjustments in expenditures so that they are as comparable as possible; this means that the definition of certain categories of expenditures differ from the published estimates (for example, the use of rental equivalence in the concordance versus the use of spending in publication estimates). This concordance is the product of joint work conducted over the past several years by BEA and BLS researchers. Earlier comparisons within the BEA and BLS were based on independently developed CE-to-PCE concordances. The joint concordance was developed using the classification system introduced by the BEA in July 2009, with the goal that the concordance would be acceptable to the BEA and BLS for data comparisons. Results presented at the Conference on Research in Income and Wealth (CRIW) in December 2011 revealed that this jointly created concordance results in CE-to-PCE ratios that are very similar to those produced by the BLS in the past (Passero et al. 2011).

Research that uses the joint concordance to build PCE-adjusted CPI, presented in Blair (chapter 2, this volume), uses a set of alternately weighted indexes created using PCE expenditure weights and CPI methodology. The CE-to-PCE concordance from this paper is used in Blair's work to map PCE items to CPI entry-level items so that the CPI can be adjusted according to PCE rather than CE expenditure levels. Conceptual differences, noted in the concordance, are used in the Blair chapter to create two PCE-weighted CPIs: one that is adjusted to match CE and CPI item definitions and one to match PCE item definitions.

The purpose of this chapter is to present similarities and differences between the CE and PCE and to present results in two ways: first, by making adjustments in published CE and PCE estimates in terms of coverage, definition, and measurement, and second, by redefining expenditure categories and restricting the expenditures to those deemed most comparable. Two questions are addressed: (1) How well does the CE and PCE match up overall and across categories? and (2) How has this relationship changed over time? The CE and PCE data from 1992 to 2010 are analyzed.

Aggregate expenditures, adjusted for differences in coverage, definition, and measurement are presented in table 6.1 for CE and PCE. Without accounting for these differences, published CE total expenditures as a percentage of PCE decreased from 71 percent in 1992 to 57 percent of PCE in 2010. After these adjustments, the aggregate published CE value of comparable items decreased from 75 percent of PCE comparables in 1992 to 62 percent in 2010. Aggregate expenditures and ratios of CE to PCE are produced for durables, nondurables, and services in tables 6.2A, 6.2B, and 6.2C. The CE aggregates in these tables have been adjusted to reduce, at a more detailed level, differences in expenditures with respect to the PCE. Through this exercise, CE aggregate expenditures have been made more comparable to PCE expenditures; CE expenditures are 84 percent of PCE aggregates for 1992 but fall

Table 6.1   Reconciliation of published Consumer Expenditures (CE) and personal consumption expenditures (PCE) (values in billions of dollars)

	1992	2010	Change 1992 to 2010	Percent change 1992 to 2010	CE-PCE disparity	Measurement differences
Personal consumption expenditures	4,236.9	10,245.5	6,008.6	141.8	—	—
Less: Final consumption expenditures of nonprofit institutions	92.3	280.2	187.9	203.4	5.1	—
Equals: Household consumption expenditures	4,144.5	9,965.3	5,820.8	140.4	—	—
Less: Coverage adjustments	28.6	67.2	38.6	135.2	0.6	—
Less: Definitional differences (net)	414.1	1,663.4	1,249.3	301.7	43.3	—
PCE not comparable to CE	1,265.3	3,518.5	2,253.2	178.1	53.1	—
Expenditures financed by government and employers	535.0	1,630.2	1095.2	204.7	29.7	—
Government social benefits	275.7	1,022.7	747.0	270.9	24.5	—
Health	260.4	949.9	689.5	264.8	22.3	—
Other	15.3	72.8	57.5	376.0	2.2	—
Employer-paid health insurance & workers' compensation	259.3	607.5	348.2	134.3	5.1	—
Imputed rental value of owner-occupied housing	468.2	1,215.1	746.8	159.5	15.2	—
Financial services and insurance	212.1	560.5	348.4	164.3	7.4	—
Financial services	174.7	511.0	336.3	192.5	8.6	—
Insurance	37.4	49.5	12.1	32.4	(1.2)	—
Net purchases of used motor vehicles	49.4	112.4	63.1	127.7	0.8	—
Food produced & consumed on farms	0.6	0.3	(0.3)	(43.5)	(0.0)	—
Less: CE not comparable to PCE	851.2	1,855.1	1,003.9	117.9	9.8	—
Expenses of owner-occupied housing	349.3	773.2	423.9	121.4	4.6	—
Used motor vehicles	80.0	134.9	55.0	68.7	(1.1)	—
Finance charges	31.0	35.5	4.6	14.8	(1.3)	—
State and local registration and license	8.3	13.5	5.2	62.0	(0.1)	—
Cash contributions incl. alimony/child support	95.8	197.8	101.9	106.4	0.5	—
Life insurance/annuity premiums	35.3	38.5	3.2	9.1	(1.5)	—
Contributions to pensions and Social Security	239.7	612.1	372.3	155.3	7.3	—
Medicare premiums	11.8	49.7	37.9	322.0	1.4	—

Equals: CE expenditures exclusive of measurement differences	3,701.9	8,234.8	4,532.9	122.4	——
Less: Measurement differences	716.7	2,408.4	1,691.7	236.0	51.1
Equals: CE total expenditures	2,985.2	5,826.3	2,841.2	95.2	——
CE total expenditures percent of PCE	70.5	56.9	(13.6)	(19.3)	——
PCE less CE total expenditures	1,251.7	4,419.2	3,167.5	253.0	——
Measurement differences as percent of total differences	57.3	54.5	(2.8)	(4.8)	——
PCE less CE comparables	716.7	2,408.4	1,691.7	236.0	——
PCE comparable	2,850.7	6,379.6	3,528.9	123.8	——
CE comparable	2,134.0	3,971.2	1,837.2	86.1	——
CE percent of PCE comparables	74.9	62.2	(12.6)	(16.8)	——
PCE-CE differences by functional category					
Food and beverages purchased for off-premises consumption	123.2	298.9	175.7	142.7	10.4
Clothing, footwear, and related services	73.0	172.1	99.1	135.7	5.9
Housing, utilities, and fuels	1.2	44.1	42.9	3,439.1	2.5
Furnishings, household equipment, and routine household maintenance	49.8	175.5	125.6	252.2	7.4
Health (including insurance)	81.1	251.4	170.3	210.0	10.1
Transportation (including insurance)	44.3	226.5	182.2	411.7	10.8
Communications	10.8	49.1	38.3	354.7	2.3
Recreation	140.0	514.5	374.5	267.5	22.1
Education	37.0	77.2	40.3	109.0	2.4
Food services and accommodations	56.4	212.6	156.2	277.0	9.2
Other goods & services	88.2	336.8	248.6	281.7	18.6

Table 6.2A Summary comparison of aggregate Consumer Expenditures (CE) and personal consumption expenditures (PCE), based on 2002 benchmark and restricted to the most comparable categories on the basis of concepts involved and comprehensiveness, 1992 and 2010 (in millions of dollars)

PCE category	1992			2010		
	PCE	CE	CE-to-PCE ratio	PCE	CE	CE-to-PCE ratio
Total durables, nondurables, and services						
Total	4,144,548	2,880,449	0.695	9,965,306	5,740,672	0.576
Comparable items	2,702,984	2,273,606	0.841	6,173,121	4,594,311	0.744
Ratio of comparable items to total	0.652	0.789		0.619	0.800	
Comparable items (adjusted for population)	2,630,940	2,273,606	0.864	6,066,251	4,594,311	0.757
Durable goods						
Total durable goods	508,082	393,010	0.774	1,085,484	594,752	0.548
Comparable durable goods	434,090	357,161	0.823	862,279	536,968	0.623
Ratio of comparable durables to total durables	0.854	0.909		0.794	0.903	
Motor vehicles and parts	204,798	203,566	0.994	340,124	306,545	0.901
Furniture and furnishings	69,274	58,009	0.837	140,960	75,230	0.534
Household appliances	24,287	15,735	0.648	40,536	32,137	0.793
Glassware, tableware, and household utensils	20,050	10,082	0.503	41,545	14,765	0.355
Outdoor equipment and supplies	1,684	413	0.245	4,788	448	0.094
Televisions	10,797	6,433	0.596	37,407	14,379	0.384
Audio equipment	9,847	6,271	0.637	19,019	4,989	0.262
Photographic equipment	2,383	1,379	0.579	2,844	3,072	1.080
Personal computers and peripheral equipment	9,112	7,346	0.806	47,355	24,689	0.521
Sporting equipment, supplies, guns, and ammunition	21,743	10,925	0.502	53,258	14,739	0.277
Bicycles and accessories	2,484	1,592	0.641	4,257	1,868	0.439
Pleasure boats	3,790	6,124	1.616	9,779	8,672	0.887
Other recreational vehicles	6,454	6,018	0.932	9,580	3,755	0.392
Recreational books	11,507	6,051	0.526	30,412	7,118	0.234
Musical instruments	2,186	1,862	0.852	4,939	1,848	0.374
Jewelry and watches	31,645	13,120	0.415	61,485	18,102	0.294
Telephone and facsimile equipment	2,049	2,235	1.091	13,991	4,612	0.330

Table 6.2B Summary comparison of aggregate Consumer Expenditures (CE) and personal consumption expenditures (PCE), based on 2002 benchmark and restricted to the most comparable categories on the basis of concepts involved and comprehensiveness, 1992 and 2010 (in millions of dollars)

PCE category	1992			2010		
	PCE	CE	CE-to-PCE ratio	PCE	CE	CE-to-PCE ratio
Total durables, nondurables, and services						
Total	4,144,548	2,880,449	0.695	9,965,306	5,740,672	0.576
Comparable items	2,702,984	2,273,606	0.841	6,173,121	4,594,311	0.744
Ratio of comparable items to total	0.652	0.789		0.619	0.800	
Comparable items (adjusted for population)	2,630,940	2,273,606	0.864	6,066,251	4,594,311	0.757
Nondurable goods						
Total nondurable goods	1,055,187	745,779	0.707	2,301,517	1,432,306	0.622
Comparable nondurable goods	983,314	690,254	0.702	2,154,925	1,349,644	0.626
Ratio of comparable nondurables to total nondurables	0.932	0.926		0.936	0.942	
Food purchased for off-premises consumption	305,188	241,497	0.791	580,641	381,772	0.658
Nonalcoholic beverages purchased for off-premises consumption	49,408	29,498	0.597	78,741	50,312	0.639
Alcoholic beverages purchased for off-premises consumption	49,294	16,511	0.335	106,649	27,473	0.258
Women's and girls' clothing	103,175	68,056	0.660	161,192	80,116	0.497
Men's and boys' clothing	63,009	45,018	0.714	95,480	46,175	0.484
Clothing materials	3,643	1,084	0.298	4,203	1,227	0.292
Shoes and other footwear	32,903	23,124	0.703	59,334	36,679	0.618
Gasoline and other energy goods	125,007	107,384	0.859	354,117	275,726	0.779
Pharmaceutical products	68,196	53,350	0.782	326,869	267,019	0.817
Pets and related products	14,756	10,572	0.716	50,068	39,653	0.792
Film and photographic supplies	3,641	2,006	0.551	2,238	213	0.095
Household cleaning products	20,689	12,861	0.622	41,287	20,676	0.501
Household paper products	16,191	9,933	0.613	40,325	20,331	0.504
Household linens	16,110	7,252	0.450	24,288	9,860	0.406
Sewing items	767	638	0.832	1,213	1,154	0.951
Personal care products	41,370	23,190	0.561	95,239	40,928	0.430
Tobacco	48,008	27,497	0.573	94,357	43,846	0.465
Newspapers and periodicals	21,959	10,783	0.491	38,684	6,484	0.168

Table 6.2C Summary comparison of aggregate Consumer Expenditures (CE) and personal consumption expenditures (PCE), based on 2002 benchmark and restricted to the most comparable categories on the basis of concepts involved and comprehensiveness, 1992 and 2010 (in millions of dollars)

PCE category	1992			2010		
	PCE	CE	CE-to-PCE ratio	PCE	CE	CE-to-PCE ratio
Total durables, nondurables, and services						
Total	4,144,548	2,880,449	0.695	9,965,306	5,740,672	0.576
Comparable items	2,702,984	2,273,606	0.841	6,173,121	4,594,311	0.744
Ratio of comparable items to total	0.652	0.789		0.619	0.800	
Comparable items (adjusted for population)	2,630,940	2,273,606	0.864	6,066,251	4,594,311	0.757
Services—household consumption expenditures						
Total services	2,581,279	1,741,660	0.675	6,578,305	3,713,614	0.565
Comparable services	1,285,580	1,226,191	0.954	3,155,917	2,707,699	0.858
Ratio of comparable services to total services	0.498	0.704		0.480	0.729	
Rent and utilities	300,537	300,378	0.999	668,759	625,584	0.935
Imputed rental of owner-occupied nonfarm housing	462,819	555,877	1.201	1,203,353	1,320,466	1.097
Other motor vehicle services	19,410	18,305	0.943	58,612	35,910	0.613
Audio-video, photographic, and information processing equipment services	42,597	28,425	0.667	102,654	83,783	0.816
Gambling	28,080	5,135	0.183	99,578	9,517	0.096
Veterinary and other services for pets	5,839	5,584	0.956	25,669	18,431	0.718
Purchased meals and beverages	247,054	174,692	0.707	533,078	322,435	0.605
Food supplied to civilians	6,573	2,609	0.397	12,501	3,325	0.266
Communication	79,093	68,262	0.863	223,385	184,529	0.826
Accounting and other business services	7,722	8,957	1.160	27,745	19,068	0.687
Funeral and burial services	10,969	6,711	0.612	18,731	7,451	0.398
Personal care services	35,661	25,273	0.709	95,870	35,037	0.365
Repair and hire of footwear	638	344	0.539	457	187	0.409
Child care	12,013	8,320	0.693	30,309	9,629	0.318
Household maintenance	26,575	17,319	0.652	55,216	32,347	0.586

to 74 percent by 2010. The second analysis reveals that nondurable categories are most alike for the CE and PCE with about 93 percent of total nondurable expenditures identified as comparable within the CE and within the PCE. Regarding trends over time and focusing on comparable goods and services only, CE-to-PCE ratios have steadily decreased. The greatest decline in CE-to-PCE ratios is for durables, with a decrease of 24 percentage points. Ratios for comparable services dropped the least, with a decrease of 10 percentage points.

The next section of the chapter focuses on coverage, definitional, and measurement differences. This is followed by information regarding the motivation for the development of the more detailed concordance, and then further results from the joint concordance. These results are presented in terms of CE-to-PCE ratios and trends in CE and PCE expenditures over time. This is followed by a summary and discussion of future directions.

6.2 Coverage, Definitional, and Measurement Differences

Coverage, definitional, and measurement differences account for the overall differences in the BEA-produced reconciliation of published CE and PCE estimates presented in table 6.1. The CE total expenditures have been consistently lower than PCE, the differences are large, and relative differences have increased substantially over time. Without accounting for these differences, CE total expenditures as a percentage of PCE decreased from 70 percent in 1992 to 58 percent of PCE in 2010. According to results that underlie table 6.1, measurement differences have accounted for more than half of the CE-PCE differences throughout the 1992 to 2010 period, with their share ranging from 53 to 60 percent. The contributions of measurement differences and of coverage and definitional differences to the widening of the CE-PCE gap from 1992 to 2010 have been about equal.

6.2.1 Coverage

The share of CE-PCE differences accounted for by coverage differences decreased from 10 percent in 1992 to 8 percent in 2010. The primary source of coverage differences is the inclusion in PCE of the final consumption expenditures of nonprofit institutions serving households (NPISHs), measured as their gross expenses less sales to households and other sectors. The NPISHs have remained in the range of 2 to 3 percent of PCE throughout the 1992–2010 period.[3] The PCE less NPISH final consumption expenditures equals household consumption expenditures (HCE). The NPISH sales to households, such as sales of education services, are included in the appropriate household consumption expenditures (HCE) categories. The remaining coverage differences have been less than 1 percent of PCE, and are accounted

---

3. This could also be treated as a definitional difference.

for by the net effect of differences in population coverage. The CE survey collects data from consumer units representing the civilian noninstitutional population residing in the United States. This includes those in noninstitutional group quarters, such as housing facilities for students and workers. Included in PCE but not in CE are expenditures of the institutionalized population, domestic military personnel living on post, federal military and civilian personnel stationed abroad regardless of the length of their assignments, and US citizens who are employees of US businesses working abroad for less than one year and whose usual residence is in the United States. Excluded from PCE but included in the CE are expenditures of students, temporary workers, and foreign nationals residing in the United States who are employees of international organizations and other countries. The PCE also includes expenditures by those who died during the year and could not be included in the CE, which asks households for their expenditures in the previous three months or week. The less than 1 percent coverage differences do not include the health care provided to the institutionalized and decedent populations through the Medicare and Medicaid programs. Including these expenditures would increase the population coverage differences to about 3 percent of PCE. Instead, all Medicare and Medicaid expenditures are treated here as definitional differences, part of third-party payments on behalf of individuals in PCE that are not part of CE.

6.2.2 Definitions

Definitional differences are accounted for by the net effect of PCE categories not comparable to CE and CE categories not comparable to PCE. The value of noncomparable PCE categories is significantly larger than for noncomparable CE categories, and relative differences between them have increased significantly over time. In 1992, noncomparable PCE was 50 percent larger than noncomparable CE, and by 2010 was 90 percent larger, at $3,518.5 billion. The share of noncomparable PCE categories increased from 30 percent to 34 percent of PCE over the 1992 to 2010 period, while noncomparable CE expenditures increased from 29 percent to 32 percent of the CE total over the period.

Exclusive of NPISHs, PCE measures out-of-pocket purchases of goods and services by households, purchases of goods and services made on behalf of households, and imputed purchases by households for some expenditure categories. The CE measures out-of-pocket expenditures by consumer units, including purchases of goods and services, interest payments, contributions to Social Security and pension plans, and cash contributions and other transfers to charitable organizations and other households.[4] Expenditures in PCE

---

4. Consumer units as defined in the CE are not identical to households, in that a household can have more than one consumer unit if groups or individuals living in the household are financially independent. The use of consumer units results in differences in average expenditures compared to the use of households, but in comparisons of aggregate expenditures, the use of consumer units versus households does not have any substantive effect.

that have no CE counterpart primarily consist of third-party expenditures by government and employers, imputed expenditures for owner-occupied rent,[5] and financial services and insurance including both direct and imputed expenditures. Together, these expenditures account for more than 95 percent of noncomparable PCE. Other noncomparable expenditures in the CE include used motor vehicles and the value net of expenses of food produced and consumed on farms.

Purchases of goods and services on behalf of households in PCE consist of purchases by government and employers. Expenditures by government primarily consist of payments for health care under the Medicare and Medicaid programs, but also include other health care expenditures and payments for education and energy assistance. These expenditures have increased very rapidly over time, and in 2010 were $1,022.7 billion, 271 percent greater than in 1992, and accounted for about one-fourth of the widening of the CE-PCE gap over that time. Purchases by employers consist of employer contributions for health insurance and workers' compensation.[6] While these are accounted for as part of personal income in the National Income and Product Accounts (NIPA) personal income and outlay account, these contributions are accounted for in PCE as well. Insurance payments for health care are included in the PCE health care categories, and premiums net of health care payments are accounted for in PCE for health insurance.[7] These accounted for about $600 billion in expenditures in 2010, but because they have not grown nearly as rapidly as have government third-party expenditures, they accounted for only about 5 percent of the widening of the CE-PCE gap.

Financial services in PCE have no CE counterpart, while insurance is considered noncomparable because of significant differences in treatment compared to the CE.[8] These services were valued at $560 billion in 2010, 164 percent more than in 1992, and accounted for 7 percent of the widening of the CE-PCE gap. Over the 1992–2010 period, PCE for financial services increased much more rapidly than insurance and more than accounted for the widening of the CE-PCE gap.

The PCE for financial services includes both imputed services and financial service charges, fees, and commissions. Imputed financial services are services furnished without payment by banks, other depository institutions, and regulated investment companies. For banks and other depository insti-

5. Although the CE program does not employ the rental equivalence concept, the BLS does use CE data to construct weights for owners' equivalent rent in the CPI.

6. Employers also make contributions for life insurance, but because life insurer expenses rather than life insurance premiums are measured in PCE, these are not included.

7. Cash benefits netted from workers' compensation premiums are not captured elsewhere in PCE, and these are accounted for as noncomparable insurance.

8. Noncomparable PCE for financial services removes bank service charges, safe deposit box rental, and credit card membership fees measured in both PCE and the CE. The value of these expenditures is 1 to 2 percent of total PCE for financial services.

tutions, these are services to depositors, and for commercial banks they include borrower services as well. For banks, the imputed charges to depositors are measured using the difference between interest paid on deposit accounts and interest that would have been paid if those assets were invested in riskless government securities. The difference accounts for the value of bank services that are not directly charged to depositors, such as book-keeping and check-clearing services. The value of these services is allocated to households in proportion to their share of deposits. The estimation of borrower services is done in a similar fashion, using the differences between interest earned by banks on loans and other assets and what those assets would have earned if invested in riskless government securities. For other depository institutions, including savings institutions and credit unions, depositor services are measured using the spread between interest earned by the institution and interest paid to depositors. Mutual fund expenses consist of expenses of regulated investment companies, largely portfolio management fees and brokerage commissions, which reduce the value of assets held. These expenses are deemed to be paid by the mutual fund holders, and are allocated to households in proportion to their share of holdings. Also included in PCE for financial services are expenses incurred by pension funds, which are deemed to be paid by households with pension fund assets. In the CE, expenditures for pension funds are measured by contributions. Financial service charges, fees, and commissions consist of fees charged by depository institutions and credit card issuers, commissions on securities transactions, portfolio management and investment advisory services, and trust, fiduciary, and custody activities. Noncomparable fees charged by depository institutions and credit card issuers are primarily penalty fees, such as overdraft fees of banks and over limit and late fees of credit card issuers. Securities commissions include both those charged directly on securities transactions and indirect charges through markups or spreads on transactions by market makers. Investment counseling fees and trust, fiduciary, and custody fees are those charged on individual accounts, and portfolio management fees are those charged on individual accounts and by hedge funds whose investors are individuals.

The PCE for insurance that are not comparable to CE include expenses incurred by life insurance companies, premium supplements on property-casualty insurance, household insurance premiums, cash benefits for property-casualty insurance, and income loss insurance.[9] Life insurance is measured in PCE by the expenses of life insurance companies in providing life insurance and annuity services, rather than by premiums, and for stock life insurance companies includes profits as well. In the CE, life insurance expenditures are measured by premiums paid. Premium supplements

9. Employer contributions for health insurance and workers' compensation have already been discussed as noncomparable third-party payments and are not considered here.

included in PCE are earnings on technical reserves of property-casualty insurance policies. Household insurance premiums are noncomparable because they include only that portion of homeowners' insurance premiums that cover household contents. Cash benefits for property-casualty insurance are a subtraction from premiums plus premium supplements and have no offset elsewhere in the PCE, unlike benefits for motor vehicle repair and health care. Premiums net of benefits of income loss insurance covering temporary disability are not comparable to CE.

Net purchases of used motor vehicles in PCE measure net purchases from other sectors through dealers and include dealer margins. They do not reflect person-to-person sales and can be alternatively measured as purchases from dealers less trade-ins and sales to dealers. The CE measure of used motor vehicles includes purchases from both dealers and persons and nets out trade-ins to dealers but not sales by persons. Using used motor vehicle sales by persons collected in the CE but not included in published CE total expenditures eliminates comparability differences between CE and PCE.

Owner-occupied housing is treated differently in PCE than in CE publications. In PCE, owner-occupied housing expenditures are defined as a service flow, and a space rental value is imputed to represent the value of that flow.[10] (For the joint concordance, a rental equivalence measure is used for CE housing in order that the CE and PCE are more comparable.) In CE publications, owners' out-of-pocket shelter expenditures are counted, which include mortgage interest and charges, property taxes, and maintenance, repair, insurance, and other expenses. In the NIPAs, these expenses are subtracted from the imputed rental value of owner-occupied housing to derive rental income of persons, a component of personal income. The rental value for owner-occupied housing remained in the range of 11 to 12 percent of total PCE throughout the 1992 to 2010 period, and accounted for about 15 percent of the widening of the CE-PCE gap, though the net effect was about 11 percent, as the contribution of the homeowners' expenses measured in the CE partially offset the PCE contribution. Using the estimated rental value of owner-occupied houses reported in the CE, but not included in CE published total expenditures, eliminates comparability differences. In the comparison of these measures, CE has been consistently higher than PCE.

Noncomparable expenditures in the CE are expenditures other than purchases of goods and services, and purchases that are measured differently than in PCE. Nonpurchases in the CE include interest payments, cash contributions including alimony and child support, contributions for Social Security and pensions, fees for licenses and registrations, and Medicare premiums. Purchases in CE that are treated differently than in PCE include homeowner

---

10. See Garner and Short (2009) for a description of the PCE method of estimating rental equivalence of owner-occupied dwellings; this description is based on communications with staff at the BEA.

expenses, used car purchases, and insurance. In the NIPAs, nonmortgage interest is included in interest paid by persons, part of personal outlays along with PCE and net private remittances. Mortgage interest is an intermediate expense of homeowners subtracted from rental value in deriving rental income of persons in personal income. Contributions to charitable organizations and other nonhousehold entities in CE are not captured in personal outlays in the NIPAs, but are captured in household outlays in the disaggregated personal sector. Transfers between households, such as alimony and child support payments, are not captured in PCE because they are offsetting among households, since payments by one household are receipts by another household. In the CE, payments are part of expenditures and receipts are part of income. Social Security contributions are treated in the NIPAs as contributions for government social insurance and are not in PCE. Private pension and retirement plan contributions are part of personal saving rather than personal outlays in the NIPAs. Motor vehicle license and registration fees and similar fees imposed by government are not purchases of goods and services, but are treated in the NIPAs as personal current taxes, which are subtracted from personal income to derive disposable personal income. Medicare premiums are paid for enrollment in Medicare Part B medical insurance and Part D prescription drug coverage. These are treated as contributions for government social insurance in the NIPAs and are not part of PCE.

6.2.3 Measurement

After removing coverage and comparability differences, remaining differences between CE and PCE are due to measurement differences for comparable items. Differences are to be expected, because the estimates are based on different sources: surveys of households for CE and reports by businesses that sell goods and services to households for PCE.[11] What is noteworthy is that CE expenditures are below PCE by significant amounts, that such differences have been observed consistently across time, that the CE understatement is observed across almost all expenditure categories, and that these differences have increased significantly over time. Based on the BEA reconciliation described above, the aggregate CE value of comparable items decreased from 75 percent of PCE comparables in 1992 to 62 percent in 2010, when the CE comparable value of $3,971.2 billion was $2,408.4 billion less than the PCE value of $6,379.6 billion. Most of the decrease in CE relative to PCE occurred from 1992 to 2003, during which the percentage decreased in 9 of the 11 years to 64 percent, 11 percentage points below its 1992 level. There was a small increase to 66 percent in 2009 before decreasing by 4 percentage points in 2010.

Explanations of the understatement of CE values relative to PCE have centered on the tendency to understatement of expenditures reported by households. Expenditure data reported by households are prone to under-

11. The PCE estimates make very limited use of CE values, accounting for about 0.5 percent of total PCE and 0.9 percent of comparable PCE.

statement because of difficulties in recalling expenditures, the deliberate underreporting or nonreporting of certain types of expenditures such as "sin" commodities (e.g., alcohol, tobacco, gambling), and what is believed to be less than full compliance with the requirements of the diary survey, which asks for the daily recording of expenditures for small, frequently purchased items for two one-week periods. In addition, there may be a tendency to underreport expenditures of household members who are not the interview respondent. The PCE estimates are also subject to error, because of sampling and nonsampling errors in the source data, which come from Census Bureau surveys and censuses and from other public and private sources, as well as in some instances the lack of complete data for deriving estimates.

The understatement of CE expenditures for this exercise is consistent with observed differences, but what is not as clear is why there would be a significant widening of the gap between CE and PCE over time. One possibility is related to the significant decline in the response rate during the period in which the gap widened. The response rate for the CE interview survey declined by from 86 percent in 1990 to 74 percent in 2010. If the decline in the response rate were "randomly distributed" with respect to income and consumption, it would have little effect on measured expenditures. However, if the increased nonresponses were accounted for disproportionately by higher income and consumption households, this could help explain the widening disparities. No direct information bears on this question, but it is clear in breaking down the differences by category that the growth in the gap has varied considerably by commodity. By broad category, the largest contributor to the widening of the disparity between CE and PCE was expenditures for recreation and entertainment, which accounted for 22 percent of the increase in the CE-PCE disparity from 1992 to 2010.[12] Within this category, major contributors were video and audio equipment, computers and peripheral equipment, and gambling. Also contributing significantly to the increased disparity, with contributions of about 10 percent each were food purchased for off-premise consumption, food services and accommodations, health care, and transportation. "Other goods and services," including personal care, personal items, social services, professional and other services, and tobacco, accounted for about 10 percent of the increased disparity. Clothing, footwear, and related services accounted for about 6 percent of the increased disparity. Together, the cited categories accounted for more than 80 percent of the increase in the CE-PCE disparity.

6.3 Motivation for a Joint CE-to-PCE Concordance

The Bureau of Economic Analysis (BEA) introduced a new classification system for PCE in July 2009 with the 13th comprehensive, or benchmark,

---

12. The categories used are PCE-functional categories shown in NIPA table 2.5.5, modified in some instances for better CE-PCE alignment.

revision of the National Income and Product Accounts (NIPAs).[13] The new system is based on the Classification of Individual Consumption According to Purpose (COICOP), a United Nations standard used in many countries. The new PCE classification system included the separation of PCE into household consumption expenditures and final consumption expenditures of nonprofit institutions serving households (NPISHs) and the reclassification of many categories of expenditures, including food and financial services and insurance. With the new system, CE-to PCE-comparisons would be affected as well as alternative weighting schemes that were based on PCE. This change offered a unique opportunity to review the assignment of CE classification codes, UCCs, and PCE line categories in the underlying detail tables used previously for CE-to-PCE comparisons, and thereby to deconstruct the CE and PCE to assess the general assumption that CE estimates should match PCE estimates both in magnitude and trend.

Over many years, reconciliations of CE and PCE have been produced, but most of these have been the products of BEA and BLS working independently; thus, the assignment of CE and PCE item codes to expenditure categories for CE-to-PCE comparisons lacked the corroboration of the other agency. With the introduction of the new classification system, staff within the BLS and BEA decided to join together to validate the assignment of UCCs for future CE-to-PCE comparisons. The major output from this joint work is the development of a new concordance of CE and PCE expenditure groups that is supported by both the BEA and BLS. A comparison of CE and PCE estimates employing this new concordance is presented in tables 6.2A, 6.2B, and 6.2C. In developing this concordance it was necessary to review the features of both the CE and PCE. These are outlined in the next section and are presented with regard to the work conducted by the BEA to reconcile the published CE and PCE regarding coverage, definitions, and measurement.

6.4 Joint CE-to-PCE Concordance

The new classification system for PCE introduced in 2009 forced BLS to revise the concordance it had established between UCCs and PCE line categories in BEA underlying detail tables that had been used to produce tables comparing aggregate estimates between the two sources. This too provided an opportunity for the BEA and BLS to develop a joint concordance. One of the features of the CE-PCE comparison tables is to show aggregate estimates for all expenditure categories and for comparable categories.

The new concordance reflects the addition of UCCs and the deletion of UCCs from previous concordances. In addition, approximately seventy UCCs exist whose expenditures should be allocated between PCE categories.

---

13. See Kunze and McCulla (2008), McCully and Payson (2009), and McCully and Teensma (2008).

Allocation proportions have been estimated for some of these UCCs and are reflected in the results presented in this chapter. More research is needed to determine the appropriate proportions for the remaining UCCs, and going forward, the frequency with which all these UCCs should be adjusted in producing a time series of comparison tables. Examples of comparables and noncomparables are presented below (see table 6.3).

The impact of this new joint concordance on CE and PCE estimates can be seen by examining tables 6.2A, 6.2B, and 6.2C, which show results for 1992 and 2010. Overall results are shown in each table with table 6.2A including those for durables, table 6.2B those for nondurables, and table 6.2C those for services. Overall, CE-to-PCE-ratios decreased from 70 percent to 58 percent for all goods and services; the ratios for comparables from 84 to 74 percent. The largest decrease was for comparable durables with a 1992 CE-to-PCE ratio of 82 percent followed by a CE-to-PCE ratio of 62 percent for 2010. Among the largest declines in CE-to-PCE ratios in the durables category are for furniture and furnishings, sporting equipment and supplies, and jewelry and watches. Increases in the ratios are present for household appliances and photographic equipment; thus, there appears to be better reporting of expenditures in the CE for these by 2010 compared to 1992.

Aggregate CE expenditures as a share of PCE expenditures fell also for nondurables. Comparable CE nondurables represented about 70 percent of PCE expenditures in 1992 compared to 63 percent by 2010. Some of the most important declines are for food purchased for off-premises consumption, alcoholic and nonalcoholic beverages for off-premises consumption, apparel, tobacco, and newspapers and periodicals. On the other hand, CE-to PCE-ratios increased from 1992 to 2010 for pharmaceutical products and pets and related products.

Aggregate comparable CE and PCE service expenditures are the most similar in magnitude of the three categories of expenditures. For this analysis, reported rental equivalence from the CE is used rather than the shelter expenditures for owners; shelter expenditures are used in section 6.2 for the comparison of published CE aggregates to PCE aggregates. Aggregate expenditures for comparable CE services in 1992 accounted for 95 percent of PCE aggregates. However, by 2010 the ratio falls to 86 percent; the CE-to-PCE ratio is still high, but falling. The CE and PCE services that are most comparable also have comparable aggregate expenditures; these include rents and utilities and imputed rents of owner-occupied nonfarm housing. Among the CE aggregate expenditures that have decreased over time relative to PCE expenditures are those for gambling, veterinary and other services for pets, purchased meals and beverages, and personal care services. Increases in CE-to-PCE expenditures, based on ratios, have resulted for services related to audio-video, photographic, and information processing.

A major factor affecting the analysis of these results over the 1992–2010 period is the sharp drop in CE-to-PCE ratios that occurred between 2009

Table 6.3   Examples of Consumer Expenditure Survey and personal consumption expenditures (PCE): Categories by comparability

UCC description	PCE title	Notes/comments
Mattress and springs	Furniture	CE and PCE comparable
Other bedroom furniture	Furniture	CE and PCE comparable
Sofas	Furniture	CE and PCE comparable
Refrigerators, freezers (owned home)	Major household appliances	PCE comparable with CE estimate adjusted to account for movable appliances included with new homes
Washing machines (owned home)	Major household appliances	PCE comparable with CE estimate adjusted to account for movable appliances included with new homes
Tenant's insurance	Net household insurance	CE and PCE not comparable. Measured as premiums plus premium supplements less expected (normal) losses.
School books/supplies & equip. for elementary/high school	Stationery and miscellaneous printed materials	CE and PCE not comparable. Contains items that can be assigned to four other PCE categories. Candidate for allocation in the future.

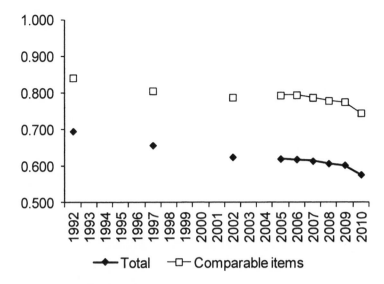

Fig. 6.1 Ratios of CE to PCE by year: Total

and 2010. The CE shows a drop in total expenditures from 2009 to 2010 of about $33 billion, while PCE shows an increase of over $379 billion. Based on recent history, there is reason to believe the PCE estimates for 2010 may be revised, leading to a change in the CE-to-PCE ratios.

The PCE data are typically revised as updated source data are received by the BEA. The 2010 PCE estimates used in the comparison came from the underlying detail table (table 2.4.5U from the BEA website) as of August 29, 2011. Based on that table, the total durables, nondurables, and services estimate was $9.965 trillion. When the 2010 PCE data were first reported in the February 2011 *Survey of Current Business*, the estimate was $10.086 trillion, about $120 billion higher than the August estimate.

If one looks at the course of PCE estimates for 2009, the first PCE estimate for total durables, nondurables, and services reported in the February 2010 *Survey of Current Business* was $9.827 trillion, a decline of about $24 billion from 2008. This estimate then declined as of March 1, 2010, to $9.823 trillion, on August 3, 2010, the estimate had dropped to $9.742 trillion, and on October 28, 2011, it had fallen to $9.586 trillion, the estimate used in deriving these ratios. In addition, these revisions increased the drop in PCE estimates between 2008 and 2009 from $24 billion to $165 billion.

Figures 6.1, 6.2, 6.3, and 6.4 show the trends in CE-to-PCE ratios from 1992 to 2010. Ratios for all goods and services and those that are comparable based on the joint concordance are presented. The declines in CE-to-PCE expenditures are clearly visible in these. The ratios for nondurables are the most level over the time period (figure 6.4).

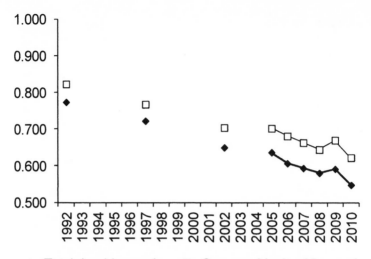

Fig. 6.2 Ratios of CE to PCE by year: Durables

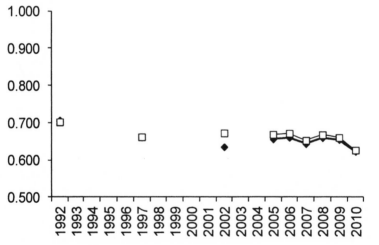

Fig. 6.3 Ratios of CE to PCE by year: Nondurables

6.5 Summary and Future Directions

The joint CE and PCE concordance, developed recently by staff within the BEA and BLS, results in a comparison of CE and PCE aggregates that are more meaningful than concordances used in the past. Results show declines in CE survey expenditures compared to PCE aggregates, even while accounting

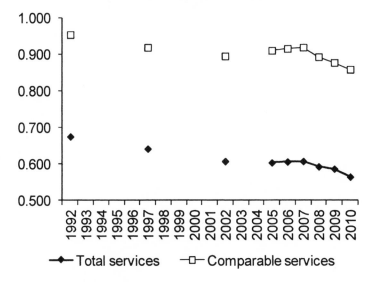

Fig. 6.4 Ratios of CE to PCE by year: Services

for comparability. The good news is that CE-to-PCE ratios for nondurables are fairly consistent over time. The bad news is that expenditures for durables are diverging at a greater rate each year, though this assumes PCE estimates will not undergo future revisions. While services have been made more similar through the concordance, the trend in CE expenditures, relative to PCE, is declining.

Future research, focused on the PCE, includes delving into the decision-making process to allocate expenditures to PCE and examining in detail the quality of the underlying data. Within the BLS, attention to allocations of expenditures across PCE categories and methods to increase data quality will continue. Although the BLS program that produces the CE is noted for the quality of its customer outreach, planning tools and its willingness to assess its products critically, studies conducted inside and outside of the BLS indicate that underreporting remains a problem for some categories of expenditures. Updated comparisons with the PCE indicate that expenditures as measured in the CE are still less than similar expenditures in the PCE. The CE program is actively working to address underreporting problems. For example, the underreporting problem with income essentially was solved through the use of imputation (see Passero 2009). Other research on methods to reduce underreporting and nonresponse is discussed in Goldenberg and Ryan (2009), Fricker, Kopp, and To (chapter 12, this volume), and in documents available on the BLS Gemini website.[14]

14. Bureau of Labor Statistics, Gemini Project website, http://stats.bls.gov/cex/geminiproject.htm.

References

Attanasio, Orazio P., Erich Battistin, and Andrew Leicester. 2006. "From Micro to Macro, from Poor to Rich: Consumption and Income in the UK and the US." Paper presented at National Poverty Center conference "Consumption, Income, and the Well-Being of Families and Children," Washington, DC, April 20.

Attanasio, Orazio P., and Guglielmo Weber. 1995. "Is Consumption Growth Consistent with Intertemporal Optimization? Evidence from the Consumer Expenditure Survey." *Journal of Political Economy* 103 (6): 1121–57.

Battistin, Erich, and Mario Padula. 2008. "Errors in Survey Reports of Consumption Expenditures." http://www.cide.info/conf/2009/iceee2009_submission_174.pdf.

Bee, Adam, Bruce D. Meyer, and James X. Sullivan. 2012. "Micro and Macro Validation of the Consumer Expenditure Survey." http://harrisschool.uchicago.edu/faculty/articles/Bee_Meyer_Sullivan_March2012.pdf.

Bosworth, Barry, Gary Burtless, and John Sabelhaus. 1991. "The Decline in Saving: Evidence from Household Surveys." *Brookings Papers on Economic Activity* 1991 (1): 183–241.

Bureau of Labor Statistics. 2008. "Consumer Expenditure Survey Compared with Personal Consumption Expenditures." *Consumer Expenditure Survey, 2004–2005*, Report 1008, 6–11. October.

Fernandez-Villaverde, Jesus, and Dirk Krueger. 2007. "Consumption over the Life Cycle: Facts from Consumer Expenditure Survey Data." *Review of Economics and Statistics* 89:552–65.

Garner, Thesia I., George Janini, William Passero, Laura Paszkiewicz, and Mark Vendemia. 2006. "The CE and the PCE: A Comparison." *Monthly Labor Review* 129 (9): 20–46. http://stats.bls.gov/opub/mlr/2006/09/art3full.pdf.

Garner, Thesia I., Robert McClelland, and William Passero. 2009. "Strengths and Weaknesses of the Consumer Expenditure Survey from a BLS Perspective." Paper presented at the NBER Summer Institute, Conference on Research on Income and Wealth, July. http://www.bls.gov/cex/pce_compare_199207.pdf.

Garner, Thesia I., and Kathleen Short. 2009. "Accounting for Owner-Occupied Dwelling Services: Aggregates and Distributions." *Journal of Housing Economics* 18 (3): 233–48.

Goldenberg, Karen, and Jay Ryan. 2009. "Evolution and Change in the Consumer Expenditure Surveys: Adapting Methodologies to Meet Changing Needs." National Bureau of Economic Research, Conference on Research in Income and Wealth, Summer Institute 2009, Cambridge Massachusetts, July 13–14.

Houthakker, Henrik S., and Lester D. Taylor. 1970. *Consumer Demand in the United States: Analyses and Projections*, 2nd ed. Cambridge, MA: Harvard University Press.

Kunze, Kurt, and Stephanie H. McCulla. 2008. "Preview of Revised NIPA Estimates for 2002: Effects of Incorporating the 2002 Benchmark I-O Accounts Proposed Definition and Statistical Changes." *Survey of Current Business* March:10–17.

Maki, Atsushi, and Thesia I. Garner. 2010. "Estimation of the Misreporting Models Using Micro-Data Sets Derived from the Consumer Expenditure Survey: The Gap between Macro and Micro Economic Statistics on Consumer Durables." *Journal of Mathematical Sciences: Advances and Applications* 4:123–52.

McCully, Clinton. 2011. "Trends in Consumer Spending and Personal Saving, 1959–2009." *Survey of Current Business* 91 (6): 14.

McCully, Clinton P., Brian C. Moore, and Kenneth J. Stewart. 2007. "A Reconciliation between the Consumer Price Index and the Personal Consumption Expendi-

tures Price Index." Bureau of Economic Analysis, Washington, DC. http://www
.bea.gov/papers/pdf/cpi_pce.pdf.

McCully, Clinton P., and Steven Payson. 2009. "Preview of the 2009 Comprehensive Revision of the NIPAs: Statistical Changes." *Survey of Current Business* May:6–16.

McCully, Clinton P., and Teresita D. Teensma. 2008. "Preview of the 2009 Comprehensive Revision of the National Income and Product Accounts: New Classifications for Personal Consumption Expenditures." *Survey of Current Business* May:6–17.

Meyer, Bruce D., and James X. Sullivan. 2009. "Five Decades of Consumption and Income Poverty." NBER Working Paper no. 14827, Cambridge, MA.

———. 2010. "Consumption and Income Inequality in the US since the 1960s." Working Paper, University of Notre Dame.

Meyer, Bruce D., and James X. Sullivan. 2011. "Viewpoint: Further Results on Measuring the Well-Being of the Poor Using Income and Consumption." *Canadian Journal of Economics* 44 (1): 52–87.

Parker, Jonathan A., and Bruce Preston. 2005. "Precautionary Saving and Consumption Fluctuations." *American Economic Review* 95 (4): 1119–43.

Passero, William. 2009. "The Impact of Income Imputation in the Consumer Expenditure Survey." *Monthly Labor Review* 132 (8): 25–42. http://stats.bls.gov/opub/mlr/2009/08/art3full.pdf.

Passero, William, Thesia I. Garner, Clinton McCully, and Caitlin Blair. 2011. "Understanding the Relationship: CE Survey, the CPI, and PCE." Presentation at the conference on Improving the Measurement of Consumer Expenditures, Washington, DC, December 2–3.

Slesnick, Daniel T. 1992. "Aggregate Consumption and Saving in the Postwar United States." *Review of Economics and Statistics* 74 (4): 585–97.

———. 1998. "Are Our Data Relevant to the Theory? The Case of Aggregate Consumption." *Journal of Business and Economic Statistics* 16 (1): 52–61.

———. 2000. *Consumption and Social Welfare: Living Standards and their Distribution in the United States.* Cambridge: Cambridge University Press.

Tucker, Clyde, Paul Biemer, and Brian Meekins. 2005. "Estimating the Level of Underreporting of Expenditures among Expenditure Reporters: A Micro-Level Latent Class Analysis." American Statistical Association, 2005 Proceedings of the Section on Survey Research Methods, Washington, DC.

The Validity of Consumption Data
Are the Consumer Expenditure Interview and Diary Surveys Informative?

Adam Bee, Bruce D. Meyer, and James X. Sullivan

7.1 Introduction

The Consumer Expenditure (CE) Survey is a vital data source. Assessing and improving the quality of the CE is a major policy and research issue for several reasons. The CE is the source of weights for the Consumer Price Index (CPI), which is used to index for inflation income tax brackets, government transfer payments such as Social Security benefits, private labor contracts, and other economic variables. The CE is also the only comprehensive source of consumption information on the US population.[1] The survey is used by government agencies for several purposes and has been extensively used by outside researchers. The CE data have been used to address a long list of research issues that would be difficult or impossible to address with another source. The survey has been available in some form for almost a century, and in its current form for over thirty years. This long history allows researchers to examine changes over a long time period.

Adam Bee is an economist at the US Census Bureau. Bruce D. Meyer is the McCormick Foundation Professor in the Harris School of Public Policy at the University of Chicago and a research associate of the National Bureau of Economic Research. James X. Sullivan is associate professor of economics at the University of Notre Dame.

This chapter does not necessarily reflect the views of the US Census Bureau. We would like to thank Tom Crossley, Thesia Garner, Steve Henderson, Clinton McCully, William Passero, and Laura Paszkiewicz for their help and participants at the CRIW/NBER conference on Improving the Measurement of Consumer Expenditures for their comments. We also thank Kevin Rinz for research assistance. For acknowledgments, sources of research support, and disclosure of the authors' material financial relationships, if any, please see http://www.nber.org/chapters/c12662.ack.

1. There are recent efforts to gather comprehensive but less detailed expenditure data as part of other surveys (see, e.g., Hurd and Rohwedder 2011; Li et al. 2010). An interesting aspect of these papers, given the focus of the current paper, is that these efforts assess the quality of their data by comparing it to that of the CE.

Many previous studies have compared the CE to other data sources. Some of these comparisons report alarming patterns. Several authors have pointed out that the weight on housing is much higher in the CPI than in the personal consumption expenditure (PCE) deflator. Bosworth (2010) argues that the housing weight is about twice as large in the CPI as the PCE because of uneven underreporting in the CE. Other authors have emphasized that the ratio of CE expenditures to PCE expenditures has declined from about 0.8 to just above 0.6 in recent decades (Attanasio, Battistin, and Leicester 2006). It is important to recognize that these earlier studies often compare expenditures that are noncomparable.

There are important gaps in our knowledge from these comparisons. A key gap is that comparisons of CE aggregates to national income account data are generally done with the integrated data that are a confusing amalgam of the two components of the CE: the interview survey and the diary survey. Researchers generally use one or the other of these components, so the benchmarking of the amalgam cannot be applied to the data that are typically used by researchers. A better understanding of the quality of spending data in each of these surveys will also inform efforts to redesign the CE, as the Bureau of Labor Statistics (BLS) is in the midst of a multiyear redesign of the surveys. The first reason given for the CE redesign in the BLS planning documents is underreporting of expenditures (Bureau of Labor Statistics 2010). To evaluate the separate components of the survey, it is necessary to compare them separately to outside sources.

In this chapter we examine comparisons of CE data to micro- and macrodata from other sources. We examine the quality of reported expenditures, which can be roughly thought of as outlays, as well as parts of consumption, which can be thought of as a flow of resources used, including the flow of resources from the ownership of durables. The rental equivalent of owner-occupied housing, while not part of expenditures, is used to determine the CPI weights and is an appropriate measure of housing consumption. In the case of vehicles, an expenditures measure would include purchases, but consumption should be based on a flow of resources consumed, which depends on the number and value of vehicles. These durable measures are crucial in calculating consumption, but their reporting has not been extensively validated. Keeping in mind that mean squared error is equal to bias squared plus variance, we also examine the variance of the data and the frequency of reports of no spending. Last, we examine the representativeness of the interview survey along a number of dimensions, including income.

We begin by examining ratios of CE aggregate data to national income account data, looking separately at the interview survey and diary survey. We rely on information from the BLS and the Bureau of Economic Analysis as to which expenditure categories are most comparable and we focus on these. We find that most of the largest categories of consumption are measured well in the interview survey, as the ratio to PCE data is close to one and has not declined appreciably over time. These categories include new vehicles, food and beverages at home, rent and utilities, the rental equivalent of owner-occupied housing, gasoline and other energy goods, and communication. Several other large categories are reported at a low rate or have seen the ratio to the PCE decline over time. These categories include food away from home, furniture and furnishings, clothing, gambling, and alcohol. There are no large diary survey categories that are both measured well and reported at a higher rate than in the interview survey. Overall, the categories of expenditures that are not reported well tend to be those that involve many small and irregular purchases. These poorly reported categories also tend to be private goods (clothing), ones that one may not want to reveal that one buys (alcohol, tobacco), and certain luxuries (alcohol, food away from home). Large salient purchases like automobiles, and regular purchases like rent, utilities, and groceries, seem to be well reported. We find that the number and value of cars compare closely to outside sources, and the time pattern of home values closely follows other data.

We also present evidence on the precision of interview and diary survey data. Coefficients of variation are noticeably higher in the diary survey than in the interview survey. Diary respondents are much more likely to report zero spending for a consumption category, and a high and increasing fraction of respondents report zero for all categories. For example, 11.9 percent of 2010 diary survey respondents report zero spending for an entire week, up from 4.5 percent in 1991.

We then compare the demographic characteristics and the income distribution reported in the CE and the Current Population Survey (CPS). The results suggest that the CE interview sample is fairly representative along many dimensions. However, Sabelhaus et al. (chapter 8, this volume) provides strong evidence of underrepresentation at the top of the income distribution and underreporting of income and expenditures at the top. They find that low-income households are well represented. The underrepresentation of high-income households and their disproportionate underreporting of expenditures means that the aggregate reporting rates relative to the PCE emphasized in the paper likely understate the underreporting problem for high-income households, but overstate the problem for low-income households.

These results have implications for the use of existing CE data and for the redesign of the CE survey. The importance of the underreporting of expenditures in the CE will depend on the purpose for which the data are used. Uses of the data that rely on aggregates are likely biased. Our results suggest the CPI is biased because the differential underreporting means that the weights do not accurately reflect consumers' purchases. However, a simple comparison of PCE and CPI weights overstates the potential bias in consumer prices because much of the PCE is not intended to be captured by the

CPI. Given evidence that the CE may be more likely to miss spending near the top of the distribution, underreporting is less of a concern for analyses that do not rely on spending at the top, such as measures of consumption poverty or median consumption. And, the high and fairly constant reporting rates for large categories of consumption in the interview survey suggest that, for some purposes, researchers can rely on these categories to address some of the concerns about underreporting.

The outline of the remainder of the chapter is as follows: In section 7.2 we describe the interview and diary components of the CE. Section 7.3 summarizes past work comparing the CE to other sources. In section 7.4 we provide our comparisons of the separate interview and diary surveys to national income account personal consumption expenditure data. In section 7.5 we provide comparisons of CE data on the ownership and value of durable goods to those from other sources. In section 7.6 we examine the precision of the data and the frequency of no reported expenditures in the interview and diary surveys. In section 7.7 we consider the representativeness of the CE survey. We discuss the implications of our results for uses of the CE survey and for survey redesign in section 7.8, and conclude in section 7.9.

7.2 The Consumer Expenditure Survey

The Consumer Expenditure survey is a national survey designed to represent the noninstitutionalized civilian population of the United States. The survey has two parts: the interview survey and the diary survey. Both components are based on the same sampling frame, but they have different questionnaires that are administered to different samples. We examine the data from both of these surveys.

The interview survey took its current form in 1980, though it began much earlier. It includes about 5,000 families each quarter between 1980 and 1998 and about 7,500 families thereafter. It is a recall survey that collects information from families (or consumer units) about their expenditures for the previous three months. The survey is a rotating panel—about 20 percent of the sample is replaced each quarter. Consumer units remain in the sample for up to five interviews—an initial bounding interview, followed by four quarterly interviews. The bounding interview collects information on demographic characteristics and ownership of major durables. Data from the bounding interview are not publicly available. The next four interviews collect detailed expenditure information in addition to demographic, employment, and income data. The interviews are generally done in person, though phone interviews have become more common in recent years. Starting in 2003, interviewers used a Computer Assisted Personal Interview (CAPI) instrument. The interview lasts sixty minutes on average.

The diary survey collects consumer unit spending through direct record-keeping. On a daily expense record, consumer units are asked to self-report spending for up to two consecutive one-week periods. This recordkeeping format is designed to capture spending on small, infrequent purchases that may be missed in a recall survey. The diary survey also includes a questionnaire that collects information on household characteristics. This questionnaire is administered by an interviewer. Since 2004, a CAPI instrument has been used for this interview. The diary survey includes about 5,000 households annually. See US Bureau of Labor Statistics (2012) for more details.

Not all types of spending are collected in both surveys (US Bureau of Labor Statistics 2012). For example, the interview survey does not collect spending on housekeeping supplies, personal care products, and nonprescription drugs, while the diary survey does not capture overnight trips expenses or credit and installment plan payments. The diary survey also does not collect information on the rental equivalent value of owned homes, which is a major component of any total consumption measure, is one of the largest PCE categories, and is weighted very heavily in calculations of the CPI. While the diary survey is designed to capture other types of spending, in practice many important categories, such as new vehicle purchases, are rarely reported.

The diary and interview surveys are also designed for different purposes (US Bureau of Labor Statistics 2012). The interview survey is designed to capture relatively large expenditures and those that occur regularly such as rent or mortgage payments. The diary survey, on the other hand, is designed to capture smaller spending categories and those purchased more frequently. Often the level of detail is much greater in the diary survey. For example, in the 2010 survey, the diary survey has more than one hundred detailed subcategories that fall under the classification of food at home, while the interview survey has only one spending classification for food at home.

7.3 Earlier Consumer Expenditure Survey Comparisons

The CE data have been compared to data from many sources, but the most extensive and heavily cited comparisons are to the personal consumption expenditure (PCE) data from the National Income and Product Accounts (NIPA). Past research (Gieseman 1987; Slesnick 1992; Branch 1994; Garner et al. 2006; Garner, McClelland, and Passero 2009; Attanasio, Battistin, and Leicester 2006; Meyer and Sullivan 2011b) has emphasized a discrepancy between CE and PCE data. In comparing the CE to the PCE data, it is important to recognize conceptual incompatibilities between these data sources.[2] Slesnick (1992), when comparing CE data from 1960–1961 through 1989, concluded that "approximately one-half of the difference between aggregate expenditures reported in the CEX surveys and the NIPA

2. See Deaton and Kozel (2005) for discussion of noncomparabilities between survey and national income account data for expenditures.

can be accounted for through definitional differences" (593-94). Similarly the General Accounting Office (1996), in their summary of a Bureau of Economic Analysis comparison of the differences in 1992, reported that "more than half was traceable to definitional differences."

A key conceptual difference between PCE and CE spending is that the CE measures out-of-pocket spending by households, while the PCE definition is wider, including purchases made on behalf of households by institutions such as employer-paid insurance or free financial services, and purchases made by nonprofits. The magnitude of this difference in how spending is defined has increased over time. McCully (2011) reported that in 2009 nearly 30 percent of the PCE was not intended to be captured by the CE, up from just over 7 percent in 1959. In 2009, these differences include imputations such as those for owner-occupied housing and financial services (but excluding purchases by nonprofit institutions serving households and employer contributions for group health insurance) that account for over 10 percent of the PCE. In-kind social benefits account for almost another 10 percent. Employer contributions for group health insurance and workers' compensation account for over 6 percent, while life insurance and pension fund expenses and final consumption expenditures of nonprofits represent almost 4 percent. Another important difference between the PCE and CE is that the CE is not intended to capture purchases by those abroad, on military bases, and in institutions.

It is also important to note that the PCE aggregates do not necessarily reflect true total spending. The PCE numbers are the product of a great deal of estimation and imputation that is subject to error.[3] One indicator of the potential error in the PCE is the magnitude of the revisions that are made from time to time (Gieseman 1987; Slesnick 1992). An indication of this is the 2009 revisions to the PCE that substantially revised past estimates of several categories. Notably, food at home, one of the largest categories, decreased by over 5 percent after the 2009 revision.[4]

One of the first evaluations of the current CE is Gieseman (1987), who reports CE comparisons to the PCE for 1980–1984.[5] He reports separate comparisons of interview survey and diary survey estimates, though the diary estimates are only for food. In these early years, published tabulations

3. The PCE estimates come from business records reported on the economic censuses and other Census Bureau surveys. These business surveys are subject to a number of sources of error and are adjusted using input-output tables to add imports and subtract sales that do not go to domestic households. These totals are then balanced to control totals for incomes earned, retail sales, and other benchmark data.
4. The 2008 value for food at home was 741,189 (in millions of USD) prior to revision and 669,441 after, but the new definition excludes pet food. A comparable prerevision number excluding pet food is 707,553. The drop from 707,553 to 669,441 is 5.4 percent. Thank you to Clinton McCully for clarifying this revision.
5. Comparisons of expenditure survey data to national income accounts data go back at least to Houthakker and Taylor (1970).

separate interview and diary data, while published data for later years are integrated.[6] Consequently, subsequent comparisons of CE to PCE almost exclusively rely on the integrated data that combine interview survey and diary survey data.[7] Gieseman found that the CE reports were close to the PCE for rent, fuel and utilities, telephone services, furniture, transportation, and personal care services. On the other hand, substantially lower reporting of food, household furnishings, alcohol, tobacco, clothing, and entertainment were apparent back in 1980–1984. In separate interview survey and diary survey comparisons for food at home, he found that the CE/PCE ratios for the interview survey exceeded that for the diary survey by 10 to 20 percentage points, but were still below 1. For the much smaller category, food away from home, the diary survey ratios exceeded the interview survey ratios by about 20 percentage points, but again were considerably below 1. The current patterns have strong similarities to these from thirty years ago.

Garner et al. (2006) report a long historical series of comparisons for the integrated data that begins in 1984 and goes up through 2002. Some categories are reported well. Rent, utilities, etc. and utilities, fuels, and related are reported at a high and stable rate over time relative to the PCE. Telephone services, vehicle purchases, and gasoline and motor oil are reported at a high rate that has declined somewhat over time. Food at home relative to the PCE is about 0.70, but has remained stable over time. The many remaining categories of expenditures have low and generally falling rates of reporting relative to the PCE, though some small categories such as footwear and vehicle rentals show increases.

The authors ultimately argue that this historical series can be replaced by a better series that focuses on categories that are the most comparable. "A more detailed description of the categories of items from the CE and the PCE is utilized than was used when the historical comparison methodology was developed. Consequently, more comparable product categories are constructed and are included in the final aggregates and ratios used in the new comparison of the two sets of estimates" (22). The authors note that aggregates from the two sources tend to be more different for noncomparable categories. The new series is reported for every five years from 1992 to 2002 in Garner et al. (2006), and updated and extended annually through 2007 in Garner, McClelland, and Passero (2009).

When this new BLS methodology on categories that are comparable between the CE and the PCE is used, and when the PCE aggregates are adjusted to reflect differences in population coverage between the two sources, the ratio of CE to PCE is fairly high, but still has tended to fall

---

6. In cases where the expenditure category is available in both surveys, the BLS selects the source for the integrated data that is viewed as most reliable. See Steinberg et al. (2010) and Creech and Steinberg (2011).

7. Exceptions include Meyer and Sullivan (2010; 2011b).

over time. The ratio for 1992 and 1997 is 0.88, while in 2002 it is 0.84 and has fallen to 0.81 by 2007 (Garner, McClelland, and Passero 2009). The share of the PCE that is comparable to the CE has also tended to fall somewhat over time, dropping from 0.57 in 1992 to 0.52 in 2007. A much larger share of the CE is comparable to the PCE, slightly over 70 percent in all years.

For nine of the larger expenditure categories, Meyer and Sullivan (2010, 2011b) report limited comparisons over time for the interview survey only. They find that for most of these major categories reporting rates are high and stable.

Some research has sharply overstated the discrepancy by comparing non-comparable categories of CE and NIPA consumption and ignoring definitional differences. In addition, almost all comparisons are based on the integrated data that combine CE diary and CE interview data, so the results are not applicable to either the CE interview data or diary data alone, as they are typically used in research. Some authors have argued that despite the incompatibilities between the CE and PCE, in the absence of definitional changes one would expect the differences between the series to be relatively constant (Attanasio, Battistin, and Leicester 2006). This conclusion is not at all obvious; one might still expect a gradual widening of the difference between the sources given their rapidly growing incompatibility as reported in McCully (2011).

There have been comparisons of the CE to many other sources. Most are summarized on the BLS comparisons web page.[8] These comparisons include utilities compared to the Residential Energy Consumption Survey (RECS), rent and utilities compared to that reported in the American Housing Survey (AHS), food at home compared to trade publications *Supermarket Business* and *Progressive Grocer*, health expenditures compared to the National Health Expenditure Accounts (NHEA) and the Medical Expenditure Panel Survey (MEPS). With the exception of health expenditures, the comparisons generally suggest that the CE does a fairly good job of reporting these types of expenditures. However, except for health expenditures, these comparisons are to categories for which the comparisons to the PCE have indicated high and roughly stable reporting, though the reporting of food at home is at a lower rate, especially in the diary survey. See Garner, McClelland, and Passero (2009) or Branch (1994) for summaries.

7.4 Separate Interview and Diary Survey Comparisons to National Income Accounts

For the purposes of assessing CE survey quality, it is important to examine the interview and diary surveys separately. Differences in spending across these two data sources provide evidence on how best to collect

---

8. http://www.bls.gov/cex/cecomparison.htm.

spending data. For some important categories there are large differences between the mean reported values in the interview and diary surveys. For example, between 1998 and 2003, average spending on food at home in the CE interview survey exceeded the average from the CE diary survey by more than 20 percent.[9]

Recognizing that not all noncomparabilities can be removed, we examine the ratio of CE interview and diary survey values weighted by population to corresponding categories of PCE data for select PCE categories.[10] We have followed the approach of Garner et al. (2006), Garner, McClelland, and Passero (2009), and Passero (2011) who select categories in the PCE and CE that are most comparable based on "concepts and comprehensiveness." These comparable categories are 56 percent of the PCE in 2010. To align each CE spending subcategory with the comparable PCE category, we have heavily relied on a concordance supplied to us by the BLS. The data appendix in Bee, Meyer, and Sullivan (2012) notes the cases where expenditure subcategories are not available in either the interview or diary survey, and appendix table 1 in that paper provides our concordance of Universal Classification Codes (UCCs) in the diary and interview survey for each of these comparable PCE categories. In tables 7.1 and 7.2, we report CE/PCE ratios for categories of expenditures for which we can define reasonably comparable CE and PCE categories for either the interview or the diary survey alone.[11] Table 7.1 summarizes the findings for the largest categories in 2010. Table 7.2 reports the results for forty-six comparable categories for 1986 and 2010. Additional years are available in appendix table 2 of Bee, Meyer, and Sullivan (2012).

Among the ten largest categories in table 7.1 (combining the BLS subcategories of clothing into one so that it is large enough to be in the top ten), six are reported at a high rate in the interview survey and that rate has been roughly constant over time. These well-measured categories are the imputed rent on owner-occupied nonfarm housing, rent and utilities, food and nonalcoholic beverages purchased for off-premises consumption (food at home), gasoline and other energy goods, communication, and new motor vehicles. These six categories are all among the eight largest. In 2010,

9. The fact that food at home from the interview survey compares more favorably to PCE numbers than does food at home from the CE diary survey does not necessarily imply that the former is reported more accurately. For example, the CE interview survey numbers may include nonfood items purchased at a grocery store. Battistin (2003) argues that the higher reporting of food at home for the recall questions in the interview component is due to overreporting, but as Browning, Crossley, and Weber (2003) state, this is open to question. We stick to the presumption that more is better, as the CE is almost always below the PCE and this criteria is largely used by the BLS in selecting which source, interview or diary, is preferred for a particular expenditure category (see Creech and Steinberg 2011).

10. We do not correct for differences in population coverage. Such corrections have averaged 2 to 3 percentage points in past analyses (Garner et al. 2006; Garner, McClelland, and Passero 2009).

11. A larger set of categories can be examined, of course, with the union of the interview and diary data.

Table 7.1   CE-PCE comparisons for ten large categories, 2010 (in millions of dollars)

PCE category	PCE	DS/PCE	IS/PCE
Imputed rental of owner-occupied nonfarm housing	1,203,053		1.065
Rent and utilities	668,759	0.797	0.946
Food and nonalc. beverages purchased for off-premises consumption (food at home)	659,382	0.656	0.862
Purchased meals and beverages (food away from home)	533,078	0.508	0.528
Gasoline and other energy goods	354,117	0.725	0.779
Clothing	256,672	0.487	0.317
Communication	223,385	0.686	0.800
New motor vehicles	178,464		0.961
Furniture and furnishings	140,960	0.433	0.439
Alcoholic beverages purchased for off-premises consumption	106,649	0.253	0.220

Notes: The PCE category name for food at home is "food and nonalcoholic beverages purchased for off-premises consumption." The PCE category name for food away from home is "purchased meals and beverages." DS = Diary Survey; IS = Interview Survey.

the ratio of interview survey to PCE exceeds 0.94 for imputed rent, rent and utilities, and new motor vehicles. It exceeds 0.80 for food at home and communication and is just below 0.80 for gasoline and other energy goods. The 2010 ratios for both the interview and diary surveys are just over 0.50 for purchased meals and beverages (food away from home) and close to 0.43 for furniture and furnishings. For clothing and alcohol, the interview survey ratios are both low and below the diary survey ratios, which are below half themselves.

While the diary survey is designed to capture most types of spending, in practice many categories are missed, including some of the largest categories. For example, no spending on new trucks, pick-ups, vans, or jeeps is captured in the diary survey between 2007 and 2010. For this reason, we do not report a diary survey/PCE ratio for new motor vehicles in table 7.1. The diary survey/PCE ratio for imputed rental of owner-occupied nonfarm housing (the largest PCE category we examine) is also missing because the diary survey does not collect information on the rental equivalent of owned homes.

Looking at the full forty-six categories reported in table 7.2, among the remaining categories outside the top ten in size, only six in the interview and five in the diary survey have a ratio of at least 0.80 in 2010. The largest of these categories reported well in the interview survey are motor vehicle accessories and parts, household maintenance, and cable and satellite television and radio services. In the diary survey, household cleaning products and cable and satellite television and radio services are reported well in 2010, though the historical pattern for both exhibits substantial variation (also see appendix table 2 of Bee, Meyer, and Sullivan [2012]). The remaining

Table 7.2 Aggregate Consumer Expenditure (CE) interview and diary survey and personal consumption expenditures (PCE), 1986 and 2010 (in millions of dollars)

PCE category	2010					1986				
	PCE	CE DS	CE IS	DS/PCE	IS/PCE	PCE	CE DS	CE IS	DS/PCE	IS/PCE
Total durables, nondurables, and services										
Total	9,965,306					2,841,379				
Comparable items (no. of categories differ for interview and diary survey)		2,315,529	3,998,836	0.57	0.74		900,434	1,502,609	0.66	0.85
Durable goods										
Total durable goods	1,085,484					421,440				
Comparable durable goods (no. of categories differ for IS and DS)		184,531	376,802	0.38	0.53		83,907	293,296	0.47	0.88
New motor vehicles	178,464		171,450		0.96	134,047		154,574		1.15
Motor vehicle accessories and parts	26,558		23,474		0.88	11,446		7,065		0.62
Furniture and furnishings	140,960	61,010	61,859	0.43	0.44	59,392	26,928	45,494	0.45	0.77
Household appliances	40,536	27,323	30,034	0.67	0.74	21,243	10,689	17,644	0.50	0.83
Glassware, tableware, and household utensils	41,545	11,822	3,402	0.28	0.08	15,142	5,653	2,983	0.37	0.20
Televisions	37,407	11,730	14,379	0.31	0.38	11,635	3,772	6,741	0.32	0.58
Audio equipment	19,019	5,703	3,086	0.30	0.16	7,247	2,480	10,290	0.34	1.42
Recording media	33,077	6,892	4,985	0.21	0.15	10,429	2,923	3,246	0.28	0.31
Photographic equipment	2,844	3,860	2,937	1.36	1.03	2,997	1,488	1,812	0.50	0.60
Sporting equipment, supplies, guns, and ammunition	53,258	12,733	16,422	0.24	0.31	13,147	6,329	7,420	0.48	0.56
Bicycles and accessories	4,257	2,338	1,868	0.55	0.44	2,114	978	1,195	0.46	0.57
Pleasure boats	9,779		6,960		0.71	4,828		4,909		1.02
Other recreational vehicles	9,580		5,245		0.55	5,446		7,235		1.33
Recreational books	30,412	4,079	5,582	0.13	0.18	7,771	3,104	4,127	0.40	0.53
Musical instruments	4,939	1,845	1,848	0.37	0.37	1,606	271	2,586	0.17	1.61
Jewelry and watches	61,485	26,774	14,320	0.44	0.23	24,333	13,354	11,329	0.55	0.47
Telephone and facsimile equipment	13,991	3,941	4,126	0.28	0.29	1,256	1,286	1,089	1.02	0.87
Nondurable goods										
Total nondurable goods	2,301,517					774,189				
Comparable nondurable goods (no. of categories differ for IS and DS)		1,008,380	1,018,800	0.60	0.70		424,127	437,329	0.66	0.77
Food and nonalc. beverages purchased for off-premises consumption	659,382	432,541	568,134	0.66	0.86	273,849	184,751	217,242	0.67	0.79

Alcoholic beverages purchased for off-premises consumption	106,649	27,016	23,452	0.25	0.22	41,670	13,899	14,252	0.33	0.34
Women's and girls' clothing	161,192	80,450	49,737	0.50	0.31	77,933	49,664	43,353	0.64	0.56
Men's and boys' clothing	95,480	44,532	31,585	0.47	0.33	44,884	30,115	26,207	0.67	0.58
Clothing materials	4,203	1,227	687	0.29	0.16	3,057	652	1,059	0.21	0.35
Shoes and other footwear	59,334	36,679	17,896	0.62	0.30	24,464	15,689	11,896	0.64	0.49
Gasoline and other energy goods	354,117	256,573	275,691	0.72	0.78	91,191	76,406	96,671	0.84	1.06
Pets and related products	50,068	28,401		0.57		10,021	6,914		0.69	
Household cleaning products	41,287	47,597		1.15		18,156	16,993		0.94	
Household paper products	40,325	12,502		0.31		11,295	4,087		0.36	
Household linens	24,288	10,767	7,070	0.44	0.29	11,020	6,102	4,077	0.55	0.37
Sewing items	1,213	1,038	1,154	0.86	0.95	574	1,224	1,030	2.13	1.79
Tobacco	94,357	29,057	43,395	0.31	0.46	32,157	17,631	21,543	0.55	0.67
Services—household consumption expenditures										
Total services	6,578,305					1,645,750				
Comparable services (no. of categories differ for IS and DS)		1,122,618	2,603,234	0.60	0.83	392,400		771,984	0.72	0.92
Rent and utilities	668,759	533,202	632,560	0.80	0.95	225,758	187,547	217,782	0.83	0.96
Imputed rental of owner-occupied nonfarm housing	1,203,053	1,281,521		1.07		304,497	340,934			
Other motor vehicle services	58,612		33,654		0.57	9,552		7,701		0.81
Cable and satellite television and radio services	79,524	64,014	77,063	0.80	0.97	10,533	4,966	10,032	0.47	0.95
Photo processing	2,388	1,456	1,383	0.61	0.58	4,110	1,558	2,265	0.38	0.55
Photo studios	7,089	2,009	2,527	0.28	0.36	3,381	709		0.21	
Gambling	99,578	9,517	6,288	0.10	0.06	15,516	3,458		0.22	
Veterinary and other services for pets	25,669	19,101	17,401	0.74	0.68	3,660	2,909	3,578	0.79	0.98
Purchased meals and beverages	533,078	270,810	281,323	0.51	0.53	161,472	116,882	104,439	0.72	0.65
Communication	223,385	153,300	178,771	0.69	0.80	55,600	41,837	44,260	0.75	0.80
Legal services	96,788	6,573	15,590	0.07	0.16	27,348	2,858	7,155	0.10	0.26
Accounting and other business services	27,745	15,921	7,934	0.57	0.29	3,729	11,137	3,192	2.99	0.86
Funeral and burial services	19,048	1,365	11,442	0.07	0.60	7,091	1,270	5,824	0.18	0.82
Repair and hire of footwear	457	416	187	0.91	0.41	449	296	351	0.66	0.78
Child care	30,309	9,270	9,629	0.31	0.32	7,983	8,081	7,126	1.01	0.89
Household maintenance	55,216	35,664	45,961	0.65	0.83	20,539	8,892	17,347	0.43	0.84

Notes: Data are from the Consumer Expenditure interview and diary surveys and the US Bureau of Economic Analysis. Reported categories are only those where the CE and PCE are most comparable. Comparable categories follows Passero (2011). The PCE numbers are from table 2.4.5U. Personal consumption expenditures by type of product, accessed on November 21, 2011.

categories that are reported poorly in both surveys with ratios below one-half include glassware, tableware, and household utensils, and sporting equipment. Gambling and alcohol are especially badly reported with ratios below 0.20 and 0.33, respectively, in both surveys in most years.

While the ratios for selected years are shown in table 7.2, the patterns for the ten largest categories of expenditures can be more easily seen in a series of figures. We discuss the categories in order of their size beginning with the largest. Figure 7.1A reports the ratio of CE-to-PCE imputed rent from 1984 onward[12] and new motor vehicles from 1980 onward.[13] These two large categories are available for the interview survey, but not the diary survey.[14] Both categories compare favorably to the PCE—they have ratios near one that have not declined appreciably over time. The imputed rental of owner-occupied nonfarm housing in the interview survey typically exceeds the PCE equivalent by about 10 percent, slightly more so in the most recent years. While some analyses of CE-to-PCE aggregates omit housing because the ratio exceeds one (Sabelhaus et al., chapter 8, this volume), we include it because selecting only those categories with low ratios would necessarily bias the overall picture. The CE/PCE ratio for new motor vehicles is overall very close to one, approximately 1.05 in the 1980s, approximately 0.97 in the 1990s, and right around one in the first decade of the twenty-first century.

Figure 7.1B reports diary and interview comparisons for rent and utilities. In the interview survey the CE/PCE ratio is just below 1, averaging around 0.95, while the diary survey ratio is about 10 percentage points lower. Food at home in the interview and diary surveys is reported in figure 7.1C. Interview food at home has a ratio just under 0.90 in nearly all years except the period from 1981 to 1987, when a different wording of the food at home question was employed.[15] The diary survey ratio is about 20 percentage points lower at 0.70. Food away from home is reported in figure 7.1D. This category has a low ratio in both surveys and one that has declined since the 1980s. The diary survey ratio is also about 10 percentage points higher than the interview survey ratio, although the two surveys give similar numbers following

---

12. Information on the rental equivalent of the home is not available in the interview survey in 1980 and 1981.

13. For the surveys administered in the fourth quarter of 1981 through the fourth quarter of 1983, the CE sampling frame only covered urban areas. For this reason, we exclude data from the 1982 and 1983 surveys. In addition, the 1981 estimates we report are not entirely nationally representative, because part of this spending comes from the fourth quarter of the 1981 survey and the first quarter of the 1982 survey.

14. The diary survey does collect data on new vehicle purchases, but we do not report ratios for this category for the diary survey because these data appear to capture a small share of purchases. See the discussion in the data appendix in Bee, Meyer, and Sullivan (2012) for more details.

15. The effect of this change in wording has been known for a long time (see Gieseman 1987). During 1980–1981, the interview survey asked usual weekly expenditure on food over the past three months, while from 1982–1987 spending on food over the previous month was asked. In 1988, the survey returned to the earlier question. Because the January to March 1982 surveys collected data for part of 1981, the change in questionnaire is partly reflected in the 1981 totals.

a change in the wording of the food away question in the interview survey in 2007.[16] The ratio for the diary survey is biased downward somewhat because the diary survey does not collect data on food away from home spending that occurs during out-of-town trips. The interview survey does collect these data; in 2010 spending on food during out-of-town trips was about 6 percent of the PCE aggregate for food away. Ratios for spending on gasoline and other energy goods are displayed in figure 7.1E. The ratio is nearly always above 0.80 in the interview survey and about 5 to 10 percentage points lower in the diary survey. The interview survey ratio did fall over the 1980s. Clothing is shown in figure 7.1F, combining the categories of women's and girls' clothing, men's and boys' clothing, and shoes and footwear. This category is the first one that is reported poorly. The reporting ratio has declined from about 0.60 to less than one-half for the diary survey, with the interview survey consistently lower. The ratio for communication is shown in figure 7.1G. The interview survey shows a ratio of about 0.80 for most years, though there is a dip to nearly 0.70 for much of the 1990s and early in the twenty-first century. The diary survey ratio has been 5 to 10 percentage points lower since about 1996. Furniture and furnishings in figure 7.1H is badly reported with a ratio in the interview survey that falls over time from about 0.75 to 0.45. The ratio for this category is more variable in the diary survey, at about 0.50 in the early years, high in the middle years, and then near the interview survey numbers in the most recent years. Alcoholic beverages purchased for off-premises consumption in figure 7.1I is a very badly reported category, with both interview and diary survey ratios that drop from 0.33 to just over 0.20.

The overall pattern indicates much better reporting in the interview survey than the diary survey. Household cleaning products is the only category among the forty-six we report where the diary survey reports expenditures at a higher rate than the interview survey and reports them well, that is, at a high absolute rate that has not declined appreciably over time. This fairly small category has a ratio of 1.15 in 2010 in the diary survey and has not declined appreciably in the past twenty years. On the other hand, there are many categories of expenditures, in particular most of the largest ones, that are reported at a higher rate in the interview survey and have maintained high and roughly stable rates.

This finding of higher reporting in an interview survey is consistent with other evidence. There is a long history of papers that have noted the presence of "diary fatigue," meaning that respondents tire of completing the diary and omit purchases. Evidence of this pattern in the CE diary survey that is frequently cited is the fact that reported expenditures fall noticeably in the second diary week (US Bureau of Labor Statistics 1983; Silberstein and Scott 1991; Stephens 2003). See Crossley and Winter (chapter 1, this

16. Starting with the second quarter of 2007, the question on food away from home changed from a query about usual monthly spending to usual weekly spending. This change resulted in a noticeable increase in reported food away spending.

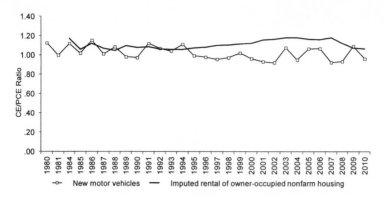

Fig. 7.1A Comparisons of CE interview aggregates to PCE aggregates, new motor vehicles and imputed rent

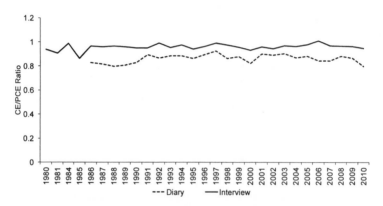

Fig. 7.1B Comparisons of CE diary and CE interview aggregates to PCE aggregates, rent and utilities

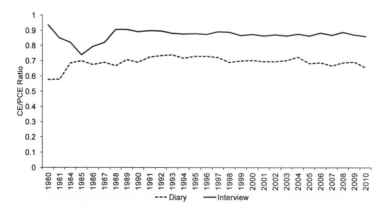

Fig. 7.1C Comparisons of CE diary and CE interview aggregates to PCE aggregates, food at home

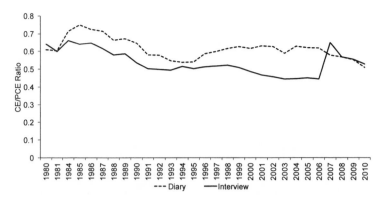

Fig. 7.1D Comparisons of CE diary and CE interview aggregates to PCE aggregates, food away from home

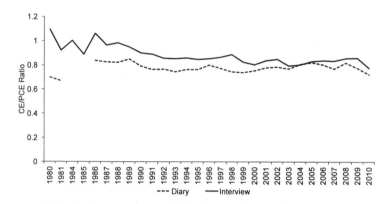

Fig. 7.1E Comparisons of CE diary and CE interview aggregates to PCE aggregates, gasoline and other energy goods

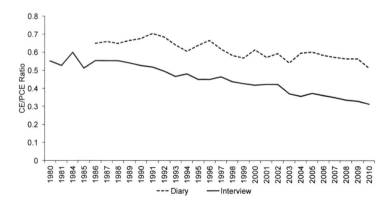

Fig. 7.1F Comparisons of CE diary and CE interview aggregates to PCE aggregates, clothing and shoes

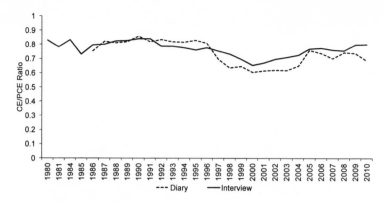

Fig. 7.1G Comparisons of CE diary and CE interview aggregates to PCE aggregates, communication

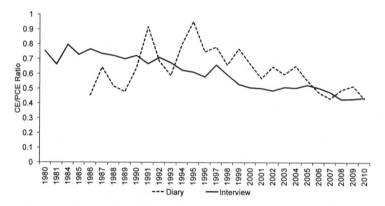

Fig. 7.1H Comparisons of CE diary and CE interview aggregates to PCE aggregates, furniture and furnishings

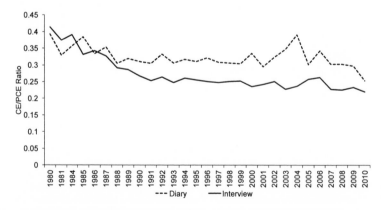

Fig. 7.1I Comparisons of CE diary and CE interview aggregates to PCE aggregates, alcoholic beverages

volume) for a nice discussion of diary fatigue and other problems with collecting expenditure data with a diary.

This pattern of lower reporting in diary surveys than interview surveys is also evident in other North American data. Statistics Canada conducted in parallel two versions of the Canadian Survey of Household Spending in 2009. One version was a twelve-month recall interview survey, while the second was the redesigned survey that gathers spending on many items through two-week diaries. The interview spending on average exceeds the diary spending for comparable categories by 9 percent for frequent expenses and 14 percent for less frequent expenses (Dubreuil et al. 2011). The authors believe the difference between the modes is not due to other features of the survey that changed, such as the elimination of balance editing. For example, balance editing tends to affect income and savings rather than expenditures. Possible reasons that this difference might arise are that insufficient motivation may lead diary respondents to omit many items to reduce the burden of the process. Consistent with this hypothesis, the Canadian Food Expenditure Survey (Ahmed, Brzozowski, and Crossley 2010) finds that the second diary week tends to have lower reported expenditures (by 11 percent) than the first, as respondents tire of the process. A recall measure from this same survey has food expenditures 14 percent higher than the two-week diary average.

In principle an attentive, motivated respondent could report better data in a diary than in a recall survey, but the evidence shows that the typical respondent does not fit this profile. The diary task also requires respondent effort at many distinct times during the two weeks, whereas an interview survey requires a single short (albeit taxing) interview. These results suggest that the presence of an interviewer may be helpful in coaxing greater compliance with the survey.

The categories of expenditures that are not reported well tend to be those that involve many small and irregular purchases. These poorly reported categories also tend to be private goods (clothing), ones that one may not want to reveal that one buys (alcohol, tobacco), and certain luxuries (alcohol, food away from home). Large salient purchases (like automobiles), and regular purchases like rent, utilities, and groceries, seem to be well reported. These patterns have been largely evident since the 1980s or even earlier. However, over the past three decades there has been a slow decline in the quality of reporting of many of the mostly smaller categories of expenditures in both the interview survey and the diary survey.

7.5 Durables in the CE

Reporting ownership of houses and vehicles is very different from reporting the small, discretionary purchases that seem to be badly reported in the CE. We begin by examining how the reported stock of cars matches that from other sources. This information does not enter expenditures, but enters consumption when we calculate a value of the services of owned cars. In table 7.3, we compare reported car and truck ownership in the interview survey to administrative data on motor vehicle registrations.

These comparisons are complicated by a number of issues. First, the CE is intended to capture only vehicles owned by households, but the registration data include commercial and publicly owned vehicles including farm trucks. We were able to obtain an estimate of the number of two types of commercial vehicles, taxis and rental cars, for four states. The taxi share ranged from 0.04 percent (Arizona in 2003) to 0.68 percent (New York in 1998). The rental car share ranged from 0.30 percent (Mississippi in 2004) to 1.54 percent (Arizona in 1998). We do not have an easy way to estimate the prevalence of corporate cars and other commercial vehicles.

Second, the registration data include leased vehicles and motor homes that are not included in the CE survey numbers. We were able to obtain estimates of the motor home shares for seven states. The share of motor homes ranged from 0.3 percent (Maine in 2007) to 1.8 percent (Oregon in 2000). The total number of leased cars and trucks in the CE survey for 2002 was 6.96 million, or about 3.75 percent of all cars and trucks. These first two complications imply that we understate the share of vehicles owned by households that are reported in the CE. Third, our survey count of vehicles will not include those that have been disposed of by the household, but have not been reported as disposed to the state or have not had their registrations expire. Conversely, registrations will not include vehicles that have not been registered. This issue, which is likely less important, could bias the measure of reporting either up or down. Fourth, prior to 1985, personal passenger vans, minivans, and utility vehicles were included in automobile registrations, while subsequently they were included in trucks. For this reason, we generally report comparisons for cars and trucks combined so that we have a consistent concept over time.

Bearing these caveats in mind, ratios of cars and trucks in the CE to those in the administrative records are reported in the bottom line of table 7.3. The ratios are consistently well above 0.80. Given that a large share of cars and trucks are commercially owned as the numbers in the previous paragraph suggest, these numbers indicate a very high reporting rate. In similar comparisons (appendix table 3 of Bee, Meyer, and Sullivan 2012), we find that the total number of reported trucks owned in the CE lines up closely with data from the Vehicle Inventory and Use Survey (VIUS)—all of the ratios of CE counts to VIUS counts are slightly over one.

We have also verified that the purchase price of vehicles in the CE interview survey is reported fairly well. Purchase prices are directly part of expenditures and also are used to determine the rental value of car ownership, which enters flow consumption. We validate the reported purchase price of new and used vehicles in the interview survey by comparing the reported values to published values in National Automobile Dealers Association (NADA) bluebook guides. For a sample of one hundred cars with a reported purchase price in each of the years 1990 and 2000, we compare the reported

Table 7.3 Comparison of vehicle ownership in the CE interview survey to motor vehicle registrations, 1972–2010 (in millions)

	1972	1973	1980	1987	1990	1992	1995	1997	2000	2002	2003	2004	2005	2006	2007	2008	2009
Automobiles																	
CE survey	89.6	80.6	105.8	120.7	121.6	120.7	121.2	116.6	113.7	116.2	118.3	114.4	106.8	106.6	107.7	108.3	108.3
State motor vehicle registrations	96.6	101.4	120.7	130.0	132.2	125.1	126.9	128.4	132.2	134.6	134.3	135.0	135.2	134.0	134.5	135.6	133.4
Ratio	0.928	0.795	0.876	0.928	0.920	0.965	0.955	0.908	0.860	0.863	0.881	0.848	0.790	0.795	0.801	0.798	0.812
Trucks																	
CE survey	10.1	9.9	25.8	33.2	39.3	42.5	52.1	56.1	63.5	69.6	74.1	86.2	87.6	89.0	90.4	91.8	92.4
State motor vehicle registrations	20.3	22.2	32.3	45.7	53.1	61.6	70.8	75.3	85.0	90.8	92.8	97.9	101.6	105.7	108.2	108.0	108.3
Ratio	0.498	0.447	0.801	0.727	0.740	0.690	0.736	0.744	0.747	0.766	0.798	0.881	0.862	0.842	0.835	0.850	0.853
Automobiles & trucks																	
CE survey	99.7	90.5	131.7	153.9	160.9	163.2	173.2	172.7	177.1	185.7	192.4	200.7	194.4	195.6	198.1	200.1	200.7
State motor vehicle registrations	116.8	123.6	153.0	175.7	185.3	186.7	197.7	203.8	217.3	225.5	227.2	232.9	236.8	239.7	242.7	243.6	241.7
Ratio	0.854	0.732	0.860	0.876	0.869	0.874	0.876	0.847	0.815	0.824	0.847	0.862	0.821	0.816	0.816	0.821	0.830

Notes: Motor vehicle registrations are from the US Federal Highway Administration, Highway Statistics. Registration numbers include all commercial cars and trucks. In 1980, personal passenger vans, passenger minivans, and utility-type vehicles are included in automobile registrations. Starting in 1990 these vehicles are no longer included in automobiles, but are included in trucks.

Table 7.4   Correlation of reported vehicle purchase price in the CE interview survey to NADA values

Survey year	1990	2000
Cars owned 6 months or less	0.956	0.912
Cars owned 12 months or less	0.937	0.790
Cars owned 24 months or less	0.879	0.779

Notes: For each of the survey years reported, we compute the correlation between the reported purchase price of a random sample of vehicles from the CE interview survey and the value of these vehicles reported in the NADA guides. Values from NADA guides were identified based on make, model, year, number of cylinders, and number of doors for each vehicle. For each survey year, we select a random sample of one hundred new and used vehicles with a reported purchase price from the CE interview survey.

vehicle values in the interview survey to bluebook data. We match these cars from the interview survey to a bluebook price based on the reported make, model, year, and number of doors for each car. We report the correlations in table 7.4. The comparisons are probably most relevant for cars that have been recently purchased. For those that have been owned six months or less the correlations are very high, 0.956 and 0.912 in 1990 and 2000, respectively. This is especially impressive given that there are many characteristics of cars that are not reported in the CE or cannot be matched to bluebook features.

Some past work has found that respondents seem to report home values fairly accurately in household surveys (Kiel and Zabel 1999; Bucks and Pence 2006). We have compared the reported rental equivalent of homes to the reported house values. The rental equivalent and home value are highly correlated, at around 0.6 in a typical year. The ratio of the rental equivalent to home value has been fairly stable, though it declined appreciably in the middle of the first decade of the twenty-first century, as one might expect during a period of rising home prices. To see whether the general pattern over time in reported home values in the CE is sensible, we plotted in figure 7.2 the average home value reported in the CE interview survey compared to the Case-Shiller house price index. The average CE rental equivalent has the same qualitative time pattern as the Case-Shiller index, but it rises faster over time. The Case-Shiller index holds housing characteristics fixed, while the CE average does not. Because many characteristics of houses are improving over time such as square footage, presence of air conditioning, and other home amenities (see Meyer and Sullivan 2011a), the CE rise should be more pronounced, which is what is evident in figure 7.2.

7.6 Precision and the Frequency of Reported Purchases in the Interview and Diary Data

We next examine the precision of expenditure reports from the interview and diary surveys. The precision of these estimates is of interest for several

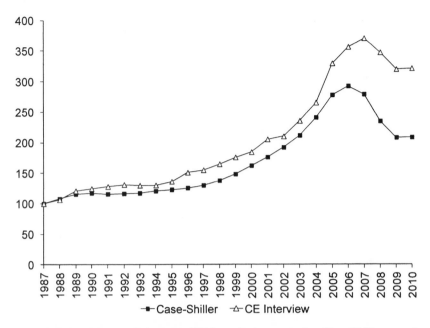

Fig. 7.2 Reported value of the home (CE interview) compared to Case-Shiller annual housing price indices (base year = 1987)

Note: The CE data exclude the following states because they are not included in the Case-Shiller index: AL, AK, ID, IN, ME, MS, MT, SC, SD, WV, and WI. In addition, the following states are excluded because of limited state information in the CE data: DE, GA, MD, and MN.

reasons. First, the precision of the consumer unit reports determines the precision of statistics calculated from the data. Second, by comparing the precision of the interview and diary components of the survey, one can determine how many diary responses are needed to obtain the same precision as one interview response. This point is important in choosing between interview and diary forms of survey administration and the appropriate sample sizes. Third, the dispersion of the various components of expenditures is informative if either of the CE survey components is going to be used to estimate distributional characteristics of expenditures, as when one is using the CE to assess inequality or poverty or in calculating percentiles for use in setting poverty thresholds as is done with the new Supplemental Poverty Measure.

To assess the precision of the CE, we examine the same forty-six categories of expenditures from table 7.2 that align closely with the PCE. We use these categories because we have verified their consistency over time. For thirty-five of these categories we have comparable data for both the interview and diary surveys. In table 7.5 we report the coefficient of variation (CV) of the quarterly interview reports and the weekly diary reports

Table 7.5   Coefficient of variation by spending category, Consumer Expenditure (CE) interview and diary survey, 1987–2010

PCE category	2010 CE DS	2010 CE IS	2010 DS/IS	1991 CE DS	1991 CE IS	1991 DS/IS	1987 CE DS	1987 CE IS	1987 DS/IS
Durable goods									
New motor vehicles		12.34			9.01			9.93	
Motor vehicle accessories and parts		4.68			4.71			5.60	
Furniture and furnishings	14.67	10.37	1.42	14.25	5.61	2.54	15.39	5.42	2.84
Household appliances	19.05	8.58	2.22	18.62	4.82	3.86	19.03	4.55	4.18
Glassware, tableware, and household utensils	6.32	8.59	0.74	20.61	5.60	3.68	9.10	7.25	1.26
Televisions	17.32	8.84	1.96	33.39	8.15	4.10	30.89	8.55	3.61
Audio equipment	16.32	10.06	1.62	22.91	6.16	3.72	18.98	5.52	3.44
Recording media	9.40	5.99	1.57	7.78	3.80	2.05	8.59	4.85	1.77
Photographic equipment	26.27	11.81	2.22	29.77	16.00	1.86	34.23	16.82	2.04
Sporting equipment, supplies, guns, and ammunition	14.03	8.84	1.59	13.33	7.64	1.75	13.86	6.26	2.21
Bicycles and accessories	29.65	17.68	1.68	35.49	14.19	2.50	33.73	10.79	3.13
Pleasure boats		80.78			51.70			30.23	
Other recreational vehicles		55.97			47.25			26.92	
Recreational books	8.91	6.20	1.44	6.89	4.52	1.52	9.41	7.21	1.31
Musical instruments	47.55	23.02	2.07	45.03	22.51	2.00	36.32	27.38	1.33
Jewelry and watches	35.99	12.43	2.90	17.01	8.22	2.07	18.41	8.81	2.09
Telephone and facsimile equipment	19.26	8.57	2.25	18.11	6.51	2.78	14.63	7.63	1.92
Nondurable goods									
Food and nonalc. bev. purchased for off-premises consumption	1.81	0.93	1.93	1.72	1.62	1.06	1.92	1.48	1.30
Alcoholic beverages purchased for off-premises consumption	4.46	4.45	1.00	4.51	4.51	1.00	3.97	3.59	1.10
Women's and girls' clothing	4.79	3.69	1.30	5.26	2.52	2.08	3.74	3.50	1.07
Men's and boys' clothing	5.31	4.78	1.11	4.34	2.84	1.53	5.06	3.27	1.54
Clothing materials	12.39	17.96	0.69	17.92	10.66	1.68	11.60	7.41	1.57
Shoes and other footwear	5.06	3.10	1.63	3.62	3.15	1.15	5.85	2.84	2.06
Gasoline and other energy goods	2.19	1.73	1.27	2.37	1.98	1.20	2.84	1.83	1.55
Pets and related products	6.56			5.68			5.22		
Household cleaning products	3.60			2.86			3.75		
Household paper products	3.37			2.96			2.85		

Household linens	6.18	4.93	1.26	7.66	5.57	1.37	7.08	4.62	1.53
Sewing items	30.73	15.88	1.93	28.75	9.10	3.16	13.69	12.21	1.12
Tobacco	6.04	5.48	1.10	3.75	3.10	1.21	3.23	3.34	0.97
Services—household consumption expenditures									
Rent and utilities	3.80	2.20	1.72	3.44	1.67	2.05	4.07	1.46	2.78
Imputed rental of owner-occupied nonfarm housing		2.08		2.86			2.76		
Other motor vehicle services		7.52		9.98			8.09		
Cable and satellite television and radio services	4.14	1.63	2.54	5.82	3.36	1.73	6.48	3.29	1.97
Photo processing	13.81	9.22	1.50	11.62	5.30	2.19	14.18	4.54	3.12
Photo studios	23.57	14.34	1.64	20.98			18.01		
Gambling	43.18	17.33	2.49	10.69			12.69		
Veterinary and other services for pets	10.70	6.75	1.59	9.43	8.52	1.11	13.67	5.79	2.36
Purchased meals and beverages	2.12	2.45	0.87	1.97	2.45	0.81	3.53	2.75	1.28
Communication	2.63	1.52	1.73	2.72	1.90	1.43	4.67	1.91	2.45
Legal services	27.21	16.41	1.66	34.45	18.46	1.87	33.79	25.15	1.34
Accounting and other business services	31.94	9.99	3.20	22.34	9.16	2.44	17.46	15.04	1.16
Funeral and burial services	38.27	17.24	2.22	77.21	15.64	4.94	60.41	16.71	3.61
Repair and hire of footwear	29.79	21.05	1.42	19.89	9.66	2.06	17.92	7.18	2.49
Child care	16.46	19.28	0.85	8.34	9.64	0.87	9.94	9.25	1.07
Household maintenance	12.13	5.52	2.20	9.13	5.94	1.54	13.35	6.82	1.96
Weighted mean (all categories)	7.07	4.32	1.63	6.30	3.67	1.72	6.71	3.75	1.79
Weighted mean (comparable categories only)	6.18	3.92	1.58	6.24	3.44	1.82	6.62	3.67	1.80
Median ratio			1.63			1.86			1.92

Notes: Data are from the Consumer Expenditure interview and diary surveys. Spending categories are the same as those reported in table 7.2. The unit of observation is a consumer unit-quarter for the interview survey and a consumer unit-week for the diary survey. The coefficient of variation is the ratio of the standard error of the mean to the mean times the square root of the sample size, where the standard error is calculated using the balanced repeated replication procedure recommend by the BLS for variance estimation in the CE survey.

for these categories of expenditures.[17] CVs for additional years are reported in appendix table 4 of Bee, Meyer, and Sullivan 2012. We focus on comparisons of quarters to weeks since a substantial share of respondents to both surveys do not complete the entire four quarters or two weeks. For example, typically about 10 percent of consumer units only respond for one of the diary weeks. For a given year table 7.5 reports the diary CV, the interview CV, and the ratio of diary to interview. Several patterns are apparent. First, the diary CVs tend to be much larger than those for the interview survey. In 2010, the weighted average of the CVs across comparable categories is 1.58 times as large in the diary survey as in the interview survey. We expect the interview survey to be more precise because it captures thirteen weeks of expenditures, as compared to just one week for the diary survey. If we make the extreme and implausible assumptions of no error in either survey, that weekly observations are independent, and simple random sampling, we would expect a ratio of CVs equal to the square root of 13 or 3.6.

Second, the diary/interview ratios vary sharply across expenditure categories. For 2010, the diary CV is over three times that of the interview CV for accounting and other business services, but the diary CV is slightly lower than the interview CV in the case of glassware, tableware, and household utensils. The ratios vary considerably, even for some of the largest categories of expenditures. For food and nonalcoholic beverages purchased for off-premises consumption (food at home) the diary CV is nearly twice as large as the interview CV, but it is smaller than the interview CV for purchased meals and beverages (food away from home).

Third, there are also noticeable changes in the CVs over time. For the diary survey, the weighted average for comparable categories falls slightly throughout the period. For the interview survey, the weighted average falls between 1987 and 1991 and then rises between 1991 and 2010. The CVs for the largest categories—food at home, purchased meals and beverages, gasoline and other energy products, rent and utilities, and imputed rent—in the interview survey tend to rise between 1987 and 1991 and then fall between 1991 and 2010, although the CV for rent and utilities rises throughout this period and the CV for purchased meals and beverages falls between 1987 and 1991. All of these categories except food away were reported at a high rate in the interview survey relative to the PCE, and these rates did not decline much

---

17. We calculate the CV as the square root of the sample size times the standard error of the mean divided by the mean. The standard error is calculated following the Balanced Repeated Replications (BRR) procedure used by the BLS to calculated standard errors for official CE tables. This BRR procedure is used to account for the CE survey's multistage sample selection process. (See http://www.census.gov/srd/papers/pdf/rr93–6.pdf for details on this procedure.) The CVs that we report are about 10 percent larger than those estimated, assuming simple random sampling design for the diary survey, and about 40 percent larger for the interview survey. We report CVs for 1987 instead of 1986 (the first year that data are available for most spending categories) because a complete set of replicate weights is not available in the public use version of the 1986 interview survey.

over time. Looking at these same categories for the diary survey (except for imputed rent, which is not available) the CVs tend to fall between 1987 and 1991, and then rise between 1991 and 2010, except for gasoline and other energy products, which falls throughout this period.

To understand what is behind these differences in the coefficients of variation across expenditure categories, surveys, and time, we look at the share of respondents who report no expenditures in a given category. It is first important to note that a substantial share of diary respondents indicate that they had no expenditures at all in a given week, and this share has been sharply increasing over time. As recently as 1991 the share of valid respondents for whom at least one of the week's expenditures was zero was 4.5 percent, but it reached 11.9 percent in 2010 (appendix table 5 of Bee, Meyer, and Sullivan 2012). In 2010, 9.4 percent of diary weeks have zero reported expenditures for the entire week. There are three reasons why a family in the diary survey would have zero expenditures for an entire week. First, the family may be on a trip for the entire week and the diary survey explicitly does not capture spending on trips. About three-quarters of the families with zero spending for an entire week in the 2010 diary survey fall into this group. Second, the family may truly have zero spending for that week, and third, the family may fail to report actual spending that occurred during the interview week. As we explain in section 7.8, regardless of the reason, the prevalence of zero expenditures, and more generally the greater dispersion of spending in the diary, has important implications for certain uses of the diary data.

In table 7.6, we report the share of reports that are zero for the forty-six categories of expenditures that we have previously considered. For each year, we report the share of zeros in the diary survey, the interview survey, and the difference between the surveys. (See appendix table 6 of Bee, Meyer, and Sullivan [2012] for additional years.) Looking at the thirty-five categories of expenditures available for both interview and diary surveys, twenty-four of the diary survey categories are zero more than 90 percent of the time, while fourteen of these same categories in the interview survey are zero for 90 percent or more of the consumer units. In 2010, 72 percent of diary survey respondents reported no spending on rent and utilities, as compared to 2 percent of interview survey respondents. Clearly these higher rates of zero reports are one reason for the higher CVs for the diary survey. The rate of reports of zero has also been rising for both surveys. Between 1986 and 2010 the majority of diary survey categories saw increases in the share of zeros. While not as pronounced, the rise in zeros is also apparent in the Interview Survey.

These results on CVs and frequency of period without any purchases have several implications for distributional analyses. In particular, the greater dispersion of weekly expenditures than quarterly expenditures, the extent to which this varies across expenditure categories and time, and the changing frequency of purchases suggest that the use of diary data to examine

Table 7.6   Fraction of consumer units with zero spending by spending category, Consumer Expenditure (CE) interview and diary survey, 1986–2010

PCE category	2010			1991			1986		
	CE DS	CE IS	DS-IS	CE DS	CE IS	DS-IS	CE DS	CE IS	DS-IS
Durable goods									
New motor vehicles		0.988			0.980			0.970	
Motor vehicle accessories and parts		0.806			0.875			0.874	
Furniture and furnishings	0.902	0.777	0.126	0.880	0.688	0.192	0.901	0.667	0.233
Household appliances	0.961	0.816	0.146	0.968	0.799	0.169	0.971	0.783	0.189
Glassware, tableware, and household utensils	0.889	0.895	-0.007	0.892	0.867	0.025	0.901	0.846	0.055
Televisions	0.997	0.957	0.040	0.998	0.959	0.039	0.997	0.950	0.046
Audio equipment	0.987	0.968	0.019	0.991	0.777	0.213	0.989	0.750	0.239
Recording media	0.954	0.811	0.142	0.942	0.703	0.239	0.963	0.768	0.194
Photographic equipment	0.994	0.976	0.018	0.995	0.976	0.019	0.996	0.969	0.026
Sporting equipment, supplies, guns, and ammunition	0.961	0.827	0.134	0.948	0.767	0.181	0.955	0.773	0.183
Bicycles and accessories	0.995	0.983	0.013	0.995	0.974	0.021	0.995	0.975	0.020
Pleasure boats		0.998			0.996			0.996	
Other recreational vehicles		0.999			0.997			0.996	
Recreational books	0.964	0.817	0.148	0.944	0.715	0.229	0.944	0.716	0.228
Musical instruments	0.996	0.987	0.010	0.995	0.977	0.018	0.996	0.975	0.021
Jewelry and watches	0.958	0.894	0.065	0.940	0.799	0.140	0.947	0.779	0.168
Telephone and facsimile equipment	0.989	0.934	0.055	0.981	0.938	0.042	0.993	0.951	0.042
Nondurable goods									
Food and nonalc. bev. purchased for off-premises consumption	0.189	0.012	0.177	0.090	0.008	0.082	0.117	0.009	0.108
Alcoholic beverages purchased for off-premises consumption	0.854	0.674	0.181	0.810	0.635	0.175	0.763	0.572	0.191
Women's and girls' clothing	0.795	0.531	0.264	0.722	0.377	0.345	0.734	0.347	0.387
Men's and boys' clothing	0.862	0.623	0.239	0.827	0.502	0.325	0.836	0.479	0.357
Clothing materials	0.983	0.972	0.011	0.963	0.916	0.047	0.966	0.901	0.065
Shoes and other footwear	0.890	0.674	0.216	0.887	0.538	0.349	0.891	0.503	0.388
Gasoline and other energy goods	0.362	0.095	0.267	0.319	0.109	0.210	0.300	0.113	0.187
Pets and related products	0.812			0.784			0.810		
Household cleaning products	0.591			0.495			0.517		
Household paper products	0.765			0.624			0.658		

Household linens	0.927	0.823	0.104	0.928	0.818	0.110	0.937	0.795	0.141
Sewing items	0.990	0.965	0.024	0.976	0.929	0.046	0.978	0.916	0.062
Tobacco	0.858	0.792	0.067	0.735	0.661	0.074	0.662	0.588	0.074
Services—household consumption expenditures									
Rent and utilities	0.720	0.024	0.696	0.629	0.028	0.601	0.708	0.034	0.673
Imputed rental of owner-occupied nonfarm housing		0.341			0.368			0.381	
Other motor vehicle services		0.750			0.748			0.737	
Cable and satellite television and radio services	0.895	0.253	0.641	0.916	0.474	0.442	0.956	0.579	0.377
Photo processing	0.985	0.931	0.054	0.973	0.745	0.229	0.974	0.747	0.227
Photo studios	0.994	0.977	0.018	0.991			0.993		
Gambling	0.955	0.898	0.057	0.935			0.948		
Veterinary and other services for pets	0.978	0.859	0.119	0.980	0.865	0.115	0.987	0.867	0.120
Purchased meals and beverages	0.304	0.194	0.110	0.254	0.166	0.088	0.246	0.162	0.084
Communication	0.729	0.055	0.674	0.701	0.050	0.652	0.676	0.061	0.615
Legal services	0.997	0.974	0.023	0.997	0.962	0.035	0.997	0.957	0.041
Accounting and other business services	0.980	0.944	0.036	0.971	0.932	0.040	0.978	0.933	0.045
Funeral and burial services	0.999	0.987	0.012	0.998	0.944	0.054	0.998	0.960	0.039
Repair and hire of footwear	0.997	0.990	0.007	0.994	0.947	0.047	0.993	0.937	0.056
Child care	0.990	0.974	0.016	0.966	0.942	0.024	0.953	0.931	0.022
Household maintenance	0.955	0.714	0.240	0.939	0.725	0.214	0.951	0.720	0.230
Mean difference			0.133			0.161			0.169
Median difference			0.065			0.110			0.120

Notes: Data are from the Consumer Expenditure interview and diary surveys. Spending categories are the same as those reported in table 7.2. The unit of observation is a consumer unit-quarter for the interview survey and a consumer unit-week for the diary survey.

poverty or inequality is problematic. We discuss these implications in more detail in section 7.8.

7.7 Representativeness of the CE

There are concerns that the CE misses certain types of households. The main method used in past studies that have assessed the bias due to unit nonresponse in the CE is comparisons of respondents contacted through more intensive methods to the remainder of respondents (Chopova et al. 2008; King et al. 2009). These studies suggest little bias. However, these analyses are not without their drawbacks, as those contacted through more intensive efforts may not be representative of those who are never contacted at all or are unwilling to respond.

To directly examine the representativeness of the CE, we compare the distribution of household characteristics in the CE to those in the Current Population Survey (CPS).[18] While the distribution of characteristics in the CPS does not necessarily reflect the true distribution in the US population, the CPS is a large survey (about 100,000 households annually in recent years) that is relied upon for many official statistics. Our results indicate that the characteristics of those in the CE line up quite closely with those of CPS respondents. These results do not necessarily confirm that the CE is representative of the US population. Rather, they indicate that any concerns about representativeness in the CE are shared with the CPS.

In addition to a base weight to account for sampling probabilities, the CE has two stages of poststratification adjustment to weights. The first stage is a "noninterview" adjustment based on region of country, household tenure (owner or renter), consumer unit size, and race of the reference person. The second stage is a "calibration factor" that accounts for frame undercoverage by adjusting the weights to twenty-four "known" population counts for region, race, tenure, age, and urban/rural status. Thus, we do not focus on these characteristics of households.

We report a number of demographic characteristics of the interview survey respondents for the years 1980–2010, as well as corresponding CPS values in appendix table 7 of Bee, Meyer, and Sullivan (2012). We examine characteristics at the individual level, rather than at the level of the family or household to facilitate comparability. The educational attainment distributions match quite closely, though the CE has slightly greater representation of those without a high school degree and this tendency has increased slightly over time. Marital status, weeks and hours worked, and age match very closely, though the CE has somewhat fewer young children. The share

18. For these comparisons we use the Annual Social and Economic Supplement, formerly called the Annual Demographic File or the March CPS.

that owns a home matches very closely, but that should not be surprising given that housing tenure is used to weight the CE data.

One of the principal concerns about unit nonresponse is that the CE may disproportionately miss households with either high or low income. Sabelhaus et al. (chapter 8, this volume) examine the representativeness of the CE interview survey by income. They match CE respondent and nonrespondent households to income at the zip-code level. They find that there is a small underrepresentation of those from the top four or five percentiles of zip-code-level income and no underrepresentation (maybe a slight overrepresentation) at the bottom of the zip-code-level income percentiles. Much more important quantitatively, they find that the income reported in the survey, either because high-income people are missing or because income is underreported at the top, is much lower than that from other sources such as the Survey of Consumer Finances and tax records. Furthermore, reported spending relative to income is very low at the top.

This evidence suggests that much of the underreporting of expenditures occurs at the very top of the income distribution, implying that the aggregate underreporting statistics emphasized in this paper likely overstate the weakness of the CE for a typical household. If much of the underreporting is due to high-income households understating spending, then spending by the vast majority of consumers is better than the averages that the aggregate numbers indicate. These results combined with those in the current chapter have several implications for various uses of the data that we discuss below.

7.8 Implications for Uses of the Current CE and for Redesign of the Survey

The results in this chapter have implications for the uses of existing CE data. Underreporting of expenditures is a first-order problem, particularly because it differs substantially across spending categories. In addition to the level of underreporting, the changes in the extent of underreporting over time have also varied across type of good. The result of these patterns is that uses of the data that rely on aggregates are likely biased. In particular, the CPI is biased since the differential underreporting means that the weights do not accurately reflect consumers' purchases. For example, as mentioned earlier, one of the principal concerns about the CE is that it causes too much weight is be put on housing in the CPI. The changes in the relative reporting of different types of good means that changes in the CPI are likely biased as well.

Fortunately, the quantitative importance of this problem may not be as severe as it first seems. A simple comparison of PCE and CPI weights overstates the potential bias in consumer prices because, as noted above, much of the PCE is not intended to be captured by the CPI. There is also research that has directly examined using PCE weights in a consumer price index (Blair chapter 2, this volume), finding only a modest bias that goes in different directions depending on how the index is constructed. It should also be noted that much of the bias may come from the plutocratic (dollar weighted as opposed to person weighted) nature of the CPI. While dollar weighting is appropriate when deflating national accounts, for many purposes of the CPI, such as indexing tax parameters and government benefits, person weighting may be more appropriate. Much of the aggregate underreporting in the CE appears to come from underreporting by high-income households who are underrepresented in the survey to begin with. While overall, the sample appears fairly representative, the dollar-weighted nature of the CPI weights means that potentially missing a small share of households that account for a large share of expenditures could significantly bias the total expenditure-based weights.

The results also indicate that certain categories of expenditures are well measured, on average, especially in the interview survey, and have not seen their reporting deteriorate. For researchers, emphasizing well-measured components may be a successful strategy to reduce bias when relying on the CE. For example, Meyer and Sullivan (2012) examine consumption poverty using "core consumption," which is based on well-measured spending categories from the interview survey: food at home, rent plus utilities, transportation, gasoline, the value of owner-occupied housing, rental assistance, and the value of owned vehicles. An important advantage of the interview survey relative to the diary survey is that the former has many more large, well-measured categories of expenditures.

One could reasonably estimate total expenditures or consumption from these well-measured categories, relying on the constancy of the relationship between these categories and total spending as measured in the 1980s, when these categories in the CE were more comparable to the PCE. For example, see Meyer and Sullivan (2010). Such a procedure will give a consistent series over time, but is unlikely to deliver an unbiased measure of the level of consumption because of underreporting that was present in the 1980s. Alternatively, scaling up total expenditures using CE/PCE ratios for all categories would be suspect given that so much of the CE is not comparable to the PCE. Methods that use CE data recognizing the nature of underreporting need to be further developed and validated.

Some uses of the CE survey rely on the distribution of expenditures. Examples include the construction of poverty thresholds for the new Supplemental Poverty Measure, and the calculation of poverty rates and inequality measures. For most of these uses, the representativeness of the CE through most of the income distribution and the concentration of underreporting among the highest income households is largely favorable for the use of the CE interview survey. Conversely, the data are ill-suited for examining the highest income households. As a corollary, analyses of inequality using CE data should focus on statistics that are not heavily dependent on spending by the top few percentiles of the distribution such as 90/10 ratios rather than variances, Gini coefficients, or spending shares at top percentiles.

The interview survey is the more appropriate data source for studies of consumption inequality or other distributional analyses. The goal of distributional analyses is typically to measure consumption rather than expenditures. Consumption differs from expenditures because one pays infrequently for goods and services that one is continuously consuming like rent and utilities. Durable goods like cars are purchased very infrequently, but their services are received over a long period of time. Even much food is in cans or boxes that may be purchased at a very different time from when it is consumed. To closely approximate consumption, average spending over a long period of time is needed. The much higher variability of weekly expenditures than quarterly expenditures is an indication of the greater deviation of weekly expenditures from consumption. The higher observed variability of weekly expenditures than quarterly expenditures could be the result of greater true variance or greater variance. Neither higher true variability nor measurement error is helpful in approximating longer-term consumption.

One might think that even though one or two weeks of expenditures are not ideal for measuring the longer-term distribution of expenditures or consumption, they have a simple, maybe even time-constant, relationship to longer-term distributions. However, such a relationship is unlikely for several reasons. Because distributional measures such as percentiles, poverty measures, and variances inherently depend on dispersion, the differing dispersion in the diary survey spending relative to longer-term spending, the differing relative dispersion across expenditure categories, and the changes in the relative dispersion over time mean that both levels and changes in distributional measures based on weekly diary data are biased. Previous studies have assumed a constant relationship between the weekly and quarterly data in order to infer longer-term distributional patterns or have not addressed the issue of the relationship between two weeks of expenditures and longer-term measures of consumption (Attanasio, Battistin, and Ichimura 2007; Attanasio, Battistin, and Padula 2012). The changing dispersion of the weekly data relative to the quarterly data for many categories indicates that this assumption is not valid. Furthermore, because aggregate spending is the sum of spending in different categories, the relationship between a given percentile in the weekly data and that of longer-term expenditures will change as spending shifts between categories with different degrees of dispersion. That the distribution of weekly expenditures differs in complicated and changing ways from the distribution of longer-term expenditures suggests there is no simple, time-invariant way to convert one to the other.

That nearly 10 percent of diary survey respondents report no spending at all in a week is also problematic. As discussed above, a family might report zero expenditures for an entire week because they are on a trip for the entire week, they have zero spending for that week, or they fail to report actual spending. However, even if these zero reports of spending are accurate, such spending is unlikely to reflect consumption accurately. The large fraction of families with zero total spending suggests that any inequality measure that depends heavily on spending at low percentiles will be misleading.

The results also have implications for the redesign of the CE survey. In deciding which type of survey, interview or diary, to emphasize in the future it is important to recognize how the current versions perform. The interview survey does well at recording many large categories of expenditures, but does poorly at others. The diary survey does better than the interview survey for some categories, particularly some small categories that the interview captures poorly, but rarely does the diary survey do well on both an absolute basis and compared to the interview survey. These results are also consistent with the evidence on diary and interview reporting from the Canadian Survey of Household Spending as well as the Canadian Food Expenditure Survey. Diary reporting seems to capture less spending than is obtained through an interview.

The greater dispersion in the diary survey means that larger sample sizes are required to obtain the same level of precision as in the interview survey. For categories of expenditures that can be compared across the two surveys, the weighted average of the coefficients of variation in the diary survey is 58 percent greater than that of the interview survey in 2010. In terms of precision, this result indicates that about 2.5 independent weekly diary survey observations approximately equal one quarterly interview survey observation.

7.9 Conclusions

In this chapter we examine the quality of consumption data in the CE interview and diary surveys. While some categories of spending are significantly underreported, our results indicate that the interview survey, in particular, does quite well in terms of a high and roughly constant share of expenditures relative to the national accounts for some of the largest components of consumption. These components include imputed rent on owner-occupied housing, rent and utilities, food at home, gasoline and other energy goods, new motor vehicles, and to a lesser extent, communication. The interview survey does poorly for food away from home, clothing, furniture and furnishings, and alcoholic beverages. Our results are less encouraging for the diary survey, which does poorly overall. There is no major category for which the diary survey has both a higher ratio to the PCE than the interview survey and the ratio is high and stable. We also find that the number and value of cars in the interview survey compares closely to outside sources, and the time pattern of home values closely follows other data.

Overall, the categories of expenditures that are not reported well tend to be those that involve many small and irregular purchases. These poorly reported categories also tend to be private goods (clothing), ones that one may not want to reveal that one buys (alcohol, tobacco), and certain luxuries (alcohol, food away from home). Large salient purchases like automobiles, and regular purchases like rent, utilities, and groceries, seem to be well reported.

While the evidence on the relative bias of the interview and diary data is compelling, the evidence on precision of the data also favors the interview survey. Coefficients of variation are noticeably higher in the diary survey than in the interview survey. We also find that diary survey respondents are much more likely to report zero spending for a consumption category. In 2010, 72 percent of diary survey respondents reported no spending on rent and utilities, as compared to 2 percent of interview survey respondents. The rate of reports of zero has been rising for both surveys. For the diary survey, we also find a high and increasing fraction of respondents reporting zero for all categories; 11.9 percent of 2010 diary survey respondents report zero spending for an entire week, up from 4.5 percent in 1991.

The CE interview sample appears to be representative along many dimensions. However, Sabelhaus et al. (chapter 8, this volume) provides strong evidence of underrepresentation at the top of the income distribution and underreporting of income and expenditures at the top. They find that low-income households are well represented. The underrepresentation of high-income households and their disproportionate underreporting of expenditures means that the aggregate reporting rates relative to the PCE emphasized in the chapter likely understate the underreporting problem for high-income households, but overstate the problem for low-income households.

These results have implications for the use of existing CE data and for the redesign of the CE survey. The importance of the underreporting of expenditures in the CE will depend on the purpose for which the data are used. Uses of the data that rely on aggregates are likely biased. Our results suggest the CPI is biased because the differential underreporting means that the weights do not accurately reflect consumers' purchases. However, we discuss several reasons why this problem might not be as worrisome as it first appears.

The evidence that the CE appears to miss spending near the top of the distribution implies that underreporting is less of a concern for analyses that do not rely on spending at the top, such as measures of consumption poverty or median consumption. And, the high and fairly constant reporting rates for large categories of consumption in the interview survey suggest that, for some purposes, researchers can rely on these categories to address some of the concerns about underreporting.

The greater dispersion of spending in the diary survey data has important implication for distributional analyses. The high and increasing fraction of zero reported spending suggests that the use of diary survey data to assess inequality trends and other distributional outcomes is likely to lead to biased and misleading results. Also, the larger coefficients of variation in the diary survey suggest that larger sample sizes are required for the diary survey to obtain the same information as in the interview survey. Furthermore, diary data may not be appropriate to capture the longer-term distribution of expenditures needed to measure consumption for distributional analyses.

References

Ahmed, Naeem, Mathew Brzozowski, and Thomas F. Crossley. 2010. "Measurement Errors in Recall Food Consumption Data." Working Paper, University of Cambridge.
Attanasio, Orazio P., Erich Battistin, and Hidehiko Ichimura. 2007. "What Really Happened to Consumption Inequality in the United States?" In *Hard-to-Measure Goods and Services: Essays in Honor of Zvi Griliches*, edited by Ernst E. Berndt and Charles R. Hulten, 515-44. Chicago: University of Chicago Press.
Attanasio, Orazio P., Erich Battistin, and Andrew Leicester. 2006. "From Micro to Macro, from Poor to Rich: Consumption and Income in the UK and the US." Working Paper, University College London.
Attanasio, Orazio P., Erich Battistin, and Mario Padula. 2012. *Inequality in Living Standards since 1980: Income Tells only a Small Part of the Story*. Washington, DC: American Enterprise Institute.
Battistin, E. 2003. "Errors in Survey Reports of Consumption Expenditures." IFS Working Paper no. 0307, Institute for Fiscal Studies.
Bee, Adam, Bruce D. Meyer, and James X. Sullivan. 2012. "The Validity of Consumption Data: Are the Consumer Expenditure Interview and Diary Surveys Informative?" NBER Working Paper no. 18308, Cambridge, MA.
Bosworth, Barry. 2010. "Price Deflators, the Trust Fund Forecast, and Social Security Solvency." Working Paper no. 2010-12, Center for Retirement Research at Boston College.
Branch, E. Raphael. 1994. "The Consumer Expenditure Survey: A Comparative Analysis." *Monthly Labor Review* 117 (12): 47.
Browning, Martin, Thomas Crossley, and Guglielmo Weber. 2003. "Asking Consumption Questions in General Purpose Surveys." *Economic Journal* 113 (491): F540–67.
Bucks, Brian, and Karen Pence. 2006. "Do Homeowners Know Their House Values and Mortgage Terms?" Working Paper, Federal Reserve Board of Governors.
Chopova, Boriana, Jennifer Edgar, Jeffrey M. Gonzales, Susan King, Dave McGrath, and Lucilla Tan. 2008. "Assessing Nonresponse Bias in the CE Interview Survey: A Summary of Four Studies." Washington, DC, US Bureau of Labor Statistics.
Creech, Brett J., and Barry P. Steinberg. 2011. "CE Source Selection for Publication Tables." In *Consumer Expenditure Survey Anthology, 2011*, 17–20. Washington, DC: US Bureau of Labor Statistics.
Deaton, Angus, and Valerie Kozel. 2005. "Data and Dogma: The Great Indian Poverty Debate." *World Bank Research Observer* 20 (2): 177–99.
Dubreuil, Guylaine, Johanne Tremblay, Jenny Lynch, and Martin Lemire. 2011. "Redesign of the Canadian Survey of Household Spending." Slide Presentation at the Household Survey Producers Workshop, June.

Are the Consumer Expenditure Interview and Diary Surveys Informative?   **239**

Garner, Thesia I., George Janini, William Passero, Laura Paszkiewicz, and Mark Vendemia. 2006. "The CE and the PCE: A Comparison." *Monthly Labor Review* 66 (September): 20–46.

Garner, Thesia I., Robert McClelland, and William Passero. 2009. "Strengths and Weaknesses of the Consumer Expenditure Survey from a BLS Perspective." Paper presented at the NBER Summer Institute, July.

General Accounting Office. 1996. "Alternative Poverty Measures." Report no. GAO/GGD-96-183R, Washington, DC, Government Printing Office.

Gieseman, Raymond. 1987. "The Consumer Expenditure Survey: Quality Control by Comparative Analysis." *Monthly Labor Review* 110 (3): 8–14.

Houthakker, Hendrik S., and Lester D. Taylor. 1970. *Consumer Demand in the United States: Analysis and Projections*, 2nd ed. Cambridge, MA: Harvard University Press.

Hurd, Michael, and Susann Rohwedder. 2011. "High-Frequency Data on Total Household Spending: Evidence from the Monthly ALP Surveys." Working Paper, RAND Corporation.

Kiel, Katherine A., and Jeffrey E. Zabel. 1999. "The Accuracy of Owner-Provided House Values: The 1978–1991 American Housing Survey." *Real Estate Economics* 27 (2): 263–98.

King, Susan L., Boriana Chopova, Jennifer Edgar, Jeffrey M. Gonzales, Dave E. McGrath, and Lucilla Tan. 2009. "Assessing Nonresponse Bias in the Consumer Expenditure Interview Survey." Paper presented in Section on Survey Research Methods-JMS 2009, American Statistical Association.

Li, Geng, Robert F. Schoeni, Sheldon Danziger, and Kerwin Kofi Charles. 2010. "New Expenditure Data in the PSID: Comparisons with the CE." *Monthly Labor Review* 133 (2): 29–39.

McCully, Clinton. 2011. "Trends in Consumer Spending and Personal Saving, 1959–2009." *Survey of Current Business* 91 (6):14.

Meyer, Bruce, and James X. Sullivan. 2010. "Consumption and Income Inequality in the US Since the 1960s." Working Paper, University of Notre Dame.

———. 2011a. "The Material Well-Being of the Poor and the Middle Class Since 1980." Working Paper, American Enterprise Institute.

———. 2011b. "Viewpoint: Further Results on Measuring the Well-Being of the Poor Using Income and Consumption." *Canadian Journal of Economics* 44 (1): 52–87.

———. 2012. "Winning the War: Poverty from the Great Society to the Great Recession." Brookings Papers on Economic Activity, Fall, 133–200.

Passero, William. 2011. "Table 1. Summary Comparison of Aggregate Consumer Expenditures (CE) and Personal Consumption Expenditures (PCE), Based on 2002 Benchmark and Restricted to the Most Comparable Categories on the Basis of Concepts Involved and Comprehensiveness, 2003–2009." US Bureau of Labor Statistics. http://www.bls.gov/cex/cecomparison.htm.

Silberstein, A. R., and S. Scott. 1991. "Expenditure Diary Surveys and their Associated Errors." In *Measurement Errors in Surveys*, edited by P. P. Biermer, R. M. Groves, L. E. Lyberg, N. A. Mathiowetz, and S. Sudman. Hoboken, NJ: Wiley.

Slesnick, Daniel T. 1992. "Aggregate Consumption and Savings in the Postwar United States." *Review of Economics and Statistics* 74 (4): 585–97.

Steinberg, Barry, Brett J. Creech, Mary Lynn Schmidt, and Patrick Falwell. 2010. "Source Selection: Selecting and Evaluating America's Expenditures." Paper presented at the Joint Statistical Meetings 2010, Section on Government Statistics.

Stephens, Melvin, Jr. 2003. "3rd of the Month: Do Social Security Recipients Smooth Consumption Between Checks?" *American Economic Review* 93 (1): 406–22.

US Bureau of Labor Statistics (BLS). 1983. "Consumer Expenditure Survey: Diary Survey, 1980–81." Bulletin 2173, US Department of Labor, September.

———. 2010. "Gemini Planning Document." Unpublished manuscript.

———. 2012. "Consumer Expenditures and Income." In *BLS Handbook of Methods*, Washington, DC: US Department of Labor.

Is the Consumer Expenditure Survey Representative by Income?

John Sabelhaus, David Johnson, Stephen Ash, David Swanson, Thesia I. Garner, John Greenlees, and Steve Henderson

8.1 Introduction

Aggregate spending in the Consumer Expenditure Survey (CE) is well below comparable personal consumption expenditures (PCE) in the National Income and Product Accounts (NIPA), and the ratio of spending in the CE to spending in the NIPA has fallen from where it was two decades ago.[1] Assuming NIPA values are a good benchmark, two potential reasons for the aggregate spending difference are that higher-income families (who presumably spend more than average) are underrepresented in the CE estimation sample, or there is systematic underreporting of spending by at least some CE survey respondents.[2] Resolving why the aggregate shortfall

John Sabelhaus is an economist in the Division of Research and Statistics at the Board of Governors of the Federal Reserve System. David Johnson is chief economist of the Bureau of Economic Analysis. Stephen Ash is a mathematical statistician in the Demographic Statistical Methods Division at the US Census Bureau. David Swanson is an economist in the Statistical Methods Division of the Bureau of Labor Statistics, US Department of Labor. Thesia I. Garner is a senior research economist in the Division of Price and Index Number Research at the Bureau of Labor Statistics, US Department of Labor. John Greenlees is a research economist in the Division of Price and Index Number Research at the Bureau of Labor Statistics, US Department of Labor. Steve Henderson is an economist in the Division of Consumer Expenditure Survey of the Bureau of Labor Statistics, US Department of Labor.

Views here do not represent those of the Federal Reserve Board, the Bureau of Economic Analysis, the US Census Bureau, or the US Bureau of Labor Statistics. The authors would like to thank C. Adam Bee for his assistance with CPS data. This chapter was prepared for the December 2011 CRIW/NBER conference "Improving the Measurement of Consumer Expenditures." For acknowledgments, sources of research support, and disclosure of the authors' material financial relationships, if any, please see http://www.nber.org/chapters/c12673.ack.

1. Crossley (2009) shows that the same basic conclusion holds for the British equivalent of the CE survey.

2. As discussed in Garner et al. (2006), there are possible components for which PCE may be overstated.

Table 8.1   Ratio of Consumer Expenditure survey aggregates to comparable NIPA personal consumption expenditure measures

| | Ratio of CE to PCE for comparable categories | | | | |
Year	All goods and services	Durable goods	Nondurable goods	Owned housing	Other services
	Garner, McClelland, and Passero (2009)				
1992	0.88	0.88	0.69	1.23	0.90
1997	0.88	0.80	0.67	1.26	0.86
2002	0.84	0.75	0.63	1.25	0.82
2003	0.82	0.79	0.61	1.26	0.80
2005	0.83	0.75	0.63	1.26	0.81
2007	0.81	0.69	0.61	1.30	0.81
	BLS published estimates based on latest NIPA crosswalk				
2005	0.80	0.69	0.67	1.16	0.75
2006	0.80	0.67	0.67	1.17	0.75
2007	0.79	0.65	0.65	1.22	0.73
2008	0.78	0.64	0.67	1.15	0.73
2009	0.78	0.66	0.66	1.10	0.73
2010	0.75	0.62	0.63	1.09	0.71

occurs is important for weighting the Consumer Price Index (CPI) and for various research questions that involve the joint distribution of spending and income, including measuring inequality, studying savings behavior, and evaluating the distributional burden of consumption taxes.

Establishing the basic facts about the accuracy of aggregate CE spending is straightforward in principle, but complicated in practice because the CE and PCE differ in terms of both spending concepts and population coverage.[3] However, piecing together the latest Bureau of Labor Statistics (BLS) estimates with the results of a study by Garner, McClelland, and Passero (2009) provides a compelling story (table 8.1). There are systematic differences across types of spending at any point in time, and there is also a general decline in the ratio of CE to PCE by about 10 percentage points between 1992 and early in the first decade of the twenty-first century. However, since 2003, the CE-to-PCE ratio has been relatively stable, both overall and within broad categories of spending.

On net, in 2010 the CE appears to be capturing 75 percent of comparable PCE. The CE is lower in most categories, but rental equivalence of owned housing is a rare exception where the CE is higher than the PCE.[4] If it is omitted, the CE's estimates of comparable spending are generally about one-third lower than the PCE. In particular, the ratios for

3. For example, PCE includes consumption spending by nonprofit institutions.
4. For a discussion of how owned-housing services are estimated in the CE, see Garner and Short (2009).

durables, nondurables, and nonhousing services are 62, 63, and 71 percent respectively.[5]

Although CE is fundamentally designed to collect expenditure data, not income data, a failure to reflect the income distribution accurately could suggest that inaccuracies occur in the spending distribution as well. There is evidence that the CE does not capture as much income as in other surveys, and the missing income seems to be at the top of the income distribution. Passero (2009) shows that the CE aggregate income is only 94 percent of Current Population Survey (CPS) aggregate income.[6] Evidence that the missing CE income occurs at the very highest income levels comes from comparing CE against other data sets. A comparison of the CE income distribution to the CPS, Survey of Consumer Finances (SCF), and tax return-based Statistics of Income (SOI) data sets suggests significant underrepresentation of the $100,000 or more income group in the CE. The CE finds fewer households in that income range, and average incomes for households that are above $100,000 are below the averages in the other data sets.

It may be that higher-income CE households are simply less likely to accurately report their incomes, but there are also good reasons to suspect that the households at the very top of the income distribution are underrepresented in the CE. The first type of evidence comes from a new approach to this question developed for this chapter. The approach involves linking all CE-sampled households (both respondents and nonrespondents) to the average adjusted gross income (AGI) in their five-digit zip code area.[7] For most of the AGI distribution there is little or no association between unit nonresponse and zip code-level AGI, but at the very top of the income distribution the unit response rate and the ratio of average CE income to mean zipcode-level AGI are both lower. That is, in the top few percentiles of households sorted by zip code-level AGI, households are less likely to participate in the CE, and those households that do participate are more likely to have incomes below the average in their zip code.

This difference in participation suggests that high-income households are underrepresented in the CE; however, underreporting of spending for at least some respondents is also quite likely. The CE tabulations (reproduced in this chapter) show that CE expenditures are lower than income, which suggests unusually high savings rates (even after accounting for measurement differences in income and spending). In addition, CE data show that the ratio of spending to after-tax income falls with income, suggesting very high savings rates at the top of the income distribution. Comparison of CE incomes to

5. Other chapters in this volume consider how more detailed categories of spending in the CE compare with external benchmarks. See Bee, Meyer, and Sullivan (chapter 7) and Passero, Garner, and McCully (chapter 6).

6. See also Meyer, Mok, and Sullivan (2009).

7. The analysis here is based on the Consumer Expenditure Quarterly interview survey (CEQ). In principle, the same exercise could be done with the Consumer Expenditure diary survey (CED).

other data sources suggests that as much as 25 or even 50 percent of income is missing in the $100,000 or more income group. As a result, if this income underreporting is simply due to underreporting for high-income households, this would imply even larger discrepancies in average savings rates between those implied in the CE data and other data sources (e.g., SCF).

Why is it important to distinguish between the possible explanations for underreporting of aggregate CE spending? The difference in CE to PCE aggregates across the broad categories in table 8.1 highlights one key reason—weighting the CPI. If there are systematic differences in how well the CE survey captures aggregate expenditures across categories, the CPI weights will be biased, and the overall index will be inappropriately affected by changes in the prices of over- or underrepresented categories.[8] Given the plutocratic nature of the CPI, the relationship of income and spending on different types of categories suggests that underrepresentation of high-income families in the CE could be biasing the CPI.

In addition to weighting the CPI, however, there are also several research areas where the ratio of expenditures to income across income groups is the crucial input, and thus distinguishing between underrepresentation of high-income families versus underreported expenditures for at least some respondents is crucial. The CE data have been used in several studies to measure differences between consumption expenditure and income inequality, with consumption-expenditure inequality shown to be consistently and dramatically lower.[9] Bosworth, Burtless, and Sabelhaus (1991) used CE data to track changes in household saving across groups and time, and the estimated patterns of low-income dissaving and high-income saving are dramatic in every period. Finally, CE data are regularly used by government agencies and other groups to measure the distributional burden of consumption taxes. Consumption taxes appear very regressive, because the ratio of spending to income falls dramatically with income.

If the source of the aggregate CE shortfall is simply underrepresentation of the highest-income households, then the inequality, saving, and tax distribution studies described above may be incomplete, but they are not necessarily biased for the range of the income distribution they represent. Even though the very highest-income households are underrepresented in the CE, Sabelhaus and Groen (2000) demonstrate that the overall underreporting of spending is partially attributable to underreporting of expenditures by at least some CE respondents.[10] If expenditure underreporting is indeed worse

---

8. See McCully, Moyer, and Stewart (2007). See also Blair (chapter 2, this volume), prepared for this conference.

9. See, for example, Johnson and Shipp (1997), Short et al. (1998), Attanasio et al. (2002), Krueger and Perri (2006), Krueger et al. (2010), and Heathcote, Perri, and Violante (2010).

10. Sabelhaus and Groen (2000) use a variety of techniques, including appealing to consumption-smoothing theory, to argue that the ratio of consumption to income for high-income families is biased down.

for higher-income households, then the results of the CE-based inequality, saving, and tax-distribution research should be revisited.

8.2 How Does the CE Income Distribution Compare to Other Data Sources?

Although the CE estimation sample reflects the actual distribution of households by income over most ranges, comparisons between the CE and other household surveys suggest that the very highest-income families are underrepresented. In this section, weighted counts of CE units and average incomes are compared against three other data sources—the Current Population Survey (CPS), the Survey of Consumer Finances (SCF), and the IRS tax-return-based Statistics of Income (SOI). The comparisons include one data set (CPS) that is similar to the CE in sampling strategy but more focused on income, one that is purely administrative (SOI), and one that employs differential sampling for high-wealth households in order to capture the top of the wealth distribution (SCF). To enhance comparability for this study, CPS and SOI incomes do not include the value of capital gains since the CE income does not include gains in income.

The overall count of sampled units in the CE, CPS, and SCF are similar. Although the CE samples "consumer units," the CPS samples "households," and the SCF samples "primary economic units," the overall counts for any given year are within 2 or 3 percent (table 8.2, last column). The count of units for the SOI is very different from the other surveys because dependent filers—usually children living in their parents' home—may have to file their own tax returns. There are also differences in the income concept in the SOI because nontaxable forms of income (mostly transfers) are not included in adjusted gross income (AGI). After adjusting for those differences, though, the four data sets are broadly consistent across the income categories.

The well-known skewness of the US income distribution shows up clearly in the CE as one moves from less than $50,000 of income (65.1 million consumer units), to between $50,000 and $100,000 (34.9 million), to $100,000 or more (18.9 million). The counts of units for the CPS, SCF, and SOI are shown as differences from the CE values, and the general impression one gets is that the differences are second order. All three data sets show the same basic shape. The SOI, as expected, finds many more units in the less than $50,000 group because of dependent filers and the fact that nontaxable transfers are not being included.

The focus of the analysis here, however, is the top of the income distribution, and although the counts of units are broadly similar in the $100,000 or more income category, the total income received by that group is much lower in the CE than in the other three data sets. For example, the CPS finds 22.1 percent more income for those households. Although much of that is because the CPS finds more households above the $100,000 line, there is no

Table 8.2   Income distribution in the Consumer Expenditure survey and three other
                   data sets, 2006

	Income category			
	Less than $50,000	$50,000 to $99,999	$100,000 or more	All incomes
Consumer Expenditure survey				
Number of units (millions)	65.1	34.9	18.9	118.8
Total income (billions $)	1,589	2,472	3,111	7,172
Differences from Consumer Expenditure survey				
Current Population Survey				
Number of units (millions)	−5.5	−0.6	3.2	−2.8
Total income (billions $)	−85	−51	688	551
Total income (percent)	−5.3	−2.1	22.1	7.7
Survey of Consumer Finances				
Number of units (millions)	−1.6	−2.7	1.5	−2.7
Total income (billions $)	11	−166	1,832	1,677
Total Income (percent)	0.7	−6.7	58.9	23.4
Statistics of Income				
Number of units (millions)	27.2	−4.9	−2.8	19.6
Total income (billions $)	210	−353	1,002	859
Total income (percent)	13.2	−14.3	32.2	12.0

Notes: The SCF and SOI income exclude capital gains.

reason to expect any divergence at all between the CE and CPS because the sampling approach and income concepts are similar.[11]

The more noticeable differences in top incomes occur when one compares CE (and CPS) to the SCF and the SOI. The SCF uses an income concept that generally matches the CE, but employs a different sampling strategy in order to capture the top of the wealth distribution.[12] The SCF finds nearly 60 percent more income in the $100,000 or more income range. To put those numbers in perspective, the nearly $2 trillion of additional income that the SCF finds at the very top is similar in magnitude to the aggregate spending mismatch that motivates this study.

11. A major difference between the CPS and CE surveys is that the CPS is focused on collecting income, while the CE is focused on spending, which could account for some of the difference in the quality of income reporting. Another difference is that CE income data are only collected in the second and fifth interviews, with the second interview values carried over to the third and fourth interviews. There are also differences between the CPS and CE in terms of imputation and top-coding procedures. See Passero (2009) and Paulin and Ferraro (1996) for a discussion of income imputation in the CE, and Burkhauser et al. (2009) for a discussion about how using the CPS without top codes affects estimates of the incomes at the very top of the income distribution.

12. For a general discussion of the SCF see Bucks et al. (2009), and for a general discussion of SCF design and implementation, see Kennickell and Woodburn (1999). The SCF sampling strategy is focused on wealth measurement, but Kennickell (2009) describes how wealth and income are related.

The conceptual differences between CE and the SOI make direct comparisons more problematic. Using an AGI income concept with the CE data will yield an even lower estimate of income. However, the SOI still finds over 30 percent more income in the $100,000 or more range even though there are fewer tax filers in that AGI range because of the differences between AGI and the more generalized income concept used in the other surveys. Thus, on net, comparing the CE to both the SOI and SCF data suggests that the very highest income households are underrepresented in the CE (and in the CPS, though to a lesser extent).

8.3 Why Does the CE Underrepresent the Very Highest Income Households?

The CE is designed to collect expenditure data and related demographic characteristics from a sample that is representative of the US civilian noninstitutional population; the weighting procedures to ensure this representativeness do not account for income. However, if the variables used to produce representative expenditure estimates are highly correlated with income, then the CE random-sampling approach should still generate an unbiased representation of the true population income distribution. However, two problems associated with sampling could lead to the underrepresentation of very high income households.

The first potential problem is sampling variability because income is highly concentrated at (and even within) the top percentiles, as indicated in both tax data and targeted surveys like the SCF. Sampling variability implies that the estimated aggregates will be very dependent on whether those probabilistically rare households are chosen to participate in the survey. The fact that CE incomes are systematically lower at the top end—and not just extremely volatile at the top end—implies that sampling variability is not the problem.

The second possible problem is differential unit nonresponse.[13] The concern here is that the highest-income households are less likely to participate in the survey when they are selected. The fact that incomes are systematically lower at the top end of the income distribution in the CE suggests that differential unit nonresponse among very high income households is an explanation worth exploring, and that is the focus of this section.

There is no direct way to assess whether or not the very highest income families are less likely to participate in the CE when they are chosen because we do not observe the actual incomes of nonparticipants. However, it is possible to make indirect inferences about survey participation using a new data set that links sampled CE units to the average adjusted gross income (AGI)

---

13. The discussion here follows a long literature on unit nonresponse. See, for example, Groves (2006) and King et al. (2009) for useful introductions to that literature.

in their five-digit zip code area. The average AGI values linked to sampled CE units are produced by the IRS Statistics of Income Division, and are available for public use.[14]

The data set built for this analysis starts with all consumer units selected for the CE for calendar years 2007 and 2008.[15] There are 104,830 units selected for participation, and 74 percent of those participated in the survey. However, the BLS excludes the first (or "bounding") interview when publishing expenditure estimates for publication, and that approach is followed here. Thus, the final data set includes 61,546 interviewed respondents out of 83,366 in-scope sampled units, which is an overall response rate of 74 percent.

The analysis here is based on sorting the sampled CE households into income groups using the average AGI for their zip code. This makes it possible to sort both respondents and nonrespondents using the same income measure, and to test for differences in response rates across AGI percentiles. Basically, the first step uses the average response rates for the CE sample in each of the 100 AGI percentile-income groups. The second step is to compare the average incomes of respondents to the average AGI for their zip code, again, by AGI percentile. Note that in both steps the percentile-cell calculations all involve several hundred observations being averaged to create the estimated response rates or the ratio of average CE income to average AGI.

8.3.1 Using Zip Code-Level AGI to Sort Households

Using zip code-level AGI to proxy "true" income of nonrespondents does raise a few concerns. First, the AGI concept itself is an imperfect measure of income because it excludes nontaxable transfers along with other tax-free income such as municipal bond interest. The idea of nontaxable transfers usually evokes images of food stamps and other income maintenance programs, but it is probably more salient to note that for most Social Security recipients, most or all of their Social Security is excluded from AGI. Thus, a retiree with $20,000 in taxable pensions and $20,000 in Social Security will show up with an AGI of $20,000, even though the CE would identify them as having $40,000 of income.

The second problem with using zip code-level mean AGI is the presence of dependent filers. As noted in the discussion of table 8.2 in the previous section, the count of SOI "units" is much higher than CE consumer

---

14. (See http://www.irs.gov/taxstats/indtaxstats/article/0,,id=96947,00.html.) To protect confidentiality, the analysis here was conducted by the authors at the Census Bureau and the Bureau of Labor Statistics using internal data with only zip code information.

15. The data set covers all units who were interviewed in the CE from the first quarter of 2007 through the first quarter of 2009, and thus will include expenditures that occurred early in 2009 or late in 2006. All income and expenditure values (including zip code-level AGI) are inflated to 2008 dollars from their reference periods using the CPI-U.

units or CPS households, because dependent children with income may file separate returns. Although the CE income calculations have been adjusted to more closely resemble the AGI income,[16] both of these problems with using AGI—that AGI excludes nontaxable income and the averages include dependent filers—imply that average AGI for the zip code is a downward biased estimate of average household income. In the first case AGI income may exclude some income components, and in the second we are splitting the household-level income across too many units. As figure 8.2 illustrates, the overall mean of CE income is about 14 percent higher than the mean of zip code-level AGI for the same zip code areas.

The third problem with using zip code-level AGI is that it excludes non-filers, but in this case there is no obvious bias in average AGI. Households who receive only nontaxable transfers will not even show up in the SOI zip code-level data file, because they are not required to file tax returns. Their exclusion from the zip code file would reduce the total number of units, but would likely not change the income ranking of the zip codes. That is, if a $20,000 per year Social Security recipient lives in the same zip code as a $20,000 per year wage earner, we would only observe the wage earner in the zip code AGI file, but the $20,000 AGI would still be a good estimate of income for both households in the zip code. Even if this is not an accurate assumption (see the next paragraph), the exclusion of nonfilers is unlikely to affect the highest income zip code areas, which are of most interest here.

The final problem with using zip code-level AGI is that zip code may not be a narrow enough geographic classifier from a socioeconomic perspective, meaning there is significant income variation within zip codes. This potential problem motivates the second step of the approach implemented here, because in addition to looking for differences in response rates by AGI percentile, we also consider the ratio of CE respondent-reported incomes to average AGI. This second step is designed to capture differences in response by income within zip codes and thus control for variations in within zip code incomes, especially at the top of the distribution where our attention is focused.

8.3.2 Response Rates by AGI Percentiles

The first question addressed using the new zip code-linked data set is whether the probability of responding to the survey, when sampled, varies systematically with income.[17] All sampled CE units are assigned the average AGI for their zip code, and the entire data set is sorted into one hundred percentile groups (0–1st, 1st–2nd, . . . 99th–100th). Although in principle

16. For the analysis in sections 8.3 and 8.4, the CE and SOI income concepts have been made more comparable (see footnote 20).

17. Note that we are not testing whether or not the probability of being sampled varies with zip code-level income, though in principle that could be accomplished by comparing the sampled CE population against the entire SOI zip code data set.

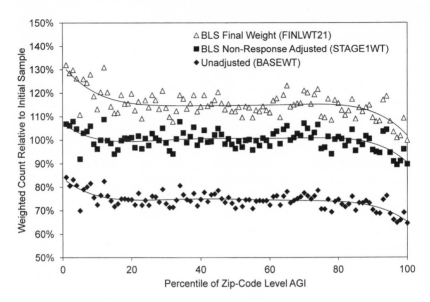

Fig. 8.1 Consumer Expenditure survey (CE) response rates by zip code-level adjusted gross income (AGI) percentile

Note: Fitted curves are fifth-order polynomials.

this is a simple calculation, because response is a binary outcome the analysis is complicated to some extent because it requires acknowledging the potential effects of existing BLS poststratification (weighting) adjustments.

The simplest calculation involves the inverse of the raw sampling probability, which BLS refers to as BASEWT. The values for BASEWT in the CE are typically around 10,000, which means that a consumer unit in the sample represents 10,000 consumer units in the US civilian noninstitutional population—itself plus 9,999 other consumer units that were not selected for the sample.[18] Using BASEWT, the simplest calculation of response by AGI involves taking the ratio of respondents (weighted by BASEWT) to sampled units (also weighted by BASEWT) within each AGI percentile (figure 8.1, lowest set of markers).

The overall response rate across AGI percentiles is 74 percent for 2007 and 2008.[19] Figure 8.1 shows that the response rate for most AGI deciles

18. There are some relatively minor adjustments to BASEWT that adjust for several types of operational and field subsampling. Examples of when subsampling is used include when a data collector visits a particular address and discovers multiple housing units where only one housing unit was expected or when more units are found in the listing than expected in rural areas that use an area frame.

19. The fact that the BASEWT response rate of 74 percent exactly matches the response rates based on simple sample counts, as noted earlier, underscores the fact that the adjustments to BASEWT are empirically very small.

is between 70 and 80 percent for most of the AGI distribution. Although the numbers exhibit a fair amount of variability, there is no clear pattern between (roughly) the 10th and 90th percentiles. The data do show lower response for the highest AGI percentiles, which confirms the hypothesized higher unit nonresponse for very high income families. Overall, the response rate for the top 5 percentiles is 66 percent, and the top 1 percent by AGI has a response rate of 65 percent.

Interestingly, the response rates by AGI are higher than average at the bottom of the AGI distribution. The overall response rate based on BASEWT is 80 percent for the bottom 5 percentiles and 84 percent in the 1st percentile. Given the very large sample sizes involved in these calculations—over 800 sampled units in each AGI percentile—these higher response rates for lower-income zip codes are noteworthy. Although we do not pursue an explanation for higher unit nonresponse by lower-income households here, it is certainly an interesting area for further research, and it is worth noting that the sample is certainly not underrepresentative for studying poverty and related topics.[20]

Although the unadjusted response rates (based on BASEWT) suggest that higher-income households are indeed underrepresented in the CE respondent sample, there are two subsequent stages of BLS poststratification that could remedy this underrepresentation.[21] The first step involves the "non-interview" adjustment factor, which involves applying differential adjustments based on estimated nonresponse patterns (this adjustment creates what BLS calls STAGE1WT). Specifically, this factor adjusts for interviews that cannot be conducted in occupied housing units due to a consumer unit's refusal to participate in the survey or the inability to contact anyone at the sample unit in spite of repeated attempts. This adjustment is performed separately for each month and "rotation group" (interview number) and yields sixty-four cells or factors based on region of the country, household tenure (owner or renter), household size, and race of the reference person.

If income is correlated with these sixty-four factors that affect unit nonresponse, then applying the noninterview adjustment factor could remedy the differential in response rates at very high (and very low) incomes. However, the correlation between zip code-level AGI and the BLS noninterview adjustment factor appears to be weak as shown in figure 8.1 (middle set of markers). The adjustment factor raises response rates nearly uniformly across AGI percentiles. The overall adjustment factors are calibrated such that the adjusted overall response rate is basically 100 percent, meaning the

20. The other key distinction between the top and bottom of the AGI distribution, explored further below, is that the average reported income in the CE at the top is well below the average AGI at the top, suggesting that the families who do participate in the top zip codes have below average income. At the bottom of the AGI distribution, reported incomes match AGI quite well.

21. The discussion of CE weighting here largely follows the Bureau of Labor Statistics, *Handbook of Methods*, available online at www.bls.gov/opub/hom/.

new weights will sum to the count of originally sampled units, but nearly the same curvature in response rates at very high and very low percentiles is observed. Hence, households in the top 5 percentiles are about 10 percent less likely to participate in the survey than households in the middle 90 percentiles, and the difference is the same regardless of whether BASEWT or STAGE1WT is used to weight the data. This suggests that the CE's noninterview adjustment is not accounting for the different response rates observed at different income levels.

Finally, BLS applies a "calibration factor" that adjusts the weights to twenty-four "known" population counts to account for frame undercoverage. These known population counts are for age, race, household tenure (owner or renter), region, and urban or rural. The population counts are updated quarterly. Each consumer unit is given a calibration factor based on which of the twenty-four distinct groups they are in (this last adjustment creates FINLWT21, the weight that CE microdata users are most familiar with).[22] Similar to the above shift shown in figure 8.1 between using BASEWT and STAGE1WT, the calibration-adjusted (using FINLWT21) response rates are shifted up again (figure 8.1, top set of markers). However, there is no qualitative change in the pattern. As with BASEWT and STAGE1WT, households in the top 5 percentiles are about 10 percent less likely to participate in the survey than households in the middle 90 percentiles.

8.3.3 Probit Analysis

An alternative approach to exploring the relationship between income and unit nonresponse involves estimating a binomial probit model in which zip code-level AGI is included as a determinant of response status along with the sixty-four-way matrix of stratifying variables used by the BLS in the weighting adjustment for nonresponse that creates STAGE1WT. Specifically, NR (in equation [1] below) is a binary variable that is equal to zero for responding CUs and one for those that did not participate in the survey. The regression also includes sixty-three dummy variables corresponding to all but one of the region-family size-race-housing tenure strata used for the nonresponse weighting adjustment in the CE. A fifth-order polynomial function in AGI is included using five variables: AGI, $AGI^2/1000$, $AGI^3/10^6$, $AGI^4/10^8$, and $AGI^5/10^{10}$.[23] The equation below is estimated using the same

---

22. Note that there are infinitely many sets of calibration factors that make the weights add up to the twenty-four "known" population counts, and the CE selects the set that minimizes the amount of change made to the "initial weights" (initial weight = (base weight) × (weighting control factor) × (noninterview adjustment factor)).

23. The functional form was chosen to match the fifth-order polynomial curves in figures 8.1 and 8.2. As in the graphical analysis, AGI and CE income data are made more consistent by subtracting capital gains income from the former and several nontaxable items from the latter: food stamp receipts, cash welfare and SSI benefits, child support receipts, and alimony payments. Using information from 2008 SOI tables, we also subtracted estimated untaxed portions of interest receipts, pension benefits, and Social Security and railroad retirement benefits.

sample of 61,546 responding and 21,820 nonresponding CUs described above, and observations are weighted by BASEWT.

Each of the five AGI variables was asymptotically significant at the 0.01 percent significance level, even with all the stratifying variables held constant. A likelihood ratio test of the significance of the five AGI variables yielded a chi-square value of 180 with five degrees of freedom, which easily surpasses any usual significance level. The probit results of interest are:

(1)   Probit (NR) = [stratification dummy terms] + 0.0104 AGI

$$- 0.1133 \text{ AGI}^2/1000 + 0.6373 \text{ AGI}^3/10^6$$

$$- 0.1605 \text{ AGI}^4/10^8 + 0.0140 \text{ AGI}^5/10^{10}.$$

This equation implies a positive impact of zip code-level AGI on the nonresponse probability, with the second derivative negative, until the highest-observed values of AGI. All five AGI coefficients were significant at the 1 percent level in a two-tailed test.

The probit approach is indicative of how one might begin to think about creating an alternative to the BLS stage-one adjustments (STAGE1WT) using AGI along with the existing BLS stratifying variables. With the probit-based noninterview adjustments, the average adjusted response rate in the top 5 AGI percentiles is only about 3 percent below that of the sample as a whole, compared to about 9 percent using the BLS STAGE1WT adjustments and 10 percent using the FINLWT21 adjustments. By giving higher weights to CUs in higher-AGI areas, the probit approach does indeed imply higher aggregate-weighted average CE incomes and expenditures, but the effects are modest.[24]

Using a revised weight based on the probit adjustment using AGI as an explanatory variable yields average income that is only about 0.37 percent higher and average spending that is about 0.19 percent higher than those using the BLS STAGE1WT. Hence, this probit analysis is able to capture the pattern shown in figure 8.1, but adjusting the weights cannot account for all of the income underreporting.

8.3.4 CE Incomes Relative to Average AGI

The previous analysis demonstrated that there is a differential nonresponse in the very high income AGI zip code areas. Although the CE income appears to be associated with zip code-level AGI, it is difficult to map these outcomes back to the univariate income distributions shown earlier (table 8.2) because CE households are being sorted by zip code-level AGI, not their

24. It is important to recognize that if the BLS actually used these probit nonresponse adjustments it would necessarily lead to different calibration adjustments. The alternative calibration factors might be expected to reduce the differences between the current and probit-based income and expenditure estimates. Unfortunately, estimating new calibration factors was not feasible for this chapter.

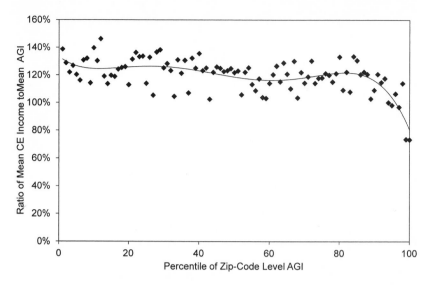

Fig. 8.2 Ratio of mean Consumer Expenditure survey (CE) income to adjusted gross income (AGI) by zip code-level AGI percentile

Note: Fitted curve is a fifth-order polynomial.

own household income (which we cannot observe for nonrespondents). The next part of the analysis provides more support for the proposition that the very highest income households are underrepresented in the CE.[25] In this second step, we compare average CE income to average AGI within each AGI percentile, and show that the ratio generally falls with income and is dramatically lower at the top of the AGI distribution.

Across all AGI percentiles in the linked data set, mean CE income for respondents (based on FINLWT21) is about 14 percent higher than mean AGI for all sampled units (based on BASEWT, though the exact weight chosen does not affect this answer). However, there is a distinct downward pattern across AGI percentiles (figure 8.2). The ratio of mean CE income to mean AGI is about 140 percent at the bottom of the income distribution, and falls steadily as AGI increases, before plummeting to below 74 percent for the top 2 percentiles of AGI. Thus, figure 8.2 complements figure 8.1 in the following sense. Figure 8.1 shows that households in the top AGI percentile zip codes are 10 percent less likely to participate than the rest of the sample, and figure 8.2 suggests that the households within the top AGI percentiles that do participate are more likely to have lower incomes than the households in that zip code who did not participate. Further, this pattern of

25. In this chapter, we use total CE income, including the incomes imputed by the BLS for consumer units who participate in the survey but who fail to respond to income questions. Imputation would have little effect on the section 8.2 comparisons.

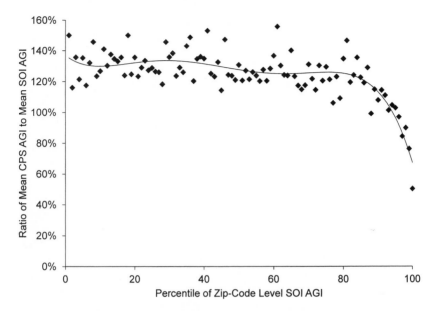

Fig. 8.3 Ratio of mean CPS adjusted gross income (AGI) to SOI AGI by zip code-level SOI AGI percentile

Note: Fitted curve is a fifth-order polynomial.

high-income areas having lower reported income may be common to many household surveys. Figure 8.3 illustrates a similar pattern using the CPS data and the AGI data by zip code. Similar to figure 8.2, figure 8.3 is based on an analysis using calendar year 2008 CPS income data that are comparable to the AGI income concept and the same SOI file by zip code used in CE analysis. Given these lower survey response rates among very high income households observed in the CE and CPS, it may be that a targeted oversampling strategy such as the one used by the SCF is the only way to get accurate representation at the top of the income distribution.

Although there are conceptual differences between AGI and CE income that make direct inferences difficult, it is worth noting that the combined insights from figure 8.1 and figure 8.2 probably go a long way toward explaining the income distribution differences presented in table 8.2. For example, the CE finds about 7 percent fewer households above $100,000 than the SCF, which is similar in magnitude to the roughly 10 percent response differentials for the top 5 percentiles shown in figure 8.1. Also, the ratio of average income in the CE to average income in the SCF for households above $100,000 is 68 percent, which is in the same ballpark as the CE income to AGI ratios at the highest AGI percentiles. Although a direct mapping from the zip code-level AGI percentile analysis to univariate income distributions requires more research, the results here suggest that differential unit nonresponse probably goes a long way toward explaining the shortfalls. To fully incorporate the effects of differential unit nonresponse into formal poststratification adjustments requires comparable income measures. A more complete analysis involves more fully reconciling the CE income and AGI concepts, which is a topic for future research. See the earlier discussion in the text about why AGI and CE income concepts diverge.

8.4 Why is Aggregate Consumer Expenditure Survey Spending So Low?

If PCE in the National Income and Product Accounts (NIPA) are viewed as the truth about what consumers actually spend in a given time period, there are two possible high-level explanations for why aggregated spending in the CE is below the corresponding PCE totals. The evidence above provides some support for the first reason, which is that the very highest income households are underrepresented. However, the observed underrepresentation of very high-income households cannot fully explain the aggregate CE spending shortfall. The most extreme estimate of the aggregate CE income shortfall above $100,000 comes from comparing the CE to the SCF. The SCF finds about $1.7 trillion more income above $100,000 than the CE, but if one applies the BLS-reported ratio of expenditures to gross income for that group (61 percent), that implies total spending would rise by 16 percent, which explains perhaps half of the overall shortfall relative to PCE totals (as shown in table 8.1).

Overall, published CE expenditures are lower than published CE after-tax incomes. For example, the ratio of published total expenditures to published after-tax income for CE respondents was 83 percent in 2006.[26] Given the relationship between aggregate spending and disposable income in the NIPA data, that ratio probably should have been much higher.[27] Based on that aggregate perspective and the conclusion that misrepresented high-income households only explains at most half of aggregate underreporting; at least some of the shortfall in aggregate CE spending seems attributable to underreporting of spending (given income) by at least some CE respondents.

---

26. These calculations are based on published BLS numbers, even though the reported values have both conceptual problems and systematic reporting errors in at least one key variable. Conceptually, for example, BLS counts Social Security taxes and employee contributions to pensions as expenditures, but they do not count mortgage principal repayments as spending. For these and other reasons the concept of after-tax income minus expenditures is not in any sense a pure "saving" estimate, but there are biases in both directions, and fixing those would require unavailable information such as net home equity extraction needed to measure net mortgage principal payments. There are also some measurement biases in the table that BLS is aware of and working on—for example, based on comparison of effective tax rates with other sources, underreporting of income taxes could account for several percentage points of the overall cash-flow discrepancy, and even more for higher-income respondents.

27. See, for example, Bosworth, Burtless, and Sabelhaus (1991) for a discussion of what is involved with reconciling aggregate and household-level saving concepts.

Knowing that the overall spending-to-income ratio seems too low for the CE survey (based on comparisons to PCE) is a starting point, but it does not help with the distributional question of whether the propensity to underreport spending varies with income itself. Researchers interested in using the CE for distributional analysis of questions about topics like consumption-expenditure versus income inequality, saving rates, or the distributional burden of consumption taxes, rely completely on the empirical joint distribution of expenditures and income. If the problem is proportional underreporting of expenditures for all CE respondents, then the simple solution is to scale up spending for all households (perhaps by type of spending) before undertaking any distributional analysis (see Slesnick [2001] and Meyer and Sullivan [2011] for a similar approach). However, if the propensity to underreport rises with spending (and thus with income), then some sort of differential adjustments are warranted.

The estimated pattern of spending-to-income ratios by income in the CE may have flaws, but if it does, those flaws are not a new phenomenon. A comparison of published BLS data for 1972–1973, 2003, and 2010 in figure 8.4 shows that the ratio of spending to unadjusted after-tax income at any given level of income has not changed much in forty years.[28] Overall, the ratio of spending to after-tax income fell from 89 percent in 1972–1973 to 84 percent in 2003 and 79 percent in 2010. While the overall spending-to-income ratios fell between 1972–1973 and 2010, the ratio across income groups remained fairly constant. This occurs because of the increase in households at the higher end of the income distribution who have lower spending-to-income ratios. Based on aggregate trends in savings rates (which are decreasing during this period), the overall spending-to-income ratio should have been higher in the last two periods than in the first. However, figure 8.4 suggests that the differences in spending-to-income ratios occur across income groups at each point in time and have not changed over time.[29]

The ratios of total expenditure to after-tax incomes by income shown in figure 8.4 exhibit a dramatic pattern, and although there are some conceptual issues and systematic reporting errors with income taxes in the BLS tabulations, those sorts of corrections do not fundamentally change that pattern. The ratio of spending to income at low-income levels seems implau-

28. Each point on the chart marks average total expenditures divided by average after-tax income, at the value of after-tax income reported in the BLS tables. Values for average after-tax income in 1972–1973 and 2003 are inflated to 2010 dollars. The year 2003 marks the first year in which BLS published "high income" tables for the modern (post-1980) ongoing CE survey.

29. The stability of spending-to-income ratios across income groups also raises concerns about the approach used by Aguiar and Bils (2011) to "correct" for bias in studies that compare consumption versus income inequality. They use the 1972–1973 CE survey to estimate Engel curves, and impute missing spending in the 1980s based on those estimated relationships and an aggregate scaling factor. If underreporting for higher-income families was just as bad in the 1970s as it is today, then they are effectively just inflating observed spending to match aggregates.

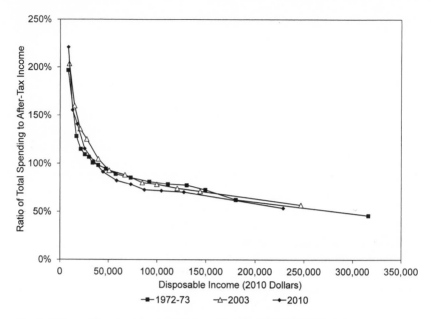

Fig. 8.4 Expenditure to after-tax income ratios in published CE data

sibly high, and the ratio of spending to income at the top seems implausibly low. There are most likely problems with both income and expenditure reporting, and sorting households by income simply highlights those errors.

In any household survey there will be measurement error, and, given that the CE is focused on spending rather than income, it is not surprising that income may be poorly reported for some households.[30] The bottom of the income distribution includes many households who underreport income (e.g., the self-employed), and hence, the high ratios of expenditure to income at low incomes can be partially explained by the presence of these households. The argument that income is missing at the bottom is reinforced by a pragmatic view of lower-income households. It is impossible to spend twice your income (figure 8.4) if you have no assets to draw down and no access to credit, which is the basic conclusion one takes away from wealth surveys like the SCF or Panel Survey of Income Dynamics (PSID). Thus, except for students, households with temporary business losses, and retirees drawing

30. Indeed, the CE data includes a number of consumer units who either refuse to answer or say they "don't know," which is why income is imputed for a significant number of cases. The CE imputation procedures, described in Passero (2009) and Paulin and Ferraro (1996), focus on preserving the consumption-to-income relationship for those households who do participate, by using expenditures as an explanatory variable in the imputation procedures. The conclusions of this chapter might suggest some reconsideration of the current imputation procedures to reflect nonrandom nonresponse.

down assets, the high rates of implied dissaving by lower-income households in the CE are already implausible and proportional scaling-up of spending would only increase these already implausibly high spending-to-income ratios.

It is also unrealistic to think that families above $100,000, on average, save the fraction of their disposable income implied by figure 8.4, using it for purchasing stocks, bonds, and other investments that are not captured by the CE. Such behavior would yield average wealth-to-income ratios for higher-income households that are much different than what we observe in wealth surveys (e.g., PSID and SCF).[31]

8.5 Conclusions

Only the very highest income households seem to be underrepresented in the CE Survey, but the overall underreported spending in the CE cannot be fully explained by that shortcoming. At least some of the shortfall in aggregate CE spending seems attributable to underreported spending by at least some CE respondents, and that has implications for research that relies on the relationship between spending and income in microdata. The observation that spending-to-income ratios fall with reported income in the CE implies that consumption-expenditure inequality will be less than income inequality, and the extent to which this ratio falls with income (and changes over time) has a dramatic impact on the estimated relationship between consumption expenditure and income inequality. Also, if this pattern in the spending-to-income ratios is partially due to measurement of total spending, then the amount of dissaving at low incomes and saving at high incomes will both be exaggerated and consumption taxes will appear (perhaps wrongly) to be highly regressive alternatives to income taxes.

Resolving whether expenditures are proportionally underreported for all CE respondents or disproportionately for higher-income (and thus higher-spending) respondents is a crucial task facing the current multiyear CE redesign effort (called Gemini). The mission of the Gemini project is to redesign the CE in order to improve data quality through a verifiable reduction in measurement error, with a particular focus on underreporting.[32]

31. Some might argue that these simple calculations ignore income fluctuations because households do not stay in the same income group from one year to the next. That is exactly the argument addressed by Sabelhaus and Groen (2000), who use data on income mobility from the PSID to test whether movements across income groups can explain the pattern of consumption to income in the CE. The answer they find is clearly no—there is not enough income mobility, even under the most extreme assumptions about consumption smoothing.

32. (For a description of the Gemini project, see http://www.bls.gov/cex/geminiproject.htm.) As part of this effort, the National Research Council, through its Committee on National Statistics (CNSTAT), has convened an expert panel to contribute to that planned redesign (see http://www8.nationalacademies.org/cp/projectview.aspx?key=49322).

Future research to examine this underreporting includes a joint effort by BLS and the Census Bureau is to examine additional variables, including income, in CE's nonresponse and calibration-adjustment processes.[33] This research will address a number of questions such as what variables are available for every household in the CE survey, both respondents and nonrespondents; what qualities characterize "good" variables for these procedures; and what variables other surveys use. An oversampling strategy such as that employed by the SCF may also be worth considering. Implementation of oversampling could be expensive, and it would not by itself address a bias problem, but if combined with revised methods for nonresponse adjustment it could be a valuable improvement. Finally, it may be the case that the demands placed on respondents in the current CE are simply too daunting because respondents are asked to remember several hundred spending items for each month in a three-month recall period. Hence, a third approach to reconciling the difference between incomes and spending across income groups might involve streamlining the collection of spending totals so that even high spenders will have a better chance to accurately estimate and report their total spending.[34] It is hoped that the results presented in this chapter will constitute a further contribution to the CE redesign program.

References

Aguiar, Mark A., and Mark Bils. 2011. "Has Consumption Inequality Mirrored Income Inequality?" NBER Working Paper no. 16807, Cambridge, MA.
Attanasio, Orazio, Gabriella Berloffa, Richard Blundell, and Ian Preston. 2002. "From Earnings Inequality to Consumption Inequality." *Economic Journal* 112 (478): 52–59.
Bosworth, Barry, Gary Burtless, and John Sabelhaus. 1991. "The Decline in Saving: Evidence from Household Surveys." *Brookings Papers on Economic Activity* 1991 (1): 183–241.
Browning, Martin, and Thomas Crossley. 2009. "Are Two, Cheap Noisy Measures Better Than One Expensive, Accurate One?" *American Economic Review* 99 (2): 99–103.
Bucks, Brian K., Arthur B. Kennickell, Traci L. Mach, and Kevin B. Moore. 2009. "Changes in US Family Finances from 2004 to 2007: Evidence from the Survey of Consumer Finances." *Federal Reserve Bulletin, 1st Quarter 2009* 95:A1–55.
Burkhauser, Richard V., Shuaizhang Feng, Stephen P. Jenkins, and Jeff Larrimore. 2009. "Recent Trends in Top Income Shares in the USA: Reconciling Estimates

---

33. In 2014, the CE will begin using a modified nonresponse adjustment that includes cells by income using the SOI public-use income data.
34. Browning and Crossley (2009) discuss the merits of collecting aggregated versus disaggregated spending data.

from March CPS and IRS Tax Return Data." NBER Working Paper no. 15320, Cambridge, MA.

Crossley, Thomas F. 2009. "Measuring Consumption and Saving: Introduction." *Fiscal Studies* 30 (3–4): 303–07.

Garner, Thesia I., George Janini, William Passero, Laura Paszkiewicz, and Mark Vendemia. 2006. "The CE and the PCE: A Comparison." *Monthly Labor Review* 129 (9): 20–46.

Garner, Thesia I., Robert McClelland, and William Passero. 2009. "Strengths and Weaknesses of the Consumer Expenditure Survey from a BLS Perspective." Paper prepared for NBER Summer Institute, Conference on Research on Income and Wealth, Joint with Aggregate Implications of Microeconomic Consumption Behavior Workshop, Cambridge, Massachusetts, July 13–14.

Garner, Thesia I., and Kathleen Short. 2009. "Accounting for Owner-Occupied Dwelling Services: Aggregates and Distributions." *Journal of Housing Economics* 18 (3): 233–48.

Groves, Robert M. 2006. "Nonresponse Rates and Nonresponse Bias in Households Surveys." *Public Opinion Quarterly* 70 (5): 646–75.

Heathcote, Jonathan, Fabrizio Perri, and Giovanni L. Violante. 2010. "Unequal We Stand: An Empirical Analysis of Economic Inequality in the United States, 1967–2006." *Review of Economic Dynamics* 13 (1): 15–51.

Johnson, David, and Stephanie Shipp. 1997. "Trends in Inequality Using Consumption-Expenditures: The US from 1960 to 1993." *Review of Income and Wealth* 43 (2): 133–52.

Kennickell, Arthur B. 2009. "Ponds and Streams: Wealth and Income in the US, 1989 to 2007." Finance and Economics Discussion Series: 2009–13, Board of Governors of the Federal Reserve System.

Kennickell, Arthur B., and Louise R. Woodburn. 1999. "Consistent Weight Design for the 1989, 1992 and 1995 SCFs, and the Distribution of Wealth." *Review of Income and Wealth* 45 (2): 193–215.

King, Susan L., Boriana Chopova, Jennifer Edgar, Jeffrey M. Gonzales, Dave E. McGrath, and Lucilla Tan. 2009. "Assessing Nonresponse Bias in the Consumer Expenditure Interview Survey." Section on Survey Research Methods, Joint Program on Survey Methods Annual Conference, 1808–16.

Krueger, Dirk, and Fabrizio Perri. 2006. "Does Income Inequality Lead to Consumption Inequality? Evidence and Theory." *Review of Economic Studies* 73 (1): 163–93.

Krueger, Dirk, Fabrizio Perri, Luigi Pistaferri, and Giovanni L. Violante. 2010. "Cross-Sectional Facts for Macroeconomists." *Review of Economic Dynamics* 13 (1): 1–14.

McCully, Clinton P., Brian C. Moyer, and Kenneth J. Stewart. 2007. "Comparing the Consumer Price Index and the Personal Consumption Expenditures Price Index." *Survey of Current Business* (November):26–33.

Meyer, Bruce D., Wallace K. C. Mok, and James X. Sullivan. 2009. "The Under-Reporting of Transfers in Household Surveys: Its Nature and Consequences." NBER Working Paper no. 15181, Cambridge, MA.

Meyer, Bruce D., and James X. Sullivan. 2011. "The Material Well-Being of the Poor and the Middle Class Since 1980." Working Paper no. 2011–44, American Enterprise Institute.

Passero, William. 2009. "The Impact of Income Imputation in the Consumer Expenditure Survey." *Monthly Labor Review* 132 (8): 25–42.

Paulin, Geoffrey D., and David L. Ferraro. 1996. "Do Expenditures Explain Income? A Study of Variables for Income Imputation." *Journal of Economic and Social Measurement* 22 (2): 103–28.

Sabelhaus, John, and Jeffrey A. Groen. 2000. "Can Permanent-Income Theory Explain Cross-Sectional Consumption Patterns?" *Review of Economics and Statistics* 82 (3): 431–38.

Short, Kathleen, Martina Shea, David Johnson, and Thesia I. Garner. 1998. "Poverty-Measurement Research Using the Consumer Expenditure Survey and the Survey of Income and Program Participation." *American Economic Review* 88(2): 352–56.

Slesnick, Daniel. 2001. *Consumption and Social Welfare*. Cambridge: Cambridge University Press.

A Comparison of Micro and Macro Expenditure Measures across Countries Using Differing Survey Methods

Garry Barrett, Peter Levell, and Kevin Milligan

9.1 Introduction

Household-level consumption lies at the center of research into many important economic questions. The measurement of microeconomic phenomena such as household poverty requires the observation of consumption choices made by households to provide useful information on economic hardship. At the macroeconomic level, the understanding of responses to booms and busts is enhanced by observing household consumption responses. Reliable consumption data are necessary to engage in meaningful empirical research in these areas.

However, there are ongoing concerns about the reliability of expenditure surveys in many countries. These concerns have led to efforts to renew expenditure survey methodology. In the United States, this activity centers on the "Gemini Project" of the Bureau of Labor Statistics, tasked with improving the Consumer Expenditure Survey.[1] In Canada,

Garry Barrett is professor in the School of Economics at the University of Sydney. Peter Levell is a research economist at the Institute for Fiscal Studies. Kevin Milligan is associate professor of economics at the University of British Columbia and a research associate of the National Bureau of Economic Research.

Paper prepared for "Conference on Improving the Measurement of Consumer Expenditures," sponsored by the Conference on Research in Income and Wealth and the National Bureau of Economic Research, December 2011. This chapter builds on joint ongoing work with Thomas F. Crossley. Cormac O'Dea assisted in the collection of the UK data. Bruce Meyer and Jim Sullivan provided some assistance with our US data. We thank the aforementioned for their contributions to this work. We also thank editor John Sabelhaus and conference participants for their suggestions for the chapter. For acknowledgments, sources of research support, and disclosure of the authors' material financial relationships, if any, please see http://www.nber.org/chapters/c12665.ack.

1. Edgar and Safir (2011) provide an overview of the Gemini Project.

the Survey of Household Spending was revised in 2010 with similar goals in mind.[2]

In this chapter, we aim to contribute to these discussions by providing an international comparison of the performance of household expenditure survey data across four "Anglosphere" countries: Australia, Canada, the United Kingdom, and the United States. Our international comparison is a useful way to gather some evidence on the potential sources of problems with expenditure surveys, as differences in experience and methodology provide sources of variation that may give insights into the importance of factors influencing the performance of expenditure surveys.

Our strategy is to compare household expenditure survey data to expenditure measured in the national accounts of each country. While this "coverage" approach is frequently adopted in country-specific studies of expenditure behavior, the novelty of our contribution is to produce comparable results across four countries.[3] Attanasio, Battistin, and Leicester (2006), in assessing the expenditure behavior of poor households in the United States and the United Kingdom, provide an assessment of microsurvey evidence benchmarked against the national accounts. In comparison to their paper, we provide more recent years of data, two more countries with differing methodology, and a more detailed accounting of the survey differences. Deaton (2005) provides a comparison of a vast array of countries, with analysis of the same kind of "survey versus national accounts" comparison we perform here.

The chapter proceeds first by reviewing the survey methods employed in the four target countries. We then discuss in more detail the construction and interpretation of household survey versus national account comparisons, and examine the trends in aggregate ratios of survey to national account data across countries. Next, we consider how survey response rates have varied across countries and relate them to our aggregate coverage measures. We then compare the coverage measures to high income concentration through time and across our countries. Finally, we look at selected subcategories of expenditure to observe how trends vary across countries.

9.2 Expenditure Survey Methodology

In this section, we provide some background on the methodology employed for the household expenditure surveys in each of the four countries in our

---

2. Tremblay, Lynch, and Dubreuil (2010) report results from a pilot project from 2007 evaluating several changes. Many of these changes have been implemented for the 2010 Survey of Household Spending.

3. Some well-known examples of this measurement approach are Slesnick (1992), Garner et al. (2006), and Garner, McClelland, and Passero (2009) for the United States. Adler and Wolfson (1988) perform a similar exercise for Canada. Passero, Garner, and McCully (chapter 6, this volume) also provide an updated approach to comparing the CE survey with PCE.

focus. We describe the target population, survey design, and other special features for each country. We begin with Australia, and proceed through Canada, the United Kingdom, and the United States. At the end of these descriptions, we provide a summary table of the key elements of the survey methodologies.

9.2.1 Australia: Household Expenditure Survey

The Australian Household Expenditure Survey (HES) has been carried out seven times: 1975–1976, 1984, 1988–1989, 1993–1994, 1998–1999, 2003–2004, and 2009–2010. The HES is conducted over a twelve-month period, typically coinciding with the financial (July–June) rather than calendar year, with households enumerated evenly over the survey period. The primary purpose of the HES is to collect comprehensive information on household expenditures along with household income and, since 2003/4, wealth. The original objective of the HES program was to provide information for the construction of commodity weights in the consumer price index (CPI)—for more details on the HES background and methodology see Australian Bureau of Statistics (2011).

Expenditures are recorded in HES on an acquisition basis, with details on most regular expenditures collected using diary methods. Regular expenditure items for each household member age fifteen years or older are recorded in a personal diary covering a two-week reporting period.[4] The fineness of the expenditure categories used in the survey has increased over time, with 660 items separately recorded in the 2003–2004 and 2009–2010 surveys.

Expenditures on infrequent, irregular, or expensive items are recorded by personal interview with each household member age fifteen years or older. The recall period for irregular purchases varies, ranging from three months for major household furniture and appliances, twelve months for motor vehicle registrations, and three years for house purchases. Items such as insurance, rent payments, and utilities bills are recorded in the interview with respondents asked the value of the last payment and the period of time that payment covered. Given the recall periods for items recorded in the household interview questionnaire, some of these expenditures will refer to time periods prior to the reference year. The public-release HES reports average weekly expenditures for all items, with expenditures on some items converted to average weekly amounts. Additional information on household demographics and income are also collected during the household interview on a recall basis.

The scope of the HES includes "usual residents of private dwellings in urban and rural areas of Australia." Excluded from the survey are resi-

---

4. The HES records regular expenditures using one-week diaries for two consecutive weeks. In the 1975–1976 and 1984 HES, the reporting period for rural respondents was four weeks.

dents of "nonprivate dwellings" such as hotels, boarding schools, boarding houses, and institutions. Further exclusions are residents of very remote districts (or indigenous communities).[5] In addition, nonusual residents of a private dwelling (e.g., visitors) are not included in the survey. Approximately 97–98 percent of the Australian population are within the scope of HES.

Sampling is based on a stratified multistage cluster design. The strata are based on census collector districts. Individual household records are weighted according to the probability of initial selection into the survey adjusted according to population benchmarks based on the demographic characteristics of household size and age composition, geographic location, and labor force status.[6] The sample size of the individual HES collections is typically 7,000 households, though the size has ranged from 4,492 in 1984 to 9,774 in 2009–2010. For the most recent survey, the response rate in the HES was 71.9 percent.

9.2.2 Canada: The Survey of Household Spending

The Survey of Household Spending (SHS) has been the primary household expenditure survey in Canada since it replaced the Family Expenditure Survey (FAMEX), starting in 1997.[7] The methodology is described in detail in Statistics Canada (2001). When relevant, we also referred to the methodological description in the user guide from the most recent SHS from 2009 (Statistics Canada 2011). A detailed comparison of the SHS with the American Consumer Expenditure Survey is provided in Brzozowski and Crossley (2011). These sources provide the foundation for the description of the SHS below. We also use the FAMEX surveys for some of our analysis, but the primary focus is on the more recent SHS.[8]

The SHS targets individuals living in Canadian private households, as well as residents of Indian reserves and Crown Lands. This definition excludes those who are official representatives of foreign countries living in Canada, as well as those who are representing Canada abroad. It also leaves out residents of institutions, hotels and rooming houses, religious orders, and members of the Canadian Forces living in camps. For the lower ten provinces, the coverage is around 98 percent of the population. For the sparsely populated northern territories, coverage is over 80 percent.

---

5. Non-Australian defence forces stationed in Australia and the diplomatic personnel of overseas governments located in Australia are also excluded.

6. The two initial HESs did not use population benchmarking.

7. The differences between the SHS and FAMEX are outlined in Statistics Canada (2000). The sample size increased, the survey became annual, population coverage broadened, and some minor changes to survey content were implemented. We include some data from the FAMEX in our work here, but primarily focus on the SHS.

8. The FAMEX surveys were conducted in 1969, 1974, 1978, 1982, 1984, 1986, 1990, 1992, and 1996. The 1984 and 1990 surveys are less comparable because in those years only residents of certain large cities were surveyed.

Sampling is based on the Labour Force Survey sample design, which uses stratified clusters. The strata are based on geography within each province. Special strata of households in areas with geographical concentrations of high- and low-income residents are also used. Clusters are chosen, and then a sample of households is chosen from each cluster. Extensive follow-up is engaged for households who refuse to comply, including further phone calls, visits, and letters. Sample size started at 18,031 in 1997. From then until 2007, the number of observations slid down to 13,939. For 2008 and 2009, budget cutbacks meant a jump down to samples of 9,787 and 10,811.

The SHS attempts to gather information on the twelve-month period from January 1st to December 31st. The information is gathered via a face-to-face recall survey of one household member in the January, February, or March following the end of the target calendar year. The survey respondents are encouraged to gather source documents such as credit card statements, mortgage statements, and their income tax records. The average survey takes one hour and forty minutes to complete. A "balance edit" is applied when the difference between expenditure, income, and savings exceeded a 20 percent tolerance level.[9] Item nonresponse is countered by imputing data based on "nearest neighbor" imputations.

For 2009, weights are provided to account for nonresponse according to cells defined by province, age, household size, and family income as measured by administrative tax data. This weighting strategy has changed several times. Importantly, starting in 1999 tax-filing data from the Canada Revenue Agency were used to match on wage and salary income.[10] This is helpful if there is a concern that lower response rates are particular to certain parts of the income distribution, as the weights can account for such systematic patterns.[11]

Major changes to the SHS were implemented in 2010, although the data have not yet been released. Dubreuil et al. (2011) report that the 2010 SHS removes the calendar year focus and now has an interview-diary format. Because income and expenditure periods no longer will match, the balance edit will no longer be used. For 2009, both the old and new SHS methodologies were employed, which will allow researchers to study the impact of the change in methodology.

9.2.3 United Kingdom: Living Costs and Food Survey

The information in this section is drawn from Office for National Statistics (2010). The Office for National Statistics (ONS) in the United Kingdom

---

9. Brzozowski and Crossley (2011) look into the impact of this balance edit in detail by examining the data from 2006 when no balance edit was imposed.

10. The income weights account for incomes in the following percentile ranges: 0–25th percentile, 25th–50th, 50th–65th, 65th–75th, 75th–95th, 95th–100th.

11. Sabelhaus et al. (chapter 8, this volume) show that response rates in the US Consumer Expenditure Survey are in fact much lower at the top of the income distribution.

has carried out some form of annual survey of household expenditures since 1957. From 2008, this survey has been known as the Living Costs and Food Survey (LCFS). Prior to this it was known as the Expenditure and Food Survey, which brought together what were two separate surveys for food and expenditure—the Family Expenditure Survey and the National Food Survey—in 2001. The survey is conducted continuously throughout the year.

Participation in the survey is voluntary. In 2009, the survey selected over 12,000 addresses, but only 5,825 of these were included in the survey. The remaining addresses were either ineligible to be included (because, for instance, the addresses were for businesses), refused to participate, or were not possible to contact. Households in Northern Ireland are sampled separately and oversampled relative to the rest of the United Kingdom in order to achieve the sample size required for separate analyses. The response rate among eligible addresses was 56 percent in Northern Ireland and 50.4 percent in the rest of the United Kingdom.

Households who are surveyed are first asked a series of questions on income, demographic characteristics, large purchases over the last year or so (on white goods, vehicles, holidays, etc.), and committed expenditures such as magazine subscription costs. Each household member over age sixteen is then given a spending diary in which they record all purchases made over the next two weeks. Simplified diaries for children age seven to fifteen have also been included since 1998. At the end of the two weeks, each adult who kept a diary is paid £10 ($16) for completing the survey (children who kept a diary are paid £5 [$8]). Spending is grossed up using weights from the most recent population census (which have in the past been carried out once every ten years—although 2011 may be the last).

Data collected in the LCFS are used for a number of official purposes. As well as being used for the construction of the national accounts, the LCFS is used to calculate expenditure weights for headline inflation measures.

9.2.4 United States: Consumer Expenditure Survey

The Consumer Expenditure Survey (CE) has been collecting information about American expenditure patterns on an ongoing basis since 1980.[12] The Bureau of Labor Statistics publishes the *Handbook of Methods*, of which chapter 16 is devoted to the Consumer Expenditure Survey (Bureau of Labor Statistics 2011b). A short summary is also provided in Bureau of Labor Statistics (2011a). A review of changes to methodology through time is provided by Goldenberg and Ryan (2009). We draw on these sources in forming our description of the CE survey in this section.

---

12. There were antecedents to the "modern" CE in 1960–1961 and 1972–1973, as well as earlier years.

The CE survey combines two one-week diaries of around 7,000 households with a series of five quarterly recall surveys of another 7,000 households. The target is the total US civilian noninstitutional population, which excludes military personnel living on base, nursing home residents, and people in prisons. Sampling takes place by choosing households from a list within each of ninety-one clusters. The list of addresses comes from the most recent census file, augmented by new construction permits. For the 2010 survey, the response rate was 73.4 percent.

The diary component starts with an interview for demographic information on the first day. The diary of expenditure is to be completed every day during the week. The diary is collected at the end of the first week and a second diary is delivered. When the second diary is picked up, more questions are used to collect information on work and income from the previous year. The data are put through edits and adjustments when being processed. Some imputations are performed as well.

The quarterly recall survey component aims to gather information on less-frequently purchased items, with a three-month recall window. The raw data from the surveys is put through various checks, with imputed values being imposed for missing data. Other adjustments, such as the splitting of mortgage payments into principal and interest components, are made. With the switch from pencil and paper to Computer Assisted Personal Interview in 2003, the time to complete the interview survey fell from about ninety minutes to around sixty-five minutes.

The survey is available annually from 1980 to 2010. For several quarters in the early 1980s, rural households were not surveyed. In our analysis below we retain these years, but they do stand out on several of the graphs for this reason.

Weights in the CE survey are calibrated to twenty-four population counts, including age, race, household tenure, region, and rural/urban. The target population counts are updated quarterly, and the demographics of the sample are assigned weights to match the population on these twenty-four factors. Of note, there is no adjustment for income.

9.2.5 Comparison

In table 9.1, we summarize the main features of the survey data in each country. The data from Canada are different in a number of ways, including the annual focus, having no diary, weighting based on administrative income data, and featuring a balance edit. In Australia, there is some weighting by income—but just the source of income is used. The recall window for the surveys varies across countries. In Australia, it goes back up to three years for some items. In the United Kingdom, one interview goes back for a period of a year. For the United States, the survey is a sequence of five quarterly focused questionnaires.

Table 9.1   **Features of the data sets**

	Australia	Canada (SHS)	United Kingdom	United States
Recall versus diary	Diary (regular) recall (irregular or large items)	Recall	Diary (regular) recall (irregular or large items)	Recall/(and diary)
Interview recall period	Varies; up to 3 years	Annual	About a year	Five quarterly surveys
Balance edit?	No	Yes	No	No
Weighting benchmarks	Age, household size, state, labor force status, income source	Age, province, earnings, household size	Age, region, and sex	Age, race, region, urban/ rural status
Typical sample size	7,000	10,000 to 18,000	6,000	7,000/(7,000)

Notes: Source is the documentation for the surveys in each of the four countries, as referenced in the text.

9.3 Aggregate Coverage Rates

The first step in our assessment of the performance of the household expenditure surveys is the examination of coverage rates of aggregate expenditure for each of the four countries. That is, we take the ratio of expenditures observed in the household survey, grossed up to the aggregate level, to the total expenditures taken from the national accounts. We compare this ratio across time and across countries.

There are several well-known reasons to expect this ratio not to be 100 percent. (See, for example, Meyer and Sullivan 2009.) The population covered by each source may differ. For example, foreigners living in the host country and nationals living out of the country receive different attention in the national accounts and the expenditure surveys, as do military personnel and native peoples. In addition, the categories of expenditure available in the national accounts may not match those available in the expenditure surveys. For example, imputed housing rent is included in the national accounts, but not in the expenditure surveys. Finally, expenditure in the household sector of the national accounts includes spending by nonprofit institutions serving households (such as charities), which does not appear in the expenditure surveys.

To make the best possible comparison, we adjust both the national accounts data and the expenditure survey data to remove items where they do not overlap.[13] For example, noncash items such as imputed rent and food grown and

13. For a detailed description of the methodology used for our UK sample, please see Crossley and O'Dea (2010).

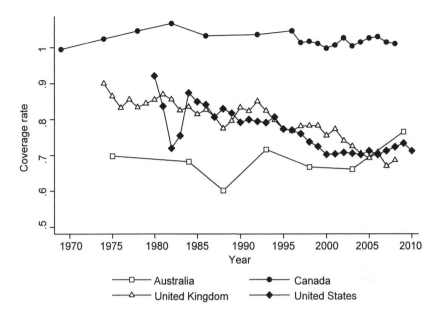

Fig. 9.1 Coverage rates

Notes: Coverage rate is the proportion of consumer expenditure in the national accounts that is accounted for in the household surveys. Calculations by authors.

consumed at home are taken out of the national accounts measure of household expenditure. Similarly, some items from the expenditure surveys, such as insurance purchases, are removed. With these adjustments made, we calculate the ratio of the grossed-up expenditures from the household expenditure survey to the aggregate from the national accounts. This ratio is referred to as the "coverage rate." This coverage calculation is performed for expenditures in aggregate (as we do here in this section) as well as category-by-category comparisons (some of which are presented in a later section).

The coverage rates are graphed in figure 9.1 for each of the four countries. In order to emphasize the nature of the decline, we have adjusted the y-axis to start at 0.5. Both the levels and trends differ sharply across countries. The Australian coverage rate stays in the 60 to 75 percent range, with no discernible trend. For Canada, the coverage rate is close to 1.0 for both the FAMEX (1969–1996) and the SHS (1997–2009) periods. There is no sign of an aggregate drop in coverage. The coverage rate for the United Kingdom drops steadily over the years, from 90 to 67 percent. Finally, the United States shows coverage rates lower than Canada, but follows a very similar trend to the United Kingdom.[14]

---

14. The extra dip down in 1982–1983 is likely related to the discontinuation of rural data collection from the third quarter of 1981 to the first quarter of 1985. We have checked our calculations against those in Meyer and Sullivan (2009) and found our coverage rates to be very similar.

In the two sections of the chapter that follow, we investigate two aspects of this decline in our four countries. First, we look at the impact of declining response rates and increasing income inequality for the expenditure surveys on coverage. Following that, we compare different categories of expenditures, looking across diary and survey categories, as well as frequently and less frequently purchased items.

9.4 Candidate Explanations for Declining Coverage

Many possible explanations for declining coverage rates have been offered. Here, we use our four countries to explore two possibilities. First, we look at declining survey participation rates. A decline in survey participation rates has been observed around the developed world, a trend that began accelerating around 1990.[15] This trend coincides with the decline in the coverage rate in the CE survey in the United States, making nonresponse a candidate explanation for the decline in coverage. Response rates are relevant for the representativeness of samples and reliability of microlevel evidence on expenditures. In particular, if the decline in response rates is not random across the population (and cannot be corrected adequately by sampling weights), then the results of the survey will no longer be representative of the population. For example, if high-expenditure households have become increasingly less likely to respond, and if weighting did not account for this change, then coverage rates would be expected to decline.[16]

The second possibility we examine is the impact of income inequality on survey accuracy.[17] The large trends in the concentration of income are documented across countries in Atkinson, Piketty, and Saez (2011). This concentration has been especially acute in the Anglosphere countries on which we focus. None of the four countries we study oversamples high-income households for the expenditure surveys.[18] If increasing concentration of income is leading to an increasing concentration of expenditures, an increasing share of expenditure may be missed if the upper tail of expenditure is not adequately included in the survey sample. We also investigate this possibility. In addition, it is possible that the income inequality effect interacts with

15. See de Leeuw and de Heer (2002) for international evidence. Tourangeau (2004) provides a discussion of the trends.
16. Tourangeau (2004) reviews the evidence on the causes of declining survey participation, but does not discuss how nonparticipation is correlated with characteristics such as income. D'Alessio and Faiella (2002) find that nonresponse in the Bank of Italy's Survey of Household Income and Wealth is more frequent among wealthier households. Finally, Sabelhaus et al. (chapter 8, this volume) show that response rates in the CE are much lower at the top of the income distribution.
17. We thank Angus Deaton for suggesting this possibility to us.
18. Canada uses the Labour Force Survey sampling frame, which does target certain high-income areas when choosing strata from which to sample. However, there is not explicit oversampling of high-income households within the survey.

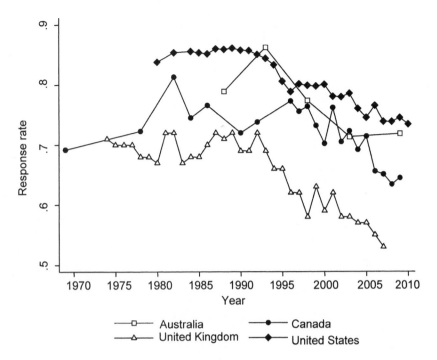

Fig. 9.2 Response rates

Source: The documentation for the surveys in each of the four countries, as referenced in the text.

Note: Response rate is the proportion of contacted households with completed surveys.

survey nonresponse. If the change in nonresponse is occurring more at the top of the income distribution, then the two effects (declining response rates and increasing income distribution) would reinforce each other.

With either survey response rates or income inequality, we will be comparing time series trends that happen to coincide with the change in coverage rates. It is prudent to be cautious in the interpretation of these results as causal. That said, we do get some mileage out of our cross-country comparison by including in our regression specification common time trends, allowing us to exploit the cross-country variation in the coverage, response rate, and inequality trends.

9.4.1 Response Rates

Figure 9.2 shows the basic response rates for the expenditure surveys for the four countries, with the y-axis starting at 0.5. Each country exhibits declining responses rates, with the steepest occurring in the United Kingdom—where the drop is from 72 percent to 53 percent. The decline begins in the early 1990s in Australia, the United Kingdom, and the United States, but is not observable in Canada until the first decade of the twenty-first century.

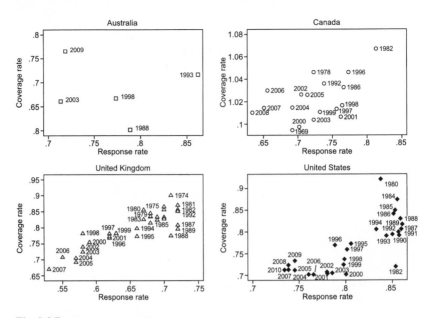

Fig. 9.3 Response rates versus coverage rates

Notes: Coverage rate is the proportion of consumer expenditure in the national accounts that is accounted for in the household surveys. Response rate is the proportion of contacted households with completed surveys. Calculations by authors.

While Canada was later starting downward, the decline exceeded 10 percentage points over the last decade.

To compare coverage and response rates, we graph the data from figure 9.1 and figure 9.2 together for each country as a scatter plot in figure 9.3. The axes are different for each country in order to highlight the nature of the relationship in each country. For Canada, the United Kingdom, and the United States, there does appear to be a positive relationship between the response rate and the coverage rate. For Canada, the positive relationship in the figure is perhaps deceptive—the variation in the coverage rate is quite small—it ranges only from just under 1.0 to just under 1.07. The United Kingdom shows a fairly tight positive relationship across the thirty-five years available. In the United States, the data are clustered in two groups that together suggest a similar positive relationship between coverage rates and response rates. For Australia, in contrast, there is no apparent relationship between response rates and coverage rates, although the limited number of surveys makes any conclusion difficult.

Figure 9.4 stacks together the data for all four countries in one plot with common axes. Looking across countries, the data display little clear relationship. However, within-country the United States and United Kingdom reveal positive relationships. Later in the chapter we can confirm these relationships in regressions.

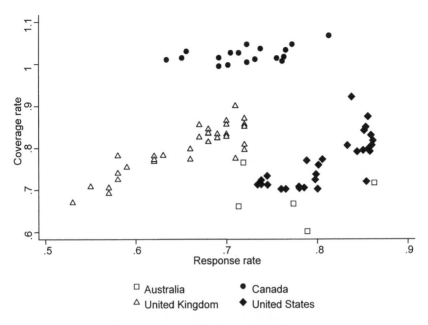

Fig. 9.4 Response rates versus coverage rates, all countries

Notes: Coverage rate is the proportion of consumer expenditure in the national accounts that is accounted for in the household surveys. Response rate is the proportion of contacted households with completed surveys. Calculations by authors.

9.4.2 Trends in High Income Concentration

The other trend we compare to declining coverage rates is the increase in income inequality. We draw on data from the high-incomes database maintained at the Paris School of Economics (Alvaredo et al. 2012). We use the proportion of income earned by those in the top 1 percent of the income distribution for our analysis here, although other high-income measures showed similar results.

Figure 9.5 shows how the top 1 percent income shares have evolved in our four countries. Through the mid-1980s there is little to be seen—although the top income share does start to rise in the United Kingdom following 1980. From around the beginning of the 1990s, there is a strong upward trend in each of the countries. The weakest of these upward trends is in Australia and the strongest is in the United States. This timing does correspond to the decline in coverage rates, which accelerated in the 1990s.

We compare the trends in top income shares to the trends in coverage rates across all four countries in figure 9.6, with separate scales for each country's axes. All four countries show signs of a negative relationship. Canada, again, has little variation in the coverage rate across years, so it

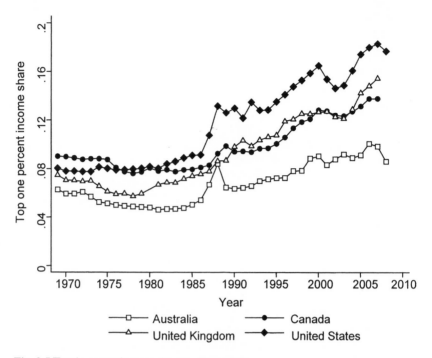

Fig. 9.5 Top 1 percent income shares, all countries

Source: Paris School of Economics World Top Incomes Database, Alvaredo et al. (2012).

Note: Top 1 percent income share is the share of total income received by those in the top 1 percent.

looks a bit different from the others. In the United States and the United Kingdom, there is a clear negative relationship between income inequality and the coverage rate.

Some parallels may be drawn here between our findings and those of Deaton (2005). In that paper, he finds that the coverage rate across countries is declining in the log of GDP, so higher-income countries are experiencing worse coverage.[19] One of Deaton's explanations is that higher-income countries tend to have higher income concentration, which may be captured less well in surveys. This is consistent with our findings here.

9.4.3 Regression Analysis

The relationships from these figures can be summarized with some basic regressions. The coverage rate is regressed on the response rate, with country and time controls using ordinary least squares (OLS). The equation takes the following form:

19. When comparing to our results, though, it must be remembered that much of the impact Deaton finds is concentrated among those countries with very low incomes.

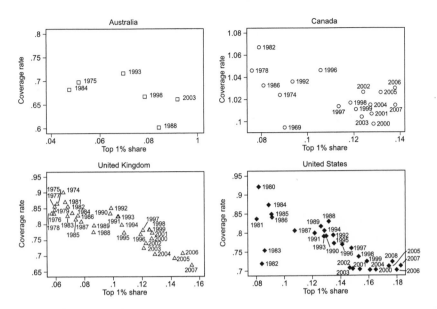

Fig. 9.6 Coverage rates versus top income shares

Source: Paris School of Economics World Top Incomes Database, Alvaredo et al. (2012). Coverage rate is the proportion of consumer expenditure in the national accounts that is accounted for in the household surveys. Source is calculations by the authors.

Note: Top 1 percent income share is the share of total income received by those in the top 1 percent.

$$Coverage_{it} = \beta_0 + ResponseRate_{it}\beta_1 + Top1\%share\beta_2$$
$$+ Country_i\beta_3 + Year_t\beta_4 + e_{it}.$$

We report these results in table 9.2. The dependent variable in all cases is the country-year coverage rate, and each column reports the results from a different specification. We report the regression coefficient, with the standard error beneath in parentheses. In column (1), we include no controls other than the constant term and the response rate variable. This effectively estimates a best-fit line through the data points as seen in figure 9.4. The small and insignificant estimated coefficient confirms the lack of relationship across countries. The second column of the table includes country fixed effects. Here, the within-country relationships are used in the estimation, essentially taking an average of the relationships shown in the country-specific scatter plots in figure 9.3. The coefficient swings strongly positive at 0.779. This suggests that for every percentage point increase in the response rate, there is a 0.779 percentage point increase in the coverage rate. Taking the United States as an example, the response rate dropped by 11.86 points from 1990 to 2008, so this coefficient explains a (0.779 * 11.86) 9.24 percentage point drop in coverage, which is larger than the

Table 9.2   Coverage and response rates

			Dependent variable: Country-year coverage rate			
	No controls (1)	Add country fixed effects (2)	Add top 1% (3)	Add interaction (4)	With linear trend (5)	Add year fixed effect (6)
Response rate	0.084	0.779	0.342	0.407	0.345	0.337
	(0.154)	(0.078)	(0.111)	(0.255)	(0.112)	(0.207)
Top 1 percent income share			−1.006	−0.642	−1.232	−1.026
			(0.203)	(1.307)	(0.362)	(0.688)
Response X top share interaction				−0.487		
				(1.731)		
Canada		0.406	0.413	0.414	0.420	0.416
		(0.020)	(0.017)	(0.018)	(0.020)	(0.028)
United Kingdom		0.237	0.197	0.199	0.204	0.191
		(0.021)	(0.020)	(0.021)	(0.022)	(0.036)
United States		0.086	0.153	0.154	0.166	0.147
		(0.019)	(0.021)	(0.022)	(0.027)	(0.047)
Linear trend					0.0007	
					(0.0010)	
Year fixed effects	No	No	No	No	No	Yes
Adjusted R-Squared	−0.009	0.912	0.933	0.932	0.933	0.928
Number of Observations	81	81	81	81	81	81

Notes: Unit of observation is a country-year. Excluded country dummy is Australia. Standard errors below each parameter estimate in parentheses. Each column represents a separate regression using the coverage rate as dependent variable.

6.85 percent drop that occurred. On this basis, we interpret this coefficient as large.

In column (3) of table 9.2 we include the top 1 percent income share variable. The coefficient on the response rate drops, but remains statistically significant and positive. The coefficient on the top income share is −1.006, which suggests that a 1 percentage point increase in the top income share is associated with a 1.006 percentage point decrease in the coverage rate, all else equal. To interpret these magnitudes differently, consider that the top 1 percent share in the United States increased by 4.69 percentage points from 1990 to 2008. Over that same period, coverage dropped by 6.85 percentage points. The −1.006 coefficient means that the decline in top income share predicts a (1.006 * 4.69) 4.72 point drop in coverage, which is 68.9 percent of the 6.85 point drop.

Column (4) includes an interaction of the response rate and the top income share. This change leads to negative (but insignificant) coefficients on the top 1 percent share term and on the interaction term. The large standard errors on both estimated effects indicate that the interaction term is not well identified from the linear effect of the top 1 percent share on coverage rates. Indeed, a joint test for significance of these two variables shows they are highly jointly significant.[20] Further, the magnitude of the partial effect of an increase in the top 1 percent share evaluated at the mean US survey response rate of 0.81 based on the estimates in column (4) is numerically very similar to the linear partial effect of −1.006 in column (3). Together, the insignificance of the interaction terms and the comparable estimated partial of income inequality on coverage rates with the two specifications indicate no evidence that the effects seen in column (3) were driven by an interaction of the two factors.

In the last two columns of table 9.2 we try alternative controls for time. Column (5) has a linear time trend. This time trend accounts for any global trend that is common to the four countries in our study. The coefficient on the response rate changes slightly to 0.345, while for the top income share the coefficient jumps up to a larger (in absolute value) magnitude. Finally, the last column includes dummies for each year of the sample, which controls flexibly for any common calendar time effects across countries. This is a fairly demanding specification given the number of observations we have and the nature of the variation we are using. Since there are only four observations per year, it may be difficult to detect any effect in this specification. The resulting coefficients remain fairly stable—but both lose statistical significance in this final specification.

---

20. The calculated F-statistic for the interaction of the top 1 percent variable and the response rate and the 1 percent variable itself is 12.19. For both main effects and the interaction, the calculated F-statistic is 50.83. For the response rate and the interaction, the joint test yields an F-statistic of 4.69. All of these are highly significant.

This graphical and regression analysis shows that the trend downward in response rates is common across all four countries, and that the decline in expenditure coverage in surveys compared to national accounts has a positive relationship with changes in survey response rates. Top income shares are also shown to be negatively related to coverage rates. Taken together, our results suggest that declining survey response rates and increasing income inequality may prove to be important determinants of the decline in expenditure coverage rates.

9.5 Coverage Rates within Expenditure Categories

The next step in our analysis is to compare different categories of expenditure across countries, looking for evidence that aligns with differences in survey methodology. Canada is the most noticeable outlier in survey methodology, as the SHS uses an annual recall survey for both frequently purchased and infrequently purchased items—with no diary component. There is also a balance edit and substantial income weighting. The four categories we consider are food at home, alcohol purchased in stores, new and used motor vehicles, and furniture appliance and household equipment.

The first category we examine is food consumed in the home. These data are collected through a diary in Australia, the United Kingdom, and the United States, but with recall in Canada. Food for consumption at home is a basic nondurable commodity that has been used as a summary measure of household welfare, and has been the focus of many studies testing predictions of consumption smoothing at the household and aggregate level. We graph the coverage rates in figure 9.7.[21] The United Kingdom shows a decline of 10 percentage points since the early 1990s. However, there is little evidence of a similar trend in the other three countries.

The second expenditure category considered is alcohol purchased in stores. This category is collected using the same methods as for food consumed at home. This category is of interest because alcohol consumption is generally viewed as socially undesirable, which may lead individuals to underreport these expenditures in a household survey. As figure 9.8 shows, it is the case that survey coverage of this item is very low—being around 50 percent for Australia[22] and Canada, and substantially less for the United States. However, conditional on the lower level of coverage, the coverage rates for this item are remarkably stable in each of these three countries. For the United Kingdom, the coverage rate is higher and has declined through time.

The final two graphs show more infrequently purchased items. In all countries, these data are collected with recall surveys. Figure 9.9 shows new and used vehicles, while figure 9.10 has household equipment, furniture,

---

21. For Canada, we now show only the SHS results, as the category-by-category analysis tends to exhibit seams between the FAMEX and SHS survey years.
22. Apart from atypically high coverage in the Australian HES in 1975–1976.

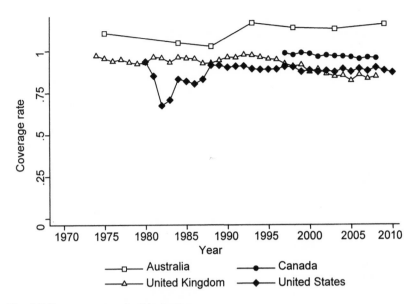

Fig. 9.7 Coverage rates, food in the home

Source: Calculations by the authors.

Note: Coverage rate is the proportion of consumer expenditure in the national accounts that is accounted for in the household surveys in this category.

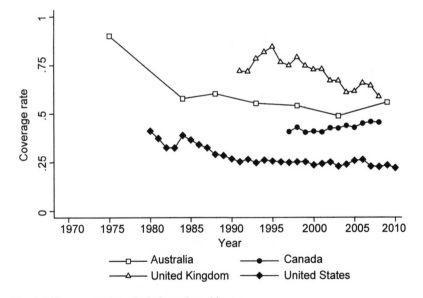

Fig. 9.8 Coverage rates, alcohol purchased in stores

Source: Calculations by the authors.

Note: Coverage rate is the proportion of consumer expenditure in the national accounts that is accounted for in the household surveys in this category.

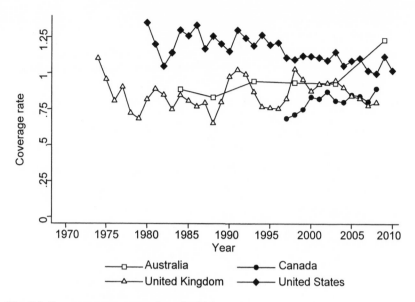

Fig. 9.9 Coverage rates, new and used vehicles

Source: Calculations by the authors.

Note: Coverage rate is the proportion of consumer expenditure in the national accounts that is accounted for in the household surveys in this category.

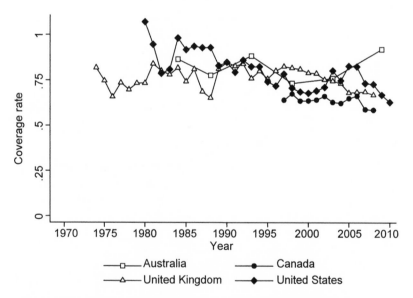

Fig. 9.10 Coverage rates, furniture, household equipment, and appliances

Source: Calculations by the authors.

Note: Coverage rate is the proportion of consumer expenditure in the national accounts that is accounted for in the household surveys in this category.

and appliances. There are no easily discernible patterns for vehicles. For Australia, coverage rates for these categories are neither consistently rising nor falling. In Canada, there is an upward trend for new and used vehicles, and perhaps small downward movement for the other two. For the United Kingdom, coverage of vehicles appears quite cyclical, but do not show a long-term decline. The series for furniture, household equipment, and appliances shows a fairly slow and steady decline, although Australia does rebound at the end.

This examination of category-by-category patterns has revealed little clear evidence about differences across countries. In all countries, the frequently consumed product (food) seems to have high coverage. In contrast, the less frequent bigger purchases appear to be much more volatile year to year, and have a more pronounced downward trend on average. This is consistent with the evidence shown previously in Meyer and Sullivan (2009) and elsewhere for the United States. The income elasticity of demand for the goods likely plays a role as well. As income concentration increases, coverage rates for goods consumed more by higher-income households may decline.

9.6 Conclusions

In this chapter we provide a comparative assessment of the performance of the household expenditure survey programs in Australia, Canada, the United Kingdom, and United States. The survey methodologies employed in each country share a number of common features while containing distinct elements. There are also differences in survey response rates and income concentration across the countries. We use this variation across countries to assess the implications for the performance of the household surveys.

After first outlining the key features of the household expenditure surveys for each country, we assess the coverage of aggregate expenditure relative to the national account benchmark. Both the survey expenditure aggregate and the national accounts data are adjusted to ensure the expenditure concepts are comparable. Coverage rates are highest in Canada and the United Kingdom; for Canada and Australia coverage remained fairly stable over the past three decades. In contrast, in the United Kingdom and the United States, coverage rates have sharply declined over the past three decades.

Next, survey response rates and top income shares were considered in tandem with coverage rates. This analysis is motivated by the widely observed decline in participation rates for household surveys over time, and the strong concentration of income that has occurred in many countries. From a series of graphical comparisons and regression models it is found that the fall in response rates over time are predictive of changes in coverage rates within countries. Further, the pattern of changes in coverage rates over time within our sample of Anglosphere countries coincided with the timing of the growing concentration of income. The prima facie evidence is that the growing concentration of income has been associated with an increasing concentration of expenditures, which has not been captured well by the microsurveys, hence contributing to declining coverage.

The last component of the analysis examined coverage rates for specific components of expenditure. Individual expenditure items considered were food at home, alcohol purchased in stores, new and used motor vehicles, and furniture, appliance, and household equipment. This list included categories that were collected using divergent methodologies (e.g., food by diary in Australia, the United Kingdom, and the United States and by annual recall in Canada) and by comparable methods (e.g., motor vehicles, furniture, and recreational equipment collected by recall in interviews in all countries). From this there was no clear pattern across countries by collection method. Rather, most evident is the high and stable coverage of regularly purchased items (such as food), along with the more volatile coverage of irregular and larger expenditure items (such as vehicles, furniture, and hold equipment). Therefore the aggregate patterns in coverage cannot be readily attributed to specific expenditure components or collection methods.

Overall, our comparative assessment of the household expenditure surveys across the four Anglosphere countries studied has shown the sharpest differences between Canada and Australia versus the United Kingdom and the United States. However, the many unique aspects of the Canadian survey methodology make it difficult to identify specific features of the methodology that are pivotal to its performance. Given the Canadian methodology changes that were put in place for 2010, some further information may soon be available about the reasons for the relative success of the Canadian data.

References

Adler, Hans J., and Michael Wolfson. 1988. "A Prototype Micro-Macro Link for the Canadian Household Sector." *Review of Income and Wealth* 34 (4): 371–92.
Alvaredo, Facundo, Anthony B. Atkinson, Thomas Piketty, and Emmanuel Saez. 2012. "The World Top Incomes Database." Accessed February 5, 2012. http://g-mond.parisschoolofeconomics.eu/topincomes.
Atkinson, Anthony B., Thomas Piketty, and Emmanuel Saez. 2011. "Top Incomes in the Long Run of History." *Journal of Economic Literature* 49 (1): 3–71.
Attanasio, Orazio P., Erich Battistin, and Andrew Leicester. 2006. "From Micro to Macro, from Poor to Rich: Consumption and Income in the UK and US." Working Paper, National Poverty Center, Gerald R. Ford School of Public Policy, University of Michigan.

Australian Bureau of Statistics. 2011. *Household Expenditure Survey, Summary of Results Australia*. Australian Bureau of Statistics, Canberra, Catalogue no. 6530.0.

Brzozowski, Matthew, and Thomas F. Crossley. 2011. "Measuring the Well-Being of the Poor with Income or Consumption: A Canadian Perspective." *Canadian Journal of Economics* 44 (1): 88–106.

Bureau of Labor Statistics. 2011a. "Appendix A: Description of the Consumer Expenditure Survey." In *Consumer Expenditure Survey Anthology, 2011*. Statistics Report 1030. US Bureau of Labor Statistics.

———. 2011b. *Bureau of Labor Statistics Handbook of Methods*. Accessed November 2011. http://www.bls.gov/opub/hom/.

Crossley, Thomas F., and Cormac O'Dea. 2010. "The Wealth and Saving of UK Families on the Eve of the Crisis." IFS Report no. R71, Institute for Fiscal Studies, July.

D'Alessio, Giovanni, and Ivan Faiella. 2002. "Non-Response Behaviour in the Bank of Italy's Survey of Household Income and Wealth." Temi di discussione del Servizio Studi, no. 462, Bank of Italy, Economic Research and International Relations Area.

Deaton, Angus. 2005. "Measuring Poverty in a Growing World (or Measuring Growth in a Poor World)." *Review of Economics and Statistics* 87 (1): 1–19.

de Leeuw, Edith, and Wim de Heer. 2002. "Trends in Household Survey Nonresponse: A Longitudinal and International Comparison." In *Survey Nonresponse*, edited by Robert M. Groves, Don A. Dillman, John L. Eltinge, and Roderick J. A. Little, 41–54. New York: Wiley.

Dubreuil, Guylaine, Johanne Tremblay, Jenny Lynch, and Martin Lemire. 2011. "Redesign of the Canadian Survey of Household Spending." Paper presented at Household Survey Producers Workshop, Washington, DC, June 1–2.

Edgar, Jennifer, and Adam Safir. 2011. "Gemini Project Overview." In *Consumer Expenditure Survey Anthology, 2011*. Statistics Report no. 1030. US Bureau of Labor Statistics.

Garner, Thesia I., George Janini, William Passero, Laura Paszkiewicz, and Mark Vendemia. 2006. "The CE and the PCE: A Comparison." *Monthly Labor Review* 129 (9): 20–46.

Garner, Thesia I., Robert McClelland, and William Passero. 2009. "Strengths and Weaknesses of the Consumer Expenditure Survey from a BLS Perspective." Draft presented at National Bureau of Economic Research Summer Institute, July.

Goldenberg, Karen, and Jay Ryan. 2009. "Evolution and Change in the Consumer Expenditure Surveys: Adapting Methodologies to Meet Changing Needs." National Bureau of Economic Research Conference on Income and Wealth, Summer Institute, Cambridge, MA, July 13–14.

Meyer, Bruce D., and James X. Sullivan. 2009. "Five Decades of Consumption and Income Poverty." NBER Working Paper no. 14827, Cambridge, MA.

Office for National Statistics. 2010. "Living Costs and Food Survey 2009 User Guide." http://discover.ukdataservice.ac.uk/catalogue?sn=6655.

Slesnick, Daniel T. 1992 "Aggregate Consumption and Saving in the Postwar United States." *Review of Economics and Statistics* 74 (4): 585–97.

Statistics Canada. 2000. "Note to Former Users of Data from the Family Expenditure Survey." Catalogue no. 62F0026MIE-00002. Income Statistics Division, Statistics Canada.

———. 2001. "Methodology of the Survey of Household Spending." Catalogue no. 62F0026MIE-01003. Income Statistics Division, Statistics Canada.

———. 2011. "User Guide for the Public-Use Microdata File, Survey of Household Spending, 2009." Catalogue no. 62M0004XCB. Income Statistics Division, Statistics Canada.

Tourangeau, Roger. 2004. "Survey Research and Societal Change." *Annual Review of Psychology* 55:775–801.

Tremblay, J., J. Lynch, and G. Dubreuil. 2010. "Pilot Survey Results from the Canadian Survey of Household Spending Redesign." Paper presented at the 2010 Joint Statistical Meetings of the American Statistical Association, Vancouver, British Columbia.

IV

**Alternative Approaches to Data
Collection**

Measuring the Accuracy of Survey Responses Using Administrative Register Data
Evidence from Denmark

Claus Thustrup Kreiner, David Dreyer Lassen, and
Søren Leth-Petersen

Measuring the Accuracy of Responses Using Administrative Register Data

10.1 Introduction

Danish administrative register data can readily be combined at the person level with survey data. This makes it possible to compare survey-based measures directly with corresponding measures based on information from administrative registers. Because register information is collected by third-party automatic reporting and completely independently from the survey collection, we believe this provides an inexpensive and powerful way to validate survey measures.

The objective of this chapter is to illustrate how Danish register and survey data may be combined at the person or household level and used for validating measures collected by survey, and we illustrate the potential of this methodology by two examples. In the first example we use administrative records about disposable income and wealth to validate the total expenditure measure collected in the Danish Family Expenditure Survey. In the second example we use third-party-reported information about gross personal income from the income tax register to validate a survey measure of gross personal income.

Claus Thustrup Kreiner is professor of economics at the University of Copenhagen. David Dreyer Lassen is professor of economics at the University of Copenhagen. Søren Leth-Petersen is professor of economics at the University of Copenhagen.

This chapter was prepared for the conference in Washington, DC, December 2–3, 2011, on Improving the Measurement of Consumer Expenditures, sponsored by the Conference on Research in Income and Wealth and the National Bureau of Economic Research, with support from the Centre for Microdata Methods and Practice. The authors would like to acknowledge that the Danish Social Science Research Council provided support for the work presented in this chapter. We are also thankful to Amalie Sofie Jensen and Gregers Nytoft Rasmussen for competent research assistance. For acknowledgments, sources of research support, and disclosure of the author's or authors' material financial relationships, if any, please see http://www.nber.org/chapters/c12663.ack.

Validating total expenditure requires assumptions as the register measure of total expenditure is itself ridden with error. The most important assumption is that the errors of the two measures are uncorrelated. This is not likely to be a restrictive assumption since the data are collected from completely independent sources. We find that total expenditure from the expenditure survey is mean unbiased, but noisy.

In the second example, where we validate survey information about gross income, the register measure of gross personal income is collected entirely from third-party automatically reported information. This is thought to be very close to the "truth" and the validation exercise therefore relies on few assumptions. We find that survey answers are noisy and mean biased. We also compare our results about the magnitude of income mismeasurement with the results from Bound et al. (1994). They compared survey responses with payroll data from a single US manufacturing company where workers are homogenous and received regular and well-defined payments. Consistent with our broader income measure and broader sample, we find larger errors than the study by Bound and colleagues.

The methodology presented in this chapter is simple but powerful. In the Danish context, it is possible to match survey and register data for any subsample of the population and it can be done at relatively low costs. In this way Denmark can be thought of as a "laboratory" for very detailed and focused validation studies to investigate the impact of survey methodology on the accuracy of survey responses so as to optimize the survey methodology across different groups and balancing this with survey costs.[1] It is possible for international researchers or statistical agencies to conduct new studies on Danish data through collaboration with researchers based in Denmark or directly with Statistics Denmark if necessary funding is available.

The next section outlines the Danish institutional setup facilitating the collection of administrative register data and the merging of register and survey records. Section 10.3 outlines the analytical framework that we use to asses the importance of measurement error in the survey data. Section 10.4 shows how income tax records with information about income, tax payments, and wealth have been used to impute a measure of total household expenditure that is then matched at the household level to data from the Danish expenditure survey in order to check how well the total expenditure measure in the survey matches the register-based imputation. The analysis presented in that section complements the analysis presented in Browning and Leth-Petersen (2003) and is based on the same data. In section 10.5 we combine income tax records with new survey data containing a measure of

---

1. Reducing measurement error is the primary mission of the Gemini project. The Gemini Project Vision Document (http://www.bls.gov/cex/ovrvwgeminivision.pdf), however, also emphasizes that the CEX budget is constant and that new initiatives to reduce measurement error should be balanced with the potential negative effects on response rates.

total gross personal income to directly validate the survey measure of gross income. Section 10.6 sums up and discusses the possibilities for future validation studies based on combining Danish register and survey data.

10.2 Matching Administrative Register Data with Survey Data

All persons in Denmark are assigned a unique personal identification number (CPR). This number is used by all government institutions to store person-specific information, including information relevant for taxation such as the information contained in tax returns, but also information about car ownership, contacts to the health care system, the educational system, and about family composition and place of residence, allowing for the construction of household units. Many administrative registers, including population registers and income tax registers, are collected by Statistics Denmark, which merges them and provides access to researchers working at authorized Danish research institutions. The data are confidential, are kept on servers at Statistics Denmark, and are accessed under comprehensive security precautions. The data must be kept at the servers and only aggregated numbers such as regression coefficients can be extracted.

The register data have many outstanding features, but the features most important in this context are that they cover the entire population and contain tax records with third-party-reported information about income and wealth. In this study we shall rely on register data from the income tax registers to validate survey information about spending and income. The income tax register is collected by the tax authorities in order to calculate the amount of taxes to be paid by all persons in Denmark by the end of each calendar year. The tax authorities collect information from many sources. Most important for this study are earnings and employers' pension contributions collected directly from employers, information about transfer income from government institutions, and information about interest payments/income and the value of assets and liabilities by the end of the year collected directly from banks. A recent study by Kleven et al. (2011) conducted a large-scale randomized tax auditing experiment in collaboration with the Danish tax authorities and documents that tax evasion in Denmark is very limited, in particular among wage earners. This means that the third-party-reported income information collected by the tax authorities is of very high quality.

The tax authorities use the information for different purposes. Information about earnings and capital income is preprinted on the tax return, whereas wealth information is used to cross-check if reported income is consistent with the level of asset accumulation from one year to the next. While the tax authorities collect this information at a high level of detail corresponding to individual entries at the tax return level for income and at the account level for wealth, this information is in some cases transferred to Statistics Denmark's research database as summary variables only; for example, we observe the sum of earnings from different employers, and for some capital income subcomponents, only net income is available. In addition to covering the entire population and being based on third-party-reported information, the income tax registers also have the attractive features that income and wealth information is not top coded and that longitudinal information can be retrieved as far back as 1980 for some variables.

A crucial feature for the present purpose is that it is possible to link to survey data via the CPR number. Matching surveys with register data is done at relatively low cost; for example, the survey used in the second part of this chapter consists of forty questions, was carried out as telephone interviews, and includes 6,000 completed interviews. The sample was randomized from the population based on register data covering the entire population, and the survey data was merged on to register data after collection. The total costs were about 200,000 USD.[2]

10.3 Analytical Framework

There are several ways of summarizing the accuracy of the survey data. In this chapter we focus on the magnitude of the attenuation bias in ordinary least squares (OLS) regressions of the register measure on the survey measure. The analytical setup is a generalization of the setup presented by Bound and Krueger (1991).

Consider

$$(1) \qquad z^S = z^* + u^S$$

$$(2) \qquad z^R = z^* + u^R,$$

where z^S is the observed survey-based measure, z^* is the true but unobserved measure, and u^S is the survey measurement error. Correspondingly, z^R is the observed register-based measure, and u^R is the register measurement error. All variables are measured in natural logarithms.[3] This amounts to assuming that the measurement error is multiplicative in levels. Subscripts identifying that each observation of $(z^*, z^R, z^S, u^R, u^S)$ pertains to an individual are suppressed. In the case of gross income we believe that the register-based measure is very close to the truth, while this is obviously not the case in the other example where we compare total expenditure from survey data with imputed measures from the register data.

2. A number of survey agencies are specialized in conducting surveys and linking to administrative register data. Two of those are SFI survey (http://www.sfi.dk/Default.aspx?ID=2832) and Epinion (www.epinion.dk) who have collected the survey used in example 2. Also, Statistics Denmark (www.dst.dk) conducts surveys that can subsequently be merged on to register data.
3. The analytical framework, of course, does not require that the variables are measured in logarithms.

Assume

(A.1) $$\text{cov}(z^*, u^R) = 0$$

(A.2) $$\text{cov}(u^S, u^R) = 0.$$

Assumption (A.1) assumes that the error of the register measure is uncorrelated with the true level. This assumption is not testable with the data used in this chapter, and may in some cases be a reasonable assumption, while in others it may not. For example, it could be that people with a low level of true income have different errors than people with a high level of true income because they have different cognitive skills that influence the quality of their answer or have total income consisting of different subcomponents and different complexity, or because low-level-income people have different amounts of undeclared income. Similarly, in the case of total expenditure, consumers with a high level of expenditures are likely to have total expenditure consisting of different types of consumption than consumers with a low level of expenditures, and this may give rise to different measurement errors if subcomponents of total expenditure have different errors. Because we assume that the measurement error is multiplicative in levels, we do allow for the level of errors being larger at high levels than at low levels of income/total expenditure, but this is entirely determined by the logarithmic functional form that we employ in the applications. Assumption (A.2) assumes that the error of the survey measure is uncorrelated with the error of the register measure. This seems to be a reasonable assumption in both of the examples as will be discussed in connection with each example.

Consider a regression of z^R on the true but unobserved measure z^*:

(3) $$z^R = \delta_0 + \delta_1 z^* + u^R.$$

Now substitute in the survey measure for the true measure

(4) $$z^R = \delta_0 + \delta_1 z^S + u^R - \delta_1 u^S.$$

Using assumptions (A.1) and (A.2), the probability limit of the OLS estimator of δ_1 can be written

(5) $$p \lim \hat{\delta}_1 = \delta_1 \lambda,$$

where $\lambda = \text{cov}\,(z^R, z^S)/\text{var}\,(z^S)$ is just the OLS regression of the register measure on the survey measure. The bias due to the measurement error in the survey measure is then $(1 - \lambda)$.

Maintaining assumptions (A.1) and (A.2), this expression covers the case with classical measurement error where u^S are *iid* and $\lambda = \sigma^2_{u^S}/(\sigma^2_{z^*} + \sigma^2_{u^S})$ but is not limited to this special case. In particular, the present framework is more general since it allows for cases where the errors are not *iid*.

10.4 Example 1: Total Expenditure

Total expenditure is one of the most important variables collected in expenditure surveys and this variable is central to numerous studies of demand and intertemporal consumption allocation. However, there is little evidence on the quality of the information collected in expenditure surveys. In Denmark it is possible to link the household-level information from the Danish Family Expenditure Survey to administrative income tax records, including third-party-reported information about income and wealth that can be used to impute total expenditure.

10.4.1 Data

The sample used consists of the households entering the Danish Family Expenditure Survey (DES) 1994–1996. The households in this survey have been contacted at different times of the year so that observations are distributed across the calendar year. Each household has participated in a comprehensive interview, where they have answered questions about purchases of durables within the past twelve months from the interview date. Furthermore, each household has kept a diary for two weeks, where they have kept a detailed account of all expenditures in the household. This information is scaled to obtain an expression of annual consumption.

For the households entering the DES administrative register, data are collected on income, tax payments, and wealth at the end of the year (corresponding to the survey year) together with wealth information for the previous year, and this is merged with the DES data. Total expenditure is then imputed from the income and wealth information by simply calculating $\hat{c}_t = y_t - \Delta W_t$, where y_t is disposable income and W_t is net wealth measured at the end of period t. While simple in theory, there are many details involved in implementing this and we refer to Browning and Leth-Petersen (2003) for details. For the analysis we use the same sample selection criteria as Browning and Leth-Petersen (2003). This leaves us with a sample of 3,352 observations.

10.4.2 Results

We start out by presenting in figure 10.1 the distributions of the two measures of total expenditure and their individual-level difference. The left panel shows that the distributions have modal points very close to each other and the right panel shows that at the individual level the differences are centered at zero. It is, however, also evident that there are important differences in the spread of the distributions of the two measures, with the register-based measure exhibiting larger dispersion. The way the data are constructed implies that a fair amount of noise is expected. First, the interviews are distributed across the calendar year, and this means that recall questions about durable purchases, for example, do not necessarily pertain to the calendar year. Moreover,

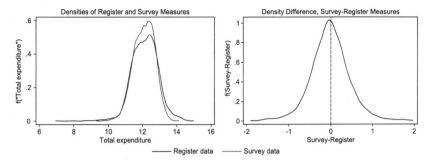

Fig. 10.1 Densities of the survey and register-based measures of total expenditure and of the individual differences

Note: The right panel includes only data in the interval –2;2. Thirty-two observations are selected away.

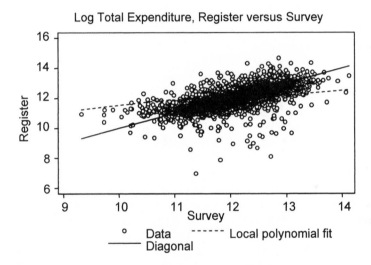

Fig. 10.2 Nonparametric regression of the register-based measure on the survey measure

Browning and Leth-Petersen (2003) show that the measurement error in the imputed measure is related to capital gains on wealth components used in the imputation.[4]

Figure 10.2 plots the data together with the diagonal and a nonparametric regression line. If the survey and the register measures coincided, all points

---

4. The Danish data hold information about the value of stocks and bonds at the household level, and this gives rise to measurement error. Without direct information about both the quantities and the prices of assets, it is not possible to distinguish active savings decisions from capital gains. Koijen, Van Nieuwerburgh, and Vestman (chapter 11, this volume) use Swedish register data with exact information about the holdings of stocks and bonds and are therefore able to address this issue.

Table 10.1   Estimates of λ

	$z^S - z^R$ unrestricted (1)	$-2 < z^S - z^R < 2$ (2)
λ	0.791***	0.816***
	(0.0148)	(0.0128)
Constant	2.519***	2.237***
	(0.1792)	(0.1546)
N	3,352	3,320
R^2	0.460	0.551

***Significant at the 1/10 of 1 percent level.
**Significant the 1 percent level.
*Significant at the 5 percent level.

would be located on the diagonal. The broken line is a nonparametric regression through the data cloud and comparing its slope to the diagonal shows the attenuation bias. One thing to notice is that the broken line is almost linear and it is also noticeable that the bias is apparent.

Table 10.1 presents the results from estimating the regression line by OLS. The estimate in column (1) shows that the bias is 0.21, suggesting that there is a fair amount of noise in the survey measure. Restricting the size of the errors does not change the estimate much, indicating that the bias is not caused by outliers. Of course, concluding that the survey measure is noisy relies on assumptions (1) and (2) being correct, in particular that the measurement errors of the two measures are uncorrelated. Since errors in the survey are related to the accurateness of the survey response and the register error is related to capital gains on the portfolio, this assumption does not appear restrictive. The assumption that the register error be uncorrelated with the true (but unobserved level) is not testable with our data and will, for example, be violated if respondents with a low level of true consumption overreport and people with high true levels of consumption underreport.

Using Swedish data, Koijen, Van Nieuwerburgh, and Vestman (chapter 11, this volume) run regressions similar to the ones presented in table 10.1 in order to quantify the amount of noise in their data, and it appears that there is more noise in the Swedish data than in our data. While there are differences between the two studies in terms of the imputation method and the timing of the surveys, it is not clear why this pattern emerges.

10.4.3 Summary, Example 1

In this example, the possibility to construct a register-based measure of total expenditure that can be compared with the survey measure is illustrated. While the validity of this exercise hinges on two important assumptions, we believe that the register approach provides an inexpensive way to get some insights on the precision of the survey measure that is difficult to obtain otherwise.

10.5 Example 2: Validating Survey Questions about Gross Income Using Third-Party-Reported Information from the Income Tax Registers

An income variable is included in almost any survey collected by social scientists, and surveying is often the only way to collect income jointly with other variables of interest. Danish register data on income are of very high quality because they are automatically third-party reported and are reported separately for different types of income. In this section we compare the responses to a one-shot recall question about gross personal income collected by telephone interview in January 2010 to the tax records of the respondents in order to assess the quality of the survey measure. As opposed to the previous example, the register information is now perceived to be close to the truth, and we therefore expect to be relying much less on assumptions (A.1) and (A.2)

10.5.1 Data

In January 2010 the authors of this chapter organized a telephone survey including 6,004 completed interviews. The purpose of the survey was to obtain information about their response to a stimulus policy implemented in 2009.[5] The sample is drawn randomly from the population of persons in employment at some point in the period 1998–2003, totaling 3.9 million persons or about 75 percent of the Danish population. As part of the survey, respondents were asked a one-shot recall question about their gross annual income in 2009. The question was:

"We are also interested in knowing about the development in your income before taxes. We are thinking about income such as earnings (including employers pension contribution), pension payments, payments from unemployment insurances, cash benefits, or other forms of transfer income. What was approximately your income before taxes in 2009?"

A total of 5,394 persons answered the question. Self-employed persons effectively self-report income to the tax authorities and we therefore do not have as much faith in the register information for this group as we have for wage earners and persons receiving transfer income. We therefore select away persons with own-business income. Finally, we deselect two observations with negative gross income[6] and are left with 4,793 observations. The survey data were subsequently merged at the person level with administrative register data about income from the income tax register covering the

5. The results are available in Kreiner, Lassen, and Leth-Petersen (2012), posted on our personal websites.
6. Negative gross income can occur because some components of capital income are available in our data set only as net measures and therefore adds negatively to gross income if the net-value is negative. This seems to be a small problem in the data set. For most people the major capital expenditure components are constituted by interest payments on bank debt and mortgages. Interest payments on bank and mortgage debt are observed, and when we take these components out, sixty-two cases are observed with negative capital income and half of these observations' negative capital income is less than 1,000 USD. We therefore conclude that this is a minor problem.

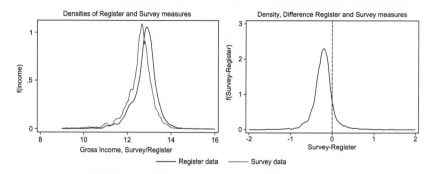

Fig. 10.3 Densities of the survey and register-based measures of gross income and of the individual differences

Note: The right panel includes only data in the interval –2;2. Sixty observations are selected away.

tax year 2009, that is, exactly the same period that the survey question was intended to cover.

10.5.2 Main Results

Figure 10.3 presents the densities of the survey and the register measure (left panel) and the density of the individual-level differences between the two measures (right panel). The left panel clearly reveals that the means of the two measures are not equal. It also suggests that the spread of the survey measure is larger, as would be expected if the survey measure carries an error and the register measure is accurate. The right panel confirms that the means are different when individual-level differences are considered, and also that individual-level errors have considerable spread, that is, that the survey measure is noisy.

Figure 10.4 graphs the register measure against the survey measure together with a smooth line through the data and a diagonal. The picture shows some very large outliers and also that the regression line has a smaller slope than the diagonal, indicating that the attenuation appears to be considerable.[7]

This is confirmed by a parametric regression reported in table 10.2. Regressing the register measure on the survey measure using the unrestricted sample yields an estimate of λ of 0.57 indicating important individual-level deviations

---

7. There is a graphically striking cluster of data points in the northeastern corner of the graph appearing to fall along a fairly tight regression line that is different from the mass of the data points. The apparent importance of this cluster is a visual deception because the cloud consists of only sixty-four observations. We have not been able to identify any significant differences between these observations and the rest of the data set apart from finding that they are, on average, four years younger than the rest of the sample. We also checked if interviewer effects could explain the pattern, but this was not the case.

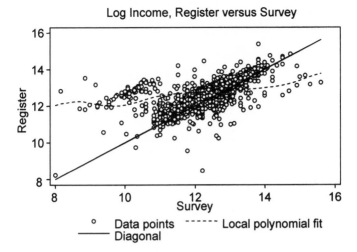

Fig. 10.4 Nonparametric regression of the register-based measure on the survey measure
Note: The graph includes only observations in the interval 8;16.

Table 10.2   Estimates of λ

	$z^S - z^R$ unrestricted (1)	$-2 < z^S - z^R < 2$ (2)
λ	0.570***	0.835***
	(0.0081)	(0.0072)
Constant	5.651***	2.283***
	(0.1024)	(0.0912)
N	4,793	4,707
R^2	0.505	0.739

***Significant at the 1/10 of 1 percent level.
**Significant at the 1 percent level.
*Significant at the 5 percent level.

between the survey and the register measure. In column (2) the errors are restricted to be within the $-2;2$ interval and this increases the estimate of λ to 0.84, suggesting that a limited number of outliers are responsible for a large part of the attenuation bias.

In table 10.3 the two measures of gross income and the individual-level errors are regressed on a set of "external" covariates. The idea is to see how the noise influences the covariance with other variables often used in empirical analyses. Comparing the numbers in columns (1) and (2) in table 10.3 suggests that the register and the survey measure have similar covariance with the set of external variables, but the parameter estimates obtained

Table 10.3   Regressing on external covariates

| | z^R | z^S | $z^S - z^R$ |
	(1)	(2)	(3)
Age	0.095***	0.114***	0.019***
	(0.0049)	(0.0066)	(0.0052)
Age^2	−0.001***	−0.001***	−0.000***
	(0.0001)	(0.0001)	(0.0001)
Woman	−0.145***	−0.232***	−0.087***
	(0.0127)	(0.0172)	(0.0136)
Single	−0.020	−0.067**	−0.047**
	(0.0162)	(0.0219)	(0.0173)
Number of children	0.012	−0.009	−0.021**
	(0.0072)	(0.0098)	(0.0077)
Education, short	0.113***	0.147***	0.034*
	(0.0160)	(0.0216)	(0.0171)
Education, medium	0.257***	0.288***	0.031
	(0.0188)	(0.0255)	(0.0202)
Education, long	0.362***	0.362***	−0.000
	(0.0241)	(0.0327)	(0.0258)
House owner	0.356***	0.245***	−0.111***
	(0.0147)	(0.0198)	(0.0157)
Constant	10.466***	9.954***	−0.512***
	(0.0980)	(0.1327)	(0.1049)
N	4,793	4,793	4,793
R^2	0.330	0.212	0.021

Note: Standard errors in parentheses.
***Significant at the 1/10 of 1 percent level.
**Significant at the 1 percent level.
*Significant at the 5 percent level.

using the survey measure do differ significantly from the parameter estimates obtained using the register measure for age, woman, number of children, single, and owner. Regressing the individual-level error on the same set of covariates suggests differences for the same variables. If one takes the register measure to be the truth, then the results of column (3) suggest that the measurement error associated with the survey measure is not classical.

10.5.3 Robustness

The survey question asks people to recall gross income including earnings, employers' pension contributions, transfer income, and capital income. Some of these are probably less salient to the respondent; employers' pension contribution is likely included in this category. This number does not appear separately on the paycheck, nor on the tax return, or the annual statement from the tax authorities since it is not liable to taxation before it is paid out. In a robustness check we subtract employers' pension contributions

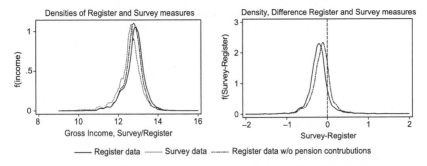

Fig. 10.5 Densities of the survey measure, the original register measure, and the register measure where employers' pension contributions are subtracted and of individual differences between the register measures and the survey measure

Table 10.4   Estimates of λ for register measure without employers' pension contributions

	$z^S - z^R$ unrestricted (1)	$-2 < z^S - z^R < 2$ (2)
λ	0.528***	0.773***
	(0.0077)	(0.0069)
Constant	6.093***	2.995***
	(0.0971)	(0.0872)
N	4,793	4,707
R^2	0.494	0.726

***Significant at the 1/10 of 1 percent level.
**Significant at the 1 percent level.
*Significant at the 5 percent level.

from the register measure and repeat the analysis of the previous section to check if the survey measure performs better when compared to the adjusted register measure. To do this we define an alternative gross income measure constructed from the registers where employers' pension contributions are deducted from the register measure used in the previous section. The idea is to investigate if respondents are more likely to have stated their income without employers' pension contributions even though it is clearly stated in the survey question that it should be included.

Figure 10.5 shows density graphs for the survey measure, the original register measure, and the register measure where employers' pension contributions are subtracted. The right panel shows densities of differences between the register measures and the survey measure. The figure shows that subtracting employers' pension contributions reduces the mean bias, but also that the spread is almost unaffected. Estimating λ by OLS reveals that this has not improved on the precision at the individual level. In fact, if anything, the estimates of λ in table 10.4 suggest that the attenuation bias has become more serious.

Table 10.5   **Regressing on external covariates**

	z^R (1)	z^S (2)	$z^S - z^R$ (3)
Age	0.086***	0.114***	0.028***
	(0.0046)	(0.0066)	(0.0053)
Age^2	−0.001***	−0.001***	−0.000***
	(0.0001)	(0.0001)	(0.0001)
Woman	−0.133***	−0.232***	−0.098***
	(0.0119)	(0.0172)	(0.0137)
Single	−0.007	−0.067**	−0.059***
	(0.0152)	(0.0219)	(0.0174)
Number of children	0.015*	−0.009	−0.024**
	(0.0068)	(0.0098)	(0.0078)
Education, short	0.102***	0.147***	0.045**
	(0.0150)	(0.0216)	(0.0172)
Education, medium	0.237***	0.288***	0.051*
	(0.0176)	(0.0255)	(0.0202)
Education, long	0.323***	0.362***	0.039
	(0.0226)	(0.0327)	(0.0259)
Owner	0.347***	0.245***	−0.102***
	(0.0137)	(0.0198)	(0.0157)
Constant	10.563***	9.954***	−0.608***
	(0.0918)	(0.1327)	(0.1053)
N	4,793	4,793	4,793
R^2	0.333	0.212	0.024

Note: Standard errors in parentheses.
***Significant at the 1/10 of 1 percent level.
**Significant at the 1 percent level.
*Significant at the 5 percent level.

Further, examining the correlation with the external covariates reveals even stronger correlations between the external covariates and the differences between the register and the survey measure. These results are presented in table 10.5. In the regression of individual-level differences between the two measures on external covariates, column (3), the parameters are now more significant, in particular in the case of education dummies. This suggests that the ability of the respondents to include employers' pension contributions when reporting their income varies across educational levels.

It is, of course, possible to construct many other concepts where other income components are subtracted. The most salient feature of income is arguably earnings and transfer income, which are received at regular intervals and where the recipient receives a letter stating the amount paid out. Capital income arrives in a less regular fashion and may therefore also be difficult to give an account for. We have experimented with subtracting capital income from the register measure, but this made little difference to the results and we therefore leave the results unreported. The calculations provided in this chapter are merely examples intended to illustrate the possibilities for identifying different subcomponents of income and how this may be used to identify what components of income respondents find it difficult to report in surveys.

10.5.4 Comparison to US Findings

The Consumer Expenditure Survey (CEX) and Panel Study of Income Dynamics (PSID) use annual recall questions about income but ask about different income components separately, for example, earned income, transfer income, and capital income. Bound et al. (1994) performed a validation study of the earnings question in the PSID by comparing answers to the PSID questions about earnings with company records for 418 workers from a single manufacturing company in 1983. This sample is called the PSID Validation Study. They find that the mean difference between the survey and the register measure is small, but that the standard deviation of the difference is substantial, amounting to 0.67 of the standard deviation of the company records. The corresponding measure in our data is 0.89. The slope coefficients from regressions of record on interview measure are similar between the two studies, 0.76 in the Bound et al. study and 0.84 in the trimmed version in our study.[8]

Both studies suggest substantial measurement error. One limitation of the Bound et al. study is that it is confined to validate the survey responses for a homogenous and small group. This could explain the smaller error. Our results suggest that the survey error is correlated with standard covariates and that the error is therefore not of the classical type. This leaves open the possibility that validation studies based on narrowly defined samples such as the PSID Validation Study do not give a complete picture of the size of the error in the main sample.

Another difference is that our study focuses on gross income including transfer income and capital income. This leaves open the possibility that our income measure is more noisy only because we include nonearned income. Gottschalk and Moffitt (2011) show evidence about the development of transitory family nonlabor income from the PSID, but to our knowledge the measures of transfer income and capital income in the PSID have not been validated.

Overall the results from the present study and the study by Bound et al. have implications for studies in many areas, but perhaps in particular for the interpretation of estimates from studies decomposing income variances into temporary and permanent components. The validation results suggest that

8. Bound, Brown, and Mathiowetz (2001) survey nine studies validating survey-based earnings measures from different US surveys against administrative records. Four of these studies report regression coefficients from a regression of the administrative record measure on the survey measure and three of these report regression coefficients in the vicinity of 0.75 using different data sets.

there is considerable noise in survey measures. This may explain why studies estimating income processes on US data collected in different ways find different results. Specifically, in a series of papers Gottschalk and Moffitt (1994) and Moffitt and Gottschalk (2002, 2011) use the PSID to decompose income into permanent and transitory variations and find that the transitory component is relatively big and increasing in the 1980s. For example, Moffitt and Gottschalk (2002) find that the variance of transitory log earnings for males is around 0.15–0.3. Kopczuk, Saez, and Song (2010) use Social Security Administration longitudinal earnings data for the period 1937–2004 and find that the transitory component is almost constant across time and relatively small, about 0.06–0.08 for the whole period and about 0.06 for the period 1980–, and that it cannot explain the increase in the variance of log earnings in the United States during the 1980s. While there are many other differences between these studies than the data collection mode, this does suggest the possibility that the size of the measurement error is important and not constant across time.

10.5.5 Summary, Example 2

The analysis of the quality of the recall question about annual gross income revealed that a one-shot recall question is inaccurate. Respondents tend to underreport their income level and the survey measure is noisy. Changing the definition of the register measure by excluding employers' pension contributions corrected for some of the mean bias, but did not reduce the spread much, and in particular did not reduce the attenuation bias in a regression of the register measure on the survey measure. The analysis also suggested that the individual-level differences between the survey and the register measure were correlated with observed characteristics of the respondents, suggesting that the errors associated with the survey measure are not of the classical type.

10.6 Summary and Suggestions for Future Work

This chapter has provided two examples illustrating how Danish third-party-reported register data can be matched at the individual- or household-level to survey records and used to validate the accuracy of responses to survey questions. The first example suggests that expenditure survey evidence on total expenditure is mean unbiased but noisy, and the second example suggests that a one-shot recall question about annual gross income is both mean biased and noisy.

The analyses presented in this chapter are possible because all persons living in Denmark are assigned a unique identification number to which all public authorities link up person-specific information and because surveys can be collected using the same person identifier. The potential of this validation methodology is big. In the Danish context, it is possible to match survey and register data for (potentially) the entire population, and it is also possible to match in the longitudinal dimension. In this way Denmark can be thought of as a laboratory where much more detailed and focused validation studies can be organized and where the impact of survey methodology on the accuracy of the survey responses are investigated so as to optimize the survey methodology across different groups and balancing this with survey costs.[9] For example, in the context of validating income questions the Danish setup allows researchers to merge survey records with tax records containing detailed information about different types of income and this provides a unique opportunity to test the ability of respondents to accurately report different types of income using different interviewing techniques and questions. Using the register data, it is also possible to consider individual as well as household units and to assess the extent to which it is important to ask all household members or just one in order to assess household income accurately. Finally, the Danish register data also contain very detailed information about car purchases with information about the exact type of car and the time of purchase. As in the Swedish case (see Koijen, Van Nieuwerburgh, and Vestman, chapter 11, this volume), this can be mapped directly to survey answers about purchases in order to test, for example, the impact of recall period length on precision of answers for that particular good.

This study focused on cross-sections of Danish households and persons. The Danish setup also allows asking the same people repeatedly and to match with panel data on income and wealth. Very little is known about the time series properties of measurement error in recall data. Bound et al. (1994) used panel data on earnings for the PSID validation study, but this is limited in size and only concerns a very narrowly defined group of people for two years. The Danish setup is much broader in scope since it potentially covers the entire Danish population with longitudinal information from the administrative registers. This provides a unique opportunity to learn about the time series properties of survey errors in the future. For example, it should be critical to understand if the size of the survey error is constant across time, if it always over/undershoots at the individual level, if the error is mean reverting but persistent, and so forth. The survey used in example 2 in this study has been repeated to cover questions concerning income in 2010 and will be repeated to cover 2011 through to 2013. When register data

---

9. For example, Olson, Smyth, and Wood (2012) explore if giving people their preferred survey mode increases the response rate. This possibility, however, potentially has a cost side to it by changing the level of precision for respondents who would have participated irrespective of the mode. Safir and Goldenberg (2008) attempts to measure this using natural data, but this approach ignores potentially important selection effects. In the Danish setting it would be possible to implement a randomized design that would be able to quantify the impact of self-selected mode choice on the precision of answers. As another example, it would be possible to asses the loss in precision by applying proxy reporting (http://www.bls.gov/cex/methwrkshp proxyrpting.pdf) by which survey responses are provided by a respondent about another member of the sampled unit or household.

have been released, we will be able to examine the time series properties of the survey errors.

The Danish setup allows matching new survey data with register data relatively easy and at relatively low costs. Matched survey and register data are kept at Statistics Denmark's servers and only researchers working at authorized Danish research institutions can get access to work with the matched data. However, researchers or statistical agencies with good research questions and appropriate funding wishing to start new research projects using combined survey and register data can do that in collaboration with Danish-based researchers. This can, for example, be done by contacting one of the authors of this chapter.

Appendix

Sample Statistics

Table 10A.1   Sample statistics, expenditure survey, and expenditure imputation from register data from example 1

	Register	Survey	Survey-register
N	3,352	3,352	3,352
Mean	12.077	12.085	0.008
Variance	0.518	0.381	0.296
Min.	6.951	9.302	−21.490
p1	10.106	10.550	−13.331
p50	12.105	12.121	−0.0210
p99	13.626	13.371	18.046
Max	14.660	14.127	46.236
Iqr.	0.988	0.875	0.551

Table 10A.2   Sample statistics, income survey, and income register data from example 2

	Register	Survey	Survey-register
N	4,793	4,793	4,793
Mean	12.804	12.561	−0.243
Variance	0.282	0.439	0.221
Min.	8.236	2.485	−8.934
p1	11.180	10.275	−0.254
p50	12.861	12.612	−0.214
p99	13.988	13.816	0.880
Max.	15.375	17.148	3.739
Iqr.	0.547	0.575	0.238

References

Bound, John, Charles Brown, Greg J. Duncan, and Willard L. Rodgers. 1994. "Evidence on the Validity of Cross-Sectional and Longitudinal Labor Market Data." *Journal of Labor Economics* 12 (3): 345–68.

Bound, John, Charles Brown, and Nancy Mathiowetz. 2001. "Measurement Error in Survey Data." *Handbook of Econometrics*, vol. 5, edited by J. Heckman and E. Leamer, 3705–830. Amsterdam: North Holland.

Bound, John, and Alan B. Krueger. 1991. "The Extent of Measurement Error in Longitudinal Earnings Data: Do Two Wrongs Make a Right?" *Journal of Labor Economics* 9 (1): 1–24.

Browning, Martin, and Søren Leth-Petersen. 2003. "Imputing Consumption from Income and Wealth Information." *Economic Journal* 113 (488): F282–301.

Gottschalk, Peter, and Robert Moffitt. 1994. "The Growth of Earnings Instability in the US Labor Market." *Brookings Papers on Economic Activity* 1994 (2): 217–72.

———. 2011. "The Rising Instability of US Earnings: Addendum." Unpublished manuscript, Johns Hopkins University, Boston College. http://www.econ2.jhu.edu/people/moffitt/jep%20addendum%20v1%202011-7-17.pdf.

Kleven, Henrik Jacobsen, Martin Knudsen, Claus Thustrup Kreiner, Søren Pedersen, and Emmanuel Saez. 2011. "Unwilling or Unable to Cheat? Evidence from a Tax Audit Experiment in Denmark." *Econometrica* 79:651–92.

Kopczuk, Wojciech, Emmanuel Saez, and Jae Song. 2010. "Earnings Inequality and Mobility in the United States: Evidence from Social Security Data since 1937." *Quarterly Journal of Economics* 125 (1): 91–128.

Kreiner, Claus Thustrup, David Dreier Lassen, and Søren Leth-Petersen. 2012. "Consumption Responses to Fiscal Stimulus Policy and the Household Price of Liquidity." CEPR Discussion Paper no. 9161, Centre for Economic Policy Research.

Moffitt, Robert A., and Peter Gottschalk. 2002. "Trends in the Transitory Variance of Earnings in the United States." *Economic Journal* 112 (478): C68–73.

———. 2011. "Trends in the Transitory Variance of Male Earnings in the US, 1970–2004." NBER Working Paper no. 16833, Cambridge, MA.

Olson, Kristen, Jolene Smyth, and Heather Wood. 2012. "Does Giving People Their Preferred Survey Mode Actually Increase Participation Rates? An Experimental Examination." *Public Opinion Quarterly* 76:611–35.

Safir, Adam, and Karen Goldenberg. 2008. "Mode Effects in a Survey of Consumer Expenditures." Bureau of Labor Statistics. http://www.bls.gov/cex/cesrvymeths safir1.pdf.

Judging the Quality of Survey Data by Comparison with "Truth" as Measured by Administrative Records
Evidence from Sweden

Ralph Koijen, Stijn Van Nieuwerburgh, and Roine Vestman

Having accurate measures of consumption is crucial for research on the optimality of household decision making, on consumption and saving behavior, on inequality, poverty, and standards of living, and for research on consumption-based asset pricing models. Our understanding of consumption behavior may well depend on how accurate the measurement of consumption really is.[1] Accurate consumption data are difficult to collect. In practice, it is infeasible to ask large numbers of households to keep track of their expenditures in great detail and over a long enough period of time. Consumption surveys instead use paper or phone interviews to ask stylized questions on spending in a few broad consumption good categories over a particular recall period. Other times, households are asked to keep track of

Ralph Koijen is professor of finance at London Business School and a faculty research fellow of the National Bureau of Economic Research. Stijn Van Nieuwerburgh is professor of finance at Stern School of Business, New York University, and a research associate of the National Bureau of Economic Research. Roine Vestman is assistant professor of economics at Stockholm University and a visiting researcher at the Institute for Financial Research (SIFR) in Stockholm.

Prepared for the conference on "Improving the Measurement of Consumer Expenditures," sponsored by the National Bureau of Economic Research and the Conference on Research in Income and Wealth, December 2 and 3, 2011, in Washington, DC. This research was supported by the National Science Foundation under grant award no. 0820105, Bankforskningsinstitutet, and Jan Wallanders och Tom Hedelius stiftelse. We thank the participants of the NBER/CRIW conference for comments, and in particular Chris Carroll (our editor), Erik Hurst, and Ari Kapteyn. For acknowledgments, sources of research support, and disclosure of the authors' material financial relationships, if any, please see http://www.nber.org/chapters/c12664.ack.

1. For example, there is debate on whether consumption inequality has gone up along with income inequality during the 1980s and 1990s, and therefore on the question of whether households' insurance opportunities have improved (Krueger and Perri 2006; Attanasio, Battistin, and Ichimura 2005; Aguiar and Bils 2011). The pattern observed in the data changes depending on the exact source of consumption data that is used.

recurrent expenditures, such as groceries, for a short period of time (a few weeks usually) in a diary. Sometimes, they are asked about large and infrequent purchases (e.g., consumer durables) over the past year in a separate interview in addition to the diary.[2]

An existing literature has found basic problems with survey-based measures of consumption, and this volume contributes to the analysis. In prior work, Ahmed, Brzozowski, and Crossley (2006) compare two measurements for the same set of households and find that recall food consumption data, which is the basis of a great deal of empirical work, suffers from considerable measurement error while diaries records are found to be more accurate. Other work has compared consumption measures across different surveys or across different waves of the same survey.[3] Measurement error is often found to be nonclassical (Bound, Brown, and Mathiowetz 2001; Pudney 2008). The measurement error in household-level consumption data, and the difficulty of estimating nonlinear models in the presence of such error, have led some to call for abandoning Euler equation estimation altogether (Carroll 2001). Bound, Brown, and Mathiowetz (2001) emphasize the usefulness of validation data in characterizing the joint distribution of error-ridden measures and their true values. It seems fair to conclude that the measurement errors are sufficiently severe to warrant exploration of alternatives.

In this chapter we develop such an alternative measure of consumption, which avoids many of the problems with standard survey-based data. The basic idea is to measure consumption as a residual from the household's budget constraint: consumption is the part of total income that was not invested. This approach imposes heavy data requirements on the measurement exercise because one needs comprehensive measures of income as well as comprehensive asset holdings and asset price data. While most countries currently do not have such data, Sweden (and a few other Scandinavian countries) collects that information as part of its tax registry. The tax registry data contain information on every stock, bond, mutual fund, and bank account each household owns at the end of the year. Housing registry data also keep track of homeownership and households' permanent address. Finally, the Swedish data also contains information on labor, transfer, and financial

2. In the United States, the Consumption Expenditure Survey (CEX) is the standard data set for consumption measurement, while the Panel Study for Income Dynamics (PSID) contains a measure of food consumption. Blundell, Pistaferri, and Preston (2008) and Guvenen and Smith (2010) impute total consumption in the PSID based on the relationship between food consumption and total consumption in the CEX. In the United Kingdom, the corresponding data sets are the Family Expenditure Survey, now called the Living Cost and Food Survey, and the British Household Panel Survey (BHPS) for food consumption. In Continental Europe, the Household Budget Surveys were recently harmonized across countries. A special issue of the Review of Economic Dynamics (January 2010) provides an excellent overview of consumption measurement in various countries.

3. See Battistin, Miniaci, and Weber (2003), Browning, Crossley, and Weber (2003), Battistin (2004), and Gibson (2002) among others.

income. The resulting series is a measure of total consumption (including durables) measured at annual frequency.[4] A final necessary condition for our exercise is that Sweden runs a standard Household Budget Survey and that we can *match* up the households in the survey to the registry data.

This setup allows us to compare registry-imputed and survey-based measures of consumption between 2003 and 2007 for thousands of households. Our first set of results study that comparison by homeownership status, age, income, and wealth. We are particularly interested in the question of whether surveys accurately measure consumption for the wealthy. To the extent that consumption of the wealthy is understated, the registry data would be useful to gauge the size of the bias. This seems relevant in light of the fact that most household budget surveys undersample the rich. Our registry-based approach does not suffer from this undersampling. We uncover discrepancies between registry- and survey-based consumption measures that increase with income and wealth. While the mean and median of the consumption distribution are similar, the survey understates the consumption of wealthy and high-income households, while slightly overstating consumption of the poorest quintile of households.

Second, we study how sensitive registry-based consumption is to an accurate imputation of returns that households are earning on their assets. The ability to calculate a household-specific portfolio return is unique to our chapter; the otherwise similar study with Danish data by Kreiner, Lassen, and Leth-Petersen (chapter 10, this volume) assumes a common, zero capital gains return. We find that incorrectly applying a broad total return measure to a household's financial asset holdings leads to substantial deviations from the properly imputed registry measure. These discrepancies are increasing in wealth. This finding is of independent interest to researchers who need to make assumptions on household portfolio returns because they lack the detailed security-level data available in Sweden (e.g., Maki and Palumbo 2001; Hurd and Rohwedder, chapter 14, this volume).

Third, we look at a subsample of households who purchased a car and find that a surprisingly large fraction of households fails to report the car purchase in the survey. The likelihood of not reporting is particularly large in the two tails of the wealth distribution. The car purchases provide validation data that establish basic problems with the survey-based measure. Finally, we study a simple measurement error model that allows for both error in survey and in registry-based imputation and we compare the relative magnitudes of the error.

---

4. While others have exploited the richness of Swedish data to study households portfolio choices (e.g., Massa and Simonov 2006; Calvet, Campbell, and Sodini 2007, 2009; Cesarini et al. 2010; Vestman 2011), or to study various topics within labor economics and inequality (e.g., Björklund, Lindahl, and Plug 2006; Domeij and Floden 2010; Lindqvist and Vestman 2011), or corporate finance (Cronqvist et al. 2009), we are the first to compute a measure of consumption based on Swedish income and asset data.

The rest of this chapter is organized as follows. Section 11.1 describes our Swedish data set. Section 11.2 describes how we construct registry-based consumption. The details of the various data sources and consumption measurement components are relegated to the appendix. Section 11.3 describes the properties of our new registry-based measure of consumption. It also compares it to the properties of survey-based consumption and discusses the correlation between the two measures for the set of households for which we observe both measures. Section 11.4 studies car transactions as an external validation tool for the survey data. Section 11.5 concludes with lessons for survey-based consumption measurement.

11.1 Data

Our analysis compares registry-based and survey-based consumption measures between 2003 and 2007. The foundation of the registry-based data is a representative panel data set LINDA (Longitudinal INdividual DAta for Sweden) of 300,000 households and their members. We add detailed registry-based data on individuals' asset holdings from LINDA's wealth supplements. Our survey-based measure is the Swedish Household Budget Survey (HBS), which tracks about 2,000 *different* households each year. Since 2003, Statistics Sweden uses LINDA as the sample frame for this survey. Therefore, it is possible to perfectly match the survey-based information with the registry-based information.[5] Appendix A describes the data sets in more detail. Along the way, we point to some measurement issues in the registry data.

It is possible to obtain detailed administrative records of Swedish tax payers for two reasons. First, each tax payer has a unique social security number and this number is used as an identifier in every administrative database. Second, the Swedish tax authority shares records with the national statistical agency, Statistics Sweden. Thus, it is possible to use all information generated in tax filings and match it with other administrative databases, such as the real estate registry or the car registry. Of particular importance is the fact that, up until 2007, Sweden levied a wealth tax on those individuals who were sufficiently rich. To establish who qualified, authorities gathered comprehensive information on all asset holdings for all households. For instance, each household reports each and every listed stock or mutual fund she holds in her tax filings. Two exceptions to this are the holdings of financial assets within private pension accounts, for which we only observe additions and withdrawals, and "capital insurance accounts," for which we

---

5. To the best of our knowledge, a similar match has only been made on Danish data by Browning and Leth-Petersen (2003) and Kreiner, Lassen, and Leth-Petersen (chapter 10, this volume).

observe the account balance but not the asset composition.[6] The reason is that tax rates on those two types of accounts depend merely on the account balances and not on actual capital gains. There is also a tax on real estate, which allows for an accurate measurement of the value of owner-occupied single-family houses and second homes (cabins). Apartment (co-op) values are less accurately measured.

11.2 Constructing Registry-Based Consumption

This section describes our approach to impute consumption expenses. We combine information from Swedish registry data on income, asset holdings, and asset returns to arrive at imputed consumption expenditure from the household budget constraint. Consumption of household i in year t is given by:

$$(1) \qquad c_{it} = y_{it} + d_{it} - (1 + r_{it}^d)d_{it-1} - a_{it} + a_{it-1}(1 + r_{it}^a),$$

where y_{it} denotes household i's labor income minus taxes plus transfers plus rental income from renting out owned houses in year t, d_{it} denotes the value of total debt at the end of year t, r_{it}^d the *household-specific* interest rate on debt between $t - 1$ and t, a_{it} denotes the total value of the asset portfolio at the end of year t, and r_{it}^a the *household-specific* holding period return on the asset portfolio held between $t - 1$ and t. Income that is not invested or used to reduce debt, declines in net asset values, and net increases in debt all translate into higher consumption. The richness of the Swedish data makes all terms on the right-hand side of equation (1) observable. When adapted to the Swedish registries, equation (1) can be spelled out in more detail as follows:

$$(2) \qquad c_t = y_t + \Delta d_t - y_t^d - \Delta b_t - \Delta v_t + y_t^y - \Delta h_t - \Delta \psi_t - \omega_t,$$

where the subscript i has been omitted for brevity. The variable y_t^d measures the interest service on debt, Δb_t are changes in bank accounts, $\Delta v_t = v_t - v_{t-1}R_t$ measures a household's active rebalancing of mutual funds, stocks, and bonds,[7] y_t^y is after-tax financial asset income (interest on bank accounts, coupons from bonds, dividends from stocks, and income from stock option contracts), Δh_t are changes in housing wealth due to active rebalancing (sales or purchases, not valuation effects), $\Delta \psi_t$ is the net change in capital insurance

6. Capital insurance accounts are savings vehicles that are not subject to the regular capital gain and dividend income taxes, but instead are taxed at a flat rate on the account balance. Hence, we do not know the exact composition of these accounts, only the year-end balance.

7. The household-specific return on this portfolio excludes any distributions (dividends, coupons): $R_t = P_t / P_{t-1}$ where P_t is the end-of-year, ex-dividend price. When the household does not change its position in a given asset but passively earns an unrealized capital gain or takes a capital loss, that asset's contribution to Δv is zero.

accounts, while ω_t are contributions to private pension accounts. Each component in equation (2) is detailed in appendix B. All amounts are denoted in real terms (with base year 2005), where the deflator is Swedish consumer price index.

11.3 Properties of Registry-Based Consumption

We now study the properties of the consumption expenditure variable, constructed from the registry data, and compare it to the corresponding consumption measure from the Household Budget Survey. This comparison is possible for the *same set* of households for the five survey years between 2003 and 2007. We recall that each household enters once in the HBS, each HBS wave is about 2,000 households, and the match rate with LINDA is 100 percent. The resulting number of matched household-year observations in our sample is 10,705. In what follows, consumption measured from the survey is denoted by c^S and consumption imputed from registry data via equation (2) is denoted by c^R.

We impose several sampling restrictions on this set of matched households to ensure stable household composition, proper identification of owners and renters, complete data on financial asset portfolios, and to eliminate outliers in terms of year-on-year wealth changes, which may be due to errors in the raw data. Appendix C describes the restrictions in detail. The final sample consists of 5,134 households, or about one thousand households per survey year on average. Of these, 1,487 are renters (29 percent) and 3,647 are homeowners (71 percent).

One important issue when comparing the HBS and the registry-based consumption measures is that they pertain to a consumption flow measured over the same time frame. Because the registry-based imputation is based on tax data, it always refers to an annual consumption measure over the period January 1 until December 31. The survey is done during a two-week period when recurrent expenditure items are recorded in a diary and when households are interviewed about big ticket purchases of cars, boats, furniture, and so forth. Thus, survey consumption conceptually refers to the fifty-two-week period ending with the last interview. This implies that survey- and registry-based measures pertain to a different one-year measurement period. In the most extreme case, households interviewed in the first two weeks of January essentially report consumption that refers to the previous registry (calendar) year. When comparing the registry-based consumption measure for a given calendar year to the survey measure, the best comparison is for households who were surveyed late in the calendar year. Our main comparison, therefore, focuses on households surveyed in December. The December sample contains 529 households, of which 159 are renters and 370 homeowners.

11.3.1 Summary Statistics

Tables 11.1 and 11.2 report our imputed consumption series for renters and homeowners, respectively. In each table, the first column shows summary statistics for the distribution of registry-based consumption. The second column reports the survey-based consumption measure for the same sample of households. Column (3) reports the moments of the distribution of the difference between registry- and survey-based measures (not the difference of the moments). Column (4) scales that difference by median registry-based consumption. Columns (5)–(8) are analogous to columns (1)–(4), but focus on the subset of households interviewed in December, a group for which the timing of consumption measurement in survey and registry is in closer alignment.

Renters. Starting with the 1,487 renters, we find average consumption of 214 kSEK (in thousands of Swedish krona) imputed consumption (about $32,300), and basically identical to the survey mean of 212 kSEK. The standard deviation is slightly higher in the registry than in the survey-based measure (130 versus 116 kSEK). In terms of the percentiles of the distribution, our imputed measure indicates lower consumption in the very bottom of the consumption distribution, equal consumption at the 25th and 50th percentiles, and higher consumption from the 75th percentiles of the consumption distribution onward. For example, the 75th percentile of imputed consumption is 283 kSEK compared to 262 kSEK in the survey, while the 95th percentile is 578 for the registry versus 525 kSEK for the survey-based measure. Despite these differences, the two consumption distributions line up remarkably well for renters. Even the 99th percentiles differ by only $8,000 on a consumption of $88,000. Columns (5) and (6) report the same statistics, but for the subset of 159 renters surveyed in December. While the December sample is obviously much smaller (the first and 99th percentiles contain only one person), the consumption distribution is similar and lines up about as well with the survey-based distribution as the full sample.

Homeowners. Turning to the 3,647 homeowners in table 11.2, we find average consumption of 328 kSEK imputed consumption (about $49,700), and noticeably above the survey mean of 292 kSEK, about a $5,500 difference. The log difference is 12 percent. The average consumption of homeowners is 53 percent higher than that of renters in the imputation, compared to 38 percent in the survey. Since homeowners are on average substantially wealthier than renters, higher consumption is to be expected. It is also a first indicator that the survey may be understating consumption of the wealthy. In addition, there is substantially more consumption inequality among owners in the registries than in the survey, and more between owners than between renters. The standard deviation of consumption is 191 kSEK in the registry versus 147 kSEK in the survey-based measure. The 5th percentile of the consumption distribution is lower in the registry-based measure (87 versus 107 kSEK), the median is higher (315 kSEK versus 270 kSEK), and the 95th percentile is

Table 11.1   Summary statistics for renters

Variable	Registry (1)	Survey (2)	Diff. (3)	Rel. diff. (4)	Registry (5)	Survey (6)	Diff. (7)	Rel. diff. (8)
Mean	214.4	211.6	-2.81	-0.015	216.1	217.6	1.52	0.008
Std.	129.8	116.2	135.9	0.71	132.7	112.4	135.1	0.69
Percentile 1	-25.8	57.6	-347.8	-1.81	-189.2	34.3	-300.8	-1.55
Percentile 5	76.4	84.7	-187.1	-0.97	56.6	75.4	-177.3	-0.91
Percentile 25	130.4	133.1	-63.7	-0.33	126.0	131.1	-61.3	-0.32
Percentile 50	185.2	192.1	-9.48	-0.05	188.6	194.7	-11.2	-0.06
Percentile 75	282.6	261.9	48.2	0.25	318.9	262.3	51.7	0.266
Percentile 95	438.5	407.3	197.6	1.03	444.0	469.9	249.9	1.28
Percentile 99	577.5	524.8	374.5	1.95	627.3	526.0	657.5	3.38
Survey month	1–12	1–12	1–12	1–12	12	12	12	12
Observations	1,487	1,487	1,487	1,487	159	159	159	159

Note: Columns (3) and (7) report the distribution of the difference between survey-based and registry-based consumption measures. Columns (4) and (8) use the median of survey-based consumption as the denominator to compute a measure of the relative difference between the two measures.

Table 11.2   **Summary statistics for homeowners**

Variable	Registry (1)	Survey (2)	Diff. (3)	Rel. diff. (4)	Registry (5)	Survey (6)	Diff. (7)	Rel. diff. (8)
Mean	328.4	291.9	-36.4	-0.135	344.2	314.4	-29.8	-0.102
Std.	191.3	147.0	184.0	0.682	185.7	146.1	165.4	0.565
Percentile 1	-93.5	75.1	-528.9	-1.96	-25.0	78.4	-526.5	-1.80
Percentile 5	86.8	107.0	-302.7	-1.12	105.6	115.4	-328.9	-1.12
Percentile 25	203.1	192.4	-123.4	-0.457	217.4	208.8	-114.9	-0.39
Percentile 50	314.8	269.9	-39.7	-0.147	323.0	292.8	23.9	-0.082
Percentile 75	426.9	364.3	49.2	0.182	444.5	389.2	60.6	0.207
Percentile 95	633.7	553.3	239.7	0.888	693.5	621.6	235.6	0.805
Percentile 99	877.3	753.0	454.2	1.68	957.9	763.7	387.6	1.32
Survey month	1–12	1–12	1–12	1–12	12	12	12	12
Observations	3,647	3,647	3,647	3,647	370	370	370	370

Note: Columns (3) and (7) report the distribution of the difference between survey-based and registry-based consumption measures. Columns (4) and (8) use the median of survey-based consumption as the denominator to compute a measure of the relative difference between the two measures.

considerably higher (634 versus 553 kSEK). The 99th percentiles of the two consumption distributions differ by 15 percent (877 versus 753), the equivalent of $18,800. Columns (5) and (6) report the same statistics, but for the subset of 370 homeowners surveyed in December. The consumption distribution is shifted up slightly (probably a Christmas-shopping effect), but the conclusions from comparing the two distributions are the same for this subset.

The understatement of consumption in the survey at the top of the distribution is consistent with Aguiar and Bils (2011), who find that consumption inequality closely tracks income inequality between 1980 and 2007 once the *relative* undermeasurement of luxury good expenditures in the CEX is corrected. The (smaller) overstatement of survey-based consumption of the poorest is a new finding. In contrast, Meyer and Sullivan (2003, 2007) and Meyer, Mok, and Sullivan (2009) argue that income transfers from welfare programs and participation in the food stamp program is understated in surveys, particularly among the poorest. This underreporting, as always, may be due to recall problems and a desire to minimize reporting burden, but in this instance, also due to confusion about the exact name of the programs and social stigma associated with participation. We speculate that, by the same token, overreporting consumption expenses among the poorest could arise from a desire to conform to the average consumption pattern (see also Bertrand and Morse 2012). In addition, it might result from an (asymmetric) inability to adjust consumption downward in the short run when faced with a negative income shock around the time of the survey.

Comparing Survey and Registries. What this comparison of consumption distributions ignores is the identity of the respondent. Next, we compute the difference, for each household, between the survey- and the registry-based consumption measures. Columns (3) and (7) report the moments of that distribution for the full sample and for the December subsample. Columns (4) and (8) express this difference relative to the median survey-based consumption. If the registry-based consumption measures are true, then the relative differences are a direct measure of the bias in the survey. We argued above that the December comparison is most meaningful because of the timing misalignment for households surveyed too early in the year. For renters, columns (7) and (8) of table 11.1 show that while the average difference is essentially zero, its standard deviation is substantial at 135 kSEK or 69 percent of median survey consumption. The difference ranges from –177 kSEK at the 5th to 250 kSEK at the 95th percentiles, or between –1 and +1 times median consumption. The statistics in column (8) can be compared to the numbers reported in table 1 of Browning and Leth-Petersen (2003), for a sample of Danish renters. Their (our) numbers are: –5.79 (–1.81) for the minimum, –0.24 (–0.32) for the 25th percentile, –0.01 (–0.06) at the median, 0.28 (0.27) at the 75th percentile, and 6.66 (4.03) at the maximum. We conclude that the two sets of deviations for Swedish and Danish renters are close. Despite the timing issues, a comparison of columns (8) and (4) shows

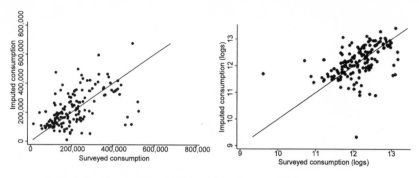

Fig. 11.1 Survey- versus registry-based consumption for renters

Notes: The left panel plots survey-based consumption in levels (horizontal axis) against registry-based consumption in levels (vertical axis) for the group of 159 renters surveyed in December. The right panel plots survey-based consumption in logs (horizontal axis) against registry-based consumption in logs (vertical axis) for the same group of households. For the purpose of this figure, we eliminated four observations with negative consumption since their log consumption is not defined. The solid line is the 45-degree line.

that the distribution of deviations looks quite similar for the full sample and the December subsample. In part, of course, this is because the full sample is much bigger and less sensitive to outliers.

Figure 11.1 shows a scatter plot of survey- versus registry-based consumption for the December sample of renters. The left plot measures consumption in levels, the right plot in logs. The figure also draws in the 45-degree line. The plot excludes four renters with negative imputed consumption. The correlation between the consumption measures in levels for all 159 December renters is 40.7 percent. Extending the sample to all 1,487 renters reduces the correlation slightly to 39.5 percent, most likely due to the timing misalignment issue alluded to above.

For homeowners, the standard deviation of the individual survey- minus registry-based differences is 165 kSEK or 56 percent of median survey-based consumption. The difference ranges from –329 kSEK at the 5th to 236 kSEK at the 95th percentiles, or between –1.12 and 0.80 times median consumption, similar to the numbers for renters. The statistics in column (8) can be compared to the numbers reported in table 2 of Browning and Leth-Petersen (2003), for a sample of Danish homeowners. Their (our) numbers are: –5.79 (–3.04) for the minimum, –0.29 (–0.39) for the 25th percentile, –0.02 (–0.08) at the median, 0.26 (0.21) at the 75th percentile, and 10.7 (1.55) at the maximum. We conclude that our Swedish registry-based measure appears somewhat closer to the survey-based measure than the Danish one, in that it seems to imply fewer large differences in the extremes of the difference distribution. Nevertheless, the two sets of deviations are close.

Figure 11.2 shows a scatter plot of survey- versus registry-based consumption for the December sample of owners. The left plot measures consumption in levels, the right plot in logs. The correlation between the consumption

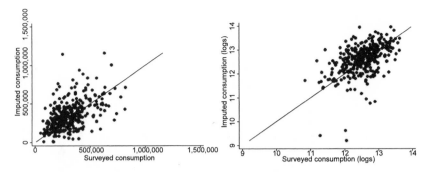

Fig. 11.2 Survey- versus registry-based consumption for homeowners

Notes: The left panel plots survey-based consumption in levels (horizontal axis) against registry-based consumption in levels (vertical axis) for the group of 370 homeowners surveyed in December. The right panel plots survey-based consumption in logs (horizontal axis) against registry-based consumption in logs (vertical axis) for the same group of households. For the purpose of this figure, we eliminated four observations with negative consumption since their log consumption is not defined. The solid line is the 45-degree line.

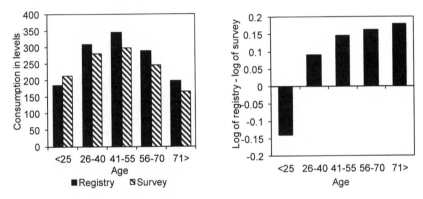

Fig. 11.3 Survey- versus registry-based consumption by age

Notes: The figure plots survey-based consumption in levels and registry-based consumption in levels for different age groups on the left panel and the percentage difference between the two measures on the right panel. Group 1 is made up of households whose head is less than twenty-five years old (180 observations), group 2 is age twenty-six to forty (1,511 obs.), group 3 is age forty-one to fifty-five (1,752 obs.), group 4 is age fifty-six to seventy (1,150 obs.), and group 5 is age seventy-one and older (456 obs.). The total sample is 5,049 observations (5,134 households minus 85 households with negative registry-based consumption).

measures in levels for all 370 December homeowners is 52.4 percent. Extending the sample to all 3,647 homeowners reduces the correlation to 43.4 percent. Combining all renters and owners surveyed in December leads to correlation between the survey- and registry-based consumption levels of 55.1 percent, while the full sample of 5,134 households results in a correlation of 46.7 percent.

Consumption by Age. Figure 11.3 plots registry- and survey-based consumption for five age groups, listed in the caption of the figure. Both measures of consumption display the well-known hump shape over the life cycle.

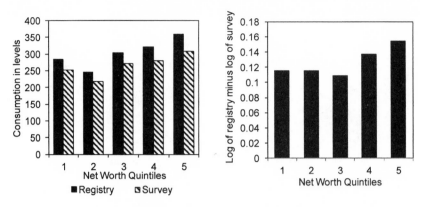

Fig. 11.4 Survey- versus registry-based consumption by wealth

Notes: The left panel plots average survey-based consumption in levels (striped bars) and registry-based consumption in levels (solid bars) for five groups of households that are ranked by wealth. Wealth is household net worth, measured as financial assets plus (primary and secondary) houses minus all debt. The right panel plots the percentage deviation (log difference) between registry-based and survey-based consumption for the same wealth groups. For the purpose of this figure, we eliminated eighty-five observations with negative consumption since their log consumption is not defined. The sample for this figure contains 5,049 households (5,134 households minus 85 households with negative registry-based consumption).

The percentage difference between the two consumption measures follows the hump-shaped profile. For the twenty-five-year-olds, registry-based consumption is minus 14 percent below survey-based consumption. For the twenty-six to forty-year-olds, it is 9.1 percent above that in the survey. That positive difference further rises with age to 14.7 percent for ages forty-one to fifty-five, and then further to 16 percent and 18 percent for the two oldest quintiles. To the extent that wealth is hump shaped over the life cycle, this is consistent with the consumption-by-wealth discussion we turn to next.

11.3.2 Role of Net Worth and Income

We now turn to the relationship between our two consumption measures and wealth. Our measure of wealth is household net worth, measured as financial assets plus (primary and secondary) houses minus all debt. Another advantage of our Swedish data is that there is no top-coding of wealth (or income). In 2007, the 10th percentile of net worth is negative, indicating debt outstripping assets (–112 kSEK), the median is 613 kSEK, and the 90th is almost 2,907 kSEK (the equivalent of $440,000), and the 95th is 3,995 kSEK (or $605,000). Table 11D.1 in appendix D reports the wealth distribution by year.

Consumption by Wealth. We sort all households with positive registry-based consumption into wealth quintiles, ranked from lowest to highest. The left panel of figure 11.4 is a bar chart of average survey- and registry-based consumption for each of these wealth quintiles. It shows that, other than a decline from wealth quintile 1 to 2, consumption increases in wealth, but

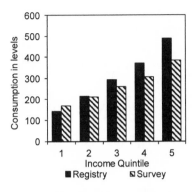 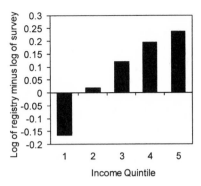

Fig. 11.5 Survey- versus registry-based consumption by income

Notes: The left panel plots survey-based consumption in levels and registry-based consumption in levels for different income quintiles. Income, y, is measured as labor income after taxes and transfers. It excludes financial income and interest payments on loans. The right panel plots the percentage deviation (log difference) between registry-based and survey-based consumption for the same income groups. The total sample is 5,049 households (5,134 households minus 85 households with negative registry-based consumption).

that registry-based consumption is steeper in wealth. The gap between the two consumption measures increases from 27 kSEK in quintile 2 to 51 kSEK in quintile 5 ($4,090 versus $7,800). The right panel plots the average *percentage* deviations between individual registry- and survey-based measures for each wealth group. This percentage deviation also increases in wealth, increasing from 11 percent for quintiles 1 to 3 to 14 percent and 15 percent for quintiles 4 and 5. In other words, the survey understates consumption, and the understatement is larger for the wealthy.

Consumption by Income. We obtain a similar picture when we study consumption by income. Figure 11.5 plots the two consumption measures for income quintiles. We use labor income after taxes and transfers, earlier defined as y_t, to group households. Registry-based consumption is lower than survey-based consumption for the lowest income quintile, similar to our results for the youngest age group. Because of the increasing life cycle profile in income, those two results reflect the same group of households to a large extent. The percentage difference between registry- and survey-based consumption turns positive for quintile 2 (2 percent) and increases further with income to 24 percent for the highest income group. This finding reinforces our conclusion that the survey may be understating consumption for the rich, as measured by either wealth or income. Results are nearly identical if we include financial income y^v and subtract interest payments on debt y^d, which are omitted for brevity.

11.3.3 Household-Specific Portfolio Returns

One major advantage of the Swedish data set, and the feature that makes it truly unique worldwide, is that it allows us to impute a highly accurate financial portfolio return for each household because we observe all holdings of financial assets at the individual security level. It is natural to ask how sensitive our registry-based consumption measure is to our ability to do this imputation correctly. Put differently, how far off would we be if we had used a different return assumption? The answer to this question seems relevant for researchers that want to follow our method for other countries (such as the United States) where such individual-specific portfolio holdings data are not available.

We explore three natural variations on the individual portfolio-return calculation. We assume that every security the individual holds earns the rate of return on a well-diversified Swedish stock portfolio (the SIXRX Stockholm stock index return). In that case, we set financial income $y_y^y = 0$ to zero but use a cum-dividend stock return in equation (2).[8] We also consider a return equal to a 50-50 weighted average of a Swedish one-year Treasury note and the SIXRX. Third, we simply consider a one-year Treasury bond yield (and $y_y^y = 0$) as the portfolio return.

Table 11.3 reports survey- and registry-based consumption measures for all 529 households, homeowners and renters, surveyed in December. Column (1) repeats the summary statistics for survey-based consumption. Column (2) is our benchmark registry-based imputation where we use the correct household-specific return. Column (3) reports using the Swedish stock index, column (4) the 50-50 stock-bond return, and column (5) uses the bond return. Comparing column (3) to column (2) makes clear that assuming that household portfolio returns equal the Stockholm Stock Exchange index return leads to an overstatement of consumption for all but the 99th percentile of the benchmark registry-based consumption distribution. The median consumption is too high by 12 kSEK, the average by 8 kSEK, and the dispersion by 7 kSEK. Using a 50-50 mix of stocks and bonds to proxy for the household-specific return leads to both an understatement and overstatement of consumption at different points in the consumption distribution. The bias in the median (mean) is –2.5 kSEK (–3.9 kSEK). Finally, using the bond return as a proxy leads to a severe understatement across the board, with median too low by 11.4 kSEK and mean consumption too low by 16.2 kSEK ($1,700 and $2,450, respectively). Using the all-bond return or the all-stock returns also leads one to overestimate the true dispersion in consumption. This fact may suggest that households may choose portfolio allocations so that they can use them to self-insure. While the sign of the bias on consumption may depend on the exact period of study (presumably, the survey bias from using an imputation benchmark based on stocks could turn positive for a sample with unusually low stock returns), the conclusions on the volatility of consumption seem always applicable.

---

8. We also explored the MSCI world index return, but it gave similar answers to using the SIXRX.

Table 11.3 Effect of portfolio returns on consumption

Variable	Survey (1)	HH portf. (2)	Stocks (3)	Stock-bond (4)	Bonds (5)	Survey (6)	HH portf. (7)	Alternative (8)
Mean	281.0	305.7	313.5	301.8	289.5	272.1	293.8	280.7
Std.	141.8	181.1	188.1	183.4	183.6	143.1	181.7	189.1
Percentile 1	60.0	−45.3	−45.4	−94.0	−141.0	43.2	−123.6	−238.5
Percentile 5	96.8	82.7	85.9	80.3	68.1	82.5	55.4	12.3
Percentile 25	176.7	172.7	175.3	170.2	160.5	162.5	163.2	154.0
Percentile 50	257.2	280.6	292.1	275.2	269.2	250.7	262.2	249.3
Percentile 75	363.1	403.9	410.8	403.3	396.6	358.9	399.3	381.6
Percentile 95	560.8	636.0	669.5	659.2	625.8	560.3	632.4	616.9
Percentile 99	722.2	872.2	925.3	880.6	838.5	741.0	839.0	841.9
Survey month	12	12	12	12	12	12	12	12
Survey year	03–07	03–07	03–07	03–07	03–07	06–07	06–07	06–07
Observations	529	529	529	529	529	195	195	195

Note: The table reports survey- and registry-based consumption measures for all 529 households, homeowners and renters, surveyed in December. Column (1) repeats the summary statistics for survey-based consumption. Column (2) is our benchmark registry-based imputation where we use the correct household-specific return. Column (3) reports using the Swedish stock index, column (4) the 50–50 stock-bond return, and column (5) uses the bond return. The bond return is a one-year government bond yield. All amounts are in thousands of Swedish krona (kSEK). Columns (6) and (7) report the same statistics as in columns (1) and (2), but only for years 2006 and 2007. Column (8) reports the summary statistics for the alternative imputation framework given by equation (3), also for the years 2006 and 2007.

We conduct a final exercise that studies data limitations that exist in other contexts. This exercise compares our approach, spelled out in equation (2), to an alternative approach that ignores the asset composition of the household portfolio and the return earned on each component. Instead, it uses the change in financial wealth between tax years, denoted by Δa_t, as a proxy. This emulates the approach taken, for example, in the Danish exercise by Browning and Leth-Petersen (2003) and Kreiner, Lassen, and Leth-Petersen (chapter 10, this volume).

$$(3) \qquad c_t^* = y_t + \Delta d_t - y_t^d + y_t^v - \Delta h_t - \omega_t - \Delta a_t .$$

Thus, instead of our "bottom-up" aggregation of security holdings to household asset balances, the alternative method relies on the aggregated asset holdings reported in the wealth supplement of LINDA. Since these data are only available for the waves 2005 to 2007, two changes can be computed in 2006 and 2007 (195 households in the December sample). Note also that the alternative measure still contains information on capital income, which consists of interest on bank accounts, bond coupons, and dividend distributions from owned stocks. But, it assumes a zero capital gain on all asset holdings. The lack of household-specific asset return information introduces measurement error in c_t^*, the latter is offset to some extent by a reduction in the type of measurement error that our approach suffers from, for example, because of incomplete or incorrect identification of securities' positions and prices.

Columns (6), (7), and (8) of table 11.3 report the results for this exercise. As can be seen in columns (6) and (7), there is substantial underreporting (21.7 kSEK) in the survey on average in 2006 and 2007, but it is confined to the top half of the consumption distribution. The average underreporting is much smaller when using the alternative registry-based measure in column (8) (8.6 kSEK). The consumption distribution in column (8) is a considerable downward shift from our preferred distribution. Even at the 5th percentile of the alternative measure, imputed consumption is just 12.3 kSEK, a difference of more than $6,530 to our measure that allows for household-specific returns. The standard deviation of the alternative measure is higher than the standard deviation of the baseline measure, implying that the utilization of the household-specific ex-dividend returns reduces the cross-sectional dispersion of consumption somewhat. This finding is in line with the reported dispersions in columns (2) to (5). Finally, the correlation between individual survey- and registry-based consumption measures is 50.1 percent in the years 2006 and 2007 for our measure, but drops substantially to 38.6 percent for the alternative measure. In sum, this comparison highlights the usefulness of our bottom-up approach of identifying individual securities, aggregation of households' asset balances, and the use of household-specific capital gain returns.

Table 11.4   **Regression diagnostic**

	Renters (1)	Owners (2)	All (3)	Owners (4)	Owners (5)
	A. Consumption in levels				
Constant	91.0	147.0	112.5	147.5	149.8
	(18.0)	(19.4)	(14.0)	(19.4)	(20.0)
c^S	0.630	0.649	0.708	0.649	0.656
	(0.076)	(0.056)	(0.044)	(0.056)	(0.058)
R-squared	0.312	0.266	0.328	0.264	0.252
	B. Consumption in logs				
Constant	5.76	4.60	4.28	4.71	4.63
	(0.077)	(0.719)	(0.542)	(0.718)	(0.711)
$\log(c^S)$	0.528	0.639	0.660	0.630	0.637
	(0.077)	(0.057)	(0.044)	(0.057)	(0.057)
R-squared	0.235	0.255	0.307	0.248	0.249
Observations	155	366	521	370	384
Change in official address	N	N	N	N	Y
Transaction of house or cabin	N	N	N	Y	Y

Notes: The table reports results from ordinary least squares (OLS) regressions of registry-based consumption on a constant and on survey-based consumption. The top panel expresses both consumption measures in levels while the bottom panel measures both in logs. The samples are the households surveyed in December. We delete eight observations with negative registry-based consumption, four renters and four homeowners. The last two columns of the table report regression results if the sampling restrictions on housing transactions are relaxed.

11.3.4 Regression Analysis

Besides the scatter plots and tables discussed above, we now turn to a more formal comparison of the two measures of consumption. We study cross-sectional regressions of registry-based consumption on survey-based consumption as an additional diagnostic of the closeness of fit.

$$(4) \qquad c_{it}^R = \alpha + \lambda c_{it}^S + \varepsilon_{it} .$$

The regressions fit the best straight line through the cloud of points reported in the left panels of figures 11.1 and 11.2. Table 11.4 reports the results. Column (1) is for the December sample of 155 renters with positive consumption, column (2) is for the December sample of 366 owners with positive consumption, and column (3) is for the combined December sample of 521 renters and owners with positive consumption. We confirm a robust positive association between the two measures for both the level measures (top panel) and the log measured (bottom panel). The top panel shows an estimated slope coefficient of 0.630 and an R^2 statistic of 31.2 percent for renters. For owners, the slope is nearly identical at 0.649, but the R^2 is lower at 26.6 percent. The R^2 for the full sample of owners and renters is 32.8 percent.

If there is (independent) measurement error in survey-based consumption, this would bias the slope down from one. Given that the two measures have about equal mean, this would result in the need for a positive intercept. This is indeed what we find. In column (3), the positive intercept is 112.5 kSEK, or about $17,000. Panel B runs the same regressions but between consumption measured in logs. The regressions in logs give a similar picture with a full-sample slope of 0.660 and R^2 of 30.7 percent. The overall conclusion from the comparison of registry-based and survey-based consumption measures is that there is a robust positive correlation among them, but that they contain either substantially different information or that there is nontrivial measurement error in one or both measures.

Under the (somewhat restrictive) assumptions of Kreiner, Lassen, and Leth-Petersen (chapter 10, this volume) that (a) both log registry and log survey consumption are noisy measures of unobserved, true log consumption; (b) the errors in survey and registry consumption are uncorrelated; and (c) that true log consumption is uncorrelated with the measurement in log registry consumption, we can say more. The bias due to measurement error in the log survey consumption is $1 - \lambda$, where $\hat{\lambda}$ is the estimated slope coefficient in equation (4). Our estimated bias is 34 percent, compared to 21 percent in Kreiner, Lassen, and Leth-Petersen (chapter 10, this volume), which shows a fair amount of noise in the survey measure. Following the Danish paper, we also look at a regression of log survey- on log registry-based consumption for the subset of households for whom the individual difference $\log(c^S) - \log(c^R)$ is between –2 and +2. This reduces the December sample from 521 to 516 households and the full sample from 5,049 to 5,000 households. In unreported results, we find that the slope λ remains constant at 0.666 while the R^2 increases from 30.7 percent to 34.7 percent. For the full sample, the slope increases from 0.617 to 0.644 and the R^2 increases from 25.1 percent to 32.6 percent. Hence, eliminating outliers increases the association between survey- and registry-based consumption measures, and under the measurement error assumptions above, reduces the bias in the survey measure only modestly (at most 2.7 percentage points).

Our analysis of the previous section shows that using household-specific returns brings survey and registry measures closer, suggesting that the lower association between the two measures in the Swedish compared to the Danish data must be due to other reasons. For example, the household budget survey itself could be noisier in Sweden. Alternatively, other features of the Swedish registry data may be noisier than the Danish registry data. For example, other elements of the budget constraint such as housing or debt could have some measurement error or there the timing of tax payments may lead to measurement error.

Effect of Sampling Restrictions Based on Housing. The last two columns of table 11.4 enlarges the sample by including households who bought or sold

Table 11.5   **Regression diagnostic—Effect of wealth and portfolio return**

	(1)	(2)	(3)	(4)	(5)	(6)
			A. Household-specific return			
Constant	112.5	110.2	121.2	112.5	131.5	84.8
	(14.0)	(38.4)	(30.0)	(16.7)	(44.1)	(54.6)
c^S	0.708	0.797	0.679	0.683	0.710	0.800
	(0.044)	(0.128)	(0.104)	(0.057)	(0.113)	(0.138)
R-squared	0.328	0.432	0.289	0.319	0.286	0.385
			B. Stock return			
Constant	114.3	110.2	120.7	116.3	146.0	97.6
	(14.7)	(38.5)	(30.1)	(17.1)	(48.3)	(66.1)
c^S	0.730	0.804	0.687	0.691	0.727	0.849
	(0.047)	(0.128)	(0.104)	(0.058)	(0.124)	(0.166)
R-squared	0.322	0.435	0.291	0.316	0.259	0.326
			C. Bond return			
Constant	125.4	114.0	123.7	110.7	138.2	93.7
	(15.2)	(38.7)	(30.1)	(17.5)	(51.6)	(66.6)
c^S	0.604	0.777	0.665	0.665	0.515	0.513
	(0.048)	(0.129)	(0.104)	(0.059)	(0.132)	(0.168)
R-squared	0.233	0.417	0.279	0.288	0.134	0.148
Observations	521	53	107	313	101	56
Range for net worth	P0–P100	P0–P10	P0–P20	P20–P80	P80–P100	P90–P100

Note: For homeowners, the most restrictive sample restrictions were used (no change in official address, no transaction of house or cabin). The ranges of net worth are specific for each year and are reported in table 11D.1. Panel A uses the framework of equation (2) to impute consumption. Panel B uses a modified version of the framework, which sets $y_t^y = 0$ and replaces the household-specific return R_t by SIXRX, the gross index of the Stockholm Stock Exchange. In panel C the term $y_t^y = 0$ and the household-specific return is assumed to equal a one-year government bond yield. As in the previous regressions, we exclude observations with negative imputed consumption (a total of eight for the full sample corresponding to the first column).

a house or cabin (column [4]) and by additionally including households who changed their official address (column [5]). The latter additionally picks up apartment purchases and sales. Comparing the results to the more restricted homeowners sample shows that the correspondence between survey- and registry-based consumption does not materially deteriorate once we include house purchasers or sellers or movers.

Effect of Wealth Distribution and Portfolio Returns. Table 11.5 explores the effect on the regression diagnostics of wealth and of the use of household-specific portfolio returns. Panel A of table 11.5 studies regression results of equation (4) for different wealth groups. Column (1) repeats the full sample result, columns (2) and (3) are for the bottom of the wealth distribution, column (4) for the middle of the distribution (20th–80th percentiles), and columns (5) and (6) for the top of the wealth distribution. Looking across columns (2) to (6), we notice that the R^2 statistics are highest for the bottom and top deciles. The R^2 is 6 percentage points higher at the top than in the full sample and both slope coefficient and R^2 are lower closer to the middle of the net worth distribution. Under the measurement error assumptions described above, the bias in the survey is largest closer to the middle $(1 - \lambda = 32\%)$. Panels B and C explore the effect of assuming different rates of return on the financial wealth portfolio. Panel B shows that using a broad stock return index results in essentially identical slope estimates for the wealthy but the R^2 statistic decreases by 6 percentage points for the wealthiest decile. Panel C shows that using the bond return leads to much worse associations between survey- and registry-based consumption measures, especially for the wealthy.

11.4 External Validation: Car Transactions

Since both survey- and registry-based consumption measures contain measurement error, many researchers have advocated finding external validation data to help understand the properties of measurement error.[9] Swedish registry data on car purchases offer an appealing source of validation data. Arguably, car purchases are one of the most salient purchase decisions households make. To the extent that recall errors plague survey data, we would expect those to be minimal for car transactions. Conversely, to the extent that there are discrepancies, they are revealing about substantial problems with survey-based data. The connection between the discrepancy and the characteristics of the household may be useful in correcting the survey, or for modeling measurement error in surveys.

Incidence of Underreporting. The Swedish car registry (discussed in the appendix) contains data on every purchase and sale of cars. The Household Budget Survey asks households about *net purchases* of vehicles (*Veh*), further broken down into cars,(*Car*), motorcycles, bikes, and other vehicles.[10] Net purchases are the difference between purchases and sales as measured over the past twelve months since the survey. To make the recall issue particularly stark, we focus on our sample of households that are both in the HBS and in the registries, and who purchased at least one car in the year they were surveyed *though at least one month before the beginning of the survey period*.[11] This results in a sample of 640 car-purchasing households (among

9. Battistin (2004) investigates the accuracy between the diary and interview samples in the US. CEX Ahmed, Brzozowski, and Crossley (2006) use two different Canadian surveys to compare recall food consumption responses. For a suggestion on how to set up a measurement error model using validation data, see section 3 in Bound, Brown, and Mathiowetz (2001).

10. In the COICOP standard, transactions of vehicles is defined by item U071 and transactions of cars by its subitem U0711.

11. As a robustness check, we tried a two-month lag as well. Our results were essentially the same as with a one-month lag. We are careful to exclude twenty-two car transactions between household members.

Table 11.6   **Car transactions in survey versus registry**

	Veh < 0 (1)	*Veh* > 0 (2)	*Veh* = 0 (3)	*Car* < 0 (4)	*Car* > 0 (5)	*Car* = 0 (6)
Mean	−40.8	78.8	0	+54.0	88.2	0
Observations	12	452	176	7	397	236
Fraction of obs. (%)	1.9	70.6	27.5	1.1	62.0	36.9

Note: The table reports the number of observations and the mean value of survey item net purchase of vehicles (*Veh*) and net purchase of cars (*Car*) for different subsamples. The sample consists of households for which at least one car purchase has been recorded in the car registry during the year of the survey, but at least one month prior to the survey month of the household. With multiple transactions, we require that at least one of the transactions occurred before the month of the survey. The amounts reported are in thousands of Swedish krona (kSEK). In sum, there are 640 households (22 transactions and gifts between different members of the same household are excluded).

the 5,134 households).[12] We then ask what those same households report in the survey about these car transactions.

Table 11.6 reports the distribution of interview responses among the car purchasers. In case of multiple purchases, we require that the first purchase occurred before the month of the survey. The table reports net purchase expenditures on vehicles (*Veh*) and on cars (*Car*), as reported in the survey. Although there is a separate category for cars in the registry, we choose to also report results for vehicles broadly defined to be able to rule out that the interviewer for convenience assigns a car transaction value only to the "vehicle item" but not to the appropriate subitem "cars." Implicit in our analysis is the assumption that, if at least one transaction has occurred, then *Veh* and *Car* should not be equal to zero.[13] The first three columns of table 11.6 show that only 72.5 percent of survey respondents report a vehicle purchase, if indeed a car purchase occurred, while 27.5 percent report a zero purchase value. For the subquestion that asks about net car purchases, we only find 62.0 percent positive responses and 36.9 percent zero responses (columns [5] and [6]).[14] We conclude that there is underreporting to the tune of 30 percent among respondents. This is a disturbingly high number, especially for such a salient item as car transactions.

12. Notice that since we require that households made their car purchase before they were surveyed, we only analyze half of the car purchasers in our sample (assuming that car purchases are distributed evenly over the year). Thus an approximation of the car purchaser fraction in our sample equals (2 * 640)/5134 = 24.9 percent. This is roughly equal to the aggregate statistics that state that in Sweden there are 1.1 million transactions of used cars every year and, in addition, 280,000 purchases of new cars. Given a population of five million households, this results in a car purchaser fraction of 27.6 percent.

13. In e-mail conversations, Statistics Sweden confirmed that this is the correct interpretation.

14. The results are similar when we confine attention to a group of households that bought one car and sold no car. Hence, our main results are not driven by a sale and purchase that exactly cancel each other out and lead to a zero net expenditure.

Table 11.7   Which households underreport?

	(1)	(2)	(3)	(4)	(5)
Age	0.0028*	–	–	–	0.0025
	(0.0015)	–	–	–	(0.002)
D(High school)	–	–0.213***	–	–	–0.178***
	–	(0.061)	–	–	(0.064)
D(College)	–	–0.161***	–	–	–0.118*
	–	(0.058)	–	–	(0.064)
D(Disp. income, 2nd quintile)	–	–	–0.057	–	–0.050
	–	–	(0.064)	–	(0.065)
D(Disp. income, 3rd quintile)	–	–	–0.067	–	–0.041
	–	–	(0.060)	–	(0.063)
D(Disp. income, 4th quintile)	–	–	–0.114*	–	–0.074
	–	–	(0.056)	–	(0.061)
D(Disp. income, 5th quintile)	–	–	–0.073	–	–0.043
	–	–	(0.058)	–	(0.065)
D(Net worth, 2nd quintile)	–	–	–	–0.094*	–0.096*
	–	–	–	(0.048)	(0.049)
D(Net worth, 3rd quintile)	–	–	–	–0.084*	–0.085*
	–	–	–	(0.047)	(0.048)
D(Net worth, 4th quintile)	–	–	–	–0.087*	–0.101*
	–	–	–	(0.048)	(0.050)
D(Net worth, 5th quintile)	–	–	–	–0.029	–0.055
	–	–	–	(0.054)	(0.057)
Year effects	Yes	Yes	Yes	Yes	Yes
Observations	640	640	640	640	640
Pseudo R-squared	0.077	0.088	0.077	0.079	0.100

Note: Probit regressions of the form $Pr(Veh = 0) = \alpha + \beta X_i + \epsilon_i$. The sample of households in the regressions is the same as in table 11.6. The table reports marginal effects.
***Significant at the 1 percent level.
**Significant at the 5 percent level.
*Significant at the 10 percent level.

Characteristics of Underreporters. Next, we ask what household-level characteristics are related to this underreporting problem. Table 11.7 estimates a probit regression of the event $Veh = 0$ on the age of the head of household, a dummy for high school and one for college education, and quintile dummies for disposable income and net worth. We find that older households are more likely to underreport. A sixty-five-year-old is 10 percent less likely to report a car transaction than a twenty-five-year-old. Higher education levels reduce underreporting compared to the omitted category of less-than-high school. As reported in column (3), higher income also reduces underreporting, but only the dummy for the middle income bracket is significant at conventional levels. Similarly, higher wealth also reduces underreporting, especially in the middle of the wealth distribution.

Table 11.8   **Regression diagnostic—Car transactors**

	(1)	(2)	(3)	(4)
Constant	103.8	175.1	158.9	155.4
	(14.1)	(35.6)	(48.8)	(48.7)
Survey (c^S)	0.672	0.660	0.868	0.678
	(0.047)	(0.100)	(0.175)	(0.128)
R-squared	0.347	0.253	0.429	0.231
Observations	386	130	35	95
Transact. in car reg.	N	Y	Y	Y
Restr. on vehicle in survey	N	N	$= 0$	< 0 or > 0

Note: The table reports results from OLS regressions of registry-based consumption on a constant and on survey-based consumption. The samples are the households surveyed in December. The last two rows indicate sampling restrictions. The sample contains 386 households with no car transactions in the registry and 130 households who bought (and possible also sold) a car in the month before they were surveyed (excluding five within-household transactions). Of those 130 households, 35 reported a zero value on the survey question on vehicle purchases (*Veh*), while 95 reported a positive or negative value.

A common feature for income and net worth is that the incidence of underreporting is U-shaped. When combined, education and wealth turn out to be the most significant explanatory variables. The pseudo R^2 is 10 percent in column (5). These effects are in line with intuition and indicate that the misreporting problem is more severe for wealth-poor, low-education, low-income, and older households. There remains substantial unexplained variation, as indicated by the low pseudo R^2.

Implications for Consumption. If a household fails to report an important purchase, such as a car, we would expect the match between survey- and registry-based consumption to deteriorate substantially. This is what we find in table 11.8. It reports the same regression as in equation (4), but splits the sample into those who did not transact a car according to the car registry (column [1]) with those who did buy or sell (columns [2], [3], and [4]). The first observation is that the fit between survey- and registry-based consumption deteriorates substantially for the subsample that does transact a car relative to the subsample that does not. The R^2 falls dramatically from 34.7 percent in column (1) to 25.3 percent in column (2).

Second, if we look at the households that do report a car transaction in the survey by answering a nonzero amount to the question on vehicle purchases, the fit deteriorates further to 23.1 percent (column [4]), and is much worse than for the households who do report a zero car transaction in the survey (column [3]). Third, the measure of survey bias $1 - \lambda$ increases from column (3) (13.2 percent) to column (4) (32.2 percent). In sum, even conditional on reporting of even salient items such as car purchases poses important problems for survey-based measures of consumption.

11.5 Conclusion

Faced with potentially severe measurement error problems in survey-based consumption, this chapter considers an alternative consumption measure derived from Swedish tax registries. Basically, we use detailed data on income, financial assets and housing, and debt to back out total annual consumption expenditures as a residual from the budget constraint. The unique feature of our data is that we observe the complete financial portfolio, which allows us to construct a household-specific portfolio return. The second important feature of the data is that we can match up the standard survey-based consumption measure and our registry-based measure for 5,134 households, surveyed between 2003 and 2007. A close comparison of both measures shows that registry- and survey-based consumption measures have the same hump-shaped life cycle profile, and that they have about the same average and median for renters. The survey-based measure understates consumption for homeowners, as well as for richer households, either measured by high net worth or high income. In the highest net worth quintile, the survey has 15 percent lower consumption, on average, while in the highest income quintile the gap is 24 percent. We also show that incorrectly approximating the portfolio return with a safe bond return leads to downward-biased consumption, especially for the wealthy. Further, approximating the portfolio return with either a stock market return or a safe bond return leads to too much consumption dispersion. We obtain a correlation between the survey- and registry-based consumption levels of 55.1 percent for our sample that combines all renters and owners surveyed in December. Similarly, a regression on registry-based and survey-based consumption illustrates that the two measures (for a given household) are far from perfectly correlated. Finally, we take a closer look at car purchases, a salient consumer item. We find that almost 30 percent of the car transactions go unreported in the survey, even though the car purchase or sale took place in the month before the survey. Reported purchase values in the survey also appear to understate the likely transaction value. Overall, the car evidence casts doubt on the quality of the interview component of the survey data.

While our exercise is hard to replicate in other countries for lack of sufficiently rich data, it nevertheless contains a number of important lessons for the measurement of consumption in the United States and elsewhere. First, surveyed consumption seems to suffer from substantial measurement error. Second, it understates consumption inequality. Third, it may be overstating consumption for low-wealth and low-income households somewhat, while substantially understating consumption of the rich. Fourth, using broad return measures instead of household-specific portfolio returns has substantial effects on the consumption distribution.

Appendix A
Registry Data: Details

LINDA

LINDA is a widely used data set in economic research. It is a joint endeavor between the Department of Economics at Uppsala University, The National Social Insurance Board (RFV), Statistics Sweden, and the Ministries of Finance and Labor. Edin and Fredriksson (2000) provide a detailed account of the data collection process for LINDA. More information on LINDA is also available from the websites of the Department of Economics, Uppsala University (http://nek.uu.se/), and Statistics Sweden (http://www.scb.se/).

LINDA is a panel data set that covers slightly more than 3 percent of the Swedish population annually. There are approximately 300,000 core individuals in the data set. The starting point for LINDA is a representative, random sample of the Swedish population in 1994, which has been tracked back to 1968 and forward to 2007. New individuals are added to the database each year to ensure that LINDA remains representative of the cross-section of Swedish individuals. In addition, the data set contains information on all family members of the sampled individual. Thus, LINDA covers all members of approximately 300,000 households in each year. The core of LINDA are the income registers (Inkomst- och Förmögenhetsstatistiken) and population census data (Folk- och Bostadsräkningen). Each wave of LINDA contains information on taxable income and social transfers (e.g., unemployment benefits) from the Income Registers in a given year. In addition, LINDA contains information on occupation, wages, and educational attainment from separate registers held at Statistics Sweden. We also use the wealth supplement of LINDA, which is available between 1999 and 2007. The wealth supplement contains information on the market value of houses, owned apartments (co-ops), cabins, plots of land, and other forms of real estate. It also reports the value of total debt and the value of student loans.

When Statistics Sweden compiles LINDA, it lacks the information to assign two people that belong to the same household but that are unmarried and without children. Such individuals are treated as two separate households. This leads to undersampling of this particular kind of household. Among the households that appear in the 2007 wave of the HBS, the number of adults reported in the HBS and the number of adults reported in LINDA agree for 85 percent of the observations.

Registry-Based Financial Asset Data

Sweden had a wealth tax in place until 2007. The Swedish tax authority, therefore, had the mandate to collect detailed information about each taxpayer's holdings of financial assets, such as bonds, stocks, and mutual funds. The data collection took place through the financial institutions. The collected data also contains information on coupon income from bonds and interest income from bank accounts. Since 1999 these data have been delivered to Statistics Sweden, which uses it for constructing the wealth supplement of LINDA. In the raw data file, each financial security and fund is identified by its International Securities Identification Number (ISIN). In rare instances, the Swedish firm ID number is reported instead, requiring a careful matching procedure by hand. For an in-depth description of this component of the data, see Calvet, Campbell, and Sodini (2007, 2009) who used this data component for the period 1999 to 2002. After matching with LINDA, we have information on all asset holdings of the LINDA respondents.

We obtain separate data on the prices, dividends, and returns for each stock, coupons for each bond, and net asset values per share for each mutual fund in the database from Datastream and from MoneyMate. We match this price and cash flow information to the holdings in order to be able to compute total returns on each asset that each individual holds. This results in a close-to-complete picture of each household's wealth portfolio.

The data set contains limited information about two kinds of financial accounts. These accounts are private pension and "capital insurance" accounts. Both types are surrounded by special tax regulations. As a result, the detailed asset composition of these accounts (regular savings accounts, stocks, mutual funds, bonds, or some other kind of financial asset) is not known. For private pension accounts, we observe the annual withdrawal or contribution to the account. Like in the United States, such private pension accounts are used to defer labor income taxes between contribution and withdrawal dates. Every year the taxpayer can deduct approximately 12 kSEK, or about $1,800. One Swedish krona is $0.15 as of November 1, 2011. It fluctuates between $0.11 and $0.17 over our sample period. We use the abbreviation SEK to denote amounts in Swedish krona and kSEK to denote amounts in thousands of Swedish krona. For our purpose of constructing annual flows of consumption expenses, the pension account reporting does not pose a limitation. For capital insurance accounts, the account balance is reported, but it is impossible to accurately impute the rate of return since the holdings in this account are unobserved. For the purpose of imputing consumption, we have to make an assumption on that rate of return. According to Calvet, Campbell, and Sodini (2007), such savings made up 16 percent of the total financial savings in 2002, making this assumption neither crucial nor unimportant. We explore different assumptions below.

Data on the balances of households' bank accounts suffers from measurement error. Until 2004, positive balances are reported only if the interest income during that year was greater than 100 SEK (roughly $15). After 2004, the balance of a bank account is reported only if it is greater than 10 kSEK (roughly $1,500).

Housing Registry Data

Housing consists of (single-family) houses, tenant-owned apartments (co-ops), and second homes (cabins). We use the national real estate registry (Fastighetstaxeringsregistret) to gain information on real estate transactions. The information on ownership and valuation of houses and cabins is more accurate than that of apartments.

The real estate registry records every purchase or sale of a house or cabin, along with the transaction date. Transactions of co-ops, however, are not contained in the real estate registry. Co-ops are registered on the title deeds of the buildings as opposed to being assigned to the individual share owners, and there is no national registry for owners of shares in co-operations. Statistics Sweden therefore needs to infer co-op membership based on the official address of the household. This method causes mistakes when a household rents an apartment in a co-op and declares this as her primary address. Consequently, the true apartment owner will not get recorded as the owner of the co-op. A third type of misclassification would occur if an owner purchases or sells one of several co-op units. This transaction goes unrecorded unless the person also changes his or her official address. In 2004, the method used to identify owners of apartments was overhauled. The reform lead to a net change of 10,000 apartment owners in a total population of nine million Swedes and 900,000 apartment owners. (As part of the reclassification, 90,000 individuals were no longer classified as owners while 81,000 were newly classified as owners, a gross change of 19 percent of apartment owners, or 1.9 percent of the population.)

Houses and cabins are valued quite accurately in the registry because there is a real estate tax on them. The tax basis, that is, the registered property value used for tax purposes, is a function of a long list of characteristics of the property, and is updated frequently. Based on transactions during the year, Statistics Sweden computes the ratio of the tax value to the market value for each of Sweden's 290 municipalities and uses this value to assign market values for all houses and cabins. Average tax-to-market value ratios are around 0.5, but they vary over time and cross-sectionally. This method implies that the aggregate stock of houses and cabins is likely to be valued accurately. The registry data, however, do not include the actual transaction price of a property, only the market value (the market-value-adjusted, property-specific tax value). Thus, property-specific changes in market values that are not accurately reflected in the property-specific tax reassessments, as well as deviations of the transaction price from the market value, are sources of measurement error.

In contrast to the relatively accurate valuation of houses and cabins, there is no national effort to collect tax values on apartments that belong to a co-op. Statistics Sweden uses the average sale value of the apartments in a co-op in a given year to assign market values to all apartments in that co-op, including to those apartments that were not transacted. However, if too few sales occurred at the co-op level, Statistics Sweden uses the average sale value in the parish instead for the imputation. This implies that there is too little variation in reported apartment values and that small apartments suffer from an upward bias in assigned values and large apartments suffer from a downward bias. Due to the inaccuracies that surround co-ops, we explore various alternative sampling restrictions described in appendix B.

From the registries, we also order a tailored dummy variable that registers whether an individual changes her official address. For the vast majority of people, the official address equals the primary residence. Some young people may rent a home on a short-term basis and may keep their official address at their parents' home. If a household member changes his or her address in the public registries, then the dummy variable takes on a value of one. The variable is helpful for identifying households that undergo a change in composition during the year (due to marriage, divorce, children moving away from home, etc.), but it is also helpful for identifying households who sell or purchase an apartment.

Car Registry Data

Finally, we add information from the car registry. Specifically, we obtain data on the characteristics of the cars that LINDA individuals purchased and sold between 1999 and 2007. Those characteristics are car brand, model (e.g., engine type, station wagon, etc.), manufacturing year, and reported mileage at the annual inspection of the car. Separately, we hand-collect data on prices of secondhand cars by brand, model, and mileage for a few common car brands (namely Audi, BMW, Mercedes, SAAB, and Volvo) from the Swedish equivalent of the Kelley Blue Book in the United States. Matching the pricing information to the LINDA data allows us to compare reported car purchases in the survey to imputed car purchases from the registry and car price data.

Household Budget Survey

Statistics Sweden produced the Household Budget Survey (Hush UTgifter) for the years 1999, 2000, and 2001. The data collection procedure was then overhauled and a new version of the survey started in 2003. The purpose of the revision was to better adhere to the guidelines of the European statistical agency, Eurostat. An important change in 2003 is that LINDA is used as the sample frame. Thus, in each LINDA wave after 2003, there is a subset of approximately 2,000 households for which we can match HBS and LINDA data. In contrast, it is not possible to identify the set of individuals and households that were surveyed in the years 1999 to 2001. Note that, in contrast to LINDA, the HBS is not a longitudinal database. Each household only appears once. As a result, the HBS does not allow for a construction of consumption growth for a household.

Table 11A.1   Data collection procedure for the Household Budget Survey

Week 50	A first letter with information is sent to subsample 1
Week 51	The first interview
	Household composition, occupation, type of home
	Purchased and sold furniture, refrigerators, microwave ovens, stoves, and other durable goods during the last twelve months
Week 52	Instructions
	Detailed instructions on the diary are given over phone
Weeks 1–2	Consumption diary
	Either the household performs the diary over fourteen days, or the household sends all the receipts to Statistics Sweden
Week 1	The second interview
	Expenses on primary residence and secondary residences such as cabins, phone, domestic services, child care, cars, insurances, and travels during the last twelve months
Week 1, 2	Follow-up phone calls
	The interviewer calls so that any issues concerning the diary can be solved
Week 3	The third interview
	Short questions about expenses. The questions are changed every quarter. The interviewer reminds the household to send the diary and any receipts
Week 3	Statistics Sweden receives the diary and any receipts

Notes: The table reports all the steps in the data collection procedure for the households who have been allotted to weeks 1 and 2 of the year. It is a reproduction from page five in the documentation of survey wave 2007, published on Statistics Sweden's website.

The HBS selects about 4,000 households, of which at least one member is between 0 and 79 years old. The response rate to the survey is about 50 percent, leaving it with a final sample of about 2,000 households each year. Data is collected via a consumption diary and a phone interview, and some auxiliary information is pulled from Statistics Sweden's registries. The sample is distributed equally over fifty-two weeks, marked by the first week of the diary, and the same procedure is used for each subsample. Table 11A.1 describes the data collection procedure for the subsample of households who keep a diary during the first two weeks in a year (weeks one and two of the calendar year).

Table 11A.2 reports summary statistics for the 2005 wave of the HBS by expense category (first column). The second column reports whether the data come from the consumption diary (D), the phone interview (I), or whether they are pulled from the registries (R). The 2005 wave consists of 2,079 households. All amounts are in current SEK (divide by seven to get approximate dollar values) and refer to annual expenditures. The first twelve rows denote the twelve (European-wide) consumption categories. Housing consumption (shelter, part of category 4) is measured as rent for renters and maintenance for homeowners. It *excludes* net mortgage interest expenses for owners because our measure of net capital income in the registry-based approach below also excludes this expense. Second homes (cabins) are treated

Table 11A.2   Summary statistics for the 2005 wave of the Household Budget Survey

	Source	Mean	Std.	Min.	Max.
01. Food and nonalcoholic beverages	D	38.9	22.0	0	348.0
02. Alcoholic beverages, tobacco, narcotics	D	6.1	8.8	0	65.0
03. Clothing and footwear	D	17.1	26.6	0	337.2
04. Housing, water, electricity, gas, etc.	I,D	51.0	33.6	0	662.2
05. Furnishings, household equipment, etc.	I,D	21.8	37.7	−55.0	690.6
06. Health	D	7.1	19.4	0	315.6
07. Transport	I,D	48.5	66.9	−155.3	699.7
08. Communications	I,D	9.8	7.4	0	156.3
09. Recreation and culture	I,D	43.3	49.7	−511.2	779.8
10. Education	D	68	923	0	27.0
11. Restaurants and hotels	D	12.3	17.8	0	231.4
12. Miscellaneous goods and services	I,D	21.8	43.5	0	1,827.0
13. Fees to unions, unempl. insurance, etc.	D,R	4.8	3.9	0	43.3
14. Taxes on vehicles	I,D	2.0	1.9	0	14.8
15. Donations	D	2.3	8.0	0	130.0
16. Cabins	I,R	2.5	9.2	0	195.4
17. Tax on benefits	R	1.9	6.5	0	63.7
18. Expenses outside of COICOP	I,D	0.5	7.5	−30.4	211.5
Total expenditure	I,D,R	295.9	164.2	−324.5	2,318.2

Notes: The expense categories follow the international COICOP standard. The number of households is 2,079. We define total expenditure as being equal to total expenditure as reported in the survey minus interest rate expenditure (COICOP category 22). As sources of the data, "D" indicates diary, "I" indicates interview, and "R" indicates registry. The registry-based expense items are: taxes on plots of land, houses and cabins, fees to labor unions, fees to unemployment insurance, and taxes that are paid for benefits received from the employer. Some households report expense items that do not fit into the COICOP standard. In such cases Statistics Sweden adds the expenses directly to total expenditure. These expenses are referred to as expenses outside of COICOP in the table. All amounts are in thousands of Swedish krona (kSEK).

analogously to primary residences and are reported separately (category 16). Transport (category 7) includes the net purchases of cars, which could be a negative number if the household sells a car but does not buy a new one in a given year. Likewise, recreation (category 9) includes the net purchases of boats—quite an important expenditure category in Sweden—which again can be negative. Finally, furnishings can also be negative if a household sells more furniture or equipment than it buys. As a result, survey-based consumption can be negative, and indeed it is for some households. Category 12 reports miscellaneous goods and services, such as hair dresser, parking tickets, funerals, bank fees, fees for ordering passports, and so forth. Categories 13, 14, 15, and 17 contain outlays on donations, vehicle taxes, taxes to unions, and taxes paid for benefits received, some of which are imputed from registries. Finally, row 18 measures other expenses that are outlays but that are not part of the harmonized European consumption expenditure standard (COICOP). Total consumption expenditure is the sum of all these categories; it includes net outlays on consumer durables (which can be negative) and excludes mortgage payments for homeowners. It refers to the consumption flow over the twelve months prior to the week following the end of the interview. Total 2005 household consumption has a mean of 296 kSEK (or about $44,400), with a considerable standard deviation of about 165 kSEK or $24,600. The minimum value is –325 kSEK (–$48,700) and the maximum value is above 2.3 million SEK ($347,700).

Appendix B
Construction of Consumption in Registries: Details

Labor Income after Taxes and Transfers

The term y_t captures labor income minus taxes on labor income plus government transfers. We compute this variable by excluding capital income from all assets, net capital gains (gains minus losses) from financial assets, and net increases in student loans (increases minus decreases) from the disposable income variable. Table 11B.1 provides the details of this computation, which changes in 2004 due to a change in the definition of disposable income in 2004. Using the 1991 definition of disposable income for 2004 and beyond would not change the results much. The variable y includes rental income from renting out (primary or secondary) owned houses.

Net Change in Debt

The term $\Delta d_t = d_t - d_{t-1}$ equals the change in total debt from the end of year $t - 1$ to the end of year t. A positive value denotes an increase in the debt balance. Debt includes credit card debt, car loans, student loans, mortgages, and other kinds of debt. We do not have a breakdown of this debt in subcategories, except for student loans, which are reported separately. The total interest payment on all debt (the debt service), y_t^d, is directly reported in the tax registries. Interest expenses lower consumption. The registry-based debt service numbers are directly comparable to the corresponding debt service numbers in the household budget survey. Table 11B.2 reports summary statistics of these two variables for the same set of households, in thousands of SEK. The table shows that the survey tends to understate interest expenses. For high interest-expense households, the bias grows in absolute terms but attenuates in relative terms. Finally, note that we are subtracting mortgage expenses as part of subtracting total interest expenses. This is consistent with the budget survey where we also excluded mortgage expenses. The alternative treatment of (a) defining housing consumption as the sum of maintenance and mortgage expenses, as in a standard-user cost approach, in the survey and (b) not subtracting mortgage expenses in the

Table 11B.1   Computing labor income after taxes and transfers

1999–2003		2004–2007	
	$y_t =$		$y_t =$
Disposable income, 1991 def.	cdisp	Disposable income, 2004 def.	cdisp04
–total capital income	–kiranta	–total capital income	–kiranta
–increases in student loans	–ismlan	–increases in student loans	–ismlan
+decreases in student loans	+uater	+decreases in student loans	+uater
–net capital gains, if positive	–max((kv–kf),0)	–gross capital gains	–kvbrut
		+gross capital losses	+kfbrut

Table 11B.2   Interest expenses from tax records and the HBS (kSEK)

	Mean	Std.	P5	P25	P50	P75	P90	P95
Interest expenses in tax registry	27.7	38.8	0	1.1	15.6	40.0	71.0	95.2
Interest expenses in HBS	21.5	29.5	0	0	10.9	31.3	59.9	81.9

Notes: This table compares total debt service (interest expenses on all debt) from the tax registry and from the Household Budget Survey. The registry variable, y_t^d, is kakuru and comes from tax form KU25. The variable for total interest expenses in the HBS is u22. The comparison is for the same set of households. The numbers are in thousands of SEK.

registry-based imputation is not possible because we do not separately observe mortgage interest expenses in the registry data.

Bank Accounts

The term $\Delta b_t = b_t - b_{t-1}$ measures the change in bank accounts (checking, savings, certificates of deposit, etc). A decline in bank accounts increases consumption, ceteris paribus. Recall that in 2006 and 2007 the balance of every single bank account is reported if the balance is greater than 10,000 SEK. In prior years, the balance of a bank account is reported if the earned interest exceeds 100 SEK.

Stocks, Bonds, and Mutual Funds

The term $\Delta v_t = v_t - v_{t-1} R_t$ measures a household's active rebalancing of mutual funds, stocks, and bonds. The household-specific return on this portfolio excludes any distributions (dividends, coupons): $R_t = P_t / P_{t-1}$ where P_t is the end-of-year, ex-dividend price. The purchase of a new fund, stock, or bond reduces consumption while the sale of an existing one increases consumption, all else equal. When the household does not change its position in a given asset but passively earns an unrealized capital gain or takes a capital loss, that asset's contribution to Δv is zero. Realized capital gains and losses are reported for tax purposes as gains and losses relative to the original purchase price. Such gains or losses do not reflect consumption-relevant cash flows. Rather, what matters for the consumption flow in a given period is the sale price of the asset rather than the difference between the sale price and the original purchase price. Our variable Δv captures the relevant capital gains and losses. Positive values for Δv reflect active increases in the financial asset position and translate in a reduction in consumption, unless they are offset elsewhere in the budget constraint. We compute income from financial assets, y_t^y, as the after-tax interest on bank accounts, coupons from bonds, dividends from stocks, and income from stock option contracts. (Total income from all financial assets is given by the variable kiranta minus four tax variables, skubank from tax form KU20 and kkuvpi, kkuvpr, and skkuvp from tax form KU21. Financial income adds to consumption, ceteris paribus.

Housing Wealth

Changes in housing wealth are given by Δh_t, which capture changes in primary residence (houses and apartments) and in second homes (cabins). Since the aim is to measure only cash flows, Δh_t differs from zero only if the household purchases or sells a house, apartment, or cabin. Parallel to the treatment of financial assets, Δh_t should reflect active rebalancing decisions and not unrealized capital gains or losses due to house price appreciation or depreciation. An increase in housing lowers consumption, unless offset elsewhere. Primary housing does not generate income. The shadow value of the housing services (rental equivalent) that the house provides is excluded both in registry- and survey-based consumption measures. If a household receives payments for renting out their second home, that rental income is measured as part of y_t. Note that, to the extent that households extract resources from their home equity through a second mortgage, cash out refinancing, or home equity line of credit, this is already captured in Δd_t.

To capture only active rebalancing on housing assets, as opposed to unrealized capital gains and losses, as well as to deal with the measurement issues in apartments described above, we set $\Delta h_t = 0$ unless at least one household member has purchased or sold a house or cabin according to the real estate registry, or unless the head of household changes her official address. A change in official address typically indicates a change of primary residence and allows us to capture active changes in ownership of co-ops that are used as primary residences. Because of measurement error in Δh_t, we also explore two sampling restrictions. In the first subsample, we exclude any household-year observations if the official address of any household member has changed in that year. Since the official address typically is equal to the address of the primary home, this set of restrictions is meant to allow households that have transacted secondary homes to remain in the sample. In a second stricter subsample, we additionally exclude household-year observations if any household member has purchased or sold any real estate according to the real estate registry that year. Effectively, the latter subsample only considers households with $\Delta h_t = 0$. These sampling restrictions offer a trade-off between maximizing sample size and minimizing measurement error. (We also considered a third subsample where we included households who report a change in official address, but whose reported value of apartment holdings are zero in the two consecutive years. The intention was to allow households that had sold or purchased a house or cabin to remain in the sample. However, since co-ops are a common form of primary housing, we lose about half the sample, and decided therefore not to report results for this subsample.) As the sampling restrictions discussed below will clarify, our main results are for the strictest subsample.

Capital Insurance Accounts

The so-called *capital insurance accounts* are savings vehicles that receive special tax treatment. Assets held in such accounts are subject to a flat 1 percent tax rate on the account balance, rather than the standard 30 percent capital gain and dividend income taxes. (To be precise, the tax rate fluctuates somewhat from year to year. It is equal to 27 percent of the average government bond yield during the year. This yield is reported every week by the Swedish National Debt Office.) Households may change the portfolio allocation within such accounts and reinvest the financial income spun off by the assets in the account, but may not withdraw funds lest they incur penalties. In our data, the account balance is reported, but the allocation to regular savings accounts, stocks, mutual funds, bonds, or some other kind of financial asset is unknown. The net change to this kind of account is imputed by $\Delta \psi_t = \psi_t - \psi_{t-1} R_t^\psi$, where R_t^ψ is the cum-dividend return on the portfolio of assets. We assume that the return on these accounts, R_t^ψ, equals the cum-dividend return on the all-share Stockholm Stock Exchange.[15] A decrease in account balances leads to an increase in consumption, all else equal.

Pension Accounts

For private pension accounts, we observe new contributions and withdrawals. Since withdrawals from private pension accounts are taxed as labor income, they are already included in income, y_t. Contributions to private pension accounts, denoted by ω_t, are reported separately in the registries and enter equation (2) as reduction in consumption.

Appendix C
Sampling Restrictions

We impose the following ten sampling restrictions on this set of matched households. Table 11C.1 lists the impact of each to the overall size of the sample.

---

15. We use the index SIXRX.

Table 11C.1   **Sample exclusions**

Type of restriction	Observations
0. Full sample	10,705
1. Excl. instable households over time (in terms of household head, number of adults)	9,711
2. Excl. farmers and entrepreneurs	8,937
3. Excl. households with inconsistent homeownership status in registry and survey	8,052
4. Excl. households who change official address or transact real estate	7,207
5. Excl. households who hold derivatives	7,078
6. Excl. households who hold securities with missing ISINs	6,965
7. Excl. households who hold mutual funds or stocks with missing prices or returns	5,283
8. Excl. households who have extreme portfolio returns (top and bottom 1 percent)	5,253
9. Excl. households who have big changes in net worth (top and bottom 2.5 percent)	5,135
10. Excl. households with negative surveyed consumption	5,134

First, we remove households whose composition changes between year ends $t-1$ and t, leaving us only with households with a stable composition. These restrictions concern the household head and the number of adults in the household. The household head is defined as the oldest male if this person is at least twenty-one years old, otherwise the oldest female if there is a female who is at least twenty-one years old, otherwise the oldest person in the household. The household head must remain the same in two consecutive waves and the number of adults (age twenty-one or older) must remain the same. This restricts the sample to 9,711 households.

Second, we exclude farmers as well as households who report more than 50 kSEK (around $7,500) in income from an own business in the registries. For self-employed households, personal and business expenditures are hard to separate, making a consumption imputation somewhat meaningless. This restricts the sample to 8,937 households.

Third, we require that households who are homeowners (renters) in the registries report to be homeowners (renters) in the survey. A homeowner (renter) in the registries is defined as a household who has positive (zero) housing wealth (i.e., apartment, house, or cabin) according to the wealth supplement of LINDA. This restriction reduces the sample to 8,052 households. These restrictions are also imposed in a similar exercise on Danish data by Browning and Leth-Petersen (2003).

In addition, we impose a set of restrictions that are aimed at mitigating potential measurement errors in households' asset changes. The fourth restriction in table 11C.1 implements the strictest criterion on changes in housing wealth, discussed in appendix B. In particular, we exclude households who change the official address or who transact a house or cabin according to the registries. This restricts the sample to 7,207 households. We explore below how our consumption measurement changes if we only exclude those who change official addresses or if we exclude neither category.

Fifth, we exclude 7,078 households where a household member owns any derivative product (including own-company stock options), which are hard to value correctly.

Sixth, we require exact identification of the entire financial asset portfolio, that is, no reported holding can have a missing ISIN in the raw data. This implies a drop of 113 households.

Seventh, we require that we carry both prices and returns for each holding of the household's portfolio. Although we are able to match nearly 95 percent of all asset positions, the restriction that all of a household's positions must be identified implies that we lose an additional 1,682 households. Approximately 600 of those are lost due to a particular harsh restriction—we require that in the case of multiple versions of a given mutual fund with the same ISIN (such as a retail version with one kind of fee structure and another version offered within the pension segment) we can establish which version of the fund that is the correct match or that the NAVs per share do not deviate more than by 15 percent from each other (in unreported results, we have verified that this restriction could in fact be relaxed).

Eighth, we drop households for which the calculated financial asset return (the portfolio of stocks, bonds, and mutual funds) is in the tails of the distribution. The lower truncation point is at the bottom 1 percent of the return distribution, while the upper truncation point corresponds to the top 1 percent of the return distribution. Specifically, the top restrictions are 111 percent (2003), 64.3 percent (2004), 67.6 percent (2005), 49.0 percent (2006), and 28.1 percent (2007). The bottom percentile restrictions on household returns are –99.9 percent (2003), –99.9 percent (2004), –99.9 percent (2005), –99.9 percent (2006), and –99.9 percent (2007). The remaining sample has 5,253 observations.

Ninth, a small number of households experience a dramatic change in net worth from one year to the next. This could happen for many reasons, among which are bequests or intervivos transfers from family members, which we do not observe. We choose to exclude households if the change in net worth is in the bottom 2.5 or in the top 2.5 percent of the corresponding year-specific distribution. At percentile 2.5, the change in net worth in thousands of SEK is as follows: –866 (2003), –663 (2004), –751 (2005), –616 (2006), and –719 (2007). At percentile 97.5, the change in net worth is 1,058 (2003), 1,116 (2004), 1,504 (2005), 1,468 (2006), and 1,397 (2007). This eliminates 118 observations.

Tenth, we delete one household for which the surveyed consumption is negative.

The final sample consists of 5,134 households, or about one thousand households per survey year on average. Of these, 1,487 are renters (29 percent) and 3,647 are homeowners (71 percent). The homeownership rate in our sample matches the rate in the Swedish population at large.

Appendix D
Wealth Distribution

Table 11D.1 reports summary statistics of the wealth distribution by year. The sample is all 5,134 households in our sample.

Table 11D.1   **Wealth distribution**

	2003	2004	2005	2006	2007
Percentile 5	−276	−280	−318	−257	−239
Percentile 10	−153	−136	−174	−124	−112
Percentile 20	−52	−31	−43	−7	0
Percentile 50	252	375	405	486	613
Percentile 80	1,061	1,274	1,412	1,551	1,903
Percentile 90	1,765	1,952	2,158	2,424	2,907
Percentile 95	2,437	2,582	2,940	3,528	3,995
Observations	1,053	1,143	1,035	936	967

Notes: The table reports summary statistics of the Swedish wealth distribution. Our measure of wealth is household net worth, measured as financial assets plus (primary and secondary) houses minus all debt. The sample is all 5,134 households in our sample. All numbers are expressed in thousands of Swedish krona (kSEK).

References

Aguiar, M., and M. Bils. 2011. "Has Consumption Inequality Mirrored Income Inequality?" NBER Working Paper no. 16807, Cambridge, MA.

Ahmed, N., M. Brzozowski, and T. Crossley. 2006. "Measurement Errors in Recall Food Consumption Data." IFS Working Paper no. W06/21, Institute for Fiscal Studies.

Attanasio, O., E. Battistin, and H. Ichimura. 2005. *What Really Happened to Consumption Inequality in the US?* Chicago: University of Chicago Press.

Battistin, E. 2004. "Errors in Survey Reports of Consumption Expenditures." IFS Working Paper no. 03/07, Institute for Fiscal Studies.

Battistin, E., R. Miniaci, and G. Weber. 2003. "What Do We Learn from Recall Consumption Data?" *Journal of Human Resources* 38 (2): 354–85.

Bertrand, M., and A. Morse. 2012. "Trickle-Down Consumption." Working Paper, University of Chicago.

Björklund, A., M. Lindahl, and E. Plug. 2006. "The Origins of Intergenerational Associations: Lessons from Swedish Adoption Data." *Quarterly Journal of Economics* 121 (3): 999.

Blundell, R., L. Pistaferri, and I. Preston. 2008. "Consumption Inequality and Partial Insurance." *American Economic Review* 98 (5): 1887–919.

Bound, J., C. Brown, and N. Mathiowetz. 2001. "Measurement Error in Survey Data." *Handbook of Econometrics* 5:3705–843.

Browning, M., T. Crossley, and G. Weber. 2003. "Asking Consumption Questions in General Purpose Surveys." *Economic Journal* 113 (491): 540–67.

Browning, M., and S. Leth-Petersen. 2003. "Imputing Consumption from Income and Wealth Information." *Economic Journal* 113 (488): 282–301.

Calvet, L. E., J. Y. Campbell, and P. Sodini. 2007. "Down or Out: Assessing the Welfare Costs of Household Investment Mistakes." *Journal of Political Economy* 115 (5): 707–47.
———. 2009. "Fight or Flight? Portfolio Rebalancing by Individual Investors." *Quarterly Journal of Economics* 124 (1): 301–48.
Carroll, C. 2001. "Death to the Log-Linearized Consumption Euler Equation! (And Very Poor Health to the Second-Order Approximation)." *B. E. Journal of Macroeconomics* 1 (1): 1–38.
Cesarini, D., M. Johannesson, P. Lichtenstein, Ö. Sandewall, and B. Wallace. 2010. "Genetic Variation in Financial Decision-Making." *Journal of Finance* 65 (5): 1725–54.
Cronqvist, H., F. Heyman, M. Nilsson, H. Svaleryd, and J. Vlachos. 2009. "Do Entrenched Managers Pay Their Workers More?" *Journal of Finance* 64 (1): 309–39.
Domeij, D., and M. Floden. 2010. "Inequality Trends in Sweden 1978–2004." *Review of Economic Dynamics* 13 (1): 179–208.
Edin, P.-A., and P. Fredriksson. 2000. "LINDA—Longitudinal INdividual DAta for Sweden." Working Paper no. 2000:19, Department of Economics, Uppsala University.
Gibson, J. 2002. "Why Does the Engel Method Work? Food Demand, Economies of Size and Household Survey Methods." *Oxford Bulletin of Economics and Statistics* 64 (4): 341–59.
Guvenen, F., and A. Smith. 2010. "Inferring Labor Income Risk from Economic Choices: An Indirect Inference Approach." NBER Working Paper no. 16327, Cambridge, MA.
Krueger, D., and F. Perri. 2006. "Does Income Inequality Lead to Consumption Inequality? Evidence and Theory." *Review of Economic Studies* 73 (1): 163–93.
Lindqvist, E., and R. Vestman. 2011. "The Labor Market Returns to Cognitive and Noncognitive Ability: Evidence from the Swedish Enlistment." *American Economic Journal: Applied Economics* 3 (1): 101–28.
Maki, D. M., and M. G. Palumbo. 2001. "Disentangling the Wealth Effect: A Cohort Analysis of Household Saving in the 1990s." Finance and Economics Discussion Series no. 2001-21, Board of Governors of the Federal Reserve System.
Massa, M., and A. Simonov. 2006. "Hedging, Familiarity and Portfolio Choice." *Review of Financial Studies* 19 (2): 633–85.
Meyer, B. D., W. K. C. Mok, and J. X. Sullivan. 2009. "The Under-Reporting of Transfers in Household Surveys: Its Nature and Consequences." NBER Working Paper no. 15181, Cambridge, MA.
Meyer, B. D., and J. X. Sullivan. 2003. "Measuring the Well-Being of the Poor Using Income and Consumption." *Journal of Human Resources* 38:1180–220.
———. 2007. "Reporting Bias in Studies of the Food Stamp Program." Harris School of Public Policy Working Paper no. 08.01, University of Chicago.
Pudney, S. 2008. "Heaping and Leaping: Survey Response Behaviour and the Dynamics of Self-Reported Consumption Expenditure." ISER Working Paper Series 2008–09, Institute for Social and Economic Research, University of Essex.
Vestman, R. 2011. "Limited Stock Market Participation among Renters and Home Owners." SIFR Working Paper, Stockholm Institute for Financial Research.

Exploring a Balance Edit Approach in the Consumer Expenditure Quarterly Interview Survey

Scott Fricker, Brandon Kopp, and Nhien To

12.1 Introduction

The US Consumer Expenditure Survey is an ongoing monthly survey conducted by the US Bureau of Labor Statistics (BLS) that provides current and continuous information on the buying habits of American consumers. The Consumer Expenditure Survey consists of two independent components: the quarterly interview (CEQ) survey and the diary (CED) survey. For the CEQ, interviewers visit sample households five times over the course of thirteen consecutive months. Each interview is conducted with a single household respondent who reports for the entire household. The first interview establishes cooperation, collects demographic information, and bounds the interview by collecting expenditure data for the previous month. This "bounding" interview is designed to limit forward telescoping, which is the process by which respondents remember and report events or purchases as taking place more recently than they actually occurred. The four remaining interviews are administered quarterly and ask about expenditures in the three-month period that just ended. In the second and fifth interview, respondents are asked additional detailed questions about household income, assets, and liabilities.

The CEQ survey presents a number of challenges for both interviewers and respondents. The interview is long, the questions detailed, and the experience can be perceived as burdensome. In part because of these challenges,

Scott Fricker is a research psychologist in the Office of Survey Methods Research of the Bureau of Labor Statistics, US Department of Labor. Brandon Kopp is a research psychologist in the Office of Survey Methods Research of the Bureau of Labor Statistics, US Department of Labor. Nhien To is an economist in the Division of Consumer Expenditure Surveys of the Bureau of Labor Statistics, US Department of Labor.

For acknowledgments, sources of research support, and disclosure of the authors' material financial relationships, if any, please see http://www.nber.org/chapters/c12671.ack.

there is concern that some CEQ data are underreported (e.g., Shields and To 2005; Bosworth, Burtless, and Sabelhaus 1991). Underreporting has been variously attributed to recall error, panel conditioning, respondent fatigue, and other causes.

To combat response errors like underreporting, some expenditure surveys have used a data quality control measure known as a "balance edit" check. Early expenditure surveys conducted by the BLS (e.g., 1935–1936 Study of Consumer Purchases; the 1950 Survey of Consumer Expenditures) used a balance edit to check for consistency among reported expenditures, income, and asset and liability totals; sample units whose expenditures exceeded income by more than 10 percent were followed up and reinterviewed or removed from the sample. This balancing procedure was eliminated prior to the establishment of the Consumer Expenditure Survey in 1972 because it was deemed "judgmental" and not operationally feasible for a (precomputer-assisted) quarterly survey (Jacobs and Shipp 1993). More recent implementations of this measure have differed across surveys, but the basic process is one in which respondents are given the opportunity to review and revise their reported expenditures, income, and changes in assets and liabilities. For example, in the 2009 Survey of Household Spending (SHS) conducted by Statistics Canada, households that had expenditures that were out of balance with the reported cash flow (i.e., spending that was significantly above or below income plus net assets and liabilities) were probed to identify and reconcile possible sources of error. There is evidence from two empirical studies that the data resulting from use of a balance edit are of higher quality than those collected by the alternative methods (Brzozowski and Crossley 2011; Hurd and Rohwedder 2010; section 12.3).

12.2 Study Objectives and Design Considerations

The current CEQ uses built-in range edit checks to flag reports that exceed normative thresholds for an expenditure category and consistency edits to flag reports that are inconsistent with data in related fields. The purpose of this study was to explore the feasibility of including a balance edit check based on a household's computed total spending relative to its income, assets, and liabilities. We conducted a small-scale lab study that addressed three basic areas of inquiry: (1) the effects of a balance edit in identifying and correcting reporting errors, (2) participants' reactions to the balance edit process, and (3) the factors that impact the quality of participants' reports or their reactions to the reconciliation process.

The study is qualitative in nature and exploratory, and there were a number of design considerations that impacted its scope and analytic objectives. One consideration was the potential increase in respondent burden that might accompany a balance edit process. The current CEQ asks an extensive battery of questions that takes an average of sixty-five minutes to administer. We were concerned that incorporating balance edits at the end of the existing CEQ would lengthen an already long and burdensome interview. Moreover, for some households the number of reports respondents would need to review could be unduly large, therefore making a balance edit process impractical to implement. In addition, in this study we wanted to be able to conduct real-time balancing checks and immediately follow up with participants during the interview. This necessitated the development of an electronic instrument that would record and tally participants' expenditure, income, asset, and liability totals, and it was not feasible to do this for the full CEQ questionnaire given the project timeline and available resources.

On the basis of these considerations, we decided to test a balance edit measure using a modified CEQ in which the detailed expenditure questions were replaced with a fewer number of global items that asked participants to report their total household spending in each of the CEQ section categories (see section 12.4 for details). We acknowledge that the use of global questions and (therefore) a shorter interview are significant departures from the current CEQ procedures, that both factors may affect the nature of response errors, and that these effects have the potential to interact with the balance edit response process. Nevertheless, we view this study as a useful first step in investigating the feasibility of implementing a balance edit, and in gathering some initial information about factors that may affect its outcome (e.g., frequency of purchase, topic sensitivity, household size and participant knowledge, conceptual clarity, cognitive difficulty, etc.).

12.3 Previous Research

Two recent surveys have implemented some form of a balance edit procedure in an effort to improve the quality of expenditure estimates—the Survey of Household Spending (SHS) conducted by Statistics Canada, and the American Life Panel (ALP) maintained by RAND Labor and Population. We briefly summarize these surveys and their use of this approach below, and discuss the studies that have examined the impact of reconciliation procedures on data quality.

12.3.1 Survey of Household Spending (SHS)

The SHS is a face-to-face survey that collects household expenditure and income data for the previous calendar year. To help combat recall errors arising from the long recall period, Statistics Canada allows respondents to report expenses for smaller and more frequently purchased items (e.g., food) on a weekly or monthly basis, and encourages respondents' use of records during the interview. In addition, the SHS has implemented a balance edit check in which respondents' reported expenditures are compared against the sum of reported income and net change of assets in the household. When expenditures were more than 20 percent different from reported income/

assets, the interviewer attempted to collect additional information to bring
the two into better balance (i.e., 15 percent or less). According to Statistics
Canada, most of the changes respondents made to their reports during
this process were to reported income and assets (personal communication,
May 2011); this is likely due to the wording of the structured probes, which
focused on these areas. The SHS households that remained unbalanced were
deemed unusable and excluded from estimates.

In 2006, SHS data collection moved to computer-assisted personal interviewing (CAPI) and the balance edit was not used in the collection phase
that year. Instead, balancing was applied at the processing phase (with no
active involvement or reconciliation by respondents), and this had the unexpected consequence of significantly increasing the number of records that
were deemed "out of balance" (from 546 in 2005 to 4,300 in 2006). This com-
prised an unacceptably large percentage of completed SHS questionnaires
for 2006 (29.4 percent), so a decision was made to reinstitute a field balance
edit feature for 2007 data collection. To assess the effect of the balance edit
on data quality, Brzozowski and Crossley (2011) compared SHS data from
2006 (no interview-based balance edit procedure) with data from 2005 and
2007. They found no differences in income or expenditure reporting across
the three years for the top fifteen income vigtiles. However, respondents in
the bottom of the income distribution (lowest five vigtiles) underreported
income when there was no field balance edit.

12.3.2 American Life Panel (ALP)

The ALP is an Internet panel of approximately 1,500 respondents who
are solicited once a month to participate in surveys typically taking less
than thirty minutes to complete. From June 2009 through December 2010,
a cohort of ALP respondents was asked to complete a monthly questionnaire that collected information about household spending in twenty-five
medium- to high-frequency purchase categories and a quarterly questionnaire that collected data on spending in eleven less frequently purchased categories. Because outliers are a problem in self-administered surveys (where
there is no interviewer to probe unusual reports), the ALP presented these
respondents with a "reconciliation" screen at the end of each survey that
provided a summary table listing the individual reported expenditures and
the spending total for the household. Respondents then were asked to review
this information and correct any items, but no automatic edit checks were
used. Examining data from this panel, Hurd and Rohwedder (2010) found
that ALP respondents corrected about 2–3 percent of entries per interview
wave, and that there were significant reductions in item nonresponse and in
the frequency and magnitude of outliers due to the reconciliation process.
There also was good agreement between the total annual spending estimates
derived from the reconciliation-aided ALP and those from CE over this time
period (i.e., ALP spending was 96 percent of CE spending).

12.3.3 Gaps in Existing Research

Although the studies by Brzozowski and Crossley (2011) and Hurd and Rohwedder (2010) provide evidence that offering respondents an efficient means of reviewing and making appropriate changes to their prior responses improves the quality of survey estimates, there is no published empirical work that has examined the cognitive underpinnings of this effect. How do respondents interpret their task? What changes do they make to their reports? (The SHS work suggests that they are more likely to change reported income and assets, but this may be an artifact of the types of probes used by Statistics Canada, which tended to focus on missed income or sources of financing for larger purchases, not expenditures.) What are respondents' reactions to being questioned about previous reports, or to seeing their household spending totals? The answers to these questions are important for understanding the quality and consequences of implementing this kind of procedure, and the present study was designed to begin to fill a gap in the literature on these and related issues.

12.4 Method

12.4.1 Design and Procedure

The study was a small-scale, lab-based test that presented participants with a modified version of the CEQ survey and a balance edit procedure for reconciling expenditure-cash flow disparities. The test sessions were conducted in the Office of Survey Methods Research (OSMR) laboratory in the Bureau of Labor Statistics (BLS). At the start of each session, a researcher explained the study's purpose and procedures and obtained informed consent from the participants. Study participants then took part in a CAPI interview that asked a brief set of demographic questions about the household, global expenditure questions for thirty-four categories (covering all of the CEQ section topics), and questions about household income and changes in assets and liabilities for the reference month.[1] All participants were given a modified version of the CEQ information booklet to refer to throughout the survey. The booklet contained a set of flashcards that provided a list of examples of the kinds of expenditures asked about in each category. All three authors served as interviewers.

Expenditures, assets, and liabilities were collected for the preceding month (one-month recall period). We used a one-month recall period rather than a three-month period (as the CEQ does) or a flexible reference period (as is done in the SHS) for two reasons. First, we needed to measure the change in

---

1. For a full set of study materials see appendixes I–III in the working paper (http://www.bls .gov/cex/cesrvymethsfricker.pdf).

assets and liabilities over the reference period (e.g., depletions/additions to savings, changes to credit card balances) to get a full picture of the household cash flow. We felt that asking participants to recall the relative change in their accounts over a longer recall period would be very difficult, especially in a lab setting in which participants had limited or no access to their household records. The second reason was practical—it was not feasible to program and administer an electronic collection instrument that allowed flexible recall periods and tailored question fills; the resulting database tracking required for the balance edit would have been too complex for this study. The drawback of using a one-month recall period is that it likely misses larger and less frequent purchases, and it is possible that these types of purchases could affect both the need for reconciliation and participants' response processes during reconciliation. We attempted to probe for this information during a postinterview participant debriefing.

For household income, we allowed participants to report using a flexible reference period (weekly, biweekly, monthly, quarterly, or annual) because there were relatively few income questions (so programming was manageable), and we felt that participants would provide more accurate information if they could choose their preferred time period. One potential problem with this approach was that our unit of measure for the balance edit check was one month. We had to aggregate up from weekly and biweekly income reports (by multiplying by four or two, respectively) or disaggregate quarterly and annual reports (by dividing by three or twelve, respectively) in order to get a one-month income value.[2] Income can naturally fluctuate for some people over time, however. The extent to which the (dis)aggregated income values differ from participants' true income for the reference period impacts the likelihood of triggering the balance edit, with potentially more effort focused on "fixing" the derived income values. Again, we examined the effect of this issue on the survey outcomes and participants' reactions to the survey.

Balance Edit. Data were recorded in an Excel workbook that calculated the ratio of participants' income-to-spending over the reference period.[3] We calculated the ratio as follows:

$$\text{Income-to-Spending Ratio} = (I_i - C_{Ai} + C_{Li}) / S_i,$$

where I_i is the (derived) monthly, after-tax household income for household i, C_{Ai} and C_{Li} are the change in assets and liabilities, respectively, for the household in the reference month, and S_i is the total spending for the household in

2. In addition to giving participants the flexibility to choose their preferred recall period for income, they could report pre-tax or after-tax income. When pre-tax income was reported, the instrument automatically calculated an estimate of the after-tax value based on current federal, state, and county tax schedules.
3. Throughout the remainder of the report we use the phrase "income-to-spending ratio" for convenience to refer to the "income-plus-net-assets-and-liabilities-to-spending ratio" unless otherwise stated.

the month. A ratio less than 1.0 indicates that the household *spent more* than its reported available income (plus net assets and liabilities). A ratio greater than 1.0 indicates that the household *spent less* than its total available income.

After all of the basic expenditure, income, asset, and liability questions were asked, the interviewer showed participants a graph depicting the ratio of their income-to-spending and read the following text:

> Thank you very much for your time so far. I'd like to take a look now at the overall picture of your household finances last month based on the information we've collected from you. This simple chart plots your reported household expenditures and your income plus any assets and liabilities. Ideally, we'd expect to see that these two figures match up pretty closely. [IF RATIO EXCEEDS THRESHOLD, READ:] However, sometimes when there is a big difference between these two amounts in a given month, it's because we missed some of your HH's expenditures or income, or need to make other changes to bring these in line.

The balance edit check was triggered by one of two income-to-spending ratios. For households with at least $30,000 in annual income, the balance edit was triggered if this ratio deviated by 15 percent or more from 1.0. For households with annual income below $30,000, the balance edit was triggered if the ratio differed by 20 percent or more from 1.0. When participants' income-to-spending ratios indicated acceptable balance at this stage of the interview (Phase 1), the interviewer terminated the interview and proceeded to the debriefing portion of the study session.

If households were out of balance (based on the criteria above), participants were given the opportunity to review a summary page of their reported expenditures, income, assets, and liabilities (individual reports and summed totals) and to make changes to their earlier reports in order to bring their ratio closer to 1.0. We recorded any changes made by participants during this review and revision phase (Phase 2), and then showed them a revised graph of their updated household income-to-spending figure. If the household was still unbalanced at that point in the interview, the interviewer administered a brief set of probes designed to capture additional sources of income and expenditures that might have been missed (Phase 3). The balance edit procedure was terminated in Phase 2 or Phase 3 when expenditures were within 10 percent of reported income plus net assets and liabilities, or when all of the CEQ items and follow-up probes had been administered.

Debriefing. Following administration of the modified CEQ (with any balance edit checks required), participants filled out a short paper-and-pencil questionnaire and then participated in a semistructured debriefing session with the interviewer. The purpose of the debriefing was to assess the following topics:

- participants' general reaction to the survey and the balance edit procedure;

- participants' perceptions of the accuracy of their reported data;
- sources of confusion or conceptual difficulty (e.g., global items, reference period, proxy reporting); and
- participants' perceptions of survey burden.

12.4.2 Participants

Participants for this study were recruited from an OSMR-maintained database of individuals who responded to advertisements for research studies placed in Washington, DC-area newspapers. We used a nonprobability-based convenience sample, but attempted to recruit participants who varied in their family size, educational attainment, household income, and employment status.[4] We interviewed twenty participants but report findings for only nineteen; one individual provided insufficient data during the survey and debriefing session. All twenty participants were paid $40 for their time. Interviews lasted approximately one hour on average—thirty minutes to administer the modified CEQ survey and balance edit, and thirty minutes to conduct the participant debriefing session.

12.4.3 Data Quality Indicators

In the next section of the chapter we present our study findings. We focus on several key results. We do not have a benchmark for "true" spending and income, so we examine the level of expenditure reporting as one commonly accepted measure of data quality. Balance edit check measures have been developed primary to reduce the likelihood of response errors due to underreporting, and thus more reporting is taken as evidence of better reporting. Another one of our primary measures of interest is the change in the household income-to-spending ratio across the interview. If the balance edit procedure implemented in this study was effective, we would expect to see those ratios improve (i.e., get closer to 1.0). Finally, we explore the qualitative responses obtained in our debriefing session to give us some additional insight into the quality of the data reported in the interview, the factors that may impact the effectiveness of a balance edit, and participants' reactions to their survey experience.

12.5 Results

12.5.1 Effect of Balance Edit on Income-to-Spending Ratios

Table 12.1 shows the distribution of participants' income-to-spending ratios at different phases of the survey. The first column shows the ratio cri-

4. We achieved reasonable balance on participant education, gender, and family size, but higher-income households and employed individuals were overrepresented in our sample. We had only two respondents with household incomes under $30,000 (sample mean: $67,800) and only three who were unemployed or retired.

Table 12.1   **Number of participants in each income-to-spending ratio group after each interview phase**

Deviation from income-spending ratio of 1.0 (%)	End of Phase 1 (main questionnaire)	End of Phase 2 (review & revise)	End of Phase 3 (additional probing)
0.0–10.0	1	3	5
10.1–15.0	0	*3*	*3*
15.1–20.0	2	*3*	*3*
20.1+	*16*	*10*	*8*

teria that we used to determine degree of balance. The second column indicates the number of participants who fell into each ratio category at the end of Phase 1 of the interview (prior to any balance edit procedures). Only one participant obtained an income-to-spending ratio good enough—0.91—to obviate the need for a balance edit. Two additional participants obtained ratios of 0.82 and 1.19 in Phase 1, respectively, but the balance edit procedure was triggered because they had annual household incomes over \$30,000 (for which "balance" was defined as a deviation of 15 percent or less from a ratio of 1.0). The remaining sixteen participants were considerably unbalanced at the completion of the basic questionnaire, with a mean deviation from unity of 43 percent (i.e., reporting 43 percent more available household income than reported spending).

The third and fourth columns of table 12.1 give one indication of the extent to which the balance edit procedure was effective. Recall that once the balance edit was triggered in this study (using the 15 percent or 20 percent deviation criterion at Phase 1), a household was deemed balanced if it achieved an income-to-spending ratio between 0.90 and 1.10. Examining the first row of the table, we see that two additional participants achieved balance after being given the chance to review a summary of their reports and make revisions (Phase 2, column [3]), and two more participants achieved balance after answering the additional expenditure and income probes (Phase 3, column [4]). Thus, a total of five participants out of nineteen obtained acceptable income-to-spending ratios by the end of the interview; one participant did so without going through the balance edit and four did so only with the help of the balance edit.

The italicized numbers in table 12.1 represent the number of participants who did not reach balance in any phase of the interview by our study criteria. Nevertheless, there is some indication in these cells that the balance edit did have a positive impact on participants' income-to-spending ratios in the aggregate. For example, the number of participants with ratios deviating by more than 20 percent from 1.0 was cut in half by the end of the balance edit process (from 16 to 8 percent). This effect is even more evident when we

Table 12.2   Distribution of the direction of ratio changes in the interview

Type of ratio change	No. of participants
Moved closer to 1.0	13
More income than spending (ratio > 1.0)	8
More spending than income (ratio < 1.0)	3
Below 1.0 to above 1.0	2
Above 1.0 to below 1.0	0
Moved farther from 1.0	1
Flipped	2
No change	2

Note: Includes only participants who were administered the balance edit (*n* = 18).

examine the pattern of changes in income-to-spending ratios for individual participants over the course of their interviews (see table 12.2).

Table 12.2 presents the number of participants whose ratios improved, worsened, stayed the same, or simply switched direction but not magnitude over the course of the interview. The majority of our participants (thirteen of nineteen) moved closer to being balanced as a result of the balance edit process. (However, despite making relative gains in their ratios during the interview, these participants' reports remained notably unbalanced, with an average deviation of 42 percent from unity.) Most of the movement toward balance in this group was the result of participants (eight of thirteen) who initially reported higher income than spending but then subsequently reported additional expenditures (these participants' ratios got smaller but remained above 1.0). Five participants initially reported significantly more spending than income and moved closer to balance throughout the interview by making small reductions to their reported spending and increases to income (e.g., reporting additional wages or forgotten tax refunds). Only one participant did worse over the course of the interview, and four individuals essentially remained unchanged (either by making no adjustments to their reports, or by flipping the sign of their ratio but not decreasing its magnitude).

12.5.2 Levels of Reporting

Table 12.3 gives a more concrete look at participants' reporting throughout the interview. The second column shows the average number of reports and average dollar amounts given by our study participants for the different survey topics in the main questionnaire (Phase 1). Consistent with our earlier findings, prior to the balance edit check our sample in the aggregate reported slightly more income (plus net change in assets and liabilities) than spending. During the initial review and revise component of the balance edit procedure (Phase 2), 61 percent of participants (*n* = 11) made changes to their reported spending (with an average of one change per participant),

Table 12.3   **Reporting incidence and level by topic and interview phase**

	Phase 1 (main questionnaire) ($n = 19$)		Phase 2 (review and revise) ($n = 18$)		Phase 3 (additional probes) ($n = 16$)	
	Average total ($)	Average no. reports	Reporting change (%)	Average change ($)	Reporting change (%)	Average change ($)
Expenditures	4,781	14	61	92	56	188
Income	5,196	2	33	589	50	973
Change in assets	67	1	22	28	n/a	n/a
Change in liabilities	49	0.5	5	−528	n/a	n/a

33 percent ($n = 6$) made changes to reported income (with an average of two changes per participant), but relatively few revisions were made to reported changes in assets or liabilities (number of changes per participant: median 0, mean 0.2).[5]

The mean dollar change figures shown on the right-hand side of the Phase 2 column reflect averages across the entire eligible sample (i.e., all participants who were administered the Phase 2 balance edit, regardless of whether a change was made or not). Restricting our analyses to only those participants who made revisions in Phase 2, the mean dollar change in expenditures was $159 ($SD_{\bar{x}} = 429) and the mean change in income was $1,866 ($SD_{\bar{x}} = $2,621$). During Phase 3, in which participants were probed about possible sources of spending and income missed earlier in the questionnaire (but not new changes in assets or liabilities), 56 percent ($n = 9$) of our sample reported additional expenditures (overall mean, $188; reporter mean, $503), and 50 percent ($n = 8$) reported additional income (overall mean, $973; reporter mean, $1,757).

12.5.3 Debriefing

Following the completion of the modified CEQ survey, participants completed a self-administered questionnaire that asked them to rate how comfortable they felt sharing expenditure, income, asset, and liability information during the interview, and how accurate they felt those reports had been. The original questions used a 5-point Likert scale—ranging from "very uncomfortable" to "very comfortable," and "very inaccurate" to "very accurate," with a neutral "neither" middle response option. We collapsed the "very" and "somewhat" categories for each dimension and omit the middle response option data for reporting purposes. Table 12.4 presents those data.

The majority of our study participants reported feeling "very" or "somewhat" comfortable providing the household financial information asked

---

5. Only one participant in this study revised her reported change in liabilities, recalling that she had paid off a business loan for $9,500 during the reference month.

Table 12.4   Participants' ratings of comfort and accuracy (%) by reporting category (*n* = 19)

	Comfort		Accuracy	
Category	Very or somewhat uncomfortable (%)	Very or somewhat comfortable (%)	Very or somewhat inaccurate (%)	Very or somewhat accurate (%)
Expenditures	5	65	5	80
Income	30	55	0	85
Change in assets	30	60	5	85
Change in liabilities	15	60	0	95

during the interview, though reporting income was more sensitive for some participants than discussing expenditures or changes in assets and liabilities. In response to a follow-up question, several participants acknowledged that they felt awkward disclosing income to a stranger, but understood the purpose of the question and believed that their responses were important and would be kept confidential. Additionally, several participants said that they were comfortable reporting income information for themselves, but had been reluctant or unable to do so for other household members.

Participants' ratings of the accuracy of their reports were very high (80–95 percent). On the one hand, this may simply reflect the effects of self-presentation management—the desire to represent oneself as a diligent and accurate participant in the data collection effort. On the other hand, a number of participants in this study evinced behavior or made explicit comments that indicated that they had engaged in effortful and thorough recall and reporting. For example, most participants followed along with the information booklet during the interview and said during debriefing that it provided definitional clarity to some of the global expenditure categories/items, and helped them recall expenditures they would otherwise have forgotten to report. Two participants spontaneously brought out their checkbooks or personal calendars during the interview to aid reporting. In addition, the balance edit process itself may have strengthened participants' perceptions of accuracy since most participants made adjustments to their reports (recalling forgotten items, revising earlier reports with greater specificity) and saw visual evidence that those efforts led to improvements in their household cash flow balance.

The self-administered questionnaire also included items to assess participants' perception of survey length and burden. We asked participants to estimate how long the interview lasted under the assumption that those estimates would exceed actual survey length if participants felt burdened (see, e.g., Block 1990). The average estimated interview duration was 32.3 minutes, about five minutes longer than the actual interview duration (mean

27.2), suggesting some degree of respondent burden. However, when asked whether the interview was "too long, too short, or about right," all participants replied that the survey length was "about right." In addition, we asked participants to rate how burdensome they felt the survey was and again the responses were uniformly positive (e.g., "It was not at all burdensome." "It was great." "It was very interesting and easy.").

Factors Affecting Accuracy. In subsequent debriefing, participants identified several factors that they felt affected accuracy. Five participants said that they could have reported more accurately if they had been given advance notice to record their expenses in some form (e.g., using an Excel spreadsheet, using their phone, bringing records to reference, writing it down on paper). The size, frequency, and saliency of expenditures was mentioned by half of the participants as contributing to their reporting accuracy, with smaller everyday expenses like food and transportation reported as more difficult to recall accurately than more stable items like income, mortgage payments, and utilities.

Participants' household composition—its size and the division of financial responsibilities—also played a role. Eleven out of fourteen participants who lived in multiperson households said that they had a "good sense" of what other people in their house bought and how much they spent, but they also identified gaps in that knowledge (e.g., food eaten out by spouses or children, gas expenditures, purchases made on other's credit cards, etc.). To a lesser extent, participants made similar comments about their knowledge of other household members' income, assets, and liabilities. In fact, four participants admitted to "forgetting" to include some or all of their other household members' expenditures and income (e.g., "I was just focused on me!"). Two of those participants were able to remedy these omissions during the balance edit, but two did not realize their mistake until the debriefing discussion.

We also asked participants whether the one-month reference period presented any reporting difficulties and if a three-month reference period would have been easier or more difficult. One self-employed participant said the one-month reference period was difficult because her income varied considerably from month to month, but none of the other participants reported difficulties with the monthly time frame. Participants' views about the efficacy of a longer reference period varied by topic. For expenditures, seventeen participants said that using a three-month reference period would be more difficult than using a one-month reference period because of the additional memory demands and the fact that some expenses are intermittent and therefore more likely to be forgotten. We asked participants how they would come up with their total household expenses for three months. The word "estimate" was used often, and many participants said that they would think of their "typical" monthly expenses and multiply by three. A few participants did say that they would think of the expenses for each specific month and try to systematically calculate an accurate three-month figure. For income, two-thirds of our study participants said reporting for a three-month period instead of one-month period would be essentially the same because their income was fairly regular and stable. For assets and liabilities, our sample was split: about half preferred the one-month and half preferred the three-month reference period. The responses depended largely on how closely the participant tracked their accounts and how regular or irregular their account activity usually was.

Reactions to the Balance Edit. We were interested in exploring participants' reactions to various features of the balance edit implemented in this study. We began by asking them about the chart they were shown at the end of the basic questionnaire that displayed their income-to-spending ratio. Opinions fell into one of three groups. The first group ($n = 3$) initially felt confused by the chart; they did not understand its purpose or what it was supposed to represent, and had a hard time comprehending the concept of income-plus-net-assets-and-liabilities. These participants indicated that the accompanying explanation about the chart provided by the interviewer was helpful in deciphering its meaning, or at least in clarifying the overall objective of the balance edit process.

A second group of participants ($n = 5$) understood the purpose of the chart and balance edit but it elicited some emotional reaction, often somewhat negative. For example, several participants said that it was somewhat surprising and uncomfortable to be confronted with a chart that showed spending in excess (sometimes far in excess) of their income. Others in this group whose reports were unbalanced initially made an inference that they must have done something wrong (e.g., "I felt a little stupid."), or that by being asked to review their previous reports that the interviewer mistrusted them in some way ("I was a little frustrated because I knew I was being truthful."). In contrast, two participants in this group whose reports were reasonably balanced and showed more income than spending expressed satisfaction upon seeing the chart (e.g., "I don't want to be balanced. I want to have more income so I can spend and save more.").

Finally, half of our participants ($n = 10$) seemed to generally comprehend the chart and the objective of balance edit, and either have no emotional reaction or be genuinely intrigued by the information presented and motivated to resolve reporting discrepancies. The participants in this group were able to clearly articulate the objective of the edit process in their own words and did not appear to have any conceptual difficulties or negative emotional reactions.

Table 12.5 shows the relationship between these subjective participant groupings and the balance edit outcomes. Given the small and disproportionate sizes of the three groups, caution should be used when making inferences based on the results in this table. However, it does appear that there is a relationship between these groupings and the magnitude of change in the

Table 12.5   Relationship between participants' initial reactions to balance edit and survey outcome

	Ratio moved closer to 1.0	Average change in ratio (%)	Achieved balance
Group 1—Initially confused (n = 3)	3	–52.3	0
Group 2—Emotional response (n = 5)	3	50.7	0
Group 3—Understood/positive response (n = 10)	7	–2.0	4

Note: Includes only those participants who were administered the balance edit (*n* = 18).

income-to-spending ratio over the interview (column [3]) and in the final balance status (column [4]).

Participants who were confused by the chart and balance edit objective (Group 1) initially reported greater income than spending. Those who had an emotional reaction initially (Group 2) reported greater spending than income. The magnitude of the average ratio change was very similar for both groups, and no participants in either group achieved balance. Participants who understood the chart and edit objective without any associated negative emotional reaction (Group 3) made smaller (or at least off-setting) changes on average during the balance edit than participants in the other two groups, and all of the balanced households came from this group.

We also queried participants on their reactions to Phase 2 of the interview in which we gave participants the chance to look over a summary page of their reports and make any corrections or additions they felt were needed. Again, reactions tended to be split. Most participants did not express any substantive opinion about this page—they simply engaged in the review process and moved on. Three participants gave only cursory examination of this page and either did not fully understand their task or chose not to exert the effort required to review the information more carefully; they made no changes on this screen. A few participants described the review and revise process as "daunting'" or "chastising" because it forced them to examine (in front of the interviewer) some hard truths about their household finances. And, finally, several other participants said that they really liked the table and task because it prompted them to consider the relative amounts reflected in each category or because the presentation triggered memories of additional items that they then could report.

Some of the most frequent adjustment and additions made on this page stemmed from participants' memories for expenditures related to landmark events (e.g., birthdays, trips, Mother's Day). Another common change that participants made stemmed from financial activities by other household members. As noted earlier, sometimes this information was neglected altogether in participants' answers to the basic questionnaire, other times it was only partially reported or participants simply provided best guesstimates. This page afforded participants the chance to refocus attention on proxy-related items they may have missed (e.g., spouses contributions to retirement accounts), or revise their estimates for other household member items in order to achieve better balance. There also were a few instances in which we believe that participants were just simply trying to improve the household balance by making seemingly arbitrary adjustments, but this was not common.

In the final phase of the interview, participants who remained unbalanced were asked a brief set of additional probes about possible sources of expenditures and income. Fifteen of the sixteen participants who received these questions said that they were clear and easy to answer. The two most common items that we picked up as a result of these probes were child care expenses and tax refunds/tax payments (the reference month in this study was April).

12.5.4 Discussion

The findings from this small study shed some light on the challenges and opportunities that a balance edit introduces to expenditure surveys. We found that eighteen of nineteen participants in this study provided reports in the initial interview that were sufficiently unbalanced to trigger the balance edit. The balance edit procedure improved income-to-spending ratios for thirteen participants, but only four individuals actually achieved balance (i.e., obtained ratios that were within 10 percent of unity). Despite the relative improvements in the ratios of the remaining nine participants, their final average deviation from unity remained quite high (42 percent). The debriefing session revealed that a sizable minority of individuals in this study either did not understand the purpose in the balance edit or had somewhat negative reactions to the process. In addition, we identified a number of factors that likely contributed to its effectiveness (e.g., participant knowledge of other household members' spending/income; the size, frequency, and salience of the expenditure category).

12.5.5 Limitations

Our study was limited by a number of factors that may have impacted the results. First, we used a small, convenience sample; a larger, probability-based sample would have strengthened our ability to generalize the results and reduced the influence of outliers introduced by individuals with very large (small) reports. Second, some of the participant confusion evidenced in this study may have stemmed from our specific implementation of the balance edit—a hybrid between the approaches taken in the SHS and ALP. In particular, the language we used to introduce the objective of the edit and to describe the chart reflecting the income-to-spending ratio likely could be improved based on what we learned in this study. In our roles as interviewers, we strove to provide participants additional task clarification as necessary, but further refinement and standardization of this feedback might have improved participant understanding. Third, some of the difficulty in achieving balance may be attributable to the use of a variable reference period for income. Half of the study participants selected reference periods other than the one-month period used for expenditures and change in assets/liabilities (e.g., biweekly or yearly). The calculations used to make these reference periods comparable (e.g., dividing yearly income by twelve) could create problems if the participant's flow of income is not steady over the course of the year. During the interview we did confirm the derived estimates for monthly income with those respondents who initially reported using a different reference period, but the differential use of flexible reference periods may have contributed to the lack of balance for these respondents. Finally, our decision to use global expenditure questions may have affected the incidence of out-of-balance households. Global questions may tend to encourage participants to provide rough estimates for many expenditure categories when other response strategies would be more optimal. Their use also may have affected participants' perceptions of the burden of the survey and the balance edit process; attempting to conduct our balance edit with the full complement of detailed, disaggregated CEQ questions likely would have been far more difficult for participants.

12.6 Priorities for Future Research

Despite evidence that the balance edit procedure used in this study led to some improvement in data quality, this methodology requires substantial additional testing. As suggested elsewhere in this report, the efficacy and appeal of a balance edit will depend largely on the overall survey design (e.g., mode, use of detailed versus global items, length, etc.) and its analytic purposes. Were the CEQ to incorporate significant numbers of global expenditure questions (which we expect are subject to significant reporting errors) and still be conducted primarily in person, then some form of a balance edit may be worth considering. If, on the other hand, the CEQ continues to be a long survey consisting of hundreds of detailed expenditure questions, and/or a significant portion of the interviews each month are administered by telephone, then we believe that this procedure is less attractive given implementation issues and the potential negative impact on respondent and interviewer burden. Additionally, we used a one-month, not a three month, reference period for this study, and we suspect that the longer time frame would reduce the quality of respondents' estimates of change in assets and liabilities, in particular. Depending on design changes under consideration for the CEQ, further research should be done on whether a balance edit is feasible over the phone, with a larger set of detailed reports, and with a longer reference period. Finally, this study was designed to examine only relative changes in respondent reporting; we had no direct measures of the actual quality of the data collected. Future research should examine measurement error more directly, for example, through the use of record validation, or studies of within-household reporting consistency/reliability (e.g., comparing reports between spouses).

References

Block, R. A. 1990. "Models of Psychological Time." In *Cognitive Models of Psychological Time*, edited by R. A. Block, 1–35. Hillsdale, NJ: Lawrence Erlbaum Associates.

Bosworth, B., G. Burtless, and J. Sabelhaus. 1991. "The Decline in Saving: Some mMicroeconomic Evidence." *Brookings Papers on Economic Activity 1:*183–256.

Brzozowski, M., and T. F. Crossley. 2011. "Measuring the Well-Being of the Poor with Income or Consumption: A Canadian Perspective." *Canadian Journal of Economics* 44:88–106.

Hurd, M., and S. Rohwedder. 2010. "The Effects of the Financial Crisis and the Great Recession on American Households." NBER Working Paper no. 16407, Cambridge, MA.

Jacobs, E., and S. Shipp. 1993. "A History of the US Consumer Expenditure Survey: 1935–36 to 1988–89." *Journal of Economic and Social Measurement* 19 (2): 59–96.

Shields, J., and N. To. 2005. "Learning to Say No: Conditioned Underreporting in an Expenditure Survey." Paper presented at the annual meeting of the American Association for Public Opinion Association, Fontainebleau Resort, Miami Beach, Florida.

Measuring Total Household Spending in a Monthly Internet Survey
Evidence from the American Life Panel

Michael D. Hurd and Susann Rohwedder

13.1 Introduction

A very extensive battery of questions about spending along the lines of the Consumer Expenditure Survey (CEX) is not feasible in a general purpose household survey because of space limitations. In the absence of panel measures of total household spending, a large number of empirical papers have been based on the panel measure of food consumption in the Panel Study of Income Dynamics (PSID).[1] However, food consumption as a proxy for total consumption has limitations for some research questions: the fraction of total consumption accounted for by food likely varies with income and with age, making it difficult to estimate life cycle models based on food consumption. An example of measuring consumption with just a few questions—but more than one—comes from the Survey of Health, Ageing

Michael D. Hurd is senior principal researcher at the RAND Corporation, director of the RAND Center for the Study of Aging, a professor at the Pardee RAND Graduate School, a fellow of NETSPAR, a research professor at the Mannheim Research Institute for the Economics of Aging, and a research associate of the National Bureau of Economic Research. Susann Rohwedder is senior economist at the RAND Corporation, associate director of the RAND Center for the Study of Aging, a professor at the Pardee RAND Graduate School, and a research fellow of NETSPAR.

We are grateful to the National Institute on Aging for research support and funding for data collection under grants P01 AG008291, P01 AG022481, P30 AG012815, and R01 AG020717. We are grateful to the Social Security Administration for funding of data collection and research support. Many thanks to the ALP team for their assistance with the data collection, to Joanna Carroll and Angela Miu for programming support, and to Alessandro Malchiodi for excellent research assistance. For acknowledgments, sources of research support, and disclosure of the authors' material financial relationships, if any, please see http://www.nber.org/chapters/c12670.ack.

1. See, among others, Hall and Mishkin (1982), Zeldes (1989), Altug and Miller (1990), and Shea (1995).

and Retirement in Europe (SHARE). The first wave of SHARE included these measures of consumption: food consumed at home, food consumed outside the home, telephoning, and total expenditure on nondurable goods and services.[2] While the data on food consumption was useful, the data on total nondurable consumption was deemed unreliable (Browning and Madsen 2005).

As an approach that tries to strike a middle ground between the extensive detail collected in the CEX and just collecting information on a handful of categories, the Health and Retirement Study introduced the Consumption and Activities Mail Survey (CAMS). Collecting total household spending in a self-administered format (mail survey), the CAMS asks about spending in thirty-six to thirty-eight categories and allows respondents to choose the length of the recall period (last month, last twelve months) for most categories. The self-administered nature of the survey has the advantage that respondents can take the time to think about their answers, even consult records if they are so inclined, without the social pressure arising from the presence of an interviewer. Hurd and Rohwedder (2009) show that obtaining useful spending data in a reduced number of spending categories is feasible. The spending totals aggregate quite closely to CEX totals and the age patterns of saving derived from the CAMS data (taking total income minus taxes minus spending) are quite close to the age patterns of savings implied by data on wealth change (Hurd and Rohwedder, chapter 14, this volume).

However, whenever respondents are asked to recall their spending over a long period of time (say, one year), recall error becomes very important (Hurd and Rohwedder 2009). This observation gave rise to the idea of attempting high-frequency elicitation of spending. Building on our experience with the CAMS data, we designed a spending module that we administered as part of the financial crisis surveys that we were conducting in early 2009 in the RAND American Life Panel. The timing for a high-frequency elicitation of spending seemed particularly suitable in view of the high volatility in the economic environment, which would make it likely that spending would be more volatile than usual as well. In fact, back in November 2008, just shortly after the large and sudden drops in the stock markets, about 75 percent of all households interviewed in the ALP reported reductions in spending in response to the economic crisis.

In this chapter we describe in detail our survey methods, including an important innovation—the spending reconciliation screen—designed to catch large outliers that can be more frequent in self-administered surveys,

2. The last item on this list included a number of cues, prompting respondents to include "groceries, utilities, transportation, clothing, entertainment, out-of-pocket medical expenses and any other expenses the household may have and to exclude housing payments (rent or mortgage), housing maintenance, and the purchase of large items such as cars, televisions, jewelry and furniture" (Browning and Madsen 2005, 318).

for example, due to typos, and no interviewer to verify unusually large numbers. The reconciliation screen allows respondents to review all of their entries and the resulting total on one screen. Beyond the catching and self-correction of outliers, the reconciliation screen also allows respondents to fine-tune their entries, most likely reducing the noise in the data and leading to more accurate reports overall. Section 13.2 provides background on the American Life Panel, the financial crisis surveys, and the specifics of the design of the spending survey module. Section 13.3 reviews unit and item response rates, and various other indicators of data quality. Section 13.4 concludes.

13.2 Data and Survey Design

13.2.1 The American Life Panel

The American Life Panel (ALP) is an ongoing Internet panel survey operated and maintained by RAND Labor and Population. It covers the US population age eighteen and over. Those who do not have access to the Internet at the time of recruitment are provided with a WebTV, including an Internet access subscription with an e-mail account.[3] Accordingly, the sample does not suffer from selection due to a lack of Internet access.[4] Post-stratification weights are provided so that after weighting, the ALP approximates the distributions of age, sex, ethnicity, education, and income in the Current Population Survey. About twice a month, respondents receive an e-mail request to visit the ALP website to complete questionnaires that typically take no more than thirty minutes to finish. Respondents are paid an incentive of about $20 per thirty minutes of survey time, and prorated accordingly for shorter surveys. Response rates are typically between 75 and 85 percent of the enrolled panel members, depending on the topic, the time of year, and how long a survey is kept in the field.

Since inception of the American Life Panel in 2006, there have been four sample recruitment efforts. In this chapter we report on high-frequency data collections that were part of the so-called financial crisis surveys, covering the period from November 2008 following the onset of the turmoil in the US financial markets up to the latest survey that was completed in October 2011. Back in 2008 the majority of active ALP panel members had been recruited from the University of Michigan Survey Research Center's Monthly Survey (MS). The MS incorporates the long-standing Survey of Consumer Attitudes and produces the Index of Consumer Expectations. The MS survey is considered to have good population representation (Curtin, Presser, and Singer 2005).

---

3. See www.webtv.com/pc/.
4. This approach has been used successfully in the Dutch CentER panel for many years.

13.2.2 The Financial Crisis Surveys

The very large stock market declines in October 2008 prompted our first financial crisis data collection. We designed a survey that was administered to the ALP in November 2008. The survey covered a broad range of topics including various dimensions of life satisfaction, self-reported health measures and indicators of affect, labor force status, retirement expectations, recent actual job loss and chances of future job loss, housing, financial help (received and given and expectations about these), stock ownership and value (including recent losses), recent stock transactions (actual and expected over the next six months), expectations about future stock market returns (one year ahead, ten years ahead), spending changes, credit card balances and changes in the amounts carried over, impact of the financial crisis on retirement savings, and expectations about future asset accumulation. We followed up with a second longitudinal interview in late February 2009 covering approximately the same topics.

In our first survey (November 2008) 73 percent of households reported they had reduced spending because of the economic crisis. These spending reductions are of substantial policy and scientific interest, and so there is considerable value in a careful measurement of the magnitude of the reductions. For example, the welfare implications of the crisis depend partially on the reduction in consumption. Furthermore, because of the lack of knowledge of how spending responds to economic shocks at high frequency, it is important to establish the empirical connection between the triggering events and the magnitude of consumption reductions. The widespread spending reductions prompted us to reorient the survey, expanding the collection of information on the components of spending.

Beginning with the May 2009 interview we established a monthly interview schedule to reduce the risk of recall error about spending and to collect data at high frequency on items such as employment, satisfaction, mood, affect, and expectations. An objective was to permit detailed sequencing of events and their consequences.[5]

Each month we ask about spending in twenty-five categories during the previous month. Every third month, beginning in July 2009, we ask about spending during the previous three months on an additional eleven categories plus seven big-ticket items. Spending in these categories tends to be less frequent, such as durables. Taken together, the monthly and quarterly surveys measure total spending over a three-month period. The categories that are queried monthly amount to about 60 percent of total quarterly spending and

5. To further reduce recall error the survey is only available to respondents for the first ten days of each month, with only minor variation (e.g., adding the weekend if the tenth falls on a Friday or to accommodate staff work schedules when the beginning or end of the survey coincides with a major holiday such as New Year's Day). Thus state variables such as unemployment refer to approximately the first ten days of a month, not the entire month.

the categories that are queried every three months account for the remaining 40 percent. This three-month schedule of two shorter monthly surveys and a longer quarterly survey has continued to the present.[6]

These surveys have several unique aspects. The first and most obvious is that they are monthly panel surveys. This design permits the observation of the immediate effects of changes in the economic environment that cannot be captured in low-frequency surveys via retrospection. A second unique aspect is our measurement of a large fraction of total spending on a monthly basis. This measurement reduces recall bias for high-frequency purchases, yet because the surveys cover an entire year, this measurement also captures low-frequency purchases. The use of a reconciliation screen in the consumption module, described in detail below, reduces noise in the spending data substantially, allowing meaningful analyses even in a small sample. Furthermore, the combination of spending data with a very rich set of covariates, elicited at high frequency, allows for a wide variety of analyses, with much more careful information on timing and sequencing of events to investigate determinants and the effects.

A total of 2,693 respondents participated in at least one of the thirty interviews from November 2008 through August 2011. The wave-to-wave retention rate has been consistently high throughout this entire period, averaging 91.0 percent without showing any decline over time. Respondents are invited to continue to participate in the surveys even if they miss one or more interviews resulting in a higher retention rate across multiple waves than would be implied by the wave-to-wave retention rate. For example, 73.0 percent ($N = 1,966$) responded to at least ten of the first fourteen interviews. Beginning with wave 15, facing budgetary constraints, we had to restrict the sample and decided to exclude the most sporadic respondents, dropping those who had responded to less than five of the first fourteen interviews, leaving us with 2,338 eligible respondents. Since then another thirty respondents either requested to be dropped from the monthly surveys or they died.

In this chapter we use data from thirty surveys covering the period May 2009 through October 2011. Calculated over the eligible sample of 2,338 respondents retained since wave 15, we obtain a unit response rate for the spending module that averages 81.7 percent ($N = 1,911$) in cross-section over thirty waves. In the interest of maintaining an adequate sample size, while at the same time basing results on an approximate panel sample, we present results for the sample of respondents who missed at most four of the thirty interviews, resulting in an average sample size of 1,440 respondents per wave, translating into an average unit response rate for this sample of 61.6 percent per wave. Restricting the sample to those who completed the spending module in all thirty waves yields a unit response rate of 35.5 percent ($N = 829$).

---

6. Information about the surveys is given in appendix table 13D.1, including survey length, fielding schedule, and response rates.

13.2.3 Eliciting Total Household Spending

Each month we asked about spending in twenty-five categories that are purchased at high to middle frequency every month. Then, every three months we asked about the purchase over the past three months of eleven less frequently purchased categories, and about seven big-ticket items. With possibly a few minor exclusions, the total of the three monthly surveys and the quarterly survey add to total spending over the quarter.

The twenty-five categories queried in the monthly surveys are shown in appendix B, grouped as they would have been displayed.[7] The grouping by broad types of spending or by frequency of spending is meant to facilitate placement of reported amounts in the proper category: respondents are sometimes unsure about category placement and they are helped by seeing other possibly relevant categories. The grouping should reduce the risk of either omission or double counting. For example, the following categories were displayed at the same time because they are associated with household operations.

Mortgage: interest and principal
Rent
Electricity
Water
Heating fuel for the home
Telephone, cable, Internet
Car payments: interest and principal

A major innovation was the development of a "reconciliation" screen. Outliers are a problem in self-administered data collection such as Internet interviewing because there is no interviewer to question extreme values. Therefore, we designed a new strategy for the ALP to help reign in outliers: following the queries about spending last month on the twenty-five items, we presented the respondent with a summary table that listed the responses and added them to produce the implied monthly spending total. The respondent was invited to review and edit any items. This produced two very favorable results: most importantly, there was a sharp reduction in outliers, which has a large impact on standard errors of the total that is constructed as the sum of these twenty-five spending categories. Also, respondents had the opportunity to improve the accuracy of their entries, including previously missing entries, which should reduce the noise in the data further. We give more details on these outcomes in the next section. See appendix D for a display of the reconciliation screen.

---

7. In November 2010 (wave 21) we added another monthly category ("other transportation expenses") in reaction to some respondents indicating difficulties allocating some of their expenses.

A natural comparison with our method is the "cash-flow reconciliation" method (Fricker, Kopp, and To 2011) or the "balance edit" that has been used in the Canadian expenditure survey (Brzozowski and Crossley 2011). These approaches have the same objective as the reconciliation screen of catching and correcting reporting errors. They compare household spending to the sum of household income and net cash flows into and out of assets, and they challenge respondent reports when there are large discrepancies between the two. One disadvantage of this approach is that just a fraction of respondents are challenged; yet, measurement error on income, spending, or on both could result in incorrectly challenging some respondents while incorrectly not challenging others. To the extent that respondents are induced by a challenge to modify possibly correct reports, the procedure will worsen the data of those incorrectly challenged. The reconciliation screen approach, on the other hand, invites all respondents to review and possibly edit their answers and therefore avoids the risk of misclassification due to measurement error. It is also worth noting that a comparison of spending with income is not practical when the reference period is one month as is the case in the ALP financial crisis surveys. This is because the concept of after-tax income in a month is not well defined, and income is more likely to fluctuate across short time periods leading to potential mismatches in the timing of the receipt of income and expenditures.

13.3 Results

13.3.1 Indicators of Data Quality

In the first ten days of May 2009, about 2,100 people responded to the survey, which was the initial survey about spending. This number was fairly constant until wave 15 (May 2010) when it declined by about 300 persons. The main reason for the decline is that due to budgetary constraints some infrequent responders were dropped from the survey.[8] Since then the number of observations has stabilized, hovering between 1,750 and 1,850 observations. In a typical wave about twenty-five people begin the survey but fail to complete it.

The measurement of spending, which is the focus of this chapter, is embedded in a longer survey of the effects of the Great Recession. For the spending part of the survey only, the median time for completion of the twenty-five monthly items, including time spent on the reconciliation screen, was about 3.3 minutes.[9] The median time to complete the additional quarterly items (ten items plus seven big-ticket items) was about 2.3 minutes.

---

8. Many analyses will use the panel aspect of the survey to study change: infrequent responders have less or no value in such analyses.

9. Mean times are not meaningful in a self-administered survey such as an Internet survey because respondents may interrupt the survey without disconnecting.

There is a very substantial age gradient: those age sixty-five or older take a little more than twice as much time as those less than forty. As for the variation over time, completion times in the first several waves were greater by roughly one minute than the typical median, but fairly quickly reached a steady level.

Item nonresponse is generally very low in the ALP and that holds also for the spending items. Respondents have two opportunities to fill in initially missing answers: first, if someone leaves a spending category blank an additional screen will appear asking the respondent to fill in the missing item(s). Then, should the respondent ignore this prompt he or she can still provide the missing value on the reconciliation screen. The average rate of remaining item nonresponse across all waves and all twenty-five monthly categories is 0.4 percent. Examining the rate of item nonresponse averaged across the twenty-five monthly categories by wave shows that this rate is fairly stable over time, ranging between 0.2 and 0.5 percent in almost all waves.[10] There is some variation across categories of spending, but it is rather small. For example, the category with the highest rate of item nonresponse is "heating fuel for the home" (0.6 percent) compared to the lowest rate of 0.3 percent for "telephone, cable, Internet." In the reconciliation screen previously missing items are replaced with the value $0. Respondents have the opportunity to correct this value on the reconciliation screen. About 13 percent of initially missing values are updated from $0 on the reconciliation screen to a positive value. In some cases it could be that the initial missing entry was due to the respondent not having that type of spending or that the respondent left the entry blank, because he or she already accounted for that type of spending elsewhere in the survey.[11] If that was the case—and one could argue that respondents affirmed this view by not updating the zeros on the reconciliation screen—then no further imputation for missing values is required. This is the approach we apply in this study when calculating total spending. Because the rates of item nonresponse are so low, any other decision on how to deal with missing information would not affect any of the statistics we present in a material manner.

The reconciliation screen invites the respondent to correct entries. In the initial wave that elicited spending (May 2009), on average 1.8 percent of the entries were corrected (modified or updated) by respondents (figure 13.1). The rate of correction declined steadily until the survey collected in February 2010. Since then it has fluctuated between 0.6 and 0.4 percent. Although this may seem like a small rate of correction, the effect on outliers can be substantial if the corrections are for entries that are extreme. In

---

10. The highest average rate of item nonresponse was recorded in August 2009 at 0.8 percent and the lowest in February 2011 at 0.1 percent.

11. A conscientious respondent may feel hesitant entering a zero when he or she had that type of spending (i.e., it was not truly zero), but had already included it elsewhere.

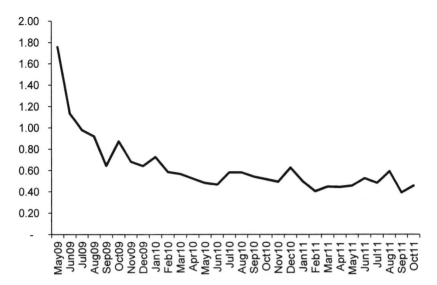

Fig. 13.1 Percent of monthly spending categories updated, unweighted
Note: Average number of observations per wave = 1,911.

the initial wave in May 2009, 17.0 percent of respondents altered at least one entry on the reconciliation screen for the monthly items. Four waves later (September 2009), this group had declined to 7.6 percent and has stayed about that size since then. The average rate of updating is smaller for the quarterly items when calculated over the entire population, which is mainly due to the fact that many more respondents have zero spending in those less frequent quarterly items and those zeros are not usually updated.[12] For the quarterly items the fraction of respondents updating any quarterly spending items has hovered around its average size of just under 4 percent all along.

The frequency and magnitude of outliers can be a problem in self-administered surveys because there is no interviewer to question extreme values. The reconciliation screen is meant to reduce this problem. A measure of the extent of the problem is the standard deviation of spending: while some fraction of the measured standard deviation reflects true variation in spending across individuals, some fraction is the result of measurement error and often it is the result of extreme outliers. We compare the standard deviation of the sum of all monthly spending items based on respondents' initial reports prior to the reconciliation screen to the same

---

12. Calculating the rate of updating conditional on positive entries (i.e., excluding the zeros) for the quarterly spending items gives an average updating rate of 0.6 percent of entries per category.

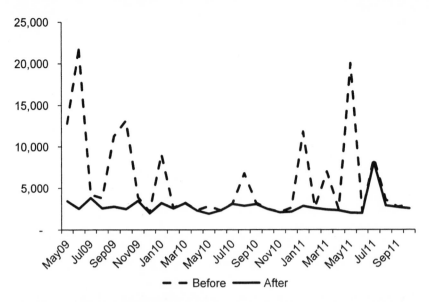

Fig. 13.2 Standard deviation of sum of twenty-five monthly items before and after the reconciliation screen, cross-section, unweighted

Note: Average number of observations per wave = 1,911. We edited twenty-two extremely large values out of 57,322 respondent-wave observations. Edits were subject to sufficient respondent-specific information being available from adjacent waves to support the determination that a value was indeed erroneous. Many consisted of shifted decimals (e.g., 10,000 instead of 100). There is a peak in July 2011 in the line depicting the standard deviation after the reconciliation screen. It is caused by two particularly large values that we decided *not to edit*. One pertains to a household that paid off the mortgage ($246,000 mortgage payment in July11 and no further mortgage payments in subsequent waves) and one pertains to a household that reports $200,000 in home repairs and $150,000 in home furnishings.

measure based on respondents' updated reports. Averaging over all thirty waves, we find that the standard deviation before the reconciliation screen is 44 percent larger than after the reconciliation screen. However, even after respondents' own corrections from the reconciliation screen there remain a small number of large outliers that dominate both the standard deviation before and the standard deviation after the reconciliation screen in some of the waves. We therefore reviewed some of the largest remaining outliers. For twenty-two very large values out of a total of 57,322 respondent-wave observations, we then edited the spending report that produced the outlier using respondent-specific information from adjacent waves. [13] We recom-

13. The edited cases were identified usually as one particularly large outlier in a wave where comparisons with that respondent's reports in prior and/or subsequent waves suggested that there was an entry mistake. In most cases there was a decimal error (e.g., $1,000 instead of $100). Both the initial report prior to the reconciliation screen and the updated report were edited and the observation was included in the calculations for figure 13.2.

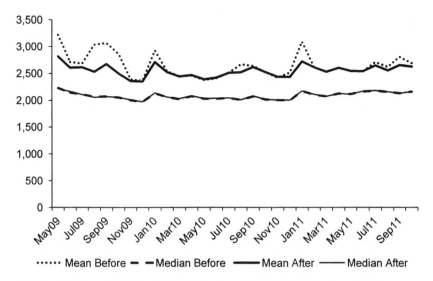

Fig. 13.3 Mean and median spending on twenty-five categories before and after reconciliation screen, cross-section, not seasonally adjusted, unweighted
Note: Average number of observations per wave = 1,907.

puted the standard deviation of total monthly spending based on initial reports before the reconciliation screen and also for the reports after the reconciliation screen. Figure 13.2 shows the standard deviation before and after the reconciliation screen conditional on the twenty-two edits.[14] In the first two waves the reduction due to the reconciliation screen was very substantial: from an average of $17.2 thousand to $3.0 thousand. In subsequent waves the reductions varied between being very small in some waves and sizeable in others, depending on whether respondents self-corrected some very large outliers. The average standard deviation (averaged over thirty waves and calculated after the twenty-two outliers were edited) was 112 percent higher before the reconciliation screen compared to after. This reduction will have a substantial effect on the standard errors in the estimation of models of spending.

Because the corrections induced by the reconciliation screen tend to involve large outliers, the corrections will reduce mean values of spending. We present the effects of the corrections on the mean (and the median) in figures 13.3, 13.4, and 13.5 for the monthly items, the quarterly items, and

14. The standard deviation includes the total mortgage payment, including repayment of principal because that is what is displayed to the respondent on the reconciliation screen. In calculating actual spending we remove principal repayments based on a follow-up question that queries the respondent about the different components of the mortgage payment (amount for principal, interest, and other expenses).

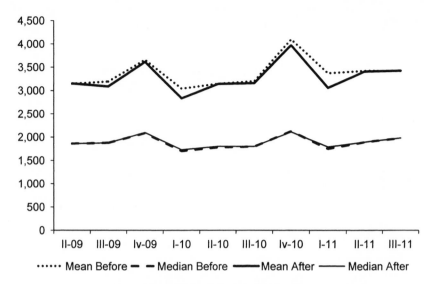

Fig. 13.4 Seventeen quarterly spending items before and after reconciliation screen, cross-section of quarters, not seasonally adjusted, unweighted

Note: Average number of observations per quarter = 1,621. Only respondents who partici-pated in every survey in a quarter are included to allow calculation of statistics of before and after reconciliation screen. Respondents may miss a quarter.

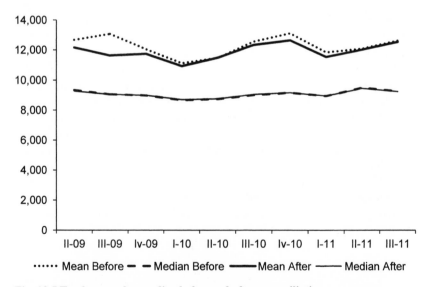

Fig. 13.5 Total quarterly spending before and after reconciliation screen, cross-section of quarters, not seasonally adjusted, unweighted

Note: Average number of observations per quarter = 1,621. Only respondents who partici-pated in every survey in a quarter are included to allow calculation of statistics of before and after reconciliation screen. Respondents may miss a quarter.

the quarterly totals (monthly plus quarterly items). The statistics in these figures are unweighted and cross-sectional to bring out the effect of the reconciliation screen.[15] The main observation from these figures is that the updates from the reconciliation screen do not affect measures of spending at the median, but they result in lower population averages at the mean in those waves where large outliers are caught.

Comparison with the Consumer Expenditure Survey

The CEX has the most authoritative survey measure of spending at the household level. Yet the level of spending as measured in the CEX is questioned because it is substantially less than household spending as measured by the National Income and Product Accounts (NIPA). Nonetheless, we will compare our measure of spending with that from the CEX because the CEX is a household survey and aims for a complete measure of household spending using similar methods to ALP (although in much greater detail). We choose the calendar year 2010 for this comparison as this is the first complete year of monthly data on household spending in the ALP. The year 2010 is also the latest calendar year for which published tables from the CEX are available. For ALP we calculate spending over a year by summing all twenty-five monthly spending items from the twelve monthly surveys and the quarterly reported spending items from the quarterly surveys referring to 2010. Average spending in 2010 as reported in the CEX was $42,736.[16] Average weighted spending in the ALP was quite close at $41,553, or 97.2 percent of CEX spending. The similarity of these levels shows that it is possible to capture approximately the same amount of spending as in the CEX but using many fewer categories of spending and, therefore, imposing substantially less respondent burden and cost.

13.3.2 Trends in Spending

To examine trends in spending over time we apply seasonal adjustments and weight the statistics.[17] We define three samples: a thirty-wave panel sample composed of those who responded to all thirty waves of the spending surveys (waves three to thirty-two of the financial crisis surveys); a twenty-six-wave panel sample composed of those who responded to twenty-six or more waves, and a cross-section sample composed of those who responded in a particular wave. When calculating population sta-

15. We have edited the twenty-two outliers as described above both in the initial reports (prior to reconciliation screen) and in the reports after the reconciliations screen.
16. We excluded from the CEX published total for 2010 outlays for "personal insurance and pensions," because we consider contributions to Social Security and pensions part of savings rather than spending. We also exclude life and other personal insurance payments because, except for insurance company profit, they represent transfers from one household to another.
17. We calculate our own seasonal adjustment factors.

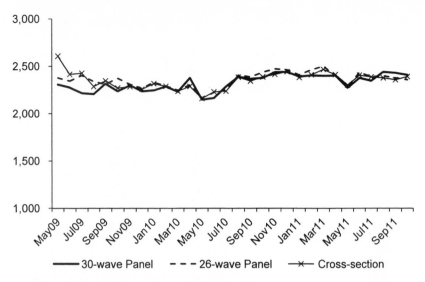

Fig. 13.6 Mean spending on twenty-five monthly items (after correction), seasonally adjusted, and weighted (three samples)

Note: Average number of observations per wave = 1,901 in cross-section, 1,440 for twenty-six-wave panel, and 829 for thirty-wave panel.

tistics we exclude from each wave a small number of observations where the respondent left many spending categories blank.[18] The respective size of these three samples is approximately 830, 1,440, and 1,900. We focus the discussion of the quantitative findings on the twenty-six-wave panel sample as it maintains close to complete panel consistency, while substantially reducing potential selection effects that a strict panel definition would entail.

Figure 13.6 shows mean spending on monthly items, seasonally adjusted and weighted for the three samples. With the exception of the first four waves all samples produce remarkably similar results both with respect to levels of spending and with respect to trends. Spending on the monthly items reached a minimum of about $2,170 (nominal) in the May 2010 survey (which measures what households spent in the month of April) and recovered after that, increasing by about 9 percent from its minimum. When adjusting for

18. Specifically, we exclude a respondent's observation on the total of the monthly spending categories if he or she did not answer six or more of the twenty-five monthly categories. For the quarterly items we exclude respondents if they did not answer six or more out of the eleven (non-big ticket) quarterly items. Because of the very low rates of item nonresponse, the resulting reductions in sample size are small: the cross-sectional sample is reduced by ten observations per wave on average; the twenty-six-wave panel and the thirty-wave panel are reduced by about twenty responses per wave on average.

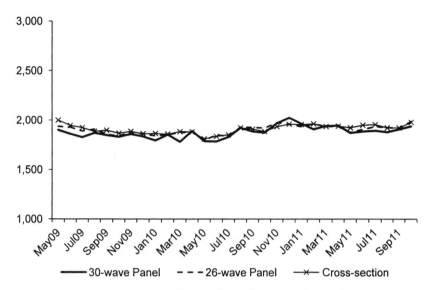

Fig. 13.7 Median spending on twenty-five monthly items (after correction), seasonally adjusted, and weighted (three samples)

Note: Average number of observations per wave = 1,901 in cross-section, 1,440 for twenty-six-wave panel, and 829 for thirty-wave panel.

inflation, the recovery since the trough in spending on the monthly items amounted to about 4.5 percent real.

There is substantial month-to-month variation most likely due to relatively high standard errors of the mean associated with our sample size. The thirty-wave sample, which has the smallest number of observations, has a standard error of 74; the twenty-six-wave sample, which has more observations, has a standard error of 60 and the cross-section, which has the largest number of observations, has a standard error of 53.[19]

Figure 13.7 shows median spending on the monthly items. The level is about $500 lower than the level of the mean but the trends and patterns over time of the two measures are similar.

These figures do not include spending on durables and other low-frequency items whose pattern and trend may differ from spending on high-frequency items. Figure 13.8 shows average total quarterly spending, which is the sum of the monthly spending items for the three consecutive months in each quarter and the quarterly spending items. The statistics are seasonally adjusted and weighted. All three samples show a decline during the first four quarters of our period of study until reaching a minimum in the second quarter of 2010; after that they all show spending increases,

---

19. The standard errors illustrate the trade-off between sample size and panel consistency.

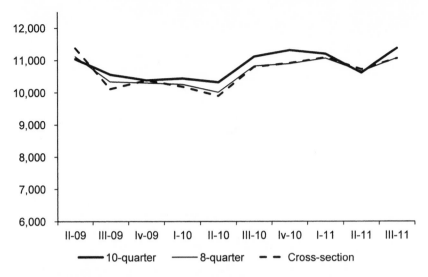

Fig. 13.8 Average total quarterly spending, seasonally adjusted, weighted (three samples)
Note: The ten-quarter panel has on average $N = 1,290$ observations per quarter. Respondents who completed at least eight quarters or more yield a sample size that averages $N = 1,594$ per quarter. Cross-sections of quarters average 1,812 observations per quarter.

indicating a recovery of household spending. Quantitatively there are some differences among the three samples. The most restrictive sample of those answering in all ten quarters shows a smaller decline, but it is also the one that is most likely to suffer from sample selection, so we focus our attention on the results from the eight-quarter panel, which are very similar to those based on the cross-sections. Average total spending declined from an initial level of $11.1 thousand in the second quarter of 2009 by about $1,100, or 9.9 percent, until it reached the minimum in the second quarter of 2010. Adjusting for inflation, the decline amounted to 12.0 percent real.[20] Over the recovery period from II/2009 through the end of our sample period, spending increased by 10.6 percent in nominal terms (as shown in the graphs), which corresponds to 6.3 percent real. Comparing the level of spending in the last quarter (III/11: $11,069) of our period of study with initial spending (II/09: $11,114), we find that despite the recovery, spending in the third

20. We note a particularly large decline during the first quarter of our survey period. This time coincides with the stock market reaching its lowest reading during this recession and rising unemployment. This large decline in spending in the first quarter of our surveys is therefore not implausible. However, the CEX disregards respondents' first quarterly reports for concerns about data quality. Our survey design and methods are very different, so CEX data quality concerns do not necessarily apply to the ALP spending data collection. To find out for sure we would have to run a large survey experiment with different parts of the sample starting to take the survey in different months.

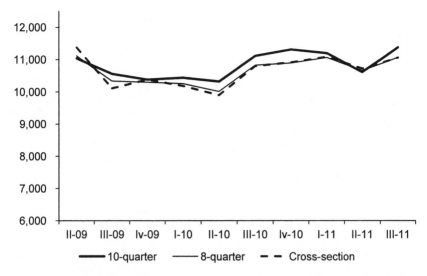

Fig. 13.9 Median total quarterly spending, seasonally adjusted, weighted (three samples)
Note: The ten-quarter panel has on average $N = 1,290$ observations per quarter. Respondents who completed at least eight quarters or more yield a sample size that averages $N = 1,594$ per quarter. Cross-sections of quarters average 1,812 observations per quarter.

quarter of 2011 was still lower compared to the second quarter of 2009, both in nominal terms (0.4 percent less) and in real terms (6.4 percent less).

Figure 13.9 has median total quarterly spending, seasonally adjusted, and weighted for the three samples. Compared to the statistics based on the mean, the median shows very similar qualitative patterns, but at a lower level reflecting the skewed distribution of spending. The medians also show a minimum in about II-10, and the recovery of spending observed until the third quarter of 2011 still remained short of the initial spending we recorded, even in nominal terms.

13.4 Conclusions

Before the initiation of our financial crisis surveys it was not clear whether high-frequency surveying about a repetitive yet complex topic such as spending was feasible. We were unsure whether respondents would respond to the survey by attriting or by providing meaningless data. Neither of these fears appears to have been warranted. Attrition was modest, and, in fact, the main reduction in sample size occurred when we dropped some 300 respondents from our sample pool. Measures of data quality such as item nonresponse, time to complete the spending module, and occurrence of outliers (after reconciliation) have been very stable over time, suggesting a steady degree of respondent cooperation over time.

The reconciliation screen has been an important innovation, especially in a self-administered survey where there is no interviewer prompting the respondent in case of unusual values. It allows the respondent to efficiently review his or her prior response and make appropriate changes. Consequently our level of data cleaning and outlier adjustment in this chapter was minimal.[21] Furthermore, the reconciliation screen also leads to corrections that do not concern outliers, but that consist of respondents' revisions of their initial entries to improve the accuracy of their reports. For example a household may correct a spending level from $1,000 to $100. This reduction of noise in the data could not be achieved by ex post data editing. Especially in small samples like ours, this effect could be important. When fitting models of spending change, these minor corrections could have a substantial effect on significance levels of estimated coefficients. A topic of future research will be to investigate the quantitative importance of such changes.

Appendix A

Basic monthly surveys are shorter, eliciting just a subset of variables. Every three months we administer a long survey (bold). The size of the initial eligible sample was $N = 2,693$. Starting with wave 15 (May10) we restricted the sample to those respondents who had participated in five or more of the fourteen prior surveys ($N = 2,338$), excluding the most sporadic of respondents. This decision was motivated by budgetary constraints. As a result, response rates among the (somewhat reduced) set of eligible respondents is higher on average in wave 15 and beyond.

21. Some surveys engage in a fairly involved "data editing" process prior to data release. In the data we presented in this chapter we did not perform any data edits beyond about twenty-two of the most obvious outliers recorded over thirty waves of data collection.

Table 13A.1   Survey schedule, survey length, and response rates

Wave	Survey	Time to complete survey Mean	Median	Field period	Completed responses (N)	Response rate (%)
1	**Nov08**	**19.1**	**16.7**	**Initially unrestricted**	**2,052**	**76.2**
2	**Feb09**	**24.6**	**21.4**	**02/24–03/16/09 = 21 days**	**2,119**	**78.7**
3	May09	14.6	11.8	05/01–05/10/09 = 10 days	2,080	77.2
4	Jun09	14.5	11.7	06/01–06/10/09 = 10 days	2,109	78.3
5	**Jul09**	**26.8**	**22.7**	**07/01–07/10/09 = 10 days**	**2,100**	**78.0**
6	Aug09	12.5	9.9	08/03–08/12/09 = 10 days	2,074	77.0
7	Sep09	12.4	9.7	09/01–09/10/09 = 10 days	2,123	78.8
8	**Oct09**	**27.9**	**23.5**	**10/01–10/11/09 = 11 days**	**2,016**	**74.9**
9	Nov09	13.9	11.1	11/02–11/11/09 = 10 days	2,056	76.3
10	Dec09	14.1	11.3	12/01–12/10/09 = 10 days	2,059	76.5
11	**Jan10**	**28.5**	**24.3**	**01/01–01/10/10 = 10 days**	**2,069**	**76.8**
12	Feb10	15.1	11.7	02/01–02/10/10 = 10 days	2,075	77.1
13	Mar10	14.0	10.7	03/01–03/10/10 = 10 days	2,057	76.4
14	**Apr10**	**27.4**	**22.9**	**04/01–04/11/10 = 11 days**	**2,019**	**75.0**
15	May10	10.4	7.9	05/03–05/12/10 = 10 days	1,861	79.6
16	Jun10	10.3	7.8	06/01–06/10/10 = 10 days	1,924	82.3
17	**Jul10**	**25.9**	**21.5**	**07/01–07/11/10 = 11 days**	**1,814**	**77.6**
18	Aug10	12.1	9.2	08/02–08/11/10 = 10 days	1,750	74.9
19	Sep10	11.8	9.2	09/01–09/10/10 = 10 days	1,836	78.5
20	**Oct10**	**27.4**	**22.6**	**10/01–10/10/10 = 10 days**	**1,797**	**76.9**
21	Nov10	12.0	9.3	11/01–11/10/10 = 10 days	1,851	79.2
22	Dec10	12.3	9.3	12/01–12/12/10 = 12 days	1,874	80.2
23	**Jan11**	**34.5**	**29.1**	**01/03–01/12/11 = 10 days**	**1,836**	**78.5**
24	Feb11	13.8	10.5	02/01–02/10/11 = 10 days	1,840	78.7
25	Mar11	12.8	9.8	03/01–03/10/11 = 10 days	1,845	78.9
26	**Apr11**	**34.2**	**29.4**	**04/01–04/10/11 = 10 days**	**1,774**	**75.9**
27	May11	16.4	12.4	05/01–05/10/11 = 10 days	1,768	75.6
28	Jun11	15.4	12.1	06/01–06/12/11 = 12 days	1,753	75.0
29	**Jul11**	**31.0**	**26.3**	**07/01–07/14/11 = 14 days**	**1,838**	**78.6**
30	Aug11	15.2	11.8	08/01–08/14/11 = 14 days	1,832	78.4
31	Sep11	14.8	11.5	09/01–09/11/11 = 11 days	1,785	76.3
32	**Oct11**	**31.6**	**26.4**	**10/01–10/10/11 = 10 days**	**1,777**	**76.0**

Notes: Time to complete the survey is calculated for completed survey responses, excluding any interviews that took two hours or longer. These respondents presumably interrupted the interview and returned to it later. The response rates for each wave are calculated over the initial eligible sample for the two periods and do not adjust for the fact that some few respondents declined future participation at some point and therefore were no longer part of the eligible sample. For example in Oct11, a total of 2,212 respondents were still eligible and active. The adjusted response rate for that wave would be 80.3 percent (= 1,777 * 100/2212).

Appendix B

Items Queried Each Month, Grouped by Actual Screen Display

Screen 1:
   Mortgage: interest and principal
   Rent
   Electricity
   Water
   Heating fuel for the home
   Telephone, cable, Internet
   Car payments: interest and principal
Screen 2:
   Food and beverages: food and drinks, including alcoholic, that you buy in
      grocery or other stores
   Dining and/or drinking out: items in restaurants, cafes, bars and diners,
      including take-out food
   Gasoline
   Other transportation expenses: parking, tolls, public transport, taxi and
      similar (please exclude spending on trips and vacations). Category
      added in wave 21 (Nov10)
Screen 3:
   Housekeeping supplies: cleaning and laundry products
   Housekeeping, dry cleaning, and laundry services: hiring costs for house-
      keeping or home cleaning, and amount spent at dry cleaners and
      laundries
   Gardening and yard supplies: yard, lawn and garden products
   Gardening and yard services: hiring costs including materials they provided
Screen 4:
   Clothing and apparel: including footwear, outerwear, and products such
      as watches or jewelry
   Personal care products and services: including hair care, shaving and skin
      products, amount spent at hair dresser, manicure, and so forth
   Prescription and nonprescription medications: out-of-pocket cost, not
      including what is covered by insurance
   Health care services: out-of-pocket cost of hospital care, doctor services,
      lab tests, eye, dental, and nursing home care
   Medical supplies: out-of-pocket cost, not including what is covered by
      insurance
Screen 5:
   Entertainment: tickets to movies, sporting events, performing arts, and
      so forth
   Sports: including gym, exercise equipment such as bicycles, skis, boats,
      and so forth

Hobbies and leisure equipment: such as photography, stamps, reading materials, camping, and so forth

Screen 6:

Personal services: including cost of care for elderly and/or children, after-school activities

Education: including tuition, room and board, books and supplies

Other child or pet-related spending, not yet reported: including toys, gear or equipment, and veterinarian

Appendix C

Additional items were queried quarterly beginning in the July survey about spending over the previous three calendar months. They include seven big-ticket items and eleven other less frequent spending categories.

Screen 1:

Big-ticket items
- Automobile or truck
- Refrigerator
- Stove and/or oven
- Washing machine and/or dryer
- Dishwasher
- Television
- Computer

Follow-up questions on big-ticket items queried amounts, and in the case of cars, how the purchase was financed.

Screen 2:

Homeowner's or renter's insurance

Property taxes

Vehicle insurance

Vehicle maintenance: parts, repairs, and so forth.

Health insurance

Screen 3:

Trips and vacations

Home repair and maintenance materials

Home repair and maintenance services

Household furnishings and equipment such as furniture, floor coverings, small appliances, and miscellaneous household equipment

Contributions to religious, educational, charitable, or political organizations

Cash or gifts to family and friends outside the household

Appendix D
Selected Screen Shots from ALP Spending Module

Sample screen shot from the monthly spending survey module

Mortgage, rent, utilities, car

Please, provide your best estimate of how much in total your household spent in the following categories. Please include spending by all members of your household, that is, by you or anyone living with you. Even if the amount your household spent last calendar month was unusual, please report that amount.

	Amount spent last month	No money spent on this last month
Mortgage	$⬚.00 OR	☐
Rent	$⬚.00 OR	☐
Electricity Water	$⬚.00 OR	☐
Heating fuel for the home	$⬚.00 OR	☐
Telephone, cable, internet	$⬚.00 OR	☐
Car payments: interest & principle	$⬚	☐

[<<Back] [Next>>]

RAND
American Life
Panel

Your household's spending total last month: **$2,838**

According to your entries your household's spending in **January** on the described categories was: **$2,838**. Below is a summary of your entries. If you would like to make any changes to your entries, you can change the amounts in the table below and then click the Update total1 button in the lower right corner of the screen to recalculate your total. Once you are satisfied with your entries, please just click 'Next1'.

As a reminder, there are some categories of spending that we DID NOT ask you about in this survey, but we will ask these in a later survey. (Click here for a list of spending categories that we will ask about in a later survey.)

Category	Amount spent last month
Mortgage	$⬚.00
Rent	$⬚.00
Electricity	$⬚.00
Water	$⬚.00
Heating fuel for the home	$⬚.00
Telephone, cable, internet	$⬚.00
Car payments	$⬚.00
Food and beverages	$⬚.00
Dining and/or drinking out	$⬚.00
Gasoline	$⬚.00
Housekeeping supplies	$⬚.00
Housekeeping, dry cleaning and laundry services	$⬚.00
Gardening and yard supplies	$⬚.00
Gardening and yard services	$⬚.00
Clothing and apparel	$⬚.00
Personal care products and services	$⬚.00
Prescription and nonprescription medications	$⬚.00
Health care services	$⬚.00

Fig. 13D.1 Sample screen shot from the monthly spending survey module (screen shot of the reconciliation screen)

Notes: This screen shot displays the top portion of the reconciliation screen. The dollar amounts stated at the top give the sum of the respondent's answers to the monthly spending questions. All dollar amount fields are filled with the respondent's previously provided entries. Any missing categories are filled with a zero. Using the usual scroll bar to the right of the screen, the respondent can scroll through the entire list of categories and edit any entries. At the bottom is a field that displays the "Total," an update button to have the total (displayed at the top and bottom) recalculated, and the usual "Back" and "Next" buttons.

References

Altug, Sumru, and Robert A. Miller. 1990. "Household Choices in Equilibrium." *Econometrica* 58 (3): 543–70.

Browning, Martin, and Edith Madsen. 2005. "Consumption". In *Health, Ageing and Retirement in Europe: First Results from the Survey of Health, Ageing and Retirement in Europe*, ed. A. Börsch-Supan et al., 318–24. Mannheim: MEA.

Brzozowski, Matthew, and Thomas F. Crossley. 2011. "Measuring the Well-Being of the Poor with Income or Consumption: A Canadian Perspective." *Canadian Journal of Economics* 44 (1): 88–106.

Curtin, Richard, Stanley Presser, and Eleanor Singer. 2005. "Changes in Telephone Survey Nonresponse Over the Past Quarter Century." *Public Opinion Quarterly* 69:87–98.

Fricker, Scott, Brandon Kopp, and Nhien To. 2011. "Exploring the Feasibility of Implementing a Cash-Flow Reconciliation Approach in the Consumer Expenditure Interview Survey." Washington, DC, Bureau of Labor Statistics.

Hall, Robert E. and Frederic S. Mishkin. 1982. "The Sensitivity of Consumption to Transitory Income: Estimates from Panel Data on Households." *Econometrica* 50 (2): 461–81.

Hurd, Michael D., and Susann Rohwedder. 2009. "Methodological Innovations in Collecting Spending Data: The HRS Consumption and Activities Mail Survey." *Fiscal Studies* 30 (3/4): 435–59.

Shea, John. 1995. "Union Contracts and the Life-Cycle/Permanent-Income Hypothesis." *American Economic Review* 85 (1): 186–200.

Zeldes, Stephen P. 1989. "Consumption and Liquidity Constraints: An Empirical Investigation." *Journal of Political Economy* 97 (2): 305–46.

Wealth Dynamics and Active Saving at Older Ages

Michael D. Hurd and Susann Rohwedder

14.1 Introduction

One of the fundamental predictions of the simple life cycle model of single persons is that, having saved when young, they will spend more than their income in old age. In the absence of a bequest motive, they aim to run down their assets to zero. However, the timing of the end of life is uncertain. Households will therefore begin to decumulate their assets when the risk of dying becomes large, while at the same time they hold on to sufficient resources so as to not run out too early. In a simple life cycle model, saving turns negative when the sum of mortality risk and the time rate of discount exceed the interest rate (Yaari 1965). Mortality risk is rather small until the late fifties but it increases approximately exponentially, becoming large late in life. For common utility function parameter values, we would expect saving to turn negative some time after age sixty-five. The exact timing is an empirical matter. A considerable body of work has investigated the empirical age pattern of saving in microdata, but many studies did not find any evidence of dissaving. With the life cycle model having become a work-horse model in the economic analysis of household behavior, the widespread fail-

Michael D. Hurd is senior principal researcher at the RAND Corporation, director of the RAND Center for the Study of Aging, a professor at the Pardee RAND Graduate School, a fellow of NETSPAR, a research professor at the Mannheim Research Institute for the Economics of Aging, and a research associate of the National Bureau of Economic Research. Susann Rohwedder is senior economist at the RAND Corporation, associate director of the RAND Center for the Study of Aging, a professor at the Pardee RAND Graduate School, and a research fellow of NETSPAR.

Financial support from the National Institute on Aging (grants P01AG08291 and P01AG022481) is gratefully acknowledged. Joanna Carroll provided excellent programming assistance. For acknowledgments, sources of research support, and disclosure of the authors' material financial relationships, if any, please see http://www.nber.org/chapters/c12667.ack.

ure of observing one of its central predictions in the data has raised doubts about the model's validity.

The most direct way of finding whether households are saving or dissaving is to study their active saving, which we define as the difference between after-tax income and spending. However, until recently no general-purpose survey collected a measure of total spending because it was thought infeasible to obtain a reliable measure of total spending without excessive burden for respondents. The Consumer Expenditure Survey (CEX), which focuses on collecting spending data, asks about some 300 categories as part of its recall interviews. Until recently the income data in the CEX were not useful for this purpose because income was calculated only for households that had no missing data in any of the income components. This selection made it difficult to extrapolate to the complete population. An additional barrier is that in the published data, taxes appear to be substantially underestimated; yet, it is the comparison of spending with after-tax income that is the relevant comparison.

An indirect method of finding whether households dissave is to study wealth change. Over long periods of time, where macro shocks should average out, households should be able to manage their spending so that wealth will decline. Because of the greater availability of wealth data, researchers have relied on studying wealth change either in panel data or in synthetic cohorts rather than active saving. Here we present results on both wealth change and active saving as complementary ways of studying the problem. An important advantage of our approach is that the data for active saving and for wealth change come from the same survey, eliminating many sources of potential differences that would arise if using data from different surveys for comparing the two approaches.

We discuss the caveats and challenges of trying to find empirical evidence of dissaving based on wealth change and contrast this with the data requirements when using data on consumption and after-tax income. We present results based on two different kinds of data from the Health and Retirement Study (HRS), a general-purpose survey that is representative of the US population age fifty-one and over. We first present life cycle saving patterns based on wealth change exploiting the panel nature of the HRS data spanning twelve years (1996 to 2008). In addition, we use data on consumption and after-tax income collected in the Health and Retirement Study. The consumption data come from a mail supplement, the Consumption and Activities Mail Survey (CAMS), which is collected separately from the HRS core data.

14.2 Challenges in the Empirical Analysis of Saving in Microdata

14.2.1 Wealth Change in Panel Data

According to the life cycle model of consumption, individuals save during their working lives and use their savings to finance consumption following retirement (Modigliani and Brumberg 1954). One could think of testing this prediction by finding wealth change as people age. An important difficulty with this approach is that wealth is measured with considerable observation error: even if the observation error is white noise, the first-difference of a variable that may have little systematic change over a short time period can consist largely of white noise (Browning and Lusardi 1996). Furthermore, wealth change incorporates capital gains, which can dominate wealth change in panel data. Thus, for example, if assets increase over several years due to an unexpected increase in their valuation, it will appear that elderly individuals engage in active saving unless the capital gains are eliminated. Both of these problems can be potentially overcome with long panels where noise and macro shocks can be averaged out. That is the approach in this chapter where we use panel wealth data over six two-year transitions.

14.2.2 Wealth Change in Synthetic Panel Data

Synthetic panel data on wealth change cover longer periods of time, hence allowing the averaging of macro shocks.[1] However, for synthetic panel results to be a valid representation of a life cycle wealth path, a fundamental necessary condition needs to be satisfied: the composition of the sample with respect to household characteristics that are correlated with wealth must stay the same over time. At older ages this is not the case in synthetic panels because persons with lower socioeconomic status (SES) tend to die earlier than those with higher socioeconomic status. As a result, population statistics computed for older ages in a synthetic panel are based on samples with higher SES than those computed for younger ages. Thus wealth can appear to increase as the cohort ages simply because those in the lower part of the wealth distribution die. All individuals and couples could be dissaving, yet cohort wealth could be flat or even increasing.

14.2.3 Consumption and After-Tax Income

Good measures of both consumption and after-tax income could be used to form a direct measure of active saving or dissaving by households. Furthermore, because of observation error, we need a fairly large sample of the older population for this method to produce reliable estimates.

In this chapter we provide empirical evidence about active saving using data on total spending to estimate directly the saving rate by individual households. The CAMS has complete measures of spending by a random sample of about 3,800 HRS households in 2001, 2003, 2005, and 2007. We use linked income data from the HRS and a calculation of taxes to find after-tax income. We compare evidence about life cycle models based on the active saving rate with evidence based on wealth change calculated over the same populations.

1. For example, the Survey of Consumer Finances.

14.3 Theoretical Background

Our thinking about saving and wealth change is guided by a life cycle model that has these features and assumptions: lifetime utility is based on time-separable utility from consumption (Yaari 1965); the only uncertainty is the date of death; resources are initial bequeathable wealth and a predetermined stream of annuities such as Social Security; bequeathable wealth cannot become negative, and, therefore, borrowing against future annuities is not allowed. As specified by Yaari, there is only one economic agent so the model is only appropriate for single people.

If a single person has no bequest motive, she will have wasted money should she die with assets: spending could have been higher earlier in life leading to higher lifetime utility. However, had spending been higher she may have been at risk of impoverishment should she have lived unexpectedly long. The theoretical solution to the problem is to spend at a high level earlier in life (to guard against dying with too much money), but then to reduce spending later in life to guard against outliving resources. Thus the theoretical prediction is that consumption will decline at advanced age as mortality risk becomes large. An implication is that the spending level should be high enough when spending is declining that wealth will also decline: if wealth does not initially decline, it will not decline in the future because consumption in the future will be even lower.[2] The result will be that the individual will die with positive wealth should she survive to the greatest age possible, violating a terminal condition of the theoretical model.

If the single person has a bequest motive, consumption will be reduced and more wealth held. Whether wealth will decline at advanced old age will depend on the details of the bequest motive.

The corresponding model for couples is considerably more complex. A couple chooses a consumption path to maximize expected lifetime utility, which includes the utility from consumption while both are alive, and the utility from the wealth that a surviving spouse would inherit.[3] Because the value of a bequest to a surviving spouse depends on the economic status, mortality risk, and other characteristics of the surviving spouse, it is difficult to quantify its effect on the slope of the consumption path. For example, even if the couple does not have a bequest motive (to others outside of their household) wealth may not necessarily decline except at advanced old age because of a reduction in Social Security benefits or defined-benefit pension income at the death of the husband. Nonetheless, a few comparative predictions are possible. For example, everything else held constant, the marginal utility of wealth is greater among the young than among the old. Thus, the value of a

---

2. This statement requires that annuity income not decline rapidly with age, which is the case for people who rely on the public pension system for annuity income.
3. See Hurd (1999) for a derivation and discussion of the couples' model.

bequest is greater to a younger spouse than to an older spouse. The greater value causes spending to be lower so that wealth should decline more slowly among couples where one spouse is substantially younger than the other.

14.4 Data

Our data come from the Health and Retirement Study. The HRS is a multipurpose household survey of the elderly population in the United States. It is collected by the Institute for Social Research at the University of Michigan. At baseline, respondents were selected from the community-dwelling population (including retirement homes, but not nursing homes). In subsequent waves, respondents were followed even if they entered an institution. The initial HRS wave took place in 1992. The sample consisted of individuals born in 1931–1941 (age fifty-one to sixty-one in 1992), plus their spouses (of any age). In 1993, a companion survey (Assets and Health Dynamics Among the Oldest-Old [AHEAD]) interviewed respondents born in or before 1923 (age seventy and older in 1993), plus their spouses of any age. Barring attrition or death, the 1992 respondents were reinterviewed in 1994 and 1996; the 1993 respondents were reinterviewed in 1995. The two cohorts were merged into a single sample with a single questionnaire in 1998, at which time the sample was augmented with respondents born in 1924–1930 (Children of the Depression Age [CODA]), and in 1942–1947 (War Babies [WB]). With provided sampling weights, the resulting 1998 sample was representative of the noninstitutionalized American population born in or before 1947 (age fifty-one or older in 1998). The HRS was reinterviewed in 2000, 2002, and 2004, and in 2004 a new cohort (1948–1953) was added to the sample to make it again representative of the population age fifty-one or over. In 2006 and 2008 all survivors were reinterviewed. They were again reinterviewed in 2010 and a new cohort of fifty-one to fifty-six-year-olds was added. The total sample size in a wave is around 20,000 individuals.

The HRS queries a wide range of topics: *demographics* (age, education, education of parents, marital status and history, veteran status); *family structure* (lots of information on household members, children, siblings, and parents); *health conditions* (whether the respondent has ever seen a doctor for various conditions, vision and hearing, pain, smoking, drinking, weight, height, depression); *cognition* (self-assessment of memory, cognitive test questions); *health care utilization and costs* (health insurance, out-of-pocket expenses, other expenses with varying detail across waves, whether anyone helped pay, Medicare number); *health status* (ADLs/IADLs, whether gets help [for each helper, gender, frequency, hours, whether paid, out-of-pocket costs, whether anyone helped pay]); *housing* (type, cost, special services); *job status* (employment status/history, earnings, hours, pension coverage, type, expected benefits, rights from previous jobs); *expectations* (chances of giving/receiving major financial assistance, inheritance, entering nursing home, major medical expenses, inflation, longevity); *income* (many sources and total, assistance from others, will); *net worth* (many asset types, IRA/ Keogh, stocks, bonds, bank, trusts); *insurance* (Medicare, Medicaid, other, whether managed, coverage and payments for long-term care, life insurance, beneficiaries); and so forth. In addition to these core questions, asked of the entire sample, there were additional topical modules asked of randomly assigned subsamples.

14.4.1 Consumption and Activities Mail Survey

The HRS has high-quality income and wealth measures, but the core survey has just a partial measure of total consumption.[4] In October 2001 the Consumption and Activities Mail Survey (CAMS), a self-administered mail survey of consumption and time use, was sent to 5,000 respondents randomly chosen from the entire age range of the HRS.[5] Only one person per household was chosen. About 3,800 HRS households responded, so CAMS 2001 is a survey of the spending of 3,800 households.[6]

The CAMS asks about the purchase of six large durables during the past year and twenty-six categories of nondurables. With a few minor exceptions, the categories were chosen to match CEX categories so as to facilitate a comparison with CEX.[7] An innovation in the CAMS questionnaire was to allow the respondent to choose the time frame for reporting on the purchases in many of the categories. A respondent may know the correct amount in one time frame but not in another. For example, rent is typically paid monthly so that the request for an annual amount requires a respondent calculation. Automobile insurance may be paid quarterly, semiannually, or annually. Clothing purchases may be made monthly by some but only rarely by others. Food is purchased weekly or monthly.

A beneficial consequence of this questionnaire design is that item nonresponse is much lower than it is for typical financial variables such as the components of wealth or income, where it can be as high as 40 percent. Furthermore, in the spending categories with the highest rate of nonresponse, we have information from the HRS core that we can use for imputation. For example, rent has almost the highest rate of nonresponse. However, we have responses in the HRS about homeownership, which we can use to impute rent. Thus, in CAMS 2001, of the 506 who were nonrespondents to

---

4. Food purchases, food consumed outside the home or delivered to the home, rent, utilities, real estate taxes, and out-of-pocket medical expenses in several major categories. These total about 40–50 percent of total consumption as measured in the CEX.

5. When referring to the HRS we mean all cohorts, including what was formerly called AHEAD, CODA, and WB (and 2004 onward, also the Early Boomers [EB]). In 2001 the age range was approximately fifty-four or older.

6. The only discernable pattern of unit nonresponse is slightly higher nonresponse among the very old.

7. Several small categories were dropped and a few were merged to reduce respondent burden.

the rent query, 420 owned a home in HRS 2000.[8] We believe we can confidently impute zero rent to these households. Based on these and similar imputations that use HRS core data to provide household-level information, in 2001 64 percent of CAMS respondents were complete reporters over all thirty-two categories of spending.[9]

We imputed the remaining missing data to account for the partial reports by assigning means within categories. Because of the low rates of item nonresponse, the amount of consumption data imputed as a fraction of the total is considerably lower than in measures of income or wealth in the HRS.

In October 2003 the same 5,000 households were sent wave 2 of CAMS.[10] It has substantially the same structure as CAMS wave 1. In October 2005 CAMS wave 3 was sent to the surviving households and to an additional 850 households to represent the new cohorts that were recruited into HRS in 2004. Item nonresponse in CAMS 2003 and 2005 was even lower than in CAMS 2001, and other indicators of data quality such as outliers were similarly improved. Additional waves of CAMS were fielded in 2007 and 2009, but we will use only CAMS data up to and including the 2007 data. Because of the financial crisis and Great Recession, consumption dropped between 2007 and 2009. In our view spending in 2009 is the result of different economic conditions and expectations than those that produced the wealth change in earlier waves of HRS. That is, we would not expect that the active saving observed in CAMS 2009 would match the wealth change that was observed in previous HRS waves.

We note that the life cycle model concerns consumption, whereas CAMS data record spending. The difference between the two mainly stems from expenditures on durables that may be purchased in one period, but whose consumption services may be enjoyed over multiple periods. We construct for our analyses a measure of consumption that makes adjustments to the recorded spending on durables to approximate the consumption value that households draw from these in a year.[11] For items like refrigerators, washing machines, dryers, dishwashers, televisions, and computers, we approximate the annual consumption value by multiplying the probability of purchasing the item in that year with the purchase price, conditional on buying one. The purchase

8. We also used HRS 2002 to check for change in homeownership.
9. All of these imputations converted nonresponses to zero values, as in the example of rent.
10. With the following exceptions: the respondent refused an interview in the HRS 2002 core, the respondent died, or the respondent had diabetes and was part of a subset that was randomly allocated to a mail questionnaire about compliance with diabetes treatment. The HRS has generated weights to account for the diabetes allocation.
11. These adjustments can make sizable differences at the household level. However, when averaging across the population, the consumption value measure and the outlay measure for these categories are about the same (by construction). At the household level the difference between consumption and spending for durables could be substantial, but at the population level the flow of new purchases of durables will average to the flow of consumption in a steady state. For example, the average consumption of durables by age will be approximately the same as average spending on durables by age. A lengthening of the time between purchases leading to a decline by age in quality-adjusted consumption will show up in the data as an age decline in spending on durables.

probability and the purchase price are each predicted from a regression with a number of explanatory variables (number of household residents, gender, age, marital status, work status, education, wealth quartiles, and income quartiles). This is to allow for the fact that both the probability of purchase and the purchase price tend to be higher for households with certain characteristics such as high wealth and income, for example. For transportation, like cars, we approximate the annual consumption value as the sum of the following components: the depreciation of the vehicles the household owns (10 percent of the total current value), the opportunity cost of capital (5 percent of the total current value) plus the amount paid for vehicle insurance.[12]

A common approach to approximate the consumption value of owner-occupied housing is to compute the rent equivalent as a function of the value of the home (that is the only characteristic of the home we observe). In this study we do not do that, because one of our objectives is to assess how saving derived from wealth change compares to saving derived from the difference between income and consumption. Including the rent equivalent of owner-occupied housing in total household consumption would impute variation in spending across households according to geographical variation in housing prices. For example, households living in areas with high housing prices would be imputed a high level of spending, leading in some cases to substantial dissaving when measured as the difference between after-tax income and spending. Yet, that level of dissaving would not match wealth change. An accounting solution would be to add into income the imputed income from housing, leaving as the difference between income from housing and spending on housing, what the household actually spent. But what the household actually spent is what enters our measure of total spending on housing. It has the following components for homeowners and renters: spending on home repairs, mortgage interest, property taxes, rent, homeowners' and renters' insurance, housekeeping supplies and services, and yard supplies and services.

In summary, our measure of total consumption is the sum of annualized spending on nondurables and services, annual spending on housing, and the consumption value derived from other durables.

Comparison with the CEX

In table 14.1 we compare CAMS totals with published totals from the Consumer Expenditure Survey (CEX).[13] We have classified by age band

---

12. We obtain the total value of the vehicles the household owns at the time of a CAMS survey as the average of the total net value reported in the two adjacent HRS core surveys (e.g., HRS 2004 and HRS 2006 for CAMS 2005 observations). The amount paid for vehicle insurance is observed in CAMS.

13. Even though the CEX measures of spending are less than the measures derived from NIPA, we believe a comparison with CEX is more relevant than a comparison with NIPA: both the CEX and CAMS are household surveys, and they use similar elicitation methods, although on much different levels of complexity.

Table 14.1   **Mean spending (thousands) in CAMS and in CEX**

	55 or over	65 or over	55–64	65–74	75 or over
2001					
CAMS	35.4	31.9	40.2	34.2	29.2
CEX	30.7	26.6	37.1	30.4	22.4
Ratio CAMS/CEX	1.15	1.20	1.08	1.12	1.30
2003					
CAMS	38.0	33.2	44.9	36.9	28.9
CEX	32.8	28.1	39.4	31.8	24.4
Ratio CAMS/CEX	1.16	1.18	1.14	1.16	1.19
2005					
CAMS	37.6	32.9	43.5	36.0	29.5
CEX	36.7	31.1	43.7	36.0	26.1
Ratio CAMS/CEX	1.03	1.06	1.00	1.00	1.13
2007					
CAMS	39.7	35.5	45.0	40.7	29.4
CEX	40.6	34.7	47.6	39.7	29.4
Ratio CAMS/CEX	0.98	1.02	0.95	1.03	1.00
Average spending ratio	*1.08*	*1.12*	*1.04*	*1.08*	*1.16*

Note: The CAMS household age is the male age, if coupled. If male age is missing for wave and surrounding waves, then female age is used.

because CAMS does not cover the entire population. In the case of couples, the age comparison is not exact because "age" in the CEX is the age of the household head. The HRS does not have that concept, so we use the age of the husband in the case of couples as an approximation.

In 2001 spending among those fifty-five to sixty years old was about $3,000 or 5 percent higher in CAMS than in the CEX. But it is notable that spending declines much more rapidly with age in the CEX than in CAMS. In CAMS spending by those seventy-five or older was 73 percent of spending by those age fifty-five to sixty-four, but it was just 60 percent in CEX.[14] While this discrepancy in the age pattern occurs in other years, it has declined. For example in CAMS 2007, spending by those age seventy-five or older was 65 percent of spending by those age fifty-five to sixty-four, whereas it was 61 percent in CEX.

When the percentage discrepancy is averaged over the four survey years as shown in the last row, spending in the fifty-five to sixty-four age band is almost identical in the two surveys, but spending in CAMS is higher at older ages. As we discuss below, the CAMS measure comes closer to matching observed wealth change than the CEX measure.

---

14. A possible reason for this discrepancy beyond age misclassification is that the CAMS includes nursing home residents who have large out-of-pocket spending, whereas the CEX is community based.

Table 14.2   **Interview schedule of HRS and CAMS and youngest age of age-eligible respondents**

	HRS core	CAMS
1996	54	
1997		
1998	51	
1999		
2000	53	
2001		54
2002	55	
2003		56
2004	51	
2005		52
2006	53	
2007		54
2008	55	

14.5 Results

In this chapter we use wealth data from HRS 1996 through 2008 to find panel wealth changes, and from CAMS waves 2001, 2003, 2005, and 2007 to find spending levels. We use the longer time period for wealth change to increase sample size and to further the aim of averaging out macro shocks. The relevant interview schedule of HRS and CAMS is shown in table 14.2 along with the lowest age among the age-eligible cohorts. Thus in CAMS 2001, the age-eligible respondents were age fifty-four or older.[15] Spending in CAMS approximately refers to the same time period as income in the following HRS wave. For example, CAMS 2001 queries about spending in the previous twelve months backward from October; HRS 2002 queries about income in 2001.

14.5.1 Wealth Dynamics

We first present results for singles because the life cycle model makes simple predictions about consumption levels and changes for singles in the absence of a bequest motive. We present three measures of wealth change:

1. $\Delta \bar{w}_t = (\Sigma w_{i,t+1} / \Sigma w_{i,t})$, where the summation is over individuals observed in two adjacent waves. Thus, this is the ratio of mean wealth for the population surviving and interviewed in two adjacent waves. We call this the "population mean" measure.

---

15. The variation in youngest age is due to the aging of the HRS respondents and the addition of a new six-year cohort every six years.

Table 14.3A   **Singles living alone, two-year percent change in wealth**

Age	Ratio of means	Ratio of medians	Median of individual change	N for ratios	N for median
65–69	1.8	0.2	−5.3	2,596	2,438
70–74	5.8	−5.4	−6.5	2,762	2,594
75–79	−3.9	−9.0	−8.9	3,079	2,918
80–84	−1.8	−10.7	−8.4	2,919	2,743
85+	−7.3	−15.8	−17.9	2,833	2,567
Total				14,189	13,260

Note: Excludes three outliers.

2. $\Delta w_t^{med} = w_{t+1}^{med} / w_t^{med}$, where again the summation is over individuals observed in two adjacent waves. This is the ratio of population median wealth in two adjacent waves. We call this the "population median" measure.

3. $(\Delta w_{i,t})^{med}$, which is the median of household wealth ratios in two adjacent waves. We call this the "individual or household median" change.

These ratios are calculated over adjacent waves between 1996 and 2008 and adjusted for price change to put the ratios in real terms. Then the ratios are averaged weighting by the square root of the number of observations in each of the ratios. By averaging over a number of wealth transitions, we aim to reduce the influence of macro shocks that would obscure anticipated or desired wealth change.

Another possible statistic, which we do not present, is $(1 / n)\Sigma(w_{i,t+1} / w_{i,t})$, which is the mean of household level wealth ratios. This statistic has considerable bias because of observation error on w, which renders some of the individual changes very large.

Table 14.3A shows the three summary measures of two-year rates of real wealth change for single persons living alone. It is important to exclude those living in extended families because we do not know the sharing of expenses. For example, the older person living with her children may spend little with the expectation that she will bequeath her remaining wealth to her children. In this case, most of the household's spending pertains to the children. The older person's wealth change would not match the saving rates derived from deducting the household's total spending from the older person's income.

In table 14.3A all three measures of wealth change show dissaving from age seventy-five on. In the other age bands there are differences depending on the measure of wealth change. In our view, the measures based on medians combine reliability and theoretical appeal in the best manner: even with averaging, the ratio of means is still vulnerable to large wealth outliers. For describing what the typical person does, the medians are more useful. Therefore we will focus most of our discussion on the median-based results.

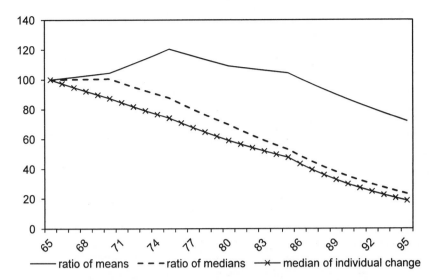

Fig. 14.1A Simulated wealth paths based on three measures of wealth change, singles living alone

Both show wealth decumulation by singles in their early seventies with the rate of dissaving accelerating with age.

The ratio of medians, which is an average of median wealth in a wave divided by median wealth in the subsequent wave where the averaging is across six wealth transitions in the HRS, indicates large rates of wealth decline: a 9 percent decline for those in their late seventies, just under 11 percent decline for those in their early eighties, and an even larger decline among those age eighty-five and older (–16 percent). The median of individual changes shows rates of wealth decline for the person in the middle of the distribution of rates of wealth change. The magnitudes are closely comparable to the ones implied by the population median with one notable difference. The median of individual changes shows wealth declines already among singles in their late sixties.

To find what these rates of wealth change imply for life cycle wealth trajectories, we have graphed the associated wealth paths beginning at one hundred at age sixty-five. The method is to apply the age-specific rate of wealth change year-by-year so as to cumulate the year-to-year changes. Thus, according to the ratio of means, a single person age sixty-six would have $100.9 (= 100 * (1 + 0.018/2))$, and a single person age sixty-seven would have $101.8 (= 100 * (1 + 0.018/2) * (1 + 0.018/2))$, and so forth. The three wealth paths are shown in figure 14.1A. Based on medians, wealth drops sharply, so that a single person who survives from age sixty-five to ninety would have 30–35 percent of initial wealth. The path implied by the median of individual changes (crossed line) indicates a somewhat steeper decline than that based

Table 14.3B   Singles living alone or with others, two-year percent change in wealth

Age	Ratio of means	Ratio of medians	Median of individual change	N for ratios	N for median
65–69	–0.2	–2.6	–7.6	4,413	4,062
70–74	3.3	–4.9	–7.4	4,231	3,912
75–79	–4.8	–8.5	–9.5	4,457	4,150
80–84	–0.7	–8.9	–10.2	4,211	3,867
85+	–4.6	–16.8	–18.3	4,075	3,593
Total				21,387	19,584

Note: Excludes three outliers.

on the ratio of medians (dashed line). The survival rate from age sixty-five to age ninety is about 21 percent, so that significant numbers would survive with that rather low percentage of initial wealth. The trajectory based on the mean initially increases and only decreases following age seventy-five.

Although demographic factors interfere with the clear predictions of the life cycle model with respect to wealth change, for completeness we present in table 14.3B the same statistics calculated over the entire population of single persons. Of immediate note is that about 30 percent of single persons over the age of seventy live with others. A prediction about saving or dissaving would require a model of intrahousehold resource flows as well as information about the other household members. Nonetheless, the general pattern is the same and the quantitative outcomes are quite similar as is shown in figure 14.1B: as measured by medians, the rate of dissaving is substantial, leading to remaining wealth at age ninety of about 30–38 percent.

These substantial rates of dissaving appear to be at odds with the results of Love, Palumbo, and Smith (2009) who state: "Our analysis of the HRS panel documents strongly rising patterns of annualized wealth in retirement. We find that the median value of annualized comprehensive wealth for the cohort of households aged 70 to 75 years in 1998 rises significantly in retirement, from about \$32,800 per person per year in 1998 to about \$42,200 per person per year in 2006—a net increase of nearly 30% in just eight years" (92). However, the measure of wealth in Love, Palumbo, and Smith, "annualized comprehensive wealth," is not a directly observed wealth amount. For single persons it is approximately the sum of annuity income and the annual income resulting from annuitizing bequeathable wealth. For most single persons annuity income is from Social Security and so is constant in real terms. Thus, the trajectory of annualized comprehensive wealth depends on the actual trajectory of bequeathable wealth, but also on the multiplicative factor that converts wealth into annuities. That factor depends on an assumed interest rate and on life tables, but it strongly increases with age: according to their table 3 for a single female it increases from 0.076 at age sixty-seven to

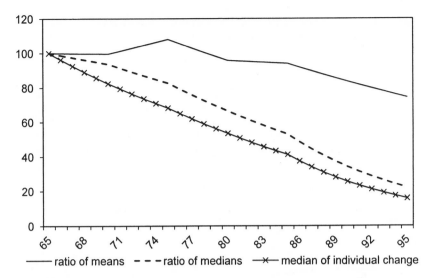

Fig. 14.1B Simulated wealth paths based on three measures of wealth change, singles living alone or with others

0.221 at age eighty-seven, a ratio of 2.91. For example, the annualized wealth from $100 of bequeathable wealth would increase mechanically from $7.60 to $22.10 over those ages. In order that annualized wealth be constant with age, bequeathable wealth would have to decline at a correspondingly high rate, about 5.3 percent per year, which is greater than what we observe for the evolution of the median wealth of single persons between age sixty-five and ninety (between 3.9 percent and 4.8 percent per year). Thus we would observe (slowly) increasing annualized comprehensive wealth for our sample of single persons, which at least qualitatively, is consistent with Love, Palumbo, and Smith. However, when annuity income is predetermined, as, for practical purposes, it is in the US population due to the dominance of Social Security and DB pension income, bequeathable wealth is what is chosen by households, not annualized comprehensive wealth. Whether annualized comprehensive wealth increases, is flat, or decreases with age is not relevant to understanding whether observed rates of dissaving are consistent with the life cycle patterns that we expect from the life cycle model.

Table 14.4A has results on wealth change for couples living alone. The reason for restricting the sample to couples living alone is the same as that in the analysis of singles. In addition, we have excluded couples where the age difference between spouses is greater than five years and who therefore have a different (longer) time horizon that would call for a different wealth decumulation path. Classifying by the age of the older spouse the median of household change in table 14.4A shows modest dissaving of between 2 and 4 percent from age seventy onward. According to the ratio of medians there

Table 14.4A   Couples living alone, spouse age difference five years or less, two-year
                       percent change in wealth

Age	Ratio of means	Ratio of medians	Median of household change	N for ratios	N for median
65–69	2.0	4.0	0.8	3,819	3,803
70–74	3.2	–0.9	–2.2	2,621	2,609
75–79	0.5	–1.9	–2.4	1,901	1,892
80 +	0.5	1.2	–3.6	1,198	1,183
Total				9,539	9,487

Note: Excludes seven outliers.

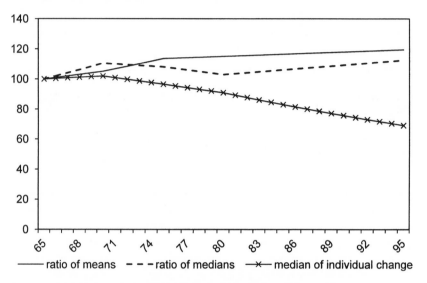

Fig. 14.2A Simulated wealth paths based on three measures of wealth change, couples living alone (age difference five years or less)

is less dissaving, and even wealth accumulation after the age of eighty, and the ratio of means does not show any dissaving at any age. In figure 14.2A we trace out the wealth paths implied by the estimated wealth changes. Wealth trajectories are much flatter than for singles. For example, according to the median household change a typical couple would still have about 83 percent of initial wealth when the oldest spouse is eighty-five. Couples retain their wealth much longer, in accordance with the predictions of the theoretical model. Note that the chances that both spouses survive until advanced old age, say eighty-five, are small and that most couple households will become single before then. Thus couples preserve wealth for the surviving spouse.

For completeness we show in table 14.4B the results for all couples, that is, those living alone and those living with others, despite the caveat of unknown

Table 14.4B   **Couples living alone or with others, two-year percent change in wealth**

Age	Ratio of means	Ratio of medians	Median of household change	N for ratios	N for median
65–69	4.1	0.3	−0.3	7,877	7,798
70–74	0.7	−1.0	−3.4	4,983	4,946
75–79	1.8	−2.4	−2.4	3,167	3,128
80 +	−1.7	−4.6	−4.3	2,154	2,117
Total				18,181	17,989

Note: Excludes seven outliers.

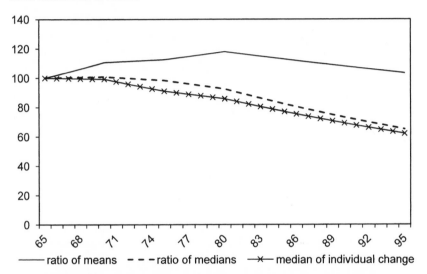

Fig. 14.2B Simulated wealth paths based on three measures of wealth change, couples living alone or with others

sharing of expenses. The estimated wealth changes turn out to be closely comparable to those in the restricted couples sample in table 14.4A only for the median of household changes. Those based on the ratio of means or on the ratio of medians are quite different. Figure 14.2B shows the implied wealth paths. Based on medians, figure 14.2B suggests dissaving by couples beginning in their early seventies, whereas figure 14.2A would suggest little, if any, dissaving.

14.5.2 Active Saving

Our second measure of saving is "active saving," which we define to be the difference between after-tax income and spending. For every wave of CAMS, we match spending with the income recorded in the immediately following HRS wave. For example, spending from CAMS 2001, which refers to the twelve months preceding October 2001, is compared with income measured in HRS 2002, which refers to income in 2001. Thus we have some discrepancy in time period between them, but the difference is relatively minor. The HRS elicits pre-tax income. To arrive at post-tax income we use the NBER tax calculator "TAXSIM."[16] Because we do not have sufficient information to calculate the taxes of household members other than the respondent and the spouse, we restrict the analysis to singles and couples living alone. Because we want to compare active saving with wealth change, we normalize active saving by wealth so as to obtain saving or dissaving as a percentage of wealth. To describe the patterns observed in the data we use the same three summary measures that we used for the study of wealth change (i.e., population medians, individual-level medians, and population means).

Table 14.5A shows results for singles living alone. The statistics are based on averages of median values across four waves of CAMS. Additional explanation of the method is found in the note to the table. We find dissaving at all ages, except for people in their late sixties, the youngest age band in our analysis. The rates of dissaving are greatest in the highest ages, just as we found for wealth change earlier. However, the magnitude of the saving rates out of wealth based on active saving is substantially smaller for singles than what we found based on wealth change. For example, the one-year change in wealth predicted by median active saving among eighty to eighty-four-year-olds is −1.7 percent, but the estimated actual change in median wealth (table 14.3A, ratio of medians) is −10.7 percent over two years or −5.3 percent per year. The qualitative result is confirmed when using the individual-level medians (table 14.5B). In contrast, the rates of saving when calculated using population means of active saving (table 14.5C) have a different pattern from rates of mean wealth change in table 14.3A, but the overall predictions about wealth trajectories are approximately the same. This can be seen in figure 14.3, which shows the wealth trajectories calculated from active saving. Whereas the paths based on active median saving lie substantially above those based on median wealth change, the path based on active mean saving is at or below the path based on mean wealth change. For example at age ninety-five, the wealth path based on mean active saving predicts that a single person living alone would have 69 percent of wealth remaining; the wealth path based on mean wealth change would predict 72 percent of wealth remaining. In principle, paths based on mean values are superior because of the adding-up characteristic of means, but those paths may be unduly influenced by outliers.

In order to facilitate the comparison of the saving rates based on active saving with those based on wealth change, we present the implied wealth trajectories side-by-side using the population median summary statistics. They are depicted in figure 14.4. The trajectory based on active saving results in much less wealth decumulation. For example, at age ninety single persons

---

16. For further information see the TAXSIM website (http://www.nber.org/taxsim/) and the paper by Feenberg and Coutts (1993) for additional background.

Table 14.5A   Singles living alone, active saving, averages of median values across four waves of CAMS

	N	After-tax income	Spending	Wealth	Saving	Saving rate, income (%)	Saving rate, wealth (%)
65–69	663	24,094	23,855	126,180	239	–0.10	–0.10
70–74	596	21,287	23,001	130,020	–1,714	–8.10	–1.20
75–79	566	19,455	21,785	148,490	–2,330	–11.90	–1.60
80–84	548	19,658	21,781	145,348	–2,123	–11.50	–1.70
85+	525	17,679	20,888	102,360	–3,209	–18.90	–3.30
Total	2,898	20,624	22,330	130,256	–1,706	–9.40	–1.50

Note: Excludes two observations due to missing data on after–tax income. "Saving" in a wave is the difference between median after-tax income and median spending all in 2008 dollars. The column entries are the averages of median values across waves weighted by the square root of N. "Saving rate, income" in a wave is "saving" divided by median after-tax income and the column entries are averages across waves. "Saving rate, wealth" is "saving" divided by median wealth.

Table 14.5B   Singles living alone, active saving, average of individual-level medians

	Saving	Saving rate, income (%)	Saving rate, wealth (%)
65–69	519	1.3	0.2
70–74	–1,198	–6.3	–0.6
75–79	–1,089	–7.3	–0.6
80–84	–831	–6.2	–0.7
85+	–1,665	–10.4	–1.5
Total	–776	–5.1	–0.5

Note: Excludes two observations due to missing data on after-tax income. "Saving" in a wave is the median of after-tax income minus spending, all in 2008 dollars. The column entries are the average across waves (weighted by square root N). "Saving rate, income" in a wave is the median of the saving rate with respect to after-tax income and "Saving rate, wealth" is the median of the saving rate with respect to wealth. The column entries are the average across waves (weighted by square root N).

Table 14.5C   Singles living alone, active saving, averages of values across four waves of CAMS

	N	After-tax income	Spending	Wealth	Saving	Saving rate, income (%)	Saving rate, wealth (%)
65–69	663	29,851	30,266	281,218	–414	–2.1	–0.3
70–74	596	27,421	29,306	304,837	–1,885	–6.6	–0.6
75–79	566	27,382	27,278	313,917	103	0.1	0.0
80–84	548	24,519	26,454	281,671	–1,936	–8.7	–1.1
85+	525	22,640	27,662	211,775	–5,022	–22.7	–2.6
Total	2,898	26,536	28,264	279,206	–1,728	–7.5	–0.8

Note: Excludes two observations due to missing data on after-tax income. Income, spending, wealth, and saving in a wave are averages in 2008 dollars. The column entries are the average across waves (weighted by square root N). "Saving rate, income" in a wave is "saving" divided by mean after-tax income and the column entries are averages across waves. "Saving rate, wealth" is "saving" divided by mean wealth.

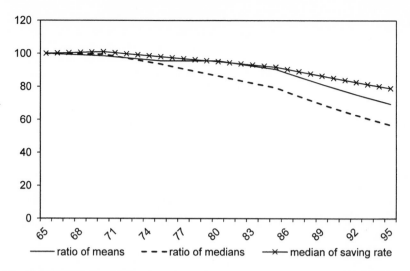

Fig 14.3 Simulated wealth paths based on three measures of active saving, singles living alone

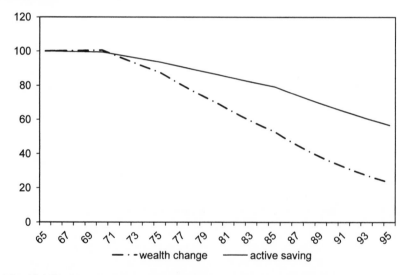

Fig. 14.4 Wealth paths from median wealth change and from median active saving, singles living alone

would have about 70 percent of initial wealth according to active saving, whereas they would only have about 35 percent of wealth remaining according to the estimates based on wealth change.

Tables 14.6A, 14.6B, and 14.6C show the summary statistics of active saving for couples living alone. For them the saving rates are positive at all ages, which implies *increasing* wealth as shown in figure 14.5. This finding

Table 14.6A   Couples living alone, active saving, averages of median values across four waves of CAMS (spouse age difference five years or less)

	N	After-tax income	Spending	Wealth	Saving	Saving rate, income (%)	Saving rate, wealth (%)
65–69	476	48,527	42,404	370,663	6,123	12.4	1.7
70–74	351	45,778	37,494	399,305	8,284	17.9	2.0
75–79	241	41,003	36,053	433,509	4,950	10.8	1.1
80 +	171	37,345	29,527	306,029	7,818	20.2	2.5
Total	1,239	44,769	38,015	382,201	6,754	14.8	1.8

Note: Excludes two observations due to missing data on wealth. "Saving" in a wave is the difference between median after-tax income and median spending, all in 2008 dollars. The column entries are the average across waves (weighted by square root N). "Saving rate, income" in a wave is "saving" divided by median after-tax income and the column entries are averages across waves. "Saving rate, wealth" is "saving" divided by median wealth.

Table 14.6B   Couples living alone, active saving, average of individual-level medians (spouse age difference five years or less)

	Saving	Saving rate, income (%)	Saving rate, wealth (%)
65–69	6,453	14.4	1.6
70–74	6,864	17.1	1.3
75–79	3,064	8.2	0.7
80 +	6,670	18.7	2.7
Total	5,704	16.6	1.8

Note: Excludes two observations due to missing data on wealth. "Saving" in a wave is the median of after-tax income minus spending, all in 2008 dollars. The column entries are the average across waves (weighted by square root N). "Saving rate, income" in a wave is the median of the saving rate with respect to after-tax income and "Saving rate, wealth" is the median of the saving rate with respect to wealth.

Table 14.6C   Couples living alone, active saving, averages of values across four waves of CAMS (spouse age difference five years or less)

	N	After-tax income	Spending	Wealth	Saving	Saving rate, income (%)	Saving rate, wealth (%)
65–69	476	67,548	53,231	726,113	14,317	21.2	2.1
70–74	351	58,152	49,071	830,334	9,081	14.6	0.9
75–79	241	49,864	48,764	599,310	1,101	2.1	0.2
80 +	171	47,469	37,022	494,040	10,446	20.0	2.0
Total	1,239	58,709	49,029	699,805	9,680	15.4	1.4

Note: Excludes two observations due to missing data on after-tax income. Income, spending, wealth, and saving in a wave are averages in 2008 dollars. The column entries are the average across waves (weighted by square root N). "Saving rate, income" in a wave is "saving" divided by mean after-tax income and the column entries are averages across waves. "Saving rate, wealth" is "saving" divided by mean wealth.

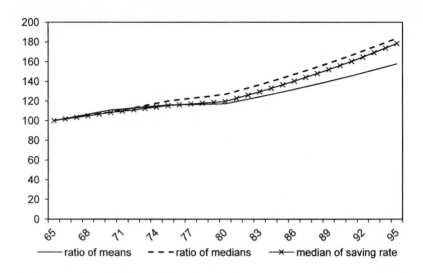

Fig. 14.5 Simulated wealth paths based on three measures of active saving, couples living alone (age difference five years or less)

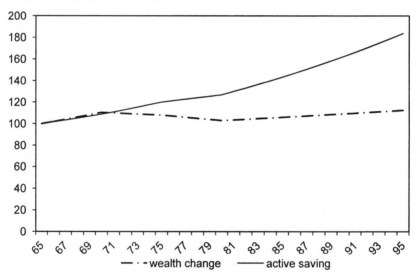

Fig. 14.6 Wealth paths from median wealth change and from median active saving, couples living alone (age difference five years or less)

is not consistent with the simple life cycle model we presented: the marginal utility of wealth to the surviving spouse should decline with age so that the household would want to consume in such a way that wealth would decrease. Figure 14.6 shows the side-by-side comparison of the wealth trajectory based on the analysis of wealth change with that based on active saving.

Both are calculated from the population medians (i.e., ratio of medians). According to the active saving path a household would accumulate about 50 percent of additional wealth by age ninety, which is in contrast to the trajectory based on wealth change, which is essentially flat (neither wealth accumulation nor decumulation).

14.6 Wealth Paths Based on CEX Spending Levels

According to the average discrepancy in table 14.1, CAMS spending levels among those age fifty-five or older averaged about 8 percent higher than spending levels in CEX. In this section, we compare wealth paths based on active saving that use CEX spending levels rather than CAMS spending levels. There are, however, a number of obstacles to such comparisons. First, we believe we must use CAMS income rather than CEX income: until recently CEX only reported income totals for households that were complete income reporters, that is, only over households that had no missing values for any income category. Because more well-to-do households have more categories of income, they are more likely to be nonrespondents to at least one income category, which would bias downward population totals. Furthermore, taxes in the CEX appear to be substantially underreported, which would cause discrepancies between pre- and after-tax income. Second, there likely are population mismatches based on age because of the use of head of household in CEX as discussed in section 14.4. An additional problem is that we cannot apply the restriction about the age difference of the spouses in the case of couples. Third, our tax calculations are for single persons and couples living alone, which is necessitated by our not having the income detail on other household members required by the NBER tax calculator. As of yet, we do not have CEX spending data by age and family composition.

Because of these problems, our method is to reduce CAMS spending by age band according to the average discrepancies between CAMS and CEX spending as reported in table 14.1. Thus we reduce observed spending by fifty-five to sixty-four-year-olds by about 4 percent, by sixty-five to seventy-four-year-olds by about 8 percent, and by seventy-five or older by about 16 percent. When compared with CAMS after-tax income, these adjustments will result in new levels of active saving, and new implied wealth paths. We calculated the new levels of active saving and wealth paths only for the measures based on means, not for the measures based on medians, because we only have mean spending in the published CEX tables. We do so for singles and couples whether living alone or with others because we do not have that demographic detail in the CEX data.

Figure 14.7 shows the wealth paths based on panel wealth changes, which is extracted from figure 14.1B, and on two measures of active saving, actual CAMS and adjusted CAMS to CEX levels. The actual CAMS (active saving)

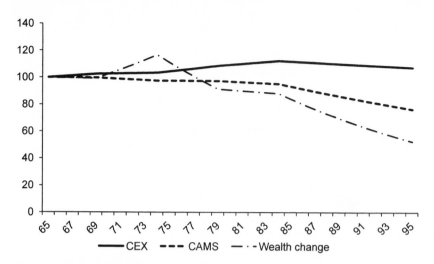

Fig. 14.7 Wealth paths from wealth change (ratio of means) and from active saving (ratio of means) for CAMS spending and CAMS spending adjusted to CEX levels, single persons living alone or with others

approximately tracks observed mean wealth change until about age eighty, when it begins to predict a flatter wealth path than actually observed. Nonetheless it shows dissaving, matching at least qualitatively observed wealth change. In contrast, CAMS active saving adjusted to CEX levels shows positive saving at all ages, resulting in increasing wealth.

Figure 14.8 has similar paths for couples. Until age eighty, the paths based on mean active saving, whether CAMS or adjusted CAMS, match fairly well the path based on mean wealth change. At older ages, the path based on wealth declines, whereas the paths based on active saving continue to increase.

14.7 Conclusions

We have shown two types of results: wealth change based on observed wealth levels in panel data and active saving rates based on observed income, calculated after-tax income and spending levels. In the case of single persons they are broadly consistent, at least qualitatively: singles dissave after age sixty-five.

Among married persons the estimate of the rate of wealth change depends on the statistic, but overall there appears to be little wealth change with age. Active saving by couples is positive in all our measures.

We conclude that the patterns of wealth change and active saving among single persons are consistent qualitatively with a simple life cycle model.

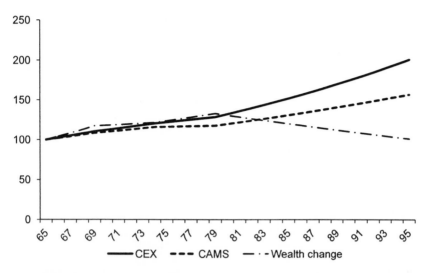

Fig. 14.8 Wealth paths from wealth change (ratio of means) and from active saving (ratio of means) for CAMS spending and CAMS spending adjusted to CEX levels, married persons living alone or with others

Among couples, the flat wealth path implies a high marginal utility of wealth of the surviving spouse. Active saving implies wealth accumulation, which is not observed in the wealth change data.

The source of the discrepancy between wealth change, which should be reliable over long periods, and active saving could arise from a number of factors. Capital gains—whether realized or unrealized—do not enter the calculation of active saving. These are empirically more important for couples than for singles, because couples hold substantially more wealth than singles at older ages. However, to the extent that capital gains are positive, they would increase the discrepancy between wealth change and active saving: taking out positive capital gains from wealth change would increase the rate of wealth decline, which is already greater than what is implied by active saving. But, it is not certain that (real) capital gains were positive over this time period. The older population holds considerable fixed-price assets which, in real terms, had negative capital gains. While the stock market recorded gains over this time period, only about one-third of older households hold stocks outside of retirement accounts. Whether house prices increased faster than the CPI depends on location: a quantitative assessment would require detailed geographic information linked to local house price indices.

A second source of discrepancy between wealth change and active saving is that measures of income in the HRS may be too large. The HRS income is somewhat larger than CPS income, but there are good reasons associated with the measurement of income from assets that would correctly lead to the greater values.[17]

A third source is taxation of withdrawals from tax-advantaged accounts. For example, consider a single person for whom after-tax income equals spending in the absence of any IRA withdrawals. Active saving would be zero and wealth change calculated from active saving would be zero. Should this person survive to advanced old age, she would have withdrawn all of her tax-advantaged wealth, paid taxes on those withdrawals and redeposited the after-tax amounts in post-tax accounts to comply with IRS rules concerning mandatory IRA withdrawals. Thus, simply by moving wealth out of tax-advantaged accounts, wealth would decline from age seventy to the end of life by the marginal tax rate. Our tax calculations do account for mandatory withdrawal of tax-advantaged savings at ages seventy and a half and older and their resulting taxation, but they do not account for any withdrawals that are necessary to finance consumption. This omission would cause an underestimate of taxes and a corresponding overestimate of active saving.

Fourth, we may be undermeasuring spending. It is difficult for respondents to remember completely their spending, and the longer the recall period over which respondents are asked to report, the larger the recall bias (Hurd and Rohwedder 2009). Underreporting is likely to be more prevalent among couples than among singles, because of the difficulties for a respondent to account for all of the spouse's spending in addition to his or her own spending. Although our measure of consumption is somewhat larger than the CEX measure, the CEX itself has been criticized as understating spending levels.

We summarize our results in table 14.7, which shows wealth at age ninety for single persons and at age eighty for couples, beginning with wealth of one hundred at age sixty-five. Because we consider medians to be more reliable than means, we only show results based on medians.

As measured by actual wealth change in panel, a single person who survives to age ninety would be expected to have 30–35 percent of age sixty-five wealth. While the other measures show smaller wealth declines, they all show declining wealth. Among married persons the results based on actual wealth change in panel suggests little wealth change to age eighty; yet, active saving predicts wealth accumulation of about 20 percent or about 1.2 percent per year. A possible reason for the difference between single persons and married persons is that active saving only incompletely accounts for taxation of withdrawals from tax-advantaged accounts. Because married persons have

17. Hurd, Juster, and Smith (2003) show that linking queries about income from assets to asset values, as was done beginning in HRS 1996, resulted in a substantial increase in income from assets between 1994 and 1996. In the CPS, queries about income from assets are asked separately from the questions about asset values, which, according to Hurd, Juster, and Smith, likely results in an underestimation of income from assets in the CPS.

Table 14.7   Percent of wealth remaining at age ninety for single persons living alone and at age eighty for married persons living alone with an age difference of five years or less

Data source	Statistic used for wealth change	
	Population medians	Medians of households
	Single persons	
Wealth change	35.1	29.8
Active saving	67.1	85.2
	Married persons	
Wealth change	103.0	90.0
Active saving	126.9	119.6

Note: Results based on population medians use the ratios of population median wealth in the case of "wealth change" and the difference between median after-tax income and median spending in the case of "active saving." Results based on medians of households use the medians of the change in wealth measured at the household level.

higher tax rates than single persons, the omission of such taxation would have a greater effect on their results.

References

Browning, Martin, and Annamaria Lusardi. 1996. "Household Savings: Micro Theories and Micro Facts." *Journal of Economic Literature* 34:1797–855.

Feenberg, Daniel Richard, and Elizabeth Coutts. 1993. "An Introduction to the TAXSIM Model." *Journal of Policy Analysis and Management* 12 (1): 189–94.

Hurd, Michael D. 1999. "Mortality Risk and Consumption by Couples." NBER Working Paper no. 7048, Cambridge, MA.

Hurd, Michael D., F. Thomas Juster, and James P. Smith. 2003. "Enhancing the Quality of Data on Income: Recent Innovations from the HRS." *Journal of Human Resources* 38 (3): 758–72.

Hurd, Michael D., and Susann Rohwedder. 2009. "Methodological Innovations in Collecting Spending Data: The HRS Consumption and Activities Mail Survey." *Fiscal Studies* 30 (Special I): 435–59.

Love, David A., Michael G. Palumbo, and Paul A. Smith. 2009. "The Trajectory of Wealth in Retirement." *Journal of Public Economics* 93:191–208.

Modigliani, Franco, and Richard Brumberg. 1954. "Utility Analysis and the Consumption Function: An Interpretation of the Cross-Section Data." In *Post-Keynesian Economics*, edited by K. Kurihara, 388–436. New Brunswick, NJ: Rutgers University Press.

Yaari, Menahem E. 1965. "Uncertain Lifetime, Life Insurance, and the Theory of the Consumer." *Review of Economic Studies* 32:137–50.

15

Measuring Household Spending and Payment Habits
The Role of "Typical" and "Specific" Time Frames in Survey Questions

Marco Angrisani, Arie Kapteyn, and Scott Schuh

15.1 Introduction

The rapid transformation of the US payment system and the increasing availability of new payment instruments have greatly changed household spending habits and use of payment methods. Understanding these trends has important policy implications. First, an assessment of consumers' preferences and financial literacy may help enact regulations, laws, and educational programs to protect and support consumer payment choices. Second, identifying which individual characteristics and personal traits drive such preferences and determine spending attitudes is critical to targeting interventions aimed at reducing households' exposure to consumer debt and boosting lifetime savings.

The Survey of Consumer Payment Choice (SCPC), developed by the Federal Reserve Bank of Boston and administered in the RAND American Life Panel (ALP), offers a unique opportunity to study these questions. While it is seldom done in practice, there seem to be clear potential advantages in allowing the respondent to choose the frequency in reporting behavior in surveys.

Marco Angrisani is an economist at the Center for Economic and Social Research at the University of Southern California. Arie Kapteyn is professor of economics and director of the Center for Economic and Social Research at the University of Southern California and a research associate of the National Bureau of Economic Research. Scott Schuh is economist and director of the Consumer Payments Research Center of the Federal Reserve Bank of Boston.

We are especially grateful to Angus Deaton, Martha Starr, and Tom Crossley for helpful comments and discussions. We also thank Barry Bosworth, Jennifer Edgar, and participants in the 2011 CRIW/NBER conference on Improving the Measurement of Consumer Expenditures. The usual disclaimer applies. The views expressed in this chapter are those of the authors and do not necessarily represent those of the Federal Reserve Bank of Boston or the Federal Reserve System. For acknowledgments, sources of research support, and disclosure of the authors' material financial relationships, if any, please see http://www.nber.org/chapters/c12672.ack.

The fundamental reason is that this gives the respondent the flexibility to select a time frame of recall that is best suited to their way of thinking and their habits. The hope is that this will provide more accurate individual results and, thus, more reliable global results. The intuition that certain payments naturally correspond to certain frequencies seems to be verified by the results of the 2010 SCPC. For example, when asked to provide information about cash expenditures in retail, 52.7 percent of respondents chose the weekly frequency, with only 10.8 percent answering on a per annum basis. An even stronger example relates to check usage for bill payments, where 67 percent of respondents answered using the monthly frequency, which might be expected as many bills are due on a monthly basis. However, when adopting such a novel survey approach, it is important to understand the nature of the collected data and how the specifics of the question might influence the response. In the SCPC, those who answered on a weekly basis on average reported 173.3 yearly cash transactions in retail, while those who reported on a monthly basis reported an average of 51.9, and those who reported on an annual basis averaged 11.2. Of course, it might be expected that the choice of reporting frequency is not independent of usage frequency, with those that use a payment type more often finding it easier to think on a weekly basis. However, the differences observed are quite large and it might be that at least part of this is due to bias imposed by the frequency choice.

Measuring the frequency with which people perform regular actions, such as purchasing consumer goods, is not a simple task. The cognitive process used by subjects to answer a frequency question, in fact, may differ substantially depending on the question content and format (Chang and Krosnick 2003). The SCPC asks respondents about their spending and payment behavior during a "usual" or "typical" period (week, month, or year). This type of question may conceivably trigger a rate-based estimation, in which individuals construct an occurrence rule and apply it to the reference time frame. An alternative approach is to elicit behavior frequency within "specific" time periods, such as past day, week, month, or year. In this case, respondents may be more likely to use episode enumeration, in which they recall and count episodes from a well-specified time frame. The reason for the SCPC to choose "typical" is that its aim is to develop aggregate US estimates of payment use that accurately reflect the trend of payment use. A concern with the use of a specific period is that it has at least two components in it—trend and non-trend, where the latter may include seasonal and other deterministic effects, cyclical effects, and idiosyncratic consumer effects. Using "typical" may help respondents focus on the trends and strip away the other sources of volatility.

Individuals tend to balance effort and accuracy in selecting formulation processes and the trade-off is often determined by the accessibility of the information in memory. The answer to a question about a specific recent period entails shorter-term recall than does one about a typical period and may therefore be subject to smaller recall error. On the other hand, it may represent a less accurate description of average behavioral frequencies, especially when sample sizes are not too large. The issue of determining the optimal recall period has a long history of study in several disciplines (for instance, Mahalanobis and Sen 1954; Deaton and Kozel 2005). In the measurement of expenditures, recall periods may vary from one day to a year. Often different periods are chosen for different types of expenditures: long periods for major purchases of durables, for instance, and short periods for small, frequently purchased items. There are various cognitive processes determining the accuracy of retrospective reports including telescoping (events that took place in the past, are reported as more recent than they really were) and straightforward forgetting. The latter is particularly relevant for the measurement of small expenditures. Deaton and Grosh (2000) and Deaton (2001) provide an extensive discussion of the effects of varying recall periods on measured consumption (and its distribution). Assessing the quality and validity of individual reports referring to specific and typical periods of different lengths is an interesting methodological question with important implications for the design of consumer spending surveys and their use for policy analysis.

With this objective in mind, we have designed and fielded an experimental module in the ALP where we ask individuals to report the number of their purchases and the amount spent by debit card, cash, credit card, and check. The experimental design features several stages of randomization. First, three different groups of sample participants are invited every month to answer the survey. Each respondent is randomly assigned to an entry month (July, August, or September 2011) and is interviewed four times during a year, once every quarter (e.g., the respondents entering in July are reinterviewed in October, respondents entering in August are reinterviewed in November, etc.). Second, for each method of payment a sequence of questions elicits spending behavior during a day, week, month, and year. At the time of the first interview, this sequence is randomly assigned to refer to "specific" time spans or to "typical" time spans. In all subsequent interviews, a specific sequence becomes a typical sequence and vice versa. Finally, the order of the time frames (day, week, month, year) within a sequence is randomly determined so as to reduce anchoring or order effects.

This design generates both between- and within-subjects variation for our research purposes. In each quarter, we will have one group of respondents answering about specific periods and another group answering about typical periods. Within these two subsamples, we will compare answers to different reference periods and evaluate the effect of shorter versus longer recall spans. Also, the randomization of the period sequence (day, week, month, year) will allow us to gauge the degree of dependency among answers referring to different time spans. For instance, is the number of payments in a typical week consistent with the number of payments in a typical day or month? At the same time, we will be able to compare, for a given reference period, reported frequencies within a specific time frame and a typical time frame.

Over two subsequent quarters, we will have individual changes from a specific to a typical period and individual changes from a typical to a specific period. By studying the direction of these changes, we will get insights on whether any of the two formats leads to systematic over- or underreporting and on whether the "intensity" of the bias differs depending on the length of the reference period (day, week, month, or year).

Over the four planned waves, we will have changes over time for each specific and typical period. Hence, we can analyze how stable answers are for different question formats. A priori, one would expect reported payment frequencies and spending amounts within typical periods to be less volatile than those within specific periods. Moreover, one would expect such differences to decrease with the length of the reference time frame. Consistency of answers could be treated as an indicator of reliability of the measurements.

An interesting output of this analysis is an assessment of how alternative measures obtained from different question formats correlate with individual characteristics such as education, cognitive ability, and wealth. We will also test the validity of such measures by evaluating their association with criterion variables (i.e., variables with which we expect spending and payment habits to correlate relatively strongly and in a specific way). Possible criterion variables among those already collected by the SCPC are household income, respondents' financial responsibility within the household, individual financial literacy and cognitive capability, and consumers' opinion about the characteristics—security, convenience, acceptance for payment, and cost—of a particular payment instrument.

The first wave of this experimental module has now been completed. In this chapter, we describe the experimental design and the characteristics of the sample (section 15.2) and provide some preliminary evidence of the role played by time frames when eliciting spending and payment habits in household surveys (section 15.3).

Our main findings are two. First, when referring to short reference periods, such as a day or a week, respondents tend to report higher number of payments and amounts spent. Differences between answers to monthly and yearly questions are relatively small. Second, the probability of reporting nonzero payments by debit cards, cash, and credit cards, is significantly higher when reporting for typical than for specific periods, while there is no differential effect for checks. At the same time, reported amounts spent are systematically lower for typical than for specific reference periods across the four payment instruments.

15.2 Data and Experimental Design

15.2.1 The Sample

The study is carried out on a sample of individuals participating in the American Life Panel (ALP), an Internet-based survey administered by the

RAND Corporation. Respondents in the ALP either use their own computer to log on to the Internet or they are provided with a small laptop or a WebTV to access the Internet. About twice a month, sample participants receive an e-mail with a request to visit the ALP URL and fill out specific questionnaires. Typically, an interview takes no more than thirty minutes and respondents are paid a monetary incentive proportional to the length of the interview (about seventy cents per minute, or twenty dollars per thirty minutes). Most respondents respond within one week and the vast majority within three weeks. To further increase response rates, reminders are sent each week. For the current study, 97 percent of the sampled individuals completed the survey within one week, 2.5 percent between two to three weeks, and only 0.5 percent took four weeks.

There are currently 5,000 members in the ALP, mainly recruited from survey programs that collect representative samples of US consumers.[1] For this study we rely on a sample of 3,285 individuals, whose characteristics are summarized in table 15.1.

15.2.2 The Experiment

About one-third of the selected sample is invited every month to answer the experimental module. Each participant is interviewed four times during a year, once every quarter. The first wave of the survey was fielded during the summer of 2011. Specifically, respondents were randomly assigned to three different entry dates—July 15th, August 15th, and September 15th—and are scheduled to be reinterviewed every three months since then. For instance, those who started on July 15th, 2011, are asked to take the second wave of the survey on October 15th, 2011, the third wave on January 15th, 2012, and the fourth wave on March 15th, 2012. (See table 15.2.)

The survey features questions about the four most common methods of payment adopted by US consumers in recent years, as documented by Foster et al. (2008, 2009). These are, in order of importance, debit cards, cash, credit cards, and personal checks. For each method of payment, sample participants are asked to report first the number of transactions made and then

---

1. Until August 2008, most participants were recruited from the pool of individuals age eighteen and older who were respondents to the Monthly Survey (MS) of the University of Michigan's Survey Research Center (SRC). The MS is the leading consumer sentiment survey that incorporates the long-standing Survey of Consumer Attitudes (SCA) and produces, among others, the widely used Index of Consumer Expectations. After August 2008, the ALP did not receive new members from the University of Michigan's MS. A subset of participants (approximately 550) has been recruited through a "snowball" sample. That is, respondents were given the opportunity to suggest friends or acquaintances who might also want to participate in the panel. These were then contacted and asked if they wanted to join the ALP. In the fall of 2009, a new group of respondents (approximately 600) was recruited from the National Survey Project (NSP), an NSF-funded panel of Stanford University and Abt SRBI. More recently, the ALP has begun recruiting from a random mail and telephone sample using the Dillman method, as well as from vulnerable populations so as to increase the representation of minorities and less affluent individuals.

Table 15.1 Sample characteristics

	Gender/age		Gender/education			Gender/income		
	Freq.	Perc.		Freq.	Perc.		Freq.	Perc.
M, age 18–34	248	7.55	M, high school or less	268	8.16	M, income < 35k	375	11.45
M, age 35–54	507	15.43	M, some college	476	14.49	M, income 35–59k	352	10.75
M, age 55+	578	17.60	M, college+	589	17.93	M, income 60k+	601	18.35
F, age 18–34	475	14.46	F, high school	426	12.97	F, income < 35k	746	22.78
F, age 35–54	774	23.56	F, some college	823	25.05	F, income 35–59k	510	15.57
F, age 55+	703	21.40	F, college +	703	21.40	F, income 60k+	691	21.10
Total	3,285	100.00	Total	3,285	100.00	Total	3,275	100.00

Note: The total number of respondents is different in panel 3 (Gender/income) due to household income being missing for ten respondents.

Table 15.2   Randomization 1: Entry date

	Freq.	Perc.
July 15th	1,067	32.48
August 15th	1,079	32.85
September 15th	1,139	34.67
Total	3,285	100.00

Table 15.3   Randomization 2: "Specific past" and "typical" recall periods

1st interview		2nd interview		3rd interview		4th interview
Specific past	→	Typical	→	Specific past	→	Typical
Typical	→	Specific past	→	Typical	→	Specific past

the amount spent in four recall periods: a day, a week, a month, and a year. At the time of the first interview, each respondent is randomly assigned to answer about "specific past" recall periods or "typical" recall periods. In all subsequent waves, those who answered about specific past recall periods in the previous interview are asked to answer about typical recall periods and vice versa. Thus, each sample participant faces two possible initial options— specific past and typical recall periods—and two possible paths over the entire survey originating from them as shown in table 15.3.

After the type of recall period (specific or typical) has been assigned, a further stage of randomization determines, at each interview and for each respondent, the order in which the four payment instruments appear in the questionnaire. Moreover, the order of the recall period sequence (day/week/month) is randomly allocated to each method of payment so as to reduce mechanical answers and systematic anchoring or order effects. Questions referring to the year are always asked after the respondent has reported about all other recall periods.[2] Table 15.4 illustrates the random assignments.

Our experiment design does not allow the respondent to choose a particular frequency (as in the SCPC), but each survey participant answers about four possible recall periods. This choice prevents us from studying how the rate of payment use (e.g., very frequent use of cash for daily purchases) induces selection into particular time frames (e.g., choosing day as a reference period when answering about cash payments). On the other hand, it

2. In a pilot test we randomized the whole period sequence (day/week/month/year). Respondents' feedback revealed strong reluctance to answer the "year" question at the beginning of the recall period sequence. We therefore decided to permute only day, week, and month, while keeping the year question at the end of the sequence for each method of payment. We acknowledge that this may cause some anchoring effects. On the other hand, however, it makes it easier for survey participants to approximate the number of payments and the amount spent over a long time span such as one year.

Table 15.4 Randomization 3: Recall period sequence and payment methods

	Specific past period					Typical period				
	Debit	Cash	Credit	Check	Total	Debit	Cash	Credit	Check	Total
Day/week/month	263	257	271	273	1,064	305	267	263	268	1,103
Day/month/week	272	261	243	277	1,053	284	287	274	287	1,132
Week/day/month	230	272	274	275	1,051	265	282	285	278	1,110
Week/month/day	309	277	252	261	1,099	274	276	279	268	1,097
Month/day/week	278	274	287	238	1,077	278	255	295	272	1,100
Month/week/day	277	288	302	305	1,172	250	289	260	283	1,082
Total	1,629	1,629	1,629	1,629		1,656	1,656	1,656	1,656	

enables us to analyze whether reporting behavior exhibits systematic differences for each method of payment across recall periods of different length. It should be noted that blocking questions by payment method and not by recall periods has the advantage of attenuating possible "seam" effects (Rips, Conrad, and Fricker 2003; Ham, Li, and Sheppard 2007; Moore et al. 2009). That is, the tendency of providing relatively similar answers for each recall period within one wave and relatively different answers across waves. This issue may conceivably arise if respondents adopt "constant responding" strategies so as to simplify the reporting task. For instance, when asked about the number of payments in a week, survey participants may be inclined to provide the same answer for all payment instruments in order to minimize the mental effort. Our design should discourage such behaviors and therefore reduce the importance of seam effects in our survey.

Defining "Specific Past" Recall Periods

In this section, we briefly discuss how specific past recall periods are defined in our study. A specific past day is determined by randomly drawing a number from one to seven, which pins down the specific recent day the respondent has to refer to. For example, if the respondent answers the survey on a Tuesday and the random number is five, he or she will have to refer to the previous Thursday when answering questions about a specific past day.

An alternative design would be to ask individuals about payments executed during the day prior to the interview. While this choice would reduce the time of recollection and perhaps increase response accuracy, it has a substantial drawback. Since sample participants are more likely to answer the questionnaire during the first three days after receiving the ALP URL, referring to the day prior to the interview would cluster the reference day on specific days of the week and, hence, reduce its representativeness.[3] For this reason, a design that randomly selects a specific day during the week prior to the interview is to be preferred.

The specific past week is defined as follows: For each interview date, an algorithm goes back seven days and pins down the reference week. Thus, if the respondent answers the interview on July 27th, the specific past week is defined as the time since July 20th. Similarly, the specific past month and specific past year are anchored to the interview date. Thus, if the respondent answers the questionnaire on July 27th, 2011, the specific past month is defined as the time since June 27th, 2011, whereas the specific past year is defined as the time since July 2010.

---

3. Among those who entered the survey on July 15th, 2011, 41 percent answered the survey during the first three days after receiving the ALP URL and 55 percent during the first five days. Among those who entered the survey on August 15th, 2011, 57 percent answered the survey during the first three days after receiving the ALP URL and 65 percent during the first five days. Among those who entered the survey on September 15th, 2011, 55 percent answered the survey during the first three days after receiving the ALP URL and 65 percent during the first five days.

Table 15.5   **Number of payments**

		Specific past period				Typical period			
		Day	Week	Month	Year	Day	Week	Month	Year
Debit	1st quartile	0	0	0	0	0	0	0	0
	2nd quartile	0	1	3	20	0	2	4	39
	3rd quartile	1	5	12	140	2	5	20	204
	Mean	1	4	13	171	1	5	15	291
	No. of obs.	1,460	1,463	1,464	1,445	1,524	1,527	1,525	1,524
Cash	1st quartile	0	0	0	0	0	0	0	5
	2nd quartile	0	1	4	24	0	2	5	50
	3rd quartile	1	4	10	100	1	5	15	200
	Mean	1	5	15	152	1	4	15	260
	No. of obs.	1,467	1,469	1,464	1,441	1,529	1,529	1,525	1,521
Credit	1st quartile	0	0	0	0	0	0	0	0
	2nd quartile	0	0	2	10	0	0	2	12
	3rd quartile	0	3	10	85	1	3	8	108
	Mean	1	3	12	161	1	3	8	135
	No. of obs.	1,464	1,464	1,467	1,448	1,529	1,529	1,530	1,530
Check	1st quartile	0	0	0	1	0	0	0	4
	2nd quartile	0	0	2	20	0	0	2	24
	3rd quartile	0	2	6	63	0	1	6	60
	Mean	0	2	6	78	0	1	5	105
	No. of obs.	1,468	1,470	1,470	1,454	1,528	1,519	1,534	1,527

Note: Statistics are computed excluding the top 1 percent of the variables' distribution.

This procedure avoids variation across individuals in the difficulty of their recall task. For instance, if we were to define the specific past month as the month prior to the one when the interview took place, we would have two persons, one answering on July 2nd, 2011, and one on July 27th, 2011, referring both to June 2011 while facing substantially different recollection times.

15.3 Results

15.3.1 Descriptive Statistics

Summary statistics reported in tables 15.5 and 15.6 reveal interesting results and, when comparison is possible, confirm the findings by Foster et al. (2008, 2009). Across all instruments, both the median and the average number of reported payments are mostly higher in typical recall periods than in specific ones. Credit cards are somewhat of an exception in that the mean number of credit card payments per year and per month is higher for specific than for typical periods. This reflects a more skewed distribution of the number of payments in specific years and months than in typical ones.

Table 15.6   **Amount spent (in current dollars)**

		Specific past period				Typical period			
		Day	Week	Month	Year	Day	Week	Month	Year
Debit	1st quartile	0	0	0	0	0	0	0	0
	2nd quartile	0	10	150	800	0	35	200	1,200
	3rd quartile	25	200	586	5,000	25	140	600	6,000
	Mean	39	141	430	4,332	17	90	409	4,864
	No. of obs.	1,475	1,475	1,466	1,466	1,542	1,542	1,543	1,543
Cash	1st quartile	0	0	0	0	0	0	0	30
	2nd quartile	0	20	75	500	0	20	100	1,000
	3rd quartile	15	95	300	2,080	10	70	300	3,000
	Mean	21	81	230	1,981	10	52	200	2,295
	No. of obs.	1,472	1,475	1,475	1,475	1,543	1,543	1,543	1,543
Credit	1st quartile	0	0	0	0	0	0	0	0
	2nd quartile	0	0	82	750	0	0	100	882
	3rd quartile	0	160	650	6,000	20	100	500	6,000
	Mean	29	162	605	5,677	15	88	477	5,560
	No. of obs.	1,475	1,473	1,475	1,475	1,539	1,522	1,540	1,542
Check	1st quartile	0	0	0	0	0	0	0	100
	2nd quartile	0	0	240	2,134	0	0	260	2,400
	3rd quartile	0	215	900	9,600	0	100	875	9,000
	Mean	47	252	727	7,282	11	86	634	6,663
	No. of obs.	1,475	1,475	1,474	1,475	1,543	1,543	1,543	1,538

Note: Statistics are computed excluding the top 1 percent of the variables' distribution.

The difference in skewness between specific and typical distributions is most pronounced when we consider the amounts spent. For all four payment instruments and for day, week, and month, average amounts are larger when we ask for specific periods than when we ask for typical ones, while median amounts are smaller. The differences between specific and typical periods decrease as the length of the recall period increases. In fact, when the reference period is a year, differences are rather modest. These patterns point to higher variances in the reported specific amounts than in the typical amounts. This is consistent with the notion that specific amounts are noisier, since these include intertemporal variation that gets smoothed out when asking for typical periods.

Across all possible payment instruments we compute that the median (average) consumer conducts twenty-two (thirty-six) transactions in the previous month, spending $1,320 ($1,839). When considering a typical month, we find a median number (average) of payments equal to and twenty-nine (forty) and median (average) spending of $1,300 ($1,599). Respondents rely more heavily on debit cards and cash to make their transactions, while credit cards and personal checks are the third and fourth most common methods of payment, respectively. As for the amount spent, survey participants indicate using mainly personal checks and credit cards for large purchases and debit cards and cash to pay for relatively smaller amounts. Such rankings appear to be robust to variations in the type and length of the recall period.[4]

Given the randomization of the sequence (day/week/month), our experimental design allows us to assess the degree of dependency among answers referring to different recall periods. For instance, is the number of payments in a specific or typical week consistent with the number of payments in a specific or typical month? Also, is the answer to a particular reference period systematically anchored by the one given in the preceding question? We investigate these issues in table 15.7, where, to help the comparison, we express reported values for day, week, and month in yearly equivalents.

Overall, answers to month and year questions are reasonably consistent, while relatively large discrepancies can be observed between spending reports referring to short (day and week) and long (month and year) recall periods. There is also evidence that answers are anchored to those given in the preceding question. Particularly for checks, the total number of payments for both specific and typical reference periods is highest for the sequence D/W/M/Y, followed by W/M/D/Y. For debit cards a somewhat similar pattern seems to emerge, but it is less uniform. Looking across reporting periods, we observe that when day is the first reference period, annualized frequencies of payments tend to be higher when based on daily reports.

The order of the recall period sequence also influences reported values. An interesting contrast emerges when comparing number of payments for checks and the total value of check payments. The annualized values across the different sequences are perfectly negatively correlated with the annualized frequencies. That is, the higher the reported number, the lower the annualized value. For cash, the amount spent tends to be higher for the "increasing" sequence day/week/month than for the "decreasing" sequence month/week/day.[5]

---

4. The Survey of Consumer Finance (SCF) is perhaps the best source of comparable information for the data collected in this study. The SCF, however, only contains information about the adoption of some noncash payment instruments and the amount spent by credit card. In the 2007 SCF, the percentage of consumers who had adopted debit cards was 67, the percentage of those who had adopted credit cards was 73, and the percentage of those who had adopted checks 89.7. Using answers to typical-year questions, the percentages of ALP respondents reporting a nonzero number of transaction by debit card, credit card, and check are 67, 63, and 77, respectively. In the 2007 SCF the average US household made $850 worth of credit card charges per month. Table 15.6 shows that the average monthly amount spent by ALP respondents in 2011 using credit cards is roughly $500 (in current dollars). Although the information collected in the two surveys is not fully comparable (SCF has household as the unit of measurement, while our analysis is based on individuals), these statistics seem reasonably in line, especially after taking into account that households have significantly decreased the use of credit cards during the recent economic turmoil.

5. For all the other recall period sequences not reported in table 15.7, there are no appreciable differences with respect to the patterns commented above.

Table 15.7   **Mean values in yearly equivalents for different recall period sequences**

		Specific past period				Typical period			
		Day	Week	Month	Year	Day	Week	Month	Year
		(number of payments)							
Debit	D/W/M/Y	612	223	247	175	430	301	225	242
	W/M/D/Y	376	381	198	134	394	275	250	255
	M/W/D/Y	243	118	164	189	272	139	92	145
Cash	D/W/M/Y	226	77	51	53	95	49	111	208
	W/M/D/Y	238	171	130	156	354	235	341	421
	M/W/D/Y	188	202	144	136	391	181	233	238
Credit	D/W/M/Y	197	143	221	136	180	124	88	125
	W/M/D/Y	98	92	239	69	88	52	61	56
	M/W/D/Y	220	172	136	162	240	163	126	156
Check	D/W/M/Y	222	158	112	141	300	242	149	183
	W/M/D/Y	98	123	92	110	153	117	97	106
	M/W/D/Y	80	75	54	64	76	57	52	56
		Amount spent							
Debit	D/W/M/Y	20,765	7,869	5,139	3,935	7,471	4,328	4,264	3,880
	W/M/D/Y	11,065	4,648	2,237	1,776	3,760	2,547	2,263	2,208
	M/W/D/Y	16,837	8,302	6,484	5,317	5,836	4,516	5,350	5,515
Cash	D/W/M/Y	27,917	12,683	8,710	8,645	4,560	3,341	7,126	6,584
	W/M/D/Y	10,649	7,609	5,179	4,153	5,527	5,001	5,848	5,844
	M/W/D/Y	6,136	4,022	2,272	1,805	3,427	2,704	2,469	1,862
Credit	D/W/M/Y	7,872	11,576	7,887	6,151	5,103	4,836	5,428	5,812
	W/M/D/Y	8,652	14,825	10,164	7,520	3,490	4,276	7,110	7,619
	M/W/D/Y	7,700	5,902	5,529	5,040	5,040	3,695	4,724	3,827
Check	D/W/M/Y	4,998	3,372	2,948	1,949	2,360	2,380	2,376	2,449
	W/M/D/Y	5,087	5,437	6,694	4,382	4,875	5,346	6,367	5,592
	M/W/D/Y	7,858	12,834	8,547	7,442	3,755	5,715	7,911	6,456

Notes: Statistics are computed excluding the top 1 percent of the variables' distribution. Reported number of payments and amount spent for day, week, and month are expressed in yearly equivalents.

15.3.2 Regression Analysis

We now turn to the analysis of the experimental data in a regression framework so as to quantify the effect that different type—specific or typical—and length of recall periods have on household spending habits as elicited by our module. Throughout this section, we will focus on two outcomes: the reported number of payments and the amount spent using one of the four payment methods in a particular time frame. As a preliminary step, we express these two variables in yearly equivalents, whenever the recall period is a day, a week, or a month. This transformation will ease the interpretation and help the comparison of estimated coefficients across recall periods of different length.

Given the experimental design described above, we have four individual reports for each method of payment, one per day, one per week, one per month, and one per year. Our strategy is to express these individual reports in yearly equivalents and regress them on question format indicators. We use relatively flexible specifications allowing the length of the reference period to interact with the type of recall frame—specific or typical—and with an indicator for the starting period in the reference period sequence. We control for a set of individual characteristics including gender, age, education, and family income, as well as for survey-specific factors such as the time it took the respondent to complete the questionnaire. In order to account for correlation between observations within each individual unit, we cluster standard errors at the respondent level.

In tables 15.8 and 15.9 we focus on the number of payments. Specifically, we first present ordinary least squares (OLS) estimates and then test hypotheses across various question formats.[6] The regression results confirm the patterns of the descriptive analysis in the previous section. Respondents report a substantially higher number of payments when referring to short time spans, such as a day or a week, than when referring to longer spans, such as a month or a year. For instance, the marginal effects (shown in table 15.10) implied by the regressions in table 15.8 reveal that individuals report fifty-one more debit card payments when referring to a week than to a month, thirty more cash payments, thirty-three more credit card payments, and twelve more check payments. These differences more than double if we compare reports referring to a day with those referring to a month. On the other hand, there are relatively small discrepancies between frequencies elicited using month and year as reference periods. Comparing typical and specific reference periods, we see that asking for the number of payments with debit cards or cash yields frequencies that are about 48 transactions higher when referring to typical periods than when we use specific periods; on the other hand, for credit cards and checks, typical periods yield respectively 18 and 24 fewer reports per annum than when asking for frequencies in specific periods. The hypothesis tests in panel A of table 15.9 show that these differences are highly significant.

Given the mixture of observations with zero and positive values for spending amounts and its different balance across the various methods of payment, we estimate a hurdle model for the reported amount spent. Compared to OLS, this approach allows us to relax the assumption that zero payments

---

6. Zero payments could reflect either nonadoption of the payment instrument by the respondent or spending inactivity by the respondent; the latter could occur even if the respondent adopted the instrument. Count data models for the number of payments give very similar results to the OLS estimates presented here. Specifically, allowing for unobserved heterogeneity, which would imply overdispersion in the number of reported transactions, we estimate a negative binomial model with quadratic variance. Moreover, in order to deal with the large number of reported zeros for short recall periods and/or for less common payment instruments (e.g., personal checks), we consider a zero-inflated negative binomial model (Cameron and Trivedi 1998), for which the process generating zero observations differs from the one producing positive values. The results of these regressions are available upon request.

Table 15.8 OLS regressions for number of payments

Recall period	Version	Sequence starting period	Debit	Cash	Credit	Check
Day	Specific	D	262.2***	216.5***	131.7***	170.7***
			(41.5)	(43.4)	(28.8)	(26.2)
		W	105.7***	77.6*	112.3***	47.7**
			(30.6)	(42.1)	(28.5)	(19.4)
		M	133.5***	82.7**	53.4**	22.0
			(32.0)	(40.8)	(21.3)	(14.9)
Day	Typical	D	306.4***	186.8***	121.5***	39.8***
			(33.1)	(35.9)	(22.0)	(13.9)
		W	203.9***	160.0***	80.6***	19.6
			(30.1)	(38.2)	(19.1)	(12.9)
		M	160.9***	132.8***	79.2***	17.5*
			(22.6)	(31.3)	(14.2)	(9.8)
Week	Specific	D	50.8*	2.9	19.3	14.1
			(26.5)	(34.8)	(18.5)	(11.2)
		W	46.2*	8.5	58.3***	55.0***
			(24.3)	(33.9)	(20.6)	(13.8)
		M	9.8	39.9	34.1	14.7
			(24.4)	(40.4)	(21.3)	(9.3)
Week	Typical	D	132.2***	66.8*	28.1*	-10.6
			(28.2)	(34.8)	(17.0)	(7.9)
		W	75.4***	35.1	15.1	-9.4
			(24.2)	(34.9)	(15.2)	(7.8)
		M	46.9**	71.6**	15.2	-6.0
			(20.8)	(33.1)	(9.8)	(6.3)
Month	Specific	D	-8.1	35.7	-22.1	-14.8**
			(26.7)	(42.1)	(15.8)	(7.4)

		(1)	(2)	(3)	(4)
Month	W	−13.4 (23.8)	0.3 (41.4)	12.3 (18.6)	10.5 (13.1)
	M	−8.9 (26.1)	−49.0 (34.3)	22.4 (22.2)	1.2 (10.5)
Typical	D	73.5*** (25.7)	37.6 (34.7)	−7.0 (14.9)	−8.6 (7.7)
	W	48.9* (27.5)	28.3 (37.2)	−16.9 (13.7)	1.2 (8.6)
	M	−32.6** (13.2)	−4.4 (24.8)	−19.2** (8.6)	−6.2 (6.3)
Year Specific	D	34.3 (30.1)	−34.5 (35.6)	15.2 (25.2)	−5.0 (10.1)
	W	−12.3 (23.7)	−36.2 (34.1)	81.7** (32.9)	2.9 (10.7)
	M	28.4 (30.5)	−50.2 (33.2)	4.3 (21.6)	2.4 (10.4)
Year Typical	D	108.5*** (31.4)	74.1* (41.2)	2.1 (15.9)	−2.6 (8.8)
	W	73.6** (30.0)	66.8* (40.6)	−4.8 (15.3)	0.2 (9.5)
Number of observations		11,905	11,918	11,932	11,941

Notes: Dependent variable: number of payments in yearly equivalents. Regressions include controls for gender, age, education, family income, and survey time. Standard errors are clustered at the individual level. The omitted category is *Year* × *Typical* × *M*.

***Significant at the 1 percent level.

**Significant at the 5 percent level.

*Significant at the 10 percent level.

Table 15.9   OLS regressions for number of payments: Testing differences across time frames

A.		Debit	Cash	Credit	Check
Specific	H_0: Day = week	***	***	***	***
Specific	H_0: Day = month	***	***	***	***
Specific	H_0: Day = year	***	***	***	***
Specific	H_0: Week = month	***	**	***	***
Specific	H_0: Week = year	**	***	○	***
Specific	H_0: Month = year	○	○	**	○
Typical	H_0: Day = week	***	***	***	***
Typical	H_0: Day = month	***	***	***	***
Typical	H_0: Day = year	***	***	***	***
Typical	H_0: Week = month	***	*	***	○
Typical	H_0: Week = year	○	○	**	○
Typical	H_0: Month = year	**	○	**	○

B.					
Day	H_0: Specific = typical	**	○	○	***
Week	H_0: Specific = typical	**	○	○	***
Month	H_0: Specific = typical	***	○	*	○
Year	H_0: Specific = typical	***	***	*	○

C.					
Day-specific	H_0: Starting D = starting W	***	***	○	***
	H_0: Starting D = starting M	***	***	**	***
	H_0: Starting W = starting M	○	○	*	○
Day-typical	H_0: Starting D = starting W	***	○	*	○
	H_0: Starting D = starting M	***	○	*	○
	H_0: Starting W = starting M	○	○	○	○
Week-specific	H_0: Starting D = starting W	○	○	*	***
	H_0: Starting D = starting M	○	○	○	○
	H_0: Starting W = starting M	○	○	○	***
Week-typical	H_0: Starting D = starting W	*	○	○	○
	H_0: Starting D = starting M	***	○	○	○
	H_0: Starting W = starting M	○	○	○	○
Month-specific	H_0: Starting D = starting W	○	○	*	**
	H_0: Starting D = starting M	○	**	**	*
	H_0: Starting W = starting M	○	○	○	○
Month-typical	H_0: Starting D = starting W	○	○	○	○
	H_0: Starting D = starting M	***	○	○	○
	H_0: Starting W = starting M	***	○	○	○
Year-specific	H_0: Starting D = starting W	○	○	*	○
	H_0: Starting D = starting M	○	○	○	○
	H_0: Starting W = starting M	○	○	**	○
Year-typical	H_0: Starting D = starting W	○	○	○	○
	H_0: Starting D = starting M	***	*	○	○
	H_0: Starting W = starting M	**	*	○	○

Notes: Tests use estimates from OLS regressions in table 15.8. The reference distribution in panels A and B is χ_3^2; the reference distribution in panel C is $N(0,1)$.

***The null H_0 is rejected at the 1% level.

**The null H_0 is rejected at the 5% level.

*The null H_0 is rejected at the 10% level.

○The null H_0 is not rejected.

Table 15.10   **OLS regressions for number of payments: Marginal effects**

	Debit	Cash	Credit	Check
Week	−135.8***	−104.1***	−67.3***	−43.4***
	(11.6)	(14.0)	(7.1)	(6.4)
Month	−186.1***	−134.4***	−100.3***	−55.5***
	(12.1)	(15.2)	(8.3)	(6.4)
Year	−157.1***	−137.8***	−79.9***	−53.0***
	(13.2)	(15.0)	(9.9)	(6.7)
Typical	47.8***	47.5***	−18.8*	−23.9***
	(13.6)	(15.5)	(10.0)	(5.2)
Starting W	−54.0***	5.9	−27.3**	2.2
	(16.8)	(18.8)	(11.9)	(6.2)
Starting M	−78.5***	−5.1	−5.8	2.7
	(16.7)	(19.0)	(12.8)	(6.2)

Notes: Marginal effects after the OLS regressions in table 10.8. Omitted categories are: "Day," for the length of the reference period; "Specific," for the type of reference period; "Starting D," for the reference period sequence starting with day. Standard errors are clustered at the individual level.

***Significant at the 1 percent level.
**Significant at the 5 percent level.
*Significant at the 10 percent level.

and positive amounts spent are produced by the same data-generating process.[7] Specifically, indicating with y_1 the number of payments and with y_2 the amount spent, we model the conditional probability of a nonzero payment as a probit:

$$(1) \qquad \Pr[y_1 > 0 \mid \mathbf{x}] = \Phi(\mathbf{x}'\beta),$$

and the expected value of a positive reported amount as a linear function

$$(2) \qquad E_{y_2 > 0}[y_2 \mid y_1 > 0, \mathbf{x}] = \mathbf{x}'\gamma.$$

The unconditional mean for the amount spent is therefore:

$$(3) \qquad E[y_2 \mid \mathbf{x}] = \Phi(\mathbf{x}'\beta) \times \mathbf{x}'\gamma.$$

We separately estimate equations (1) and (2) and compute the combined marginal effects for a discrete explanatory variable x_j using

$$(4) \quad E[y_2 \mid \mathbf{x}]_{x_j=1} - E[y_2 \mid \mathbf{x}]_{x_j=0} = [\Phi(\mathbf{x}'\beta) \times \mathbf{x}'\gamma]_{x_j=1} - [\Phi(\mathbf{x}'\beta) \times \mathbf{x}'\gamma]_{x_j=0}.$$

7. Model specifications addressing these issues are discussed, among others, by Deaton and Irish (1984), Blundell and Meghir (1987), Chesher and Irish (1987), and Robin (1993). The literature on consumer payment choice addresses the zero payment problem using a Heckman two-step selection model by estimating adoption of a payment instrument (e.g., getting a credit card) in the first step and estimating payment use for adopters only in the second step (but without controlling for zero payments by adopters). For example, see Schuh and Stavins (2010) and references therein.

In tables 15.11 and 15.13 we report average partial effects defined as:

$$(5) \qquad \frac{1}{n} \sum_{i=1}^{n} \{[\Phi(\mathbf{x}_i'\hat{\beta}) \times \mathbf{x}_i'\hat{\gamma}]_{x_{ij}=1} - [\Phi(\mathbf{x}_i'\hat{\beta}) \times \mathbf{x}_i'\hat{\gamma}]_{x_{ij}=0}\},$$

with i indicating the ith observation from a sample of size n.[8]

The estimated coefficients of the hurdle model provide some insights on the mechanisms driving reporting behaviors. First, as one would expect, the probability of reporting a positive number of payments increases with the length of the reference period. However, the extent to which this happens varies substantially across payment methods. The likelihood of reporting positive purchases by debit card when referring to a week, month, and year is, respectively, 16, 23, and 27 percentage points higher than when referring to a day. For transactions using checks, differences are on the order of 30, 55, and 60 percentage points. Within a typical framework, the probability of reporting positive purchases increases by 9 percentage points for debit cards and cash and by 4 percentage points for credit card. On the other hand, there is no differential effect for personal checks.

Second, conditional on nonzero payments, answering about short recall periods significantly increases the reported amount in yearly equivalents. After computing the marginal effects implied by the estimates in table 15.11, we find that, when they refer to a week, respondents report about $2,500 more spent by debit card and cash, $3,000 more spent by credit card, and $6,000 spent by check than when they refer to a month. These differences are much more pronounced when answers to questions about the day are compared to those about the month. On the other hand, less marked discrepancies are observed between answers to a month and to a year, ranging from $1,000 for debit cards to $2,000 for checks.

Third, with the exception of checks, a typical framework increases the probability of reporting nonzero payments by 8–9 percentage points. At the same time, it lowers the reported amount spent, conditional on it being positive. Specifically, individuals who conduct a nonzero number of transactions report $9,000 less spent by check, $6,500 less spent by debit and credit card, and $3,000 less spent in cash when they are asked to refer to a typical rather than to a specific past period (comparison of average partial effects for specific and typical periods computed taking all interactions into account).

The combination of these mechanisms produces the results in table 15.12. Panel A shows that the length of the reference period greatly affects household reporting behavior. Answers to shorter time spans are systematically different from those to longer ones. Within either a specific or a typical framework, this is true across all four payment instruments. Discrepancies between answers to monthly and yearly questions tend to be economically

---

8. Estimated coefficients for the probit model in equation (1) and the OLS regression in equation (2) are available upon request.

less sizable and not statistically significant when respondents are asked to refer to typical periods.

Panel B in table 15.12 reveals that the question frame matters as long as the length of the reference period is short enough. That is, answers referring to a specific day or week are systematically different from those referring to a typical day or week. On the other hand, answers about month and year are fairly similar independently of the question frame. The tests in panel C confirm that the order of the reference period sequence has very little effect on individual answers. We only find evidence that respondents report higher frequencies and amounts when they are asked about daily payments and the day features as first in the sequence of reference periods. Respondents exhibit a similar behavior when they are asked to recall payments during a specific past week and the sequence of reference periods starts with week instead of month.

Since different question frames affect the propensity with which positive payments are reported, treatment variables in equation (2) could potentially be correlated with unobserved characteristics driving reporting behavior. In other words, if there is selection on unobservables, the estimated coefficients on treatment variables in equation (2) may be biased. A Heckman selection model would allow for selection on unobservables. The absence of plausible exclusion restrictions, however, makes the estimation of such a model entirely dependent on functional form assumptions. Rather than relying on arbitrary exclusion restrictions, we prefer a different approach. As is well-known, if the errors in the probit equation and the amount equation are correlated this leads to the addition of a Mills ratio to equation (2), where its coefficient is the product of the correlation between the error terms and the standard deviation of the error term in the amount equation. We calculate the Mills ratio from the probit equation and add it to equation (2). Next, we vary the size of the correlation coefficient from 0 to 1. We find that although the estimated marginal effects do vary as the size of the correlation coefficient increases, these changes are not dramatic and in no case is the sign of a statistically significant coefficient reverted.[9]

In table 15.13 we report the estimated coefficients for the control variables used in the hurdle model regressions.[10] The coefficients on income and education have the expected sign. Compared to those whose income is less than $35,000 and accounting for the probability of reporting nonzero payments, individuals with more than $60,000 spend $2,000 more by debit card and about $5,500 more by credit card and check. At the same time they rely

---

9. For correlation values up to 0.4, estimated marginal effects change very little. For larger values of the correlation parameter, some of the magnitudes change substantially more, but that is only true for a small minority of (typically not statistically significant) coefficients. The results of this exercise are available upon request.

10. The same set of controls was used for the OLS regressions commented above, but the corresponding estimated coefficients were omitted for brevity.

Table 15.11   Hurdle model: Average partial effects

Recall period	Version	Sequence starting period	Debit	Cash	Credit	Check
Day	Specific	D	5.16***	1.68***	1.11	0.92
			(1.26)	(0.58)	(0.99)	(1.31)
		W	0.40	-0.02	-0.30	-3.16***
			(0.92)	(0.46)	(0.88)	(1.03)
		M	0.80	-0.02	-1.43*	-3.27***
			(0.93)	(0.45)	(0.80)	(1.02)
Day	Typical	D	0.08	-0.55**	-1.75***	-6.29***
			(0.56)	(0.27)	(0.54)	(0.41)
		W	-1.32**	-0.80***	-2.30***	-6.56***
			(0.52)	(0.26)	(0.50)	(0.41)
		M	-1.01***	-1.07***	-2.07***	-6.52***
			(0.39)	(0.20)	(0.38)	(0.36)
Week	Specific	D	1.63**	0.41	0.62	-0.57
			(0.81)	(0.40)	(0.79)	(0.90)
		W	2.59***	1.34***	2.76***	3.58***
			(0.82)	(0.44)	(0.87)	(1.18)
		M	0.08	0.01	-0.28	0.10
			(0.68)	(0.33)	(0.66)	(1.02)
Week	Typical	D	-0.48	-0.65***	-1.36***	-5.03***
			(0.48)	(0.24)	(0.50)	(0.43)
		W	-0.63	-0.17	-1.66***	-4.66***
			(0.49)	(0.28)	(0.48)	(0.46)
		M	-0.99***	-0.40**	-0.84***	-4.27***
			(0.29)	(0.16)	(0.32)	(0.36)
Month	Specific	D	-0.27	-0.08	0.33	-0.67
			(0.58)	(0.31)	(0.66)	(0.68)
		W	0.25	-0.44	1.47**	0.92
			(0.60)	(0.29)	(0.71)	(0.88)

Month	Typical	M	1.10* (0.66)	0.15 (0.34)	1.89** (0.74)	0.94 (0.88)
		D	-0.12 (0.50)	-0.41* (0.23)	0.05 (0.55)	-0.89 (0.63)
		W	0.14 (0.52)	-0.34 (0.25)	-0.64 (0.51)	-0.13 (0.69)
Year	Specific	M	-0.11 (0.24)	-0.41*** (0.13)	-0.05 (0.24)	0.03 (0.35)
		D	-0.48 (0.59)	-0.73*** (0.26)	0.29 (0.64)	0.30 (0.78)
		W	-0.17 (0.60)	-0.70*** (0.25)	0.84 (0.63)	0.65 (0.86)
Year	Typical	M	0.47 (0.62)	-0.43 (0.29)	0.24 (0.59)	-0.48 (0.68)
		D	0.05 (0.51)	-0.16 (0.25)	0.30 (0.58)	-0.45 (0.65)
		W	0.37 (0.54)	-0.49** (0.24)	-0.43 (0.52)	0.17 (0.69)
Number of observations			12,021	12,048	12,043	12,046

Notes: Combined average partial effects from probit and OLS regressions are reported. The dependent variable for probit is an indicator for nonzero number of payments. The dependent variable for OLS is the amount spent in yearly equivalents expressed in 1,000 dollars. Regressions include controls for gender, age, education, family income, and survey time. The omitted category is $Year \times Typical \times M$. Bootstrap standard errors (500 replications) are clustered at the individual level.

***Significant at the 1 percent level.

**Significant at the 5 percent level.

*Significant at the 10 percent level.

Table 15.12   **Testing differences across time frames (hurdle model)**

A.		Debit	Cash	Credit	Check
Specific	H_0: Day = week	***	***	***	***
Specific	H_0: Day = month	***	***	***	***
Specific	H_0: Day = year	***	***	**	***
Specific	H_0: Week = month	***	***	***	**
Specific	H_0: Week = year	***	***	**	**
Specific	H_0: Month = year	o	***	***	**
Typical	H_0: Day = week	**	***	***	***
Typical	H_0: Day = month	***	***	***	***
Typical	H_0: Day = year	***	***	***	***
Typical	H_0: Week = month	***	o	***	***
Typical	H_0: Week = year	***	***	***	***
Typical	H_0: Month = year	o	***	o	o

B.					
Day	H_0: Specific = typical	***	***	***	***
Week	H_0: Specific = typical	***	***	***	***
Month	H_0: Specific = typical	o	o	***	o
Year	H_0: Specific = typical	o	*	o	o

C.					
Day-specific	H_0: Starting D = starting W	***	***	o	***
	H_0: Starting D = starting M	***	***	**	***
	H_0: Starting W = starting M	o	o	o	o
Day-typical	H_0: Starting D = starting W	**	o	o	o
	H_0: Starting D = starting M	*	*	o	o
	H_0: Starting W = starting M	o	o	o	o
Week-specific	H_0: Starting D = starting W	o	*	**	***
	H_0: Starting D = starting M	*	o	o	o
	H_0: Starting W = starting M	***	***	***	***
Week-typical	H_0: Starting D = starting W	o	*	o	o
	H_0: Starting D = starting M	o	o	o	*
	H_0: Starting W = starting M	o	o	o	o
Month-specific	H_0: Starting D = starting W	o	o	o	*
	H_0: Starting D = starting M	**	o	**	*
	H_0: Starting W = starting M	o	o	o	o
Month-typical	H_0: Starting D = starting W	o	o	o	o
	H_0: Starting D = starting M	o	o	o	o
	H_0: Starting W = starting M	o	o	o	o
Year-specific	H_0: Starting D = starting W	o	o	o	o
	H_0: Starting D = starting M	o	o	o	o
	H_0: Starting W = starting M	o	o	o	o
Year-typical	H_0: Starting D = starting W	o	o	o	o
	H_0: Starting D = starting M	o	o	o	o
	H_0: Starting W = starting M	o	**	o	o

Notes: Tests use estimates from the hurdle model in table 15.11. The reference distribution in panels A and B is χ^2_3; the reference distribution in panel C is $N(0,1)$.

***The null H_0 is rejected at the 1% level.

**The null H_0 is rejected at the 5% level.

*The null H_0 is rejected at the 10% level.

°The null H_0 is not rejected.

Table 15.13   **Hurdle model: Individual characteristics**

	Debit	Cash	Credit	Check
Female	0.82**	−0.44**	−0.82**	−0.58
	(0.33)	(0.19)	(0.39)	(0.49)
Age 35–54	−0.50	−0.48*	0.11	2.30***
	(0.42)	(0.26)	(0.51)	(0.66)
Age 55+	−3.54***	−1.30***	0.31	5.33***
	(0.37)	(0.26)	(0.49)	(0.74)
Income 35–59k	1.66***	−0.96***	0.73	3.51***
	(0.40)	(0.22)	(0.47)	(0.60)
Income 60k+	2.07***	−0.67***	5.53***	5.92***
	(0.42)	(0.22)	(0.51)	(0.63)
Some college	0.87*	−0.52*	0.07	0.14
	(0.46)	(0.27)	(0.49)	(0.64)
College+	−0.35	0.01	4.35***	1.79***
	(0.46)	(0.27)	(0.52)	(0.67)
ST q2	1.38***	0.68***	2.39***	1.75***
	(0.49)	(0.26)	(0.56)	(0.67)
ST q3	1.00**	1.11***	3.43***	3.12***
	(0.45)	(0.29)	(0.57)	(0.76)
ST q4	1.92***	1.08***	4.37***	6.26***
	(0.51)	(0.32)	(0.67)	(0.94)

Notes: Average partial effects for the control variables used in the hurdle model regression (table 15.11). The $ST\ q(k)$ is an indicator for the kth quartile of the survey time distribution. The omitted categories are Income < 35k, Education ≤ high school, $18 \leq Age < 35$, and the indicator for $SurveyTime \leq q1$. Bootstrap standard errors (500 replications) are clustered at the individual level.
***Significant at the 1 percent level.
**Significant at the 5 percent level.
*Significant at the 10 percent level.

substantially less on cash payments spending, on average, $700 less. Having a college degree appears to have a combined positive effect for credit card and check payments, but it seems to have no impact on the use of debit cards and cash.

The estimated coefficients on age dummies reveal an interesting pattern, too. Relatively older respondents are found to use debit cards and cash less frequently, while relying more on personal checks.[11] Specifically, being in the group of those age fifty-five and over decreases the amount spent by debit card by $3,500, but increases the amount spent using checks by $5,300.

A further interesting result is the effect of survey time on reported payment frequencies and spending habits. As mentioned above, we include in our regression a control for the time taken by the respondent to complete

11. This is consistent with the trends in the use of paper checks documented by Schuh and Stavins (2010).

the questionnaire.[12] We observe a strong, positive relationship between such a variable and both the likelihood of reporting nonzero payments and the amount spent conditional on it being positive. These two effects produce sizable and statistically significant coefficients for the survey time indicators in table 15.13. For instance, passing from the first quartile ($ST q1$ corresponding to five minutes) of the survey time distribution to the fourth ($ST q4$ corresponding to fourteen minutes) increases the reported amount of debit card charges by $2,000 and the one of credit card charges by $4,400. Needless to say, these effects are not necessarily causal. Someone who reports more transactions may need more time to think about the correct number of transactions and the correct total amount than someone whose total number of transactions is lower.

15.4 Conclusion

In this chapter we investigate the role of different time frames (specific or typical recall periods of different length) in survey questions measuring household payment and spending habits. For this purpose, we have designed and fielded an experimental module in the American Life Panel (ALP) where we ask individuals to report the number of their purchases and the amount spent using four common payment instruments, debit cards, cash, credit cards, and personal checks. Three different groups of sample participants are randomly assigned to an entry month (July, August, or September 2011) and interviewed four times during a year, once every quarter. For each method of payment, a sequence of questions elicits spending behavior during a day, week, month, and year. At the time of the first interview, this sequence is randomly assigned to refer to specific time spans or to typical time spans. In all subsequent interviews, a specific sequence becomes a typical sequence and vice versa.

Accounting for all possible payment instruments, we compute that the median (average) consumer makes twenty-two (thirty-six) transactions in the previous month, spending $1,320 ($1,839). In comparison, when asked to refer to a typical month, respondents report twenty-nine (forty) transactions, spending $1,300 ($1,599). Respondents rely more heavily on debit cards and cash to make their transactions, while credit cards and personal checks are used less frequently to pay for relatively large expenses.

---

12. We computed that the questionnaire could be completed in five to ten minutes, depending on the number of payment instruments adopted by the respondent. This is confirmed by the data. The median respondent answered in eight minutes, while respondents at the first and third quartile of the survey time distribution answered in five and fourteen minutes, respectively. In our analysis we exclude all those who completed the questionnaire in less than two minutes— forty-eight—and those who did so over multiple days—187 (in the ALP respondents can pause the survey and resume it later as long as the survey is still "open").

Regression analysis shows that, when referring to short reference periods, such as a day or a week, respondents tend to report higher numbers of payments and amounts spent. Differences between answers to monthly and yearly questions are relatively small. Within a typical framework the probability of reporting nonzero payments increases significantly for debit cards, cash, and credit cards, while there is no differential effect for checks. At the same time, reported amounts spent are systematically lower for typical than for specific reference periods across the four payment instruments.

The present analysis is very preliminary as it only uses the data from the first completed wave of our survey. Further evidence will be provided as data from subsequent waves will become available. Notably, given our experimental design, we will exploit in the future both cross-section and within-subject variations to assess the effect of different time frames on individual reporting behavior.

References

Blundell, R., and C. Meghir. 1987. "Bivariate Alternatives to the Tobit Model." *Journal of Econometrics* 34:179–200.

Cameron, A. C., and P. K. Trivedi. 1998. *Regression Analysis of Count Data*. Cambridge: Cambridge University Press.

Chang, L., and J. A. Krosnick. 2003. "Measuring the Frequency of Regular Behaviors: Comparing the Typical Week to the Past Week." *Sociological Methodology* 33:55–80.

Chesher, A., and M. Irish. 1987. "Residual Analysis in the Grouped and Censored Normal Linear Model." *Journal of Econometrics* 34:33–61.

Deaton, A. 2001. "Survey Design and Poverty Monitoring in India." Working Paper, Research Program in Development Studies, Princeton University.

Deaton, A., and M. Grosh. 2000. "Consumption." In *Designing Household Survey Questionnaires for Developing Countries: Lessons from Ten Years of LSMS Experience*, edited by M. Grosh and P. Glewwe, 91–133. Oxford: Oxford University Press.

Deaton, A., and M. Irish. 1984. "Statistical Models for Zero Expenditures in Household Budgets." *Journal of Public Economics* 23:59–80.

Deaton, A., and V. Kozel. 2005. "Data and Dogma: The Great Indian Poverty Debate." *World Bank Research Observer* 20 (2): 177–99.

Foster, K., E. Meijer, S. Schuh, and M. Zabeck. 2008. "The 2008 Survey of Consumer Payment Choice." Public Policy Discussion Paper no. 09-10, Federal Reserve Bank of Boston.

———. 2009. "The 2009 Survey of Consumer Payment Choice." Public Policy Discussion Paper no. 01-1, Federal Reserve Bank of Boston.

Ham, J., X. Li, and L. Sheppard. 2007. "Correcting for Seam Bias When Estimating Discrete Variable Models, with an Application to Analyzing the Employment Dynamics of Disadvantaged Women in the SIPP." Working Paper, University of Southern California.

Mahalanbois, P. C., and S. B. Sen. 1954. "On Some Aspects of the Indian National Sample Survey." *Bulletin of the International Statistical Institute* 34 (2): 5–14.

Moore, J., N. Bates, J. Pascale, and A. Okon. 2009. "Tackling Seam Bias through Questionnaire Design." In *Methodology of Longitudinal Surveys*, edited by P. Lynn. Hoboken, NJ: John Wiley & Sons.

Rips, L., F. Conrad, and S. Fricker. 2003. "Straightening the Seam Effect in Panel Surveys." *Public Opinion Quarterly* 67 (4): 522–54.

Robin, J. M. 1993. "Econometric Analysis of the Short-Run Fluctuations of Households' Purchases." *Review of Economic Studies* 60:923–34.

Schuh, S., and J. Stavins. 2010. "Why Are (Some) Consumers (Finally) Writing Fewer Checks? The Role of Payment Characteristics." *Journal of Banking and Finance* 34:1745–58.

The Potential Use of In-Home Scanner Technology for Budget Surveys

Andrew Leicester

16.1 Introduction

In-home scanner expenditure data are collected via a barcode reader installed in the home. Information about purchases is collected when participants scan the barcodes of any items brought home. Matched with information on prices, stores, and the characteristics of participants, such data offer in principle a detailed, complete record of purchasing behavior. Scanner data have long been used for marketing studies, and increasingly in the economics literature to explore questions relating to consumer, retailer, and manufacturer behavior (recent examples include Griffith et al. [2009]; Broda, Leibtag, and Weinstein [2009]; Aguiar and Hurst [2007]). For researchers, the appeal of scanner data lies both in the detailed purchase information and in the fact that the data are typically longitudinal (see Parker, Souleles, and Carroll [chapter 3, this volume] for a discussion of the virtues of longitudinal data for research purposes). Panel expenditure data sets are comparatively rare. National budget surveys are usually a cross section, and

Andrew Leicester is a manager in the public policy practice of Frontier Economics.

Funding from the ESRC Centre for the Microeconomic Analysis of Public Policy (RES-544-28-5001) at IFS is gratefully acknowledged. The author would like to thank Chris Carroll and participants at the December 2011 NBER-CRIW conference on Improving the Measurement of Consumer Expenditure in Washington, DC, for useful comments; Kantar Worldpanel for supplying the data on which much of the analysis is based; Kate Davies, Gareth Clancy, and Neil Price from the UK Office for National Statistics (ONS) for advice on national accounts and retail sales data; and Giles Horsfield of the ONS for information on the use of scanners by the ONS. Data from the UK Living Costs and Food Survey 2001/2–2009 are collected by the Office for National Statistics and distributed by the Economic and Social Data Service. Crown copyright material is reproduced with the permission of the Controller of HMSO and the Queen's Printer for Scotland. Views and mistakes are those of the author alone. For acknowledgments, sources of research support, and disclosure of the author's material financial relationships, if any, please see http://www.nber.org/chapters/c12669.ack.

measures of spending in panel data (such as the UK Household Longitudinal Study) tend to be limited and highly aggregated. Panel data offer the chance to explore changes in purchasing behavior in response to shocks or policy interventions. For example, Harding, Leibtag, and Lovenheim (2012) use scanner data to explore the impact of changes in cigarette taxes on prices and consumption. There is also growing interest among policymakers in what can be learned from scanner data. The UK Department for the Environment, Food and Rural Affairs carried out a study of ethical shopping decisions in conjunction with a commercial scanner data collector (DEFRA 2011). Scanners are also starting to feature in noncommercial surveys: the US Department of Agriculture is planning to use scanners, alongside other data collection methods, to record detailed food purchase behavior as part of the Food Acquisition and Purchase Survey (FoodAPS).[1]

The main aims of this chapter are to consider what role home scanner data could play for collecting household expenditure information as part of budget surveys such as the US Consumer Expenditure Survey (CE) or the UK Living Costs and Food Survey (LCF).[2] A limited role is validation. Comparisons of budget survey data to aggregate data have led to increasing concern about the quality of survey expenditure data. However, there has been little scope to make microlevel comparisons since few surveys (besides the budget survey itself) collect detailed spending information. Scanner data offer such a possibility. They also record household expenditures over long periods of time, which allows us to explore how the time-limited nature of budget surveys (the UK LCF records spending over just two weeks) affects the spending patterns that are observed.[3]

A more involved role for home scanner data in budget surveys might be as part of the data collection process itself (Mathiowetz, Olson, and Kennedy 2011). This could involve scanners being used in place of or alongside current survey methods such as paper diaries and recall questions. The key question for statistical agencies is to understand the modal effect of using scanners on the data that is obtained. Comparative studies between scanner and other expenditure data offer some insights here, but fully disentangling modal effects from other differences between surveys (such as demographic and sampling differences) is likely to require experimental methods. Scanner data could also be used for imputation. As a way to reduce respondent burden, some commentators (e.g., Tucker 2011) have suggested asking only limited questions about aggregate category-level expenditure in budget surveys.

---

1. See http://www.ers.usda.gov/Briefing/SNAP/food_aps.htm and Cole (2011).
2. The discussion here represents a condensed version of Leicester (2012), which provides further detail and analysis in a number of areas.
3. This has important implications for attempts to use short-run spending information to make inferences about the distribution of living standards (for example, Attanasio, Battistin, and Leicester 2006; Brewer, Goodman, and Leicester 2006).

Information from other sources such as scanner data could then be used to break these down into detailed spending patterns using imputation methods.

This chapter focuses on how statistical agencies might make use of established home scanner surveys collected by market research companies. An alternative would be for statistical agencies to establish and maintain their own scanner data. While costly, this would offer a number of advantages. It would override concerns about outsourcing part of the data collection process to commercial organizations. It would allow controlled experimentation to explore modal effects. It would ensure that the information on demographics and the statistical properties of the data were of sufficiently high quality to be useful for national statistics and research purposes. We offer some thoughts on the scope for establishing a separate scanner survey in the conclusions.

The rest of the chapter is organized as followed. Section 16.2 describes the data sets that underlie most of our analysis: the UK LCF and home scanner data from Kantar Worldpanel. Section 16.3 briefly surveys the existing literature comparing home scanner data to other data. In section 16.4, we compare food expenditures reported in home scanner data, budget survey data, and national accounts data. We assess the impact of using budget shares taken directly from the budget survey and scanner data as basket weights in calculating food price indices, in place of current weights derived from aggregate expenditure data. We also explore how expenditure patterns vary with the duration for which we observe household spending. Section 16.5 explores the prospects for using detailed spending patterns from home scanner data to impute budget shares for households when all we observe are total expenditures. Section 16.6 offers some overall thoughts and conclusions.

16.2 Data

16.2.1 Living Costs and Food Survey

The Living Costs and Food Survey (LCF) is the main UK source of household budget information. Collected by the Office for National Statistics (ONS), it is an annual cross section of around 6,000 households. The survey has been renamed twice, each time undergoing some structural changes (though the coverage and main methods of the data have remained essentially unchanged). Until 2001 it was the Family Expenditure Survey (FES). It then merged with a second, related survey recording nutritional intake at the household level and became known as the Expenditure and Food Survey (EFS). It was then renamed the LCF in 2008. We use LCF throughout to refer to this data. Sampling is carried out via stratified random sampling, with strata based on region, socioeconomic status, and car ownership. Northern Ireland is oversampled, but survey weights are provided to ensure the weighted sample is nationally representative. The response rate in 2010 was 50 percent; this has declined substantially in recent years.

The data are made up of two main parts. The first is a two-week diary issued to all household members age sixteen and over. Children age seven to fifteen receive a simplified diary.[4] Participants record all their expenditures over the period, attaching till receipts where possible to reduce the extent to which handwritten records of spending have to be maintained. A £10 incentive (£5 for children) is paid for successful completion of the diary. Household members are also interviewed to obtain detailed demographic and income information, as well as data on large irregular purchases (such as furniture and holidays) and regular expenses like household energy and housing payments. Data from the diary and the questionnaire are coded into a large number of separate spending items for each household, all of which are reported on a per-week basis. Details of methods and the main findings are collated each year into an ONS publication *Family Spending.*[5]

16.2.2 Kantar Worldpanel

Kantar is a market research company that operates a number of surveys of consumer behavior, including Worldpanel, which is collected in a number of countries. In Britain, one use of Worldpanel data is to estimate market shares of the major supermarkets.[6] A large, representative sample of households is active in the data at any one time. Until 2006 the average sample size was around 15,000, since then it has risen to around 25,000. Participants are recruited from a range of address sources using quota sampling, though Northern Ireland is excluded. Household weights are derived that ensure that the weighted sample (over a particular period of observation) of active households is representative based on household size, housewife age, social class, and region.

Households can participate for as long as they wish, and receive points redeemable for consumer goods as an incentive to do so. Participating households are issued a barcode reader, which is installed in the home, and are asked to record the purchases of all barcoded products brought home. Our data contain information on "fast-moving consumer goods"—essentially food and grocery products, including things like cleaning products and personal care items. Alcohol (purchased off-licence) is included, but tobacco is not. Leicester (2012) estimates that the set of products contained in the Worldpanel data make up something like 18 percent of all nonhousing expenditure.[7]

---

4. Children were first asked to keep a diary in 1995/6. We use LCF data including spending reported by children, since in principle children's purchases should also be captured in scanner data.

5. The report on the 2010 LCF data is available from http://www.ons.gov.uk/ons/rel/family-spending/family-spending/family-spending-2011–edition/family-spending-2011–pdf.pdf.

6. See http://www.kantarworldpanel.com/.

7. His analysis suggests that just over one-third of all spending would be amenable to in-home scanning.

Purchases from all retailers, not just supermarkets, are in principle recorded, as are online grocery purchases. The data are at the transaction level—typically up to a million separate transactions are recorded in a week of data. Detailed information on the characteristics of the products purchased is recorded, including the macronutritional composition of food items. Until 2006, all households were asked to report nonbarcoded food and grocery purchases using a booklet of generic barcodes. Details of the product characteristics for these items (such as weight, country of origin, flavor, and so on) were also entered manually via the scanner device. This increases responder burden, and so since 2006 some households were no longer required to report these items and were issued with a simpler scanner unit. Information on the price paid is obtained from till receipts that are mailed in to Kantar, who match the price to the purchase record. Where no receipts are available, prices are taken from centralized databases of store- and product-specific prices, or otherwise imputed. The data also record any promotional deal attached to a purchase. Information on the store visited is recorded by the participants.

Household demographic characteristics are recorded in a baseline telephone interview, and then updated every nine months or so. The set of demographic questions is typically much less comprehensive than those recorded in the LCF, and an interview is held only with the "main shopper" in each household rather than with each household member separately. All household members should, though, report their expenditures.

16.2.3 Mapping Kantar Expenditure Data to LCF Data

The Kantar data are reported at the barcode level. There are more than 568,000 individual products. The LCF records household-level expenditures in a large number of fairly disaggregated expenditure codes. Making comparisons requires us to match individual products from the Kantar data into equivalent LCF expenditure codes. We use detailed information on the sorts of products that make up each expenditure code supplied with the LCF documentation, and the detailed product characteristics in the Kantar data, to make this match as accurately as possible, though inevitably there is some judgement in this process. Having created this mapping, we then further aggregate expenditures into commodity groups to match those defined in the UK Consumer Prices Index (CPI). This definition matches the level at which disaggregated expenditure information is available from the national accounts, making comparisons to aggregate data more straightforward. Our analysis covers only food and drink purchases.

In principle, of course, when making comparisons across data sets, we could look at much more disaggregate commodity groups. The LCF includes seventy-three distinct food and drink codes, so this would be the most disaggregate comparison possible.[8] Finer disaggregation may be useful to under-

---

8. Statistical agencies would, of course, have access to even more disaggregate budget survey data.

stand exactly where differences between scanner and other data sets arise and what might be driving that. However, as discussed in Leicester and Oldfield (2009), the more disaggregate the comparison the less confident we can be about the mapping between Kantar and LCF expenditures. The problems are particularly acute where it is not clear in the Kantar product information whether meats, fish, fruits, and vegetables are "fresh" (largely meaning unadulterated, so including, for example, plain frozen fish fillets) or "processed" (largely meaning they are preprepared or flavored in some way). Fresh and processed products have distinct LCF codes but fall into the same CPI groups, such that at the CPI level of aggregation there is more certainty that we are comparing like-with-like (spending on fish or meat, say).

16.3 Previous Research

This chapter adds to a small but growing literature exploring data quality issues for home scanner data. There is a parallel literature on "storescan" data collected from items passing through tills. There are clearly complementarities between store-level and consumer-level scanner data. Store-level scanner data might be employed for some of the uses to which budget survey data are put. In a previous NBER volume, Feenstra and Shapiro (2003) considered the possible usefulness of store-level scanner data for measuring prices and price indices, and provides a good introduction to such data.

A number of previous studies have compared home scanner data to budget survey data. Any regularities that emerge from these comparisons would be strongly suggestive of survey mode effects from the use of scanners. However, definitive statements about modal effects would require experimental evidence, which held, as far as possible, other factors constant. Such evidence does not appear to exist at the moment. A valuable contribution from statistical agencies collecting their own scanner survey data would be the ability to carry out controlled experimental analysis.

The strongest common finding is that average expenditure levels are markedly lower in scanner data than in budget survey data. Duly et al. (2003) compare AC Nielsen Homescan data to CE diary survey data from 2000. Overall, scanner expenditures were about two-thirds of the budget survey level. Alcohol and tobacco expenditures were about half the budget survey level in the scanner data. Using British data from Kantar Worldpanel and the Living Costs and Food Survey, Leicester and Oldfield (2009) find that, in 2005, weekly total food expenditures in scanner data were about 20 percent below those in budget surveys on average. Using comparisons of nutritional intake, Griffith and O'Connell (2009) find that the number of calories reported in British scanner data were around 23—52 percent lower than in budget survey data depending on the household type studied. They find strong evidence, as do we below, that a large part of this gap is driven by weeks in which no food at all is purchased in scanner data, though it does not account for all of the difference.

Previous studies have not found common results on the extent to which this under-reporting in scanner data is consistent across product categories. Using US data from 2002–2005, Zhen et al. (2009) find scanner expenditures 50 percent below CE levels for a number of commodity groups, particularly categories where nonbarcoded items are common such as meat, fruit, vegetables, and fish. For groups where almost all items are barcoded, such as confectionery and processed fruits, they find essentially no differences in expenditure. In contrast, Leicester and Oldfield (2009) find little evidence in British data of significant differences across groups, with the exception of alcohol. One likely reason for the difference is that in the US data, only 20 percent of households were required to record nonbarcoded items, whereas all households in the British data were asked to do so. Leicester and Old-field (2009) can explore this directly, since from 2006 only some households were asked to report nonbarcoded purchases. They find this has a substantial effect. Households reporting their nonbarcoded purchases recorded 24 percent less expenditure on fruit than found in budget surveys; those not reporting them recorded 44 percent less spending.

There is also disagreement on the extent to which demographic differences between samples help account for the lower expenditures in scanner data. Zhen et al. (2009) use a regression model to strip out observable demographic differences between data sets and argue that, in combination with the nonbarcoded items issue, they largely account for the spending differences. Leicester and Oldfield (2009) conclude that demographic differences *accentuate* the gaps between data sets. They estimate a "propensity weight" for each household in the Worldpanel data, which reflects how similar its observed demographics are to those of LCF households. Using this weight, they find that the average gap between total spending in the two data sets rises from 20 percent to 25 percent. These contrasting findings probably result in part from differences across countries in the relative sample compositions between scanner and budget survey data. For example, in the United States, scanner households appear to have fewer members on average than those in the budget survey (Huffman and Jensen 2004) while the reverse is true in Britain (Leicester and Oldfield 2009). The contrast may also reflect differences in the set of observable demographics common to scanner and budget survey data sets. The demographic information available in scanner data is often much less comprehensive than that found in budget surveys. Kantar Worldpanel, for example, did not routinely collect information on household incomes until 2008, and even then only a banded measure of gross total income is collected from a single question asked of the main shopper. By contrast, the LCF contains detailed questions on unbanded incomes by source for each household member. Similarly, information in the Worldpanel on education and employment status are not consistently collected for each adult household member, and common variables like tenure are also not always reported.

A particular problem noted by Leicester and Oldfield (2009) was poor reporting of demographic *transitions* over time in the Kantar data. For example, using data from 2002 to 2005, they find that among a sample of households headed by someone employed and age fifty or over, just 2.9 percent were observed to be unemployed a year later. This compared to 11.4 percent of a similar sample constructed from the British Household Panel Survey (BHPS), the main panel data set in the United Kingdom. There does not appear to be similar evidence from any study of other scanner panels that would shed light on whether this issue was common to scanner data in general or particular to the Kantar Worldpanel.

The main lessons from these findings seem to be that scanner data record less spending than budget surveys, but differences in methods across scanner data sets lead to different conclusions about the extent to which this is driven by observable factors rather than being a modal effect of scanner data *per se*. Thus any statistical agency (or indeed researcher) planning to use scanner data ought to be aware in detail of the methods that underlie its collection and what that might mean for the data that are collected. There would appear to be a strong case for collaboration between statistical agencies, researchers, and data collectors to better understand these issues. Without experimental methods, the next best approach to tease out modal effects may be to try and make comparisons of scanner and budget survey data across countries that follow, as closely as possible, identical methodologies to see which findings are robust.

Aside from comparisons to budget survey data, some papers have attempted to explore reporting issues in scanner data more directly. Einav, Leibtag, and Nevo (2008) perform a detailed matching exercise of shopping trips at a particular store, comparing purchases reported in Homescan data to what should be the same shopping trips in loyalty card records. They find that 20 percent or so of trips recorded in Homescan were not found in the retailer data, and that around half the trips that were reported in the retailer data were not observed in Homescan. On matched trips, the scanner data reported on average 10–15 percent fewer items, mostly small consumables that may be consumed before entering the home. The authors found significant problems in reporting prices in scanner data. The price reported in the Homescan record failed to match the loyalty card recorded price about half the time. However, this appears to be a particular problem with the way in which prices are imputed into Homescan data based on centralized records of chain week-level prices. This means store- or consumer-specific prices are missed in Homescan. In British Worldpanel data, prices are taken from till receipts and are rarely imputed.[9] Einav,

---

9. Where receipts are not sent in, imputation methods may be used. Since national supermarket chains in the United Kingdom all use national pricing, this imputation should still capture chain-level deals and promotions, though individual discounts from coupons or loyalty cards would be missed.

Leibtag, and Nevo (2008) recommend that a similar approach be adopted for Homescan.

With in-home scanners, there may concern about people taking some time to adapt to the technology before they report reliable data. Leicester and Oldfield (2009) find that reported expenditures were highest in the first few weeks of participation. After about six months, households spent about 5 percent less than in their first week, on average. This might be evidence of survey fatigue, with households being less assiduous about reporting all their spending after the initial novelty wears off. It might also be evidence of a settling-in process in which households make small errors early on (multiple recording, say), which inflate expenditures relative to their true values. It could also be a genuine behavioral reaction to participation. For statistical agencies thinking about scanner data for budget surveys, the interesting comparison is with the current survey approach. Ahmed, Brzozowski, and Crossley (2006) find that in the Canadian Food Expenditure Survey, spending drops by 9 percent between the first and second week, on average.

A further issue relates to quota sampling methods used in scanner data (Tucker 2011; Zhen et al. 2009; USDA 2009; Harris 2005) rather than random probability or stratified sampling used in budget surveys. Westat (2011b) and Perloff and Denbaly (2007) are both critical of commercial scanner data collectors for releasing little information on sampling methods, response rates, attrition rates and so on, and suggest caution in relying on existing scanner data for these reasons.

A final point relates to *unobservable* differences in the characteristics of households who participate in scanner data and budget surveys. If significant, such differences could have important repercussions for spending records and researchers. Lusk and Brooks (2011) find that households in two large US scanner samples, Homescan and IRI, appear to be more price responsive than the population at large, even conditional on observable characteristics. They offer two possible explanations. First, participating in scanner data may make households more aware of their purchasing behavior and thus more price sensitive. Second, those who agree to participate in scanner data may be a self-selected sample of more price conscious households. Of course, these findings do not tell us whether the participation and self-selection effects are greater in scanner data than in budget surveys, which would be an interesting extension. A fascinating study would be to estimate demand models using budget survey data and scanner data aggregated to the same level to see whether they give similar results.

16.4 Comparing Scanner and Other Expenditure Data

Surveys of household expenditure are prone to error. Participants could deliberately or accidentally misreport their purchases, or change their usual shopping behavior as a result of participation. Data validation is therefore vital. Without any clear way to obtain a "gold standard" benchmark of actual expenditures against which to compare surveys, the most promising approach to validation is to compare data sources against one another to see whether they provide different impressions of spending levels, patterns, and trends.

In this section, we make two distinct sets of comparisons. First, we compare survey data from Kantar Worldpanel and the LCF to aggregate data from the ONS national accounts. Second, we make microlevel comparisons between the two surveys. In each case we explore not just total spending, but also expenditure patterns. Differences in total spending will matter for issues like living standards and inequality where spending is used as a measure of well-being. But in some cases it is the pattern of spending that matters— for example, in deriving expenditure weights for price indices or estimating demand models. Comparisons of both are therefore important.

16.4.1 Comparison to National Expenditure Aggregates

Several recent papers explore the quality of budget survey data by comparing them to aggregate expenditure data. Examples in the United States include Triplett (1997), Slesnick (2001), Attanasio, Battistin, and Leicester (2006), and in the United Kingdom include Tanner (1998), Blow, Leicester, and Smith (2004), Attanasio et al. (2006), and O'Dea and Crossley (2010). Key findings from these studies are:

- Spending reported in the US CE makes up about 70 percent of aggregate levels. In the UK LCF, the figure is around 80 percent. Both have worsened over time. The decline in UK coverage is particularly noticeable from the early 1990s.
- Similar trends occur for food at home. In the United States, coverage fell from more than 75 percent in the 1980s to around 65 percent early in the first decade of the twenty-first century. In the United Kingdom, coverage fell from more than 95 percent in the 1970s to less than 90 early in the first decade of the twenty-first century.

We focus on food at home and off-licence alcohol expenditures in the UK National Accounts (NA) and compare them to spending reported in the LCF and, for the first time, Kantar Worldpanel data.[10] We are not aware of other papers that have made similar comparisons of scanner data to national spending figures in this way. Our interest is not just in how much total aggregate expenditure is reported in the surveys, but also in whether trends over time are similar. There are a number of reasons why we would expect food spending to be higher in NA data than survey data. The NA figures include expenditures by people living in nonhousing accommodation (student halls,

---

10. For information on data used to compile NA expenditure figures, see Office for National Statistics (2010a).

old age homes, army barracks, and so on) and spending by tourists in the United Kingdom, which are not included in the surveys. The NA figures are also based on UK-wide expenditures (including Northern Ireland). Since the Kantar data covers only Great Britain (excluding Northern Ireland), for consistency across surveys we also look at LCF data for Great Britain.

To make the comparisons, we need to aggregate the LCF and Kantar survey data to national totals. The LCF reports weekly household-level expenditure by commodity group and provides sampling weights for each household, which gross up the data to national figures. Thus we convert weekly expenditure figures to annual figures (multiplying by fifty-two) and use the weights to generate national annual expenditures. In the Kantar data, sampling weights are provided for each household covering different periods of time (e.g., four weeks, fifty-two weeks). Households who fail to report expenditures consistently over that period are assigned a zero weight, with the weights of other households adjusted such that the figures gross up to national totals. We calculate total aggregated expenditures by commodity over a series of four-week periods using the appropriate weights. These are then further aggregated into annual totals by adding up the thirteen four-week periods that generate a fifty-two-week "year," which closely (though not perfectly) covers a single calendar year.[11] We convert aggregated figures to weekly averages.

Figure 16.1 shows average total weekly food and drink expenditure in the NA and the survey data sets between 2002 and 2009, the period for which full-year comparisons can be made. Figure 16.2 reports year-on-year growth rates.

Levels of spending in the LCF are about 79 to 81 percent of those in NA data.[12] Those in the Kantar data are about 51 to 53 percent of NA values. Looking at growth rates, there is much more volatility in the LCF. Aggregate spending on food and drink grew by around 8 percent between 2005 and 2006, a spike not seen in other data. The NA and Kantar figures suggest a sharp slowdown in spending in 2009, but this is not reflected in the LCF data. There is no evidence that the Kantar data perform worse than the LCF when compared to NA data. Indeed, the larger sample size in the Kantar data mitigates the volatility in growth rates observed in the LCF. Such volatility cautions against making year-on-year inferences about changes in living standards from consumption changes in the LCF.

Table 16.1 disaggregates total food expenditures in the surveys and NA into groups based on CPI commodity definitions. Figures are shown for

---

11. For example, the period labeled 2002 in the Kantar figures covers Jan. 7th 2002—Jan. 5th 2003.

12. This is not simply because of geography—the absence of Northern Ireland from the survey data is not nearly enough to account for the lower spending. In 2009, for example, we find LCF expenditures are 81 percent of those reported in the NA; adding Northern Ireland back in raises this to just 83 percent.

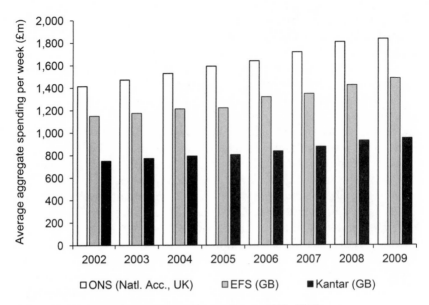

Fig. 16.1 Gross weekly food and drink expenditures, 2002–2009
Source: Calculated from UK Office for National Statistics Data, LCF data, and Kantar Worldpanel.

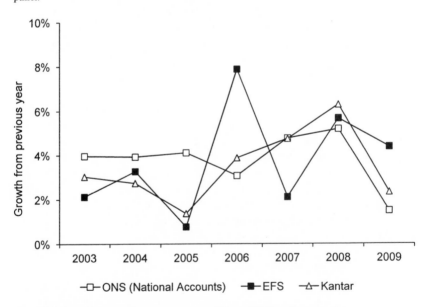

Fig. 16.2 Growth rates of aggregate expenditure, ONS and survey data
Source: Calculated from UK Office for National Statistics Data, LCF data, and Kantar Worldpanel.

Table 16.1   Gross expenditures by commodity in national accounts, LCF, and Kantar data (2002 and 2009)

| | £ million/week | | | | | | Ratios | | | | | |
| | 2002 | | | 2009 | | | LCF/NA | | Kantar/NA | | Kantar/LCF | |
	NA	LCF	Kantar	NA	LCF	Kantar	2002 (%)	2009 (%)	2002 (%)	2009 (%)	2002 (%)	2009 (%)
Total	*1,413.6*	*1,149.3*	*749.0*	*1,833.5*	*1,484.0*	*951.2*	*81*	*81*	*53*	*52*	*65*	*64*
Food	**1,057.5**	**922.4**	**620.9**	**1,377.3**	**1,209.3**	**787.5**	**87**	**88**	**59**	**57**	**67**	**65**
Bread and cereals	176.9	177.9	120.5	230.8	234.0	156.4	101	101	68	68	68	67
Meat	248.3	227.3	155.2	315.7	284.1	182.4	92	90	62	58	68	64
Fish	46.1	44.4	27.8	56.6	58.3	35.7	96	103	60	63	63	61
Milk, cheese, and eggs	145.6	125.6	84.1	210.0	180.7	120.2	86	86	58	57	67	67
Oils and fats	24.2	21.1	15.4	28.7	28.5	20.7	87	99	64	72	73	73
Fruit	87.2	74.1	47.8	125.6	99.4	59.5	85	79	55	47	65	60
Vegetables	166.5	142.3	97.6	208.5	182.8	118.9	85	88	59	57	69	65
Sugar and confectionery	134.8	66.3	43.4	160.9	80.4	56.4	49	50	32	35	66	70
Other food	27.9	43.3	29.0	40.6	61.3	37.3	155	151	104	92	67	61
Beverages	**141.7**	**86.3**	**58.8**	**183.9**	**103.1**	**71.4**	**61**	**56**	**41**	**39**	**68**	**69**
Coffee, tea, and cocoa	35.1	25.7	18.3	47.3	29.5	21.4	73	62	52	45	71	73
Fruit juices and soft drinks	106.6	60.6	40.4	136.6	73.7	50.0	57	54	38	37	67	68
Alcohol	**214.4**	**140.5**	**69.3**	**272.3**	**171.6**	**92.3**	**66**	**63**	**32**	**34**	**49**	**54**
Spirits	55.8	28.1	18.9	74.9	32.7	24.4	50	44	34	33	67	75
Wines, cider, and perry	103.2	75.8	34.8	131.1	98.3	49.0	74	75	34	37	46	50
Beer	55.4	36.6	15.7	66.4	40.6	19.0	66	61	28	29	43	47

Source: Author's calculations from ONS, LCF, and Kantar Worldpanel data.

Notes: NA = national accounts, LCF = Living Costs and Food Survey. The LCF and Kantar data are for Great Britain, while NA data are for the United Kingdom (including Northern Ireland). The LCF and Kantar data are converted to gross national annual totals using supplied household sampling weights; all data are then expressed as weekly average expenditures.

2002 and 2009, the start and end of our comparison period. Food items are better reported than either alcohol or nonalcoholic beverages in both survey data sets. The relative underreporting of drinks compared to food is striking.[13] Interestingly, the LCF data appear, if anything, relatively worse at recording nonalcoholic drinks than alcoholic drinks, while the reverse is true in the Kantar data. Within food, spending on bread and fish appears to be particularly well captured in survey data. There appears to be some issue in how sugar and confectionery products are reported as well as "other food." Given what appear to be high relative reports of survey expenditure on other food and low reports of sugar and confectionery, it could be some coding issue where items that are included in the NA definition of confectionery are included in the LCF definition of other food. It is not clear what drives this, and we cannot drill down into the NA figures in more detail. In principle, the LCF expenditure codes should map directly on to the NA commodity codes, since both use the COICOP (Classification of Individual Consumption by Purpose) categorization method. Since we map the Kantar products onto LCF codes, these too should then translate directly into comparable NA commodities.

Comparing across the LCF and Kantar data sets, those commodities that are relatively well reported in one also tend to be relatively well reported in the other. The most notable differences come in alcohol, where reported Kantar spending is relatively lower than reported LCF spending. Within alcohol there are differences, too: for example, the LCF does comparatively badly at recording spirits purchases, capturing just 44 percent of NA expenditure (compared to 61 percent for beer and 75 percent for wine). In the Kantar data, it is beer that is least well recorded (29 percent of NA spending). This could be due to the way the data is collected. In the LCF, each household member has an individual diary to fill out. In the Kantar data, while in principle each household member should record items brought home, in practice it may be that main shopping trips are well reported while those carried out by secondary shoppers are less well captured. If main shoppers are mostly female and men buy more beer, this might explain this finding.

{insert table 16.1 about here}

Comparing results for 2002 and 2009 tells us where survey expenditure measures have grown more or less quickly than those in the NA. A noticeable shift occurs for oils and fats, where spending growth was much faster in the both surveys than the NA. This is driven by a sharp fall of around 15 percent in spending between 2008 and 2009 in the NA, with much smaller declines in the surveys. There is also a relative decline in both surveys for

13. By 2009 only 54 percent of soft drink expenditure in the NA was captured in the LCF, compared to 75 percent of wine expenditure and 61 percent of beer expenditure. Much attention has been paid to the relative underrecording of alcohol in surveys, but these results show the same is also true of soft drinks.

fruit spending. Again, this is driven mostly by a single year: fruit spending grew by more than 16 percent in 2005 in the NA data, but only by around 7 percent in the two surveys. Detailed figures for spending ratios and growth rates in each year for each commodity are available on request, but broadly the conclusion from earlier that (a) spending growth is more volatile in the LCF than either the NA or Kantar data sources and that (b) there is no clear "winner" between the LCF and Kantar as to which tracks growth rates observed in the NA holds across commodities as well.

16.4.2 Comparing Scanner and Budget Survey Expenditure Data

We now make detailed comparisons between the survey measures of spending from Kantar and the LCF. This analysis is useful not only as a way to compare, contrast, and validate the different expenditure surveys, but also to inform us about how useful existing scanner data might be for imputing detailed expenditures into budget survey data (see section 16.5). If we find that expenditure *patterns* are very different in the Worldpanel and LCF, we might be less confident about using scanner data to try and predict detailed expenditures in the survey data given high-level information on total outlays.

When making cross-data set comparisons, it is important to bear in mind that they are collected in very different ways. The LCF is recorded over two weeks based on diaries kept by each household member. Respondents are contacted at least once during the two-week period to check for any problems filling in the diary, and a thorough check is made of the diaries at the end of the period to ensure they have been properly completed (Ayers, Hossack, and Payne 2010). In the Kantar data, each household can participate for as long as they wish. They are contacted every nine months or so to check that demographic information is up to date, but in general attempts to ensure good compliance are limited. Thus if we want to compare average spending levels and patterns in the LCF to those in the Kantar data, the crucial issue is what sample of households we select from the Kantar data, over what period of time we choose to observe them, and how we deal with seeming periods of noncompliance. Leicester and Oldfield (2009), for example, look at average weekly expenditures in the Kantar data among households who report spending in at least four separate weeks (not necessarily consecutive) in a given year. They include only those weeks in which some spending is observed. On this basis, they find that average total food and drink expenditures were about 25 percent lower in the Kantar data than in the LCF data in 2005, once observable demographic differences in the samples were taken into account.[14]

---

14. They find a smaller gap of around 16 percent when comparing the first two full weeks of expenditure for households newly signed up to the Kantar data (again excluding cases where either week includes zero expenditure). This could reflect the fatigue issue mentioned earlier, which sees recorded spending drop off slightly with the length of participation.

Sample Selection

Our main comparisons between LCF and Kantar data cover calendar year 2009.[15] In the LCF, we exclude all households in Northern Ireland to ensure the geographical coverage of the two data sets is comparable. This gives a sample size of 5,220 households.

In the Kantar data, a total of 26,655 separate households are observed making at least one purchase in 2009. We look first at households who, according to the dates at which they signed up to and dropped out of the survey, were active during the whole period. This gives a "nondropout" sample of 21,093 households (79.1 percent of the full sample). As an additional selection, we also condition on households who have no reporting gap (period during which no food and drink expenditures at all are recorded) exceeding six weeks.[16] While this threshold is somewhat arbitrary, the intention is to try and exclude households who do not appear to be fully compliant over the whole year. Shorter periods of nonreporting might be reconciled as holiday periods, for example, but it seems somewhat unlikely that many households would legitimately purchase no food items for that long.

This "regular reporter" sample includes 15,781 households. Leicester (2012) shows that households excluded by this sample selection are significantly more likely to be in London, be headed by someone under forty or over sixty years of age, be headed by a female, to have larger numbers of adults or children, and to have missing demographic information either on income, employment status, or the number of cars. Households who are not required to report nonbarcoded items are significantly *more* likely to be part of the regular reporter sample, which suggests that the reduced respondent burden may encourage households to report spending consistently. Income and employment status have no independent effects on the likelihood of selection into this sample. The fact that our preferred regular reporter sample is clearly a nonrandom set of all Kantar households should be kept in mind when comparing raw expenditures. Later in this section, we condition on observable demographics across the data sets to see how far they can explain spending differences.[17]

Comparisons of Average Expenditure and Budget Shares

Table 16.2 shows average expenditures per week, by CPI commodity, from the LCF and Kantar data during 2009. To strip out the effects of household

15. As in the comparison to national accounts aggregates, we use a fifty-two-week Kantar period, which does not quite overlap with the calendar year, running from December 29th, 2008, until December 27th, 2009.
16. We do not consider whether or not households buy nonfood items during this period.
17. In the Kantar data, we observe household spending over a full-year period. We have demographic data once a year for each household that are updated roughly each November. For the 2009 sample, then, the demographics refer to November 2008 values.

Table 16.2   Weekly average equivalized expenditure levels by CPI commodity group, LCF, and Kantar (2009)

	LCFS		Non-dropouts		Kantar					
	2 weeks		2 weeks		Regular reporters				Longest continuous	
					2 weeks		52 weeks			
	Mean	SD	Mean	SD	Mean	SD	Mean	SD	Mean	SD
Bread and cereals	8.51	5.20	5.65	4.63	6.34	4.54	6.36	2.98	7.17	3.24
Meat	10.65	8.73	6.78	6.86	7.64	6.94	7.60	4.64	8.54	5.17
Fish	2.25	3.43	1.33	2.20	1.50	2.28	1.51	1.40	1.70	1.65
Milk, cheese, and eggs	6.75	4.48	4.38	3.71	4.96	3.67	4.97	2.55	5.61	2.77
Oils and fats	1.08	1.23	0.78	1.07	0.88	1.11	0.88	0.61	0.98	0.71
Fruit	3.81	3.94	2.19	2.91	2.48	3.04	2.48	2.25	2.83	2.57
Vegetables	6.81	4.87	4.32	3.95	4.86	3.94	4.88	2.70	5.56	3.08
Sugars, confectionery	3.01	3.32	2.06	2.90	2.34	3.03	2.34	1.76	2.61	2.04
Other food	2.23	3.46	1.35	1.65	1.50	1.67	1.51	0.91	1.69	1.11
Food	*45.10*	*24.03*	*28.82*	*20.82*	*32.50*	*19.87*	*32.53*	*13.56*	*36.70*	*14.32*
Coffee, tea, and cocoa	1.15	1.68	0.82	1.51	0.94	1.58	0.94	0.85	1.05	0.99
Mineral water, soft drinks	2.58	2.77	1.78	2.35	1.98	2.40	1.98	1.67	2.24	1.92
Beverages	*3.73*	*3.31*	*2.60*	*2.95*	*2.92*	*2.99*	*2.92*	*1.92*	*3.29*	*2.19*
Spirits	1.36	4.69	0.94	4.05	1.06	4.32	1.09	3.07	1.17	3.48
Wine	3.81	10.44	1.90	5.32	2.17	5.67	2.17	4.17	2.42	4.82
Beer	1.45	3.89	0.77	2.97	0.86	3.19	0.85	2.04	0.96	2.43
Alcohol	*6.63*	*13.05*	*3.61*	*8.40*	*4.10*	*8.88*	*4.11*	*6.52*	*4.56*	*7.44*
Total spending	**55.46**	**31.28**	**35.03**	**26.03**	**39.52**	**25.03**	**39.56**	**17.18**	**44.56**	**18.29**
No. of households	5,220		21,093.00		15,781		15,781		15,781	
Percent zero weeks	2.7		21.7		13.2		13.2		0.0	
Avg. nonzero weeks/hh	1.95		1.57		1.74		45.13		25.10	

Source: Author's calculations from 2009 Kantar Worldpanel and LCF 2009.

Note: Expenditures are equivalized using the before housing costs–modified OECD scale.

composition, expenditures are equivalized using the before housing costs-modified Organisation for Economic Co-operation and Development (OECD) equivalence scale.[18] We look at a number of different Kantar samples. First, we take the "no dropout" sample and pick a random consecutive two-week period (matching the LCF diary period) over which to observe expenditures. This approach assumes that weeks in which households record no food spending are accurate reflections of true purchasing behavior. We then make the additional selection described above and drop households with long reporting gaps. Within this sample, we look at average weekly spending when we choose observation periods of different length.[19] Finally, for each Kantar household in this sample, we select the longest consecutive set of weeks containing any recorded expenditure at all. This, in effect, assumes that all weeks in which zero spending is recorded are inaccurate. The mean duration of observation in this sample is 25.1 weeks.

Average household weekly equivalized food and drink expenditures in 2009 were £55.46 in the LCF. Expenditures in the Kantar data were lower for all samples. For the no dropout sample observed over two weeks, expenditures were £35.03, almost 37 percent below the LCF figure. Excluding those with long gaps in reporting, average spending rises to £39.52 (29 percent below the LCF figure) when households are observed over a random two weeks or £39.56 observed over the full fifty-two weeks. It is striking how little difference there is in average expenditures when households are observed for a full year rather than a single two-week period, though the standard deviation of expenditures falls markedly. We return to this issue shortly. Finally, once we ignore zero spending weeks altogether, average spending rises to £44.56, a gap of just under 20 percent compared to LCF levels.

These figures make clear that the treatment of weeks in which zero expenditure is reported is hugely important. Around half of the gap between Kantar and LCF expenditures is eliminated once we strip these weeks out. The greater propensity for zero spending weeks in the Kantar data than the LCF is striking and should be a priority for further analysis. It could reflect households who have effectively attrited but not formally dropped out. However, many households have reporting behavior that is not consistent with this—for example, they report nothing for a few weeks then start scanning again. Understanding what drives this in scanner data would be useful.

Table 16.3 shows Kantar expenditures relative to LCF expenditures for various sample definitions, and table 16.4 shows the expenditures in terms of budget shares. Even if average expenditures are lower in the scanner data, if the extent of underreporting is quite consistent such that the patterns of expenditure are similar, this acts as a useful validation (of both data sources)

18. See appendix A of Jin et al. (2011) for details of equivalence scales.
19. Results over two and fifty-two weeks are shown; figures for periods of four, twelve, and twenty-six weeks essentially show the same results and are available on request.

Table 16.3   **Kantar as a proportion of LCF expenditure (2009)**

	All	Regular reporters		
	2 weeks (%)	2 weeks (%)	52 weeks (%)	Longest (%)
Bread and cereals	66.4	74.5	74.7	84.3
Meat	63.7	71.7	71.4	80.2
Fish	59.1	66.7	67.1	75.6
Milk, cheese, and eggs	64.9	73.5	73.6	83.1
Oils and fats	72.2	81.5	81.5	90.7
Fruit	57.5	65.1	65.1	74.3
Vegetables	63.4	71.4	71.7	81.6
Sugars, confectionery	68.4	77.7	77.7	86.7
Other food	60.5	67.3	67.7	75.8
Food	*63.9*	*72.1*	*72.1*	*81.4*
Coffee, tea, and cocoa	71.3	81.7	81.7	91.3
Mineral water, soft drinks	69.0	76.7	76.7	86.8
Beverages	*69.7*	*78.3*	*78.3*	*88.2*
Spirits	69.1	77.9	80.1	86.0
Wine	49.9	57.0	57.0	63.5
Beer	53.1	59.3	58.6	66.2
Alcohol	*54.4*	*61.8*	*62.0*	*68.8*
Total spending	**63.2**	**71.3**	**71.3**	**80.3**

Source: Author's calculations from 2009 Kantar Worldpanel and LCF 2009.

Note: Expenditures are equivalized using the before housing costs-modified OECD scale.

and gives us more confidence in trying to use scanner data as a means to impute detailed budget shares from aggregate expenditure data.

From table 16.3, several features emerge. The average proportion of LCF expenditures reported in the Kantar data rises for all commodities as we remove the impact of zero-spending weeks. Once again, observing households for two weeks or fifty-two weeks makes little difference to the average proportion. Using the "longest uninterrupted" measure of Kantar spending (right-most column of table 16.3), relative to LCF spending, Kantar expenditure levels match up most closely for nonalcoholic beverages and least closely for alcohol. Food spending is somewhere between. There are differences across disaggregate commodities: for example, the Kantar data picks up about 75 percent as much spending on average for fish, fruit, and other foods than the LCF, but about 90 percent of the expenditure on oils and fats, and coffee and tea. Differences across alcohol types are particularly clear.

Expressed as shares of the total food and drink budget, table 16.4 makes it clear that the particular sample selected from the Kantar data makes very little difference to the pattern of expenditure observed. Comparing LCF budget shares to those from the uninterrupted Kantar sample also reveals relatively small differences. For any single commodity, the largest difference

Table 16.4   Food and drink budget shares, by survey (2009)

| | LCFS | Kantar | | | |
| | | All | Regular reporters | | |
	2 weeks (%)	2 weeks (%)	2 weeks (%)	52 weeks (%)	Longest (%)
Bread and cereals	15.3	16.1	16.0	16.1	16.1
Meat	19.2	19.4	19.3	19.2	19.2
Fish	4.1	3.8	3.8	3.8	3.8
Milk, cheese, and eggs	12.2	12.5	12.6	12.6	12.6
Oils and fats	1.9	2.2	2.2	2.2	2.2
Fruit	6.9	6.3	6.3	6.3	6.4
Vegetables	12.3	12.3	12.3	12.3	12.5
Sugars, confectionery	5.4	5.9	5.9	5.9	5.9
Other food	4.0	3.9	3.8	3.8	3.8
Food	*81.3*	*82.3*	*82.2*	*82.2*	*82.4*
Coffee, tea, and cocoa	2.1	2.3	2.4	2.4	2.4
Mineral water, soft drinks	4.7	5.1	5.0	5.0	5.0
Beverages	*6.7*	*7.4*	*7.4*	*7.4*	*7.4*
Spirits	2.5	2.7	2.7	2.8	2.6
Wine	6.9	5.4	5.5	5.5	5.4
Beer	2.6	2.2	2.2	2.1	2.2
Alcohol	*12.0*	*10.3*	*10.4*	*10.4*	*10.2*

Source: Author's calculations from 2009 Kantar Worldpanel and LCF 2009.

in budget share is for wine, which makes up on average 5.4 percent of food and drink spending in the Kantar data, but 6.9 percent of spending in the LCF. In the opposite direction, bread and cereals make up 16.1 percent of total Kantar food and drink spending compared to 15.3 percent of LCF spending.

These results are for 2009, but figures from earlier years are not very different. Figure 16.3 shows average equivalized weekly expenditures in the Kantar data (based on the uninterrupted sample definition) as a proportion of LCF values each year between 2002 and 2009. There is a small increase over time. In 2002, Kantar households reported 78.5 percent as much spending as LCF households on average. This rose to 80.3 percent by 2009.

More noticeable is what appears to be a step increase between 2006 and 2007 for beverages, from about 84 percent to 90 percent, and a longer-term upward trend for alcohol beginning in 2006 (though stalling somewhat in 2009). This may be related to the introduction of a new scanner technology for some Kantar households in 2006, who were no longer required to scan nonbarcoded items. If this made compliance costs lower it may have increased reporting of barcoded items—likely to cover almost all spending on alcohol and nonalcoholic drinks—at the cost of reducing reporting of some other categories of

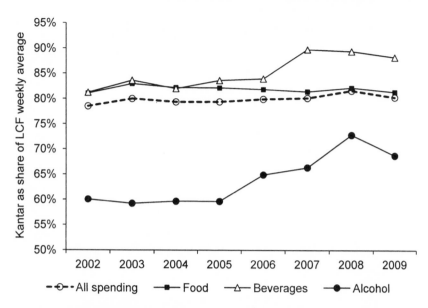

Fig. 16.3 Average Kantar expenditures as a proportion of LCF by year and broad commodity aggregate, 2002–2009

Source: Author's calculations from Kantar Worldpanel and LCF data.

Note: Kantar figures relate to "longest uninterrupted" period of Kantar reporting among households that are active across the full calendar year and have no single reporting gap in excess of six weeks.

spending.[20] More detailed analysis lends some support to this: Between 2005 and 2009, for example, weekly average spending on meat in the Kantar data fell from 82.5 percent to 80.2 percent of the LCF average, for dairy products (including cheese) from 85.0 percent to 83.1 percent, for fruit from 77.1 percent to 74.3 percent, and for vegetables from 83.7 percent to 81.6 percent.

Table 16.5 uses the 2009 data and makes a direct comparison between households who report nonbarcoded products and those who do not. We focus on the longest uninterrupted spending period. Households who do not record nonbarcoded items spend on average £1.65 per week more than those who do, a statistically significant difference. The largest effects are for beer (28 percent higher spending), soft drinks (22 percent), other food (14 percent), and wine (13 percent). Spending is lower in only two categories: fruit (22 percent lower) and vegetables (3 percent). This leads to quite different expenditure patterns across the groups. We explore below the extent to which these differences might also be attributed to demographic differences between the groups, as well as the technology they use.

20. This hypothesis does not really explain what appears to be quite a sustained improvement in alcohol reporting, at least between 2005 and 2008, however.

Table 16.5   Weekly expenditure comparisons, LCF and Kantar "uninterrupted" sample 2009, by reporting of nonbarcoded items

	Average weekly spending				Budget shares				Kantar/LCFS		
	LCFS	Kantar (longest continuous)			LCFS (%)	Kantar (longest continuous)			All (%)	Yes RW (%)	No RW (%)
		All	Yes RW	No RW		All (%)	Yes RW (%)	No RW (%)			
Bread and cereals	8.51	7.17	6.99	7.44	15.3	16.1	15.9	16.3	84.3	82.1	87.4
Meat	10.65	8.54	8.42	8.73	19.2	19.2	19.2	19.2	80.2	79.1	82.0
Fish	2.25	1.70	1.69	1.71	4.1	3.8	3.8	3.8	75.6	75.1	76.0
Milk, cheese, and eggs	6.75	5.61	5.55	5.71	12.2	12.6	12.6	12.5	83.1	82.2	84.6
Oils and fats	1.08	0.98	0.98	0.99	1.9	2.2	2.2	2.2	90.7	90.7	91.7
Fruit	3.81	2.83	3.10	2.41	6.9	6.4	7.1	5.3	74.3	81.4	63.3
Vegetables	6.81	5.56	5.63	5.45	12.3	12.5	12.8	12.0	81.6	82.7	80.0
Sugars, confectionery	3.01	2.61	2.53	2.73	5.4	5.9	5.8	6.0	86.7	84.1	90.7
Other food	2.23	1.69	1.60	1.83	4.0	3.8	3.6	4.0	75.8	71.7	82.1
Food	*45.10*	*36.70*	*36.50*	*37.01*	*81.3*	*82.4*	*83.1*	*81.3*	*81.4*	*80.9*	*82.1*
Coffee, tea, and cocoa	1.15	1.05	1.01	1.11	2.1	2.4	2.3	2.4	91.3	87.8	96.5
Mineral water, soft drinks	2.58	2.24	2.06	2.52	4.7	5.0	4.7	5.5	86.8	79.8	97.7
Beverages	*3.73*	*3.29*	*3.07*	*3.63*	*6.7*	*7.4*	*7.0*	*8.0*	*88.2*	*82.3*	*97.3*
Spirits	1.36	1.17	1.17	1.18	2.5	2.6	2.7	2.6	86.0	86.0	86.8
Wine	3.81	2.42	2.30	2.61	6.9	5.4	5.2	5.7	63.5	60.4	68.5
Beer	1.45	0.96	0.87	1.11	2.6	2.2	2.0	2.4	66.2	60.0	76.6
Alcohol	*6.63*	*4.56*	*4.33*	*4.90*	*12.0*	*10.2*	*9.9*	*10.8*	*68.8*	*65.3*	*73.9*
Total spending	**55.46**	**44.56**	**43.90**	**45.55**					**80.3**	**79.2**	**82.1**
No. of households	5,220	15,781	9,508	6,273							
Avg. nonzero weeks/hh	1.95	25.10	25.06	25.14							

Source: Author's calculations from 2009 Kantar Worldpanel and LCF 2009.

Note: Expenditures are equivalized using the before housing costs–modified OECD scale. "Yes RW" are households who report random-weight (nonbarcoded) products; "No RW" are households who do not.

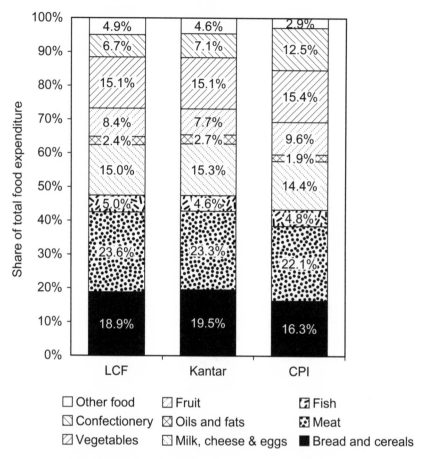

Fig. 16.4 Food commodity weights, LCF, Kantar, and CPI, 2009
Source: Author's calculations based on 2009 Kantar Worldpanel, LCF, and ONS data.

One way to illustrate the economic significance—or otherwise—of differences in spending patterns across data sources is to ask what food inflation rates would have looked like had CPI weights for different food groups been drawn directly from the LCF or Kantar surveys, rather than based (as now) on the national accounts aggregates. Figure 16.4 shows the 2009 food budget shares based on Kantar data (using the longest uninterrupted sample for all households), LCF data, and from the CPI expenditure weights.[21] Note that

21. Note that CPI weights are based on national accounts expenditure aggregates, which are in turn based on slightly outdated expenditure data from the LCF. For example, 2010 weights in the CPI are heavily influenced by LCF data from 2008 and 2009. Our estimates based on LCF and Kantar data use contemporaneous data (e.g., the 2009 weights are based on 2009 data).

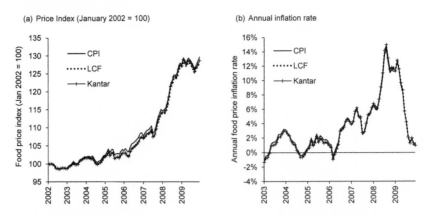

Fig. 16.5 CPI food price indices and inflation rates based on CPI, LCF, and Kantar expenditure weights, 2002–2009

Source: Author's calculations based on 2002–2009 Kantar Worldpanel, LCF, and ONS data.

we look only at food (a higher-level CPI aggregate) and exclude drinks. The differences between LCF and Kantar data are small: the Kantar basket more heavily weights bread, dairy, fats, and confectionery while the LCF basket more heavily weights fruit, fish, and other food. There are larger differences between the weights based on survey data and those from the CPI basket. Weights for bread, meat, fairy, fats, and other food are lower in the CPI than either of the survey baskets, while weights for confectionery and fruit are higher. The much lower spending on other food in the CPI accords with the much higher expenditure on other foods observed in the surveys than the national accounts aggregates in section 16.4.1.

Figure 16.5 shows the different inflation rates for food that result from applying survey- and year-specific commodity weights. The left-hand panel gives the results as index numbers between January 2002 and December 2009; the right-hand panel as annual inflation rates starting in January 2003.[22] Overall, the effect of reweighting the food CPI using LCF and Kantar-specific commodity weights is small. Over the whole period, the food CPI rose by 29.6 percent, whereas an index based on LCF weights rose by 28.1 percent, and one based on Kantar weights rose by 28.6 percent. The average annual food inflation rate between 2003 and 2009 was 3.8 percent based on CPI weights, and 3.7 percent based on weights from both surveys. The largest absolute gap for any single month between the CPI-weighted inflation rate and the LCF-weighted rate was 0.5 percent. The largest gap

22. Figures were calculated by calculating within-year price indices for each food subgroup based at 100 in January and using the different weights to calculate a within-year food index. These indices are then "chained" to give a series over the whole time period. See section 2.5 of Office for National Statistics (2010b) for more on chaining.

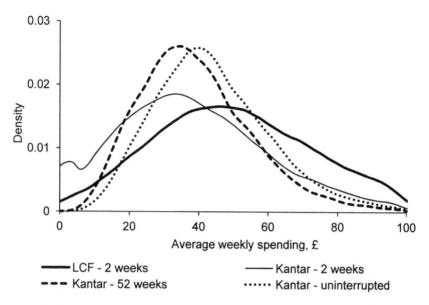

Fig. 16.6 Distribution of equivalized weekly food and drink expenditures, 2009
Source: Author's calculations based on 2009 Kantar Worldpanel and LCF data.

comparing CPI-weighted and Kantar-weighted inflation rates was 0.7 percent. The largest gap comparing LCF-weighted and Kantar-weighted inflation rates was just 0.3 percent.

Distributions of Spending and Budget Shares

The comparisons so far have focused on average spending levels and budget shares. However, looking at their distribution across households is informative. It helps to understand what might be driving differences in the averages. Further, even if (as we saw above) changing the period over which we observe Kantar households makes little difference to the average budget share or spending level, it may still affect the distribution. For issues like poverty and inequality, it is the distribution that matters. Figure 16.6 shows a density plot of the distribution of average equivalized weekly food and drink spending in 2009 for the LCF, and regular reporter Kantar households observed over two weeks, fifty-two weeks, and for the longest uninterrupted number of weeks.

The distribution for LCF households is relatively smooth over the range of spending shown. However, when we observe Kantar households for just two weeks, there is a bulge in the distribution at zero, reflecting the high prevalence of zero expenditure weeks. Observed over longer periods, the distribution of expenditures in the Kantar data become more smoothly distributed though clearly skewed somewhat more toward lower expenditures than the LCF figures. There are notably far fewer high-spending households in the Kantar data than the LCF.

Even more interesting is the impact of the observation period on commodity-level budget shares. One problem with observing expenditure over a short horizon like two weeks is that households may purchase and consume some goods relatively infrequently. To take a stylized example, imagine that all households shop once a week and consume one can of beer per week. Beer is only sold in four-packs, which sell for £5. Households therefore spend £5 on beer once every four weeks, and average weekly beer consumption is £1.25. If we took a random two-week period, we would observe half of households buying beer (consuming £2.50 per week) and half of households buying no beer (consuming £0 per week). The average value of consumption across all households would be right, but the distribution would be wrong. Given the wide availability of freezer and refrigerator space and the ability to store some food and drink items (like canned goods) for a long time, there is also scope for households to engage in stockpiling: buying goods when they are cheap (perhaps on a temporary special offer) for consumption over a long period. The longer the horizon over which we can observe spending patterns, therefore, the more accurate a record of true consumption that data is likely to represent.

Leicester (2012) takes the regular reporter Kantar sample and shows that, observed over a full year, almost all households are observed to purchase from all CPI commodity groups whereas observed over two weeks, large numbers report zero expenditure. The exception is alcohol—over a year, around 39 percent of households do not buy spirits, 32 percent do not buy beer, and 16 percent do not buy wine. However, over just two weeks the proportions not observed to buy are 89 percent, 84 percent, and 71 percent, respectively. For researchers interested in estimating price responsiveness or demand models, the ability to observe spending over an extended period is a key advantage of scanner data, since it drastically reduces the problem of how to deal with zero expenditure values.

Aside from the impact on the likelihood of observing zero expenditure, increasing the duration over which spending is recorded substantially reduces the variance in the distribution of household-level budget shares of each commodity. Figure 16.7 illustrates this for four different commodities (clockwise from top left for bread and cereals, meat, vegetables, and fish; figures for other goods available on request). This is crucial for some applications. For example, past research in the United Kingdom has used data from the two-week LCF to estimate household-specific expenditure patterns from which household-level inflation rates have been estimated (Leicester, O'Dea, and Oldfield 2008; Levell and Oldfield 2011). If at least some of the variation in household budget shares is driven by the short period of observation, then these studies would overstate the variation in household-specific inflation rates across different types of household groups.

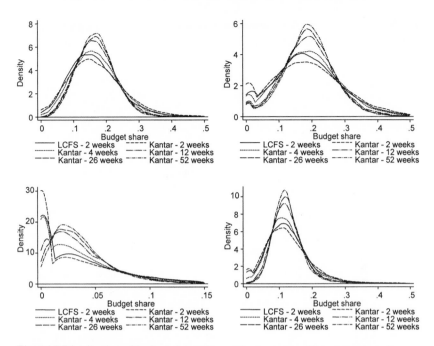

Fig. 16.7 Distribution of budget shares for particular commodity groups based on period of observation, 2009

Source: Author's calculations based on 2009 LCF and Kantar Worldpanel data.

Notes: Commodities shown, clockwise from top left, are bread and cereals, meat, vegetables, and fish.

The Impact of Demographics

Are differences in expenditures across scanner and budget survey data driven by demographic effects? Recall that we select a particular nonrandom sample of households from the scanner data—those who do not drop out of the sample in a given year and have no long gap in their reported expenditures. If the households in this sample have characteristics that would typically make them low spenders on food at home (for example, being poorer), then this could account for the spending gap between the data sets.

Appendix A compares the observable characteristics of the LCF and Kantar (regular reporter) samples in 2009.[23] There are relatively few demographics common to both data sets. To the extent that we can strip out the effects of these common demographics, there may well be a large set of

---

23. In these results and for the rest of this section, we exclude a small number of households from the Kantar sample who report missing information on the number of cars they own or the employment status of the household head, and households in either survey who report equivalized average weekly spending on food and drink (over two weeks in the LCF sample, and over the longest uninterrupted reporting period in the Kantar sample) of less than £5.

unobserved demographics or variables observed in one data set but not the other, which affect expenditures but on which we cannot condition. To summarize the key differences, we find that:

- Kantar households tend to have lower income. Among those with non-missing incomes, only 12.5 percent (3.7 percent) of Kantar households have gross annual household income in excess of £50,000 (£70,000) compared to 20.8 percent (9.9 percent) of LCF households.
- Kantar households are much more likely to own a home computer: 89.5 percent of the Kantar sample do so compared to 75.6 percent of the LCF sample. This probably reflects the fact that many Kantar households also participate in online surveys run by Kantar, and many use personal computers (PCs) to upload their expenditure records to Kantar from the scanner units.
- Only 12.9 percent of Kantar households do not own a car, compared to 21.6 percent in the LCF.
- The regional composition of the two data sets is similar. In the Kantar sample the southeast and east of England are more heavily represented. Scotland appears to be slightly less represented.
- Kantar households are noticeably more middle aged: only 2.7 percent of the Kantar sample is headed by someone age eighty or over compared to 7.1 percent of the LCF sample. Less than 1 percent of Kantar households are headed by someone age twenty-four or under compared to 3.0 percent of the LCF sample.
- Fifty-six percent of Kantar households are headed by a female, compared to 25 percent of the LCF sample.
- Kantar households are much more likely to be headed by someone who is not working (11.3 percent compared to 8.6 percent in the LCF) or part-time employed (15.8 percent working less than thirty hours, compared to just 6.1 percent in the LCF).
- Kantar households are much more likely to contain three or more adult members. This accords with information received from discussions with Kantar that they oversample multiple adult households because of difficulties in obtaining purchase information from secondary shoppers.
- Kantar households have about the same number of young (preschool age) children as LCF households on average, but slightly older children.

Ex ante, it is not clear what these demographic differences imply for expenditures. Kantar households are poorer, on average, and less likely to be headed by a full-time employee, which might mean we would expect them to spend less than LCF households. But along other dimensions they are better off: for example, being more likely to have cars and computers, and more likely to be middle aged (where life cycle expenditures peak). Thus an empirical study is needed. We first pool observations from the LCF and Kantar samples in 2009. We take average total food and drink weekly spending figures over two weeks from the LCF and from the longest uninterrupted spending period from the Kantar sample.[24] We regress the log of expenditure on a dummy variable, which takes the value 1 for households from the Kantar sample, to give the raw average proportional difference between the surveys. We then add a vector of common demographic controls from the surveys to strip out observable demographic effects and see what happens to the coefficient on the Kantar dummy. Table 16.6 reports the key results, including separate results for households who do and do not report random weight items in the Kantar survey.

Across all households, the raw gap between the LCF and Kantar surveys is just over 9 percent—this is markedly less than the 20 percent seen earlier in this section, but our analysis here is based on a different (unequvalized) measure of spending and drops households with very low average food spending of less than £5 per week. Those who are asked to report random weight purchases spend 12 percent less than LCF households, while those who are not asked to do so have a raw spending difference of less than 5 percent. As above, this suggests that reducing respondent burden increases expenditures in scanner data.

Adjusting for demographic differences between the surveys, however, gives very different results. The coefficient on the Kantar dummy across all households almost doubles, suggesting a conditional expenditure gap of more than 18 percent. This is consistent with Leicester and Oldfield (2009), who found the gap between Kantar and LCF spending in 2005 rose from 20 percent to 25 percent once observable demographics were taken into account. They also concluded that controlling for demographics made little difference to overall spending patterns, suggesting that the effects are similar for each commodity group. From our results, it is notable that once we adjust for demographics, there is no difference at all in the Kantar dummy among the groups asked or not asked to report random weight items. This suggests that much of the seeming improvement in reported spending is attributable to demographics.

To investigate the impact of demographics further, we repeat the above analysis, but now interact common observable demographics across the surveys with a Kantar dummy. The coefficients on these interactions tell us which household groups report relatively higher spending in the Kantar data than the LCF.[25] Table 16.7 shows the main significant interaction terms. The base group is households in the southeast of England, with incomes between

24. As we now control for demographics, including household composition, here we use unequivalized expenditure figures.

25. This follows the approach of Zhen et al. (2009), equation (1), and Leicester and Oldfield (2009), table 9. Zhen and colleagues note that in their results, "[the] coefficient on the Homescan indicator variable (H) provides a measure of the average difference in reported expenditures between Homescan and CES for the reference group. Interestingly, this coefficient is not statistically significant for any of the five [commodities]. These results suggest that much of the differences in mean expenditures [between Homescan and CES] are correlated with the observed household characteristics" (479). However, this interpretation is not quite right—as they say, the insignificant Homescan dummy tells us that there is no difference between CES and Homescan *for the reference group* (in their study, households under twenty-five with income under $5,000 of "other race" living in the northeast in 2002, and so on). To compare Homescan and CES for other groups requires a test of the joint significance of the Homescan coefficient and the interaction between Homescan and the other group dummy variable.

Table 16.6   Coefficients on Kantar dummy from regression of log average weekly food and drink expenditures, pooled Kantar and LCF sample, 2009

	All households	Records random weight	No random weight
No demographic controls	-0.093***	-0.123***	-0.047***
	(0.011)	(0.011)	(0.012)
R^2	0.005	0.010	0.002
Controlling for common observed demographics	-0.182***	-0.179***	-0.179***
	(0.009)	(0.010)	(0.013)
R^2	0.406	0.412	0.414
N	20,875	14,643	11,382

Source: Author's calculations based on 2009 LCF and Kantar Worldpanel data.

Notes: Expenditure figures are unequivalized. Households with missing information on number of cars or employment status are dropped, as are those spending less than £5 (equivalized) per week, on average, in either survey. Demographic controls are household gross annual income group, number of cars, region, age group of household head, sex of household head, employment status of household head, number of adult males, number of adult females, numbers of children in age groups birth to four years, five to ten years, eleven to seventeen years, and numbers of people age sixty-five or over. Standard errors are robust. Full results are available on request.

***Significant at the 1 percent level.
**Significant at the 5 percent level.
*Significant at the 10 percent level.

Table 16.7   **Interaction terms between Kantar dummy and demographic groups**

Variable	Coefficient	Variable	Coefficient
Income £0–£10k	+0.101***	Head <25	–0.019
Income £20–£30k	–0.032	Head 25–29	+0.058
Income £30–£40k	–0.049	Head 30–34	+0.003
Income £40–£50k	–0.087**	Head 35–39	+0.039
Income £50–£60k	–0.041	Head 40–44	–0.006
Income £60–£70k	–0.106**	Head 50–54	–0.036
Income £70k+	–0.220***	Head 55–59	–0.019
		Head 60–64	–0.087**
0 adult males	–0.095*	Head 65–69	–0.093
2 adult males	+0.019	Head 70–74	–0.070
3+ adult males	–0.205***	Head 75–79	–0.146*
		Head 80+	–0.121
0 adult females	+0.100***		
2 adult females	–0.052	Female head	+0.106**
3+ adult females	+0.022		
1 child age 0–4	–0.127***	1 person age 65+	+0.080
2 children age 0–4	–0.033	2 people age 65+	+0.137**
3+ children age 0–4	–0.330***	3+ people age 65+	–0.065
N	20,875	R^2	0.413

Source: Author's calculations based on 2009 LCF and Kantar Worldpanel data.

Notes: Left-hand side variable is the log of total weekly household average food and drink expenditure (unequivalized). Other variables controlled for are region, numbers of children age five to ten and eleven to seventeen, head of household employment status, number of cars and presence of a PC in the household. Households with missing information on number of cars or employment status are dropped, as are those spending less than £5 (equivalized) per week on average in either survey.
***Significant at the 1 percent level.
**Significant at the 5 percent level.
*Significant at the 10 percent level.

£10,000 and £20,000 per year, with one car and a home computer, where the head is a male age forty-five to forty-nine and full-time employed, where there is one adult male and female but no children or anyone over sixty-five years of age. For this group, average spending is 9 percent lower per week in the Kantar data than the LCF. The coefficients in table 16.7 show the additional difference in the Kantar/LCF gap for other demographic groups; significantly positive figures suggest that households who differ from the base group only in terms of that characteristic report relatively higher expenditures in the Kantar data. Demographic variables, which had no significant effects on the interaction terms, are not shown.[26]

26. Region is not shown. There is one significant coefficient of –0.087 in the East Midlands. Full results are available on request.

A striking finding is that lower-income households report relatively higher spending in the Kantar data, while higher-income households report relatively lower spending. If we take LCF spending levels as "true" (though in general we should be wary of doing so), this result is consistent with poorer households fully reporting their spending in the scanner data, and richer households being more prone to underreporting. This might reflect the higher opportunity costs of time faced by high-income participants. It could also simply reflect poorer households buying less overall and thus requiring less time and effort to scan their purchases. Notably, there is no effect of employment status on relative Kantar expenditures, which we might also expect to be related to the opportunity costs of time.[27]

Household composition also matters. Households with young children report relatively lower expenditures than those without—again, this seems plausibly related to time constraints. The coefficients on the interaction terms for older children are negative but insignificant. The number of adults also affects relative Kantar expenditures, though in different ways according to gender. For example, having three or more male adults in the household is associated with much lower relative reported spending, but there is no similar effect for three or more female adults. In general, we would tend to expect that households with multiple shoppers would report relatively low spending in the scanner data compared to the LCF to the extent that spending is better reported by the main shopper than other adults; however, the evidence for this based on these figures is quite weak.[28]

Age effects are interesting: there is some (albeit not particularly significant) evidence that relative spending is higher for households headed by younger people and lower for those headed by older people. This might be interpreted as a modal effect—for example, older households may find using the scanner technology more difficult than younger households. However, it is worth noting two things that go against this conclusion. First, these results are based on the sample of Kantar households who report spending consistently—presumably households who cannot use the technology will not be included. Second, the regression also includes a variable for the number of people age sixty-five or over in the household (which is the UK retirement age for males). Discussion with Kantar suggests that they believe older households to be relatively more diligent recorders of their spending, perhaps because they have more time.

---

27. Recall, too, that these estimates are based on the subset of Kantar households who report for the whole year without large spending gaps. If time costs are important, then richer or full-time employed households might be less likely to be part of this sample—though as we saw earlier (and detailed in appendix A) there is no significant effect of income or employment status on being part of this selected sample.

28. Leicester and Oldfield (2009) perform a similar exercise using 2005 data from Kantar and the LCF; they find no evidence of household composition effects on relative expenditures. Unlike our estimates, they find that unemployed households report relatively more spending, but this may proxy for income that was not observed in their estimates.

A brief comparison to the results of a similar exercise in Zhen et al. (2009) is worthwhile. They compare AC Nielsen and CE commodity-level expenditures, regressing spending on demographic variables interacted with a Nielsen dummy. They find a number of demographic effects on relative expenditures, which are different from the findings here: for instance, they find no significant effect of the number of children, a negative impact of households with female heads, significant regional effects, and generally positive effects for older ages. Other findings are more comparable: for example, lower relative spending for high-income households and no clear employment status effects. What this suggests is a point raised in section 16.3: findings from one particular comparison of scanner and other data sets do not necessarily translate across countries or surveys. If there were clear modal effects of scanner technology we might expect the results to be quite similar across countries; instead, it seems that the particular features of each data set might be most crucial in driving findings in different countries. Of course, the comparison we make here is not identical to that made in Zhen et al. (2009) in terms of the covariates for which we can control or the selection of households, for example. One area for future work might be to explore cross-country comparisons of scanner and budget survey data using, as far as possible, identical methods. Regularities that emerge from this exercise might be more credibly assigned to modal effects.

The Relationship between Total Food Expenditures and Expenditure Patterns

The results so far in this section have indicated that, on average, food-spending levels in scanner data are lower than those in budget survey data, but that spending patterns are very similar, certainly once we strip out alcohol purchases. There may be two explanations for this. First, the Kantar and LCF surveys could be sampling similar types of households, but those in the scanner data are underrecording their spending on each broad commodity group at roughly the same rate, on average. Alternatively, the Kantar data could be sampling lower-spending households, on average, but food-spending patterns vary relatively little with total food expenditures.

To explore this latter possibility, one approach is to estimate Engel curves for each food group in the two data sets. Engel curves relate the share of total food expenditure devoted to each food commodity to the log of total food spending. For the purposes of how scanner data may be useful for statistical agencies, as discussed earlier (and detailed in section 16.5), one option may be to use detailed expenditures from scanner data to impute spending patterns into budget survey data if all we knew were total spending—which is precisely this Engel relationship. Therefore, a key issue is whether or not the Kantar and LCF surveys give a similar impression as to how food expenditures break down as the total food budget increases. If so, we might be more confident in making this kind of imputation. If not, it may shed more light on where particular problems in measuring expenditures arise.

This exercise is carried out in Leicester (2012) (see, in particular, appendix C). He imposes no particular restriction on the shape of the Engel curves, but finds them to be approximately linear for most food groups. Most importantly, he concludes that the relationship between food expenditures and commodity-level budget shares is very similar across data sets. The slopes of the Engel curves—where they have any slope at all—are the same. Necessities within the food budget (goods with downward-sloping Engel curves) are bread and dairy products. Luxuries (with upward-sloping curves) are meat, fish, and fruit. For fats, vegetables, confectionery, and other food and beverages, the Engel curves are broadly flat. Perhaps the biggest divergence in the Engel relationship between data sets is for other food, which shows some evidence of being a luxury in the LCF, but where the budget share is essentially flat in total spending in the Kantar data. However, there are certainly no clear cases where one data set suggests a commodity to be a luxury and the other data set a necessity. These findings are quite reassuring that the scanner and budget survey data sets tell similar stories about how spending patterns change with total food outlays.

16.5 Using Detailed Scanner Data to Predict Budget Shares from Aggregate Spending

Our analysis so far has focused on how scanner data compare to spending information from aggregate data and other expenditure surveys. These sorts of comparisons are useful as a source of validation for budget survey data and to inform statistical agencies of possible issues in using scanner methods as part of the data collection process.

We now assess the potential for using scanner data to impute detailed expenditures given only knowledge of total spending. A redesigned CE could decide to reduce respondent burden by asking people only about their total expenditures (or total category-level expenditures such as food spending), and then use detailed expenditure records to estimate how this breaks down. These records could come from a subset of households who agree to provide a more detailed account of their expenditures (whether using scanners, till receipts, diaries, or whatever), or from external data sets like commercial scanner data. This section aims to provide evidence on how successful such an approach might be. We use scanner data to predict household-level budget shares for each commodity as a function of total expenditure and observable demographics. How well these predictions compare to actual budget shares gives a sense of how well observable demographics predict expenditure patterns, and thus how successful such an imputation approach might be. One advantage of using scanner data for this exercise is that we have detailed information on where people shop. This is useful as spending patterns appear to vary by store, so performing this exercise separately for different store types may improve the results.

We take an agnostic view on how the information on total expenditures is obtained. One approach would be a series of questions that first ask about how much households typically spend in total over a given period and then how this breaks down into broad commodity aggregates like food, clothing, leisure, and so on. Further questions could be asked about the proportion of food spending in different store types, such as supermarkets, corner shops, and specialist food stores. Another approach would be to use individual bank records and credit card statements to get total store-specific expenditures. This becomes more feasible as cash spending, which cannot be attributed to a particular store, declines in importance.[29]

We base our analysis on the regular reporter sample in the 2009 Kantar data (see section 16.4.2), restricting attention to households who record random weight purchases. We exclude fourteen households from this sample who have missing demographic information on cars or employment status to give a sample size of 9,494 households. We focus attention on food and nonalcoholic beverages, and use the CPI commodity categories, which have formed the basis of our analysis so far, to define the patterns of expenditure we wish to impute. This gives eleven categories in total.

We look at expenditures in eight different types of store. UK food retailing is dominated by the "big four" supermarkets—Tesco, Asda, Sainsbury, and Morrisons (together accounting for almost 80 percent of expenditure in our data)—and we look at each of these stores separately.[30] Other supermarket chains are grouped according to quality segment: discount supermarkets (Aldi, Lidl, Netto, Cash and Carry stores), quality supermarkets (Waitrose, Marks & Spencer), and other supermarkets (Co-op, Somerfield, Iceland, other chains). Remaining stores are then grouped together into a single category for local and high street expenditures—largely shopping in specialist food retailers (butcher shops, delicatessens, and so on) and corner shops. These account for a low share of spending, suggesting there is little to be gained from disaggregating them still further. Table 16.8 shows the eight store types considered and their market shares by expenditure. Figure 16.8 shows how total food and drink expenditure breaks down for each store across the eleven commodities we consider.[31]

There are some differences in expenditure patterns across stores. Notably, in discount supermarkets, soft drinks and confectionery account for a larger share of spending than across all stores, while dairy and meat products account for smaller shares. In quality supermarkets, fruit, vegetables, meat,

29. Figures from the UK Payments Council (2010, 2011), for example, suggest that about 68 percent of retail purchases by value were on credit and debit cards in the second quarter of 2011, compared to about 61 percent in 2008.
30. Spending in the big four supermarkets includes spending in all formats of stores (e.g., Tesco Extra, Tesco Express). Online expenditures are allocated to the appropriate store.
31. These estimates are based on the full 2009 Kantar sample, rather than the selected "good reporter" sample.

Table 16.8   Store types in the analysis and market shares, 2009

Store	Market share (%, by expenditure)
Tesco	31.5
Asda	18.8
Sainsbury	14.8
Morrisons	13.6
Other supermarkets	7.2
Discount stores	6.0
Quality stores	4.5
Local/High Street stores	3.7

Source: Author's calculations based on 2009 Kantar Worldpanel data.

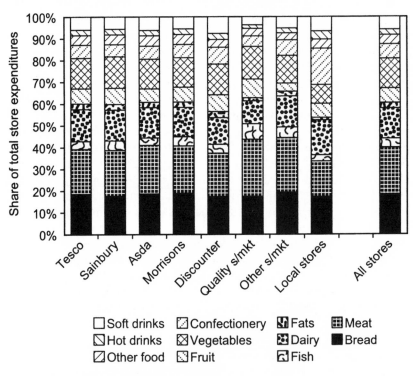

Fig. 16.8 CPI commodity budget shares by store type, 2009
Source: Author's calculations based on 2009 Kantar Worldpanel data.

and fish account for a larger share and dairy, confectionery, and soft drinks account for lower shares. The most striking differences are in local stores— for example, across all stores confectionery accounts for about 6.5 percent of expenditure, but in local stores the share is 16.7 percent. This probably reflects the different sorts of shopping done in local stores that are more associated with top-up and impulse purchases.

If households systematically underreport different types of expenditure in scanner data, imputed budget shares would be biased. A useful check would be to compare expenditure patterns at the store level obtained from store data to those seen in the in-home scanner data. The former would presumably be complete, accurate records of store-specific sales patterns. We do not have access to such data and are not aware of any comparisons having been made of this nature. It would, though, be a useful line of inquiry for statistical agencies thinking of using in-home scanner data.

Using the Kantar sample, we calculate total annual household-level spending during 2009 across each of the store types defined above, broken down by the eleven CPI food and drink commodities. This gives us household-store specific budget shares. Weighting these by the share of each household's spending in each store type gives the household's overall observed budget share for each commodity. We then use seemingly unrelated ordinary least squares (OLS) regression methods to estimate a system of equations for store-specific budget shares for each commodity:

$$w_{ij}^k = \alpha + \beta \ln(X_{ij}) + Z_i'\gamma + \varepsilon_{ij}^k,$$

where w_{ij}^k is the budget share of household i in store j for commodity k, X_{ij} is the total spend of household i in store j, and Z_i is a vector of observable demographic household characteristics.[32] The system is run separately for each store type, allowing for store-specific Engel curves and for demographic effects to vary across store types. From the equation we predict the expected budget share $\hat{w}_{ij}^k$. To ensure the predicted budget shares add up to 1, we estimate the results for ten of the eleven commodities, excluding "other food," for which the predicted budget share is estimated as a residual. These predicted shares are then weighted into an overall predicted household-specific budget share for each commodity using the household-store specific expenditure weights.

Detailed regression results for each store type are available on request. As a summary of the predictive power of these regressions, Table 16.9 reports

32. The model includes gross household income, region, household composition (numbers of adult males, females, children in different age groups, and people age sixty-five and older), the age band and sex of the household head, the employment status of the household head, the number of cars, and whether or not there is a home computer. Because we use annual expenditures, we do not include any seasonal controls. We experimented with various specifications, including adding a squared term on total expenditure to allow store-specific Engel curves to be nonlinear, but found this not to be important. We also experimented with including the share of total food spending by household i in store j as a right-hand-side covariate, the idea being to capture variations in budget shares among households who rely on a particular store type for most of their shopping against those who use the store more as a top-up or secondary store. We found this had little additional explanatory power for the model, but led to a substantial rise in the number of predicted budget shares that were negative. Similarly, conditioning the regression estimates on households who spent more than some minimum amount in each store type made the predicted number of negative budget shares much larger, presumably because the model did not perform well out of sample for those with low total store expenditures.

Table 16.9   Explanatory power (R^2) of store-specific commodity budget share model

	Tesco	Sainsbury	Asda	Morrisons	Discount	Quality	Other	Local
N	7,988	6,026	6,558	5,970	6,054	4,736	7,109	7,512
Bread	0.055	0.055	0.039	0.045	0.021	0.078	0.029	0.028
Meat	0.038	0.044	0.038	0.050	0.046	0.064	0.050	0.085
Fish	0.034	0.032	0.025	0.036	0.028	0.047	0.018	0.025
Dairy	0.013	0.017	0.019	0.023	0.023	0.032	0.019	0.090
Fats	0.037	0.021	0.021	0.026	0.018	0.018	0.020	0.012
Fruit	0.045	0.029	0.026	0.041	0.028	0.023	0.030	0.063
Vegetables	0.028	0.028	0.021	0.025	0.017	0.036	0.012	0.015
Sugars	0.029	0.034	0.024	0.020	0.030	0.036	0.017	0.109
Hot beverages	0.026	0.019	0.018	0.019	0.019	0.016	0.014	0.020
Soft drinks	0.037	0.035	0.033	0.045	0.038	0.024	0.08	0.070

Source: Author's calculations based on 2009 Kantar Worldpanel data.

the R^2 estimates by store and commodity (the number of observations varies because the equations are estimated only for households with positive expenditures in each store during the year). The key conclusion is that observable characteristics, including total store expenditures, have little predictive power for store-specific commodity budget shares. This implies that there is a large amount of unobserved heterogeneity in within-store spending patterns. Of course, our estimates here are somewhat constrained by the limited set of demographic variables available in the Kantar data, though our covariates include most of the usual explanatory variables such as age, household composition, and income that would feature in demand models.

Appendix B shows the distribution of actual and predicted household-level budget shares resulting from this modeling exercise. Broadly, this approach captures the average shares quite well, but not the distribution: the modeled shares lie over a much narrower range than is observed in the data.

One way in which we might be able to capture some of this unobserved heterogeneity is to use the variance of the error terms from the model to predict a (mean-zero) vector of random "noise" for each store-specific budget share, which is then added to the predicted share. We could also use more sophisticated imputation and econometric methods to predict the budget shares. For example, a particular problem with the OLS approach is that households do not buy from each commodity group at each store type they visit. This is particularly problematic once we condition on store type: for example, more than half of households who ever use local stores buy no meat, fish, fats, or hot beverages at all, even over a year. Even within the big four supermarkets, more than 30 percent of shoppers never buy from the hot beverage category, more than 25 percent buy no fish, and more than 20 percent no fats. This problem might suggest running a system of Tobit equations for each store to help better model the zero shares. This would also mean predicted shares could not be negative: in our estimates, around 16 percent of households are predicted to have at least one negative budget share (these households are dropped from the results in appendix B). However, the main intention of this exercise is to assess the extent to which observable covariates are able to explain variation in within-store spending patterns, for which these simple OLS estimates provide initial evidence. If this approach were taken further by statistical agencies, then more attention should be paid to the precise econometric methods used.

The findings in this section suggest that attempts to use detailed store-level expenditure patterns to impute household-specific budget shares, if we observe only total spending, may not be particularly successful. There is a large amount of unobserved heterogeneity in store-specific expenditure patterns not captured by the usual demographic covariates commonly featured in models of household spending. We may be able to do a reasonable job of predicting average budget shares but would be unlikely to replicate the distribution of actual budget shares, though, of course, more sophisticated econometrics may get us further toward that goal. While from the perspective of estimating CPI budget shares getting the average right is the key objective, from a research perspective having accurate household-specific budget shares is vital (for example, in demand modeling and accurately estimating household responsiveness to price shocks, or in estimating the distributional consequences of policies, or how inflation rates vary across households). A consumer budget survey that relied heavily on imputed expenditure patterns might therefore be very undesirable. At the very least it would seem important to have a large enough subset of respondents provide detailed expenditure data without imputation, even if imputation were used to "fill in" the spending patterns for households unable or unwilling to provide more than broad aggregates.

16.6 Summary and Conclusions

In-home scanner data offer a hugely exciting opportunity for researchers to explore detailed questions about household expenditure behavior and firm-pricing decisions. Scanner data sets and scanners as a method of data collection are also potentially of interest for statistical agencies in terms of how they might inform, or be integrated into, budget survey data. Existing scanner data typically only cover a relatively narrow subset of total expenditures. Nevertheless, in terms of the potential for using existing commercial scanner data sets, organizations like the ONS or BLS may see three key opportunities:

1. Comparison and validation—Do expenditures reported in scanner data tell a different story to those reported in budget survey data, and what can we learn from a more micro analysis of differences in spending across households?

2. Detail—having full knowledge of precisely what is bought helps inform the choice of representative items for inflation measurement, the weights that should be given to these items at the lowest level of disaggregation in inflation calculations, the importance of product turnover (particularly in dynamic sectors like grocery retail), and so on.

3. Duration—scanner data report spending over a long time period whereas budget surveys collect detailed spending only for a short duration. The scanner data can therefore give insight into whether short observation periods are appropriate even for nondurable commodities like food and whether the distribution of spending patterns across households is well measured.

However, crucial for any use of scanner data is an understanding of data quality. Researchers and data collectors have, over a long period, developed a good knowledge of the strengths and weaknesses of budget survey data. Scanner data are more novel. The evidence in this chapter and the previous literature point to some consistent differences between scanner data and budget survey data collected via diaries—in particular, that expenditures are lower in scanner data, that expenditures appear to be particularly low for certain commodity groups like alcohol and soft drinks, that it matters whether or not participants have to record nonbarcoded products, and that there are differences in the relative underreporting across household groups (in particular relating to income and numbers of children, which plausibly reflect time constraints). These differences point to modal effects. However, in some cases, differences between scanner and budget survey expenditures, which might in isolation be attributed to survey mode may, in fact, be specific to the particular data sets studied. This implies that researchers and data collectors would need to be aware of the features and methods of the particular scanner data they are using in order to assess its likely benefits. Detailed cross-country comparisons of scanner and budget survey data which, as far as possible, apply common methods would be a useful way to tease out modal effects. Collaboration between national statistical agencies and researchers in different countries to share knowledge and carry out such research would be desirable. For example, statistical agencies have access to much more disaggregate information about households and shopping trips from the budget survey than are made available to external researchers. This information could give more detailed insight into the differences between diary-based and scanner expenditures, and so should be made available for this kind of analysis. Another possibility would be for statistical agencies and commercial data collectors to collaborate directly. For example, to address issues around sample representativeness in scanner surveys, agencies could supply a household sample drawn at random from the population and ask the data collectors to try and incorporate them into the sample, seeing who refuses, who drops out quickly, who appears to cooperate effectively, and so on. In some countries, notably Nordic ones, detailed population-level data linked to identification records is maintained that would allow for detailed analysis of these sorts of issues to be carried out.

Our comparisons between scanner data and budget survey data point to a number of key conclusions. Most notably, scanner data are prone to large numbers of weeks in which no purchases at all are recorded, even by ostensibly active households. We do not have a clear understanding of what drives this, but these zeroes explain a large part of the raw gap between scanner and budget survey expenditures. However, even when we restrict ourselves to a sample of households who are faithful reporters, and eliminate zero spending weeks altogether, a large expenditure gap remains. Evidence from British data suggests that this gap is not accounted for by observable demographic differences between samples. More reassuringly, patterns of spending across surveys are similar even though the levels are different, and reweighting the food CPI using survey-specific budget shares has very little impact on inflation rates. The relationship between total expenditures and commodity-level budget shares is also very similar across surveys.

We find compelling evidence that asking households to record detailed expenditures over a short horizon leads to an inaccurate picture of the distribution of commodity-level budget shares, but not average spending patterns. The two-week duration of budget diaries both in the LCF and the CE is probably not long enough to get a good measure of true food consumption patterns, generating too much variability in the distribution of budget shares and too many zero expenditures for particular commodities.

We also consider the possibility that scanner data may be useful to "drill down" into aggregate store-level expenditures and impute commodity-specific expenditures. We find substantial differences in expenditure patterns across store types, which supports breaking down spending by store rather than imputing based on total spending in all stores. However, we find very little relationship between expenditure patterns and observable covariates. Thus, while an imputation approach might get the averages broadly right, the distribution of imputed budget shares is much less dispersed than the distribution of observed budget shares. More sophisticated imputation or econometric methods may help, and we could also be hamstrung in this analysis by the relatively limited set of demographic information in the scanner data. In general, though, it would not appear to be sensible to rely too heavily on imputation methods to obtain detailed measures of spending.

As mentioned in the introduction, rather than relying on existing commercial scanner data, agencies like the BLS or ONS might be interested in the idea of establishing their own panel of households using scanner methods to record their spending on an ongoing basis. If this were integrated with the budget survey, there would be clear benefits in terms of immediately stripping out demographic differences as a source of variation between scanner and other expenditure data, and in ensuring that the scanner sample were collected using proper random sampling methods. It would also allow, for the first time, detailed scanner data for particular commodities to be linked to more general expenditure patterns. Existing scanner data sets are limited in coverage to food at home and a small number of nonfood purchases. Knowing how much households spent on food out, as well as other expenditure categories, would be extremely beneficial, as would any other links that could be made between the detailed information in scanner data and wider household characteristics relating to health, dwelling characteristics, durable ownership, and so on. A new data set collected by a statistical agency would also enable experimental analysis of the impact of survey mode, different scanner devices, different reporting requirements (e.g., nonbarcoded items), different incentives for participation, and so on. By providing "gold standard" evidence of these issues using randomized trials, this would be extremely valuable not just for the agencies themselves, but also for researchers into survey design and data users.

We end by offering some thoughts, based on this chapter and previous studies, on other ways in which new scanner data could improve on existing commercial data sets. First, one of the major limitations of the Kantar Worldpanel relative to the LCF (and other data sets collected by statistical agencies and used frequently by researchers) is the relatively poor demographic information. Scanner data are collected for commercial marketing and market research purposes. The main clients are retailers and grocery manufacturers who may need only relatively basic demographic profiles of the households in the sample. While the data follow the same households over time, one of the key findings from previous analysis of the Kantar data is that important demographic transitions such as changes in employment status are not well recorded. This may not be true of scanner data sets in general, but we are not aware of research that has looked at this question for other data. Improperly recorded transitions hugely restrict the usefulness of the panel nature of the data (for example, in analyzing how detailed food-spending behavior changes around retirement or in response to unexpected income shocks). New scanner data collected by statistical agencies could presumably obtain much more detailed demographic information about household members to match the kinds of data familiar in budget surveys, and ideally would also take more care to ensure changes in demographics were captured if the same households were followed for an extended period. This should extend not only to knowing whether a transition occurred, but also when.

Second, a key unresolved problem with scanner data is the high prevalence of weeks in which no expenditures are reported. This does not match up to budget survey data. Understanding this better would be a key contribution of a new scanner data set. For example, if no expenditures are recorded over a week or a fortnight, households could be prompted with some form of contact from the statistical agency to see what has driven this, and then code this into the data. This would allow the agency and researchers to distinguish genuine zeroes—holidays, weeks in which households simply used stocks of food or ate out and so on—from nongenuine ones where trips were made but not reported for whatever reason. Indeed, it might be possible in this latter case to get retrospective information (from till receipts or recall questions) or to impute missing trips altogether.

Third, it seems important that any scanner data aims to be, as far as possible, a complete record of the shopping trip. Most existing panels now require only a subset of respondents to report nonbarcoded purchases. In the Kantar data, this was justified by better reporting compliance for nonbarcoded items. However, our analysis suggests that this result is at least partly driven by demographic differences between those who do and do not report nonbarcoded purchases. It may also be differences in the type of scanner device, rather than the lack of random weight reporting that gives this result. Our preference would be that households were asked to record random weight purchases as well, since not doing so risks substantial bias in estimating consumption of certain commodities, particularly fruit and vegetables. The aim should be to minimize the additional burden imposed by this requirement. One problem for commercial scanner data is the need to include very detailed product characteristics, which needed to be manually input by respondents for random weight items (e.g., the country of origin of different fruits, whether organic, the weight purchased). To the extent that such details are not needed by statistical agencies they could be dispensed with altogether, or taken where available from till receipts, or imputed. If recording random weight items simply required scanning a barcode from a generic booklet or tapping an icon on the barcode reader itself, then it may be little more onerous than recording barcoded products.

Finally, we would certainly advocate that any new scanner data made use of till receipts as well as the in-home scanner. Studies of Nielsen data highlighted the problems of relying on imputed prices obtained from centralized store-level databases given the growth of personalized pricing through vouchers and loyalty cards, as well as store-specific special offers. Participants should be encouraged to send in receipts, and it may be that technology could enable this to be done digitally (scanned receipts or optical character recognition devices attached to computers) to integrate it with the data collection process more closely.

Appendix A

Observable Demographic Comparisons

The tables below compare observable demographic characteristics of the LCF 2009 sample (excluding Northern Ireland) and the Kantar 2009 regular reporter sample (see section 16.4.2). Respective sample sizes are 5,150 and 15,752 households.

Table 16A.1   Gross annual household income

	All		Excluding unknown		
	Kantar (%)	LCF (%)	Kantar (%)	LCF (%)	K ÷ LCF
Unknown	18.1	0.0			
< £10,000	9.9	13.4	12.1	13.4	0.90
£10,000–£19,999	22.4	23.9	27.3	23.9	1.15
£20,000–£29,999	17.7	17.9	21.6	17.9	1.20
£30,000–£39,999	13.1	13.6	15.9	13.6	1.17
£40,000–£49,999	8.6	10.4	10.5	10.4	1.01
£50,000–£59,999	4.9	6.6	5.9	6.6	0.90
£60,000–£69,999	2.3	4.3	2.9	4.3	0.67
≥ £70,000	3.1	9.9	3.7	9.9	0.38

Table 16A.2   **Computer in the household?**

	Kantar (%)	LCF (%)	K ÷ LCF
No	10.5	24.2	0.43
Yes	89.5	75.8	1.18

Table 16A.3   **Number of cars**

	Kantar (%)	LCF (%)	K ÷ LCF
Zero	12.9	21.6	0.59
One	50.7	45.0	1.13
Two or more	36.5	33.4	1.09

Table 16A.4   **Region**

	Kantar (%)	LCF (%)	K ÷ LCF
Northeast	4.8	4.5	1.07
Northwest	11.6	11.2	1.04
Yorks & Humber	8.8	9.2	0.95
East Midlands	8.5	7.5	1.13
West Midlands	9.2	10.1	0.91
East of England	10.8	9.6	1.13
London	8.5	8.8	0.96
Southeast	15.1	13.4	1.12
Southwest	9.5	10.0	0.95
Wales	5.1	5.2	0.97
Scotland	8.2	10.4	0.79
Northeast	4.8	4.5	1.07

Table 16A.5   **Gender of household head**

	Kantar (%)	LCF (%)	K ÷ LCF
Male	44.0	74.7	0.59
Female	56.0	25.3	2.21

Table 16A.6   Age of household head

	Kantar (%)	LCF (%)	K ÷ LCF
<25	0.6	3.0	0.20
25–29	4.0	5.3	0.75
30–34	7.5	7.1	1.06
35–39	10.1	8.7	1.15
40–44	11.6	9.9	1.16
45–49	10.6	10.1	1.05
50–54	10.3	9.0	1.14
55–59	10.6	9.7	1.09
60–64	9.9	9.6	1.03
65–69	8.3	7.7	1.08
70–74	8.6	6.8	1.26
75–79	5.4	6.0	0.90
≥80	2.7	7.1	0.38

Table 16A.7   Employment status of household head

	Kantar (%)	LCF (%)	K ÷ LCF
Works 30+ hours	41.8	51.5	0.81
Works 8–29 hours	13.7	5.7	2.42
Works < 8 hours	2.1	0.4	5.68
Unemployed	1.9	3.9	0.50
Retired	28.6	29.1	0.98
Full-time education	0.5	0.9	0.60
Not working	11.3	8.6	1.32

Table 16A.8   Number of adults (age eighteen and older)

	Males			Females		
	Kantar (%)	LCF (%)	K ÷ LCF	Kantar (%)	LCF (%)	K ÷ LCF
Zero	16.5	22.7	0.72	9.4	13.5	0.69
One	71.6	69.2	1.03	79.7	78.7	1.01
Two	10.1	7.1	1.43	9.6	6.8	1.40
Three+	1.8	1.0	1.89	1.4	1.0	1.45

Table 16A.9   **Number of children**

	Ages 0–4			Ages 5–10			Ages 11–17		
	Kant (%)	LCF (%)	K ÷ L	Kant (%)	LCF (%)	K ÷ L	Kant (%)	LCF (%)	K ÷ L
Zero	87.9	87.7	1.00	84.4	87.5	0.96	82.9	85.5	0.97
One	9.4	9.6	0.97	11.4	9.0	1.27	11.7	9.6	1.22
Two	2.6	2.4	1.10	3.8	3.3	1.16	4.7	4.3	1.10
Three+	0.1	0.3	0.52	0.4	0.3	1.59	0.7	0.6	1.13

Table 16A.10   **Number of people age sixty-five and older**

	Kantar (%)	LCF (%)	K ÷ LCF
Zero	71.0	70.9	1.00
One	16.5	18.6	0.89
Two	12.5	10.5	1.19
Three+	0.0	0.1	0.33

Appendix B

Actual and Predicted Household-Level Budget Shares by Commodity, 2009

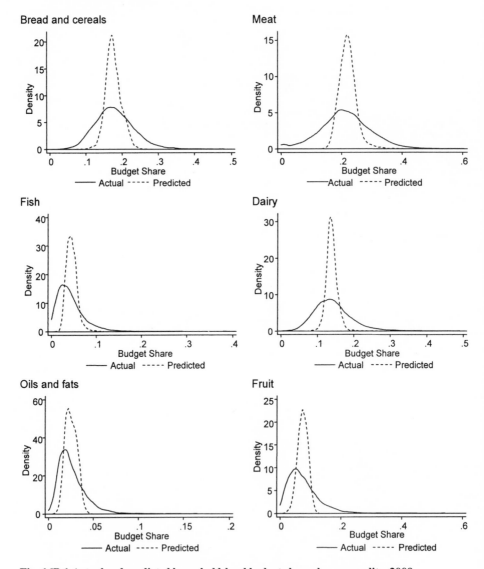

Fig. 16B.1 Actual and predicted household-level budget shares by commodity, 2009

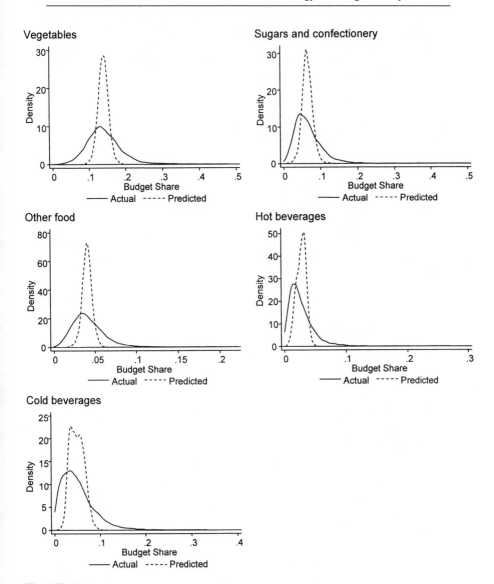

Fig. 16B.1 (cont.)

References

Aguiar, M., and E. Hurst. 2007. "Life-Cycle Prices and Production." *American Economic Review* 97:1533–59.

Ahmed, N., M. Brzozowski, and T. Crossley. 2006. "Measurement Errors in Recall Food Consumption Data." IFS Working Paper no. 06/21, Institute for Fiscal Studies. http://www.ifs.org.uk/publications/3752.

Attanasio, O., E. Battistin, and A. Leicester. 2006. "From Micro to Macro, from Poor to Rich: Consumption and Income in the UK and the US." Conference Paper, National Poverty Center, University of Michigan. http://www.npc.umich .edu/news/events/consumption06_agenda/Attanasio-Battistin-Leicester.pdf.

Ayers, R., P. Hossack, and C. Payne. 2010. *Living Costs and Food Survey Technical Report for the Survey Year January—December 2009*. Newport, South Wales: Office for National Statistics.

Blow, L., A. Leicester, and Z. Smith. 2004. "Consumption Trends in the UK, 1975– 99." IFS Report no. 65, Institute for Fiscal Studies. http://www.ifs.org.uk/comms/ r65.pdf.

Brewer, M., A. Goodman, and A. Leicester. 2006. *Household Spending in Britain: What Can It Teach Us about Poverty?* Bristol, England: The Policy Press. http:// www.jrf.org.uk/sites/files/jrf/9781861348555.pdf.

Broda, C., E. Leibtag, and D. E. Weinstein. 2009. "The Role of Prices in Measuring the Poor's Living Standards." *Journal of Economic Perspectives* 23 (2): 77–97.

Cole, N. 2011. "Design of the National Household Food Acquisition and Purchase Survey (FoodAPS)." Presentation to Committee on National Statistics Household Survey Producers Workshop. http://www.bls.gov/cex/hhsrvywrkshp_cole.pdf.

Department for Environment, Food & Rural Affairs (DEFRA). 2011. *Attitudes and Behaviours around Sustainable Food Purchasing*. London: DEFRA. http://www .defra.gov.uk/statistics/files/defra-stats-foodfarm-food-attitudes-report-110406 -mainreport.pdf.

Duly, A., T. Garner, E. Keil, S. Reyes-Morales, and C. Wirth. 2003. "The Consumer Expenditure Survey and AC Nielsen Survey: A Data Comparison Study." Unpublished manuscript, Bureau of Labor Statistics.

Einav, L., E. Leibtag, and A. Nevo. 2008. "Not-So-Classical Measurement Errors: A Validation Study of Homescan." Stanford Institute for Economic Policy Research Discussion Paper no. 08–07, Stanford University. http://www-siepr .stanford.edu/repec/sip/08-007.pdf.

Feenstra, R. C., and M. D. Shapiro, eds. 2003. *Scanner Data and Price Indexes*. Chicago: University of Chicago Press.

Griffith, R., E. Leibtag, A. Leicester, and A. Nevo. 2009. "Consumer Shopping Behavior: How Much Do Consumers Save?" *Journal of Economic Perspectives* 23 (2): 99–120.

Griffith, R., and M. O'Connell. 2009. "The Use of Scanner Data for Research into Nutrition." *Fiscal Studies* 30 (3–4): 339–65.

Harding, M., E. Leibtag, and M. Lovenheim. 2012. "The Heterogeneous Geographic and Socioeconomic Incidence of Cigarette Taxes: Evidence from Nielsen Homescan Data." *American Economic Journal: Economic Policy* 4 (4): 169–98.

Harris, J. M. 2005. "Using Homescan Data and Complex Survey Design Techniques to Estimate Convenience Food Expenditures." American Agricultural Economics Association Conference Paper. http://ageconsearch.umn.edu/bitstream/19344/1/ sp05ha07.pdf.

Huffman, S., and H. Jensen. 2004. "Demand for Enhanced Foods and the Value of Nutritional Enhancements of Food: The Case of Margarines." American Agricultural Economics Association Conference Paper. http://ageconsearch.umn.edu/ bitstream/20205/1/sp04/hu05.pdf.

Jin, W., R. Joyce, D. Philips, and L. Sibieta. 2011. "Poverty and Inequality in the UK: 2011." IFS Commentary no. 118, Institute for Fiscal Studies. http://www.ifs.org .uk/comms/comm118.pdf.

Leicester, A. 2012. "How Might In-Home Scanner Technology Be Used in Budget Surveys?" IFS Working Paper no. 12/01, Institute for Fiscal Studies. http://www .ifs.org.uk/wps/wp1201.pdf.

Leicester, A., C. O'Dea, and Z. Oldfield. 2008. "The Inflation Experience of Older Households." IFS Commentary no. 106, Institute for Fiscal Studies. http://www.ifs.org.uk/comms/comm106.pdf.

Leicester, A., and Z. Oldfield. 2009. "An Analysis of Consumer Panel Data." IFS Working Paper W09/09, Institute for Fiscal Studies. http://www.ifs.org.uk/publications/4468.

Levell, P., and Z. Oldfield. 2011. "The Spending Patterns and Inflation Experience of Low-Income Households over the Past Decade." IFS Commentary no. 119, Institute for Fiscal Studies. http://www.ifs.org.uk/comms/comm119.pdf.

Lusk, J. L., and K. Brooks. 2011. "Who Participates in Household Scanning Panels?" *American Journal of Agricultural Economics* 93 (1): 226–40.

Mathiowetz, N., K. Olson, and C. Kennedy. 2011. "Redesign Options for the Consumer Expenditure Survey." Unpublished manuscript, National Academy of Sciences. http://www.bls.gov/cex/redwrkshp_pap_abtsrbirecommend.pdf.

O'Dea, C., and T. Crossley. 2010. "The Wealth and Saving of UK Families on the Eve of the Crisis." IFS Report no. 71, Institute for Fiscal Studies. http://www.ifs.org.uk/comms/r71.pdf.

Office for National Statistics. 2010a. *Consumer Trends, Q2 2010.* Newport, South Wales: ONS. http://www.ons.gov.uk/ons/rel/consumer-trends/consumer-trends/q2-2010/consumer-trends-no—57.pdf.

———. 2010b. *Consumer Price Indices Technical Manual: 2010 Edition.* Newport, South Wales: ONS. http://www.ons.gov.uk/ons/guide-method/user-guidance/prices/cpi-and-rpi/consumer-price-indices-technical-manual—-2010.pdf.

Perloff, J. M., and M. Denbaly. 2007. "Data Needs for Consumer and Retail Firm Studies." *American Journal of Agricultural Economics* 89 (5): 1282–87.

Slesnick, D. 2001. *Consumption and Social Welfare.* New York: Cambridge University Press.

Tanner, S. 1998. "How Much Do Consumers Spend? Comparing the FES and National Accounts." In *How Reliable is the Family Expenditure Survey? Trends in Incomes and Expenditures over Time,* edited by J. Banks and P. Johnson. London: Institute for Fiscal Studies. http://www.ifs.org.uk/comms/r57.pdf.

Triplett, J. 1997. "Measuring Consumption: The Post-1973 Slowdown and the Research Issues." Federal Reserve Bank of St. Louis Review (May/June):9–42. http://www.brookings.edu/~/media/Files/rc/articles/1997/0702useconomics_triplett/19970702.pdf.

Tucker, C. 2011. "Using Multiple Data Sources and Methods to Improve Estimates in Surveys." Presented at Bureau of Labor Statistics Household Survey Producers Workshop, June 2011. http://www.bls.gov/cex/hhsrvywrkshp_tucker.pdf.

UK Payments Council. 2010. *The Way We Pay 2010: The UK's Payment Revolution.* http://www.paymentscouncil.org.uk/files/payments_council/the_way_we_pay_2010_final.pdf.

UK Payments Council. 2011. *Quarterly Statistical Report Q2 2011.* http://www.paymentscouncil.org.uk/files/payments_council/minutes_of_payments_council_board/statistical_release_2011_q2.pdf.

United States Department of Agriculture (USDA). 2009. *The Consumer Data and Information Program: Sowing the Seeds of Research.* http://www.ers.usda.gov/publications/ap/ap041/ap041.pdf.

Westat. 2011. *Redesign Options for the Consumer Expenditure Survey.* http://www.bls.gov/cex/redwrkshp_pap_westatrecommend.pdf.

Zhen, C., J. L. Taylor, M. K. Muth, and E. Leibtag. 2009. "Understanding Differences in Self-Reported Expenditures between Household Scanner Data and Diary Survey Data: A Comparison of Homescan and Consumer Expenditure Survey." *Review of Agricultural Economics* 31 (3): 470–92.

Contributors

Marco Angrisani
Center for Economic and Social
  Research
University of Southern California
635 Downey Way
Los Angeles, CA 90089-3331

Stephen Ash
US Census Bureau
4600 Silver Hill Road
Washington, DC 20233

Orazio Attanasio
Department of Economics
University College London
Gower Street
London WC1E 6BT England

Garry Barrett
School of Economics
H04-Merewether
The University of Sydney
Sydney NSW 2006 Australia

Adam Bee
US Census Bureau
4600 Silver Hill Road
Washington, DC 20233

Caitlin Blair
US Department of Commerce
1401 Constitution Avenue, NW
Washington, DC 20230

Laura Blow
Institute for Fiscal Studies
7 Ridgmount Street
London WC1E 7AE England

Christopher D. Carroll
Consumer Financial Protection Bureau
1700 G Street, NW
Washington, DC 20552

Thomas F. Crossley
Department of Economics
University of Essex
Wivenhoe Park
Colchester, UK, C04 3SQ England

Scott Fricker
Bureau of Labor Statistics
Office of Survey Methods Research,
  PSB Suite 1950
2 Massachusetts Avenue, NE
Washington, DC 20212-0001

Thesia I. Garner
Bureau of Labor Statistics
2 Massachusetts Avenue, NE
Washington, DC 20212

John Greenlees
Bureau of Labor Statistics
2 Massachusetts Avenue, NE
Washington, DC 20212

Steve Henderson
Bureau of Labor Statistics
2 Massachusetts Avenue, NE
Washington, DC 20212

Michael D. Hurd
RAND Corporation
1776 Main Street
Santa Monica, CA 90407

Erik Hurst
Booth School of Business
University of Chicago
Harper Center
Chicago, IL 60637

David Johnson
Bureau of Economic Analysis
1441 L Street NW
Washington, DC 20230

Arie Kapteyn
Center for Economic and Social
  Research
University of Southern California
635 Downey Way
Los Angeles, CA 90089-3331

Ralph Koijen
London Business School
Regent's Park
London NW1 4SA England

Brandon Kopp
Bureau of Labor Statistics
2 Massachusetts Avenue, NE
Washington, DC 20212

Claus Thustrup Kreiner
Department of Economics
University of Copenhagen
Øster Farimagsgade 5, building 26
DK-1353 Copenhagen, Denmark

David Dreyer Lassen
Department of Economics
University of Copenhagen
Øster Farimagsgade 5, building 26
DK-1353 Copenhagen, Denmark

Valérie Lechene
Department of Economics
University College London
Gower Street
London WC1E 6BT England

Andrew Leicester
Frontier Economics
71 High Holborn
London WC1V 6DA England

Søren Leth-Petersen
Department of Economics
University of Copenhagen
Øster Farimagsgade 5, building 26
DK-1353 Copenhagen, Denmark

Peter Levell
Institute for Fiscal Studies
7 Ridgmount Street
London WC1E 7AE England

Clinton McCully
Bureau of Economic Analysis
1441 L Street NW
Washington, DC 20230

Bruce D. Meyer
Harris School of Public Policy Studies
University of Chicago
1155 E. 60th Street
Chicago, IL 60637

Kevin Milligan
Department of Economics
University of British Columbia
#997-1873 East Mall
Vancouver, BC V6T 1Z1 Canada

Jonathan A. Parker
MIT Sloan School of Management
100 Main Street, E62-642
Cambridge, MA 02142-1347

William Passero
Bureau of Labor Statistics
2 Massachusetts Avenue, NE
Washington, DC 20212

Luigi Pistaferri
Department of Economics
579 Serra Mall
Stanford University
Stanford, CA 94305-6072

Susann Rohwedder
RAND Corporation
1776 Main Street
PO Box 2138
Santa Monica, CA 90407

John Sabelhaus
Board of Governors of the Federal
   Reserve System
20th and C Streets, NW
Washington, DC 20551

Scott Schuh
Federal Reserve Bank of Boston
600 Atlantic Avenue, T-9
Boston, MA 02210

Nicholas S. Souleles
The Wharton School
University of Pennsylvania
2300 Steinberg Hall-Dietrich Hall
Philadelphia, PA 19104-6367

James X. Sullivan
Department of Economics
447 Flanner Hall
University of Notre Dame
Notre Dame, IN 46556

David Swanson
Bureau of Labor Statistics
2 Massachusetts Avenue, NE
Washington, DC 20212

Nhien To
Bureau of Labor Statistics
2 Massachusetts Avenue, NE
Washington, DC 20212

Stijn Van Nieuwerburgh
Stern School of Business
New York University
44 West 4th Street, Suite 9-120
New York, NY 10012

Roine Vestman
Department of Economics
Stockholm University
SE-106 91 Stockholm, Sweden

Joachim K. Winter
Department of Economics
LMU Munich
Ludwigstr. 33
D-80539 Munich Germany

Author Index

Subject Index